Understanding the Sources of Early Modern and Modern Commercial Law

Legal History Library

VOLUME 25

Studies in the History of Private Law

VOLUME 14

The titles published in this series are listed at *brill.com/shpl*

Understanding the Sources of Early Modern and Modern Commercial Law

Courts, Statutes, Contracts, and Legal Scholarship

Edited by

Heikki Pihlajamäki
Albrecht Cordes
Serge Dauchy
Dave De ruysscher

BRILL
NIJHOFF

LEIDEN | BOSTON

Cover illustration: The planet Mercury and his influence on the world, Johann Sadeler (I), after Maerten de Vos, 1585 (Rijksmuseum, Amsterdam).

Library of Congress Cataloging-in-Publication Data

Names: Pihlajamaki, Heikki, 1961- editor. | Cordes, Albrecht, editor. | Dauchy, Serge, editor. | Ruysscher, Dave de, editor.
Title: Understanding the sources of early modern and modern commercial law: courts, statutes, contracts, and legal scholarship / edited by Heikki Pihlajamaki, Albrecht Cordes, Serge Dauchy, Dave de Ruysscher.
Description: Leiden ; Boston : Brill/Nijhoff, 2018. | Series: Legal history library, ISSN 1874-1793 ; volume 25 | Includes bibliographical references and index.
Identifiers: LCCN 2017059783 (print) | LCCN 2017059945 (ebook) | ISBN 9789004363144 (E-book) | ISBN 9789004360457 (hardback : alk. paper)
Subjects: LCSH: Commercial law--History. | Commercial law--Netherlands--History.
Classification: LCC K1006 (ebook) | LCC K1006 .U43 2018 (print) | DDC 346.07--dc23
LC record available at https://lccn.loc.gov/2017059783

Typeface for the Latin, Greek, and Cyrillic scripts: "Brill". See and download: brill.com/brill-typeface.

ISSN 1874-1793
ISBN 978-90-04-36045-7 (hardback)
ISBN 978-90-04-36314-4 (e-book)

This book is printed on acid-free paper and produced in a sustainable manner.

Contents

List of Illustrations

Tables

Charts

Notes on Contributors

Anja Amend-Traut
is Professor of Legal History, Civil Law, and Canon Law at the Julius-Maximilians-Universität of Würzburg. Her research focuses on the history of commercial law and the history of jurisdiction in early modern Europe.

Albrecht Cordes
is Professor of Medieval and Early Modern Legal History and Civil Law at the Goethe University in Frankfurt am Main. His research is especially focused on the history of commercial law, Hanseatic legal history, and the history of conflict resolution.

Ricardo Galliano Court
is an early modern economic historian and Director of Undergraduate Studies in Political Science at the University of Wisconsin-Madison. His research focuses on informal commercial networks, trustworthiness, and reputation in early modern Italy.

Serge Dauchy
is Research Director at the CNRS (Lille-France) and Professor of Legal History at the University Saint-Louis of Brussels. His main research topics are the history of civil procedure, comparative history of central courts, and the history of Québec.

Dave De ruysscher
is Associate Professor at Tilburg University and at Vrije Universiteit Brussel. He specializes in the history of commercial and private law of the early modern period and the nineteenth century.

Olivier Descamps
is Professor of Legal History at the University of Panthéon-Assas, Paris. His research focuses on history of private law.

Eberhard Isenmann
is Professor emeritus of Medieval History at the University of Cologne. His research focuses on the legal, economic, and social history of late medieval and early modern German cities and the Empire.

Mia Korpiola
is Professor of Legal History at the University of Turku. Much of her research focuses on the legal history of medieval and early modern Sweden from a comparative perspective.

Peter Oestmann
is Professor of German Legal History and Private Law at the University of Münster. His research focuses on the history of courts and litigations in the middle ages and early modern times.

Heikki Pihlajamäki
is Professor of Comparative Legal History at the University of Helsinki. His research focuses on comparative legal history of the early modern period and the nineteenth century.

Margrit Schulte Beerbühl
is Professor of Modern History at the University of Düsseldorf. Her main research interests include early modern global trade and speculation.

Edouard Richard
teaches at the University of Rennes. His research focuses on the history of commercial law.

Guido Rossi
is Lecturer in European Legal History at the University of Edinburgh. His research is mainly focused on medieval and early modern European law.

Boudewijn Sirks
is Emeritus Regius Professor of Civil Law at the University of Oxford. His research focuses on Roman law, and the legal and intellectual history of Europe.

Bram Van Hofstraeten
is Associate Professor at the Faculty of Law, University of Maastricht. His research focuses on the history of commercial law in early modern Europe.

Alain Wijffels
is Professor of Legal history and Comparative law. He teaches at the universities of Leiden, Leuven, and Louvain-la-Neuve. He is also a senior research fellow of the French CNRS (at the Centre d'histoire judiciaire, Lille).

Justyna Wubs-Mrozewicz
is Senior Lecturer in Medieval History at the University of Amsterdam. Her research interests include the Hanse and premodern conflict management in northern Europe.

CHAPTER 1

Introduction

Heikki Pihlajamäki, Albrecht Cordes, Serge Dauchy and Dave De ruysscher

The history of commercial law is one of the most interesting and fastest-growing sub disciplines of legal history. The history of commercial law is also an interdisciplinary field *par excellence*, as it attracts not only legal historians, but also general historians and economic historians. Since commerce has always crossed national boundaries, its legal history also lends itself more than naturally to a comparative approach.

This volume is an attempt to present the history of early modern commercial law in Western Europe as an interdisciplinary and comparative enterprise, capable of being approached from various different angles and with many methodologies. The early modern period, for our purposes, is a long one, stretching from the fifteenth to the end of the nineteenth centuries. This is arguably the period which has received the least amount of attention so far in the study of commercial law in England, Italy, and Germany. The medieval period, not least because of the discussions on *lex mercatoria*, has attracted more attention in these countries, and the same can be said for the past two centuries, which has seen much research focused on the formation of modern law, although even in these two periods, scholarly work has mainly concentrated on national histories of commercial law. In France, however, the medieval history of commercial law has been less studied, but its history in the early modern period has received much more attention.

There is also a difference between legal and economic history. For England, Italy, and Germany, a great deal of legal historical research has been carried out on commercial law, but this is less the case for the Low Countries and France. Commercial-economic themes concerning nineteenth-century France (apart from for the codification era) have been mostly the territory of economic historians, not legal historians. The same is true for the Low Countries and in all periods. There, and especially on the Northern Netherlands, economic historians have covered the seventeenth and eighteenth centuries well. Much the same applies to Scandinavian research on the history of commercial law. As for the United States and the United Kingdom, the distinction between legal and economic history is less rigid.

 | DOI 10.1163/9789004363144_002

The book is based on papers presented at the workshop 'Historiography and Sources of Early Modern Commercial Law', which was organized in September 2014 in Helsinki. This was the first in a series of five workshops with different themes: 'Small, Medium-Sized and Large Companies in Law and Economic Practice (Middle Ages – Nineteenth Century)' (Brussels, May 2015); 'The Influence of Colonies on Commercial Legal Practice' (Fiskars, Finland, January 2016); 'Migrating Words, Migrating Merchants, Migrating Law' (Frankfurt am Main, September 2016); and 'The Historiography of Commercial Law: Past, Present, and Future' (Helsinki, September 2017).[1]

This first workshop invited the speakers to choose subjects that dealt with either the sources of commercial law or historiographical themes. All but one contributor chose the former, and accordingly we decided to limit this volume to the sources of commercial law and to devote the final conference to the historiography. One of the red threads that runs through this present volume is the extent to which historical sources reflect sources of law.

In this study the aim is to demonstrate the wide variety of sources that are necessary to grasp fully the numerous facets of early modern commercial law. It is not appropriate to limit the understanding of 'sources' to normative sources, although their central role is self-evident in legal history. The most important of these are codifications, both comprehensive ones such as the French *Ordonnance de Commerce* and the more selective ones; and court records, which become more extensive during the late Middle Ages and the Early Modern periods. However, in order to approach the reality of commercial life and commercial law, these normative sources need to be seen in the context of the day-to-day business routine: official and private registers and account books, contract charters, letters, and wills. Educational literature, manuals on law and bookkeeping, arithmetic books, and similar sources which are not strictly normative complete the picture.

If we take law in commercial matters to mean something more than simply legislation and state-derived norms, the problem of normativity enters the picture and we unavoidably touch upon legal-theoretical debates. For example, if one defines law as 'living law', in the spirit of the legal sociologist Eugen Ehrlich, then cultural practices and shared mentalities can be identified as belonging to 'merchant law'. Established practices and customs are, however, difficult to distinguish in conceptual terms. This then triggers the question of to what

1 The conferences were organized by the Project 'The Making of Commercial Law: Common Practices and National Legal Rules from the Early Modern to the Modern Period'. The Project Leader is Heikki Pihlajamäki, and the Steering Group consists of Albrecht Cordes, Serge Dauchy, and Dave De ruysscher.

extent merchants were legally literate and articulate, with regard not only to official law, but also vis-à-vis their own 'ways of doing things'. Did they, for example, consider accounting practices that were shared among merchants as 'law'? Were sanctions more than a (temporary) loss of reputation? Analysis of different historical sources can yield answers to such questions. However, it is only by focusing on the detailed scrutiny of historical sources and on what they can tell us that we will arrive at conclusive views. Therefore, this book contains contributions in which diverse historical sources stemming from within mercantile milieus, such as letters, merchant manuals, newspapers, and others, are held up to the light.

The concept of commercial law is notoriously elusive, and especially so in the early modern period. The Dutch law for example, as Boudewijn Sirks shows, had no commercial law separate from private law before the early nineteenth century. Thus, there existed no special body of rules applicable to merchants and/or special courts. Nevertheless, there were specific commercial regulations, contract forms of special importance for commerce and even courts, which in practice dealt mostly with commercial problems. Hence, when dealing with the early modern period we must allow ourselves a certain degree of pragmatism in deciding what we recognize as 'commercial law', if we wish to be able to compare the law on commercial activities in different parts of Europe and the world. Our concept of commercial law is a practical one, as it refers to all forms of legal regulation that had to do with merchants and their business. Commercial law thus encompasses commercial contracts, bankruptcy, commercial courts and procedure, and company law.

As Justina Wubs-Mrozewicz shows, international commercial conflicts were not solved based on legal sources and legal practice only. Economic and political interests were deeply intertwined in the resolution of commercial conflicts, which is why diplomatic sources are indispensable when trying to understand premodern commercial conflict solving at the international level. Alain Wijffels emphasizes the links between commercial law and public policy. Using the practice of the Grand Council of Mechlin as an example, he demonstrates how important it is to see commercial law not only as private law between merchants, but also in connection to public governance. High courts, such as the Grand Council of Mechlin, are important here because of their nature as 'institutions where the interface between public governance on trade and the private interests of merchants was put to the test'.

Ricardo Court's chapter on the sixteenth-century merchant customs uses the commercial letters of a Genoese merchant as a primary source. The letters of Gio Francesco di Negro contain important information, not easily found in the traditional legal sources, on the 'written and unwritten rules governing long-distance trade in the Western Mediterranean'. Guido Rossi explains, in his contribution on sixteenth-century insurance practice, how different sources (written rules, insurance manuals, and documents such as policies, mercantile correspondence, and judicial or arbitral decisions) must often be used to complement each other in order to form a coherent picture of insurance law. Comparing Dutch, English, French, and Italian practices regarding the institution of abandonment, Rossi shows how different sources can be understood in context.

Notaries were, at least in some parts of Europe, at times involved in the drafting of partnership agreements. Bram van Hofstraeten's contribution demonstrates how notarial practice evolved in the sixteenth-century Low Countries. He demonstrates that notarized partnership agreements were primarily concerned with the internal organization of the partnerships, and only little with external liability issues. Notarial guidebooks or *formularii* formed a branch of practical legal literature, as did merchant guidebooks, which Dave De ruysscher discusses in his article. During the period ranging from 1490 to 1600, over a hundred *ars mercatoria* manuals were published in Antwerp alone. De ruysscher, however, cautions against reading merchants' manuals as descriptions of valid mercantile law, but rather as expressions of individual thought. He is doubtful regarding to what extent early modern commercial practices can be described as normative at all, given, for instance, the scarcity with which customary law is mentioned in sources. Customs as binding legal norms are not frequent in the early modern *consilia* either, as Eberhard Isenmann writes in his article on the fourteenth- and fifteenth-century German legal, moral-theological, and economic expert opinions on commercial matters. Instead of usages, customs, or moral arguments, legal professionals preferred Roman law and legal literature. Nevertheless, a wide range of commercial legal issues were discussed in the opinions, such as bookkeeping, trademarks, contracts, and just prices.

Anja Amend-Traut's article shows the wealth of normative material also contained in the commercial case files of the Imperial Chamber Court and the Aulic Court, the two highest courts of the Holy Roman Empire of the German Nation. Although the decisions themselves were lacking *rationes decidendi*, expert opinions and law faculties' opinions included in the case files contain interesting legal argumentation. In addition to this, the Aulic Council granted privileges and formulated trade policy decisions with a general normative character.

Unfortunately, the wealth of sources we encounter in continental Europe is largely absent in some of the European fringe areas such as Scandinavia. As Heikki Pihlajamäki shows, the Swedish early modern commercial law can nevertheless be researched at least through case files of the lower courts and high courts. However, since these were not specialized commercial courts, commercial cases are far from frequent. Legal literature on commercial law is also scarce, and there are no notarial deeds or *consilia* to be found in the archives. Swedish law was, from early on and compared to other parts of Europe, statute-based to a great extent, and thus centralized. The statutory development of the seventeenth century offers, therefore, one important insight into commercial law in early modern Sweden. Mia Korpiola's contribution then offers a view into the practice of Sweden's first royal appellate court, the Svea Court of Appeal, in its very first years. Starting its functions in 1614, the Court received few commercial cases in its first year. Their number then gradually increased, the main part consisting of simple credit notices (*manebrev*) and – in accordance with Alain Wijffels's observations concerning the Grand Council of Mechlin – controlling the observance of public trade regulations.

Margrit Schulte Beerbühl, writing on the speculation bubble of 1799, adds another significant source to those mentioned above, which gains significance from the seventeenth century onwards: newspapers. She approaches her topic, however, not only by way of newspaper publicity, but also through court records and other sources.

Modern commercial law emerged in the nineteenth century. It is often presented as the period of rising legal positivism, and France is often given as the prime example. However, Edouard Richard demonstrates with various examples the French paradox in which, despite the prevailing post-revolutionary *légicentrisme*, commercial customs, and usages could still thrive, and sometimes even clearly *contra legem*. One of the reasons behind this phenomenon was the poorly drafted Commercial Code of 1807, the preparation of which Olivier Descamps analyses in his contribution.

For most of the nineteenth century, Germany was in stark contrast to France politically. Steps towards legal unification were nevertheless taken before the unification in 1871. Peter Oestmann presents in his essay the founding history of the *Oberappellationsgericht Lübeck*, the most significant of the German nineteenth-century courts dealing with commercial affairs. The Lübeck court was founded in 1820 as the superior court for the free cities of Bremen, Frankfurt am Main, Hamburg, and Lübeck, and the court functioned until 1879. Although the Lübeck court did not specialize in commercial law, a large proportion of the cases dealt *de facto* with commerce. Most of the case files and printed decisions of the court still exist and are easily accessible.

The most important message of this volume is the following. We hope that the contributions here show something of the wealth of sources on which historians of commercial law can, and indeed often should, use to approach their subject. Depending on the subject, historical research on mercantile law must be ready to open up to different approaches and sources in a truly imaginative and interdisciplinary way. This is the case, of course, in all legal historical research. It is, however, even more the case in a field such as commercial law. This, more than many other branches of law, has always been largely non-state law. This remains so even despite the fact that it is vital to take public concerns into consideration if one wishes to grasp the workings of commercial law and changes in it. Mercantile law rising out of situations and the practices of commercial life, often gradually and piece-meal, may sometimes call for its historian to employ a different set of sources than, say, were one to write a history of procedural or criminal law. Merchants themselves, usually without legal training, have always been instrumental in shaping the rules governing their activity. Normative, 'official', sources are important in commercial law as well, but other sources are often needed to complement them. Though it may not be a complete study, the articles here hopefully present a good assemblage of those sources.

We are thankful to all the authors for their contributions. Besides the authors, we would sincerely like to thank the Academy of Finland and the Finnish Cultural Foundation for their generous grants. Without them, our project and this publication would never have been possible. With great accuracy and speed, Sara Elin Roberts copy-edited the manuscript and corrected the English – we are enormously thankful for that. Many thanks to Jussi Sallila and Katja Tikka for their valuable help in the workshop arrangements, and to Sofia Söderholm for her efficient technical assistance in the final phases of the book production. Finally, we thank Anita Geritz for preparing the indexes.

CHAPTER 2

Mercantile Conflict Resolution in Practice: Connecting Legal and Diplomatic Sources from Danzig *c*.1460–1580

Justyna Wubs-Mrozewicz

1 Introduction

Commercial law evokes the image of a venerable monument, which has been gradually built up with local and imported material of laws and customs, and which bears witness to the growing expertise of its constructors. As such, it is firmly rooted in the historiographical and empirical legal tradition of studying the development of commercial law. However, since commercial law deals with trade and thus with negotiation, another metaphor will be used here for the late medieval and early modern period, namely that of a coin. Premodern commercial law can be seen as the 'head' side of a coin which changed hands; the other side is the practice of mercantile conflict resolution. This 'tail' side of the coin has left its impression on a broader category of sources than strictly legal ones: next to legal proceedings, letters of individual traders and of town councils, contracts and entries in town books are of importance. Some of these sources on the practice of mercantile conflict resolution have been studied by legal historians, usually zooming in on specific cases.[1] Also, this broader category of sources has, relatively recently, attracted the attention of economic historians, as part of the New Institutional Economics, or in reaction to it. In this approach, the economic and social mechanisms behind mercantile conflict resolution are central, and the researchers usually zoom out in order to arrive at a generalization.[2] The different research interests and the approaches

1 A good overview of the authors, topics and bibliography is to be found through the articles in Albrecht Cordes and Serge Dauchy (eds.), *Eine Grenze in Bewegung: Öffentliche und private Justiz im Handels- und Seerecht* (München: Oldenbourg, 2013).

2 Douglass North, *Institutions, Institutional Change and Economic Performance* (Cambridge: Cambridge University Press, 1990); and Douglass North 'Institutions, Transaction Costs, and the Rise of Merchant Empires', in James D. Tracy (ed.), *The Political Economy of Merchant Empires: State Power and World Trade, 1350–1750* (Cambridge: Cambridge University Press, 1991), 22–40; Avner Greif, Paul Milgrom and Barry R. Weingast, 'Coordination, Commitment and Enforcement: The Case of the Merchant Guild', *Journal of Political Economy* 102:4

 | DOI 10.1163/9789004363144_003

of legal and economic historians are the reasons why late medieval and early modern commercial law and the practice of mercantile conflict resolution are rarely studied systematically together. This has also been the case for maritime law and maritime legal practice, and legal proceedings in general.[3]

Yet there is a 'third side' to this metaphorical coin which determined its value: the political and economic context in which it was put on the table. Individual commercial conflicts were set in a framework of intertwined large-scale interests: for instance, wars breaking out and disrupting the market, privateers attacking foes and sometimes also friends, or legal proceedings which were connected to peace negotiations. Traders strove to recover their losses and continue trade, by means of mediation, arbitration and law, that is, tools which were available in a given context of time and space of their towns and states. Conversely, individual mercantile conflicts could seriously aggravate relations between these town councils and rulers, or even unleash large-scale violence. These interrelationships are reflected in yet another category of sources: letters to rulers and between rulers, instructions to envoys, reports of war and diplomatic negotiations, as well as copies of privileges, which were attached to these documents. These sources have been traditionally viewed as the main corpus of diplomatic history, and are mainly used by political and military historians.[4] In the context of the North Sea and the Baltic in the medieval and early modern period, the connections between the mercantile practice of conflict resolution and the resolution of large-scale conflicts where commerce played an important role have been studied in only some aspects, most notably prize law and the power struggle over the seas.[5] Alain Wijffels has cast light on instances

---

(1994), 745–776; Sheilagh Ogilvie, *Institutions and European Trade: Merchant Guilds 1000–1800* (Cambridge: Cambridge University Press, 2011); Oscar Gelderblom, *Cities of Commerce: The Institutional Foundations of International Trade in the Low Countries, 1250–1650* (Princeton: Princeton University Press, 2013).

3 Edda Frankot, *'Of Laws of Ships and Shipmen': Medieval Maritime Law and Its Practice in Urban Northern Europe* (Edinburgh: Edinburgh University Press, 2012), 2; Peter Oestmann, *Rechtsvielfalt vor Gericht: Rechtsanwendung und Partikularrecht im Alten Reich* (Frankfurt am Main: Klostermann, 2002), 5–20. Commercial law and practice was the topic of the conference 'The Merchant and the Law: Mind the gap?' held at the Faculty of Law, University of Maastricht (30–31.03.2015).

4 Maurits Ebben and Louis Sicking, 'Nieuwe diplomatieke geschiedenis van de moderne tijd: Een inleiding', *Tijdschrift vor Geschiedenis* 127:4 (2014), 541–552; John Watkins, 'Toward a New Diplomatic History of Medieval and Early Modern Europe', *Journal of Medieval and Early Modern Studies* 38:1 (2008), 1–14.

5 Karl-Heinz Böhringer, *Das Recht der Prise gegen Neutrale in der Praxis des Spätmittelalters* (Hamburg: Alfred Metzner, 1972); Jan H.W. Verzijl, *International Law in Historical Perspective:*

in English-Hanseatic relations where law and diplomacy were intertwined in a particularly interesting way, and discussed the position of diplomats.[6]

In this paper, I am focusing on the 'tail' side of the coin, and on its position on the bargaining table. In other words, my point of departure are primary sources on the *practice* of mercantile conflict resolution and sources on the resolution of large-scale conflicts related to trade. The argument that I am advancing is that when these sources are studied together, several interdependencies appear. Small- and large-scale conflicts were often connected, or the dynamics of their development and resolution ran parallel. Specifically, (a) there are intersections between the beginnings and endings of these conflicts; (b) the same people are involved in it; and (c) the language of conflict resolution indicates that they were part of the same imagery of conflict and conflict resolution. I therefore seek to demonstrate how juridical and diplomatic sources together can contribute to our understanding of the practice of commercial conflict resolution.

This paper, and the research on the primary sources conducted for it, is anchored in the NWO (Netherlands Organization for Scientific Research) VENI postdoctoral project on mercantile conflict resolution in Danzig c. 1450–1580,

Part 9C, The Law of Maritime Prize (Dordrecht: Martinus Nijhoff, 1992); Cornelius G. Roelofsen, 'Early Dutch Prize Law: Some Thoughts on a case before the Court of Holland and the Grand Council of Mechelen (1477–1482)', *Netherlands International Law Review* 27:2 (1980), 218–226; Rudolf Häpke, *Die Regierung Karls V. und der europäische Norden* (Lübeck: Schmidt, 1914); Aksel Christensen, *Dutch Trade to the Baltic about 1600: Studies in the Sound Ttoll Register and Dutch Shipping Records* (Copenhagen: E. Munksgaard, 1941); Artur Attman, *The Struggle for Baltic Markets: Powers in Conflict 1558–1618* (Göteborg: Kungl. Vetenskaps- och Vitterhets-samhället, 1979); Louis Sicking, *Neptune and the Netherlands: State, Economy and War at Sea in the Renaissance* (Leiden: Brill, 2004).

6 Alain Wijffels, 'History and Law: The case for the German Hanse against the English Merchants Adventures (1603–1604)', in Ignacio Czeguhn (ed.), *Recht im Wandel- Wandel des Rechts: Festschrift für Jürgen Weitzel zum 70. Geburtstag* (Köln: Böhlau, 2014), 427–452; Alain Wijffels 'Le déclin de la Hanse au fil des négociations avec l'Angleterre (1474–1604)', in Jean-Marie Cauchies (ed.), *Publications du Centre Européen d'Etudes Bourguignonnes (XIVe–XVIe s.)* (Neuchâtel: Centre Européen d'Etudes Bourguignonnes, 2013), 275–289; Alain Wiffels, 'International Trade Disputes and Ius Commune: Legal Arguments on the "Gdańsk Issue" during the Hanseatic Eembassy to London in 1553', in Albrecht Cordes and Serge Dauchy (eds.), *Eine Grenze in Bewegung: Öffentliche und private Justiz im Handels- und Seerecht* (München: R. Oldenbourg Verlag, 2013), 65–89; Alain Wijffels, 'Le statut juridique des ambassadeurs d'après la doctrine du XVIe siècle', in Jean-Marie Cauchies (ed.), *Les relations entre Etats et principautés des Pays-Bas à la Savoie* (Neuchâtel: Centre européen d'études bourguignonnes, 1992), 127–142.

a Hanseatic town under the Polish Crown.[7] In this project, the policy (development of norms), practice (employment of strategies and legal practice), and perception (contemporary evaluation) of conflict resolution are combined. Moreover, conflicts on three levels of individuals, groups, and finally towns and states are investigated. In order to keep the analysis of the very rich archives in Danzig (supplied by research in Copenhagen, Brussels, the Hague, London, and Lübeck) and the published primary sources feasible, the lens of the interaction of Danzigers with foreigners has been applied. This means the focus was on dealings with burghers from other towns, most notably Hansards, Hollanders and Zealanders, Englishmen and Polish nobility involved in the grain export from this Baltic metropolis. The research has resulted in several conference papers and publications, where the findings have been presented focusing on specific conflict cases,[8] or uncovering the mechanisms which can be found in various cases.[9] Here, I will combine the methodologies. One case which illustrates the connections of legal and diplomatic sources particularly well, the conflict of Tomasso Portinari with Danzig and the Hanse, will be presented shortly in this introduction and then used as a connecting thread in the three parts. Moreover, examples from other conflicts will be employed to buttress the main argument. I will develop further arguments which have been put forward in earlier articles of this project.

The starting point is the chronological structure of the Portinari conflict case. In 1473, a Florentine galley under the Burgundian flag was captured by the Danzig privateer Paul Beneke on its way from Bruges to London. Its very valuable goods were confiscated and some members of the crew were killed, injured or thrown overboard. A second galley managed to escape. The context of the incident was the war between the Hanse and England (1469–1473), and the attempt to block any trade which might benefit England. However, the seized galley and its contents, among them Hans Memling's masterpiece *The Last Judgement*, proved to be a troublesome prize of war. The Florentine magnates the Medici, through Tomasso Portinari, their manager in Bruges,

7 On the Hanse in general, see Justyna Wubs-Mrozewicz, 'The Hanse in Medieval and Early Modern Europe: An Introduction', in Justyna Wubs-Mrozewicz and Stuart Jenks (eds.), *The Hanse in Medieval and Early Modern Europe* (Leiden: Brill, 2013); and Donald J. Harreld (ed.), *A Companion to the Hanseatic League* (Leiden: Brill, 2015).

8 For instance Justyna Wubs-Mrozewicz 'Mercantile Conflict Resolution and the Role of the Language of Trust: A Danzig case in the Middle of the Sixteenth Century', *Historical Research* 88:241 (2015), 417–440.

9 For instance Justyna Wubs-Mrozewicz, 'Kopieergedrag: De vormen en functies van afschriften in het laatmiddeleeuwse politieke briefverkeer van de Hanzesteden', *Tijdschrift voor Geschiedenis* 127:4 (2014), 603–624.

the Burgundian duke Charles the Bold and even the Pope got involved in claims for the restitution for incurred commercial losses. The moot point was who was to be made liable for these losses: the privateer Paul Beneke, his home town Danzig, or the whole Hanse. Tomasso Portinari was inclined towards the latter, and was eager to pursue legal action against the Hanse. Yet one of the fundamental principles of this organization of towns and traders was that one town was not to be legally responsible for the actions of another, in order to avoid reprisals. These legal principles were explicitly presented during the peace negotiations with England in 1474, and in the talks with the Burgundian sovereign, in the by now emblematic elaboration of what the Hanse was not.

Until 1477, when Duke Charles the Bold died, the threat of legal action was in the air, but this subsided due to the changed political circumstances, and due to the commercial interests which the Burgundian Netherlands had in trade with Danzig and the Hanse. The approach to this individual commercial conflict case was thus directly dependent on the large-scale political and commercial interests. This is also clearly apparent in the second stage of the conflict: in 1492, with the backing of the new ruler Philip the Fair, Tomasso Portinari seized his chance to recover the losses. After unsuccessful negotiations with the Hanseatic Kontor in Bruges, he sued the Kontor in Bruges, and the whole Hanse, before the Great Council of Mechlin. The outcome of it was a sentence with a sky-high restitution to be paid to the Florentines. It would seem that this was the end of the conflict case in the juridical sense, even though the possibility of appealing to the imperial *Kammergericht* was discussed. The end phase of the conflict, however, unfolded in a surprising way, politically and economically. The town council of Bruges, fearing that the Hanseatic merchants would leave the town, offered to pay the damages to the Portinari party. The condition was that the Hanseatic Kontor would not be moved to Antwerp. When in the sixteenth century, as history would show, the weight of international commerce moved to the Brabantian centre and the Hanseatic merchants adopted the tongue twisting title 'of the Bruges Kontor, residing nowadays in Antwerp', the threat of legal proceedings was again looming.[10]

---

10 Most relevant sources on the case were published in the third volume of the third series of the source edition *Hanserecesse/Hanserezesse* (Leipzig, 1870–1970), 4 series and a total of 26 volumes (henceforth HR). In the context of the Hanse, the most extensive discussion can be found in Otto Meltzing, 'Tomasso Portinari und sein Konflikt mit der Hanse', *Hansische Geschichtsblätter* 12 (1906), 101–123; and from the perspective of Paul Beneke and Beata Możejko, *'Peter von Danzig': Dzieje wielkiej karaweli 1462–1475* (Gdańsk: Wydawnictwo Uniwersytetu Gdańskiego, 2011); Sander Nicolai, 'De denkbeeldige vijand van Tomasso Portinari: Een conflict naar aanleiding van de diefstal van een Florentijns/ Bourgondisch galeischip door hanzeatische kapers, 1473–1499' (BA thesis, Leiden

2 Beginnings and Endings

Large-scale conflicts where commerce played an important role, and small-scale commercial conflicts, rarely started and ended at the same time. Still, several individual Danzig cases, when viewed in the context of interchanging periods of political turmoil and periods of relative peace in the Baltic and North Sea areas, show a clear connection. The beginnings and endings of the two seemingly separate categories of conflict often depended on each other.

A good place to start is the hilltop perspective. First of all, the outbreak of war necessarily led to individual mercantile losses. It could be as a result of blockades, sea battles, seizure by privateers, downright robbery on water or land which went hand in hand with political chaos, or augmented prices. Town councils warned their own and foreign merchants of the risks.[11] Trade contacts could be severed when the partners suddenly found themselves on two different sides and even had to take up arms against each other. For instance in the 1455–1466 war between Danzig and Poland on the one hand, and the Teutonic Order on the other hand, the Livonian Hanseatic towns had to follow the commands of the Master of the Teutonic Order. This meant that despite their aversion to this conflict and their efforts to halt it, they had to act against the fellow Hansards in Danzig and declare themselves their enemies. The Livonians warned that individual traders were in danger of being captured by privateers. Even Lübeck, which officially kept aloof of the conflict, turned into a perpetrator and victim of mercantile losses during this war, a complexity

---

University, 2014), under my supervision, awaits publication in a shortened form. In an international context, the case has attracted attention due to the role the Florentines played in it, see Raymond A. de Roover, *The Rise and Decline of the Medici Bank 1397–1494* (Cambridge: Harvard University Press, 1963); and art historians have also explored the background: Florence Edler de Roover, 'A Prize of War: A Painting of Fifteenth Century Merchants', *Bulletin of the Business Historical Society* 19 (1945), 3–12; Barbara G. Lane, 'The Patron and the Pirate: The Mistery of Memling's Gdańsk Last Judgement', *The Art Bulletin* 93 (1991), 623–640. For the Hanse and England context, as well as the self-description of Hansards in negotiations, see Stuart Jenks, 'A Capital without a State: Lübeck caput tocius hanze', *Historical Research* 65 (1992), 134–149; and Nils Jörn, *'With money and bloode': Der Londoner Stalhof im Spannungsfeld der englisch-hansischen Beziehungen im 15. und 16. Jahrhundert* (Köln: Böhlau, 2000).

11 For instance in 1576, the Danzig town council called in all Hollandish skippers and traders to a meeting at the town hall, and distributed a leaflet with information on how to proceed in the context of the Dutch Revolt, see the Archiwum Państwowe w Gdańsku [State Archives in Gdańsk] (henceforth APG) 300,93/551 fols. 100 and 110.

which had to be resolved diplomatically.[12] One of the best examples (in terms of available sources) on how a large-scale conflict affected an individual trader is the case of Hinrick van Resen, a Danziger who used to be one of the administrators in the Bruges Kontor. During the 1520s conflict which involved some Hanseatic towns, Hollanders, and Danes, a Hollandish ship was seized by privateers from Danzig. As an act of reprisal, the goods of Hinrick van Resen were arrested in Dordrecht, and he himself was imprisoned and faced a trial before the Great Council of Mechlin.[13] The sources bear witness to the very intensive and concerted attempts of the council of Danzig, Lübeck, and the Kontor in Bruges to resolve the matter, since it was connected to large-scale politics. The energetic Hinrick, who kept sending letters from prison, was even ordered to hold his tongue and stay his quill if he wanted to have the backing and goodwill of the towns. The Danzig council impressed upon him that it was not an individual mercantile case anymore, and future damage needed to be prevented (*Hierumbe beuehle wy jw jn dieser sake fordan stille tho staen sso ferne gy vnse hulde hebben willen vnd yw vor thokunftige schaden gedencke tho hoeden*).[14] In the Portinari case, presented in the introduction, Florentine merchants were transporting their goods under a neutral (Burgundian) flag during the war between the English and the Hansards. The individual mercantile loss was thus directly caused by somebody else's conflict, Portinari argued, and therefore compensation was due. In other words, the ship could not be seen as a prize of war. The fact that the ship was sailing to an English harbour did complicate matters from the Hanseatic point of view, and made the individual seizure part of the large-scale conflict.[15] A final telling example is that in 1546, a Deventer ship sailing with grain from Danzig was captured by Scottish privateers immediately after the outbreak of hostilities between the Habsburg Netherlands and Scotland. Two years later, after the ship had changed hands and had become the property of a merchant from Antwerp, the traders from Deventer started a lawsuit undermining the property rights. The argument was

---

12 HR 2:4 nr. 325: '*Aldus de Lifflandeschen steden hebben gescreven den van Dantzig darut is to merkende, dat ze vyende zint*'; HR 2:4 nr. 377; HR 2:4 nr. 603; HR 2:5 nr. 24; HR 2:5 nr. 29. The role of Lübeck in the conflict is important, because the town councillors became mediators in the conflict, see HR 2:4 nr. 612.

13 APG 300 D 20/401, 403, 405; APG 300, 27/10 fols. 129–130; APG 300, 27/11 fols. 18–19v; 300,27/11 fols. 321v–322; HR 3:8, 794 note 1; HR 3:9 nr. 133 § 5; HR 3:9 nr. 598; HR 3:9 nr. 598 § 39; Rudolf Häpke (ed.), *Niederländische Akten und Urkunden zur Geschichte der Hanse und zur deutschen Seegeschichte*, 2 vols. (München: Duncker & Humblot, 1913), (henceforth NAU) 1 nr. 58.

14 APG 300, 27–11, 268–268v.

15 HR 3:3 nr. 176.

that they were unaware of the new war with Scotland: a line of reasoning that was rejected at the court in Amsterdam, in appeal at the Hof of Holland, and most probably at the last instance, the Great Council of Mechlin. The frame of reference was prize law and the politics of the day, not a loss which could be seen as an isolated legal case.[16] Individual merchants were affected by large-scale conflicts, and the resolution of their conflicts had to happen within the framework of the large conflict, whether they liked it or not.

The compensation of some of these losses, such as goods which were taken by privateers, was often settled during or after a peace or truce. The long lists of merchant names and marks, sent around to rulers, as well as diplomatic negotiations in the late fifteenth and in the sixteenth centuries, bear witness to the practice. It was often a central element of the bargaining on the conditions of a peace or truce.[17] This meant that a hard line could be followed from the top down for even a minor, individual loss. Yet the large-scale context could also have an adverse effect. For instance, in 1473, Hansards suggested to the English king that some new individual claims, which were brought before various courts, should be dropped in order to avoid endangering peace negotiations.[18] Another example: during the war between Danzig and the Polish king (1576–77), ships from Enkuizen were taken by Danziger privateers. William of Orange, as the leader of this part of the Netherlands at this point in the Dutch revolt, negotiated the repayment of damages. But having to take larger economic and political interests into account, he decided against pursuing the case.[19] Such cases exemplify once again that the examination of juridical sources of conflict resolution alone is not enough: sources on legal proceedings can end with a cliff-hanger, while the actual end mark was put at the negotiation table.

Here, one has to note that this agreement might have been formulated explicitly in the diplomatic sources, such as reports from the meetings, letters, circulating copies or *cedulae* (loose notes inserted into letters, which could be slipped out of the official letter if need arose) which have survived to this day.[20] However, the agreement also could have been oral and general for all similar

16 Algemeen Rijksarchief, Brussels (henceforth ARA Brussels) Grote Raad van Mechelen A 105 nr. 461.

17 For instance the case of Herman Wynberg, HR 4:2 nr. 625.

18 HR 2:7 nr. 173.

19 APG 300, 53/796 fols. 29, 33–34; 45–51, 57–59; 65–71, 73–74, 77, 83–87; 89–90; 133–134; Maria Bogucka, 'Zatarg z Batorym', (The conflict with Batory) in Edmund Cieślak (ed.), *Historia Gdańska vol. II* (The History of Gdańsk) (Gdańsk: Wydawnictwo Morskie, 1982), 579–585.

20 Bastian Walter, *Informationen, Wissen und Macht: Akteure und Techniken städtischer Außenpolitik: Bern, Straßburg und Basel im Kontext der Burgunderkriege (1468–1477)* (Stuttgart: Franz Steiner Verlag 2012); Wubs-Mrozewicz, 'Kopieergedrag'.

cases, so the outcome of the individual case can only be derived indirectly from the peace settlement. From a different angle, the inability to settle the repayment of losses incurred by the activity of Hollandish and Wendish privateers in the first half of the fifteenth century, and by war altogether, was the reason behind the diplomatic stalemate between the parties. Instead of putting an end to the conflict, namely by a peace treaty, truces were prolonged for decades. The positive side to this was that trade could continue.[21]

Next to the possibilities and constrictions which diplomacy entailed for the settlement of individual conflicts embedded in large-scale conflicts, there was also the legal route to pursue. Sources show that it could go either from lower courts up to the highest instances, such as the Deventer merchants who lost their ship to Scottish privateers, or that politicized cases could be brought directly before a high court, such as the Tomasso Portinari case before the Great Council of Mechlin. Letters, reports and instructions, which were in fact non-juridical sources, reveal that it was the large-scale conflict context which was crucial in opening up possibilities for litigating at such forums. Also, the Portinari case sources indicate that such a court was as much a political forum, where large-scale interests were being weighed, as a legal one.[22] The next step, which cannot be considered here but which is pertinent, is the consequence such politicised practice of commercial conflict resolution could have on the formulation of commercial law.

The perspective will now be changed and we will take small-scale conflicts as a starting point. Seemingly petty mercantile conflicts between two individuals from various towns or territories, traders or shippers on foreign waters, or foreign merchants ignoring the policy of a town could unleash serious political conflicts. This usually happened as a chain reaction, when more and more towns and rulers were persuaded to support the claims of their burgher. I have investigated it in depth in a Danzig-Deventer-Mecklenburg case from the late 1550s–1560s. A very brief summary: a trader from Danzig borrowed a substantial sum from a visiting friend from Deventer, without giving written proof of the debt. He then left town on the sly, which spurred his friend to look for him. Once the debtor had been found in Mecklenburg, a recognizance was demanded. Thereafter, the Danziger tried to default once again by bringing a criminal charge of kidnapping and robbery against his former friend to the Danzig town council court, and later to the Dukes of Mecklenburg.[23] A declaration of

---

21 Justyna Wubs-Mrozewicz, 'The Close "Other": Medieval and Modern Perspectives on Hollanders and the Hanse', *German History* 31:4 (2013), 453–472.

22 HR 3:3 nr. 175.

23 Wubs-Mrozewicz, 'Mercantile Conflict Resolution'.

reprisals for all Deventer burghers followed, and the regent of the Netherlands became involved. The matter almost turned into an armed conflict, and high-profile mediators such as Albrecht, the Duke of Prussia, were sought.[24] Another example is a case where Hollandish salt ships and their crews were arrested during the Northern Seven Years War (1563–1570) and tried in Danzig at the instigation of the Danish king. The legal proceedings turned into a political tug-of-war and peace between the rulers of Denmark and Poland on the one hand, and the Hollandish regent on the other hand.[25] Taking a step back in time, a Kammergericht case is illustrative. In the 1480s, grain was scarce in Prussia and the councils of Danzig and Elbing decided to stop the export of it. The wealthy merchant Thomas Jodecke apparently paid no heed to the export ban and as a result, 43 ships carrying his cargo were arrested. Eventually, Jodecke brought his case to the *Kammergericht* in 1497. Since the town councillors did not react to the citation, the emperor imposed an imperial ban (*Reichsacht*) on the towns. This was a decision the councillors vehemently contested as the cities were under the Polish king, and not the emperor. Political tensions ensued, and the issue returned several times in the sixteenth century, even after the ban was lifted in 1515.[26]

In all these conflicts, both legal and diplomatic tools were used in an attempt to resolve the conflict, along with extrajudicial means such as arbitration and mediation. When a conflict escalated, diplomacy up to the highest level was needed, but it does not mean that there was necessarily a sequence of arbitration-lawsuit-diplomacy. The Portinari case shows that diplomacy and mediation could be attempted in the first place, then followed by a lawsuit and simultaneously by backchannel diplomacy, namely when the Bruges council decided to pay the due sum. In the salt ships case embedded in the Nordic Seven Years War (1563–1570), diplomatic games concerning the participation of the Habsburg Netherlands in the war preceded the lawsuit. This

24 Geheimes Staatsarchiv Preußischer Kulturbesitz (henceforth GStPK) XX HA, EM, 28 m nr. 33 9r–12v.

25 Justyna Wubs-Mrozewicz and Alain Wijffels, 'Diplomacy and Advocacy. The Case of the King of Denmark v. Dutch Skippers before the Danzig City Council (1564–67)', *The Legal History Review* 84 (2016), 1–53; and from a political and economic point of view, Justyna Wubs-Mrozewicz, 'Neutrality before Grotius. A City, a State and Seven Salt Ships in the Baltic (1564–67)', *Journal of Early Modern History* (forthcoming).

26 GStPK XX HA, OBA, nr. 18012 and 20715; APG 300D 20/362-364; HR 3: 4 nr. 76; nr. 79§259; 81§26; nr. 138; nr. 170; HR 3:7 nr. 113 §113; H. Samsonowicz, 'Rola Gdańska w życiu stanowym Prus Królewskich', (The role of Gdańsk in Royal Prussia) in Edmund Cieślak (ed.), *Historia Gdańska* vol. II (The History of Gdańsk) (Gdańsk: Wydawnictwo Morskie, 1982), 278.

context makes it very clear that the legal proceedings were a political handmaiden of the Danish and Polish kings in this conflict.[27] Similarly, the lawsuits filed by the Danish Christian II at the *Kammergericht* against the towns of Danzig and Lübeck earlier in the sixteenth century were not so much an attempt to resolve mercantile problems, but to make a political mark.[28] This intertwining of cases shows clearly that in order to understand the practice of mercantile conflict resolution, there is a serious need for all types of available sources for analysis.

Could the end of an individual legal case prompt the end of a war or another serious large-scale conflict? The evidence I examined suggests that this probably hardly ever happened: apparently, it was not a way of regaining control in a large-scale conflict. If, however, we look at the cases where rulers and other towns became more and more involved, one observation can be made. The resolution of such individual conflicts attached to larger controversies could be indicative of the larger interests at stake, such as in the Portinari case when the town of Bruges decided to pay the compensation which the Hanse was due according to the Great Council verdict, on the condition that the Hansards would stay in town. It was an attempt to prevent a permanent move of this economic potential to Antwerp, and thus an attempt to end a political-economic crisis in a town.[29] The same case showed that Hollandish towns were eager to mediate in the conflict in the hope of bringing it to an end, their economic interests being connected both to the Hanse and to Flanders.[30] Also, in the Hinrick van Resen case, the way the lawsuit was approached from both sides showed the precocity of Hollandish-Hanseatic relations, and the desire not to let political and legal differences stand in the way of economic exchange.[31] Finally, the wrapping up of a (seemingly) individual commercial case could also be a litmus test for the balance of power at the highest level. The way a ruler influenced the closure of a case, such as the decision of the Polish king to release the Hollandish ships and goods despite Danish protests in 1567, could be symptomatic of his own change of mind during a conflict. Indeed, with the revelation of the insanity of the Swedish king Eric XIV and the possibility of passing the throne to his brother John III (who at the same time was the

27 Wubs-Mrozewicz and Wijffels, 'Diplomacy and Advocacy'.

28 APG 300, 28/103 fols. 1–34v; HR 3:8 nr. 30, 114, 130.

29 Gelderblom, *Cities*, 174–175; HR 3:6 nr. 188§120.

30 APG 300D 20/294 XX 226; APG 300D 20/295 XX 227; HR 3:3 nr. 180.

31 APG 300,27/11, fols. 18–19v, 41v–42, 55v–56, 152v–153, 185–185v, 231–232, 253–253v, 263v, 268–268v, 321v–322, 357–358v; APG 300, 53–794, fols. 115–121.

husband of a Polish princess), as well as increasing problems with Russia, the Polish king was keen to end or withdraw from the war.[32]

A final observation concerns the connections between small-scale mercantile conflict resolution, and large-scale conflicts with a commercial component. In both categories, a clear end-point was sought, often with symbolic underpinning. This was, on the one hand, a reconciliation with the help of mediators or arbitrators, registered before the town council, or in the case of Danzig, in the *Schöffenbuch*. In the more juridical variant, it was a legal sentence, often followed by an *Urfehde*. And on the other hand, a peace treaty marked the end of a large-scale conflict. Sources for these end points manifest themselves in the solemnity of the content, and the decorative elements within them underline the care with which they were drafted. Apart from the desire to end a conflict, the various symbolic actions which resulted from it were also to have a performative character. They were an attempt to prevent further conflict, be it between individuals, or between towns and states.[33]

3 People

The second category of connections and similarities between juridical and diplomatic conflict resolution which pertained to merchants and trade, which I intend to deal with in this paper, concerns the people involved. These people shaped the course of mercantile conflict resolution in terms of legislation, jurisdiction and external diplomacy, including mediation between towns.

If we look at those who had a direct impact on diplomacy and jurisdiction, the most noteworthy feature is that the very same people – or the same type of people – were responsible for the practical side of conflict resolution. This is discernible for the whole of the period analysed, in the Hanse area as well as outside of it. For the towns in northern Europe, the root of this duplicity lay in the internal and external comprehension of power and representation. As is well known, in pre-modern Europe there was no formal separation of

32 Robert I. Frost, *The Northern Wars: War, State, and Society in Northeastern Europe, 1558–1721* (Harlow: Longman, 2000), 23–44, 74–81; Jacek Wijaczka, 'Prusy królewskie: Dzieje polityczne do 1660' (Royal Prussia: Political History until 1660), in Edmund Kizik (ed.), *Prusy Królewskie: społeczeństwo, kultura, gospodarka 1454–1772* (Gdańsk: Muzeum Narodowe w Gdańsku, 2012), 131–202; Paul G. Schwarz, 'Die Haltung Danzigs im nordischen Kriege 1563–1570 mit besonderer Berücksichtigung der Beziehungen zu Schweden', *Zeitschrift des westpreussischen Geschichtsvereins* 49 (1907), 1–101.

33 APG 300,27/13; APG 300,53/794; APG 300,53/794 fol. 62.

municipal powers into legislative, judiciary and executive branches. Town councillors both formulated laws (or adapted existing law codes), and judged according to them, but as the legal practice shows, they also did so according to political circumstances. In the Portinari case, in 1499 it was the councillors of Bruges who came up with the aforementioned political solution to a problem which at that time was clad in a juridical form: paying the due sum of the sentence of the Great Council of Mechlin instead of the Hansards. The Bruges councillors explicitly stated that they did it in order to maintain relations with the 'Oestlant'.[34]

The intertwining of power in the Hanse area is also clearly apparent in the fact that it went beyond a single town: at Hanseatic Diets, the same councillors were involved in creating shared regulations, for instance on the shipment of goods;[35] in furthering specific cases of merchants tried in Hanseatic towns or elsewhere;[36] and in devising a shared foreign policy towards the rulers.[37] When a merchant was excluded from the Hanse as a result of breaches of law or political agreements in one town, the councillors communicated this decision to all the other towns.[38] Thereby the legal and political side of the commercial Hanse network was activated by its decision makers. Burgomasters and councillors were also envoys to the courts of rulers in Scandinavia, the Netherlands or England, to negotiate trading privileges and the legal position of the Hanseatic merchants abroad, or to reach a peace settlement after a war.[39] For instance in 1537, Hanseatic envoys were invited to the coronation festivities in Copenhagen, which included eight days of *ritterlichen stechspilen*. At first, exasperated that no negotiations could take place because of all the jousting, they eventually decided to make use of the time to draft a full list of arrested goods and present it to the king afterwards. One gets a vivid image of diligent

34 HR 3:4 nr. 157. See also HR 3:3 nr. 735; HR 3:4 nr. 72; HR 3:6 nr. 188 § 120; compare HR 3:3 nr. 677, where the councillors of Bruges stated that they could not prevent the legal action itself.

35 Carsten Jahnke (ed. and trans.), *Flandrischer Copiar Nr. 9. See- und Schiffrechtsbestimmungen* (Lübeck: Schmidt Rømhild, 2003).

36 For instance the Hinrick van Resen case, see note 31.

37 HR 2:4 nr. 589; Justyna Wubs-Mrozewicz, 'Alle goede coepluyden…'. Strategies in the Scandinavian trade politics of Amsterdam and Lübeck c. 1440–1560, in Hanno Brand (ed.), *The Dynamics of Economic Culture in the North-Sea and Baltic Region* (Hilversum: Verloren, 2007), 86–101.

38 Justyna Wubs-Mrozewicz, 'Hinrick van Hasselt: Rebell und Bergenfahrer aus Deventer. Problemlösung im Kontor in Bergen in den 40er Jahren des 16. Jahrhunderts', *Hansische Geschichtsblätter* 124 (2006), 1–20.

39 For instance HR 2:5 nr. 255–258, HR 4:1 nr. 102, HR 4:2 nr. 625.

merchant diplomats scribbling away, while medieval knightly culture carries on in the background.[40] The same type of people were brokers in international politics, for example Danzigers were conducting talks with their sovereign, the Polish king, about the conflicts of the Hanseatic towns with Denmark in the 1520s.[41]

In a similar way, the administrators in the Hanseatic Kontore in London, Bruges, Bergen and Novgorod combined juridical and diplomatic power in their hands. They adjudicated some issues according to the Kontore statutes (for instance insubordination, revealing secrets, defaulted payment of taxes), and forwarded others to the hometowns of Hanseatic merchants, thus coordinating the commercial life of the settlement and the links with the Hanseatic towns.[42] Yet their diplomatic role, namely as intermediaries between the foreign rulers and the Hanse towns, was at least as important. They combined inside knowledge of the local politics of the settlement, and of their Hanseatic hometowns, and were therefore hubs of communication. For instance, they explained to their fellow Hansards in Lübeck that in the Burgundian Netherlands, *de heren und princen doen hiir, wat se willen, mitten steden*. This statement showed that the Hanseatic view on how relations *should* be with the overlord was slightly different.[43] In the Portinari case, the Kontor administrators played a crucial role in steering the course of resolution of this conflict. First, they attempted to contain the damage for the whole Hanse (in line with the task the Kontor had in the Hanse organization) by corresponding with Danzig on the liability for the seizure of the Florentine ship. When the Danzig councillors declined to take the brunt of the cost, the Kontor advised the town on how to proceed with the Burgundian ruler during the diplomatic negotiations, and once Charles the Bold had died, urged them not to pursue the matter further in any way. In the second phase of the conflict, the Kontor administrators were essential in navigating the matter between postponement and action, and eventually in providing information during adjudication before the Great Council of Mechlin. Behind the scenes, the administrators were also negotiating the deal with the Bruges councillors on dropping the charges,

40 HR 4:2 nr. 611 § 29.

41 HR 3:8 nr. 257; HR 3:8 nr. 356; HR 3:8 nr. 452; HR 3:8 nr. 505; HR 3:8 nr. 577; HR 3:9 nr. 116.

42 Nils Jörn, 'Die Herausbildung der Kontorordnungen in Novgorod, Bergen, London und Brügge im Vergleich – 12.–17. Jahrhundert', in Doris Ruhe and Karl-Heinz Spiess (eds.), *Prozesse der Normbildung und Normveränderung im mittelalterlichen Europa* (Stuttgart: Steiner, 2000), 217–235; Mike Burkhardt, 'Kontors and Outposts', in Donald J. Harreld (ed.), *A Companion to the Hanseatic League* (Leiden: Brill, 2015), 127–161.

43 Wubs-Mrozewicz, 'Kopieergedrag'; HR 3:9 nr. 387§6, nr. 388; HR 3:3 nr. 552.

and eventually on keeping the Hanseatic residence in Bruges in return for the payment of the damages to the Portinari party: *wii hebben mit de van Brugghe vele woirde gehat*. Thereby the backchannel diplomats had an impact on the legal outcome of this case, and helped to maintain the nebulous legal status of the Hanse: the actual question of Hanseatic liability was left as unanswered as it was before the litigation.[44]

In large-scale matters which had a commercial and thus also a wider economic underpinning, it is telling that those who held the three power lines in their own hands were eager to act as mediators or arbitrators. This pertained both to rulers of states and to town councillors. While mediation relied more on diplomatic tools of conflict resolution, arbitration was a way to discuss justice outside a court room. The choice between the two depended on the context, but it involved the same people. For instance in a conflict in the 1480s between Danzig on the one hand, and Rostock and Wismar on the other, concerning the confiscation of goods and which resulted in reprisals, both mediation at a Hanse meeting, and the arbitration by three chosen town councils was discussed.[45] When mediation was suggested, even in such complex contexts as the Portinari case, the emphasis was on the mutual relations (i.e. implicitly in the value of maintaining good relations), rather than on the problem.[46] This squares with the insights on how choices are still made nowadays between litigation, arbitration and mediation.[47]

Moreover, it is noteworthy that at the time when the legislative, juridical and diplomatic functions were in the hands of rulers, burgomasters, councillors and administrators of commercial settlements abroad, there was also a firm conviction that this was the correct order of things. In the Hanse area, this appears from the discussions around the position of the secretaries at the Hanseatic Diets and as envoys. From the mid-fifteenth century onwards, most Hanse towns had at least one secretary, often holding a law degree from one of the universities. In this sense, he had enjoyed more specialist training in conflict resolution than the generalist councillors had. At the same time he was

44 HR 3:3 nr. 175; HR 3:3 nr. 181; HR 3:3 nr. 188; HR 3:3 nr. 552; HR 3:3 nr. 678; HR 3:4 nr. 157; HR 3:4 nr. 158; HR 3:4 nr. 189; HR 3:6 nr. 188§§120, 129.

45 HR 3:1 nr. 326, nr. 334§§23–24, 41, 44; nr. 338.

46 HR 3:3 nr. 188.

47 See for instance Stephen B. Goldberg, *Dispute resolution: Negotiation, Mediation, Arbitration, and other Processes*, 6th ed. (New York: Wolters Kluwer Law & Business, 2012); Christopher W. Moore, *The Mediation Process: Practical Strategies for Resolving Conflict*, 4th ed. (San Francisco: Jossey-Bass, 2014); Jacob Bercovitch, *Conflict Resolution in the Twenty-first Century: Principles, Methods, and Approaches* (Ann Arbor: University of Michigan Press, 2009).

able to follow the practice of small- and large-scale conflict resolution from a closer point, being involved in the dealings of the council. Still, his role was far more limited: at the end of the fifteenth century, councillors meeting at Hanseatic Diets expressed great displeasure when a secretary was sent instead of a councillor or burgomaster. The reason was that he did not have equal decision-making power in all the areas required, as the other attendees of the Diet had. The secretary had to leave the room when some matters which were to remain secret were discussed.[48]

However, it does not mean that the category of people involved in conflict resolution related to trade was unchangeable: rather, changes in diplomacy went hand in hand with changes in jurisdiction. The advancement of stronger states, and changes in the way law was perceived, taught and practiced from the sixteenth century on, had a visible impact on how commercial conflicts were resolved. Territorial rulers such as the Polish king had more say on the internal urban policy, administration and law, and towns like Danzig had to take royal politics into account. Changes in litigation within the towns in the sixteenth century developed in a parallel way with changes in external diplomacy. The sources in Danzig show there was an advance in Roman law, a gradual increase the number of academically educated (often meaning trained in law) members of the town councils, advocates started to be used as auxiliaries, and there was renewed use of Latin during trials. Also in diplomacy, legal training started to be a prerequisite for representing a town like Danzig or the interests of all Hanse towns, for instance in negotiations about privileges with the Danish king in 1550 and 1560.[49] This means that the changes affected all people involved in practising juridical and diplomatic conflict resolution. Mercantile issues, both within a town and on a political stage, were dealt with by people who did not necessarily practice trade themselves. The implications of this gradual change deserves detailed examination in its own right.

Finally, we will return to the sources on commercial conflict resolution. The argument advanced in this section has an implication for biographic or prosopographic research on the people behind juridical and diplomatic conflict resolution. Even when a researcher is interested in only one of the two aspects, it is necessary to consult a broad range of sources in order to determine the range of power and the motivations of the conflict fixers, and the challenges and choices they faced. The role of a figure such as the Danish prosecutor Christof Schiffer, who brought Hollandish shippers (and the merchants who freighted

48 HR 2:3 nr. 288§49; HR 3:1 nr. 334§§23–24; HR 3:3 nr. 352§§23, 114, 116–119; HR 3:7 nr. 39§§14–22; HR 3:7 nr. 40§§4–5; HR 3:7 nr. 45§§14–18.

49 Wubs-Mrozewicz, 'Alle goede coepluyden'.

their ships) to court in Danzig in 1565 in the salt ships case, can only be understood when reading the legal proceedings, various types of correspondence and also the instructions he had. Next to litigation on behalf of the Danish king, which was in any case very political in content, he was also to exert diplomatic pressure on the Polish king and the Danzig council. This double role is not surprising when taking into account the long tradition of combining such roles, but various types of sources are needed to see the full extent of it.[50]

4 Language of Conflict and Conflict Resolution

The topic of the language of historical conflict resolution, and more generally that of conflict management, is a vast subject which would deserve a separate monograph. Theory has mostly been formulated on the basis of very recent conflicts.[51] On the other hand, medieval and early modern political conflicts have been studied from the communication angle.[52] Here, I will focus on

---

50 Wubs-Mrozewicz and Wijffels, 'Diplomacy and Advocacy'.

51 Dan Smith, 'Language and Discourse in Conflict and Conflict Resolution', *Current Issues in Language & Society* 4:3 (1997), 190–214. Research on communication and conflict (resolution) focuses mostly on information transfer and communicative strategies, see for instance Robert M. Krauss and Ezequiel Morsella, 'Communication and Conflict', in Morton Deutsch, Peter T. Coleman and Eric C. Marcus (eds.), *The Handbook of Conflict Resolution: Theory and Practice*, 2nd ed. (San Francisco: Jossey-Bass, 2006), 144–157. Peace linguistics is focused on specific words and expressions, and is to a large extent programmatic, see Patricia Friedrich, *Language, Negotiation and Peace: The Use of English in Conflict Resolution* (New York: Continuum, 2007); and Patricia Friedrich, 'English for Peace: Toward a Framework of Peace Sociolinguistics', *World Englishes* 26:1 (2007), 72–83; Francisco Gomes De Matos, 'Language, Peace, and Conflict Resolution', in Morton Deutsch, Peter T. Coleman and Eric C. Marcus (eds.), *The Handbook of Conflict Resolution: Theory and Practice*, 2nd ed. (San Francisco: Jossey-Bass, 2006), 158–175.

52 See for instance the contributions in the recent volumes Mark Häberlein and Christof Jeggle (eds.), *Materielle Grundlagen der Diplomatie. Schenken, Sammeln und Verhandeln in Spätmittelalter und Früher Neuzeit* (Konstanz: UVK Verlagsgesellschaft, 2013); Oliver Auge et al. (eds.), *Bereit zum Konflikt. Strategien und Medien der Konflikterzeugung und Konfliktbewältigung im europäischen Mittelalter* (Ostfildern: J. Thorbecke, 2008); Romy Günthart and Michael Jucker (eds.), *Kommunikation im Spätmittelalter: Spielarten, Wahrnehmungen, Deutungen* (Zürich: Chronos, 2005); Cecilia Nubola and Andreas Würgler (eds.), *Formen der politischen Kommunikation in Europa vom 15. bis 18. Jahrhundert: Bitten, Beschwerden, Briefe* (Berlin: Duncker & Humblot, 2001); see also Gerd Althoff, *Spielregeln der Politik im Mittelalter: Kommunikation in Frieden und Fehden* (Darmstadt: Primus Verlag, 1997).

political and juridical aspects of language which tie in with the previous two sections of the article.

First of all, the outbreak of a war, a diplomatic crisis or taking legal steps was described and explained as being inevitable. The crucial factor was the past: the history of the relations would be drawn in as the handmaiden of politics, or as a way of presenting the context of a legal case. It could range back several decades, or refer to recent past. In the Portinari case, the first phase was the fierce reaction of the Duke of Burgundy in 1473 to the fact that a ship under his neutral flag had been disrespected. In other words, he had no choice but to react.[53] This was a skilful ploy by Tomasso Portinari in the background, who was counting on a diplomatic reaction by a ruler to the action of a privateer. On the other hand, the Hansards argued that the skipper had no choice but to attack a ship heading to an enemy (English) harbour. Moreover, they claimed it was a usual way to proceed during a conflict. They buttressed the argument with references to how the Duke forbade trade with his own enemies in the past, captured ships which did not follow the orders, and waved off any ensuing claims for damages.[54] Such 'historical' rhetoric was recurrent in other conflicts to underpin the statement of inevitability. In the relations between Hansards and Hollanders, the issue of the payment of damages from the first half of the fifteenth century still played a role one hundred years later.[55] The history of this discord was evoked when politically convenient. Another example, in reference to rulers: in the 1520s, when the Hanseatic towns were at war with the Danish king Christian II, his deeds (and those of his privateers) were portrayed as cruel and outrageous in the letters to other European rulers. It was necessary to legitimize the war, especially directed at the regent of the Netherlands, Margaret of Austria, who was a relative of Christian II, and also for Danzig, directed towards their Polish sovereign.[56] Conversely, one of the privateers of Christian II, Severin Norby, claimed that because Lübeckers and Swedes had thrown 300 of his men overboard, without any regard to the fact that some of them were noblemen, he had no choice but to wage war and arrest ships.[57] During the Northern War (1563–1570), the Danish king Frederick II closed the Sound to the east-west traffic with the argument that there was no other way to stop the expansion of the Swedish king.[58]

53 HR 2:7 nr. 28, 29.

54 HR 3:3 nr. 176; HR 3:3 nr. 181.

55 HR 4:2 nr. 120; HR 4:2 p. 441.

56 HR 3:8 nr. 371; HR 3:8 nr. 422; HR 3:8 nr. 455.

57 HR 3:8 nr. 560.

58 APG 300,208/104 fol. 188.

In addition, sources connected to legal proceedings show that bringing the case before one of the juridical fora was also often presented as an inevitable, ultimate step, when all other means had failed. This was for example the case with the debt conflict between a Danzig trader, Jacob Dembker, and his friend from Deventer, Henrick Wenterschwieck, in the 1550s. The very detailed account of the deterioration of their relationship, with attempts to solve the matter directly and then through mediation, bears witness to a reluctance to litigate. But once in court, both parties argued that it was unavoidable.[59] In several cases where widows of shippers and merchants turned to the Danzig town council or to the bench of alderman for legal assistance in securing an inheritance, the necessity of this step was underlined. The driving force was the *grote nodt* and *elend* of the families left behind, and explicit appeals were made to the *christlich Mithleiden*.[60] Finally, in cases when law and diplomacy intersected, namely when the Danish kings started legal proceedings as a means of applying pressure in what were primarily political conflicts, the urgency of such a choice was brought to the fore. This took place in the 1520s, when Christian II decided to sue the towns of Lübeck and Danzig before the imperial *Kammergericht*,[61] and in the 1560s, when Frederick II prosecuted Hollandish shippers before the Danzig town council court for allegedly giving provisions to his enemy.[62] It is telling that both war, and the legal proceedings, could be called war (*Krieg*): it was presented as an ultimate step in a conflict where other means of conflict resolution had failed. Whether this corresponded with the reality is a different matter.[63]

Another analogy is that conflict, be it large- or small-scale, could be presented as threatening and burdensome. In the Low German sources I have investigated, the same adjective was often used for ongoing war and legal proceedings: floating (*schwebend*), i.e. hanging like a dark cloud above those who had little influence on the course of the conflict. In reference to war, it was used for instance when an armed conflict raged nearby, or when it was affecting the local economic situation.[64] When describing legal proceedings with this

59 Wubs-Mrozewicz, 'Mercantile Conflict Resolution'.

60 For instance the 1550s case of the Hamburg widow Armgard Wyneke, APG 300, 53/936 fols. 51, 55–56. See also APG 300 D 31/882 and APG 300,1/4 fols. 192–193.

61 APG 300,28/103 fols. 1–34v; HR 3:8 nr. 30, 114, 130.

62 Wubs-Mrozewicz and Wijffels, 'Diplomacy and Advocacy'.

63 In the juridical context: APG 300, 44/30 fols. 4–5; see also *Deutsches Rechtswörterbuch* online, '*Krieg*' III.

64 For instance when it was in the vicinity: APG 300, 10/1 fol. 356v '*in diesem benachpartem schwebende Kriege*' or in reference to the Dutch Revolt in 1576, APG 300, 93/55a fol. 110 '*jn diesenn schwebenden Kriegsempoerungen in den Niderlanden*'.

term, it denoted a protracted conflict which could have grave political repercussions, such as the salt ships case from the 1560s or the case of an English commercial representative of king Henry VIII, who was seeking justice in Danzig and complained that it took forever.[65] It was also used for the lengthy conflict between the Hanse and Tomasso Portinari.[66]

Furthermore, both types of conflict were frequently described as costly and altogether disastrous for commerce.[67] When parties were drawn into such conflicts without having much choice otherwise, for instance when the Hanseatic towns in Livonia suddenly became the enemies of the Prussian Hanseatic towns in 1455 (during the war the Prussians waged against the Teutonic Order, who remained the overlord of the Livonian towns), they were eager to underline the fact that they considered it unfortunate (*leit*).[68] For neutral towns and states, for example the Habsburg Netherlands and Danzig during the Northern War in the 1560s, expressing their aloofness from the troublesome war in a variety of ways was crucial for maintaining commercial relations with the warring parties in the long run.[69] Finally, when the allegiance of a warring seafarer was uncertain, for instance the infamous shipper Clement, who was connected both to the banished king Christian II and to the town of Amsterdam, the resolution of the commercial problems (among other issues) he had caused to to a Danzig trader proved particularly daunting. The language of conflict resolution had to be chosen with care. Pursuing the legal course would write him off as a pirate and absolve the ruler and the town from responsibility, but it would minimize the chance of regaining the losses. Describing him as privateer, on the other hand, could worsen the crisis in the relationship between Danzig and Holland. One way or another, it was a conflict where *fele misshegelicheit vnd affgunst sso hieruth erwassen kunde*.[70] The costs of conflict and conflict resolution in commercial cases were both economic, and relational.

The relational part of conflict and conflict resolution was very important in terms of wording, both in war and in litigation. From the large-scale perspective, it determined who was to be seen as a participant in a conflict and thus was liable for the commercial losses. In the Portinari case, this was an obvious struggle between Portinari and the Hanse on the one hand, but also of the

---

65 APG 300,28/104 fol. 61v '*erortunge dieser schwebendenn Rechfertigunge*'; APG 300,53/746 fol. 7.

66 HR 3:1 note 1 p. 373; HR 3:4 nr. 72.

67 HR 3:8 nr. 452; HR 3:9 nr. 128; NAU 2 nr. 195; 300, 27/11 fol. 274; Wubs-Mrozewicz, 'Neutrality'.

68 HR 2:4 nr. 325; HR 2:4 nr. 765.

69 Wubs-Mrozewicz, 'Neutrality'.

70 APG 300, 27/12 fol. 298v.

Hanse internally. The Danzig council was very adamant in avoiding forms of communication (specifically, not wanting to spread copies) which would make it possible for Portinari to sue the town individually. Instead, the councillors stressed the collective political responsibility of the Hanse over the problem. They did not want the issue to be *alleyne up unnsen back gelecht warden*. Lübeck, on the other hand, wrote about the captor of the ship as *eynen schippren der Dutzschen hanze, Pawell Beneke genomet, to den tiden vormiddelst de van Dantzick uppe de Engelschen uthgeredet.*[71] This was a complex approach since the Hanse denied a collective legal liability towards rulers or external parties. The very careful choice of formulations shows that in the diplomatic and legal conflict resolution on mercantile matters, language and forms of communication was seen as a useful, but potentially also dangerous, tool.[72]

The rhetoric of the inevitability of a conflict, and the concern with the costs of it, certainly depended on the position of a warring party or a litigant in the conflict, i.e. whether the participation was an active choice or more or less haphazard. Yet it also depended on the phase of the conflict: in many of the cases investigated, there was a crucial shift in the language of conflict resolution, perceptible both in large-scale conflicts and in small-scale discords. Proceeding from the past, where the inevitability of the outbreak of a conflict was stressed, the central phase and thus the present tense of the language of the conflict revolved around threats towards enemies, assurances or demands of reciprocity towards allies, and on what was perceived to be the core of the problem.[73] Once a decision was reached by at least one of the active parties that peace or settlement was to be sought, the focus was shifted towards a discussion of the costs of continuing the conflict and on what it could mean for future relations. The phrase that attempts were made to resolve a matter 'in friendship' (i.e. through dialogue or mediation, rather than armed conflict or law), was recurrent. Even in the Portinari case, the Kontor administrator in Bruges underlined in writings to the Duke of Burgundy that they hoped they would '*redelick in vrundscop to verlikene* (…) *alle moyete van processe und rechtganghe to sparene*'.[74] Both in diplomatic negotiations and in individual cases where mediation was applied, the importance and value of peace was addressed very explicitly. For instance, in the context of the Hinrick van Resen case and the repercussions of the 1520s clash between some of the Hanseatic towns and Holland, the regent of the Netherlands underlined that she was a

71 HR 3:3 nr. 183, 186; HR 3:4 nr. 72; Wubs-Mrozewicz, 'Kopieergedrag'.

72 HR 3:3 nr. 175–179; HR 3:3 nr. 183, 187 § 2; Wubs-Mrozewicz, 'Kopieergedrag'.

73 NAU 1 nr. 453; NAU 2 nr. 195; APG 300 D 20/365.

74 APG 300, 53/794 fol. 34; HR 3:3 nr. 181.

peace lover (*vnss wo leffhebbern fredes*).[75] To add extra weight to it, it was often put in the context of Christian faith.[76]

The language of conflict resolution also referred to the people who were in charge of it. Whether functioning as diplomats and mediators in a large-scale conflict where a considerable issue could be commercial interests, or as mediators, arbitrators or witnesses in individual mercantile conflicts, clear expectations were voiced regarding the persons involved. The interesting aspect is that these expectations overlapped, and can be summarised here in a few adjectives: 'trustworthy', 'of good reputation', and 'of adequate standing and rank'. The latter was of particular importance in the negotiations with foreign rulers; for instance during the Northern War, there was an extensive discussion on who was to be sent from the Netherlands to Copenhagen to conduct talks with the Danish king. Eventually, a suggestion was made that suitable ambassadors were to stay permanently in Denmark to safegurd the crucial access to the Baltic for the Netherlandish traders and shippers.[77] Such persons were also to be 'knowledgeable' of the economic and political circumstances. In the towns of the Hanse rank (in the sense of nobility or of great wealth) was of lesser relevance than it would have been at royal or princely courts or in the Italian towns. Instead, trustworthiness, reputation and experience were central concepts, both for the administrative and the juridical functions that the town councillors had to fill.[78] The oath formulae from the sixteenth century in Danzig show that good intentions to govern and to judge in a proper way were also perceived as being crucial.[79] Similar requirements were expected of the administrators of the Hanseatic Kontore abroad, particularly in Bruges and London.[80]

Finally, we shall examine the language of conflict resolution as language in the stricter sense of this word. In the sixteenth century, a shift took place both in diplomacy and in litigation on commercial matters. On the one hand, there was the increasing use of Latin for the most formal settings, and more

75 APG 300, 27/11 fol. 358. Such an expression could also be a thinly veiled threat, for instance from the regent of the Netherlands to the Hanse towns in 1542, NAU 1 nr. 418.

76 APG 300, 1/4 fols. 192–193; APG 300, 27/28 fols. 153r–154r; Wubs-Mrozewicz, 'Mercantile Conflict Resolution'.

77 NAU 2 nr. 504.

78 Dietrich W. Poeck, *Die Herren der Hanse: Delegierte und Netzwerke* (Frankfurt am Main: Lang, 2010); Thomas Behrmann, *Herrscher und Hansestädte: Studien zum diplomatischen Verkehr im Spätmittelalter* (Hamburg: Kovac, 2004); and Johannes L. Schipmann, *Politische Kommunikation in der Hanse (1550–1621)* (Köln: Böhlau, 2004).

79 APG 300 D/ Bb 28 XVI fol. 3.

80 Jörn, 'Die Herausbildung der Kontorordnungen'; Burkhardt, 'Kontors and Outposts'.

formulaic language can be observed in contexts where the vernacular or other languages would previously have been employed. This has been explained in research as being due to the fact that Roman law was further permeating the court rooms and that more and more often, town councillors enjoyed a classical university training.[81] In the case of contact with the English, in 1465 Hansards expressed regret with the fact that in the past, German was sufficient, but now a 'middelsprake', i.e. Latin, was needed.[82] In the second phase of the Portinari case, the Kontor decided to address the Great Council of Mechlin in writing in Latin, to enhance the formal character of the petition.[83]

On the other hand, however, both diplomatic sources and sources of legal practice from the late fifteenth and the sixteenth centuries offer a very rich rendition of the vernacular. For commercial cases, many versions, perceptions and wordings of the same conflict case can be found. And when witness hearings are examined, the researcher comes as close as it is probably possible to get in northern Europe to the spoken, living contemporary language.[84] This development in part bridges the gap with southern Europe, where commercial private correspondence can be analysed in detail in terms of language from the Middle Ages onwards.[85] In the north, private commercial correspondence has not been preserved to such an extent, so the appearance of more extensive official records is very valuable.[86] The change to the writing of proceedings has much to do with the explosive growth of writing in towns and chanceries, which

81 Dave De ruysscher, *'Naer het Romeinsch recht alsmede den stiel mercantiel': Handel en recht in de Antwerpse rechtbank (16de–17de eeuw)* (Kortrijk-Heule: UGA, 2009); Mark Häberlein, *Brüder, Freunde und Betrüger: Soziale Beziehungen, Normen und Konflikte in der Augsburger Kaufmannschaft um die Mitte des 16. Jahrhunderts* (Berlin: Akademie Verlag, 1998), 260.

82 HR 2:5 nr. 712.

83 HR 3:3 nr. 175; HR 3:3 nr. 182.

84 See for instance the hearings discussed in Wubs-Mrozewicz, 'Mercantile Conflict Resolution'.

85 Ricardo Court, 'Januensis Ergo Mercator': Trust and Enforcement in the Business Correspondence of the Brignole Family, *The Sixteenth Century Journal* 35:4 (2004), 987–1003; and Ricardo Court, 'The Language of Trust: Reputation and the Spread and Maintenance of Social Norms in Sixteenth Century Genoese Trade', *Rime* 1 (2008), 77–96; Sebouh Aslanian, 'The Salt in a Merchant's Letter': The Culture of Julfan Correspondence in the Indian Ocean and the Mediterranean, *Journal of World History* 19:2 (2008), 127–188.

86 For the Hanse, the well preserved correspondence of Hildebrand Veckinchusen with more than 500 letters is an exceptional source, see Wilhelm Stieda (ed.), *Hildebrand Veckinchusen. Briefwechsel eines deutschen Kaufmanns im 15. Jahrhundert* (Leipzig: Hirzel, 1921).

was at least in part related to the availability of cheaper paper.[87] Apparently, if there is something that is worth writing about a great deal, it is conflict: either a large-scale or a small-scale conflict.

5 Conclusions

A common adage has it that a conflict has many sources. The main point of this article has been to demonstrate that in order to understand how commercial conflicts were resolved, many historical sources should be used. Sources of law and legal practice are natural twins. Yet there is more to be found. In this article, I have argued that sources on legal practice (legal proceedings, letters of individual traders and of town councils, contracts and entries in town books) should be combined in analyses with diplomatic sources (letters to and between rulers, instructions to envoys, reports of war and diplomatic negotiations, privileges and their copies). The resolution of commercial conflicts was at the heart of the law, legal practice, and the economic and political interests of towns and rulers of medieval and early modern states. Since these spheres were not treated as separate, there were several interrelations and parallels between large- and small-scale conflicts which affected traders.

On the basis of sources connected to the commercial activity of Danzigers c. 1450–1580, I have analysed these links in terms of the beginnings and endings of conflicts, the people involved in conflict resolution, and the language of conflict resolution. The result of the analysis is that there were causal relations in the outbreak and resolution of conflict which went both ways, and accordingly, both diplomatic and legal tools were used. In the case of small-scale commercial conflicts, it has been the aim to demonstrate that the sometimes surprising, unpredictable endings were caused by the large-scale political and economic climate. A shared trait is that a symbolic ending was pursued in both types of conflict. The parallels can also be found when examining people who attempted to resolve conflicts: members of town councils, administrators of settlements abroad or representatives sent by rulers were involved in large- and small-scale conflict resolution. Moreover, the requirements posed to them changed in a parallel way in reference to both legal and diplomatic conflict resolution. Finally, the language shows several analogies between individual

87 See the research project by Megan Williams (University of Groningen): http://www.paperprinces.org/ and her article 'Unfolding Diplomatic Paper and Paper Practices in Early Modern Chancellery Archives', in Arndt Brendecke (ed.), *Praktiken der Frühen Neuzeit* (Köln: Böhlau Verlag, 2015), 496–509.

commercial conflicts, and large-scale conflicts where economy and commerce in particular played an important role. These are: expressions of the inevitability of the outbreak of the conflict (due to the history of the relations, the outrageous behaviour of the other party, the lack of choice since other means of conflict resolution and prevention had been exhausted); perceptions of conflicts as threatening and burdensome; careful choice of wording in conflict resolution with the view of the legal and political responsibility for losses during the conflict; and shifts from the problem towards the importance of relations and the value of peace, when a solution was desired.

If we follow the premise that premodern commercial law builds upon legal practice, then this analysis shows that the sources of commercial law include sources of commercial conflict resolution, and of commercial diplomacy. For all the interested parties, there is a wide river in which to fish.

CHAPTER 3

Justitia in Commerciis: Public Governance and Commercial Litigation before the Great Council of Mechlin in the Late Fifteenth and Early Sixteenth Century

Alain Wijffels

1 Introduction: Summary and General Thesis

There is a risk that legal historiography considers commercial law too narrowly as a branch of private law, or too exclusively as rules governing merchants as private individuals in their mutual professional dealings. The practice of late medieval and early modern courts in the context of the present contribution, specifically at the Great Council of Mechlin, shows, however, that because trade was then, as it still is today, a central issue of public governance, trade regulations which would nowadays be labelled as parts of public law and public international law played an important part not only in the relations between public authorities and merchants (as individuals or corporations), but also in any commercial venture a merchant was considering. Because justice and its administration were an essential feature of what was considered, from medieval times onwards, to be good public governance – a fundamental element of legitimacy for any ruler – merchants who were dissatisfied with the regulations of trade and their implementation would seek redress before the ruler's court. A review of cases involving merchants and merchants' interests before the Great Council during the last decades of the fifteenth century and the first decades of the sixteenth century shows that even in proceedings where primarily private parties were litigating, public policy considerations were often at stake and were duly taken into account as such, i.e. with an eye for the broader public interests the specific case could affect. A considerable number of cases which obviously fit such a characterization are proceedings on a wide variety of taxes, duties and restrictive measures. During the period of reference, violence at sea, in particular through robbery, piracy and privateering, was also a cause for merchants to seek remedies from a public authority, often through court proceedings, and the central authority could see its own advantage in extending its jurisdiction to such cases. Thus, much of what

 | DOI 10.1163/9789004363144_004

qualifies today as 'public law' was part of the costs, risks and profits calculations which were anticipated by merchants in the preparation of their more ambitious ventures, or on which they fell back when a venture went wrong. This strengthened even further the relation between the principles of good governance and commercial regulations. Any historical study of commercial law has therefore to include public governance to perceive the broader picture.

2 Preliminary Caveat

'Commercial litigation' in the title of the present contribution should be understood in a broad and flexible sense. During the period under review, there was arguably not yet a precisely defined branch of the law which can be referred to as 'commercial law', nor was commercial law in a modern sense included in any other specific branch of the law. Since medieval times, however, it had been recognised that trade, the legal status of merchants and their business relations, agreements arising from or pertaining to trade, as well as litigation on all such issues, could justify to a greater or lesser extent a distinctive approach with regard to regulation, substantive law to be applied, the determination of the forum, and the proceedings before that forum. Depending on the geographical, political, social and cultural context, the degree of that recognition could vary. In a centre where trade played a significant part in the polity's life and economy, the disposition to recognise distinct features in merchants' dealings and conflicts would obviously be greater than elsewhere. Admittedly, practically every city in the middle ages would have depended to a greater or lesser extent on its industry and trade, so that specific rules on trade may be found almost everywhere. The character of trade in any specific jurisdiction – local, regional, international – would also play a role. A specific legal literature on commercial issues only started developing during the second half of the sixteenth century.[1] For other legal authorities, such as statutes, customs, or treaties, specific (clusters of) rules on commercial issues appear much earlier.

1 The collection of treatises *De mercatura seu mercatore tractatus* by Benvenuto Stracca (1509–1579), first published in 1553, was one of the first, if not the first, legal imprint dealing specifically with merchants' law. On Stracca, see the entry by Vito Piergiovanni in *Dizionario biografico dei giuristi italiani* (*XII–XX secolo*), vol. 2 (Bologna: Il mulino, 2013), 1920–1922; on *De mercatura*: Charles Donahue Jr, 'Benvenuta Stracca's *De Mercatura*: Was There a *Lex Mercatoria* in Sixteenth-Century Italy?', in Vito Piergiovanni (ed.), *From lex mercatoria to commercial law* (Berlin: Duncker & Humblot, 2005), 69–120. See, in Donahue's article, the two appendices offering an outline of the *Tractatus*'s contents: the general structure appears to be inspired by that of the Roman law Institutes (*personae, res, actiones*), with, generally

By the time the Burgundian-Habsburg Great Council in the Low Countries developed into a more or less autonomous court during the second quarter of the fifteenth century,[2] industry and trade were a major feature of the economic, social and political life in the Low Countries' key-cities and territories, in particular the seafront counties of Flanders, Zeeland and Holland, and the (politically) landlocked Duchy of Brabant.[3]

3 Trade, Merchants, and Public Governance

As will be emphasized further on in the present contribution, trade – along with justice, economic policies, including monetary policies, taxation and the organisation of industry – belonged to the core areas of public governance. Whether a ruler's government was a form of *buon governo* or *gutes Regiment* depended on the virtues and effectiveness of his governance in those areas. It is therefore hardly surprising that justice, economic policies and trade make up a substantial and essential part of the growing legislation of late-medieval and early-modern princes. Trade, moreover, unlike justice, was not an area which belonged only to the home affairs of the ruler's polity: because it also affected international trade, one finds that statute law on interregional trade within the polity was supplemented by an increasingly important body of international instruments in which the interests of merchants, both subjects of the ruler and foreign merchants, and the general commercial interests of the polities involved, were at times regulated in great detail.[4] Comparatively few provisions in that statute law for domestic use and

speaking, an emphasis on private law (substantive law and legal proceedings in commercial cases). Today, the work is most easily accessible through the reprint: Benvenutus Straccha, *Tractatus de mercatura, seu mercatore* (Lugduni, Apud Sebastianum de Honoratis, 1558; reprint Goldbach: Keip, 1997), which also includes the *Tractatus de sponsionibus et assecurationibus mercatorum*, an earlier example of a monograph-type work on a more specific range of merchant law topics (Toon Van Houdt, 'Petrus Santerna, pionnier de l'assurance', *Bulletin du Crédit Communal* 180 (1992), 15–25), and other texts on commercial law by Ioannes Nider, Baldus de Ubaldis and Rodericus Suarez.

2 Jan Van Rompaey, *De Grote Raad van de hertogen van Boergondië en het Parlement van Mechelen* (Brussel: Paleis der Academiën, 1973); Alida J.M. Kerckhoffs-de Hey, *De Grote Raad en zijn functionarissen 1477–1531* (Amsterdam, 1980).

3 On the Duchy of Brabant's attempts to gain sovereign access to the sea for its maritime trade: Alain Wijffels, 'Emergence et engloutissement judiciaires du "Brabant maritime". Les prétentions territoriales sur l'Escaut occidental durant la seconde moitié du XVe siècle', *Publication du Centre européen d'études bourguignonnes (XIVe–XVIe s.)* 42 (2002), 55–73.

4 The sophistication of such instruments is illustrated by (e.g.) the *Magnus Intercursus* (1496), which remained a reference for generations, and the *Malus Intercursus* (Thomas Rymer (comp.), *Foedera, conventiones, literae, Et cujuscunque generis acta publica inter Reges*

in international treaties deal with issues of commercial law as the body of law governing the professional and business relations between merchants only as private individuals. Consequently, the law on trade as a characteristic branch of public governance law, dealing primarily with the merchants' commercial interests and the polity's general interest, has been mostly left out from historical studies focusing on the history of commercial law understood as the private law of merchants and business.

The whole range of normative principles of conduct, from business practice to positive written rules of law governing the commercial operations between merchants was of course a substantial part of the 'frame of reference' merchants had in mind when planning and putting into effect their trade. However, in the balancing of costs and profits which a commercial operation or larger venture entailed, that private law of merchants may not in most cases have been the primary concern of a merchant. From the merchants' perspective, many issues which would now be regarded as political or public law issues, would play an even more important part in the calculation of expected costs and profits: political stability in the region where the commercial operation would take place, various forms of taxation on the journeys to and from the regions where the operations were planned, export and import restrictions, the status and protection of foreign merchants (including legal and judicial means of defending one's claims), access to the local markets and so on. All these areas linked to domestic or foreign trade belonged to the responsibility of a ruler's good public governance – whether the ruler was a monarch, an ecclesiastical office-holder, or a city council.

4 Legal Authorities on Trade-related Issues

Legal rules specifically relating to merchants, their trade and the solution of conflicts involving merchants in their professional or business capacity reflect, characteristically for the way late-medieval and early modern law worked, a measure of jurisdictional complexity. Customary law and statute law were the most important authorities.[5] The learned *ius commune* tradition of civil

Angliae, et alios quosvis imperatores, reges, pontifices, principes vel communitates, ed. tertia, vol. 5, Part 4 [*Hagae Comitis, Apud Joannem Neaulme*, 1741], respectively on pages 81–87 and 223–227).

5 Arguably, norms which could be regarded as rules of professional ethics and business practice, but possibly not as customary rules in a strictly legal sense, also played a major role. However, such norms remain almost by definition to a large extent beyond the sources of legal history, and once they do enter into the horizon of legal history, these norms have often

and canon law was relevant, especially in the higher courts, where university-educated jurists were employed, for providing general principles and concepts, rules of construction, procedural rules, and occasionally – and in theory only as a subsidiary authority – rules of substantive law (e.g. the sections on the S.C. Velleianum, in discussions on the capacity of married women).[6] The authority of *ius commune* could also work indirectly. Until the sixteenth century, and for the Low Countries even until the beginning of the seventeenth century, legal works based on *iura propria* were comparatively scarce. And although the *ius commune* only produced major works on merchants' law from the mid-sixteenth century onwards, e.g. in the Netherlands, P. Peck's civil law commentaries on maritime trade,[7] the general commentaries included *sedes materiae* which could be topical on commercial issues. Moreover, specifically relevant legal literature could already be found at an earlier stage in particular sections of the collections of legal consultations and in the civil law style reports (*Decisiones*). Particularly for the second half of the sixteenth century, both such consultations and law reports in printed form remain at present the most accessible source-material in order to gain a first-hand insight into the practice of the higher courts.[8]

In general, the early-modern practice of the superior courts appears to be following the principles of the theory of legal authorities[9] established by late medieval scholarship.[10] Inevitably, however, in legal practice – including

---

been going through a process turning them into legal – *viz.* customary – rules. That was usually the result of their use by professional lawyers who had been trained in a law faculty.

6 The S.C. Velleianum is quoted here because it is, in the context of a merchant's family business arrangements and liability, a recurrent theme in Belgian practice-orientated legal literature of the sixteenth and seventeenth centuries; see for that literature Alain Wijffels, 'Business Relations Between Merchants in Sixteenth-Century Belgian Practice-Orientated Civil Law Literature', in Vito Piergiovani (ed.), *From Lex Mercatoria to Commercial Law* (Berlin: Duncker & Humblot, 2005), 255–290.

7 On Petrus Peckius, *Commentaria in omnes pene iuris civilis titulos ad rem nauticam pertinentes* (*ed. pr.* Lovanii, Petrus Colonaeus, 1556), see the corresponding entry by Dave De ruysscher in Georges Martyn et al. (eds.), *Books That Made the Law* (forthcoming).

8 Wijffels, 'Business Relations Between Merchants'; that literature is now being thoroughly researched by Mr Wouter Druwé (Leuven) in the context of his PhD dissertation on credit, money lending and interest; several of the papers he has presented while this paper was written are now likely to be in the press.

9 Wolfgang Wiegand, *Studien zur Rechtsanwendungslehre der Rezeptionszeit* (Ebelsbach: R. Gremer, 1977).

10 Alain Wijffels, *Qui millies allegatur, Les allégations du droit savant dans les dossiers du Grand Conseil de Malines (causes septentrionales, ca. 1460–1580)* (Leiden: E.J. Brill,

the consultations by academic jurists submitted in the course of litigation – counsel would ply that theory and those principles for the opportunistic purpose of their clients' interests. Legal arguments in *consilia* involving merchants' litigation nonetheless show a tendency to narrow down applicable *iura propria* (customs and statutes) to a particular law *ratione loci* (for the sixteenth century, when a large part of commercial litigation appearing in printed consultations originated in Antwerp, the Antwerp custom),[11] rather than a regional or international *lex mercatoria*. That argumentative device made it possible to apply primarily the local rule, but also to adjust it according to *ius commune* principles of construction. A common argument consisted of asserting the congruency between the alleged *ius proprium* rule and, as that rule was being construed, the *ius commune*. For example, in a *consilium* by Leoninus, a professor in the law faculty at Louvain, the central legal issue was whether an insurance against a past risk was valid or not.[12] Counsel for the opponents referred to various foreign customs which declared such a contract void, implying perhaps that this was a general rule applicable among merchants. Leoninus, on the contrary, maintained that under some circumstances, such an insurance would stand and that the practice was admitted by Antwerp (merchants') custom. Moreover, he argued that *ius commune* agreed with the Antwerp particular rule.

A degree of specificity granted to the merchants' *ius proprium* was further enhanced through two other devices which had already been developed by late medieval and canon law scholarship: on the one hand, the adjustment of rules through the concept of a specific type of equity, *aequitas mercatoria*;[13] and, on the other hand, taking into account policy considerations. The concepts of equity and policy considerations could, to some extent, overlap.[14]

Universitaire Pers Leiden, 1985), [*necnon in*: *Verzamelen en bewerken van de jurisprudentie van de Grote Raad*, Nieuwe Reeks, X (Amsterdam, 1985)].

11 Wijffels, 'Business Relations Between Merchants', 264–265.

12 Elbertus Leoninus, *Centuria Consiliorum* (Antverpiae: Ex officina Christophori Plantini, 1584), Cons. 22, pages 132–136, discussed in Wijffels, 'Business Relations Between Merchants', 256–259.

13 Charles Donahue Jr, 'Equity in the Courts of Merchants', *Tijdschrift voor rechtsgeschiedenis* 72 (2004), 1–35; Wijffels, 'Business Relations Between Merchants', 276–282 (*aequitas mercatoria*).

14 Wijffels, 'Business Relations Between Merchants', 283–288; and Alain Wijffels, 'Argumentationsmuster in belgisch-niederländischen Konsiliensammlungen des 16. Jahrhunderts. "Policy considerations" in der *ius commune*-Tradition', in Albrecht Cordes (ed.), *Juristische Argumentation – Argumente der Juristen* (Köln: Böhlau, 2006), 55–73.

5 Higher Judicature and Public Governance on Trade

Since medieval times, a thriving trade has been viewed as one of the typical benefits of good public governance.[15] Both for practical policy considerations and because of the underlying ideology of public governance in the Western tradition, rulers have therefore been expected to include the development and protection of trade as one of their main priorities. To some extent, the rise of early-modern sovereigns who succeeded in eliminating or subordinating competing political actors, many of whom had played a prominent part in medieval times, was due to the fact that those early modern sovereigns were able to impress on their subjects that they were in a better position than local or regional government to defend their interests and thus provide a more efficient governance. In the Low Countries, the Burgundian and Hapsburg rulers were on the whole quick to acknowledge that their power and the success of their domestic and foreign policies would largely depend on their capacity to enhance the industrial and commercial potential of their territories in the Netherlands. Law and justice, as essential features of what was understood to be necessary in order to achieve good governance, was a prominent part of their legislative and institutional programme.

In the central institutions created under the Burgundian regime, litigation where merchants were involved occurred frequently. The superior, but not always supreme or sovereign, provincial courts were mostly courts of appeal, but they would also in many cases have jurisdiction in first-instance proceedings.[16]

15 One famous example is the representation of the *buon governo* by A. Lorenzetti in the town hall of Siena, especially the fresco on the positive effects of good public governance, which shows a thriving agriculture, trade and industry. Alain Wijffels, 'Van *buon governo* naar *public governance*: Juristen en openbaar bestuur in de Westerse rechtstraditie', *Ars Aequi, juridisch maandblad* 62 (2013), 776–785.

16 In the main principalities mentioned above, there was (apart from special cases) a three-tier system of courts: a local court (e.g. of the city), a provincial court, which since the personal union of the Dukes of Burgundy expressed the ruler's supreme jurisdiction within the principality (e.g. the Council of Flanders in Ghent, for the County of Flanders; the Council of Brabant in Brussels, for the Duchy of Brabant; the Court of Holland in The Hague, for the county of Holland; all these courts had both first-instance and appellate jurisdiction). The Great Council of Mechlin had been intended to act as a 'central' paramount court for all the territories in the Burgundian Low Countries, and for a while it functioned as such, both in first-instance cases and as an appellate court (as well as, in some cases, as a court of revision). However, by the early sixteenth century at the latest, some principalities objected to having the decisions of their provincial supreme court challenged before the Great Council: that was notably the case of Brabant. The situation in the County of Zeeland (which was bound in a personal union with Holland, as it were,

The supreme court of appeal in the Low Countries, the Great Council of Mechlin, combined both first-instance and appellate jurisdiction. First-instance jurisdiction (as a *privilegium fori*) was claimed in favour of, among several other categories, foreign merchants.[17] In addition, politically sensitive cases – and most cases involving wider issues of trade beyond the private interests of the individual litigants would have been deemed to be politically sensitive – could also be (and, it seems, were often effectively) dealt with, either at a preliminary stage or while the case was already pending before an inferior or superior court, by the Privy Council, which had developed wide-ranging quasi-judicial powers parallel to its administrative and governmental tasks.[18]

A comprehensive understanding of how public governance was reflected in the practice of the superior courts of the Netherlands would require systematic research into the records of those superior courts. That is unlikely to be feasible in the foreseeable future. For Brabant, the main first-instance court for commercial litigation during the sixteenth century was the Antwerp

---

within the more general personal union of the Low Countries) was still different, for that county did not have its own provincial court: Zeeland litigants could either appeal against decisions of their local courts to the Court of Holland (with the possibility of a further appeal to Mechlin), or challenge the local court's decision directly before the Great Council (a procedural remedy called 'reformation'). During the sixteenth century, the Privy Council developed a strong jurisdictional activity of its own, which could act as a parallel supreme judicature along that of the Great Council, or even in a superior position to the Great Council. Because the Privy Council sat in Brussels, the Brabant privilege of not having Brabant subjects forced to appear in a court outside the duchy did not prevent the Privy Council to enforce its jurisdiction in the duchy. Alain Wijffels, 'Grand Conseil des Pays-Bas à Malines (vers 1445–1797)', in Erik Aerts et al. (eds.), *Les institutions du gouvernement central des Pays-Bas-Habsbourgeois: 1482–1795*, vol. 1 (Bruxelles: Archives générales du Royaume, 1995), 448–462.

17 Cf. Art. I.11 of the 1522 Ordinance on the Great Council: '*Item, auront lesdits président et gens de nostre grand conseil la cognoissance en première instance de tous marchans estrangiers, vivans pardechà soubs prévilège, on ayans aucuns domiciles, ou de plusieurs marchans, aussi estrangiers, résidens en divers lieux, soubs divers ressors et pour la connexité des causes et matières ou pour obvier à multiplication de procès*'. The section is discussed by Cornelis H. (Remco) van Rhee, *Litigation and Legislation: Civil Procedure at First Instance in the Great Council for the Netherlands in Malines (1522–1559)* (Brussels: Algemeen Rijksarchief, 1997), 36–38: whether the last part is a ground of competence in its own right. See also, van Rhee, *Litigation and Legislation*, 41, n. 64, the jurisdiction of the Council of Flanders with regard to some categories of foreign merchants in the County of Flanders. The section in the 1522 ordinance was repeated in the Ordinance of 1559 (art. I.10).

18 Hugo de Schepper, 'Conseil Privé (1504–1794)', in Erik Aerts et al. (eds.), *Les institutions du gouvernement central des Pays-Bas-Habsbourgeois: 1482–1795*, vol. 1 (Bruxelles: Archives générales du Royaume, 1995), 287–317.

court, the records of which, as far as they have been kept for that period, have recently been researched by D. De ruysscher.[19] For the provincial, appellate and sovereign court of Brabant, which would have dealt with appeals from the local Antwerp court, direct systematic access to commercial cases may prove to be more cumbersome. The records of the Privy Council's judicial practice remain largely *terra incognita*. For the Great Council of Mechlin, calendars of the judgements (until approx. 1585) and inventories for some series of case-files are available,[20] but the Council had no jurisdiction for the Duchy of Brabant from the early years of the sixteenth century onwards, and for the appeals from the County of Flanders, only a relatively small part of the records can be retrieved, whereas on the other hand, the records of the provincial Council of Flanders have been calendared. As a result, commercial litigation in the sixteenth-century practice of the Great Council can to some extent be traced systematically through the existing calendars, but a similar study is more difficult for the Council of Brabant and the Privy Council. Some insight into the practice of the Great Council can be gained from case-studies which combine records and, when available, printed *consilia* and *decisiones*.[21]

19 Dave De ruysscher, *'Naer het Romeinsch recht alsmede den stiel mercantiel': Handel en recht in de Antwerpse rechtbank (16de–17de eeuw)* (Kortrijk-Heule: UGA, 2009).

20 Alain Wijffels, 'Dutch Litigation before the Great Council of Mechlin: An Additional Calendar of the "Appeals from Holland"', *Tijdschrift voor rechtsgeschiedenis* 77 (2009), 539–550, with further references. For a recent overall survey of the records of the Great Council of Mechlin: Dirk Leyder, *Les archives du Grand Conseil des Pays-Bas à Malines (vers 1445–1797)* (Bruxelles: Archives générales du Royaume, 2010).

21 Some of the single case-studies based primarily on Great Council records (and sometimes combined with printed *consilia* or *decisiones*) which I have written deal directly or indirectly with merchants or commercial interests. Alain Wijffels, 'Een prince ende heere van justitie: Un avis de G. Mudaeus sur l'organisation d'une table de prêt', *Tijdschrift voor Rechtsgeschiedenis* 64 (1996), 113–139; Alain Wijffels, 'Flanders and the Scheldt Question: A Mirror of the Law of International Relations and its Actors', *Sartoniana* 15 (2002), 213–280 (Part I); Alain Wijffels, 'Toll-Free Navigation on the Honte ca. 1466–1468: A Legal Consultation by J. Boods, Pensionary of Antwerp', *Bulletin* 50 (2009) [= 2012], 175–201; Alain Wijffels, 'Ius commune and International Wine Trade, A Revision (Middelburg c. Antwerp, 1548–1559)', *Tijdschrift voor Rechtsgeschiedenis* 71 (2003), 289–317, and its sequel: 'A Consultancy on Wine Imports', *Tijdschrift voor rechtsgeschiedenis* 73 (2005), 321–355; Alain Wijffels, 'Une consultation de Wamèse sur une question de droit fiscal', in *Liber Amicorum Jacques Malherbe* (Bruxelles: Bruylant, 2006), 1169–1194; Alain Wijffels, 'Vicarious Liability for the Carrier by River?', *Tijdschrift voor rechtsgeschiedenis* 75 (2007), 333–353.

6 Case Studies

Some of the case-studies already available show that judicial proceedings were instrumental in managing and adjusting conflicts of trade interests involving several regions. The cases reflect not only conflicts of private interests i.e. of private merchants or professional corporations, but also inter-regional conflicts of interests which affected the general domestic and international trade policies of the central government, and hence the Habsburgs' economic governance in the Low Countries. Here, two examples may briefly illustrate the point.

The first example is a litigation from 1566–1574 between merchants from Oudenaarde in the southern part of the County of Flanders and the Corporation of Free Shippers in Ghent.[22] The claimants had suffered damage when a ship run by members of the Corporation carrying the goods of the former capsized in the river. The central legal issue was whether the Corporation could be held vicariously liable for the damage caused through the negligence of one of its members. There was a *prima facie* case in favour of the Corporation's vicarious or at least subsidiary liability on the grounds of s. 20 of Charles V's 1541 ordinance on the carriage of goods on the rivers Scheldt, Leie and Lieve, which seemed to phrase the Corporation's liability in broad terms. However, counsel for the Corporation, assisted by two consultants from the Louvain law faculty, were able to argue that the section had to be construed restrictively in the light of the ordinance's purpose. Their argument went back to the circumstances in which the statute had been enacted, at the time when the Emperor was meting out a series of punishments towards Ghent after the city had rebelled in 1536–1540. At the same time, the central government had taken the opportunity to regulate commercial shipping on the rivers of Flanders and its neighbouring provinces. Thus, in litigation about private interests, learned lawyers were able to interpret an ordinance in the light of the public policies it was intended to serve. The ordinance itself had been enacted in 1541 through a quasi-judicial process involving the various interest-groups who were affected by transport by river in Flanders and the neighbouring Hapsburg dominions.

The second example is drawn from litigation between the rival cities of Middelburg in Zeeland and Antwerp in Brabant in 1548–1559.[23] The issue of tolls and other imposts levied on the estuary of the Scheldt river had already been a source of litigation between Zeeland and Brabant interest-groups before the

22 The case is discussed in detail in Wijffels, 'Vicarious Liability for the Carrier by River?'

23 Wijffels, 'Ius commune and International Wine Trade', and 'A Consultancy on Wine Imports'.

Great Council in the fifteenth century and during the first years of the sixteenth century, ending in 1504 with the Council's judgement in favour of the Count of Zeeland's right to levy a toll on the Scheldt estuary. The toll did not prevent the rise of Antwerp as a major international harbour and trade centre, but throughout the sixteenth century and until the 1580s, when, as a consequence of the Dutch revolt, the Scheldt estuary was closed for navigation to and from Antwerp, the commercial rivalry between Zeeland and Brabant – and in particular between the cities of Middelburg and Antwerp – continued to be a source of conflicts and, at times, litigation. During the 1540s, Middelburg, which claimed a crane privilege and a gauge-privilege, used those privileges to interfere with Antwerp-bound navigation on the Scheldt and the import of goods. The case led to protracted proceedings, including extraordinary revision proceedings, and ended with a judgement in favour of Middelburg. That, however, was not the end of the controversy, as Antwerp appealed to the States of Brabant to lobby the central government for a new, more favourable legislation. At first sight, the legal proceedings started around fairly simple facts, when a foreign ship with a cargo of wine was set off course by a storm on its way to Antwerp, and had to submit to the crane-duty exercised by Middelburg in Zeeland. The issue was whether an involuntary and temporary stop in Zeeland would justify Middelburg's levy of duties which would otherwise only have been due at the port of the ship's final destination, *viz.* Antwerp. Both cities submitted consultations by Louvain law professors – Leoninus for Middelburg; Mudaeus and Peckius for Antwerp. In this case, too, a large part of the legal arguments focused on the interpretation, through *ius commune* rules, of the statutes on which Middelburg relied. Both parties also argued on the strength of policy considerations, anticipating the negative effects for the sovereign's income and for international trade in the Low Countries if their opponent's claims were to be admitted. Middelburg also argued that the duties it levied were necessary for maintaining the waterways in the Scheldt estuary, from which navigation to and from Antwerp therefore benefited. The close link between public governance and general welfare, policy considerations and commercial interests can be appreciated in the following quotations from Leoninus's consultation on behalf of Middelburg: 'For no harm is done by the application of this statute to the general trade or to the freedom of navigation, but it simply provides a proportionate remedy against fraud, and it rules out uncertainty. That is consistent with the law and with distributive justice, and it relates to both the highest degree of reason and equity itself'.[24] Middelburg's privileges were

24 *'Nam publicis commerciis aut libertati navigandi nihil per observantiam dictae Constitutionis detrahitur, sed duntaxat aequabili remedio adversus fraudes providetur, et incertitudo*

justified because they were said to be 'in the interest of the commonwealth and for the Prince, and in order to maintain more strongly justice in trade'.[25] Mudaeus and Peckius ventured onto more dangerous grounds when they challenged the extensive interpretation of the statutes granting privileges to Middelburg, because of the inherent qualifications associated by late-medieval legal principles to the exercise of the ruler's *plenitudo potestatis* – not perhaps, under the rule of Charles V of Philip II, the politically most effective line of argumentation, as the concept of sovereignty had by then much evolved since it had been dealt with by the Italian jurists in their medieval city-states.[26] In any case, the judicial decision in favour of Middelburg did not prevent the development of Antwerp's supremacy as a commercial centre. Therefore, competition and rivalry between the city and Zeeland interests continued to dominate their conflictual relations. It is an example where neither judicial nor administrative proceedings and decisions could put an end to the conflict of interests: such proceedings were not instrumental in conflict resolution, but rather in conflict management. That was the lawyers' main contribution to the public governance of their time.

Beyond individual case-studies, thematic studies based primarily on cases i.e. final judgments and/or case-files, may contribute to help tease out features transcending the individual circumstances of a particular case, however characteristic and representative of wider issues these may be. For example, the Great Council records for the late fifteenth and sixteenth centuries document several legal proceedings involving cities from Holland and Zeeland entangled in disputes about inter-city and interregional beer trade.[27] The fact that even though the interests of private enterprises were often on the forefront of controversies, the cities came up as the principal litigants in most cases, and this shows that public interests were at stake. That was not only true for legal proceedings originating in internal disputes e.g. between an

---

excluditur; quod juri et justitiae commutativae est consentaneum, et cum summa ratione ac ipsa aequitate conjunctum. [...]' (quoted in Wijffels, 'Ius commune and International Wine Trade', 305, from Elbertus Leoninus, *Consilia*, Cons. 8).

25 '...*utilitati reipublicae et Principi, et ad magis conservandam justitiam in commerciis*' (quoted in Wijffels, 'Ius commune and International Wine Trade', 308, from the same *consilium* as above, previous note).

26 Alain Wijffels, 'Early-Modern *Consilia* and *Decisiones* in the Low Countries: The Lost Legacy of the *mos italicus*', in Paola Maffei and Gian Maria Varanini (eds.), *Honos alit artes: Studi per il settantesimo compleanno di Mario Ascheri*, vol. 1 (Firenze: Firenze University Press, 2014), 125–137.

27 Alain Wijffels, 'Gelehrtes Recht und Wirtschaftsordnung: Niederländische "Bierkriege" im 15. und 16. Jahrhundert', *Zeitschrift für Neuere Rechtsgeschichte* 25 (2003), 177–203.

individual brewer or trader and the city authorities, or between brewers or traders within the same city, but also for proceedings involving different cities from the same region or province, or cities in inter-provincial disputes, and proceedings between a city and the central government. A characteristic feature in those cases was that, although the counsel's legal arguments were rarely very sophisticated, they often referred to the general welfare or interest (*utilitas publica*) in order to buttress their client's position. The general welfare proved to be a flexible notion: whereas in a local dispute, it could be identified as the common good of the city, a higher level of general interest had to be sought and asserted when the litigation involved different cities or the central government. Ultimately, the highest general interest was deemed to be represented by the prince, and in the dynamics of late-medieval and early modern state formation, cities had therefore to align gradually ever more the common welfare they were supposed to stand for with that of the prince. It illustrates how the legitimacy of public governance in trade regulation shifted from the cities to the polity's ruler – and, incidentally, how those shifts in economic governance contributed to early modern state formation. Cases about the beer trade show that the more the city's trade interests extended beyond its own city walls, the more the city became dependent on the prince's power and authority for protecting its trade and its competition with rival interests.

7 The Impact of Public Governance on Commercial Litigation, and Vice Versa

Preliminary studies on proceedings before the Great Council, for example involving Portuguese litigants and interests, several of whom were merchants and related to trade disputes, may illustrate the points briefly made in the previous pages. It may strengthen the main thesis in particular, *viz.* the relevance, even when looking at commercial law from the vantage-point of private merchants at the time, of the incidence of public governance and legal regulations with regard to the public governance of trade, on day-to-day commercial practice.[28] Within the limits of this brief contribution, which will discuss a few

28 For a good contextualisation of the presence of Portuguese merchants in the Low Countries at the end of the Middle Ages, see Flávio Miranda, 'Before the Empire: Portugal and the Atlantic Trade in the late Middle Ages', *Journal of Medieval Iberian Studies* 5:1 (2013), 69–85, which includes a rich bibliography. Miranda's article shows that well before they developed an overseas colonial empire, the Portuguese had worked out for centuries a commercial network northwards along the Western coasts of France and in England and

Portuguese cases in the context of commercial litigation in general (before the Great Council), what follows barely scratches the surface of the wealth of information historians may find in the court's records. Most of the cases referred to in this fragmentary survey are drawn from the last decades of the fifteenth century and from the first decades of the following century.[29]

A first category[30] of cases where merchant or merchants' interests were at stake may be broadly described as those where the application of a specific

the seafront provinces of the Low Countries. That network (with shifts: for example, from England to Flanders towards the end of the fourteenth century) could then be connected to the Portuguese trade beyond Europe during the fifteenth century.

29 The cases referred to here are mainly drawn from the 'extended sentences' (judgments) of the Great Council, the records of which have been calendared by Jacobus Th. de Smidt et al., *Chronologische Lijsten van de geëxtendeerde sententiën en procesbundels (dossiers) berustende in het archief van de Grote Raad van Mechelen, vol. I: 1465–1504* (Brussels: Ministère de la justice, 1966) and *vol. II: 1504–1531* (Brussels, 1971). For a selection of Portuguese cases, extending the period up to 1580, I rely on Robert van Answaarden, *Les Portugais devant le Grand Conseil des Pays Bas (1460–1580)* (Paris: Foundation Calouste Gulbenkian, Centre culturel portugais, 1991). The author was active during the 1980s in Professor de Smidt's project of calendaring the records of the Great Council; his introduction to the volume (pages 31–88) provides useful information on the characteristics of commercial litigation by Portuguese before the Great Council. References are to the decisions of the Great Council (hereafter abbreviated as GCM): the date makes it possible to trace the full reference to the records in one of the volumes of the *Chronologische Lijsten*.

30 I have not attempted here to present a typology of cases involving merchants. The two categories mentioned in this paper stand out because of their frequency in Great Council proceedings between 1470 and 1530. Of course, several categories related to commercial interests (e.g. companies, transport contracts, sureties, insurance etc.) are also represented. The most important single category with regard to mainly 'private' merchants interests which I have identified deal with what may be designated under the very broad term of 'debts' – a general characterisation which of course would require further nuances and specification. However, in the context of the main theme of the present contribution, it may be pointed out that even for such cases which pertain essentially to private merchant interests, there is often a strong link with public governance, because in many such proceedings, a procedure of distraint highlighted the need for a creditor to be able to rely on public authorities in order to secure the interests of his suit (cf. also on this last point van Answaarden, *Les Portugais devant le Grand Conseil des Pays Bas, o.c.*, 84). For a more developed typology, see Flávio Miranda, 'Commerce, conflits et justice: les marchands portugais en Flandre à la fin du Moyen Âge', *Pays de Bretagne et des Pays de l'Ouest* 117:1 (2010), 1–14. Another aspect which is omitted here is that of the financial dealings, including loans, between merchants and public authorities: see for example van Answaarden, *Les Portugais devant le Grand Conseil des Pays Bas, o.c.*, 191–194, where an agent of the King of Portugal sued Bruges with respect to a loan taken by the future emperor Maximilian. The reimbursement was complicated because of the financial difficulties of Bruges at the

regulation was at stake. Within that broad category, tax regulations, unsurprisingly, take a major place. Apart from accusations of tax fraud,[31] many cases were triggered by claims of tax exemptions. In such cases, both individual merchants[32] and corporations (professional corporations, but also cities), depending on the foundations of the alleged exemption or on the broader interests at stake, could appear as litigants. If the tax or duty was levied by a city, that city would in most cases appear as a party or join the main litigant.[33] The cases are manifold, on the one hand because of the variety of taxes and duties,[34] and on the other hand because of the variety of privileges and exemptions which were claimed.[35] Moreover, the late-medieval system of taxation reflected the jurisdictional complexity of the polities in the Low Countries. Some taxes and duties were a prerogative of a public corporation, often granted by privilege, or public authority.[36] Taxes which remained a non-delegated prerogative of the central government ('central' within a principality or central within the personal union) were often farmed out, and in such cases the toll-farmers faced with unwilling tax-payers had to litigate in person,[37] but, because of the long-term interests at stake, could be joined by the Proctor-General acting on behalf of the ruler.[38] Some of the corporations which levied duties were

time, which had obtained (as had many other cities in the Low Countries) a delay for its repayments.

31 See (e.g.) GCM 22.11.1513.

32 For example GCM 05.11.1471, a wine merchant attached to the ducal court claiming tax-exemption when selling wine at Abbeville.

33 There are many examples, but it was not necessarily so; see e.g. GCM 03.12.1529, which opposed a merchant from Bruges to the collector of taxes on cloth in Menen.

34 For example, the staple-duties. On the Dordrecht staple, see (e.g.) GCM 10.11.1475; GCM 10.10.1504; in GCM 20.07.1521, Norwegian shippers, backed by the city of Den Briel, denied that they had been in breach of the Dordrecht staple, because their first port of call had been Briel, which referred to a privilege of 1280. Other examples illustrated in litigation are the 'quayside-duties' in Flushing (GCM 25.05.1484), 'pole-money' (*paalgeld*) levied by Amsterdam (16.11.1498); 'loading-money' (*ladeghelt*) levied by a corporation on exports by foreign merchants, but forbidden by the Bruges city authorities (GCM 23.12.1514).

35 Conversely, cloth merchants protested in Haarlem that a tax on cloth would affect only them and not the whole of the city's citizens (GCM 24.07.1500 and First-Instance Proceedings 174).

36 GCM 19.12.1480 (two judgments rendered on the same day).

37 On a case where an individual's right to levy toll had been repealed by the municipal authorities of Damme: GCM 02.12.1514.

38 Several cases relating to the toll of Iersekeroord (see already in 1468, First-Instance Proceedings 2673), GCM 07.09.1499; GCM 11.10.1504; GCM 22.10.1513; GCM 26.06.1517; GCM 15.01.1518 ns; GCM 05.12.1523; GCM 12.06.1529. On the Grevelingen toll: 11.12.1500. See also GCM 02.12.1514 (Mechlin relying on a toll freedom granted by Charles the Bold).

merchants' corporations, for example on commercial operations involving their members.[39] Only exceptionally did a regulating or tax-levying authority outside the Low Countries appear in litigation before the Great Council.[40]

Not all the (public) regulations which were at the heart of commercial litigation were strictly tax-related. A significant part of the litigation may be styled as 'restrictive practices' from the perspective of private merchants. These cases could be ordinary disputes of competition between different professional corporations: for example, when the fishmongers of Bruges challenged local professional carriers of goods (*lastdragers* and *mandedragers*), in an attempt to limit the number of those who would be entitled to sell fish.[41] In Saint-Omer, sellers of haberdashery challenged a decision in favour of the apothecaries by the local tribunal which had forbidden them the sale of syrup.[42] The competition could also be one between similar professional groups from different cities: in 1504, the corporation of shippers of Bergen op Zoom unsuccessfully sued their counterparts in Bruges, Middelburg and Arnemuiden with regard to their alleged rights on the transport from Arnemuiden to Bruges and Middelburg of imported goods.[43] Similarly, the shippers' corporation of Delft unsuccessfully sued the shippers' corporation of Middelburg with regard to shipping goods to places other than Delft.[44] Middelburg and Arnemuiden were also successful in fencing off similar claims from their fellow city Zierikzee in Zeeland.[45] The appellate courts also ruled in cases where the regulation by a city council with regard to the activities of a specific corporation was being challenged,[46] or when the implementation of an ordinance by the prince proved controversial.[47]

39 Bruges office of the Hanse: GCM 06.03.1470 ns and 09.09.1471. See also hereafter on the litigation involving Portuguese merchants.

40 See also the case where a former officer of the Portuguese Mint was being prosecuted in the Low Countries, but was eventually discharged: van Answaarden, *Les Portugais devant le Grand Conseil des Pays Bas, o.c.*, 197–207.

41 GCM 12.03.1490 ns, the Great Council established a regulation largely in favour of the defendants.

42 GCM 03.031497 ns (appeal dismissed).

43 GCM September 13, 1504. Arnemuiden was the advanced port of Middelburg, and the latter claimed (successfully) a privileged right of loading and shipping for its own shippers.

44 Here again, the Great Council upheld the Middelburg claim for preferential shipping in favour of Middelburg shippers (GCM 03.08.1498 and 19.11.1518, and further records in the series GCM First-Instance Proceedings 215).

45 GCM 21.10.1519.

46 For example GCM 01.04.1531.

47 In GCM 29.01.1530, the Bruges authorities had seized English cloth, the importation of which had been prohibited in a statute issued by the prince in 1498 – the Great Council confirmed the seizure, which had first been challenged before the Council of Flanders.

Other litigation pertained to what may be seen to be a form of quality control of goods.[48] In one case of 1522, the *schout* of Vere had wanted to impose a fine on an Antwerp merchant accused of acting in breach of a statute of the Duke of Brabant prohibiting certain transactions in favour of students; the *schout* won before the court in Vere, but the merchant appealed successfully to the Court of Holland, and that judgment was confirmed by the Great Council.[49]

In 1470, the agent of the King of Portugal in Bruges sued a Portuguese merchant in the same city for acting in breach of a king's ordinance on the trade of ivory. The Great Council referred the case to the Council of the King of Portugal.[50]

The Spanish and Portuguese 'nations' were also involved in litigation with regard to contributions, sometimes called *avaries*, from their members. In 1516, the apparently last remaining Portuguese merchant in Bruges who had refused to pay his contribution to the Portuguese corporation of merchants in Antwerp won his case before the Great Council.[51] More protracted were the proceedings on the payment of *avaries* on transport of goods by Spanish ships. These duties were claimed by Spanish officials, but in 1515, the Great Council decided that only Genoese merchants had to pay the duties.[52] The Genoese consul and merchants opposed the enforcement of the decision, but their opposition was rejected by the Great Council after further proceedings.[53] Nevertheless, the enforcement pursued by the Spanish continued to be challenged by the Genoese, and the Great Council was willing to hear their arguments.[54] The Genoese brought the case before the Privy Council, which allowed revision proceedings before the Great Council. The latter had to have issued an interim injunction pending those revision proceedings.[55] The Spanish (Biscay) nation proceeded against the decision of the Privy Council, which had suspended the 1515 judgment of the Great Council and had forced the latter to

48 Possibly GCM 02.12.1496, on a prohibition of buying reject scraps of wool (but the case also involved the non-payment of the Grevelingen toll).

49 GCM 21.11.1522.

50 GCM 04.09.1470; van Answaarden, No. 4.

51 GCM 10.10.1516; van Answaarden, No. 24.

52 GCM 28.07.1515 (the first judgement on that day in the proceedings of the Spanish consuls against Italian merchants, the second in parallel proceedings opposing the Spanish consuls, on the one hand, and those of Genoa, Florence, Venice and Lucca, joined by the Proctor General, on the other).

53 GCM 22.05.1518.

54 GCM 13.07.1518.

55 GCM 28.11.1523.

provide a clarification of its decision in 1523. The Genoese then challenged the Great Council's declaration.[56] The consuls of Biscay nonetheless still needed to proceed further and obtain an explicit confirmation of the Great Council allowing them to enforce the judgment against the reluctant consuls of the Genoese nation.[57]

A second substantial part of merchants' litigation before the Great Council originated in violence and robbery at sea, covering both privateering and piracy. In addition, another substantial part of litigation in which merchants were involved was related to the effects of warfare. For the period 1470–1530, most cases of robbery at sea which are recorded among the extended judgments date from the late fifteenth century, reflecting perhaps a degree of anarchy, or at least ineffective authority of the Low Countries' rulers over adjacent sea territories.[58] Moreover, one may wonder to what extent the cases recorded through these judgments reflect the whole reality of the disturbances suffered, and sometimes inflicted, by merchants on the seas. The vast majority of the judgments appear to offer remedies to the victims of robbery.[59] Such an outcome may only have been possible in a comparatively small number of cases, which would not be representative of the predicament of most merchants who had been robbed. Among the prerequisites for successful proceedings against privateers, pirates or their accomplices, a lawsuit supposed that a defendant could effectively be brought to justice. The next hurdle a merchant then had to take was that of the evidence: evidence of the circumstances of the capture

56 GCM 31.03.1525 ns.

57 GCM 06.10.1526; see also van Answaarden, *Les Portugais devant le Grand Conseil des Pays Bas*, *o.c.*, 221–222.

58 A selection of cases has been studied by C.G. Roelofsen, *Studies in the History of International Law: Practice and Doctrine in Particular with Regard to the Law of Naval Warfare in the Low Countries from circa 1450 until the Early 17th century* (Diss. Utrecht, 1991); for a selection of case studies in the broader context of the (re-) organisation of admiralty in the Low Countries under Burgundian and Habsburg rule: Louis Sicking, *Zeemacht en onmacht: maritieme politiek in de Nederlanden, 1488–1558* (Amsterdam: De Bataafsche Leeuw, 1998); see also Jacques Paviot, *La politique navale des ducs de Bourgogne, 1384–1482* (Lille: Presses universitaires de Lille, 1995).

59 GCM 21.11.1470; GCM 24.031472 ns; GCM 24.07.1472 (seized ship after capture released in favour of the owner); GCM 13.07.1476; GCM 25.08.1478; GCM 12.02.1479 ns; GCM 27.03.1579 ns; GCM 19.05.1479; GCM 08.10.1479; GCM 29.02.1479 ns and GCM 25.03.1480 ns; GCM 27.07.1484; GCM 11.09.1489; GCM 16.10.1489; GCM 21.1.1491 ns; GCM 09.09.1491; GCM 30.03.1492 ns; GCM 07.12.1492; GCM 08.03.1493 ns; GCM 11.12.1495 (possibly no privateering, but a case of fraud); GCM 05.08.1496; GCM 24.10.1500; GCM 06.04.1501 ns; GCM 29.10.1501; GCM 28.04.1503; GCM 20.05.1519; GCM 20.04.1520; GCM 23.05.1523; GCM 28.01.1527 ns.

of his ship and goods,[60] but often also of the value of the cargo.[61] If he was seeking recovery from a third party who had acquired the goods, the complications of an action in *revendication* or compensation could be even greater.[62] And if the merchant obtained a judgment in his favour, the whole procedure (in the case of Great Council judgments, often in second- or third-instance proceedings) had only been worth initiating if sufficient property was available to recover the losses and costs. The cases nonetheless make it clear that robbery was one of the risks which any maritime commercial venture had to take into account in the costs and profits calculation of the enterprise or voyage.[63] The possibility of recovering part of the losses through legal proceedings would only have attenuated the risk calculation to a limited extent. On the other hand, the cases also show that because of the importance of international trade for the effectiveness of public governance, the administration of justice was part of the means set in action by the authorities in order to ensure

60 Cf. the case of missing witnesses in van Answaarden, *Les Portugais devant le Grand Conseil des Pays Bas, o.c.*, 186–187.

61 The latter issue, following *ius commune* authorities, was often solved by relying on the victim's oath with regard to the value lost (cf. Alain Wijffels, 'References to Judicial Precedents in the Practice of the Great Council of Malines (c. 1460–1580)', in *Miscellanea Consilii Magni III* (Amsterdam: Universiteit van Amsterdam, Faculteit der Rechtsgeleerdheid, 1988), 165–186.

62 See (e.g.) GCM 11.06.1479 (compensation of the value of ship and cargo by the buyers); GCM 27.07.1484 (restitution of the buyers who had paid out some compensation to the owner of the property which had been captured at sea); GCM 08.03.1493 (buyer ordered to perform restitution, even though he had bought the goods at the privileged market of Dordrecht); GCM 06.04.1501 (*mala fide* buyer). In a case opposing a Portuguese merchant established at Middelburg to a merchant from Valencia in Aragon, the issue presented the additional feature that the buyer claimed that he had bought the wares at a public auction, and was therefore immune from any claim by the original owner. During the proceedings, several commercial practices were referred to. Both the Court of Holland and the Great Council decided against the buyer (GCM 11.12.1495, van Answaarden, *Les Portugais devant le Grand Conseil des Pays Bas, o.c.*, 178–182).

63 The outcome was not a foregone conclusion, even if the prerequisites mentioned above were fulfilled, for in a few cases, the Great Council decided that a privateer had acted legitimately, e.g. GCM 30.03.1484 ns (capture of enemy goods on a neutral ship); GCM 06.02.1489 (privateer had a valid commission); GCM 24.12.1524: capture of a French ship carrying goods from Brazil by Spanish privateers; the agent of the Portuguese Crown seized the goods, but the seizure was undone by the Great Council (van Answaarden, *Les Portugais devant le Grand Conseil des Pays Bas, o.c.*, 231–238). See also the dismissal of the claims for restitution or compensation in GCM 04.08.1497; GCM 12.08.1502.

some degree of protection to the merchants' interests.[64] Among the actors of maritime warfare (and sometimes piracy), some cities also played a role.[65] The Great Council's practice shows that by the early sixteenth century, these public actors, too, were gradually being more strongly subordinated to the prince's political authority, and the justice system which adjudicated in his name.[66] Since these cities involved in maritime warfare had themselves major interests in maritime trade, they may also have appreciated the advantages of a system of effective public governance transcending particular local and regional jurisdictions.[67]

A late-fifteenth century case involving a Portuguese merchant emphasises the importance of the Great Council as an institution which was perceived to combine the expertise and authority to deal with complex issues. The merchant's ship and cargo had been captured while on his way from Honfleur to Zeeland. The authors of the capture justified their action by asserting that during the troubles in Flanders during the late 1480s, they had been commissioned by the military commanders to attack any ships providing support to the rebels, and that the claimant had in fact planned to sail to a port held by those rebels. The deputy of the admiral, confronted with the technicalities of

---

64 In a few cases, this is apparent through the coercive measures which benefit the victim who obtains a judgment in his favour: e.g. GCM 23.06.1475 (confirmation of reprisals on Scottish ships for the capture of a Hollandish ship near the Scottish coast); GCM 13.02.1478 (hostage-taking [*gijzeling*] of a Frenchman in Bruges, in order to obtain compensation for the loss of a ship taken by French privateers or pirates); 09.07.1501 (seizure unsuccessful because enforced in privileged area). Forms of reprisals between burghers of different cities in the Low Countries also occurred: see e.g. van Answaarden, *Les Portugais devant le Grand Conseil des Pays Bas, o.c.*, 152–160.

65 GCM 08.10.1479 (warship of Gouda); GCM 09.11.1479 (Haarlem); GCM 29.02.1480 and 25.03.1480 (Haarlem and Rotterdam); GCM 20.04.1520 (Amsterdam).

66 Examples are GCM 08.10.1479; GCM 09.11.1479; GCM 29.02.1480 ns; GCM 20.05.1519 (Amsterdam to pay compensation for the losses caused by shippers acting in the service of the city); GCM 20.04.1530; GCM 23.05.1523 (Court of Holland, confirmed by Great Council, ordered Dordrecht and Den Briel to make an end to hostilities and Dordrecht to give back ships from Den Briel).

67 This may be illustrated in a 'voluntary condemnation' (i.e. a settlement between the parties confirmed in the form of an executory judgment) between Middelburg, Amsterdam and Enkhuizen (GCM 16.10.1512) with regard to a capture of a cargo from the latter two cities by ships from Brittany twenty-six years earlier, and for which Middelburg had acted as a surety.

the case and proceedings, was moved to have the case deferred to the Great Council, which ordered the defendants to refund the claimant.[68]

Other war-related issues or *post-bellum* issues which affected merchants' interests also highlight the importance of the appellate courts in order to limit arbitrary decisions.[69] However, the circumstances and policies of wartime allowed for a certain degree of opportunism and sometimes exceptional exactions. Cases of confiscation were strongly influenced by the political context, as were the conflicts of interests generated by the repression of collaboration with the enemy.[70] Military expediency seems also have had to be taken into account,[71] though occasionally, plundering of (non-enemy) merchants' goods had to be corrected.[72] The validity of *lettres de marques* was in some cases subjected to judicial review.[73] This was for example the case in litigation opposing Portuguese merchants to Spanish and Genoese insurers. Both the claimants and the defendants were established in Bruges. The Portuguese had lost a ship during a voyage from Lisbon to the Low Countries. The ship had suffered damage in a storm and sailed to Laredo for shelter. There, ship and cargo were seized by the local authorities, apparently by virtue of *lettres de marques* issued as reprisals for the capture of a Spanish ship by a Portuguese privateer. Although the central issue of the case was primarily one of private law, *viz.* whether the loss in such circumstances was covered by the insurance, the insurers' argument that the risk of reprisal was never covered by an insurance led to a debate about the validity of the *lettres de marques*. A procedural question about the admission of ambassadors who were called as witnesses gave the insurers an opportunity to bring the case before the Great Council, which dismissed the Portuguese merchants' claim.[74]

68 GCM 15.11.1593, van Answaarden, *Les Portugais devant le Grand Conseil des Pays Bas, o.c.*, 160–169 and 184–185.

69 A local official in Zeeland had taken hostage a twelve-year old French boy when a war with France started; a Zeeland merchant who feared for the safety of boys from the Low Countries in France, and for his own goods in La Rochelle challenged the official's conduct before the court in Middelburg. When the decision of the Middelburg court was ignored by the official, the merchant brought the case before the Great Council which ordered the release of the French boy (GCM 18.02.1531 ns).

70 GCM 03.07.1472; GCM 16.01.1478 ns; GCM 12.09.1480.

71 GCM 27.10.1488.

72 GCM 07.11.1494.

73 GCM 04.07.1494; GCM 11.08.1497; GCM 13.10.1497.

74 GCM 08.04.1478, van Answaarden, *Les Portugais devant le Grand Conseil des Pays Bas, o.c.*, 136–148.

The jurisdiction of the prince over adjacent waters was not only applicable in cases of robbery. When a merchant from Cadiz claimed compensation against Portuguese defendants for causing the loss of his ship during a storm, the jurisdiction of the Middelburg city court was challenged because it was said that the alleged delict had been committed on the *stroom* (the sea territory) of the Count of Flanders. The further proceedings are only partly documented, but it appears that the referral to the Great Council was effectively pursued.[75]

8 Concluding Remarks

Now that legal historiography has (re)discovered how, for example, the French *Code civil* and other comparable legislative achievements are not only monuments of private law, but were also critical instruments of public policy, and that many other policy instruments associated with a restrictive concept of private law were very much tools of public governance, legal historians should not be deceived into focusing on commercial law as a mainly private normative system of merchants. Private law remains a distinctive feature of the specificity of the *lex mercatoria* – or, more accurately, the *leges mercatoriae* – as a set of intertwined particular laws within a system of relative self-governance. However, the reality of commercial law was much broader than that system, and is in many regards unintelligible unless considered in connection with the 'public dimension' of commercial law. The relationship between merchants' communities and political rulers was governed from the middle ages onwards by both a quasi-continuous or recurrent conflict of short-term interests and a recognition of long-term mutual interests. The tension could be attenuated in the governance of cities where the leading political classes represented the interests of the city's trade and industry, but even in the polity governed by a prince whose understanding of the public interest was bound to transcend the economic and cultural priorities of merchants' communities, the advancement of business was a shared perception of a successful commonwealth.

Higher courts established by the prince or which had developed within the ambit of his court, such as the Great Council, were institutions where the interface between public governance on trade and the private interests of merchants was put to the test. As the cases referred to in this contribution illustrate, proceedings before the Great Council (in some cases also running back

75 GCM 13.03.1495 ns, van Answaarden, *Les Portugais devant le Grand Conseil des Pays Bas*, *o.c.*, 169–178.

and forth to the more politically oriented Privy Council) allowed with some leeway the implementation *in concreto* of general regulations, which were often viewed as fact-sensitive regulatory compromises. Moreover, when an existing regulation created too strong a tension because of a conflict of interests (between merchant groups, or between some merchant interests and public policies), they also offered an opportunity for considering the controversial policies and to seek alternative legal remedies if the legitimacy of the public governance was being seriously challenged. On the whole, however, the Great Council seems to have been able to maintain its role as a forum for dispute resolution which remained acceptable (if not attractive) to individual merchants and merchant companies, merchants' communities and cities with marked commercial interests.

Among the cases decided during the last third of the fifteenth century and the first third of the sixteenth century by the Great Council of Mechlin and in which merchants or merchants' interests were at stake, two broad categories stand out. Tax litigation entailed in a complex polity a risk of arbitrariness. Access to the higher provincial courts and the Great Council could contribute to attenuating the arbitrary or at least unchecked practice of tax-collectors representing different levels of local and regional authorities. Privateering and piracy offered rulers an opportunity to legitimize their authority over sea territories. The practice of the Great Council suggests that when merchants who had been robbed off-shore or on the high sea could produce a strong case, the ruler's administration of justice was inclined to acknowledge their rights and to grant them compensation or restitution.

Justice – as a principle of policy, but also in its practical form of administration of justice – was understood as an essential feature of good public governance. Moreover, one of the essential benefits of good public governance was associated with a flourishing industry and trade. Commercial relations were therefore an area of particular relevance to rulers who wished to advertise their public governance. Not only were their policies were supposed to reflect and implement the virtues of good governance, but they also had to ensure that merchants would have access to the ruler's courts for protection and the implementation of their legitimate claims. The princely courts which were strongly developed in the Netherlands during the transition from the middle ages to the sixteenth century were instrumental in ensuring the balance between public governance, justice and commercial interests.

CHAPTER 4

Honore et utile: The Approaches and Practice of Sixteenth-century Genoese Merchant Custom

Ricardo Galliano Court

1 Introduction

A view into the social, professional, and legal world of sixteenth-century Mediterranean trade is revealed in the letters of Gio Francesco di Negro, by his successes, his failures, and the language he used. A 'language of trust' acted simultaneously as the linguistic fabric of his economic agreements, and the social thread that tied his network together. His claims of trustworthiness could be effectively and efficiently gauged, fostering a robust, low-cost regime of informal contract enforcement. In Gio Francesco's world, there was much to lose by cheating and much to gain by being honest. Relationships were valuable. Revealing his world provides context for the noted shift in praxis in the seventeenth century,[1] when Spanish banking failure and resulting bankruptcies caused the value of these commercial relationships to collapse in the 1620s. Genoese merchants became willing for the first time to invest in costlier institutional arrangements, including Venetian style state-run commercial fleet and insurance.

Traders like Gio Francesco were embedded in networks. This meant that no one, no matter how successful, was immune to economic downturns. War, bad harvests, and epidemics caused frequent economic collapses. Traders adept at cooperative behaviours were able to weather downturns because of their ability and willingness to communicate cooperative behaviour. In their own words, sixteenth-century merchants described successive waves of failures that struck everyone and the importance of cooperation, honesty, and honour to bouncing back. This culled dishonest and incompetent merchants from the population, leaving a critical mass of co-operators. Honest traders were preserved as a durable majority, and honour and profit proliferated.

The inner workings of these networks stands in stark contrast to presently accepted mechanisms of public punishment of moral hazard as the

1 Thomas Allison Kirk, *Genoa and the Sea: Policy and Power in an Early Modern Maritime Republic (1559–1684)* (Baltimore: Johns Hopkins University Press, 2005), Chapters 3–5.

 | DOI 10.1163/9789004363144_005

socio-economic force that ensured informal contractual agreements. However, when one searches contemporary communications for such public mechanisms, they are difficult to perceive. Giovanni Francesco's letters show that moral hazard was kept at bay, not by the punitive decisions of individual merchants, but by a preponderance of trustworthy behaviour. It is well known that young merchants copied letters, took dictation, and entered accounts. They must also have been indoctrinated into the mentality of their elders at the same time. In the letters studied below, Gio Francesco di Negro lectures his young associates on *honore et utile*, the behaviours that preserve it and the offences that undermine it.

2 A Privileged Perspective of the Sixteenth-century Commercial Landscape

The viewpoint of an actual practitioner of early modern commerce provides a privileged perspective on sixteenth-century mercantile praxis. The manuscript *Registro di lettere* (1563–1565) of Giovanni Francesco Di Negro, a noble Genoese merchant, preserved in the Archivio Doria in Genoa is a fascinating repository of the merchant's *consuetudine,* the written and unwritten merchant custom governing long-distance trade in the Western Mediterranean. It is also one of the rare examples of the merchant's *koinè* with which merchants strove to assert their expectations, declare their trustworthiness, and justify their shortcomings. Within the trades, remittances, and bills of exchange we can discern elements of merchant custom and practice that are typically hidden from view. That privileged viewpoint offers a great deal to the study of early commercial law and offers to fill lacunae in our understanding.

There has been extensive scholarship on early-modern merchants; however, our view of the merchant ethos is incomplete. Christian Bec's research focus on fourteenth-century Tuscan family or memory books reproduces the rules of the different actors running an activity both within the family and within their civic class, framing the merchant's identity in the public square.[2] Bec paints a portrait of the merchant, by analysing the language of their private memoirs as if it constituted a high literary style belonging to an unexplored literary genre. Vittore Branca spoke of a *ragion di Mercatura* not dissimilar in coldness to the *ragion di stato*.[3] Armando Petrucci has argued that the merchant manuscript in its varied forms – letter-register, account-book,

2 Christian Bec, *Les Marchands écrivains à Florence 1375–1434* (Paris: Mouton & Co., 1967).

3 Vittore Branca, *Mercanti scrittori: ricordi nella Firenze tra Medioevo e Rinascimento* (Milano: Rusconi, 1986). Branca seems to have taken non-merchant writers' views of merchants at face

notebook – contains meaning beyond its functional purposes. Alberto Tenenti and Ruggero Romano,[4] esteemed Leon Battista Alberti's *Libri familiae* and the intimate professional and familial world he depicted, rather than relegating it to the 'middlebrow'. As a result, informal memoirs and family books have begun to be considered a literature genre, though of lower profile and limited to a peculiar time and place. This study seeks to add to this landscape by examining the culture, language, and above all, the practice and custom of merchants. Previous approaches concentrate on what merchants and non-merchants had to say about mercantile practice, rather than what they said when they talked to each other. The few surviving contemporary *copialettere* reflect the language, vocabulary, and mentality explored here. Few survive but we can be reasonably certain, given the precise form and clear usage as an aid to and proof of memory, that all of Gio Francesco's peers kept one.

Tuscan merchant writers strove to narrate events and advice for future generations. Genoese merchants had a different custom. Genoese commercial letters not only aimed at recording what had been ordered, but also aimed at registering many shifting orders and conditions that also acknowledged that orders might arrive late, or never at all. Merchants like Gio Francesco sometimes expressed their relief that their orders had not been followed, conditions, having changed, rendering the original operation a losing prospect. The figures reported in the master ledger do not express the flexibility of transactions. The *copialettere* contains contracts in flux and the letters register expectations at the time of writing rather than strict orders. Beyond their pragmatic function, they were also crucial in establishing, rebuilding, reiterating, and otherwise preserving professional relationships.

The *paterfamilias* imposed expectations of behaviour in the 'public square' on his family and junior associates; he negotiated expectations with his peers and obsequiously subscribed to his superiors. This study argues that the merchant's place in society was maintained and appreciated continuously, and that the negotiation of place was embedded in the very language and vocabulary that he chose. Gio Francesco reinforced accepted norms among his juniors, all but lecturing them on proper conduct. The ethical concerns of the merchant, the *honore* in *honore et utile,* are embedded in the letters. Bad behaviour (e.g. gambling, usury, illicit relationships, laziness, and intemperance) could jeopardize the credibility – the *credere* – of a family firm. The letters make clear that

value, rendering merchants into two dimensional stereotypes of greed and suspicion, fearful of any whiff of risk.

4 Ruggiero Romano and Alberto Tenenti (eds.), Leon Battista Albert, *I libri della Famiglia* (Torino: Einaudi, 1980).

a reputation for engaged trustworthiness required constant cultivation by all members of an enterprise. Gio Francesco lectured his juniors that no one, no matter how powerful or successful, could survive a loss of confidence. For Gio Francesco, *Honore et Utile* was a virtuous circle that established and reiterated complex expectations of courtesy, service, and obligation among members of the merchant community.

After a cross and an invocation to Jesus, each letter listed the date, recipient, and destination. A salutation (*Nobile, Nobile honorando, Illustre Signor Osservantissimo*, etc.) was followed by an inventory of the letters received from the addressee, the dates they had arrived, and to which specific letter this particular one was a response (e.g. I have three of your dearest letters dated 12, 16, and 25 May to which I am content to respond…). The formal conventions describe distance and travel-time between locations. The keeping of a *copialettere* was an important element of the merchant custom, an activity expected of every merchant by every other merchant, and is a good place to look for the written traces of the unwritten rules.[5]

3 Merchant Custom vs. Lex Mercatoria

This study occupies an uncomfortable place between theorists of related disciplines. Many noted economists, most famously Avner Grief,[6] claim that historical evidence supports a theoretical framework in which trustworthiness in pre-modern contracts was enforced by the broadcasting of bad behaviour that punished cheating with higher transaction costs. More simply put, a merchant who has been chastised and alienated from the mercantile community would not be welcomed back until he reformed. This theory is bolstered with an array of elegant mathematical models that are calculated to seem without reproach. These studies are strong on models, lack actual examples of the attitudes and customs of merchants. Archival documents are cited only when the text seems to illustrate the theory.

5 Though, there are very few other surviving analogous collections stored in public archives. There are also few analogous documents known to be held in private collections the Fieschi Archive; Durazzo-Pallavicino's private archive in Genoa; the Brignole-Sale's Archive at the Archivio Civico di Genova; the Spinelli Archive, split between the Archivio di Stato in Florence and the Beinecke Library at Yale University. The form, terms, and usage in all of these sources is strikingly similar, suggesting not only a common vocabulary but also a common mentality.

6 Avner Greif, 'Reputation and Coalitions in Medieval Trade: Evidence on the Maghribi Traders', *The Journal of Economic History* 49 (1989), 857–882.

On the other hand, for decades legal historians have produced a copious scholarship surrounding the Medieval and early modern *Lex Mercatoria*,[7] a self-generated and self-regulated system of universal rules, customs, and norms that, according to the claim, did not need government intervention in markets and indeed is said to have solved many economic problems caused by governments. Studies seem to cite each other in circles. They exploit the language found in historical statutes and merchant manuals to argue for a libertarian economic ideology in the present. Worryingly, these studies also conduct only the most superficial examination of the surviving documentary examples of merchant practice. Both of these academic practices have discouraged important historical work in early commercial history. After all, if the mechanisms have already been discovered, why subject oneself to the slog of reading hundreds of accounts, bills, or letters?

Other legal historians, most recently Emily Kadens, focus solely on legal documents including court cases and written contracts in order to make the contrary statist claim on the origin of commercial law.[8] Again, the focus is on documents connected with, but not central to commercial practice in the period. In this, they ignore commercial correspondence, and in so doing they miss some of the most compelling features of early-modern commercial practice. It is useful, therefore, to highlight the practice and customs of early-modern merchants as interesting and worthy of study, and perhaps by doing so, influence these lines of inquiry.

Early modern merchants did not subscribe to customs to solve theoretical moral hazard problems, as economists would have one believe, nor to establish fundamental legal issues, as legal scholars stress. They cooperated with each other to trade. It is true that local rules applied to transactions generally and not just to long-distance trade, as critics of the *Lex Mercatoria* illustrate, however mercantile culture, customs, and practice did solve problems specific to long-distance trade in ways that were not in conflict with established law. The persistent and incorrect idea that local officials knew little of trade and thus represented an obstacle to trade should have been long dispelled by the

7 Coined in the classic, Levin Goldschmidt, *Handbuch des Handelsrechts* (Stuttgart: Verlag von Enke, 1891). Others took on the mantle, William Mitchell, at the turn of the twentieth century, Berthold Goldman in the 1960s, Harold Berman in the 1980s, and Leon Trakman and Bruce Benson in the 80s and 90s. Each one cites the last in chronology all the way back to Goldschmidt.

8 Emily Kadens, 'The Myth of the Customary Law Merchant', *Texas Law Review* 90 (2012), 1153–1206.

scholarship;[9] all indications suggest that local rules and jurisdictions worked very well for merchants. The primary problem in long-distance trade was one of maintaining consistent and coordinated effort from afar, and not the prevention of dishonesty.

Laws and norms differed from location to location and this created obvious problems for merchants. The custom of sixteenth-century Genoese merchants solved these problems by framing interactions with an overtly aristocratic rhetoric. *Honore et utile,* honour and profit, were two sides of the same coin. Neither was possible without the other. The mercantile custom apparent in Gio Francesco di Negro's letters constitutes a set of norms and expectations that were transmitted between locations. Merchants were given frequent opportunities to reiterate accepted rules, assert expectations, and express disappointments or present mitigating circumstances when things did not go as planned. Rules did not have to be created, transmitted, or maintained in any uniform way assumed by a *Lex Mercatoria.* This is not to say that early modern merchant activity did not differ from local contracts, even if the form of those contracts was very similar or subscribed to the same laws. Merchant custom created an environment in which those 'contracts' could be drawn up after the business described in them had already been concluded. Locals dealt with each other in face-to-face transactions, just as medieval traveling merchants had done. In contrast, Genoese merchant custom was conducted by way of correspondence. These merchants bought and sold in local markets face-to-face, but dealt with each other almost exclusively by long-distance communications. There were no international law codes governing commerce. Finely gauged reputations expressed in aristocratic terms no doubt derived norms from the study and application of Roman law in Renaissance Italian cities including Genoa. Rights and responsibilities defined in these terms, however, differ greatly from both from statist and private-order economic models.

Commercial instruments, such as bills of exchange, bills of lading, futures contracts, or insurance, left gaps that needed to be filled by custom and practice. This is where the risks of concentrating on concluded contracts or assuming that transactions were always formally expressed becomes most apparent. Unwritten rules are formalized when they are broken and affected parties protest.[10] The protest could take many forms, from the denigration of one's

---

9 Mary Elizabeth Basile et al., *Lex Mercatoria and Legal Pluralism: a Late Thirteenth-Century Treatise and its Afterlife* (Cambridge MA: Ames Foundation, 1998).

10 'Many jurists contended that the demonstration of tacit consent required someone to behave contrary to the usage and consequently to incur the objection of others'. Kadens, 'The Myth', 1165–1166.

reputation, to financial or even corporal sanction. The merchant custom had its own specialized vocabulary: Bad behaviour affected Genoese merchants' *honore* (honour) and damaged their *utile* (profits). Their protestation of *obligo* (obligation) would not be believed and the lack of *credere* (faith) in them would cause other merchants to retreat from them financially, withdrawing the *servizio* (service) and *fatica* (effort) crucial to merchant activities. The system of unwritten rules and norms that constitute the Genoese custom described below required repeated articulation, but it did not require any system of retribution.

Part of the confusion in regards to the intersection of private- and public-order institutions derives from a hazy distinction between laws, customs, and techniques. The Genoese merchant custom lies somewhere between them, overlapping in interesting ways. Bills of lading, insurance documents, letters of exchange, and even merchants' account books and letter registers were afforded respect similar to notarial documents and formalized contracts. These are business techniques; however, they were so similar in form and use that by the sixteenth century they had been given the force of law. The customs and techniques that constitute the merchant custom allowed for open-ended arrangements, for flexible agreements that did not have to be fixed at the issuing of orders. Correspondents would pledge, should conditions change in the weeks it could take a merchant letter to arrive, *Serverò i vostri interessi se fossero i miei propri* (I will serve your interests as if they were my own). In the frequent case that exchange rates, commodities supply or conditions, the availability of shipping, or numerous other things had changed, the correspondent was expected to ignore orders in the letter and apply the merchant's capital as if it were his own. Serving the other's interests as they were one's own was not a contract in the sense that it would stand up in any court. Everything about the letters communicated that the agreement, no matter how fungible the terms, was binding.

Both statist and private-order theories require repeated transactions for trustworthiness and creditworthiness to be maintained; social sanctions in the form of damage to reputation leading to interruptions of those transactions providing enforcement. Though as stated above, merchants did not create networks or norms to solve moral-hazard problems. They created them to trade. Part of the appeal to the Genoese custom was that it created a means to conduct discontinuous trade with a variety of trading partners and an ideology that allowed for coordinated action without resorting to forms of agreement or enforcement that restricted rapid reaction to economic changes. Merchant letters and bills may have initially solved the problem of insufficiency, inconvenience, or even the danger of using specie, but the greatest value of the techniques and customs of the merchant custom was in creating opportunities and surmounting difficulties and not in enforcing contracts to the letter. This allowed traders to create transactions without explicitly laying out the details of their deal with an understanding that whatever was expressed in any given agreement was contingent on local conditions. Asynchronous cooperative behaviour was achieved without a detailed consent *ex ante*, and with 'contracts' that were 'drawn up' in the form of accounts receivable and payable *post facto*. Local statues and customs applied to everything merchants did in the buying and selling of goods and commodities in a particular locale. Private-order institutions like the Genoese merchant custom bridged locales, spanning time and space, travel-time and delay, enabling decisions to be made that were very similar to those merchants might make, had they been able to be in two places at once. Far from being at odds with each other as the debate has us believe, private- and public-order institutions worked hand in glove.

4 An Essential Glossary of a Mercantile *koiné*: *fatica*, *obligo*, *servizio*, *cortesia*, and *credere*

There are five terms that illustrate the professional ethos, praxis, and mentality of sixteenth-century merchants. These five words that comprise a glossary of trust. *La fatica*/fatigue, *l'obbligo*/obligation, *il servizio*/service, *la cortesia*/courtesy, and *lo credere*/faith, were almost always reserved for cultivating relationships with non-kin (when they were used with kin, it denoted a large gap in social position). As many of Gio Francesco's communications were with merchants who were not closely allied to the di Negro enterprise, the five terms serve as ideal vehicles to examine the Genoese merchant custom. Gio Francesco used all five terms to modulate the tone and tenor of his rapport with collaborators with whom he had weaker, more volatile ties.[11] Merchants were not afraid to ask each other for an effort (*fatigue*) for which they felt strongly obligated (*obligato*) and for which they promised greater service (*servizio*) in

11 It is striking that mercantile relationships, which consist of exchanges of valuable goods and money, should be weak and volatile and still yield trustworthy results. Because weak ties are crucial to successful trade networks, and because weak ties in evolving social networks universally exhibit volatility (Gueorgi Kossinets and Duncan Watts, 'An Empirical Analysis of an Evolving Social Network', *Science* 311 (2006), 88–90.), it serves to reason that coping with associative volatility is one of the fundamental functions we should expect the Genoese merchant custom to do well. The value of an empirical study like this one is that we are forced to look for the cultural, social, and importantly, the linguistic underpinnings of trust in such a dynamic and complex environment, rather than rely on what we intuitively 'know' about human nature vis à vis honest or dishonest behaviour.

the future; they were encouraged by the courtesy (*cortesia*) shown them by other merchants in whom they had strong faith (*credere*). Together, these five examples of the mercantile lexicon neatly reflect Adam Smith's *Theory of Moral Sentiments* (1759).

Beyond Adam Smith's observation that people understand each other 'by conceiving what we ourselves should feel in the like situation', merchants use this vocabulary to impose their sentiments on each other, telling them what the other should feel about a given transaction. According to Smith, morality derives from human empathy, which diminishes with distance. Thus it is no surprise that we find Gio Francesco and his compatriots weaving proximity into their letters with their trading partners in remote locales among the quotidian account balances, bills of lading, exchange contracts, purchase orders for commodity futures, and insurance.[12] It is not incidental that we find genuine expressions of emotional sentiment embedded in the merchant custom.

Fatica

The term *fatica* is a false friend for the modern reader. Sixteenth-century merchants would not have recognized the distinctions or the multiple modern definitions of the word fatigue. For Gio Francesco *fatica* was synonymous with

---

12 Adam Smith, *The Theory of Moral Sentiments* (Edinburgh: Kincaid & Bell, 1759), Part 1, Section 1, Chapter 1, paragraph 2: Of Sympathy. Personal morality for Smith was dominated by that person's self-interest and ability to act morally with others despite 'natural selfishness and rapacity'. Smith rejected the idea of an innate 'sense' of moral good, pointing instead to morality derived from neighbours in any given person's close proximity. Smith's insight is that empathy works to prompt us to help our neighbours, but attenuates with social distance: 'that we should be but little interested, therefore, in the fortune of those whom we can neither serve nor hurt, and who are in every respect so very remote from us, seems wisely ordered by Nature'. The ability and desire to empathize with one's neighbours 'provide the basis both for specific benevolent acts and for the general social order'. Recent discoveries in neuroscience are bolstering Smith's insights about the crucial role of empathy in human sociality and morality, but even Smith himself would perhaps have been taken aback by the degree to which we find that moral perception, behaviour, and attitudes are malleable and subject to change in accordance with others in one's proximity. That one can consistently impose moral sentiments on others has been borne out experimentally in a very insightful experiment by Lisa Shu, 'Dishonest Deed, Clear Conscience: When Cheating Leads to Moral Disengagement and Motivated Forgetting', *Personality and Social Psychology Bulletin* 37/3 (2011), 331–349. Almost as an afterthought, Shu observes that which is at the heart of the mercantile *modus vivendi*: 'although dishonest behaviour motivated moral leniency and led to forgetting of moral rules, honest behaviour motivated moral stringency and diligent recollection of moral rules'. It seems that people's 'natural state' is whatever social context they happen to be in at that moment, and that morality is not only relative, but dynamic.

task. We do not find the modern sense of the word in the seventeen letters where we find Gio Francesco asking for or taking on a *fatica*. When he writes the word it is always understood in the sense of work. I think it prudent to assign a precise definition to the term: a job, a task, a duty, an office, a commitment, or an activity done by one merchant for another without a particular reward beyond a nominal restitution of costs. Being able to ask for an effort to be extended on one's behalf was a fundamental element of the Genoese merchant custom for which Gio Francesco could assert: *Non mi estendendo in pigliarvi scusa di questa fatica*/I will not beg your pardon for this effort.[13]

By asking for a *fatica*, a merchant was requesting that a simple task be performed, but there was something more imbedded in the request. Often the request followed a set formula. As formulaic as these requests were, I do not believe that they were ever insincere; nor were promises of greater service in the future contained within them empty platitudes. This remained true despite the fact that offers of future service were necessarily indeterminate. Beyond the narrow utility of the particular task, the purpose of requesting a *fatica* was also to motivate, to cultivate, and even to impose a rapport of friendship or of exchange. A request for a *fatica* can be seen as a unilateral offer of reciprocity that genuinely signalled future availability. At the beginning of any relationship, the powerful are able to ask for a *fatica;* in so doing, they activate the opportunity for serial exchanges. The weak, in turn, were only in the position to advertise piecemeal services for small commissions.

In one example of a mundane request, the purchase of a pair of spectacles, Gio Francesco declares '*vi ringrazio della fatica offertami per voi molto maior cosa* /I thank you for the effort offered me [and I promise] for you a much greater thing'.[14] Gio Francesco took the opportunity to declare his friendship, to promise to return the favour with some service to be defined in the future, and to explicitly express his continued availability. The offer of assistance would not have been seen as an obligation in the sense of a negotiable asset, yet it recognized openly that the value of the service provided was more than the nominal reimbursement paid. It also recognized the friendly exchange as a 'gift' offered willingly, and acknowledged an obligation for that gift. Whenever they were able, merchants acknowledged the necessity of such gifts for anyone's success in commerce. Even if the individual *fatiche* merchants extended to each other were rather small, in the aggregate the work accomplished was not at all trivial. Along with thanks for the *fatica*, a merchant promised a corresponding gift of 'a much greater thing' when the need arose. Of course,

13 March 14, 1565.

14 February 15, 1563.

taken word for word, the offer is a bit exaggerated, though Gio Francesco's affability cannot be called into question. The expression of gratitude, cordiality, and accessibility was the main objective. In reality, Gio Francesco was only promising 'a much greater thing' if there had been an equivalent increase the volume or value of the exchange between him and his trading partners. This was not always, nor even often, the case. However, he optimistically openly expressed his willingness to expand their joint activities, should it prove mutually beneficial.

Connecting a favour he was requesting to favours he had enjoyed in the past, Gio Francesco wrote to Johann d'Acer, a merchant in Antwerp,

> *La presente sara per darvi un poco di fatica scondo il mio solito haverdomi la vostra cortesia invitato à ricorrer da voi in quanto per giornata mi accade bisognare*/the present letter will give you a bit of effort, as is typical of me, having been invited by your courtesy to rely on you whenever my needs arise.[15]

The timeframe of the three letters above extends beyond the now; past, present, and future are encapsulated in each phrase. In the first, Gio Francesco does not apologize for the effort expended on his behalf, yet an apology is precisely what he is communicating. In the second excerpt, he knowingly makes an offer that no other merchant would ever believe in its literal reading; he would need to be able to predict the future to make it true. In the third excerpt, Gio Francesco circumscribes the central idea while never touching on it, namely that the two merchants were on friendly terms and exchanged favours serially. The jocular phrase makes fun of the relationship without cynicism, and in this way declares a warm and fruitful collaboration. Gio Francesco quips, 'I write to make your day difficult, but you only have yourself to be blamed, since the friendship you have shown me has invited me to do it'.

Gio Francesco flattered Johann by characterizing their relationship as one that had become so close and so infused with trust that it was as if the cordiality between them knew no limit, as if it could support infinite effort and offer infinite service. The exaggeration was as humorous as it was untrue, as we shall see. We must acknowledge the possibility that these letters could be a succession of empty platitudes; but if we insist that they are, we must also contend with the fact that these fibs set in motion the movement of real goods and real money: they triggered both written and physical activity, justified real risk, and produced real earnings.

15 September 4, 1563.

The imposition of a *fatica* is the confirmation of an ongoing, highly-functional relationship. The healthy running of a commercial enterprise required the continual exchange of favours between merchants. The relationships that could support repeated *fatiche* were those in which each trader recognized and appreciated the contribution of the other. The mere recognition of the efforts done on one's behalf was integral to the trust relationship. The message communicated by the quotations below shines through: I appreciate your efforts on my behalf; I await the moment in which I may return the favour; I will take any opportunity that is offered to me to lessen your efforts. Each request for a favour, no matter how trivial, was an opportunity to declare a willingness to collaborate and not a simple *quid pro quo*. The offer to reciprocate was not a reward, but a gift.

Elaborately, Gio Francesco declared,

> *La cortesia vostra mi da fidutia de darvi questa poca fatica la quale vi prego a pigliare volontiere asicurandovi che sono prontissimo a pigliarne molto maggiore in vostro servicio*/Your courtesy gives me faith to give you this little fatigue, which I pray you take willingly assuring you that I am most ready to provide much greater in your service.[16]

Gio Battista Spinola was simply being asked to sell a Spanish bond for Gio Francesco. The incongruence between the task and the elaborate thank you would have been apparent to the recipient of the letter. We could read this as formulaic and completely insincere. Instead, Gio Battista would have seen cordiality. His optimistic phrase of increase indicates that Gio Francesco was willing to continue and possibly to increase the value of the relationship, declaring that the value of the relationship greatly exceeded the trivial value of the goods and services exchanged.

Gio Francesco was also willing to offer a merchant's *fatica* to a third party as if it were a negotiable commodity.

> ...*essendo persona honorata et riputata è chiaro ve lo utiliterà molto masime che secondo me havete uffici favourevole et non dubito della cortesia et amorevolezza sua acetterà questa fatica se lo richiderete*/...being an honoured and regarded person it is clear that he will be very useful to you especially, in my view, since you [will] have favourable offices [at your disposal] and I do not doubt of his courtesy and friendship, he will accept this effort if you request it.[17]

16 March 14, 1565.

17 August 2, 1565.

Gio Francesco finds himself in the middle of the social hierarchy, dancing between the deferential act of offering a service to his superior and imposing a *fatica* on his social inferior. Notwithstanding being addressed to his brother-in-law, the letter's rhetoric is consistent with those written to unrelated acquaintances. The opening salutation shouts submissiveness: *Molto magnifico signor cugnato osservatissimo*/The very magnificent and most esteemed gentleman brother-in-law. This is the only example in the *copialettere* of *fatica* applied to a kinsman. When kinship and *fatica* coincide in the same communication, we encounter a sign of great social distance. In the example above, Gio Francesco offers up his the services of his son-in-law to his brother-in-law. It seems out of step with all of the other examples in the register, especially when referring to a kinship tie to declare the willingness to collaborate, which one would assume among kin.

Even a trivial necessity could become an opportunity for traders to reaffirm their deference and to renew a promise of fidelity:

> …*non mi estendendo in pigliarvi scusa di questa fatica perche mi parrebbe quasi farvi segno de dovere havere le vostre moleste et in vero non è cosi, e percio* v'*offero l'opera mia in ogni vostro comodo*/I will not beg your pardon for this fatigue because it seems to me almost to show you a sign of fealty to [be able to] bother you, and in truth it isn't like that, and for this I offer you my own work to accommodate your every need.[18]

Gio Francesco did not see the need to apologize to 'the great' for asking for a favour because being in a position to provide favours is precisely what makes one *Magnifico*, *Honoratissimo*, or *Osservantissimo*. He acknowledged this when he dealt with his own inferiors. He felt free to assign them tasks, knowing full well that they would be well compensated by his larger network of associates and by his greater reach. The *magnifici* provided bridges between localities, asking the *nobili honorati* for their efforts and availability in exchange. The serial *fatiche* great and small – including the verbal dance used to ask for them – were crucial to the constant cultivation and conservation of networks of trust.

Obligo

The word 'obligation' has different connotations in Gio Francesco's correspondence: first, it indicates the divine obligation that children owed their fathers, that everyone owed to Christian charity; it is the obligation to send goods ordered by someone or to remit an agreed upon payment; and finally, in the sense considered here, obligation referred a merchant sentiment of feeling

18 March 14, 1565.

obliged to reciprocate the generosity of another. Obligations could take many forms. As in modern English, *much obliged* is another way to say *thank you*. In considering the merchant custom it is useful to explore whether the promise of a recompense for a favour constituted an enforceable obligation, or whether it was indicative of a more sentimental bond of mercantile friendship. *Amico*, or 'friend', had a specific meaning in sixteenth-century trade. *Amici* were merchants related neither by blood nor marriage nor were they otherwise formally allied with the family enterprise. They were nonetheless trusted acquaintances. Interactions with certain *amici* were often few and far between. The capacity for merchants to start and stop these friendly relationships after long intervals shows that it was not necessary, as commonly assumed, to conduct a series of recent transactions in order to maintain a consistent and trusting relationship. This kind of trust, was best expressed in the words *obligo, obligato, obligatissimo*.

Gio Francesco uses a rhetorical flourish the opportunity to express his sense of obligation while performing a favour for the Barcelona merchant Lazaro Gherse, *...e non accade reputiate restarmi obligatissimo per cosi poco servitio, perche vorei fare molto piu acomodo vostro*/and it is not the case that you consider yourselves most obliged to me for so little service, because I want to do much more to accommodate you.[19] He insists that Lazaro not feel obliged for this particular favour because Gio Francesco already feels much more indebted to the Catalan for past *fatiche* and *cortesia* on his behalf. Gio Francesco's sense of obligation could be pure fiction, or perhaps more precisely, the assertion of a claim. We do not have the means to judge how fitting this specific claim was, but accuracy was certainly not the point of Gio Francesco's insistence. At no time do we find any discussion of a tit-for-tat series of exchanges, nor discussions of the relative value of favours done, nor any discounting of favours of unequal value. The sentiment of gratitude and obligation appears even in thanks for the most trivial matters. Gio Francesco says that he is motivated to reciprocate Lazaro's courtesies in the future, but he was certainly not compelled to do so. The purpose of the letter was to speak of an obligation where none could be enforced. The sentiment of an obligation took the place of a contractual obligation. The sentiment was not, however, an empty one. It was the sense of obligation that when necessary worked in the future as a real obligation. The claim might very well become a self-fulfilling prophecy.

A letter to Johann D'Acer in Antwerp contains the most complex and prolix reproach for a lack of attention to a task found in Gio Francesco's *copialettere:*

19 April 22, 1564.

> you will find in [the box] half a dozen loaves of quince paste and two dozen and a half *ramaggi* of peach paste in sugar such things you should enjoy in my name, accepting these present things as a sign of friendship that, besides, are small and still one does greater diligence as you have well done, I desire an occasion to demonstrate to you a greater sign of the benevolence considering myself obliged by your great courtesy, however, up to now you have not taken care of that work of mine [that I sent you to do].[20]

If theories of private order institutions are to be believed, Gio Francesco could have, should have, or even have been compelled to take Johan D'Acer to task for his inattentiveness, perhaps even broadcasting his laziness to their mutual trading partners. However, instead of seeking to chastise him publically – as the theory of 'enforcement mechanisms' goes – to increase Johan's cost of doing business until he mended his ways, Gio Francesco sent him a gift. This exchange illustrates how the merchant custom was not a mechanism built to avoid moral hazard (though it was quite good at doing just that), but rather a social environment cultivated to conduct trade. This gift of sweetmeats was a generous gesture, but how do we gauge it? Perhaps it was true that he desired 'an occasion to demonstrate [to you] a greater sign of the benevolence considering myself obliged by your great courtesy', but how do we reconcile that sentiment with the cold fact that he states, 'up to now you have not taken care of that work of mine?' Gio Francesco and Johan D'Acer doubtless felt obliged to each other. However, Gio Francesco seems to ask, 'And, now what?' It is interesting that this letter was not written to reprimand, which he was very capable of doing with his own son. Unlike his interaction with his wayward son there is no talk here of duty or what he is owed. Instead Gio Francesco sought to 'sweetly' nudge his *amico* into action. In terms of positive and negative incentives, there seems to be a carrot here, but no stick. Did the presence of a carrot always imply a stick? Was a stick even possible in such a situation? What could Gio Francesco have done if Johan D'Acer had failed to complete the requested service? In the short term there is nothing at all Gio Francesco could do about it. In the long term, however, neglecting their relationship would compromise countless future opportunities and inestimable amounts of *honore et utile.* After tasting the gift – no doubt a sweet gesture – how could Johan D'Acer ignore the future fruits of their collaboration?

Gio Francesco felt obliged to do the tasks requested by richer and more powerful merchants. Addressing a merchant as *Magnifico* or *Onoratissimo*

20 November 18, 1564.

expressed deference and submission. Gio Francesco himself would have been accustomed to being addressed in this fashion by his social and professional inferiors. When addressing kinsmen who were much more powerful and richer, a merchant needed to mirror the pledges typically directed at weakly connected trading partners. In this case, pledges of obligation, offers of greater service, and praise of past courtesy were identical to those asserted with non-kin.

This parallel rhetoric is fascinating and surprising, especially in light of how scholars assume that kin and non-kin were historically distinguished: the former were assumed to be trusted without reservation, the latter were assumed to be trusted only to give precedence to their own selfish interests. Here we can observe that the use of trust words in general must have been understood as a sign of sincerity, authenticity, and respect, and not as an empty gesture. Otherwise, being addressed with empty gestures by a social inferior would have been quite insulting indeed! The deference that Gio Francesco extends his powerful kinsmen stands in stark contrast to the lack of deference extended to him by his own son, Geronimo. In both cases Gio Francesco placed particular stress on obligations. To Gio Battista Spinola he regarded himself 'obliged' in the sentimental sense; but with Geronimo, he was frustrated by his son's refusal to recognize the obligation 'for divine commandment sons owe their fathers'. Did the bond he felt toward his brother-in-law or the one he felt with his peer-merchants carry a similar religious moral force? Gio Francesco would have to respond unambiguously in the affirmative.

This kind of complexity and subtlety is little explored by present theories of 'enforcement mechanisms'. Admittedly, moral sentiments do not easily lend themselves to economic formality; yet not for lack of rigor. Read literally, these assertions of obligation only make sense if we read them as a kind of ceremonial. Reading between the lines we can decipher who felt obligated to whom and why. The uncertainty about any given transaction was no risk to a general rapport. This fact was indicative of the strength of a relationship. The sense of obligation fundamental to the merchant custom was not subject to the success or failure of any given exchange.

Servizio

Gio Francesco used the word *servizio*/service and *servire*/to serve to indicate when he assumed the interests of another merchant *come i miei fossero* – as if they were my own. To provide a service in the sixteenth century comprised an activity that could fall across a broad spectrum, from the delivery of an important letter by hand, to the purchase or sale of high quantities of bulk goods, or of small extraordinarily valuable objects, to critical autonomous decisions on trades, on what goods to purchase at what price, or to purchase nothing at all. Service could run completely contrary to explicitly delineated orders. Letters allowed merchants to 'be served' by a sum of money, or to 'be served' by a quantity of grain, or to 'be served' as if (*se fossero*) their interests were the other correspondent's private ones. The mechanical elements of service are easy enough to characterize. Those elements, however, do not add up to the sum total of the definition of the word *servizio*. Merchants defined 'rendering service' as doing everything in the interests of another. When he was 'rendered service' a merchant was able to rely on a like mind who he could be sure would act as he himself would act if he were temporally and geographically present. To render service, therefore, was to be the other merchant by proxy.

Gio Francesco offered haste as an element of good service, and much more:

> *In observantione del vostro ordine apparevame consista il tutto nella celerita et siete molto ben servito come vederete*/In observation of your order which seems to me to have consisted of every alacrity and you will be very well served as you shall see.[21]

Being *molto ben servito* included the motivation to earn his client a higher profit, the ability and inclination to apply his experience and know-how, and the dedication to keep his attention on every detail, seeking out mistakes big and small before they became intractable problems. Rendering service meant being trustworthy, but being trustworthy meant much more than being honest. Well-provided service consisted of a marriage between honesty and competence. Above all, rendering service required a dedication to remaining flexible and positively disposed to a continuing exchange of goods, effort, and friendship. *Servizio* was kind of mercantile levitation, by which they moved tons of goods and vast wealth over long distances with a few scratches of the pen.

> *Mi piace, perseveri alli servitii di quelli signori con satisfactione loro perche dal pigliare bona pratticia de quello negotio te ne risultera honore et utile*/I am pleased that you persist in the service of those gentlemen to their satisfaction because getting good experience in that business will [earn] you honour and profit.[22]

Profit, honour, know-how, and service were interconnected. Together, these embodied *lo credere*/mercantile faith, which is the fifth trust word to be discussed below. Service and its *bona pratticia* were the way par excellence to gain

21 May 27, 1563.

22 July 8, 1563.

honour in the eyes of others, as well as to earn one's daily bread or even to become rich. Gio Francesco pledged continued service into the indefinite future recognizing at the same time his reliance on the other merchant:

> *La molta vostra cortesia col prontissimo mio desiderio a pigliarne per voi, e farvi ogni servicio mi danno aiuto de ricorrere da voi in li mei bisogni.*/Your great courtesy with my most ready desire to provide for you and do you every service helps me to recur to you for my needs.[23]

Though he speaks of an ongoing relationship, Gio Francesco speaks only in the present tense. Your courtesy and my service provides for my needs, rather than, our past makes me trust you progressively more in the future.[24] A contemporary understanding of trust follows a demonstration of progressively greater resistance to temptation. Someone who was trusted with certain amount in the past could be trusted with more in the future; trust was the amount of risk above and beyond the amount goods that trustees had already shown themselves trustworthy to possess, the degree of resistance to moral hazard. Aside from misplaced trust, where trust was unwarranted, there seems no downside to trust. It seems intuitive and reasonable to conclude that this is the way trust works; after all, how would one otherwise earn the privilege of being trusted with greater volume or greater value of another's assets? Eventually, this kind of trust would have increased transaction costs by progressively restricting the number of possible traders to those with whom one has had progressively valuable relationships. The seeming rationality of this proposition also obstructs keeping us from asking how one initiated trust in the first place. If someone were not to be trusted with another's goods from the start, then what could fundamentally change over time other than the amounts placed at risk? What prevents another person from reaching a point where temptation will get the better of them disposing them to steal? At what point would a merchant give in to temptation? Starting at certain sum where would a merchant's trustworthiness break? At twice the sum, ten times, one hundred? Is there a 'natural' limit to human trustworthiness? Did merchants' piety increase that limit? By how much? *Servizio* solves these potential problems. The logic behind a theory of progressive trust based on past transactions is forced and non-falsifiable. This was not how Gio Francesco trusted, nor would simply increasing values over time have ever been sufficient for him to increase trust by the same

23 March 5, 1565.

24 Robert Axelrod's 'shadow of the future' in Robert Axelrod, *The evolution of cooperation* (Ann Arbor: Institute of Public Policy Studies, University of Michigan, 1980).

increments. Gio Francesco's trustworthiness was a sentimental attachment to service. Trust is initiated by trusting; the barriers of trust are surmounted by the expression of sentiment.[25] Thus, Gio Francesco's *copialettere* represents a more accurate and faithful representation of the early modern way of doing business that the oft-cited Tuscan family books, the authors of which express a cynicism that seems at odds with actual practice.[26]

Cortesia

It is curious that sixteenth-century Mediterranean merchants would use the word 'courtesy'. Courtesy expressed the essence of courtly or chivalrous behaviour, an ethos completely and explicitly at odds with profit-seeking or economically competitive behaviour. These men were, after all, not courtiers. They worked in the counting house, the quay, and the *bottega*. There was no prohibition in Italy against mercantile activities that elsewhere forced merchants to choose between their noble status and their businesses. Still, Italian merchants' high social position limited the nature of businesses in which they were eligible to participate. As we might expect, merchant businesses had to be *al ingrosso*/wholesale and not *al minuto*/retail. Mercantile activities were suspect everywhere; goods were expected to be improved before they could be resold at a higher price than they had been purchased for in order for the sale to be considered licit. Merchants sold their goods unaltered and for a profit. This should have made merchants no better than thieves. Even theologians from Jerome[27] and Aquinas onward were forced to begrudgingly agree that

25 Only recently have the implications of trust, examined in psychological and behavioural studies, been applied to the macro sphere in any systematic way. Bill McEvily, Vincenzo Perrone and Akbar Zaheer, 'Trust as an Organizing Principle', *Organization Science* 14/1 (2003), 91–103, outlines the benefits and downsides of trust in an organizational setting. One downside of trust is felt when relationships can be unchanging in the face of shifting conditions. The 'probabilistic leap of faith' (Mark Granovetter, 'Economic Action and Social Structure: The Problem of Embeddedness', *American Journal of Sociology* 91 (1985), 481–510) required to initiate a trusting relationship may lead the trustor to delay changing relationships as conditions change. The epistolary expression of mitigating circumstances has been misunderstood by Avner Grief and others, as an attempt to damage reputation, despite the fact that in none of these researchers has shown that complaints were widely broadcast.

26 This cynicism is at the basis of Branca's *ragion di mercatura* and its dog-eat-dog vision of merchant activity.

27 Jerome's dictum was subsequently embedded in canon law by the twelfth century, '*Eiiciens Dominus vendentes et ementes de templo significavit, quia homo mercator vix, aut numquam potest Deo placere. Et ideo nullus Christianus debet esse mercator, aut, si voluerit*

merchants fulfilled a necessary social need, and that their skills and industry were required for that social good to occur. Merchants provided goods that would not otherwise have been available without their activities.

Nonetheless, theirs was a profit-making business and not a charity. They moved goods from where they were plentiful to where they were scarce, and this effort legitimately deserved remuneration. Merchants were able to reconcile making money and demonstrating their honour. The word 'courtesy' did not enjoy a special definition restricted to the mercantile arena that would have been obscure to anyone not conducting commerce. Merchants used the word courtesy in precisely the same way as aristocrats of their day and this reveals much about the attitudes of sixteenth-century merchants towards their peers. Merchants acknowledged their interdependence and their nobility through the word courtesy. The definition of sixteenth-century courtesy offered by the *Vocabulario degli Accademici della Crusca* – the first Italian dictionary of 1612 – matches very well how Gio Francesco used the word *cortesia:*

> Courtesy is the disposition of the soul to benefit, and to grace, without any personal comfort, and the benefit and the grace itself. Liberality here is called courtesy, for reason of humanity and sweetness. It is said courtesy that was first observed in the Courts of Princes. Here one should note, that courtesy is, according to the philosopher of the Ethics, a virtue that suppresses greed and sharpens munificence. Courtesy is the benign inclination to charity that a man has toward his neighbour, for which a man does good for his neighbour.[28]

Modern prejudice might not lead us to expect that humanity, sweetness, suppressed greed, and sharpened munificence were the elements of trade. The way merchants used the word courtesy tells us that they thought it was impossible in the long run for anyone to make money without explicitly doing good. Was it really the disposition of the 'mercantile soul' to benefit and do good for

---

esse, proiiciatur de ecclesia Dei'. Eltjo Schrage, 'Mercatura Honesta', *Fundamina: A Journal of Legal History* 8 (2002), 190–202.

28 Cortesia, *Vocabolario degli Accademici della Crusca* (Venice: Giovanni Alberti, 1612). The 'benign inclination' that is courtesy to Smith's assertions of the invisible hand: 'In spite of their natural selfishness … they are led by an invisible hand … and thus without intending it, without knowing it, advance the interest of the society'. Smith, *Moral Sentiments,* Part IV, Chap. 1. Although, in light of Gio Francesco's courtesy, he may have made little of this assertion. For Gio Francesco courtesy and commerce were inseparable. He clearly intended and knew that he was both advancing his own interests and advancing the interests of his community and society.

his neighbour without personal comfort? The sceptic might assume that courtesy was an empty and formulaic platitude, however, the mercantile use of the word courtesy seems to conform to the aristocratic definition in the *Crusca*. In his *copialettere,* Gio Francesco seems to use the word entirely in earnest. Mercantile courtesy transformed personal interests into common interests: *se fossero interessi proprii*/as if they were personal interests. The motivation to assist another merchant was not solely an exercise in networking to build the basis for future earnings, because they profited from them in the present. Courtesy was never presented by merchants as being functional, and they took pains against expressing it in such a blunt way.

Denying the functional nature of courtesy and entertaining a more aristocratic view allowed merchants to expend time, effort, and money on behalf of another merchant without insisting on a quid pro quo; merchants did not keep 'favour ledgers' on the shelf next to their account books. Every merchant inevitably paid someone back, in some future transaction for every favour the received. They would not have accepted a lowly, base, or mean concept of doing favours in exchange for money; their 'noble self-esteem' would prohibit such cynicism. Courtesy was a virtue in excess of its utility and Gio Francesco would have seen it as actual kindness. Courtesy was boastfully altruistic. Merchants saw courtesy, therefore, as a profoundly moral exchange, and not just material one. Courtesy was intimately tied with claims of honour and with claims of moral superiority. Courtesy, in the sixteenth-century view of it, was seen as a generous interaction between gentlemen who conducted trade, and none of them would have been able to prosper any other way.

Gio Francesco declares himself committed to an aristocratic ethos of service and courtesy that was both altruistic and self-serving, containing both *honore* and *utile*. This ethos was altruistic in the sense that traders gave gifts of courtesy to each other without a mechanism of recompense. Like-minded merchant nobles were assured of reducing their costs and increasing their *utile*. Gio Francesco says explicitly that the greater the *honore* greater the *utile*. Despite the frequent use of *fatica* or *servizio,* and *cortesia* in the same phrase, courtesy was not a *quid pro quo* but an expression of benevolence and friendship, a true moral sentiment and not an empty platitude. By meticulously recognizing courtesy in others, Gio Francesco signalled his ideological dedication to it and his willingness to treat another merchant's interests as his own.

As described below, Gio Francesco's rebellious son threatened the reputation of the family enterprise.

> *Perche gia* v'ho *scritto che troverlo disubidente doveste anche dar avertimento ali altri li quali per loro cortesia mi faccimo volontieri piacer di detta*

> *mia volonta*/Because I have written already that I find [Geronimo] disobedient you will avert others who, for their courtesy, will willingly do me the pleasure of [conforming to] my will.[29]

Gio Francesco openly describes as 'courteous' those who agreed to show no courtesy his disobedient son. Courtesy could be defined as extending commercial services, but in this strange example, it is also defined as not extending any service at all! In this astonishing fragment, the 'courteous' offered no refuge to the defiant. The courteous helped Gio Francesco to isolate the threat to his reputation, helping him preserve his credibility, his *credere*.

Lo Credere

Lo credere, or faith, embodied reputation, confidence, and faith in another merchant's skills and trustworthiness. *Credere* never meant certainty. The accounts in merchant ledgers were not publicly available information. To the contrary, ledgers were full of closely held secrets. The actual solvency of a merchant remained a mystery, whose silent opacity was broken only by whispers of those who did or did not have confidence in him, and by the merchant's offers of effort, service, and courtesy. Lacking any certainties, the maintenance of public image of a merchant was crucial. The wanton and disloyal attitude of the son did not only reflect badly on him, it was a blemish on his father's reputation and the whole family enterprise. The merchant was sober, unflustered, and reliable. He was credible. *Lo credere* and credit and that credibility had the same root. Creditworthy was not the limit of the definition of *lo credere*. *Lo credere* required a robust public image. That merchants relied on their reputations should be a surprise to no one.

Gio Franceso implies that it was perfectly normal put the money in the hands of near strangers in more peaceful times. Indeed, expanding the number of acquaintances and cultivating them into *amici* with offers of *servizio* was the well-worn path to *honore et utile*. In times of financial turmoil, however, there persisted an environment in which *lo credere* was obscured.

> I urge and implore you not to put much of your money in the hands of strangers and less in those in whom you do not have faith, because as you can see every hour there are new bankruptcies and I believe that it is a good proposition that you do not increase your exposure especially since you have the latitude to do otherwise.[30]

29 September 15, 1564.

30 May 7, 1563.

Gio Francesco warned that having faith in anyone save few close associates had become impossible. In this moment, cascading bankruptcies created uncertainty as to who was exposed to them. Courtesy and service in moments of total uncertainty never offered enough assurance for trust to prevail. Even in the best of times there were never any guarantees of another merchant's solvency. What we see in this letter is a crisis causing Gio Francesco's trust network to temporarily shut down. Gio Francesco warned his young associate to carefully wait out the crisis. The current tempest would punish the profligate, the miserly, and the greedy – those of lesser capacities. Those who had survived the moments of strife could rightly claim that their skills, know-how, and their honour had been validated. Instability ebbed and flowed, and quiet always followed the storm. In the midst of turbulence, no one was able to trust anyone, no matter the courtesy. As soon as calm was restored, trust was reinvigorated. Soon enough everyone would return to trusting everyone else since those who deserved *credere* would survive.

The anomalous – the crisis in which trust breaks down – serves to illuminate the normal, which to Gio Francesco and his peers would have been too obvious to merit description. The normal exercise of trust, courtesy, and service became obscured behind a veil of fog. Only when conditions darkened, and trust became impossible did merchants implore their young associates to exercise caution. Later that summer, Gio Francesco warned another young associate in the clearest possible terms.

> Conduct your dealings much more cautiously, which is more important in all things, so many bankruptcies have occurred that it is almost as though one does not know from whom one needs to protect oneself. You, however, will take care not to send much of your [money] around at least not until this great fog clears up. Protect yourself very well and do not send your money with those who you do not hold in faith.[31]

In times of crisis it was more important than ever to give the impression of solid reliability. The merchant who seemed 'pummelled and wrought by his circumstances', or who was 'excessively avaricious', could not inspire faith, and was therefore not worthy of being extended credit. No merchant would enter into joint ventures with him, and no one would risk their goods or their money with him. Without being able to collaborate with one's peers, a trader could do nothing but fail. Judging by Gio Francesco's anxiety, *lo credere* or the lack of it could easily become a self-fulfilling prophecy.

---

31 August 3, 1563.

> Know how such sad jabs do damage to one's effects and reputation and from that results new damage, since people do not deal willingly with he who has been pummelled or who shows himself swollen with the desire for gain.[32]

In a merchant's lexicon, effort/*fatica,* obligation/*obligo,* service/*servizio,* courtesy/*cortesia,* and faith/*lo credere* substantiated more than just words. For the scholar, they are five concepts that function as powerful lenses through which we can examine the professional ethics among merchants. When we study the moral sentiments of particular and specific merchants empirically, we can begin see the emotions, dedication, and openness that made long-distance trade possible in the first place. Each lens magnifies its own portion of the mercantile milieu. Together they bring into view a set of norms and mores that we can starkly contrast to the strange affair of the immoral, profligate, and dissolute life of Geronimo di Negro, Gio Francesco's only son. Using Geronimo as a counter-example, the purpose of mercantile mentality and its indispensable collaborative ethos come brightly into view. Gio Francesco struggled to protect his hard-earned place in the wondrously cooperative and collaborative mercantile world; Geronimo and his cupidity threatened everything Gio Francesco di Negro held dear.

5 The Merchant's Prodigal Son

By all accounts, Geronimo di Negro was a difficult son. Analysing the concept of trust in economic-historical terms, one of the most important questions we can ask is, who should be considered a reliable partner? It is taken as a given that kin always act more reliably than non-kin. If we assume that the family members are always the most dependable and the most accessible, what did a trader do when his kinsman turned out to be lazy, or stupid, or in the case of Geronimo, stubborn, spendthrift, profligate, and perhaps, even a usurer?

Since only outgoing letters survive part of the story has to be pieced together. Regrettably, none of Geronimo's letters have survived. Gio Francesco openly declares that his son has neither the ability nor the desire to take care of business and that he neglects his own and the family's 'honour and profit'. He feels the bitterness of misplaced hope that Geronimo would be convinced 'not to miss such good an occasion to propel himself ahead', and, by so doing, would care for the family business. Instead, he will complain that Geronimo desired only to feed 'his own appetites'.

---

32 August 3, 1563.

In late 1563, Gio Francesco reluctantly sent his son to act as his agent in the Sicilian city of Messina. Geronimo must have paused for a time at home in Genoa on his way south. We can only imagine the discussion that must have ensued between father and son about moving to Sicily or about the expectations that father had of his son. Once there, he immediately came into conflict with his father over his lifestyle, which contrasted dramatically from that promoted and applied by his father. Geronimo had shown signs of difficulty in accepting his father's guidelines even before arriving at Messina. That summer, Gio Franceso sent Geronimo to the Besançon exchange fair to learn the profession of exchange banker under the tutelage of his uncles. Geronimo soured on banking quickly. Four months later, we read that Geronimo had left Besançon abandoning his short vocation as a banker. On one page we find Gio Francesco unwilling to even entertain his son quitting the exchange fair, on the very next page we find Geronimo on a galley rowing south.

> Geronimo has tired of Besançon, and since our Nicolò di Negro is already travelling there for the negotio delli cruzada, he desires to accompany him, and they embarked on the galleys which were in port in Livorno on November 7 and they should still be there, may our Lord God guide them safely, when he is there your duty will be to advise me minutely on his progress, persuading him to be obedient to Nicolò from whom he will have nothing but the best advice.[33]

In a letter to a nephew and collaborator Gio Francesco addresses his grudging resignation at his son's change in vocation.

> Geronimo who has found himself there for months but does not take care to learn that business as I want him to for his own good. In time he would regret not having done it and not having the usefulness of it, though in that respect he has not quit it. If he has written to persuade you, and because I think you made mention of it in the letter you wrote to him, I resolve not to send him there [to Sicily] and not cast him into some vain fantasy since it is not appropriate to give in to him. I desire that he resolve to govern himself in everything, and I approve that you have written him encouraging his involvement in that business to his honour and profit...[34]

33 November 12, 1563.

34 July 8, 1563.

Apparently, Geronimo did not possess the qualities of a good exchange banker, and soon began to urge that his father to transfer him to Sicily to conduct the family's commercial activities on the island. In his letter to his cousin Battista Toriglia, Gio Francesco shows but a spark of optimism as he writes that that one day his son will repent his prodigality and stop giving in to his sloth. Gio Francesco enlisted Battista to advise Geronimo, as if the young man needed only a modicum of encouragement from someone who was not his father. Even this glimmer of hope would soon fade, as we shall see. Geronimo was not prone to listen to the advice of anyone. Even while Gio Francesco expressed doubts about the reliability of his son, he ultimately consented to send Geronimo to Sicily – a decision he would soon lament.

Geronimo was placed under the tutelage of his two cousins: Nicolò di Negro alongside him in Messina, charged with giving advice, and Battista Toriglia, charged with watching him from Palermo. The register does not convey any news of Geronimo until six months later when, responding to a letter sent by Nicolò on 29 April detailing Geronimo's 'lifestyle', Gio Francesco replies with disapproval giving precise instructions on how to encourage a change in attitude:

> I understand what you have written about Geronimo, and it pains me that he perseveres in his error, I shall not neglect to advise him and admonish him to reconcile with God and to satisfy me … keep your eyes open down there and beseech him where it seems useful, and I pray that our Lord God wants to illuminate him from within.[35]

The early modern merchant's conduct was closely connected to a pious and moral standard of behaviour. There is no doubt that Gio Francesco's religious devotion and exhortations were sincere, but clearly public behaviour also had pragmatic import, namely, the protection of his reputation. The pious and practical elements of a merchant's reputation were inexorably intertwined. Tellingly, Gio Francesco combines both into a single phrase: 'I shall not neglect to advise him and admonish him to reconcile with God and to satisfy me', as if satisfying his father's practical demands and realigning himself with the Lord were synonymous. Gio Francesco insists that any behaviour in the public square, even behaviour that had nothing to do with business, reflected directly upon a merchant's reputation for honesty and reliability in commerce.

If Geronimo repented balancing his divine accounts 'inside', he would also stop corrupting his image, and therefore the family's image, as honest, trustworthy, and solvent. Merchants outwardly worthy of *lo credere*, reflected their

35 May 17, 1564.

inner moral disposition. Gio Francesco and his contemporaries genuinely and explicitly believed that God himself would scrutinize their account books and compare the bottom lines to those in the divine ledger. For Gio Francesco and his brothers, cousins, and in-laws, Geronimo's dissolute life was not only objectionable; it was fundamentally opposed to the smooth operation of business. Alas, we do not find in any letter a precise description of Geronimo's violation, which Gio Francesco calls *la carogna*, the corpse.

The traditional historiography of Mediterranean merchants from Roberto Lopez to Frederick Lane[36] tells us that one of the most marked characteristics of family enterprises is that factors and agents always followed their orders to the letter. Further, only kinsmen could be free of motivations that diverged from those of the *paterfamilias*; and, finally, to the contrary, this historiography assumes that conflicts of interest with non-kin merchants always lay just below the surface. At the same time, the doyens of Mediterranean commercial history insist on the self-evident importance of reputation, which is so intuitive to need no explanation at all. If non-relatives were, by definition, not to be trusted, then how can we explain the importance of cultivating and guarding a good reputation? Why does Gio Francesco put so much stock in *lo credere?* The example of Geronimo di Negro shows that a merchant could not have unconditional trust in the motivations of subordinate employees, including close kin. We cannot assume that kinsmen always subvert their motivations to those of the *capofamilia.* However, we cannot assume that non-kin can only trust each other when their interests perfectly align. If family solidarity cannot reasonably be seen as the peerless carrier of trust, then something else is at work. No merchant ever prospered by placing unconditional trust in kinsmen, nor did any ever succeed without placing conditional trust in non-kin. In fact, *lo credere* could take priority even over a filial relationship.

Dramatically, Gio Francesco began to widen the circle of informed people outside the family or *amici* to include friends of friends in a plea for help:

> adopt all that is possible with your friends to make him execute my order and if necessary tell him that if he perseveres in his disobedience, you have my commission to make plain his disobedience and to inform everyone that as a favour to me they shall not support him in his needs or upkeep, they will do me the favour not to support him even with one shilling, as such you will execute the effect, and he shall see how, abandoned by me, he will not have the means to resist.[37]

---

36 Robert S. Lopez, *The Commercial Revolution of the Middle Ages* (New York: Prentice Hall, 1971); Frederic C. Lane, *Venice, a Maritime Republic* (New York: Longitude, 1973).

37 July 21, 1564.

By delegating the power to reprimand his wayward progeny to another by granting him permission to tell his network of 'friends' Gio Francesco dramatically brought the conflict, which previously had been private, into a very public context. It is remarkable that Gio Francesco wanted many to know of his son defects. For Gio Francesco to communicate his disapproval to people who were not strictly members of the family may have served to insulate his own reputation and that of his business, widening the circle of those who knew of the conflict. Such a public airing of dirty family laundry presumably had a cost.

The litany of outrage in this message is obvious and the expressions are very strong: 'I remain very angry' (*resto di lui malissimo*) fails to capture the sharpness of this letter that marks a drum-beat of accusations: Geronimo is lost to the 'corpse' or 'carcass' of his deviance (*perduto apreso la carogna*), Gio Francesco is willing to say publicly (*dicosi publicamente*) that he has conspired and plotted (*coiuniarsi*), that this filth (*di questa spurtitia*) injures his honour, life, and soul, (*grave error lo quale è indetrimento dela roba del honor de la vita et del'anima sua*) that is, both his internal and external image, and that it is plain to see as if it were a physical scar across his face (*cosi oprobrioso fregio del volto*), a traditional punishment and public shaming for adultery. For Gio Francesco, Geronimo's behaviour was so inappropriate and so obviously outside of the norm that it was comparable to a self-inflicted wound on his face, a shame that would injure his ability to interact in the merchant's world.

Not only did Gio Francesco threaten to cut off Geronimo from his living allowance, he also threatened to go public with the split, cutting him off from any alternate source of livelihood, declaring to take grave offence at any aid extended to him. The growing litany of sin rises as his hope fades. Gio Francesco not only broadcasted his private dilemma to the world, itself a remarkable thing for a merchant who feasted and starved by his own image; but he also aggressively asserted that he would be personally offended by anybody who thwarted his attempt to punish his wayward son.

> Because his nature does respond to kindness, my son will take this occasion rather to harden himself in his ostentation and since we are only speaking of his good or ill, in which he cannot do harm except to himself, I think it a lesser evil that lets him know by experience that alone one cannot support oneself, and moreover, that he has a great obligation to all those who advise and admonish him to change his way of life.[38]

Geronimo remained in Messina, but the money gradually ran out. Since dramatically reducing contact between the company and the errant son by

38 August 25, 1564.

warning friends and allies of what had happened, Gio Francesco was able to declare: 'He cannot do harm except to himself, I think it a lesser evil that lets him know by experience that alone one cannot support oneself'. He was able to do this publicly because Geronimo's isolation greatly reduced the danger of damaging the reputation of the family enterprise. The very public airing of the scandal was crucial to preserving *lo credere* of the di Negro. Alone, no merchant, even the rich and successful could sustain themselves without a network of collaborators. This mutual dependence greatly strengthened social cohesion among merchants. If someone like Geronimo lacked the will to 'govern himself', then he was missing this most fundamental element of trade.

The maintenance of a commercial network – commercial interaction in all of its social complexity as well as financial – required an adherence to collectively held norms. An individual merchant worked for his own *honore et utile*; but in addition, he worked toward the shared objectives of the community because 'alone one cannot support oneself'. Geronimo's mendacity signalled his inability to act as a partner merchant.

Until such time as he decided to repent, he would be judged not worthy to participate in the common enterprise. It seems that Gio Francesco was shocked by ease with which his son lied especially when faced with the prospect that Gio Francesco 'would no longer intercede on his behalf'. Gio Francesco admits to being at a loss for words and ideas about how to proceed. If the son would not behave and did not recognize the true wellspring of his own happiness, then perhaps he would when other merchants withdrew and he found himself 'in desperation'. It is difficult to overemphasize the point: Geronimo was not just a misbehaving son, and Gio Francesco was more than a strict, moralizing parent. These letters are testimony of a father stunned by a son who seemed incapable of understanding how his family derived its livelihood or what minimally acceptable behaviour was required to participate in their enterprise.

Aid of even a *quattrino* (literally a quarter of a clipped penny, a farthing) was to be denied, leaving Geronimo *squattrinato*, not only from family members and close allies, but also from anyone who hoped to do business with Gio Francesco or his allies in the future. The key to this strategy was not just to deprive Geronimo of funding for his loose living, it also served to deprive him of his autonomy to act in any way. By the past participle *abbandonato* Gio Francesco really meant abandoned and cut off from family, friends and profession and not merely from money. If Geronimo refused to align his interests with those of the enterprise, his father would exclude him from the mercantile world. Gio Francesco strengthens his orders with thinly veiled threats to his young collaborators: none of them should dare to 'feign ignorance of his orders'.

Beyond his willfulness, Geronimo's obstinacy struck Gio Francesco as genuinely insane (*impazzito*). To lesser sins against morality Geronimo had added those against the *paterfamilias* and the collective will of his family. Geronimo was guilty of ingratitude toward the goodwill and support he had enjoyed, and guilty of indifference to the divine order of family, society, and propriety. He had turned his back on all welfare and his own *honore et utile*. Geronimo seems to have done the unforgivable: 'He has so little brains ... he intends to find help from strangers'. Geronimo sought financial help from complete strangers to avoid having to do what he had been ordered. By seeking such assistance, Geronimo had irretrievably separated himself from his family. Gio Francesco's reaction was to wash his hands of him, *de lui lavarei le mani*. It seems before Gio Francesco had washed his hands of him, Geronimo had already gone. Those who would turn their backs on Geronimo would do so willingly in order to show they were courteous. *Cortese* had a precise connotation rich with ethical and moral overtones.

However immoral Geronimo's activities were, they seem also to have been illegal:

> Petro Rovo writes me that ... he found himself under an injunction ordering him to leave the concubines and promise to leave that carcass, and since an injunction is terrible for he who cannot bail himself out with money, perhaps God will have put him in anxiety and fear and thus he will let himself be persuaded to retreat to Palermo.

It is unlikely that the injunction – the *bando* that was posted publically for all to see – was levied against someone whose crime was that he frequented prostitutes. Prostitution was common and perhaps even tolerated; however his adventures might have been financed by the practice of usury. Had Geronimo become a 'notorious' usurer? If Geronimo did not want to repent his past behaviour even when abandoned, what might have done if harassed by the police, or worse, if thrown in jail? Geronimo could not be *impazzito* enough to choose prison over compliance, but perhaps the threat provided the necessary anxiety and fear to convince him to take the straight and narrow path.

One might rightly ask how much more convincing Geronimo required: his financial support had been cut off, his honour impugned, he had been shut out of the commercial network, threatened with jail, and thrown out of his family; on the positive side, sweet-talking cousins were ready to welcome him back into the fold and were willing to lie to him in order to nudge him along. Despite all of this, Nicolò had already departed for Palermo without Geronimo, had to interrupt his own dealings and return to Messina to try to drag Geronimo from his unnamed filth. Gio Francesco readily admits that there is no guarantee that his son would take to the virtuous path. Petro sends good news that at last he has convinced the wayward son to respond to his father's letters. Gio Francesco, however, had been repeatedly disappointed and so unconvinced that any desire to have open communication with his son and agent had long since fled.

> I do not care to have a response while he perseveres in this infamy and does not obey me. I am absolutely resolute not to consider him my son and not have him with me and as such he will begin to reap the bitterest fruits of his default and his opprobrious life.

Lo bando, or the injunction against Geronimo, is compelling. Here we learn that perhaps Geronimo had a partner in crime. 'That dishonest [woman]', *quella dishonesta,* may have been caught up in the legal dragnet as well, which had placed her in a well-earned anxiety. Who was *quella dishonesta* with whom Geronimo seemed to have had a well-known and public love story? What did she want? What was Gio Francesco accusing them of? What was ordered by 'command of the Viceroy' in the injunction? Who had asked for the injunction to be called? Was it by request of Gio Francesco himself? Had Geronimo become infamous and sought by the law completely on his own? Was he in hiding? Gio Francesco was in a position to make the promise that Geronimo would only do harm to himself, and that promise did not come from his religious convictions. He was in the position to have such theological certainty only because he had successfully cut off Geronimo from the rest of the familial concern. Gio Francesco had aligned all his forces to conserve the enterprise (and their *credere*). Despite the rhetoric to the contrary, the redemption of Geronimo's eternal soul retained a lower priority. While citing the will of God and admitting to Christian charity, Gio Francesco had anticipated the reckoning in this world rather than waiting for it to come in the next. Impenitent, Geronimo would be deprived of the provident welfare of the community of merchants, and would be plunged into obscurity and poverty in disgrace before God and men.

Between 6 October, 1564 and 18 May, 1565 we have no news of Geronimo. If Gio Francesco wrote another letter, he did not record it in the *copialettere.* Finally, just before 18 May, he arrived at Palermo. 'Geronimo has arrived safe, thus far he has not taken that resolution, which would be expedient to him, we shall see what he does, praying to God to illuminate him with his grace'. Gio Francesco might have been receiving letters reporting on his son's progress, but none of those have survived. We know that Gio Francesco wrote private letters to his son which he mentions throughout his correspondence but which do not show up in the *copialettere*. It is certainly curious that he would record the torrid affair in such an important document. Perhaps letters that refer to business transactions and non-familial partners had to be placed in the register. It is possible that once Geronimo was under the tutelage of his kin, letters written about him no longer had to be recorded in the *copialettere*. In the end, some combination of dissimulation, threats, stripping of income, and involvement of the Viceroy had finally convinced Geronimo to move away from his *carogna*. Did *carogna* refer to Geronimo's sins? His lover? His profligate life? All of the above? It is still unclear exactly what Gio Francesco had wished to signal by using such a charged word. By July Geronimo was back conducting business for his family.

Gio Francesco must have feared that his son could easily backslide into 'filth'. Since the Geronimo's debtors knowingly had lent him the money that facilitated his disobedience, they could not claim a repayment after son and father had reconciled. In a legal world where the debts of dependents were the debts of the *paterfamilias,* and in a juridical world where the sins of the son were also the sins of the father, an obvious question emerges: to what degree Geronimo's creditors would have tolerated this declaration? The financial mess continues unresolved to the very end of the letter register. This is not the only unresolved confusion. 'Geronimo … perseveres in wanting to do things his way and to his greatest prejudice, God be praised in everything'. This enigmatic sentence is the last that mentions Geronimo in the register. No doubt there were plenty of other references to the troubles caused by Geronimo, but sadly they are lost in the nine-year lacuna between volumes. It seems that the ceasefire of the conflict between the difficult son and the bewildered father was only temporary.

CHAPTER 5

The Abandonment to the Insurers in Sixteenth-century Insurance Practice: Comparative Remarks and (A Few) Methodological Notes

Guido Rossi

1 Introduction: Making Sense of Insurance Sources

As is the case with most types of early commercial practice, early modern insurance sources are patchy. The lawyer seeking such sources would hope to find clear rules grouped systematically and coherently, only to realise – and fairly soon – that this is not the case. Making sense of the subject therefore becomes somewhat more complex, for it involves coordinating and especially integrating different kinds of sources together.

The starting point is compilations of written rules. Those rules were enacted by individual cities, typically those most involved in maritime trade. From the late fifteenth century, and particularly in the sixteenth, such regulations become both more complex (one would be tempted to use the term 'systematic') and widespread. Rather unsurprisingly, however, they were intended for merchants involved in the business, not for lawyers studying it. As a consequence, they often say very little about the actual working of a rule. To understand that aspect, we have to turn to practice.

There are two main kinds of practically oriented sources. First, insurance manuals. For the early modern period, few of them are particularly elaborate. Nonetheless, they may provide invaluable insights to help us to appreciate the rationale of the rules, and most of all to understand the logic of the merchants who used those rules. It is however important to stress the great difference between practical manuals and learned treatises. We are not concerned with the latter, written by lawyers for lawyers, but exclusively with the former, written by merchants for fellow merchants. The two kinds of writings are altogether different. For understanding early modern commercial practice, lawyers are of little use – especially on the subject of insurance.[1] Apart from a few manuals, practically oriented sources consist of commercial and legal documents:

1 Guido Rossi, 'Civilians and Insurance: Approximations of Reality to the Law', *Tjidschrift voor Rechtsgechiedenis* 83 (3–4) (2015), 323–364.

 | DOI 10.1163/9789004363144_006

policies, related documentation, mercantile correspondence and arbitral or judicial decisions. If rules are the 'bones' of the body we are trying to reconstruct, documents represent the 'muscles'. They allow us to understand how those 'bones' could have moved: in what direction, and to what extent.

Even after this operation, one still has the problem of making sense of the overall picture. To do so, it is necessary to use a comparative perspective. Among lawyers, comparative analysis is typically considered to be an 'added value' of sorts, a further dimension to better appreciate the differences and similarities among neatly defined institutions. This, however, presupposes full understanding of the original institution which is to be compared. But that is not the case for our subject: despite our best efforts, there are still gaps (often large ones) in our knowledge. Sometimes we may know a rule, but not its practical application. Other times, we may be aware of a practice, but are unsure as to whether that was the customary position or just an isolated episode. Most of the time we do not know whether a rule continued to apply in the form which was attested, and if so, for how long. Often there is not much we can do: we have to resign ourselves to an overall picture. It is at this point that the comparative analysis becomes crucial.

Insurance was one of the commercial instruments that evolved more rapidly. This swift development was greatly encouraged by fast exchanges, as well as by competition. Large commercial centres, in growing connection with each other, were exposed to the influence of the different rules which were applied in one of the other main trading centres. Smaller centres typically borrowed the rules of the nearest large centre, and applied them with few changes. The great commercial cities were not all equally receptive to foreign influences, but growing competition often forced them to open up to innovations. A merchant did not necessarily have to insure his cargo in the port of departure. He could well insure at the place of arrival, or he could turn to a specialised market, and do so even in the absence of any connection with the voyage of the ship. Mutual influence, sustained by growing competition, resulted in some degree of similarity among insurance rules – as long as political constraints allowed as much.

Needless to say, insurance did not develop in a legal vacuum. The closer we move to modern times, the more local, and especially national, legislation becomes an important player that cannot be overlooked. Until a certain period (and this varied depending upon the location), however, the growth of legislation did not result in a progressive divergence of insurance rules from country to country. Economic reasons strongly discouraged deep differences. Another factor that contributed to the preservation of the overall normative affinity among different rules was the way they were implemented on a practical level.

This similarity among different insurance markets must not to be overemphasised – in insurance practice, similarity never meant uniformity. But this similarity was pronounced enough to enable us to fill some of the gaps in our knowledge of a system by looking at the rules and practices applied in another system. As long as we treat them as guidelines, and not as universal rules of a phantom *lex mercatoria*,[2] it is possible to use those other rules – or at least their rationale – to make (partial) sense of some gaps in our knowledge of other systems.

Lastly, the overall affinity among different insurance systems allows us also to perform the opposite operation: making sense of the differences. Insurance markets were all in close competition with each other, and the main factors attracting (or discouraging) customers and underwriters alike were both the reputation and the rules of a market. If we find a significant difference between insurance systems, therefore, we cannot simply accept it as a curiosity but we must find a clear explanation for it. The similarity (in some cases, even uniformity) among different systems was markedly pronounced at the level of principles. At the sub-level of specific rules, however, there were significant divergences. As long as the market was relatively open in terms of access, and commercial relations with other markets thrived, its system of rules remained 'permeable', receptive to external influences. In this situation, significant divergences between different rules cannot simply be considered as historical accidents (most accidents in commercial rules were progressively overcome), nor simply as the product of primitive versus advanced rules (for market competition would increasingly press for the substitution of the less efficient rules with more sophisticated ones). The reasons for significant normative differences are typically the product of broader economic (or sometimes political) considerations.

Even when it is not immediately apparent, the interplay between rules furthers a certain equilibrium within a system. This equilibrium of course may be more or less economically efficient. But such equilibrium may lend considerable strength to inefficient rules, allowing them to resist the pressure for change. For the change of single rules might require deeper changes in the broader interplay with other principles (hence the temptation to call those sets of rules 'systematic'). Because of its impact on the whole system, the cost of replacing inefficient rules may well exceed its advantages, at least in the short run. And the perspective of any system tends to be a short term one – unless

2 The literature on the subject is bountiful. It will suffice to refer to Emily Kadens, 'The Myth of the Customary Law Merchant', *Texas Law Review* 90 (2012), 1153–1206, both for her excellent study and for its extensive bibliography.

change is imposed on it from the outside. Thus, by and large, the longer a set of rules applies, the harder it becomes to alter its components. This is of course different from saying that the continued application of a single rule shelters it from change. When the rules (at least, the principal ones) of a system stay in place for a long time, the system tends to crystallise. At that point, it is difficult that any significant alteration occur from within. Typically, the system tends to remain stable overall, until a higher authority (government or high courts) forces it to change.

The purpose of this paper is to give a practical example of reconstructing a subject through the combined reading of different kinds of sources, comparing its application in different jurisdictions, and trying to understand its peculiarities and the reasons (both normative and economic) for its resilience. The subject chosen is a particular feature of insurance practice, the abandonment of the insured item to the insurers. The reason for choosing this specific topic is both practical and methodological. Practical, because it provides a good example of how to use different sources to make sense of a very elusive institution, on which there are few and scattered rules. Methodological, because its pragmatically-oriented nature, and the scattered evidence we have, both require a bottom-up approach. Further, the resilience of commercial customs may be best appreciated by looking at very specific (and highly practically-oriented) institutions, not at general rules. Unless forced by factors exogenous to the system – and it is worth remembering that, by and large, lawmakers and law courts were exogenous to the early modern economic system – general rules change only when prompted to by the pressure from below, by the combined strength of a number of specific, bottom-level rules. More often, however, those bottom-level rules pulled, so to say, in different directions. The resulting 'general rules' were therefore the product of this equilibrium, with all the constraints of the case. Changes in any single bottom-rule would thus trigger a series of other changes, not all of them welcome or indeed beneficial to the system. This was often the main reason for the overall resilience of the system, and (to a lesser extent) also for the long-lasting affinity between customs of different countries.

As already said, the study of a specific and patchy commercial custom attested in several countries requires constant comparisons. One of the problems of comparing incomplete sets of rules, however, is that there is a risk of being misled by what is seen. The problem is hardly new, but we tend to think about it with regard to discrete time periods, and less so with regard to prolonged timeframes. To understand the development of rules – first of all commercial ones – it is necessary to compare diachronically. This is particularly important when one cross-examines the development of commercial customs with the economic and financial conditions of the markets in which those customs are attested. It may happen that the same rule is applied in two different markets in the same period. But those markets may well be moving in very different – sometimes even opposite – directions. Thus, the same rule may be found in both emerging and declining markets. To understand the reason for that rule in each of the two markets it is therefore necessary to stretch the chronological boundaries of the comparison.

Ultimately, the reason for looking at very specific and practically oriented mercantile customs is that the 'bigger picture' is a false friend. Looking at it first and entering into details only later is often seriously misleading. With jigsaws, at least there is the huge advantage of having the full picture printed on the box. Creating a box to explain the jigsaw is tempting, but not advisable. That has been done too often already.

2 The Abandonment to the Insurers

In insurance practice, the payment to the insured in case of mishap could take two forms: either 'average' or 'abandonment'. In the first case (average), the insured was entitled to receive compensation for the actual damage to the insured goods. In the second case (abandonment), the insured did not seek compensation for the damage, but rather transferred the ownership of the thing-at-risk to the insurers in return for the full amount they had underwritten. Thus, abandonment had two main advantages over average. First, the insured would recover the entire amount of the insurance, not just a part. Second, he would avoid the lengthy process of liquidation of damages and receive the payment at once.

Abandonment was therefore a very important element of insurance. And yet its importance barely appears in our first kind of sources, the compilations of written rules. Very few commercial ordinances of the sixteenth century provided expressly for abandonment, mainly the Burgos Ordinances of 1538 and 1572 and, if one were to be flexible with time limits, the Antwerp mercantile compilation of 1608, so-called *Compilatae*.[3] But, to limit ourselves to the

3 The text of the Burgos Ordinances of 1538 may be read in Eloy Garcia de Quevedo y Concellon (ed.), *Ordenanzas del Consulado de Burgos de* 1538, 2nd ed. (Burgos Diputación Provincial, 1995); that of the Burgos Ordinances of 1572 in Consulado de Burgos (ed.), *Ordenanzas del Consulado de Burgos*, anastatic reprint of the 1572 edition (Valladolid: Lex Nova, 1988). The Antwerp 1608 *Compilatae* may be found in Guillaume de Longé (ed.), *Coutumes du Pays et Duché de Brabant, Quartier D'anvers*, 7 vols. (Bruxelles: F. Gobbaerts, 1870–78), 4:198–334.

most important compilations, there is nothing in the Florentine statutes of the 1520s, in the Genoese legislation of 1588, in the Ordinances of both Seville and Bilbao (respectively of 1556 and 1560). Equally silent are the important Antwerp compilations preceding the 1608 *Compilatae* (the 1571 *Antiquae* and the 1582 *Impressae*), as well as the by-laws of Amsterdam (1598) and Rotterdam (1604).[4]

Because of the importance of the subject, it would be very unlikely that abandonment was allowed only in a few insurance markets and forbidden in many others. So, we must look at other sources to fill this gap in our knowledge. The first source to take into account is mercantile manuals. For the late sixteenth century (as well as the early seventeenth) the most important is probably the *Guidon de la Mer* of Rouen, especially its seventh chapter, on abandonments (*Des Delais*).[5] The *Guidon* provides valuable insights on abandonment, and shows its reader how mistaken he would be to draw any conclusion on the subject from its poor treatment in most compilations. Then, finally, one should start looking at the available documents. The researcher would soon realise that the subject frequently appears also in the available policies of most insurance markets that failed to regulate it expressly. The most important documentary source in our case, however, does not consist of insurance policies but of declarations of abandonment, often to be found in notarial records. Available judicial records are unfortunately scarce on the subject – considerably more research is needed. The combined reading of these different sources allows us to get a better picture of abandonment. Perhaps we can appreciate its working by looking at a practical case.

3 Abandonment in Context

On 14 February 1589 the Venetian ship *Santa Croce* (Holy Cross) was mooring at Cape St Vincent, in Southern Portugal. The ship was carrying fine wine from

4 The Florentine statutes are presented in Ascanio Baldasseroni (ed.), *Delle Assicurazioni Marittime*, 3 vols. (Florence, 1786), 3:500–514. The relevant parts of the Genoese legislation of 1588 are in Jean-Marie Pardessus (ed.), *Collection de Lois Maritimes antérieures au 18 Siècle*, 6 vols. (1828–45), 4:526–534. For the Seville Ordinances of 1556 see the same Pardessus, *Collection de Lois Maritimes*, 6:76–103. The 1560 Bilbao Ordinances are in Teofilo Guiard y Larrauri (ed.), *Historia Del Consulado y Casa de Contratación de la Villa de Bilbao*, 2 vols., 2nd ed. (Bilbao, 1972), 1:598–621. The insurance-related parts of the Antwerp compilations of 1571 and 1582 may be found in de Longé, *Coutumes*, 1:598–605 and 2:400–413 respectively. Both the Amsterdam by-law of 1598 and the Rotterdam one of 1604 are in Pardessus, *Collection de Lois Maritimes*, 4:122–135 and 4:152–164 respectively.

5 *Gvidon, Stile Et Vsance Des Marchands Qvi Mettent À La Mer*, 2nd ed. (Roven: Mesgisser, 1619), 32–39.

Crete to London. On the same day, part of the fleet of Francis Drake happened to pass by the Cape. In principle, England and Venice were on good terms with each other. But privateering for the Queen was thirsty work. Threatening the Venetians, the Englishmen demanded a written document for 200 casks of their wine, eventually settling for 120. The English fleet then escorted the Venetian ship to Plymouth, where they arrived on 11 March. Upon arrival the Englishmen took the casks and promptly consumed their content. While not happy about this, the captain of the Venetian ship was not overly distressed either: his cargo was insured. We do not know for exactly how much, but the number and importance of the insurers involved would probably suggest a considerable amount.[6]

The captain needed evidence of what had happened, so he asked an English notary to take the deposition of his crew. Upon his return to Venice, he produced the document before the insurers and abandoned the insured cargo to them.[7] At first sight, it might appear strange that the insured sought payment by way of abandonment and not of average – after all, the insured thing was no longer in existence. But the consummation of the wine was unlawful, so it gave rise to a legal claim against its perpetrators. As such – in principle – the insured had a claim of at least the same value as the insured value. Pleading average and pocketing the insurance money might have been problematic, for there was a chance that he would also receive compensation by the perpetrators (or, more probably, their government). From the perspective of the insured party, it was easier to abandon his proprietary rights in the insured thing to the insurers and claim full recovery. This way, the claim for compensation would pass on to them, the insurers.

Abandonment entailed the passage of ownership to the insurers. Upon abandonment, the insurers would proceed either to the recovery of the insured thing (typically, the wrecked cargo or the ship), or to the enforcement of their claim (the original claim of the insured, which passed to the insurers upon abandonment). In either case, the insurers needed to act with full proprietary rights. And they needed to act swiftly – especially when there was some chance of recovering the insured thing, either in part or in full. To this end, a simple notice of abandonment, even if done by a public officer, might not be sufficient title, especially when the recovery had to be effected abroad.[8] What the insurers really needed to avoid delays was an authorisation from the insured to deal with the insured thing in as full a manner as possible, irrespective of any ownership issue. Accordingly, it was a widespread practice for the

6 Document of May 31, 1589, Archive Corsini of Florence (hereafter ACF), Room II, unnumbered.
7 Copy of the declaration of abandonment, date missing, *ibid.*
8 See esp. *Gvidon*, cap. 7, 33–34.

insured to give special mandate to the insurers, granting them permission to deal with the insured property as they wished. To ensure prompt compliance from the insured, many insurance markets required them to grant the mandate together with the declaration of abandonment. For instance, the Antwerp *Compilatae* of 1608 required the insured to issue the *procuratie* contextually with the declaration of abandonment.[9] The same is attested in Florentine practice.[10] In Rouen, the mandate was to be given within three days after the abandonment.[11] In Venice and Ragusa (now Dubrovnik) the insured could not receive the payment from the insurers until he waived his rights to them and instituted them as his procurators.[12] This combination of abandonment and mandate was better than the simple transfer of ownership, as it provided the insurers with a more effective tool to act swiftly, especially when they had to act in a different country from that of the contract.

When English privateers spoiled ships of neutral or friendly countries (an event far from uncommon), the usual *modus operandi* was to petition the Queen for compensation. In our case, the Venetian insurers chose a London representative well connected with the government, the merchant Bartholomew Corsini. We have other petitions by Corsini to the Privy Council for similar cases (he was particularly trusted by the Venetians),[13] but not the one concerning the ship *Santa Croce*, so we do not know whether the insurers managed to recover anything. But that is not the point of this story. The point is that there was virtually no difference at all between abandonments done in England and those done in Venice. Had the ship been English, and insured

9 Antwerp *Compilatae*, pt. iv, tit. 11, Sec. 7, art. 249.

10 See e.g. the declaration of abandonment of May 9, 1591, on a policy of January 2, 1591, ACF, Room II, unnumbered.

11 *Gvidon*, cap. 7, 33–34.

12 For Venice see the declarations of abandonment transcribed in Giuseppe Stefani, *Insurance in Venice: From the Origins to the End of the Serenissima*, (trans.) Dawson Amoruso, 2 vols. (Trieste, 1958), vol. 1, doc. 20–22 and 27, pages 273–276 and 280–281 respectively, and vol. 2, doc. 9, pages 339–340. Cf. also Claudio Schwarzenberg, *Ricerche sull'Assicurazione Marittima a Venezia: Dal Dogado di Pasquale Cicogna al Dogado di Paolo Renier* (Milan: Giuffrè, 1969), 119, note 79. For Ragusa see Giovanni Cassandro, 'Note Storiche sul Contratto di Assicurazione', *Assicurazioni, Rivista di Diritto, Economia e Finanza delle Assicurazioni Private* 26 (1959), 16–57, at 53–54.

13 See e.g. Stefani, *Insurance in Venice*, vol. 1, doc. 25–26, pages 278–280, on the appointment of the same Corsini for the release of a Venetian cargo captured by the 'excellent generals of the of the most serene Queen of England' (presumably, some privateers) in 1590. On the relations between Venice and Corsini see also Guido Rossi, 'Florence and the Great Fire: New Sources on English Commerce in the Late Sixteenth Century', *The Journal of Legal History* 33 (2012), 93–100, at 96.

in London, its spoiling by Venetians would have triggered the very same procedure. The same is true for most of Europe. Throughout the vast majority of Western Europe, and often beyond that, the abandonment to the insurers followed the same principles and shared the same practice.

4 The Need of Uniformity and the Role of the Notary

An important common feature of this almost pan-European practice was the role of the notary. Abandonment and mandate to the insurers were typically done with the assistance of a notary. Despite the increasing geopolitical divergences and the growing differences among legal systems, early modern international commerce continued to rely on notarial documents. So, for example, 'imperial notaries' in London continued to authenticate the translation of Continental documents, written by notaries in other countries, long after the rupture with Rome. It is difficult to imagine how things could have been different. On insurance matters, both abandonment and mandate had to pass through the notary because their object was typically in another country. Differences between legal systems were easily circumvented with broad statements. In the case of the Venetian ship, for instance, the mandate was shaped in its amplest possible form. This allowed the appointed mandatee – Corsini – to act as the insurers' attorney in London, since the usual way to give mandate in England was to appoint the mandatee as the mandator's attorney.[14]

The need for a uniform practice was particularly important given that abandonment often entailed multilateral relationships: the insurers relied on their business associates abroad. Depending on the business contacts, some further passages could be necessary. If the insurers had no trusted associate in the country where recovery had to take place, they would involve someone in a third country who did have good connections in the country of the recovery. Our case of the Venetian ship and the thirsty Englishmen is of some interest in this respect. It would seem that the insured (the Venetian captain) had closer contacts in England than the insurers had. Because of that, he was in a better position to appoint someone locally so as to proceed with the recovery. This is probably why the insurers did not appoint Corsini directly. Rather, after the insured had abandoned the goods in their favour, they appointed him as their

14 This was not an uncommon practice in insurance, and it is attested also for the sale of the insured merchandise after the policy had already been subscribed (selling the insured goods, on the contrary, would have avoided the policy). See e.g. ACF, Room II, bill of January 7, 1592 (on two policies of November 13, 1591 and November 24, 1591, *ibid.*).

representative to proceed with the recovery. The mandate was broad enough to also encompass the right to appoint a proxy. So, upon receiving the mandate from the insurers, the insured appointed Corsini to act on his behalf.[15]

Another example is a further mandate in favour of the same Bartholomew Corsini of London. The Corsinis were business partners of some merchants from Cremona, who supplied them with Italian cloths. In 1586 one such shipment was captured by Dunkerque pirates while crossing the Channel. The merchants from Cremona asked Corsini to recover the cargo or its value, and Corsini appointed two merchants of Antwerp (incidentally, one was French and the other Spanish). As the Antwerp merchants had to act locally, the mandate was written in Dutch. We do not have the Dutch text but its English translation, authenticated by an English notary.[16]

A better solution was to use Latin from the beginning: this way no certified translation was needed. With specific regard to our subject, it is common to find the declaration of abandonment and the mandate to the insurers written in Latin, especially so when the recovery was to take place in a different country. Another case involving English privateers offers a good example. This time the case begins in Tuscany. On 2 January 1591 some Spanish merchants had some Oriental drapes insured (in two different policies) by their business correspondent in Pisa, and shipped from Leghorn to Alicante and Cadiz. However, the ship was intercepted and captured by Englishmen in the waters between Barcelona and Alicante, and the cargo was brought to England. The Tuscan merchant who had insured and shipped the drapes then went before a notary in Florence and abandoned the cargo to the insurers. The declaration of abandonment consists of a lengthy document. The document first reproduced the insurance policies and the bills of lading (attesting that the insured cargo was effectively loaded onboard the captured ship), then it gave a summary explanation of the mishap, and finally it proceeded with the declaration of abandonment and the mandate to the insurers. While policies and bills are reproduced in the vernacular (Italian), the remainder of the document (description of the mishap, abandonment and mandate) is in Latin.[17] The reason is that the insurers appointed two London merchants as representatives, because the recovery of the insured cargo or its value had to take place in England. Hence, Latin was a more appropriate choice. The same solution is also attested in another document, concerning the same ship. A few days before the above

15 *Ibid.*

16 Document of September 1, 1586, ACF, Room II, unnumbered. Transcription *infra*, Appendix i.

17 *Ibid.*, document of May 9, 1591. Transcription *infra*, Appendix ii.

policies, on 22 December 1590, another Pisan merchant insured some Italian drapes and Milanese halberds for his Spanish correspondent on the same ship. Here as well, policy and bill of lading are in Italian, whereas abandonment and mandate to the insurers are in Latin.[18] In both cases, the mandate to the insurers is framed in a significantly broad manner. As added precaution for both documents, the insurers had a second notary authenticating the notarial document itself. This was not ordinary practice. It is probable that the insurers did so to avoid any objection as to the mandate's authenticity when it had to be executed in England. The insurers were thinking of the most practical solution for a prompt recovery, so upon receiving abandonment and mandate they proceeded immediately with the appointment of their representative in the place where the recovery had to be effected. As such, we have a third document, but it refers only to the first one, the two policies of 2 January 1591. This third document is written entirely in Latin, and in all probability it had to be attached to the first one, because it contains neither policies and bills of lading nor abandonment and mandate, but focuses only on the appointment of the insurers' representatives. Here as well, the representatives are given an extremely broad mandate.[19]

The broad terms in which abandonment and mandates (both that of the insured to the insurers, and especially that of the insurers to their representative) were shaped allowed the instrument to retain its uniformity among different countries despite the local differences as to the specific rules on abandonment. It was a two-way relationship: the document had to be broad precisely because of the differences from country to country. Yet, those differences did not concern the main principles on abandonment. On the contrary, the 'ductility' of the instrument contributed to the preservation of the overall uniformity despite the local differences.

5 Common Principles and Local Differences

Let us now focus on some of those differences. A first difference concerns the rules customarily applicable to the mandate to the insurers in different countries. To understand them properly, we have to look at other rules beyond abandonment. We have seen that abandonment to the insurers entailed the transfer of ownership in the object of the insurance, and that giving mandate to the insurers contextually to the abandonment was a remarkably widespread

18 *Ibid.*, document of May 16, 1591. Transcription *infra*, Appendix iv.

19 *Ibid.*, document of May 9, 1591. Transcription *infra*, Appendix iii.

practice. However, the insurance policy might be subjected to compulsory underinsurance. When that was the case, the abandonment entailed the passage of ownership from insured to insurers only for the part of the thing-at-risk covered by the policy. Where, on the contrary, there was no compulsory underinsurance, in principle the insured could abandon the entire value of the thing-at-risk to the insurers.

In the sixteenth century most Italian customs, particularly those of Venice and Florence, had no compulsory underinsurance.[20] This meant that the rules on abandonment worked on the assumption that the merchant might well insure the whole cargo, not just a part of it. So, the moment the insured abandoned in favour of the insurers, in principle they could receive the entire cargo (or ship), and not just a quota of its value. As a result, in those Italian regions the mandate was given for the whole of the cargo or ship insured. The possibility that the policy did not cover the entire value of the thing-at-risk was of course taken into account. In that case, both abandonment and mandate would simply mention that the insured retained ownership of the uninsured quota of the thing-at-risk. Still, and crucially, the mandate was given for the whole of it.[21] This avoided complex negotiations between the parties in a situation in which time was of the essence. Immediately upon receiving mandate, the insurers were free to act as they saw fit. The choice of whom to appoint as representative was only of the insurers. The insured had in principle no say on that, for the object of the insurance was no longer their property. As just said, the same applied even when the policy did not cover the entire value of the thing-at-risk. In such a case, the insured could rely on the simple fact

20 There is a general trend among insurance markets to progressively relax underinsurance provisions, first lowering the caps and then abolishing them altogether (either by statute or simply by desuetude). For Venice see Stefani, *Insurance in Venice*, 1:239; Giulio Giacchero, *Storia delle Assicurazioni Marittime: l'Esperienza Genovese dal Medioevo all'Età Contemporanea* (Genoa: Sagep, 1984), 59. For Florence see Guido Bonolis, 'Contributo alla Storia delle Assicurazioni in Firenze', *Archivio Storico Italiano* serie V, 22 (1898), 312–321; Livio Piattoli, 'Le Leggi Fiorentine sull'Assicurazione nel Medioevo', *Archivio Storico Italiano* serie VII, 18 (1932), 205–258, 208–209; Federigo Melis, *Origini e Sviluppi delle Assicurazioni in Italia (Secoli XIV–XVI)* (Rome: Istituto nazionale delle assicurazioni, 1975), doc. 37, 232–233.

21 See e.g. the Venetian policies of February 7, 1565, February 9, 1565, March 2, 1565, March 24, 1569 (all in Fondazione Mansutti di Milano, hereafter FMM, unnumbered), December 23, 1578, January 24, 1583, August 1, 1585, and two policies of May 25, 1589 (all transcribed in Stefani, *Insurance in Venice*, vol. 1, doc. 1–5, pages 249–256). See also the work of Wilfrid Brulez, *Marchands Flamans à Venise*, 2 vols. (Bruxelles-Rome, 1965–1986), where an extraordinary number of abandonments may be found.

that, for once, his interest in the matter was the same as that of the insurers, since they were now co-owners.

Such a practice was efficient as far as the mandate was concerned. But it was not efficient in other respects. When the insured merchant did not accompany the insured cargo, often his factor did. This meant that the insured party could be in a better position to act promptly than the insurers were, who had still to hear of the mishap and to appoint someone to deal with it. But if the insured was no longer the owner of the insured thing, then he had no incentive to act either – not least since the insurers might disapprove of his expenses and refuse to reimburse him. Still, these consequences were heavily dependent upon the imposition of compulsory underinsurance. Without it, they could not develop spontaneously by way of customary changes to current practice. Most Venetian and Florentine policies, at least from the mid-sixteenth century, state that in case of mishap the insured is more than welcome to recover and preserve the insured thing at the insurers' expenses (the so-called 'sue and labour' clause).[22] But very often this simply did not happen. When describing the Venetian wine taken by Englishmen, it was mentioned that the Venetian captain was probably insured for a considerable amount. This was a deliberate reference. Because it would seem that he did not do anything to recover the value of the wine until he returned to Venice and abandoned it to the insurers. Looking at Venetian records, this was hardly an isolated case. It is probable that the insured availed himself of the faculty to recover the insured cargo only (or mainly) when the insurance covered just a part of its value. It is commonplace to say that full coverage increase the insured's moral hazard. Whether it is true or not, it certainly did not encourage him to spend time and money to rescue the insured thing or to enforce his claim in case of destruction. He simply lacked the incentive to do so.[23]

Where on the contrary underinsurance was required, the same rules on abandonment and mandate worked differently. Let us look at Norman and Dutch practice. There, just as in Italy, the insured was given the faculty of

22 For Florence see the policies of December 24, 1588, January 13, 1589, January 23, 1589, October 25, 1589 (all in ACF, Room II, unnumbered) and August 6, 1602 (in FMM, unnumbered). As with the abandonment to the insurers, the 'sue and labour' clause was not present in sixteenth-century Florentine legislation. For Venice see the policies of February 7, 1565, February 9, 1565, March 2, 1565, March 24, 1569 (all in FMM, unnumbered), January 24, 1583 and May 25, 1589, both in Stefani, *Insurance in Venice*, vol. 1, doc. 2 and 5, 250–251 and 255–256 respectively.

23 It might not be fortuitous that the 'sue and labour' clause developed with significant delay in Florentine insurance practice, as it is not attested before the mid-sixteenth century. The scarce incentive of the insured might have slowed the reception of this clause.

recovering and preserving the insured thing at the insurers' expenses. But, unlike in Italy, it would seem that the insured took this faculty more seriously. He did so because, despite the insurance, he still had a considerable interest in the thing-at-risk. In both Normandy and the Low Countries, the merchant could not insure more than 90 per cent of the value of the cargo or ship.[24] There, the problem was not persuading the insured to do something, but making sure that he would not overdo it, because with the abandonment a good part of the thing-at-risk now belonged to the insurers. The solution was typically found in placing a cap on the refundable expenses the insured could incur. The amount of the cap varied from country to country – in Rouen it was 25 per cent of the cargo's value;[25] in Antwerp, 10 per cent.[26] Both customs had their logic: Rouen applied the same cap on the insured's expenses in the case of ransom as well as in that of recovery of the insured thing. In Antwerp the cap on the insured's expenses was the same as the compulsory underinsurance, so the insured could not overspend in respect of his remaining quota of the thing-at-risk.

A possible reason why Italian customs did not move spontaneously towards the position attested in Antwerp and Rouen was that, while it solved a basic problem, it also created a new one. Even when the insured intended to abandon, he would still remain interested in the preservation of the insured thing because he could not abandon the whole of its value. But since the abandonment was always limited to a portion of the value of the thing, the insured was reluctant to give mandate to the insurers for the whole. In other words, since both parties necessarily had an interest in the thing-at-risk, they had to work together even after the abandonment.

The appointment of a common representative for all the insurers was already complex and time-consuming enough as it was. First, each insurer had to be asked whether he wanted to contribute to the expenses. Then, the insurers who accepted the expenses had to agree on whom to appoint as their common representative.[27] The choice of the representative necessarily had to follow the individual enquiry to see who wanted to contribute to the recovery, for the representative was typically elected among the insurers who

---

24 For the Netherlands, see the Dutch *Placcaaten* of 1550 (cap. 22), 1563 (tit. VII, s. 11), and 1571 (s. 3), as well as the Amsterdam *Placcaat* of 1598, s. 2; for Belgium, see the Antwerp *Compilatae* of 1608, pt. iv, tit. 11, Section 1, art. 2; for Normandy, see the *Gvidon*, cap. 2, 8–9. The Dutch *Placcaaten* may be read in Pardessus, *Collection de Lois Maritimes*, 4:38–119.

25 *Gvidon*, cap. 7, 34–35. Cf. *ibid.*, cap. 6, 28–29.

26 Antwerp *Compilatae* of 1608, book iv, tit. 11, para 7, art. 252. Cf. Johan P. Van Niekerk, *The Development of the Principles of Insurance Law in the Netherlands from 1500 to 1800*, 2 vols. (Cape Town: Juta, 1998), 2:1299–1300.

27 Antwerp *Compilatae* of 1608, book iv, tit. 11, para 7, art. 249–254.

agreed to the expenses.[28] It was precisely because of the length of such operations that the customs of Rouen opted for a considerably higher cap on the expenses the insured was allowed to incur on behalf of the insurers. Given the insured's interest in the preservation of the cargo or ship, he would proceed with the recovery immediately after the mishap, so as to minimise the loss. He would act on behalf of both parties – himself and the insurers.[29] The amount he could spend (a quarter of the total value of the thing insured) considerably exceeded the uninsurable quota (of 10 per cent), but was not sufficient to encourage him to engage in inefficient (uneconomical) operations. Still, without a formal authorisation signed by all the insurers, the insured could not be certain of their approval about the way the money was spent – and so about future reimbursement.

As such, neither approach was fully satisfactory. In Antwerp, it was unsatisfactory because of the time needed for the insurers to agree on the representative to appoint, and the subsequent need to coordinate with the insured for the uninsured quota. In Rouen, because of the uncertainty of the insured as to his effective powers, both in terms of the kinds of operations and of the amount that could be spent. In this respect, it was simply more efficient for the insured to give full mandate to the insurers, including also the part of the cargo not covered by the policy – precisely the solution adopted in a large part of Italy. However, the 'Italian' solution required a mandate for the whole cargo because it moved from the assumption that the insured would no longer have any interest in it. And allowing the insured to divest himself of any interest in the insured thing was not an efficient rule to begin with. In other words, neither side – the 'Italian' or the 'Northern' one – was particularly efficient in abstract terms. But both adapted their specific rules so as to increase overall efficiency, given their normative framework. While the principles on abandonment were the same, the specific rules diverged. And this difference depended on the interaction with a different set of rules – namely, on compulsory underinsurance. A thorough revision of the entire institution of abandonment therefore would have been possible only if accompanied by a similar revision of the rules on underinsurance.

This is what happened in London in the late sixteenth century. It is not clear whether London insurance customs originally had any cap on the insurable quota. Given the strong links with Italy (on insurance matters, especially

28 *Ibid.*, art. 250.

29 The procedure for the appointment of a common representative would commence only if the insured refused to do so, and it would follow the underwriting values in descending order (the highest underwriter would be asked first, and so on). *Gvidon*, cap. 7, 35.

Florence), it is however likely that no compulsory underinsurance applied. After the mid-sixteenth century, however, the growing influence of Northern European markets (Antwerp in particular) resulted in major changes to London insurance practice.[30] The introduction of a 10 per cent compulsory underinsurance was one of them.[31] The moment the merchant was no longer allowed to insure the whole of his cargo, the abandonment could no longer apply to the entire value of the thing-at-risk. So, it became necessary to introduce some rules on the election of a common representative of both insurers and insured to proceed with the recovery of the cargo or the ship insured.

On the subject, London was probably influenced by both Rouen and Antwerp. From Antwerp it took the 10 per cent cap on the expenses the insured was allowed to incur without authorisation from the insurers.[32] As in Antwerp, the rationale of this cap was to protect the latter from unwelcome expenses – the insured could spend no more than the value of his quota left uninsured. At the same time, London carved out an exception to this rule. The insurers' approval was not required for higher expenses if the part of the cargo left uninsured was higher than the quota covered by the policy.[33] This exception, not attested elsewhere, might have depended on experience, as Italian merchants proved particularly active towards the preservation of the insured cargo when the policy covered a small portion of its value. If London borrowed the Antwerp 10 per cent cap rule, however, it sought to avoid the associated cumbersome procedure for the appointment of the common representative, and opted for the Rouen model instead. As such, the insured would act as common representative also for the insurers by default.[34] This hardly amounted to a blank cheque to the insured though. Not only was he subjected to a stringent expense limit, but also – and moreover – the insurers kept the right to elect a representative of their choice and to prevent the insured from acting on their

30 On the changes to London insurance customs during the late sixteenth century see David J. Ibbetson, 'Law and Custom: Insurance in Sixteenth-Century England', *Journal of Legal History* 29 (2008), 291–307; and Guido Rossi, 'The London "Booke of Orders": a 16th Century Civil Law Code in England', *Maastricht Journal of European and Comparative Law* 19 (2012), 240–261.

31 London, British Library MSS Harleian 5103, art. 59, fol. 170*r*–*v*, and Additional 48023, [art. 65], fol. 262*r*.

32 In all probability, the Antwerp influence was mediated through the Ordinances of the Spanish Consulate in Bruges: see Guido Rossi, *Insurance in Elizabethan England: The London Code* (Cambridge: Cambridge University Press, 2016).

33 London, British Library MSS Harleian 5103, art. 85, fol. 175*v*, and Additional 48023, [art. 93], fol. 266*r*.

34 *Ibid.*

behalf for the insured quota, if they wished. In such a case the insured and the insurers' representative would have to coordinate the operations of recovery and preservation of the cargo together.[35]

Whether this new system worked smoothly – or, at least, significantly better than the others we have seen – we do not know. But it would not seem likely. The mercantile community seems to have sought to reconcile the impossible. On the one side, this new system envisaged a prompt start of the recovery operations – which necessarily meant putting the insured in charge. On the other side, there were stringent limits to the same insured, both as to the amount he was allowed to spend without the approval of the insurers, and with regard to the possibility that the insurers would appoint a different representative.

What is important to our purposes, however, is that these deep changes in the structure of abandonment – moving from a Mediterranean (Italian) model to a Northern (Antwerp-Rouen) one – were possible because the changes in London also extended to the insurable quota. Without that, a thorough revision of the abandonment would not have been possible. At most, London merchants could have sought to improve the overall efficiency of their system working within its existing normative framework, not replacing it.

6 Deceptive Affinities

Other differences between insurance markets may be fully appreciated only by looking at their economic context. To explain this point, we will now examine the scope of abandonment, looking in particular at the specific restrictions imposed on its exercise in London and Antwerp.

The abandonment clearly worked to the benefit of the insured, who recovered the value of their goods in full, irrespective of whether the insured thing was completely lost, partially damaged, or perfectly intact but in someone else's possession. As such, it was necessary to put some limits to its scope. Those limits were meant to redress the balance of interests between the parties. According to the scope of those restrictions, a custom might be more or less permissive on abandonment, and so more or less favourable to the insured. Comparing those restrictions, one can better appreciate how common principles resulted in diverging practical rules, and how such divergence depended on different balances of interests. Three examples follow.

First, partial abandonment. Most insurance customs allowed partial abandonment, that is, abandoning to the insurers only the merchandise that

35 *Ibid.*

suffered damage or loss, and not the entire cargo insured.[36] Partial abandonment was considerably widespread.[37] Only a few customs forbade it, mainly the Antwerp *Compilatae* of 1608,[38] which sought to discontinue a pre-existing practice, probably allowed in Antwerp until then.

Second, ship's unseaworthiness. Another restriction to abandonment (although a less common one) applied to the case of the ship's unseaworthiness. During navigation, it might happen that the ship had to stop for repairs or it had to be abandoned altogether. In those cases, several insurance customs allowed the immediate abandonment of the cargo.[39] Again, Antwerp customs sought progressively to limit the scope of this case of abandonment. While until the 1580s the insured could abandon at once,[40] from the early seventeenth century he had to wait for a whole month.[41] This limitation was meant as an encouragement to the insured to trans-ship the cargo onto another vessel instead of relinquishing its property to the insurers. On the subject, London customs underwent a more drastic change. Initially, the insured was free to abandon for unseaworthiness of the vessel. During the second half of the sixteenth century, however, this changed and the insured was expressly prohibited from doing so.[42] The prohibition was not simply a forced delay in the exercise of the insured's right – as in Antwerp – but an outright revocation of that same right.

Third and last, there was abandonment for damages. A particularly important limitation to abandonment might be imposed for the case in which the mishap did not result in the total loss of the cargo, but only in some damages to it. Also in this respect, both Antwerp and London customs placed stringent limits on the scope of abandonment during the late sixteenth century – more than most coeval insurance customs. While allowing abandonment for damages in principle, in practice London restricted it with so many exceptions that it left very little scope for its actual application.[43] In Antwerp no restriction

36 Two basic restrictions are however typically attested on partial abandonment. First, the abandonment applied to the whole kind of merchandise that suffered damage or that was lost, not just a part of it. Second, the loss was rated on the whole insured cargo.

37 E.g. BL MSS Harleian 5103, art. 86, fols. 175*v*–176*r*, and Additional 48023 [art. 94], fol. 266*r*; *Gvidon*, cap. 7, 36–37; Burgos Ordinances of 1538, ord. 79; Bilbao Ordinances of 1560, ord. 57.

38 Antwerp *Compilatae* of 1608, book iv, tit. 11, para 7, art. 226.

39 E.g. Seville Ordinances of 1556, ord. 55; Amsterdam *Placcaat* of 1598, s. 25.

40 Antwerp *Antiquae* of 1571, tit. 29, and *Impressae* of 1582, tit. 54, s. 14.

41 Antwerp *Compilatae* of 1608, book iv, tit. 11, para 7, art. 225.

42 BL MSS Harleian 5103, art. 29, fol. 163*v*, and Additional 48023 [art. 30], fol. 225*r*.

43 BL MSS Harleian 5103, art. 4, 23, 41–42, 44–46, 50, fols. 158*v*–168*v*, and Additional 48023, [art. 6, 24, 47–48, 50–51, 52, 56], fols. 247*r*–260*v*.

applied in the *Antiquae* of 1571, but the *Compilatae* of 1608 wholly prohibited it.[44] Restrictive positions on the subject were not uncommon,[45] but the timing of the change in Antwerp and London does not appear to be fortuitous, as we will now see.

The three examples above attest the shift towards a more restrictive approach on insurance in the markets of Antwerp and London. At first, this shift would seem substantially similar for the two markets: both the timing and the normative content of the changes were nearly identical. However, the opposite is true. For the same shift was the product of different stages in the 'financial life' of their respective markets. The position of Antwerp in the early seventeenth century was that of a market in decline. The main reason for that lies in the blockade of the Scheldt by the Dutch fleet, which progressively strangled Antwerp's economy. Markets in difficulty tend to shift towards more restrictive positions, and Antwerp was no exception. The relationship between a stagnating economy and restrictive normative attitudes is particularly evident in early modern insurance markets, for the contraction of the economy meant difficult credit access. In such conditions, even a single unlucky underwriting could prove fatal to the insurer. This was the reason why, a few decades earlier than Antwerp, in 1572, the Spanish Consulate of Burgos brought some changes to its insurance customs (of 1538) to better protect its insurers. The difference between the Burgos customs of 1538 and those of 1572 is less conspicuous than that between earlier and later customs of Antwerp. But that is probably due to the fact that Burgos was remarkably restrictive (and so, 'pro-insurer') from the outset. The changes in its rules on insurance were not so pronounced only because there were not many additional limitations that could be reasonably imposed on the insured. But the very fact that some further restrictions were introduced, despite an already stringent set of limitations to the insured, would seem quite revealing. The same need to protect the insurers led to a similar change in Antwerp. Unlike in Burgos, in Antwerp the change was more evident because of the previously more 'liberal' attitude of its insurance customs.

---

44 Contrast the Antwerp *Antiquae* of 1571, tit. 29, with the *Compilatae* of 1608, book iv, tit. 11, para 6, art. 186.

45 In Rouen the abandonment for damages was excluded in principle, except in the situation where the damage amounted to half or more of the insured value, or the merchandise had a value at destination of less than half of the expected value (*Gvidon,* cap. 7, 32 and 37 respectively). In Venice, abandonment for damages was already customarily excluded in the fifteenth century. See Karin Nehlsen-von Stryk, *L'assicurazione Marittima a Venezia nel XV Secolo*, (trans.) Carla Vinci Orlando (Rome: Il Veltro, 1988), 408–431.

The reason for London's shift from 'liberal' to protective (i.e. pro-insurer) measures is entirely different to Antwerp's. The markedly pro-insurer attitude of London was not the product of a declining market, but rather of a very young one. Earlier insurance customs were considerably more permissive (and so, ultimately, pro-insured). But they were customs applied mainly by foreign merchants for their transactions in England. In a way, therefore, they were 'English' only because they were attested in England, not because they were customarily applied by English merchants. English merchants began to take an interest in insurance only during the first half of the sixteenth century, and until the 1550s the whole insurance market was still in the hands of foreigners. Only then did the English insurance market become properly English. But the transition needed time. By the late sixteenth century most investors were still simply 'trying their luck' with one-off underwritings. Few ever took out a policy themselves. Such an environment betrays a considerably high risk aversion, where bad news could easily trigger panic and deter from further underwritings. Hence the interest in protecting potential insurers at the expenses of the insured.[46]

Thus, the ultimate reason for the increasingly restrictive (and 'pro-insurer') attitude of both London and Antwerp depended on the increased risk aversion of merchants. But while in Antwerp this was probably due to restricted (that is, more expensive) credit access, in London it depended on the lack of familiarity with the insurance instrument. The same phenomenon had very different reasons, which could only be explained by taking into account the specific economic environment. A simple comparison between the two customs would not suffice. Worse than that, it would lead to the wrong conclusions.

Appendix

i Mandate to Recover the Cargo, 1 September 1586, ACF, Room II, Unnumbered

An English merchant's mandate to his Antwerp business correspondents for the recovery of some fustian shipped from Hamburg to London but which was captured by Dunkerque privateers. Authenticated English translation of the original Dutch text.

Translated owte of Duche

46 Cf. Guido Rossi, 'England 1523–1601: the Beginnings of Marine Insurance', in Adrian B. Leonard (ed.), *Marine Insurance: International Development and Evolution* (London: Palgrave Macmillan, 2015), 139–140.

In the name of God Amen: By this *pre*seunte publyke Instrumente of Procuracion be it knowne and manifeste vnto all menne that on the firste daye of the moneth of September in the yeare of our Lorde Jesus Chryste on thowsande Fyvehondreth Fowreskore and Sixe [1586] And in the Eyght&twentieth yeare of the Raigne of our moste gracious Lady & Queene Elizabeth Before me Cornelius Spirink Notary & Tabellion publyke dwelling in the citie of London by the authority of the saide Queenes Ma*ies*ty admitted & sworne & in the *pres*ence of the witnesses vnderwritten Parsonally appeared the wourshippfull Phillip Corsini m*er*chaunte florentin dwelling on this Citie of London (vnto me Notary well knowne) w*hi*ch aforesaide appeareth (assuming for his brother Bartholmew Corsini beinge absente) hath in the beste forme & manner vnto him possible by lawe authorised & constituted even as he doeth authorise & constitute by theis *pre*seunt*es* Baptiste de Sottovelasques and Fraunch Tassis both merchant absent as yf they were *pre*seunte, Iointly & severally, Gyvinge vnto them full power authority & special chardge For and in the name of the saide Bartholmew Corsini to pursue the recovery of Tenne Bales of Millian fustians beinge marked with the markes in the margent, which now of late have bene laden at hambarowe [Hamburg] in the shippe of Richarde Powlter Englisheman for to be transported from thence toward*es* this Citie of London and the same shippe following her voyage hath bene taken (as he constituant affirmed) on the Seas by those of dunkerke in flanders where the saide good*es* nowe remaynem Lykewyse yf it be possible to compounde & agree w*i*th those w*hi*ch have taken the saide bales w*i*th fustians or ells to buy the same agayne for the saide Bartholmewe Corsini for suche a som*me* of mony and to moste profit of the saide Bartholmew vnto him possible / To gyve & acknowledge acquytance, to swere in the sowle of him Constituante (even as already he hath donne in the hands of me Notary) that the same fustians are belonging & app*er*tayninge vnto the said Bartholmew Corsini his brother John Battista Toncis And Jerome Superletto m*er*chaunt*es* of Cremona And yf neede be for the recovery of the saide tenne bales of fustians or any parte thereof to sue the Lawe To appeare before whatsoever Lord*es* Iudges & Iustices to sue the Lawe To oberve all dayes & termes of Lawe & further for the sute to doe & discharge all that w*hi*ch therevnto shalbe necessary & requyred according to Lawe style & vse or custome of the place / And concerning the premises & dependences thereof to doe procure & administer all that w*hi*ch he constituant or his aforesaide brother beinge p*er*sonally *pre*seunte myght doe allthowgh the matter dide requyre more special power then theis p*resentes*, w*i*th power also one or more Attorneys w*i*th lyke or limited power to Substitute Them agayne to revoke remayninge neverthelesse these p*resentes* in full strength & vertew Promysinge the saide constituant in the hand*es* of me the saide Notary that he the saide Bartholmew Corsini his brother for ever shall have & holde for good fyrme & of valewe all that w*hi*ch by his sayde Attorny and Substitut*es* shalbe donne procured & administred in & abowte the *pre*misses, To staunde to the lawe and to fulfill that w*hi*ch shalbe adIudged yf neede be, Byndinge therevnto his p*er*son and all & singular his good*es* moveable vnmoveable p*re*sente & to come Even thus donne & passed in the cittie of London in the p*re*sence of Barnarde Geimi & Aron deens inhabitans of the saide citie witnesses herevnto called & requyred, Subscrybed per me Filippo Corsini

Haec translatio concordat substantialiter cum Registro
Ita attestor Cornelius Spirink Notarius publicus
1 Sep. 1586

ii Abandonment to the Insurers, 9 May 1591, ACF, Room II, Unnumbered

The document contains a copy of the two policies and the respective bills of lading, of the declaration of abandonment to the insurers and finally of the mandate to the insurers. Policies and bills of lading are in Italian, abandonment and mandate in Latin.

Cum sic, quod sub die secunda Januarij proxime praeteriti fuerint factae infras*cri*ptae securitates viz

A di 2 di Gennaio 1590 in Firenze[47]
Noi a pie di questa scritta sottoscritti assicuriamo le somme da noi dichiarate al Mag*nifi*co Diego della Torre sopra tre balle di rasee di Firenze, et sopra ogn'altra sorte di Mercantie saluo le prohibite da S*ignori* Off*itia*li di sicurta attenente à detto Diego della Torre, et à Cristofaro de Aldara de Siuilla, et altri sua amici carichi, o da caricarsi nel Porto, o spiaggia di Liuorno per le mani di Gio*vanni* Batt*ist*a Pezzini d'ordine di Gio*vanni* Maria Rucellai & *soci* di Pisa per commissione del detto Diego della Torre alla nave nominata santo Rocco Padrone Pietro di Gio*vanni* Vadopia Raugeo le quali rasee assicuriamo da che saranno cariche con el nome di Dio in detto Porto, o spiaggia di Liuorno, in detta nave sino à che saranno scariche in terra a buono saluamento in Cadiz contentandoci in virtù della p*rese*nte scritta correre ogni sorte di risico sop*ra* le dette rasee come se la fussi scritta publica di securtà fata per mano, et con interuento di publico mezzano, et uolendo habbia la medesima forza et uigore, et con li meesimi patti, et capitoli et conuentioni, che si contengono in le scritte ordinarie di sicurta dando la medesima forza, et uigore, et sottomettendoci ad ogni risico, et caso generale et particolare nella istessa forma et modo, che si contengano in dette scritte di sicurta

47 The policies in both Appendices ii and iv are written in the Pisan style. Unlike Florence, where the policy opened with the party who wanted to be insured, in Pisa the subject of the policy were the underwriters. It is remarkable that the Pisan style survived so long, despite the fact that Pisa had long become a secondary insurance market, gravitating around that of Florence. The reason why these policies are written in the Pisan style despite being made in Florence is probably because the insured were Pisan merchants.

fatte p*er* mano di pubblico mezzano sottomettendoci ad esse in ogni loro parte in tutto e per tutto promettendo nel osseruanza inuiolabilmente q*uesto* di et anno in Firenze

sc. 600 d'oro	Noi Rede di Federigo de Ricci & s*oci* di banco assecuriamo p*er* scudi secento d'oro di li*re* sette et mezzo per sc*u*do et auiamo ricevuto Il risico a noue percento Dio la salui detto di 2 di gennaio 1590 ab Incanatione Domini
sc. 150 d'oro	Io Franc*esco* Velluti assecuro per sc*udi* centocinquanta d'o*ro* et ho ricevuto il premio questo di soprad*etto* Idio la salui
sc. 120 -	Io Tommaso di Antonio scarlattini assicuro per sc*udi* centouenti d'o*ro* come di sopra di che ho riceuuto il premio questo di sudetto Iddio la salvi

A di 2 gennaio 1590 In Firenze
Noi a piè di questa scritta, sottoscritti assecuriamo le somme da noi dichiarate al Mag*nifi*co Diego della Torre sopra Drappi di oro e di seta di ogni sorte attenenti à Lorenzo di Castro di Valla*doli*d et sopra dua tauole di ciambellotti di levante attenente à Christofano Penndosa di M*edin*a del Campo, et sopra ogni altra sorte di mercantie saluo le prohibite da S*ignori* Offi*tia*li di sicurta attenente al detto Diego della Torre, et altri sua amici cariche, o da caricarsi nel porto, o spiaggia di Liuorno per le mani di Gio*vanni* Batt*ist*a Pezzini di ordine di Gio*vanni* Maria Rucellai & s*oci* di Pisa p*er* commissione del detto Diego della Torre alla nave nominata santo Rocco padrone Pietro di Gio*vanni* Vadopia Raugeo; le quali mercantie assicuriamo da che saranno cariche con el nome di Dio in detto porto, o spiaggia di Liuorno in detta nave sino a che sarannno scariche in terra a buon saluamento in Alicante contentandoci in virtu della p*rese*nte scritta correre ogni sorte di risico sopra li detti drappi e ciambellotti come se la fussi scritta publica di sicurta fatta per mano, et con interuento di publico mezzano, et uolendo habbia la medesima forza, et uigore et con li medesimi patti, et capitoli, et conuentione, che si contengano in le scritte ordinarie di sicurta, dannoli (*sic*) la medesima forza, e uigore, et sottomettendoci ad ogni risico, et caso generale, e particolare nella stessa forma, e modo, che si contengono in dette scritte di sicurta fatte per mano di publico mezzano sottomettendoci ad esse in ogni loro parte in tutto, et per tutto promettendone l'osservanza inuiolabilmente questo di, et anno in Firenze

sc. 700	Noi Rede di Federigo de Ricci & s*oci* di banco assicuriamo per sc*udi* settecento di li*re* sette & dieci p*er* sc*udo* e auiamo ricevuto cinque per c*en*to detto di 2 gennaio 1590 – idio la salvi
sc. 200	Io Francesco Velluti assicuro per sc*udi* dugento d'o*ro* come di sopra, et ho ricevuto il premio questo di sopradetto dio la salvi

sc. 250 Io Tommaso d'Antonio Scarlattini assicuro come di sopra per sc*udi* dugento cinquanta d'o*ro* di che ho ricevuto il premio q*uesto* di sud*etto* idio la salui

sc. 200 Io Gio*vanni* Francesco Sini assicuro per sc*udi* dugento d'o*ro* come di sopra, et ho ricevuto il premio questo di sopradetto idio la salui

s. 270 Io Franc*esco* sassetti assicuro come di la e detto per sc*udi* dugento settanta d'o*ro* di li*re* 7 ½ per sc*udo* et ho ricevuto il premio q*uesto* di 3 di gennaio 1590

et cum sit quod postea, et sub die 8 et x eiusdem mensis Ianuarij prox*imi* preteriti fuerint onust*ae* dictae raseiae, et drappi aurei, et ciambellotti super dicta naui, et propterea fuerint factae infra*scr*iptae Apodissae onerationis viz

A di 8 di Gennaio 1590
Ha carico col nome di Dio, et di buon saluamento in questo Porto di Liuorno Gio*vanni* Batista Pezzini di commissione del Mag*nifi*co Gio*vanni* Maria rucellai di Pisa et lui disse d'ordine del Sig*nor* Diego della Torre di Firenze sopra la naue nominata san Rocco capitano Pietro di Giovanni Vadopia raugeo per consegnare in Cadiz a Christofano di Aldara di Siuilla, o, a chi per lui –

3 balle tre in elle quali dissene esser pezze dodici di rasee nere segnate di auanti segno nº 6 . 7. 8 auolte in canovaccio e ben conditionate il qual capitano promette consegnare come sopra pagando di nolo reali cento quarantaquattro per tutte, et in fede sara firmato la p*rese*nte poliza con tre altre simile, che consegnando per l'una l'altre restino di nulla ualore idio la salui – Io Luca di Gio*vanni* scriuano di detta nave affermo quanto di sopra disse esser

IHS A di x di gennaio 1590
Ha carico con nome de Dio e di buon saluamento in questo Porto di Liuorno Gio*vanni* Batt*ist*a Pezzini di commiss*io*ne del M*agnifi*co Gio*vanni* Maria rucellai di Pisa, et lui disse di ordine del S*ignor* Diego della Torre di Fior*en*za sopra la naue nominata san Rocco, Capitano Pietro di Gio*vanni* Vadopia raugeo p*er* consegnare in Alicante a Gio*vanni* Auigliano come roba di conto di Christofano Pennalosa –

2 tavole dua nelle quali dissero esser pezze trenta di ciambellotti per tauola segnate di avanti segno nº 14 . 15 e ben conditionate il qual capitano promette consegnare come sopra pagando di nolo reali trenta per tauola cui fede sarà firmato la p*rese*nte poliza con tre altre simile, che consignando p*er* l'una l'altre restino di nulla valore idio la salvi – Io luca di Gio*vanni* scriuano di detta nave affermo q*ua*nto di sopra disse essere

IHS A di x di gennaio 1590
Ha carico col nome di dio e di buon salvamento in questo porto di Liuorno Gio*vanni* batt*ist*a Pezzini di commiss*io*ne del Mag*nifi*co Gio*vanni* Maria Rucellai di Pisa, et lui

disse d'ordine del S*ignor* Diego della torre di Fior*en*za sopra la naue nominata san Rocco Capitano Pietro di Gio*vanni* Vadopia Raugeo per consegnare in Alicante à Gio*vanni* Auegliano di conto di Lor*en*zo di Castro di Vill*adoli*d –

1 cassetta una nella quale dissero essere pezzi quattro di drappo d'oro, segnate de auanti segno n° 27 e ben conditionate il qual Cap*ita*no promette consegnare come sopra pagando di nolo reali ottanta castellani, e in fede sara firmato la p*rese*nte poliza con tre altre simili, che consegnando p*er* l'una l'altre restino di nulla ualore idio la salui – Io Luca di Giovanni scriuano di detta nave affermo quanto di sopra disse essere

Cum que sit quod de eodem mense Januarij, siue alio ueriori tempore eade*m* nauis nuncupata sancto Rocco patronizzata per dictu*m* Petru*m* Joannis vadoppia Rauseum fuerit capta, siue depredata ab Anglis in ea plaga maris, quae est inter Barcinonem, et Alicantem, et merces in naui *prae*dicta onustae fuerint ab Anglis *prae*dictis transvectae in Insula Angliae, et propterea uenerit casus solutionis summarum *prae*dicta*rum*, ut supra respectiue assicuratar*um*, et ipsi assicuratores uelint, prout parest, illas soluere, et infra*scr*iptam cessionem Iurium impetrare – Hinc est quod constituti in p*raesen*tia mea et testium dicti et et infra*scrip*ti D*omi*ni assicuratores, quorum nomina inferius describentur, actualiter et in prompta, et numerata pecunia dederant, soluerunt, et numerauerunt dicto D*omino* Didaco siue Diego della Torre p*raese*nti, et ad se realiter et actualiter trahenti infra*scr*iptas summas, et quantitates ab infra*scrip*tis Assicuratoribus viz

Ab haeredibus Federici de Riccijs et socijs banci pro prima securitate sc*utos* sexentum viz sc*utos* 600
A Francisco de Vellutis pro eadem prima securitate sc*utos* centumquinquaginta viz sc*utos* 150
A Thommasio Antonij de scarlattinis pro dicta prima securitate sc*utos* centumuiginti viz sc*utos* 120
Et pro secunda securitate a dictis haeredibus Federici de Riccijs, et sociis banci sc*utos* septingenti*um* viz sc*utos* 700
Et ab eodem Franc*isco* de Vellutis pro dicta *secun*da securitate sc*utos* duecentum viz sc*utos* 200
Et a dicto Thommasio Antonij de scarlattis pro d*icta secun*da securitate sc*utos* duecentu*m*quinquaginta viz 250
Et a Ioanni Franc*isco* Sini p*er* dicta s*ecun*da securitate sc*utos* duecentu*m* viz sc*utos* 200
Et a Franc*isco* de sassettis pro dicta *secun*da securitate sc*utos* duecentumseptuaginta viz sc*utos* 270

De quibus respectiue summis dictus D*ominus* Diegus della Torre uocauit se bene solutum tacitum et contentu*m*, et ad cautelam renunciauit exeptioni nonnumeratae pecuniae. Et qui D*omino* Diegus della Torre ante dictarum pecuniaro (*sic*) solutionem per se et suos heredes omni in illud que potuit et potest cessit transtulit, et mandauit omnia Iura ipsi quomodolib*et* competentia, et competitura in, ad et super dictis raseijs, ciambellottis ed drappis aureis ut supra dictum est assicuratis, et quae fuerunt onusta super dicta naui, et postea ab Anglis fuerunt depraedata, cessit in quam (*sic*), dicta Iura dicti (*sic*) D*ominibus* assicuratoribus p*rese*ntibus, et recipientibus et cuilibet eoru*m* procurata ut supra per eos respectiue soluta, constituens se dicta Iura, uel quasi tenere pro dictis assicuratoribus, et constituens illos et quemlibet eoru*m* p*raese*ntes Procuratores ut in re ipsoru*m* propriam, et promittens dicta Iura esse penes eum salua integra, et illaesa et nemini cessa, et talia manutenere, et p*rae*dicta omnia Iura fuerant ad integram gabella*m* dictoru*m* D*ominorum* Assicuratoru*m* a qua promiserunt conseruare indemnem d*ictum* D*o*minu*m* Diegum pr*aesen*tem qu*ae* omnia promisit att*ine*re pena dupli quemquem pro quibus obligauit renunciauit cui per guarantigiam Rogantes

Actum Forentiae in Apotheca Actis iurici M*agnifi*cu*m* Haeredu*m* Federici de Riccijs iuxta proprie Forum nouu*m* D.I. Anno mill*esi*moquinq*uagintesi*monag*esi*moprimo Indictione quarta [1591]. Die vero nona mensis Maij Greg*orio* IX P.M. et Ser*enissi*mo Ferdinando Medici etrurie magno Duce dominante. Pr*aese*ntibus Joanne Baptista Michaelis de Guardis, et Raphaele Joannis Baptistae de Grandozzijs Ciuibus Florentinis Testibus

Ego Laurentius Mutius q*uondam* Cammilli filius imperiali auctoritate iudex ordinarius, notariusque publicus florentinus de praedictis in*petra*nti et alijs tribus proxime praecedentibus paginis manu misi fidi scriptis rogatus fui, et in fidem subscripsi, ac mei notariatus signum apposui

Nos Jacobus de spezialibus ciuis et not*arius* publicus fl*orentiae* nec non ad pr*aese*ns Praeconsul vniuersitatis iudicum et notarioru*m* Ciuitatis Flor*entiae* fidem facimus, et attestamum sup*radic*tum p*er* Laurentiu*m* mutiu*m* q*ui* de sup*radic*to instrumento solutionis, et cessionis fuit rogatus, et illud subscripsit fuisse, et esse legalem authenticu*m*, et fidedignum notariu*m* publicu*m* Florentinu*m*

Flor*entiae* die 15 maij 1591

iii Mandate to the Insurers' Representatives in London, 9 May 1591, ACF, Room II, Unnumbered

Immediately upon receiving the insured cargo from the insured and paying the insurance value in full, the insurers gave mandate to their representatives in London to proceed with the recovery of the cargo or of its value.

I.H. Dei nomine Amen. Anno ab incarnatione D*omi*ni nostri Iesu Ch*ris*ti Millesimo quingentes*imo* nonagesimo primo ind*ictio*ne 4 Die uero nona mensis Maij Greg*orio* 14 P.M. et Ser*enissi*mo Ferdinando Medice Etruriae magno Duce dominante. Actum Florentiae in foro nouo mercatoru*m* p*raesen*tibus Franc*isc*o Ioannis bart*olom*ei di quaratensibus et Mario Petri di Perinis ciuibus flor*enti*nis t*es*tibus

Multum mag*nifi*ci Domini Vincentius de Riccijs nobilis ciuis et senator florentinus socius et institor, ac administrator societatis, et rationis Florentiae uigentis, et caritatis in haeredes Federici de Ricciijs, et socios banci de Florentia Franciscus de Vellutis similiter ciuis, et mercator florentinus, Tommas Antonij de Scarlattinis similiter ciuis et Mercator florentinus, Ioannes Franciscus de Sinis similiter ciuis, et Mercator florentinus ut et tamquam assicuratores quarumdam rasciarum, ciambellottorum, et drapporum auri (*sic*) onustorum p*er* Ioannem baptistam de Pezzinis in portu liburni de commissione D*omini* Diegi de la Torre Florentiae residentis sup*er* naui nuncupata Sancto Rocco capitanata p*er* Petrum Ioannis Vadoppia Rauseum pro consignando in Alicante Ioanni de Auellano, quae res una cum reliquis mercibus onustis sup*er* dicta naui fuerit depraedata ab Anglis, et qui Domini assicuratores summas p*er* eos assicuratas, propter depraedationem praed*ic*tam dicto Domino Diego della Torre soluerunt, et ab eo cessionem iurium sup*er* dictis rebus impetrauerunt, prout constat instrumento rogato manu mea notarij infra*scrip*ti sub hac p*raese*nti supra*dic*ta

Dicti inquam superius nominati domini assicuratores, et cessionarij ut et tamq*uam* assicuratores, et cessionarij praedicti tam coniunctim quam diuisim, et omni alio meliori modo uia, iure, causa, nomine, et forma, quo, qua, et quibus magis, et melius potuerunt, et possunt, fecerunt, constituerunt, et solemniter ordinauerunt eorum, et dictorum heredu*m* Federici de Riccijs ueros, certos, leg*iti*mos, et indubitatos procuratores, actores, factores, et negocioru*m* suorum infra*scrip*torum gestores et certos nuncios generales, et speciales ita tamen quod generalitas specialitati non deroget, nec e contra viz mag*nifi*cos D*omi*nos P*hi*lippum de Corsinis, et Bernardu*m* de Gerinis nobiles florentinos Londini residentes, et quemlibet eoru*m* in solidum licet absentes, ita tamen quod non sit melior conditio primitus occupantis, nec deterior subsequentis, sed quicquid unus eorum incoeperit, id alter prosequi finire, et cum effectu terminare prosit, et ualeat, specialiter, et expresse ad nomine, et pro parte dictoru*m* Dominoru*m* constituentiu*m*, et cuiuslibet uel alterius eoru*m* petendu*m* habendu*m*, exigendum, et recuperandum, uel si habuisse, et recepisse confitendum dictas rascias, ciambellottos, et drappos auri sup*er* dicta naui nuncupata sancto Rocco per dictum Petrum Ioannis Vadoppia patronizzata, siue capitaneata, et quae rasciae, et ciambellotti, et drappi aurei fuerunt per eosdem D*omi*nos constituentes assicurati, et pro quibus impetrauerunt cessionem à dicto D*omi*no Diego della Torre, fuit dictaru*m* reru*m* preciu*m*, et ualorem exigendum a quacum*que*, et quibuscum*que* persona, et personis loco comune corpore, collegio, societate, et uniuersitate in cuius potestate sunt uel erunt, et ad quos restitutio, et consignatio dictaru*m* reru*m* pertinet, et spectat tam*quam* res, et mercimonia ad dictos D*omi*nos constituentes mercatores florentinos pertinentes et qui propter assicurationes praedictas damnum ex depraedatione dictaru*m* reru*m* sentiunt: et de habitis, et receptis ex actis, ac recuperatis, et de his, quae dicti eoru*m* procurators habebunt, exigent, et recipient, quamcum*que* finem quietationem, absolutionem, et pactum perpetuu*m* de amplius non petendo faciendu*m* cum solemnitatibus oportunis: Et pro recuperatione, et ex pactione praedicta si opus erit ad comparendum coram Ser*enissi*ma D*omi*na Regina Angli*ae*, et coram quocum*que* Gubernatore administratore, Iudice, Magistratu, et Tribunali, et alijs quibusuis hominibus, et personis quomodolibet ad ius, et iustitia deputatis, uel deputandis, quocum*que* nomine nuncupantur, et quocum*que* fungantur officio uel regimine, et coram quibuscum*que* alijs hominibus, et p*er*sonis coram quibus comparendu*m* esset, et dicta Ser*enissi*ma D*omina* Regina et alijs quibus opus erit supplicandu*m*, et quascum*que* preces, siue petitiones porrigendu*m* pro ricuperatione dictaru*m* rasciaru*m* ciambellottoru*m* et drapporu*m* auri, siue eoru*m* ualoris, et precij, et quasqum*que* scripturas, et probationes exhibendum, et quaecum*que* iuramenta licita tamen, et honesta in animas, et sup*er* animas dictoru*m* Dominoru*m* constituentiu*m* praestandu*m*, et subeundum, et quoru*m*cum*que* rescripto*rum* exequutionem petendum, et etia*m* si opus erit ad fieri faciendum quascum*que* citationes, requisitiones, protestationes, capturas, carceratones, grauamenta, staggimenta, sequestrationes, subhastationes, et demu*m* omnes, et quascum*que* exequutiones tam reales, quam personales, quae erunt necessariae, aut quomodolibet oportunae pro recuperatione praedicta, et ad agendu*m*, causandum, et defendendum et omnes et singulos actus faciendum, qui sub uerbis agere, et causari ueniunt, et comprehenduntur, cum clausula ad lites, et causas in forma amplissima et secundum magis amplum stilum notarioru*m* Ciuitatis londini, siue loci, et locorum, ubi praedicta fieri co*n*tigerit. Item ad substituendum, et loco ipsorum ponendum unu*m*, uel plures procuratores cum eadem, uel magis limitata facultate et substitutos reuocandum totes quoties ipsis D*omi*nis procuratoribus principalibus uidebitur, et placebit. Et generaliter ad faciendum in praed*ic*tis et circa praedicta Omnia et singula necessaria, requisita, et oportuna, et quae dicti Domini constituentes facere possent, si praemissis o*mni*bus et singulis p*raese*ntes, et p*er*sonaliter adessent, etia*m* si talia forent, quae mandatu*m* requirent magis speciale, quam p*raese*ntibus sit expressum, Dantes, atcque concedentes dictis eoru*m* p*ro*curatoribus, et cuilibet eoru*m* in solidu*m* et substituendis ab eis plenu*m* liberu*m* generale, ac speciale mandatu*m* faciendo, et exerciendi praedicta, et quodlibet p*rae*dictorum Promittentes sub hypoteca vel Releuantes vel Rogantes etc. ‡ et E*go* Franciscus de Sassettis ciuis et mercator florentinus

Ego Laurentius Mutius q*uondam* Cammilli filius imperiali auctoritate iudex ordinarius, notarius*que* publicus florentinus de praedictis rogatus in fidem sub*scripsi* ac mei notariatus signu*m* apposuit approbando remissum ut supra sub hoc signo ‡ factum, quia per errore*m* omiseram nomen dicti Francisci de Sassettis, qui in p*raese*nti mandato interuenit una cum alijs assicuratoribus

Nos Jacobus spezialiis ciuis et notarius publicus floren*tiae* nec non ad pr*aesens* Praeconsul vniuersitatis iudicum et notariorum Ciuitatis fl*orentiae* fidem facimus, et attestamus supra*dic*tum p*er* laurentiu*m* mutium q*ui* de supra*dic*to mandati instrumento fuit rogatus, et illud subscripsit fuisse, et esse legalem authenticum, et fidedignum notarum publicum flor*entinum*

Florentiae die 15 maij 1591

iv Abandonment to the Insurers, 16 May 1591, ACF, Room II, Unnumbered

The document contains a copy of another policy (on merchandise to be carried on the same ship as the previous two policies), of the two bills of lading of the merchandise insured, and of the declaration of abandonment to the insurers together with the mandate to deal with the insured cargo. Policy and bills of lading are in Italian, abandonment and mandate in Latin.

In Dei nomine Amen Cum sit quod usq*ue* sub die 22 mensis Decembris proxime praeteriti fuerint factae infrascriptae securitates per infrascriptus de infrascriptis vasseijs, armis, et rebus, et super id fuerint exlibrata, et subscripta cedula dictoru*m* assicurationum tenoris, et continentiae infrascripta viz

Addi 22 di Dicembre 1590 Noi à pie di q*ue*sta scritta sottoscritti assicuriamo le somme da noi dichiarate al Mag*nifi*co Pietro Fernandez di Salinas sopra raserie di Firenze nere, et mistie, et sopra alabarde, et drappi d'oro di Milano, et sopra ogn'altra mercantia di qual sorte essersi uoglia saluo le prohibite da S*igno*ri offitiali di sicurta attenente al detto Piero Fernandez de salinas, à Andrea de Solorzano à bernardo Cliores Martinez, à Diego de basal, et altri sua amici cariche, et da caricarsi nel porto, o spiaggia, di liuorno per le mani di France*s*co et Antonio Bersighelli d'ordine di Francesco, et Bartolomeo Bersighelli e *soci* di Pisa per commissione del detto Pietro Fernandez di salinas alla naue nominata san Rocco padrone Pietro di Giouanni Vadoppia ragugeo, le quali mercantie assicuriamo da che saranno cariche in terra a buon saluamento in Cadiz contentandoci in virtu della p*rese*nte scritta correre ogni sorte di risico sopra li detti drappi, raserie, et altro, come se la fussi scritta publica di sicurta fatta per mano, et con interuento di publico mezzano, et uolendo habbia la medesima forza, et uigore, et con li medesimi patti, et capitoli, et conuentioni, che si contengono in le scritte ordinarie di sicurta dandoli la medesima forza, et uigore, et sottomettendoci à ogni risico, et caso generale, et particolare nella stessa forma, et modo, che si contengono in dette scritte di sicurta fatte per mano di publico mezzano sottomettendoci ad esse in ogni parte loro in tutto et per tutto, et promettendone l'osseruanza inuiolabilmente questo di, et anno in Firenze

Io Domenico Berti assicuro per sc*udi* nouecento d'*o*r*o* et ho riceuuto il risico questo di 22 di d*ecem*bre 1590. In Firenze Dio la salvi

Io lottieri di Gio*vanni* Franc*esc*o Gherardi assicuro per sc*udi* trecento d'*o*r*o* Dio la salui et cum sit quod postea, et sub die 7mo et 9na mensis Ianuarij immediate post dictum mensem *decem*bris subsequentis anni ab Incarnatione D*om*ini 1590 et a Natiuitate 1591 [7 and 9 January 1591] ex commissione et mandato dicti D*omini* Petri Fernandez salinas fuerint in portu siue piaggia liburni oneratae infra*scrip*tae raseiae, arma *et* telae sup*er* dicta naui nuncupata sancto Rocco capitaneata per Petrum Ioannis Vadoppia Raguseum, et fuerint factae infra*scr*iptae apodissae onerationis viz

A di 7 di Gennaio 1590
Ha carico col nome di Dio et di buon saluamento una uolta tanto in porto di Liuorno, Francesco, et Antonio Bersighelli di commissione di Francesco, et Bartolomeo Bersighelli di Pisa, et loro dissero d'ordine, et commissione di Pier Fernando salinas di Firenze sopra la naue nominata san Rocco Capitano Pietro di Gio*vanni* Vadoppia Ragugeo per consegnare in Cadiz à Andrea di Soleriano (*sic*), o chi per lui, et sono di conto suo et d'altri –

3 Balle tre in che dissero essere pezze 12 di raserie, le noue nere, et tre mistie segnate d'auanti segno nº 1 . 2 . 3 auuolte in canouaccio, et incerato immagliate, e ben conditionate pagano di nolo reali dodici Castigliani per pezza Dio la salui Io luca di Giovanni scriuano di detta naue affermo quanto di sopra disse essere

A di 7 gennaio 1590
Ha carico col nome d'Iddio, e di buon saluamento una uolta tanto in porto di liuorno Francesco, et Antonio Bersighelli, di commissione di Francesco, et Bartolomeo Bersighelli di Pisa, et loro dissero d'ord*i*ne et commissione di Pietro Fernandez di salinas di Fiorenza sopra la naue nominata santo Rocco Capitano Pietro di Giouanni Vadoppia Ragugeo per consegnare in Cadiz à Michele Martinez de Iaureguì, et Gir*ola*mo de Iaureguì, che sono per conto di Bernardo cliores Martinez di Haeera (*sic*) et d'altri -

1. Balla una in che dissero essere pezze quattro di raserie nere fine segnate d'auanti segno nº 3 auuolte in canouaccio, et incerato ammagliata, e ben conditionata paga di nolo reali dodici cast*iglia*ni per pezza iddio la salui –

A di 9 di gennaio 1590
Ha carico col nome de Iddio, e di buon saluamento una uolta tanto in porto di liuorno Francesco, et Antonio Bersighelli di commissione di France*sco* et Bartolomeo Bersighelli di Pisa, et loro dissero d'ordine, et commi*ssion*e di Pier Fernandez salinas di Firenze sopra la naue nominata san Rocco Capitano Pietro di Giouanni Vadoppia Ragugeo per consegnare in Cadiz à Michel Martinez de Iauriguì, et Hieronimo (*sic*) de Iauriguì, o chi per loro per conto di detto della sala[48] –

48 Presumably, Pier Fernandez Salinas.

1. Cassa una in che dissero essere sei Alabarde

1. Cassettina una in che dissero esser un taglio di tela da giubboni segno inuolte in canouaccio ammagliate, et bene conditionate pagano di nolo reali quindici Castigliani per tutto Dio la salui – Io Luca di Giouanni scriuano di detta naue affermo q*ua*nto di sopra disse essere

Cumq*ue* sit quod de eodem mense Ianuarij eiusd*em* anni 1591 a Natiuitate ab Incarnatione uero 1590 – seu alio ueriori tempore dicta nauis nuncupata sancto Rocco patronizzata per d*ictum* Petrum Ioannis Vadoppia Ragugeum fuerit capta siue depredata à quibusdam Anglis in ea plaga maris quae est int*er* Barcinonem, et Alicantem, siue alio ueriori loco, et merces sup*er* naui pr*aedicta* onustae fuerint ab Anglis p*rae*dictis transuectae in Insulam Angliae, et propterea uenerit casus solutionis summaru*m* praedictarum ut supra respectiue assicuratar*um*, et ipsi assicuratores uelint (prout aequum est) illas soluere, et infras*cr*iptam cession*em* iurorum impetrare. Hinc est quod constituti in p*raese*ntia mea, et testium dicti Dominicu de Bertis, et Lotterius de Gherardis Ciues Florentini actualiter, et in prompta et numerata pecunia soluerunt, et numerauerunt d*icto* D*omino* Petro Fernandez salinas Florentiae residenti p*raese*nti, et ad se realiter, et actualiter trahenti infras*cr*iptas summas, et quantitates pecuniarium à dictis et infras*crip*tis assicuratoribus viz à dicto Dominico de Bertis summam et quantitatem sc*u*toru*m* nonagentor*um* auri, et à dicto Lotterio de Gherardis summam scutor*um* trecentoru*m*; De quibus respectiue summis dictus D*ominus* Petrus Fernandez salinas uocauit se bene solutum tacitum, et contentum, et ad cautelam renunciauit exceptioni non numeratae pecuniae – Et qui D*ominus* Petrus Fernandez salinas ante supra dictaru*m* pecuniaru*m* solutionem omni meliori modo quo potuit et potest cessit, trastulit, et mandauit dictis Dominis assicuratoribus praesentibus, et recipientibus, et cuiuslibet eorum pro rata sua ut supra per eos respectiue soluta omnia Iura sibi quomodolibet competentia in ad et super dictis raseijs, armis, et telis ac alijs ut supra assicuratis, et super dicta naui oneratis, et à dictis Anglis depraedatis Constituens se dicta Iura, uel quasi tenere pro dictis assicuratoribus, et constituens illos, et quemlibet eorum p*rese*ntes Procuratores ut in re ipsorum propria, promittens dicta Iura esse penes se salua integra, et illaesa, et nemini cessa, et talia manutenere promisit / quae omnia promisit attendere pena dupli quae qua pro quibus obligauit renunciauit cui per guarantigiam Rogans Actum Florentiae in Domo dicti Dominici de Bertis anno ab Incarnatione D*omini* n*ostri* I*esu* Chr*is*ti millesimo quingentesimo nonag*esi*mo primo Indictione quarta die uero Decima sexta mensis Maij Greg*o*rio xiiii P.M. et Ser*enissi*mo Ferdinando Medice Etruriae magno Duce Dominante, Praesentibus Christophoro Buoni de Rinuccis, et Antonio Pauli de Carnesecchis Ciuibus Florentinis Testibus.

Ego laurentius Mutius q*uondam* Cammilli filius, imperiali auctoritate iudex ordinarius, notariusq*ue* publicus florentinus de praed*ict*a solutione, et iuriu*m* cessione manu alterius mihi ficti in p*rese*nti, et alijs duabus prox*ime* praecedentibus paginis scriptis rogatus fui, et in fidem subscripsi, ac mei notariatus signum apposui

Nos Iacobus de spezialibus ciuis, et notarius publicus florentinus nec non ad pr*aesens* Proconsul uniuersitatis iudicum et notariorum Ciuitatis florentie fidem facimus, et attestamus supra*dic*tum Laurentium Mutium quod de supra*dicto* solutionis, et cessionis instrumento fuit rogatus, et illud subscrpsit fuisse, et esse legalem authenticum et fidedignum notarium publicum florentinum[49]

49 The seal covers place and date.

CHAPTER 6

Historiographical Opportunities of Notarized Partnership Agreements Recorded in the Early Modern Low Countries

Bram Van Hofstraeten

1 Introduction

At the end of the sixteenth century, Jacques Thuys, an Antwerp notary, published his *Ars Notariatus* (1585).[1] Although largely plagiarised, the book was reprinted numerous times and continued to play a key role within the notarial world of the Low Countries.[2] As a *formularium*, intended to help notaries in their daily activity of drafting deeds, it also contained a fictitious example of a partnership agreement. As such, Thuys indirectly provides an overview of those clauses that seemed to be commonly used by early modern merchants while establishing a private partnership.[3] The contracting parties are identified along with the object or line of industry of the company under discussion, while at the same time it makes reference to the intended duration of the partnership together with the respective contributions of the contracting parties to the establishment of the company. In addition, a proportional distribution of the profits or losses is agreed upon. The example also addresses the external relationship between the constituting partners with regard to obligations concluded with third parties, as it stipulated that such contracting always required the mutual consent of all the partners. Besides the *Ars Notariatus* of Thuys, a comparable significance is generally attributed to the *Notarius Belgicus* (1663) of Joan Baptist Joseph Huygens, at least in the Low Countries.[4] Unlike Thuys, who merely provided a fictitious example of a partnership agreement, Huygens stated that four elements had to be agreed upon explicitly in the partnership

1 Jacques Thuys, *Ars Notariatus: Dat is conste ende stijl van notarischap, begrepen in theorijcke ende practijcke* (Antwerp: Arnout s'Conincx, 1590).

2 Anton Fl. Gehlen, *Het notariaat in het tweeherig Maastricht: een rechtshistorische schets van de inrichting en practijk van het Maastrichtse notariaat vanaf zijn opkomst tot aan het einde van de tweeherigheid over de stad (1292–1794)* (Assen: Van Gorcum, 1981), 97.

3 Thuys, *Ars Notariatus*, 189–191.

4 Joan Baptist Joseph Huygens, *Notarius Belgicus oft Ampt der Notarissen verdeelt in theorie ende practyque*, 2nd ed. (Brussels: t'Serstevens, 1745), 141–146.

 | DOI 10.1163/9789004363144_007

instrument: the object of the partnership, the exact input of the respective partners, the intended duration of the company, and finally, the way in which profits or losses would be divided between or borne by the constituting partners.[5]

In reality, however, the contractual freedom that contracting parties had at their disposal usually rendered the notarized partnership agreements in a much lengthier document than one would expect from the basis of the writings of the aforementioned authors. By means of a quantitative analysis of the various kinds of contractual clauses, that can be found in a considerable number of preserved partnership agreements recorded by notaries in the early modern Low Countries, this article will evaluate the historiographical opportunities offered by such contracts.

The data set supporting this assessment consists of 162 notarized partnership agreements in total, of which 126 had been drafted and recorded in sixteenth-century Antwerp (1480–1620), 16 in seventeenth-century Liège (1575–1705), nine in seventeenth-century Maastricht (1650–1700), six in seventeenth-century Amsterdam (1595–1650), and five in seventeenth-century Rotterdam (1630–1680).[6] Almost all of them are structured and subdivided into an introductory part, a centre section, and a closing clause.

5 Huygens, *Notarius Belgicus*, 141–146.

6 Bram Van Hofstraeten, 'The Organization of Mercantile Capitalism in the Low Countries: Private Partnerships in Early Modern Antwerp (1480–1620)', *Tijdschrift voor Sociale en Economische Geschiedenis* 13:2 (2016), 1–24; Bram Van Hofstraeten, 'Private Partnerships in Seventeenth-century Maastricht', in Bram Van Hofstraeten and Wim Decock (eds.), *Companies and Company Law in Late Medieval and Early Modern Europe* (Louvain: Peeters, 2016), 129–166; Simon Van Brakel, 'Ontbrekende schakels in de ontwikkeling van ons vennootschapsrecht', in Sybrandus Johannes Fockema Andreae et al. (eds.), *Rechtshistorische opstellen aangeboden aan Mr S.J. Fockema Andreae, hoogleraar aan de Rijksuniversiteit te Leiden* (Haarlem: De Erven F. Bohn, 1914), 153–194; Simon Van Brakel, 'Een tiental vennootschapsacten uit de 17de eeuw', *Bijdragen en mededeelingen van het Historisch Genootschap* 37 (1916), 182–231. The partnership agreements with regard to seventeenth-century Liège will be studied more extensively in the next volume of this series on *The Making of Commercial Law*, entitled *Small, Medium-sized and Large Companies in Law and Economic Practice*. Notwithstanding the considerable size of the data set at our disposal, one has to keep in mind that there may be a potential bias because of three phenomena. Firstly, the study was exclusively based on partnership agreements that had been registered by notaries. Consequently, privately drafted and oral contracts, which were still a very popular means for establishing private partnerships, could not be included. The same is true in the case of those partnership agreements that may have been recorded officially by other municipal institutions. Secondly, the preserved notarial archives are not comprehensive either, for there are various notaries whose protocol books did not survive. Finally, there is the assumption that strangers in particular, as opposed to partnerships created between family members exclusively, resorted to notarized partnership agreements.

2 Introducing the Constituting Partners and a Partnership's Object

In general, the introduction of notarized partnership agreements opens directly with the date on which the agreement had been drafted and recorded by the notary working on it. As becomes apparent in Table 6.1, the introductory part is primarily instructive on the identity – in the broadest sense – of the contracting parties. It not only expresses the names of the contracting parties, it also identifies them in light of their geographical, professional and social background.[7]

From a geographical perspective, the focus lies on the contracting parties' current place of residence or activity – which does not necessarily correspond with their place of origin – while statements on the parties' birthplaces start

TABLE 6.1 *Identifying the contracting parties.*[a]

	An – 126	L – 16	M – 9	Am – 6	R – 5
Names	126	16	9	5	5
Origin 1: place of birth	11	0	0	0	0
Origin 2: place of origin	23	2	1	0	0
Origin 3: place of residence/activity	42	6	1	3	5
Profession	62	10	3	2	2
Family ties 1: with outsiders	30	1	2	0	2
Family ties 2: with fellow partners	35	3	3	3	3
Social status	20	7	5	0	0

a In this and all upcoming tables, 'An' refers to Antwerp, 'L' to Liège, 'M' to Maastricht, 'Am' to Amsterdam, and 'R' to Rotterdam. The numbers next to these abbreviations represent the respective city's total number of extant notarized partnership agreements.

7 From a legal point of view, the importance of the introductory part lies in the fact that contracting parties express their willingness and reciprocal consensus to conclude a private partnership in an unstrained and voluntary manner. As such they distinguish their co-operative relationship from a mere *communio*. See also Henri Lévy-Bruhl, *Histoire juridique des sociétés de commerce en France aux XVIIe et XVIIIe siècles* (Paris: Domat-Montchrestien, 1938), 18.

to disappear from the middle of the sixteenth century onwards. Together with the description of the partnership's object, which also appears in most introductions, the geographical data with regard to the contracting parties provide a better understanding of the geographical range of those commercial and industrial activities in which a specific city was involved during a certain period of time. As such, the degree of international cooperation in cities like Liège and Maastricht during the course of the seventeenth century proved to be less extensive than that which could be observed in sixteenth-century Antwerp.[8]

So, the introduction of notarized partnership agreements proved to be of interest to economic historians in the first place. A similar conclusion can be drawn with regards to the inclusion of the partners' professional and family background in the introductory part. Whereas the presence of a partner's profession in the introduction provides an overview of those professional categories that favoured the use of notarized partnership agreements, the inclusion of indications on the contracting parties' family ties within the partnership structure is primarily helpful in providing an evidence-based contribution to the historiographical debate on the familial and domestic character of early modern private partnerships.[9] Although it has been generally assumed that notarizing a partnership agreement was more or less restricted to the field of partnerships between non-relatives, whereas businesses based upon a family unit primarily resorted to oral agreements or privately drafted contracts, our data, as presented in Table 6.1, shows that, from the second half of the sixteenth century onwards, notarized partnership agreements gained importance among related partners as well. In Antwerp, for example, more than one third of all notarized partnership agreements had been concluded exclusively between family members by 1600: father and son(s), brothers, mother and son(s), father and daughter(s), mother and son-in-law, cousins, etc. Despite a growing number of family-based partnership agreements in the sixteenth

8 Van Hofstraeten, 'The Organization of Mercantile Capitalism', 17–18; Van Hofstraeten, 'Private Partnerships in Maastricht', 141–146.

9 See for example: Paul D. McLean and John F. Padgett, 'Obligation, Risk and Opportunity in the Renaissance Economy: Beyond Social Embeddedness to Network Co-constitution', in Frank Dobbin (ed.), *The Sociology of the Economy* (New York: Russell Sage Foundation, 2004), 193–227; Amalia D. Kessler, *A Revolution in Commerce: The Parisian Merchant Court and the Rise of Commercial Society in Eighteenth-Century France* (New Haven: Yale University Press, 2007), 141–151; Falah Hassan Abed Al-Hussein, 'Trade and Business Community in Old Castile Medina del Campo, 1500–1575', (Unpublished doctoral dissertation, East Anglia University, 1982) 205–216; Jeroen Puttevils, 'The Ascent of Merchants from the Southern Low Countries: From Antwerp to Europe, 1480–1585' (Unpublished doctoral dissertation, University of Antwerp, 2012) 191–238.

century, one cannot ignore the fact that almost two thirds of the contracts still established partnerships between non-related contracting parties. As already suggested by Puttevils, this observation is most likely to be explained by the essential nature of notarized documents. Supported and enforced by Antwerp law, notarized partnership agreements accommodated the need for more certainty and trust for non-related contracting parties, because of the absence of familiarity.[10]

The category 'Social status' in Table 6.1 refers to a contracting party's designation in the agreement as a burgher (*poorter*, *ingesetene*, *bourgeois* etc.) of a specific city. So far, early modern partnership agreements in the Low Countries have not produced evidence of the participation of members of other social strata such as, for example, the nobility and the clergy.[11] Nevertheless, recent studies have shown that the inclusion of such social categories in the partnership agreement may lead to significant conclusions regarding the use of (limited) partnerships by members of specific social groups. Amalia Kessler, for example, has shown how, in eighteenth-century France, clerics and noblemen welcomed limited partnerships as a means of participating secretly in mercantile affairs in order to make profitable the idle financial assets.[12]

As mentioned earlier, most introductions specify the partnership's activity or object concisely. These specifications help to provide insights into the particular use of private partnerships, for its preferred field of application is not necessarily the same in each town, city or region. Whereas the city of Antwerp showed an unmistakable preference for the use of private partnerships in the framework of commercial activities, the Liège partnership agreements indicate that the city's inhabitants primarily used notarized partnership agreements in organising their mining and metallurgical operations, whereas Maastricht citizens showed an increased interest in partnership agreements regarding the exploitation of local taxes that had been farmed out by the

10 Puttevils, 'The ascent of merchants', 200.

11 In opposition to the situation in the early modern Low Countries, such social groups did play a significant role in establishing private partnerships in French and Italian mercantile centers. Philippe Wolff, *Commerces et marchands de Toulouse (vers 1350–vers 1450)* (Paris: Plon, 1954), 490; Maurice Carmona, 'Aspects du capitalisme toscan au XVIe et XVIIe siècles: Les sociétés en commandites à Florence et à Lucques', *Revue d'histoire moderne et contemporaine* 11 (1964), 81–108, 84–85. The available data on the early modern Low Countries does demonstrate a noteworthy involvement by women and under-aged children in creating private partnerships.

12 Amalia D. Kessler, 'Limited Liability in Context: Lessons From the French Origins of the American Limited Partnership', *Journal of Legal Studies* 32 (2003), 511–548.

municipal government.[13] Such variations in the most favoured application of notarized partnership agreements still need more research. In so doing, one might wonder whether different fields of application (commerce, mining, tax farming, industry, etc.) called for different elaborations of early modern company law.

It goes without saying that mining, metallurgical and tax farming activities are capital-intensive enterprises, so that opting for a corporate structure is self-evident. As regards commercial and small-scale industrial companies – which did not necessarily call for a huge starting capital – the choice of private partnerships is less obvious, and here, one should take into consideration other underlying motivations that stimulated merchants to contract private partnerships, such as, for example, reducing fixed and monitoring costs or assuring the continued survival of the family business.[14] Unfortunately, notarized partnership agreements tend to refrain from stating explicitly why contracting parties had opted for a private partnership in particular. Most agreements do express the partners' duty to generate as much profit as possible and to avoid potential losses. In various instances, such profit-driven objectives served a further goal, which can only be identified by means of an in-depth analysis of the content of the contract and a careful evaluation of the identities of the partners, their personal and professional relationship, and their respective financial and physical contributions to the organisation at hand. As such, other motivations may become clear. Besides merely generating a daily income for the survival of a merchant and his family, private partnerships could also be used to advance a marriage, to render the possessions of under-aged children profitable, to introduce one's children to the world of commerce and nurture their professional development as a merchant-to-be, to generate a pension-like income for older people and physically incapacitated merchants, etc.[15]

Finally, and in opposition to early modern partnership agreements in Augsburg, the agreed duration of the partnerships established in the early modern

13 Van Hofstraeten, 'The Organization of Mercantile Capitalism'; Van Hofstraeten, 'Private Partnerships in Maastricht'. As far as commercial companies established in sixteenth-century Antwerp, are concerned, one should point out that the specification of the object of the company merely occurs in generic terms. Most partnership agreements establishing commercial companies describe their business as trade "in all kinds of profitable merchandise".

14 Cf. Kessler, *A Revolution in Commerce*, 142–151.

15 Bram Van Hofstraeten, 'Limited Partnerships in Early Modern Antwerp (1480–1620)', *Forum Iuris Historiae*, 5th of November 2015, http://www.forhistiur.de/en/2015-11-van-hofstraeten/.

TABLE 6.2 *Duration-related clauses.*

	An – 126	L – 16	M – 9	Am – 6	R – 5
Duration 1: fixed	98	7	3	3	3
Duration 2: undetermined	17	9	2	1	2
Duration 3: one venture	6	0	4	1	0
Prolongation clause	6	0	0	0	1

Low Countries is not necessarily mentioned in the introduction.[16] Nonetheless, most of the contracts did contain a clause on their intended duration, whether it be a partnership agreement concluded for a fixed term, a private partnership established for an undetermined duration, or a so-called one-venture partnership (Table 6.2). Very few contracts included explicit arrangements about a potential prolonging of the contract after it had expired.

3 Establishing a Partnership's Profitability

The middle part of notarized partnership agreements, recorded in the early modern Low Countries, essentially centred on the most fundamental objective of every private partnership, i.e. its proceeds. Therefore, most clauses which made up the centre section defined all kinds of rights, obligations, privileges and/or restrictions that aimed at (1) establishing, securing and maximizing a partnership's profitability, while reducing potential risks; and (2) distributing the eventual earnings (or potential losses) as equitably as possible.

First of all, the establishment of a private partnership required investments from the constituting partners. Such individual contributions could take various forms. Whereas commercial companies were primarily established on the basis of cash, a shop or retail space, and/or merchandise; industrial or artisanal enterprises also required labour, tools, a workshop or manufactory, raw materials, and sometimes, the input of exceptional, industry-specific skills and/or business secrets. Mining and tax farming companies, for their part, called for the additional acquisition of extraction or tax rights.

16 Joachim Riebartsch, *Augsburger Handelsgesellschaften des 15. und 16. Jahrhunderts: eine vergleichende Darstellung ihres Eigenkapitals und ihrer Verfassung* (Köln: Verlag Josef Eul, 1987), 206.

Since the mutual, quantitative relationship between these respective contributions served as a determinant for the manner in which the profits or losses were to be distributed among the partners after the conclusion of the partnership, the nature and size of the respective inputs were set out meticulously in most of the extant partnership agreements. Table 6.3 provides an overview of the number of partnership agreements that specified the initial fixed capital of the company in a well-defined amount of cash, or in goods with an exact monetary value.[17] Economic historians might be tempted to employ these amounts – which occur particularly in partnership agreements establishing commercial companies – for a size-related, synchronic, as well as diachronic comparison between the various enterprises that were created as such in the early modern Low Countries. Yet, one may not ignore the fact that commercial partners tended to increase their working capital by means of additional credit facilities such as, for example, deposits made by themselves, but also by outsiders.[18] In particular, those deposit investments made by third parties were not included in the partnership agreement. Therefore, the usefulness of the original capital contributions of the constituting partners has to be put into perspective, and should only be used as a mere index to the partners' initial ambitions, rather than an indicator of the scale of the eventual enterprise.[19]

TABLE 6.3 *The financing and cost management of a private partnership.*

	An – 126	L – 16	M – 9	Am – 6	R – 5
Fixed capital in agreement 1: limited	63	7	4	3	2
Fixed capital in agreement 2: unlimited	6	0	0	0	0
Specification of corporate and personal costs	62	9	3	3	3

17 In sixteenth-century Antwerp, six partnership agreements stipulated that the contracting parties were to invest 'all their capital'. See Table 6.3: Fixed capital in agreement 2: unlimited. It remains unclear, however, to what extent these partnerships resembled a so-called *societas omnium bonorum*.

18 See Puttevils, 'The Ascent of Merchants', 193–194.

19 Richard A. Goldthwaite, *The Economy of Renaissance Florence* (Baltimore: Johns Hopkins University Press, 2009), 78–79.

It goes without saying that bringing about substantial profits required an efficient management of the company's expenses. Therefore, partnership agreements contained arrangements that specified and distinguished between costs at the expense of the company, and those to be paid by the individual partners personally. Such costs generally concerned the housing of the respective partners as well as the enterprise, their household expenses, travel costs, insurances, wages of servants, the purchase of raw materials and tools, etc.

As soon as the availability of the means that were necessary to get the partnership up and running had been assured, the corporate activities could take off. In general, standard private partnerships allowed all constituting partners to execute, manage and administer all the various aspects of the corporate undertakings. By contracting a partnership agreement, partners implicitly authorized each other to do so. As becomes apparent in Table 6.4, such mutual authorization or mandate no longer required an explicit formulation in the partnership agreement. However, various partnership agreements did stipulate that partners could only act on behalf of the company with the mutual consent of the constituting partners. These general partnerships, with equally authorized partners who were all simultaneously active in the same or a distinct location, appeared to be the most frequently established ones by means of a notarized partnership agreement recorded in the early modern Low Countries.[20] Only exceptionally is one able to identify a partnership agreement in which some of the partners were being assigned or mandated explicitly as authorized administrators (*bewindhebbers*) of the company.[21] The practice does seem to become more recurrent in seventeenth-century Amsterdam. At the same time, partnership agreements drafted in the seventeenth-century Dutch Republic show a growing importance in the majority rule in the corporate decision-making process.

Besides partnership agreements establishing companies that were composed of active partners exclusively, various contracts stated explicitly the

20 Van Hofstraeten, 'The Organization of Mercantile Capitalism'. As far as general partnerships combining partners that were operative in distinct locations are concerned, the preserved notarized partnership agreements provide a further insight into the trade movements between the Low Countries and the rest of the world. The same is true as regards the agreements by means of which a one-venture partnership is established that sends out one or more partners on a specific journey or mission.

21 As in sixteenth-century Salamanca, but in opposition to fifteenth-century Florence, notarized partnership agreements in the early modern Low Countries hardly created complex, hierarchical corporate structures. See Table 6.4; Francisco Javier Lorenzo Pinar, 'La formación de compañías comerciales en Salamanca en el siglo XVI', *Obradorio de Historia Moderna* 22 (2013), 283–314, 293; Goldthwaite, *The Economy of Renaissance Florence*, 81.

TABLE 6.4 *The distribution of tasks.*

	An – 126	L – 16	M – 9	Am – 6	R – 5
Explicitly authorized partners (equally)	3	0	1	1	1
Explicitly authorized administrators	3	0	0	3	1
Acting with mutual consent	16	5	1	1	0
Majority rule	0	0	0	1	1
Passive capital-providers	22	4	0	3	1
Delegation of well-defined tasks	22	7	2	4	2

passive role of partners who were merely capital-providing. Together with those partnership agreements that present one or more contracting parties as mere capital-providers, without stating their passivity explicitly, these partnership agreements represent useful opportunities in order to identify limited partnerships in the early modern Low Countries in a more indirect way. For example, by making use of various other distinctive criteria – apart from the presence of explicit clauses on the limited liability of silent partners in the partnership agreements – I was able to identify 25 limited partnerships that were created, established and operative in the Antwerp market in the course of the long sixteenth century.[22]

In addition, contracting parties were free to include stipulations in the partnership agreement that introduced deviations from the aforementioned default organisation through the assignation of well-defined tasks – such as bookkeeping, travelling, producing, selling, etc. – to certain partners and/or relieving other partners from specific operational duties. By means of such clauses on the organisational structure and division of tasks within a specific company, notarized partnership agreements can become most instructive on the level of the complexity of the enterprises that had been established in the Low Countries in the course of the sixteenth and seventeenth centuries. As such, these contractual arrangements are primarily of interest to business historians – despite the almost complete absence of prescriptions on strictly operational matters – as well as legal historians who aspire to clarify the emergence of limited partnerships in a specific geographical area.

22 Van Hofstraeten, 'Limited Partnerships'.

4 Securing the Accumulation of Profit

After establishing a most effective organisational structure and assuring the provision of the appropriate means, by means of which the contracting parties aspired to generate profits, they generally agreed upon additional arrangements in order to secure, and even maximize, the profitability of the enterprise.[23]

It goes without saying that successful business management required proper accounting. The extant partnership agreements suggest that the contracting parties considered such a necessity to be self-evident. Only a handful of the preserved notarized partnership agreements did include a separate clause that obliged the respective partners to keep their accounts properly and/or to safeguard the mutual openness of the books from one partner to another (Table 6.5).[24] In the early modern Low Countries, notarized partnership agreements did not elaborate on the specific way of accounting that was required by the contracting parties, nor did they distinguish in a consistent manner between the three most commonly used types of accounting books: the memorandum, the journal, and the ledger.

In the light of securing a company's profitability, contracting parties did stipulate contractually the need to communicate, inspect and settle the respective accounts of the constituting partners on a regular basis, or as soon as such intermediate settlement was required by one of the partners. It enabled them to evaluate the current profitability of the company and helped them to decide on whether it was still appropriate to continue the partnership or not.

---

23 Evidently, the financial contributions of the respective partners to the establishment of the company were to remain in the partnership for as long as it existed. See also Elmar Lutz, *Die rechtliche Struktur süddeutscher Handelsgesellschaften in der Zeit der Fugger*, 2 vols. (Tübingen: Mohr, 1976), 1:253–254. Consequently, such a commonly accepted requirement is hard to find as a separate clause in the extant partnership agreements. Only exceptions to this rule were included in the contract explicitly, yet, only exceptionally.

24 The preserved partnership agreements suggest that sixteenth-century accounting was still a matter of individual accounting in the first place. In Antwerp, for example, only thirteen partnership agreements make reference to 'the company's books'. In six cases, one of the partners was assigned to keep the revenues of the company in a 'common cash register'. The observation that bookkeeping was still an individual duty of all the operating partners is confirmed by the scarcity of clauses in which it was agreed upon to whom the initial contributions of the respective partners had to be paid, as well as the frequent occurrence of clauses requiring partners to communicate their individual accounts, with regard to those obligations concluded on behalf of the company, on a regular basis in order to assess the current state of the affairs.

TABLE 6.5 *Securing profits and reducing risks.*

	An – 126	L – 16	M – 9	Am – 6	R – 5
Accounting requirement	15	4	1	5	1
Reciprocal openness of accounts	6	2	0	0	2
Intermediate settlements of accounts	66	4	2	1	1
Capacity to act 1: prohibitions	20	0	0	1	1
Capacity to act 2: mutual consent	16	5	1	1	0
Clauses on premature leaving	36	3	1	3	1
Confidentiality clause	3	0	0	0	0

The length of the prescribed interval between two settlements can be interpreted as an indication of the level of trust between the partners, as well as the risks inherent to the corporate undertakings at hand.

Besides intermediate settlements of the accounts, early modern partnership agreements inform us of two additional ways of securing a partnership's profit. Firstly, risks were being reduced by means of contractual restrictions on the capacities to act of one or more, mostly young and inexperienced, members of a partnership. Most often, such constraints entailed a prohibition to act as a guarantor for third parties, and to a lesser extent, to accept loans or deposits on behalf of the partnership and to sell goods on credit.[25] Similarly, various partnership agreements limited the overall capacity of all constituting partners to act, by prescribing mutual consent as a necessary requirement in order to act on behalf of the company. Secondly, safeguarding a company's continuous profitability was achieved by the inclusion of prescriptions that protected the partnership from a premature dissolution. In order to do so, contracting parties included clauses that forbade or discouraged them – by imposing substantial financial penalties – from leaving the partnership prematurely. Despite the observance of an overall reluctance towards prematurely leaving partners in the extant partnership agreements, some of these clauses do offer

25 Cf. Abed Al-Hussein, 'Trade and Business Community', 217–221.

TABLE 6.6 *Maximizing profits.*

	An – 126	L – 16	M – 9	Am – 6	R – 5
Competition clause	43	4	2	6	2
Fuori del corpo	14	0	0	0	1

instructive opportunities with regard to the grounds that were considered to be reasonable in order to accept one of its members leaving prematurely.[26]

As regards the maximization of profits, one type of contractual clause manifests itself as predominant, and that is the so-called competition clause, by means of which contracting parties forbade one, several or all partners from conducting any, or at least partnership-related, business on their own in addition to their activities on behalf of the company (Table 6.6). Likewise, contracting parties ruled out unnecessary competition, while at the same time, they avoided future disputes on the question of whether certain transactions, profitable or not, had been executed on behalf of the company or at a partner's personal risk. After all, such quarrels could arise easily, since (1) corporate accounting still seemed to be primarily a matter of private accounting, and (2) hardly any of the early modern partnership agreements, drafted by notaries in the Low Countries, included explicit statements on the name (of the company) that was to be used by the partners while contracting on behalf of the partnership.[27]

Another means of enhancing a partnership's profitability was provided by the so-called *fuori del corpo*. Originally distinctive of medieval Florentine companies, it referred to the right of a partner to invest or deposit an additional amount of capital in the company in return for an annual interest.[28] The presence of such clauses in the preserved partnership agreements, recorded in the Low Countries, but also elsewhere, gives proof of the European dissemination of Italian practices within the field of late medieval and early modern

26 See Bram Van Hofstraeten, 'Jurisdictional Complexity in Antwerp Company Law (1480–1620)', in Seán Patrick Donlan and Dirk Heirbaut (eds.), *The Laws' Many Bodies, Studies in Legal Hybridity and Jurisdictional Complexity, c1600–1900* (Berlin: Duncker & Humblot, 2015), 57–80.

27 Cf. *infra*, Table 6.9.

28 Goldthwaite, *The Economy of Renaissance Florence*, 66. As regards sixteenth-century Castile and eighteenth-century France, see Abed Al-Hussein, 'Trade and Business Community', 222; Lévy-Bruhl, *Histoire juridique des sociétés de commerce*, 112.

company law. Besides these additional investments by constituting partners, a partnership could also increase its stock of capital by means of deposits by outsiders. Unfortunately, notarized partnership agreements in the Low Countries refrained from stating such investments explicitly. There is, however, no doubt that such deposits constituted a significant part of the total working capital of early modern companies in the Low Countries.[29]

5 Distribution of Profits or Losses

At the beginning of the eighteenth century, the Supreme Court of Holland, Zeeland and West-Friesland had to decide, in three different cases, on the actual existence of a private partnership. Each judgement confirmed the opinion that taking part in the profits of the partnership was the distinguishing criterion for the existence of a private partnership.[30] Cooperating parties, who had been working together for some time, while even using the name of the company in their commercial activities, were not acknowledged as being true partners for as long as they were merely remunerated by means of a salary instead of having a share in the partnership's profits. For Huygens too, notarized partnership agreements were to provide for contractual arrangements on an equitable distribution of profits (or losses) among the members of a partnership.[31] Of course, the distribution of profits was the most fundamental goal of every kind of private partnership. So, it is not surprising that arrangements on the distribution of profits (or losses) were among the most frequently used clauses in early modern notarized partnership agreements (Table 6.7).

These stipulations not only inform us about the generally accepted ways of profit distribution in relation to the partners' original contribution to the partnership, but they also enlighten us on the potential reception of more complex – often Italian – distribution methods such as, for example, the one by means of which the actual working capital was divided into fictitious shares and the eventual profits were to be divided proportionally to the number of shares held by each constituting partner. So far, such a distribution method has not been identified in the extant notarized partnership agreements.[32]

---

29 Puttevils, 'The Ascent of Merchants', 193–194.

30 Martijn Punt, *Het vennootschapsrecht van Holland: Het vennootschapsrecht van Holland, Zeeland en West-Friesland in de rechtspraak van de Hoge Raad van Holland, Zeeland en West-Friesland* (Deventer: Kluwer, 2010), 124–128.

31 Cf. *supra*, Introduction.

32 Also with regard to sixteenth-century Castile, Abed Al-Hussein could only identify two such-like examples. Abed Al-Hussein, 'Trade and business community', 227–228.

TABLE 6.7 *Distribution of profits or losses.*

	An – 126	L – 16	M – 9	Am – 6	R – 5
Distribution of profits or losses	124	13	8	4	4

6 Anticipatory Measures

By means of its focus on generating, securing, maximizing and distributing the potential profits of the enterprise, early modern notarized partnership agreements in the Low Countries addressed the functioning of the partnership-to-be in normal circumstances. However, these circumstances could change drastically during the existence of the partnership. The occurrence of specific events, such as the sudden death, unexpected emigration, temporary absence, unfortunate imprisonment, inability to work, or the marriage of one of its members, could have a significant impact on the survival, size and composition of the partnership. In order to avoid internal disputes that might arise because of these far-reaching incidents, various partnership agreements already included prescriptions on how one should deal with such changing circumstances. As shown in Table 6.8, handling the premature death of one of the partners during the functioning of the partnership was, by far, the contracting parties' main concern. Here, contracting parties had to decide in advance on the continued existence of the company and the respective role of the heirs in the partnership, or they could agree upon procedures for an early termination of the corporate activities.[33]

In addition to such altering circumstances, notarized partnership agreements could also address in advance the future admission of an extra partner and the transfer of a partner's part in the company to a third party, while stipulating the extent up to which the members of the partnership enjoyed pre-emption in the latter case.

In case disputes between the members of a partnership did arise, the warring parties had the option of taking recourse to arbitration (by so-called *goede mannen* or *hommes de bien*) instead of legal procedures before a court. Whereas partnership agreements in early modern Southern Germany as well as in sixteenth-century Lyon often stated explicitly the contracting parties' preference for a settlement of internal disputes by means of self-selected arbiters, their

33 Van Hofstraeten, 'Jurisdictional Complexity', 68–71; Van Hofstraeten, 'Private Partnerships in Maastricht', 135.

TABLE 6.8 *Anticipating altering circumstances.*

	An – 126	L – 16	M – 9	Am – 6	R – 5
Death	47	5	2	3	5
Marriage	12	0	0	0	1
Emigration/Temporary absence	6	1	1	2	1
Imprisonment	5	1	0	1	0
Illness/Inability to work	6	2	1	0	0
Extra partner(s)	5	0	0	0	0
Transfer of share	0	1	0	1	1
Right of pre-emption	0	1	0	1	0
Arbitration clause	2	4	0	1	2

counterparts produced in the early modern Low Countries, and those drafted in sixteenth-century Antwerp in particular, barely contained such arbitration clauses.[34] In seventeenth-century Liège, Amsterdam and Rotterdam, such clauses can be found more often 'to avoid litigation in court' (Table 6.8). To some extent, the inclusion of such stipulations in the partnership agreement can be interpreted as representing the contracting parties' belief in the expertise of local jurisdictions with regard to commercial disputes, as well as their speediness in settling the disagreements. Sometimes, the identities of the arbiters were already agreed upon in the contract, and in case these arbiters could not succeed in reconciling the conflicting parties, most agreements allowed them to choose an extra *superarbiter*. The arbitration clauses in Amsterdam and Rotterdam partnership agreements also express the condition that the arbiters have to judge 'by equity' instead of the law. Hardly any of the observed arbitration clauses allowed for an appeal or a *reductio ad arbitrium boni viri* against the arbiters' final decision.

7 Externally Oriented Clauses?

From an overall perspective, notarized partnership agreements in the early modern Low Countries were mainly concerned with the internal.[35] As far

34 Richard Gascon, *Grand commerce et vie urbaine au XVIe siècle: Lyon et ses marchands (environs de 1520 – environs de 1580)* (Paris: Mouton, 1971), 282; Lutz, *Die rechtliche Struktur*, 1:469–478.

35 See also eighteenth-century France: Kessler, *A Revolution in Commerce*, 172.

as the agreements did address the external interactions of the constituting partners with third parties, such statements primarily expressed restrictions on the respective capacities to act of partners who were mostly young and inexperienced.[36] In addition, only a small number of partnership agreements stipulated openly the (im)possibility of partners binding their co-partners for the obligations they had run into with third parties on behalf of the company, and/or the extent up to which the respective partners were to contribute to the repayment of these contracted debts (Table 6.9). None of the extant partnership agreements contained clauses specifying the individual partners that could or could not be addressed and held liable by the partnership's creditors.[37]

The low occurrence of such externally oriented clauses confirms that a partner's possibility of binding his fellow partners for obligations with third parties – in other words, the idea that they had mandated or authorized each other mutually to do so – was already a well-established practice for some time among early modern merchants in the Low Countries, and that the acknowledgement of a joint and several liability no longer required a contractual expression.[38] Nevertheless, one may still wonder about the conditions that ought to be fulfilled in order to classify a specific obligation or debt as one that had been concluded on behalf of the company, and was thus capable of binding the fellow partners in a joint and several manner. Such requirements could, for example, take the form of contracting *in re societatis*, contracting *in loco societatis*, contracting *in nomine societatis*, or combinations of these formal conditions.

Again, notarized partnership agreements in the early modern Low Countries remained silent on such conditions, however, with few exceptions (Table 6.9). These exceptional clauses, in particular, present us with a manifest preference, among contracting parties in the Low Countries, for contracting *in re societatis*, i.e. in accordance with the line of industry for which the partnership was originally established, as the quintessential requirement in order to bind

36 Cf. *supra*, Table 6.5.

37 The lack of stipulations on external relationships in the preserved notarized partnership agreements renders them quite useless as regards the common desire of present-day scholars to categorize early modern private partnerships on the basis of an external liability criterion. Clearly, early modern contracting parties did not think in such categories, which is also demonstrated by the alternate and inconsistent use of terms by means of which they designated their private partnerships. In addition, the lack of interest in external relationships is demonstrated by the absence of clauses that regulated the ranking of private creditors and corporate creditors in case of bankruptcy, or the extent up to which private creditors can lay claim to the working capital of the partnership of a bankrupt partner.

38 Goldthwaite, *The Economy of Renaissance Florence*, 65; Kessler, *A Revolution in Commerce*, 163.

one's fellow partners.[39] As such, early modern partnership agreements do prove useful with respect to a critical assessment of the level of conformity between early modern commercial practice and contemporaneous jurisprudential and legislative sources, for the latter started to have an increasing interest in these conditions from the late medieval period onwards.[40] As far as the city of Antwerp is concerned, there is a striking dissimilarity to be observed with regard to the identification mechanisms in order to typify a specific obligation as one on behalf of the company. Opposed to the observations in the extant partnership agreements, the city's statutes of 1608, the so-called *Consuetudines compilatae*, postulated – under the influence of Genoese practice and ditto legislation – that, in order to bind the other partners in a joint and several way, the obligation had to be concluded *in nomine societatis*, i.e. while using the name of the company or *firma*.[41]

The assumption that contracting *in nomine societatis* was not a fundamental requirement in order to bind one's fellow partners in the early modern Low Countries manifests itself too by means of the quasi-complete absence in the extant partnership agreements of clauses defining the composition of the *firma* that was to be used while contracting on behalf of the company. In total, the data set of 162 partnership agreements only contains four contracts in which such a clause had been included (Table 6.9).

8 Notarized Partnership Agreements and the *Lex mercatoria*

The very scarce *firma* clause allows notarized partnership agreements to offer historiographical opportunities with regard to the scientific debate on the so-called law merchant or *lex mercatoria*, i.e. the hypothesis that from the medieval period onwards merchants created, from the bottom up, and independent

39 Van Hofstraeten, 'Jurisdictional Complexity', 61–64.

40 Bram Van Hofstraeten, 'Antwerp Company Law around 1600 and its Italian Origins', in Bram Van Hofstraeten and Wim Decock (eds.), *Companies and Company Law in Late Medieval and Early Modern Europe* (Louvain: Peeters, 2016), 29–56.

41 In the course of the seventeenth century, one can observe a growing importance in the *firma*-criterion as a requirement to bind one's co-partners jointly and severally for obligations on behalf of the company. The Antwerp data set contains two partnership agreements in which it was agreed upon that all obligations on behalf of the company had to be signed 'while using both names of both constituting partners'. Both examples date from after the year 1600. In addition, the seventeenth-century Liège, Amsterdam and Rotterdam source material merely mentions the use of the *firma* as a condition to bind one's fellow partners, as far as such conditions are discussed explicitly.

TABLE 6.9 *Clauses on the external relationship of partners with third parties.*

	An – 126	L – 16	M – 9	Am – 6	R – 5
Possibility of binding co-partners	7	0	0	0	0
Conditions in order to bind co-partners	5	0	0	1	0
Contribution to repayment of debt	6	1	0	0	0
Limited liability clause	0	0	0	1	0
Name of the company – *firma*	1	1	0	1	1

of all kinds of government involvement and on the basis of their mercantile practices, a distinct set of gap-filling rules which, by their uniformity and universality, facilitated international trade.[42]

Although the idea of a *lex mercatoria* has received major criticism over the last years, one cannot ignore the fact that partnership agreements in late medieval and early modern Europe, apart from in the Hanseatic area, often took similar forms and contained many analogous kinds of clauses.[43] As such they provided for some sort of a universal and uniform way of creating partnerships across Southern and Western Europe. Indeed, the aforementioned analysis of notarized partnership agreements, recorded in the early modern Low Countries, has shown a substantial level of conformity between the ways of contracting in the cities at hand. Although not following a standard model, the constituting clauses were usually much the same from one contract to another.[44] Despite the modesty of the data at our disposal, one could argue that such similarity also existed on an international level. In late medieval and early modern European countries too, like Italy, Spain, France and the southern part of the

42 For a comprehensive historiographical overview on the *lex mercatoria*-debate, see Emily Kadens, 'The Myth of the Customary Law Merchant', *Texas Law Review* 90 (2012), 1153–1206, 1153–1159.

43 See also Kadens, 'The Myth', 1160.

44 The same is true regarding partnership agreements that were concluded in late medieval Toulouse, sixteenth-century Medina del Campo, and fifteenth-century Florence. Wolff, *Commerces et marchands de Toulouse*, 493; Abed Al-Hussein, 'Trade and Business Community', 217; Goldthwaite, *The Economy of Renaissance Florence*, 65.

Holy Roman Empire, partnership agreements were primarily concerned with the partners' contribution to the working capital, their share in the profits, the partnership's duration, its line of industry, competition clauses, the provision of intermediate accounts, the payment of operational costs, etc.[45]

There is, however, one vital difference between notarized partnership agreements drafted in the early modern Low Countries, on the one hand, and contemporary partnership agreements that were recorded in Italy, Spain, France, and to some extent also the southern part of the Holy Roman Empire, on the other hand. As opposed to early modern Italian, Spanish, French, and Southern German merchants, sixteenth- and seventeenth-century merchants in the Low Countries were not concerned at all with the (composition of the) name of their company. As mentioned earlier, only four contracts contained a clause by means of which the official name of the company was agreed upon contractually. This observation not only goes against the previously suggested belief in a shared way of contracting partnerships among European merchants, it also provides a substantial starting point for debunking the assumption of a universal and uniform *lex mercatoria* existing in late medieval and early modern Europe. Whereas uniformity and universality are generally acknowledged to be core elements of such a customary law merchant, our analysis of notarized partnership agreements, recorded in early modern Europe, provides proof for the existence of significantly different approaches as regards the customarily recognized ways of binding one's co-partners for obligations with third parties. In sixteenth-century Antwerp, for example, one could hardly observe any *firma* clauses, while at the same time, the extant partnership agreements demonstrated a manifest preference for contracting *in re societatis* as the most fundamental requirement in order to bind one's fellow partners. On the other hand, Italian practice favoured contracting *in nomine societatis* as the necessary condition for binding one's co-partners, and this was already the case from the twelfth century onwards.[46] Subsequently, the condition found its way into the field of Italian statutory legislation at the beginning of the fourteenth

---

45 Wolff, *Commerces et marchands de Toulouse*, 493; Abed Al-Hussein, 'Trade and Business Community', 217; Goldthwaite, *The Economy of Renaissance Florence*, 65. In the Hanseatic territories, however, partnership agreements tended to present themselves as significantly distinctive. Cf. Pierre Jeannin, 'Entreprises commerciales lubeckoises au milieu du XVIe siècle', in Pierre Jeannin (ed.), *Marchands du Nord: Espaces et trafics à l'époque moderne* (Paris: Presses de l'Ecole normale supérieure, 1996), 63–102, 77–78. The article is a translation of the 1963 article: Pierre Jeannin, 'Lübecker Handelsunternehmungen um die Mitte des 16. Jahrhunderts', *Zeitschrift des Vereins für Lübeckische Geschichte und Altertumskunde* 43 (1963), 19–67.

46 Ralf Mehr, *Societas und universitas: Römischrechteliche Institute im Unternehmensgesellschaftsrecht vor 1800* (Köln: Böhlau, 2008), 154.

century (in Florence, Modena, Arezzo, etc.). In the course of the sixteenth century, the condition spread out from the Italian peninsula towards various neighbouring mercantile areas. Elmar Lutz noticed a growing concern about the *firma* and contracting *in nomine societatis* in partnership agreements establishing Southern German commercial companies towards the middle of the sixteenth century.[47] At the same time, various merchant cities, situated in the southern part of the Holy Roman Empire, gradually incorporated the condition in their municipal statutes (Nurnberg 1564, Frankfurt 1578).[48] Regarding Spain, Burckhardt Löber stated, on the basis of the work of Manuel Basas Fernandez on sixteenth-century Castilian partnership agreements, that from the second half of the sixteenth century more and more partnership agreements started to contain clauses on the composition of the name of the company.[49] Likewise, Falah Hassan Abed Al-Hussein noticed that notarized partnership agreements recorded in Medina del Campo between 1500–1575, always had a separate clause for the definition of the *firma*.[50] In France, Philippe Wolff did not mention the *firma*-clause in his dealings with medieval merchants in Toulouse (1350–1450), whereas Richard Gascon noticed a strong Italian influence on contracting in sixteenth-century Lyon where clauses defining the name of the company were no longer an uncommon feature.[51] By the eighteenth century, partnership agreements drafted in France did contain a similar clause.[52]

So, taking into account the aforementioned preference of contracting parties in sixteenth-century Antwerp for the less sophisticated 'contracting *in re societatis*' (as a condition to bind one's co-partners) as well as the quasi-complete absence of clauses on the composition of the name of the company in the extant partnership agreements that were drafted in the early modern Low Countries, one may conclude that there existed substantial differences within sixteenth-century Europe as regards the formal requirements to bind one's fellow partners for obligations with third parties on behalf of the company. Consequently, one cannot speak of the existence of a universal and uniform

47 Lutz, *Die rechtliche Struktur*, 1:451–452.

48 Frank Thomas, *Die persönliche Haftung von Gesellschaftern von Personengesellschaften in der historischen Entwicklung der Neuzeit* (Berlin: Duncker & Humblot, 2003), 119–123, 126, and 128–130.

49 Burckhardt Löber, 'Das spanische Gesellschaftsrecht in 16. Jahrhundert' (Unpublished doctoral dissertation, Freiburg im Breisgau, 1967), 80; Manuel Basas Fernandez, 'Contratos de compañias mercantiles castellanas del siglo XVI', *Revista de derecho mercantil* 78 (1960), 375–412, 393.

50 Abed Al-Hussein, 'Trade and Business Community', 220–221.

51 Gascon, *Grand commerce et vie urbaine*, 284, 289.

52 Lévy-Bruhl, *Histoire juridique des sociétés de commerce.*

set of rules – at least not with regard to sixteenth-century European company law – that might have facilitated international trade.

The previous overview of how the typically Italian condition to contract *in nomine societatis* dispersed itself over its neighbouring territories, and likewise contributed eventually to the establishment and universal acceptance of a uniform approach in Southern Europe, does confirm Emily Kadens' conviction that universal and uniform rules, governing long-distance trade, usually arose from contract and legislation rather than from custom, and that this was due to the limited transferability of the latter.[53]

9 Closing a Partnership Agreement

By means of conclusion, notarized partnership agreements ended with the formulation of a closing clause. It expressed the commitment of the contracting parties to respect the content of the agreement. Therefore, they obliged themselves *se et sua*, i.e. with their persons and all their belongings, both present and future, as well as their movable and immovable property. In addition, the closing clause identified the witnesses to the contract, and stated the geographical location where the partnership agreement had been notarized.

As shown in Table 6.10, a considerable number of the agreements renounced explicitly all legal instruments, both *beneficia* as well as written and customary rules, that the contracting parties might make use of as a means to privilege themselves with regard to the content of the agreement. Such *beneficia* comprised, for example, the *senatus consultum Velleianum* and the *Authentica si qua mulier* for women, as well as the *senatus consultum Macedonianum* for under-aged children.

Until 1560, numerous closing clauses of notarized partnership agreements in Antwerp imposed a financial penalty on contracting parties who did not comply with the agreement. Afterwards, such penalty clauses became much more exceptional, whereas in seventeenth-century Liège, Maastricht and Rotterdam, they have disappeared altogether.

From an overall perspective, the closing clauses proved to be the most instructive with regard to the nature and development of contracting practices,

53 Kadens, 'The Myth', 1158–1161. Regarding the diffusion of the requirement to contract *in nomine societatis*, the recorded *decisiones* of the Genoese *Rota* (1582) played a crucial role. Mehr, *Societas und universitas*, 154. This was also confirmed recently by an in-depth analysis of the legal sources that shaped Antwerp company law as it was recorded in the city's statutes of 1608. Van Hofstraeten, 'Antwerp Company Law'.

TABLE 6.10 *The closure of a notarized partnership agreement.*

	An – 126	L – 16	M – 9	Am – 6	R – 5
Renunciation clause	47	1	4	2	1
Penalty clause	19	0	0	1	0
Bearer clause	0	7	3	0	0

or contract law in general, in the various regions of the early modern Low Countries. Such an observation is also illustrated by the emergence of a bearer clause with regard to notarized partnership agreements in seventeenth-century Liège and Maastricht. Whereas such bearer clauses, for example, the authorization of a debtor to pay his debt to a third party (limited interpretation) or the procuration of a bearer to act on behalf of a creditor in court (extended interpretation), are generally associated with the repayment of letters obligatory or bills of exchange, the Liège and Maastricht source material give proof for such bearer clauses within the framework of notarized partnership agreements.[54] Here, the bearer clause constitutes the authorization of 'all bearers of the contract' to act in court in order to assure the realization and observance of the content of the partnership agreement.

10 Conclusion

The quantitative analysis of the content of notarized partnership agreements, recorded in the early modern Low Countries, has revealed a wide range of clauses demonstrating the contractual freedom that allowed contracting parties to formalize their case-specific corporate structures without being hampered by legislative prescriptions or being limited by the straightjacket offered by contemporaneous *formularia* of notarial deeds. Such liberties significantly widened the present-day historiographical scope of notarized partnership agreements.

However, it has become clear that, in designing private partnerships, contracting parties were mainly concerned with their internal relationships within the organizational boundaries of the company. Notarized partnership agreements primarily served as a means of determining and formalizing the

54 Cf. Philippe Godding, *Le droit privé dans les Pays-Bas méridionaux du 12e au 18e siècle* (Bruxelles: Académie royale de Belgique, 1987), 425–426.

internal organization that one considered to be most effective in establishing and maximizing the enterprise's profitability in a specific situation. Most clauses, at least in the centre part of the agreement, consisted of or defined all kinds of rights, obligations, privileges and/or restrictions that aimed at (1) establishing, securing and maximizing a partnership's profitability, while reducing potential risks, and (2) distributing the eventual earnings (or potential losses) as equitably as possible. In addition, the extant partnership agreements gave proof for numerous clauses stipulating anticipatory measures that were chiefly directed at guaranteeing the continuous existence of the partnership. As such, notarized partnership agreements proved to be primarily instructive for business historians as well as for their legal counterparts interested in the history of company law, whereas the introductory part in particular offers significant historiographical opportunities for socioeconomic historians in general.

Since notarized partnership agreements mainly dealt with the internal, legal historians may deplore the scarcity of clauses addressing the external relationships of the respective partners, in particular because legal historians tend to categorize medieval and early modern private partnerships on the basis of the external liability criterion. Such liability, however, does not seem to have been the main concern of the contracting parties. Likewise, the extant partnership agreements serve as an invitation to rethink present-day categorization approaches. Despite the paucity of such externally-oriented clauses, those few examples that can be identified do offer opportunities to understand and explain local practices with regard to the manner by means of which one was able to bind one's co-partners for obligations with third parties on behalf of the company. Such rare instances provide occasions for evaluating the level of conformity between early modern practices, on the one hand, and contemporaneous legislation or jurisprudence, on the other hand, as well as the extent up to which the latter exercised a modifying influence on the former. In addition, the observed requirements in order to bind one's fellow partners externally allow the identification of similarities or discrepancies from a broader, European perspective. As such the quasi-complete absence of the requirement to contract *in nomime societatis* in sixteenth-century Antwerp, as well as the scarcity of clauses on the *firma* of the company, provide a valuable contribution to the debunking of the idea of a *lex mercatoria* existing in early modern Europe.

Of course, notarized agreements merely represent the tip of the iceberg of all private partnerships that had been established in the early modern Low Countries, and one might even wonder to what extent these notarized partnership agreements can be regarded as true representations of traditional corporate practices in the territory at hand. After all, their official recording by a notary in particular, which seems to have been more the exception than the rule, might imply that these partnership agreements were deviating from the standard and that for that reason in particular they needed to be recorded by a notary. So, it goes without saying that studying and reconstructing early modern company law calls for the exploration of additional kinds of historical sources. In this regard, major opportunities are believed to be hidden away in the preserved jurisdictional archives.

CHAPTER 7

How Normative were Merchant Guidebooks? Of Customs, Practices, and … Good Advice (Antwerp, Sixteenth Century)

Dave De ruysscher

1 Introduction

Trade instruction books of the later Middle Ages and early modern period have attracted much attention. Since the publication of the comprehensive bibliography by Pierre Jeannin, Jochen Hoock and Wolfgang Kaiser in 2001,[1] late medieval and early modern professional literature for an audience of merchants has become more accessible, and these works of the *ars mercatoria* have been cited more often in historical studies. Over recent years, the question has been raised as to whether these merchant manuals, which are in and of themselves a diffuse category, not only reflected but also prescribed behaviour. In response, the instructional contents of these guidebooks have mostly been identified as touching upon trustworthiness and professional standards that were closely linked to virtues, values, self-esteem and a sense of belonging.[2] Questions on the nature of the relationship between merchant manuals and law, however, have been asked less often.[3] Yet this problem deserves more attention.

1 Jochen Hoock, Pierre Jeannin and Wolfgang Kaiser (eds.), *Ars Mercatoria: Handbücher und Traktate für den Gebrauch des Kaufmanns. Manuels et traités à l'usage des marchands, 1470–1820: Eine analytische Bibliographie in 6 Bänden*, 4 vols. (Paderborn: Schöningh, 1991–2001).

2 Without presuming to create an exhaustive list, one can think of publications by Nathalie Zemon Davies, Pierre Jeannin and Jochen Hoock. See also Jaume Aurell, 'Reading Renaissance Merchants' Handbooks: Confronting Professional Ethics and Social Identity', in Josef Ehmer and Catharina Lis (eds.), *The Idea of Work in Europe from Antiquity to Modern Times* (Farnham: Ashgate, 2009), 71–90 (instructional literature conferred a sense of belonging to a group of professional merchants, and it contained corresponding standards and ethics); Jeroen Puttevils, *The Ascent of Merchants from the Southern Low Countries: from Antwerp to Europe, 1480–1585* (PhD thesis, University of Antwerp, 2012), 171–184 (merchant manuals listed conventions concerning mutual trust). On the importance of trust in business relations, see also the chapter by Ricardo Court in this volume.

3 Drawing a link between guidebooks on bookkeeping and canon law, in particular usury legislation, see James Aho, *Confession And Bookkeeping: The Religious, Moral, And Rhetorical*

 | DOI 10.1163/9789004363144_008

The nature of norms in late medieval and early modern commerce is still very much debated among economic and legal historians. A keen but implicit point in the discussions is the dividing line between practices and (facilitating and restricting) institutions, among them legal norms.[4] As the following pages will illustrate, merchant guidebooks constitute an indispensable aid for shedding more light on this problem. They were written for a merchant audience, and they highlighted constraints of different types. However, legal historians must handle trade instruction books with care because often they cannot be considered a historical source for mercantile practices or commercial law.

This chapter will assess to what extent *ars mercatoria*-literature contained normative wording, defined in what follows as imposing or structuring conduct. In addition, it will analyse whether such phrasing was based on customs,[5]

Roots of Modern Accounting (Albany: State University of New York Press, 2005) (stressing the rhetorical use of double-entry bookkeeping and manuals concerning it, in order to justify credit against the background of ecclesiastical usury laws); Bruce G. Carruthers and Wendy Nelson Espeland, 'Accounting for Rationality: Double-Entry Bookkeeping and the Rhetoric of Economic Rationality', *American Journal of Sociology* 97:1 (1991), 31–69, 38–39 (merchant bookkeeping and instruction books on the theme served a rhetorical and cognitive purpose, not a strictly rational efficiency-dependent one; the rhetorical purpose partly comprised an aim to neutralize concerns over usury); John E. Dotson, 'Commercial Law in Fourteenth-century Merchant Manuals', *Medieval Encounters* 9 (2003), 204–213 (merchant guidebooks lacked information on official law, even though the data included referred to a legal framework). Other authors relate early modern *ars mercatoria*-literature to legislation, customs and academic law: Emily Kadens, 'The Myth of the Customary Law Merchant', *Texas Law Review* 90 (2012), 1153–1206, 1171–1173 (pointing at the virtual absence of customs and other rules in merchant handbooks); Francesca Trivellato, *The Familiarity of Strangers: The Sephardic Diaspora, Livorno, and Cross-Cultural Trade in the Early Modern Period* (New Haven: Yale University Press, 2009), 153–177 (merchant manuals gradually interacted with academic doctrine with respect to the evidential value of business correspondence).

4 The literature on the subject is abundant. Some excellent appraisals can be found in Albrecht Cordes, 'À la recherche d'une Lex mercatoria au Moyen Âge', in Otto G. Oexle and Pierre Monnet (eds.), *Stadt und Recht im Mittelalter: La ville et le droit au Moyen Âge* (Göttingen: Vandenhoeck & Ruprecht, 2003), 117–132; Kadens, 'The Myth', 1153–1206; Karl O. Scherner, 'Lex mercatoria – Realität, Geschichtsbild oder Vision', *Zeitschrift der Savigny-Stiftung für Rechtsgeschichte. Germanistische Abteilung* 118 (2001), 148–167.

5 For the remainder of the text, the term 'custom' is understood to mean a repeated practice or convention based on a normative belief within a group of persons. This definition conforms with the early modern definition of *consuetudo*, which jurists construed as consisting of *usus* (a durable practice) and *tacitus consensus* (implied consent as to its normativity). In the sixteenth century, a *consuetudo* was legally binding if it was reasonable and not explicitly prohibited in legislation. See Roy Garré, *Consuetudo: Das Gewohnheitsrecht in der Rechtsquellen- und*

standard forms of contract, and rules of official law (i.e. legislation or norms imposed through the verdicts of courts). Furthermore, it will examine whether the publication of merchant manuals containing instructions was controlled or solicited by authorities. In search for answers, this chapter focuses on the case of sixteenth-century Antwerp, where many mercantile guidebooks were published and where municipal law was frequently adapted in order to make it fit with contracts that were in use among merchants.

2 Trade-orientated Guidebooks in Sixteenth-century Antwerp

Between 1490 and 1600, no less than 103 *ars mercatoria*-manuals rolled off the printing presses in Antwerp. In this period, this production made the city the second-largest centre for such editions, closely following Venice (136), and well ahead of Frankfurt (76). The majority of the Antwerp merchant books were published after 1540, when Antwerp was experiencing its heyday as a leading commercial metropolis of the West, until its Golden Age ended around 1565. Antwerp printers such as Simon Cock and Jan van Waesberghe produced several guidebooks, even though it would be an exaggeration to consider them publishers specializing in this genre. The majority of the merchant manuals published in Antwerp between 1490 and 1600 dealt with letter writing and translation (30.77 per cent): they were dictionaries and books containing common phrases in several languages. Other popular subjects were coins and currencies (20.39 per cent), and mathematics and bookkeeping (25.96 per cent).[6] Apart from some printed versions of princely laws regarding marine insurance, which were brought onto the market for more than just merchant use,[7] there were virtually no other publications on the subjects of official law or merchants' customs. Some treatises contained summaries of academic or imperial (German) law, but their purported audience was clearly not a mercantile one.[8]

Methodenlehre des späten ius commune in Italien (16.–18. Jahrhundert) (Frankfurt am Main: Vittorio Klostermann, 2005), 66–72, 145–160; Kadens, 'The Myth', 1163–1166.

6 Puttevils, 'The Ascent of Merchants', 175.

7 A Dutch version of the princely ordinance of October 31, 1563 was printed by Willem Silvius and Willem van Parys. Dutch and French versions of the princely statute of October 11, 1570 and of January 20, 1571 were printed by Christopher Plantin. See Henry L.V. De Groote, *De zeeassurantie te Antwerpen en te Brugge in de zestiende eeuw* (Antwerp: Marine Academie, 1975), 29–30.

8 In 1560, Simon Cock published *Den Spieghele der Recht: uut den natuerlijcken, bescrevenen, gheestelijcken, wereltlij*cken*, ende anderen ghebruyckelycken rechten…*, which was a translation

Moreover, municipal law that was imposed by the Antwerp government was almost never printed. Occasionally, municipal bylaws were issued in print, but they did not concern topics of commerce.[9] The first printed edition of Antwerp municipal law containing chapters on mercantile contracts dates from 1582,[10] long after Antwerp's glory had passed.

The numbers mentioned above only relate to published guidebooks, which were also called *manuali*. However, there were also private instructional books, read within the circle of one family or firm only. For this genre, the term *zibaldoni* is often used.[11] An example of a *zibaldone* was the *Regula transporti* by Willem van der Lare. It was most probably written in the early 1530s. Parts of it reflect commercial dealings of the 1520s; others were meant to be advice and guidelines for trade. Those latter sections might additionally consist of excerpted fragments from older, unknown manuals. The *Regula transporti* lists information on weights, currencies and taxes in diverse locations, as well as warnings on trading costs.[12] Comparable manuals were still common in the seventeenth century. Treatises of this type were read among the staff and partners of large firms, and in particular by trainees.[13] As such, *zibaldoni* and *manuali* may yield further information about which rules, applied in the Antwerp market, their authors thought it necessary to provide. The rest of this chapter will focus primarily on these *manuali*, in order to answer the third of the aforementioned research questions, namely, that concerning the influence of authorities on the contents of locally printed *ars mercatoria*-literature.

---

of Justin Göbler's *Der Rechten Spiegel*, which had been published in Frankfurt in 1552. In 1556, Cock had also issued *Keyserlycke statuten, ordinantien, costumen, en ghewoonten, ende bisonder elcker stadt rechten, principalijck den keyserlijcken landen aengaende*, which was a translation of Göbler's *Keyserlicher und des h. Reichs rechten* (Frankfurt, 1552). In the introduction of both works, Cock stressed that the books were intended for administrators and judges. Their content as to mercantile issues is minimal.

9 Bylaws concerning procedure in the Municipal Court were regularly printed; the most important are those dating from March 1565 (ns) and May 1576.

10 *Rechten, ende costumen van Antwerpen* (Antwerp, 1582).

11 The distinction between *zibaldoni* and *manuali* was first made in Peter Spufford, 'Spätmittelalterliche Kaufmannnotizbücher als Quellen zur Bankengeschichte: Ein Projektbericht', in Michael North (ed.), *Kredit im spätmittelalterlichen und freuneuzeitlichen Europa* (Köln: Böhlau, 1991), 103–120.

12 Antwerp, Plantin-Moretus Museum, Manuscripts M 318.

13 For an overview, see Jean Denucé, *Koopmansleerboeken van de XVIe en XVIIe eeuwen in handschrift* (Brussels: N.V. Standaard-boekhandel, 1941).

3 Did Merchant Manuals Stipulate Legal Requirements? The Example of Jan Ympyn's *Nieuwe Instructie*

With regard to intersections between municipal law and the prescriptive content of instructional books, a recent thesis on the functionality of bookkeeping manuals of the later fifteenth and in the sixteenth centuries, in Antwerp and elsewhere, is important. In 2013, Oscar Gelderblom argued that in these periods, handbooks on accounting not only facilitated the application of double-entry bookkeeping, but they also had a normative function. Even though a high number of such manuals were published, they still did not suffice to promote the technique; acquiring the skills of double-entry bookkeeping was dependent on the teaching and tutoring by specialists. Thus, the repeated publication of manuals, according to Gelderblom, mostly served the purpose of setting standards as to the form that accounting books should have in order to be considered sufficient evidence in courts. Over the course of the early sixteenth century, the municipal government of Antwerp had accepted books and letters as lawful proof of debt. Thenceforth, Gelderblom claims, the Antwerp authorities started stipulating what merchant books should look like. Formal requirements for double-entry books were communicated by means of locally printed instructional tracts, among them the *Nieuwe Instructie* by Jan Ympyn.[14]

3.1 *The 'Right Manner' for Keeping Books*

The *Nieuwe Instructie* was printed and offered for sale in Antwerp in 1543, on behalf of Jan Ympyn's widow, after he had passed away in September 1540. Jan Ympyn was a mercer who had spent some years in Italian cities, particularly in Venice, where he became acquainted with Luca Pacioli's work. In 1494, Pacioli had published his seminal *De computis et scripturis* on double-entry bookkeeping. Ympyn continued gathering information on bookkeeping after his return to Antwerp around 1519, and acquired knowledge of the recent literature as well.[15] In her introduction to the *Nieuwe Instructie*, Ympyn's widow Anna Swinters mentions that several renowned and rich merchants had asked Ympyn to write a treatise on the double-entry variety of bookkeeping 'for the benefit and utility of all merchants residing in this country'. She anticipated controversy over the contents of the manual, insisting that her husband had practiced

14 Oscar Gelderblom, *Cities of Commerce: The Institutional Foundations of International Trade in the Low Countries, 1250–1650* (Princeton: Princeton University Press, 2013), 94–100.

15 Raymond De Roover, 'Een en ander over Jan Ympyn Christoffels, de schrijver van de eerste Nederlandsche handleiding over het koopmansboekhouden', *Tijdschrift voor Geschiedenis* 52 (1937), 163–179.

double-entry bookkeeping since his youth, and that while writing the book he had received help from experts. Moreover, before applying for a printing privilege, Anna had consulted councillors of a princely council (the Council of Finance, or perhaps the Council of Brabant). They in turn had sought advice from merchants, who had argued in favour of publication.[16]

At the start of the *Nieuwe instructie*, Ympyn states that his treatise serves to bring the 'profitable and laudable art and science' of double-entry bookkeeping to Antwerp, because in his view it was badly practiced, for example, among partners.[17] Ympyn writes that accounting books are 'the mirror held up to the merchant': bookkeeping is an instrument that keeps one aware of the loss of money.[18] Thereafter, Ympyn contends that among those who might profit from the book are teachers, tax collectors, legislators and judges. Ympyn mentions that judges can use his guidebook when deciding disputes and lawsuits that come from badly kept books.[19] It is precisely this statement that Gelderblom takes as his main argument for underpinning the presence of an official rule as

16 Jan Ympyn Christoffels, *Nieuwe Instructie ende bewijs der looffelijcker consten des rekenboecks, ende rekeninghe te houdene nae die Italiaensche maniere* ... (Antwerp: Gillis Copyns van Diest, 1543), fol. 1r. A translation of this introduction can also be found in the French edition, which dates from 1543 and which was co-authored by Anna Swinters. Jan Ympyn Christoffels, *Nouvelle instruction et remonstration de la tres excellente science du livre de compte* ... (Antwerp, 1543), fols. 1r–v. There are some interesting differences between both editions: the French introduction does not say that Anna herself finished the manuscript, for example. There is also an English edition, dating 1547, in which the introduction by Anna Swinters does not figure. It is indeed very possible that Anna was herself involved in the teaching of accounting or arithmetic. New research has brought to light the fact that schoolmistresses were very common in sixteenth-century Antwerp. See Ad Meskens, *Practical Mathematics in a Commercial Metropolis: Mathematical Life in Late Sixteenth-Century Antwerp* (Dordrecht: Springer, 2013), 214–215.

17 Ympyn, *Nieuwe instructie*, fol. 2r; Ympyn, *Nouvelle instruction*, fol. 2r.

18 Ympyn, *Nieuwe instructie*, fol. 4v *'maer dese ordinantie, die den spiegel des coopmans is houwende...'*; Ympyn, *Nouvelle instruction*, fol. 7r *'par ceste ordonnance, qui est le mirroir des marchans...'.*

19 Ympyn, *Nieuwe instructie*, fol. 2r *'Als inden eersten allen wethouderen ende iusticieren, op datse hier af kennisse hebbende weten te discerneren, ende rechtelijck moghen handelen tusschen ende in die differencien ende geschillen, dewelcke onder die cooplieden dagelijcx geschien ende rysen, so by fauten van qualick boeck houden, als anders, soe men doet in Italien...'*; Ympyn, *Nouvelle instruction*, fol. 5r *'Et premierement a tous iusticiers, affin quilz ayent cognoissance de ce que dessus dit est, pour discerner tous differendz & altercations meues, & qui iournellement se meuuent entre les marchans, tant par faulte de tenir mal leurs livres de comptes que aultrement. Comme on faict en Italie...'*. The English version has 'very commodious & profitable to all iusticiaries, because theie maie have knowledge to discerne al differences and alteracions that daily happeneth emong marchantes, as well

to the formal requirements of account books in Antwerp, and which he claims was proffered for the first time in Ympyn's tract. Upon closer examination, however, it becomes clear that what Ympyn meant was that his text would allow judges to discover the fraudulent use of accounts; when reading the *Nieuwe instructie*, that is, they would acquire the expertise to sense whether allegations of fraud regarding entries in books had any ground. In point of fact, then, Ympyn's manual was not reflecting a legal standard but rather advising caution and honesty in keeping books. Bookkeeping practices were very diffuse still in the 1540s, and what Ympyn presented as a viable method ('manner') consisted of both abstract principles and concrete instructions. Few of them were shared among groups of merchants and, interestingly enough, many were the author's creation.

Ympyn speaks of the *rechte maniere* ('the right manner') to keep books[20] and he sets forth guidelines that at the same time warrant the efficient use of the books and protect the reputation of the merchant drafting them. The language of Ympyn's treatise stands in a tradition of describing the ideal merchant as a diligent and prudent individual. The 'right manner' referred to the correct application of techniques of bookkeeping, which had the purpose of ascertaining how much was on hand and what was due. Ympyn linked instructions on the 'right way' of keeping accounts to an optimal behaviour by merchants doing so. Ympyn says that the merchant must be 'like a cock, who is vigilant day and night',[21] and who insists that books are kept up-to-date.[22]

In spite of references to a 'manner', Ympyn's tract is not legal, or even normative. When occasionally it mentions a 'custom', his manual describes 'best practices', as it were, followed in order to avoid confusion or allegations afterwards.[23] When using the term 'custom', Ympyn does not refer to what, in literature regarding the history of commercial law, is often referred to as 'customs of merchants'. Such customs are practices that are normative and shared

by faute of evil kepyng of their bokes of accomptes as otherwise (as is used in Italy)'. See Jan Ympyn Christoffels, *A notable and very excellente woorke* ... (s.l., 1547), fol. 4.

20 Ympyn, *Nieuwe instructie*, fol. 3v and fol. 11r.

21 Ympyn, *Nieuwe instructie*, fol. 5r.

22 Ympyn, *Nieuwe instructie*, fol. 4v.

23 Ympyn, *Nieuwe instructie*, fol. 4r '*die goeden costume van den Italiaenen...*' ('the good custom of the Italians...'); fol. 8r '*is oock een costume ende groote redene*'. References to customs could have an extraterritorial flavour. In the introduction (fol. 4r), Ympyn refers to the '*maniere ende usantie van Venegien*' ('the manner and usage of Venice [of bookkeeping]') and he states that '*door middele van welcker costumen men lichtelijck comen sal totter kennissen vande usantien van allen anderen steden*' ('on the basis of this custom one will easily gain knowledge of the usages of all other cities').

among groups of traders: if a merchant failed to honour the custom, he was exposed to sanctions in one way or another.[24] Even if these terms possibly hinted at some 'usual' conduct by bookkeeping merchants (in Italian cities, for example), Ympyn did not consider the phrases referring to them as mandatory or as setting boundaries to possible behaviour.

Some of Ympyn's lines certainly contain stronger wording, particularly when they touch upon fraud. For example, Ympyn states that it was common practice in Italy to put the symbols for *livre, sou* and *denier* before the number of the amount, and not behind it, because otherwise the numbers of debts 'could be obfuscated'.[25] Errors in entries should not be expunged but were to be supplemented with a new entry or new writing, which would 'prevent the appearance of fraud or carelessness'.[26] Yet even from these warnings it is evident that Ympyn did not envisage some sort of formal standard for double-entry bookkeeping. Instead, his treatise relied for the most part on a general principle of carefulness, which would ensure that any damage to reputation would be avoided.

3.2 *The Lack of Uniformity and Detail in Accounting Practices and Rules*

There is no evidence that the Antwerp municipal administrators (aldermen) were involved in the publication of Ympyn's treatise, or that the Antwerp government imposed or even desired standards as to the form of account books in one way or another. The printing privilege, which was far from unusual for 'technical' monographs such as Ympyn's book, was for four years. It was granted by Charles V, Lord of the Netherlands and Holy Roman Emperor, following examination of the manuscript by members of government. It is unlikely that the Antwerp magistracy was involved in the reviewing or publication process.

Moreover, evidence suggests that the Antwerp aldermen, who were also the judges in the city's Municipal Court, did not care too much about the exact formal structure of accounting books. Ever since the last decade of the fifteenth century, private documents could be submitted to the Antwerp aldermen-judges as proof. They could include acknowledgments of debt, accounts and account books. In the Municipal Court of Antwerp a document that had been written by the claimant, and which was presented as evidence of a debt, could

24 The literature on the subject is abundant, yet unsatisfactory in many respects. For a recent and critical appraisal, see Kadens, 'The Myth'.

25 Ympyn, *Nieuwe instructie*, fol. 15v.

26 Ympyn, *Nieuwe instructie*, fol. 19r.

be reinforced by means of his oath.[27] In the 1490s and in the early sixteenth century, the oath was required because private documents were still considered to be 'half-proof' (*probatio semiplena*), though reservations of this type disappeared throughout the 1520s and 1530s. Nevertheless, the prevalent rule of academic doctrine remained, namely, that *libri rationum* had to be confirmed with an oath in order to be acknowledged as full evidence,[28] such that this argument was still raised in the Municipal Court of Antwerp well into the later sixteenth century.[29] In the compilations of Antwerp municipal law, which were made in 1548, 1570, 1582 and 1608, no detailed rules as to the form of account books, required for their evidential value, are mentioned. There are no traces of official rules on that subject. These compilations acknowledged the use of books, for example, in seizure and bankruptcy proceedings,[30] but they did not stipulate specific formal requirements. In the 1608 collection, it was only said that 'merchant books' served as valid proof among merchants of honour, if they had been well kept, if the cause of the debt had been registered in the entries, and if the claimant presenting his books was willing to confirm their genuine nature under oath.[31] Therefore, during most of Antwerp's Golden Age, account books could be used as proof, as could other documents mentioning a debt; they could, as could any other evidential material, be contested on the basis of charges of forgery or manipulation as well. However, in regard to the contents of account books, the aldermen-judges relied on general and mainly undetailed principles.

The absence of subsequent publications of Ympyn's book, which in 1543 had received a printing privilege for four years, additionally argues against Ympyn's book providing any standard of evidence by law. Moreover, later bookkeeping

27 Antwerp, Municipal Archives (hereafter AMA), Vierschaar (hereafter V) 1237, fol. 16r (October 21, 1542). This had been done in the 1490s as well: AMA, V1231, fol. 121v (June 14, 1490) and V1231, fols. 129v–130v (July 26, 1491). For the learned-procedural context of this oath *in supplementum probationis*, see Jean-Philippe Lévy, *La hierarchie des preuves dans le droit savant du Moyen Âge depuis la renaissance du droit romain jusq*u'a *la fin du XIVe siècle* (Paris: Librairie du Recueil Sirey, 1939), 106–127.

28 Maura Fortunati, *Scrittura e prova: I libri del commercio nel diritto medievale e moderno* (Roma: Fondazione Sergio Mochi Onory per la Storia del Diritto Italiano, 1996), 111–116, 127–138; Lévy, *La hiérarchie*, 78.

29 AMA, *Processen*, M9993, *salvatiën* (February 20, 1592), s. 32.

30 *Costuymen 1570*, 522 (seizure of claims is allowed), *Costuymen 1582*, 530–532; *Costuymen 1608*, 388 (insolvents should refrain from changing or transferring their books).

31 *Costuymen 1608*, 656 (s. 42). The description in the 1608 law book comprised any type of book (one-entry, double-entry, inventory…).

manuals issued by Antwerp publishers in the 1550s and 1560s did not contain the same guidelines as found in Ympyn's manual.[32] This difference corresponds with the introductory parts of Ympyn's treatise, which, as was mentioned, are defensive. Ympyn's widow even states that it was to be expected that the book would meet with opposition 'from people with bad intent that will criticise it for its novelty'.[33] Ympyn himself explains why practices pertaining to the Venetian method that he follows, are in his opinion to be preferred over others.[34] This Venetian approach consisted of guidelines, but they were also rather abstract in many ways. Pacioli most probably devised instructions when making general principles and best practices more concrete. Likewise, Ympyn sometimes followed his own intuition, or responded to new problems; at many points he advised in a different way to Pacioli.[35] Ympyn goes some way to admitting to this divergence himself in the first pages of his tract. He mentions that since not every detail can be answered in the manual, and because 'every day more and more is coming to the light of day' in the art of bookkeeping, every reader is advised 'to use his head'.[36]

In summary, then, Ympyn did not perceive his guidebook as imposing detailed instructions that were to be followed in order to preserve the legal-evidential value of account books in the Municipal Court of Antwerp.[37] Instead,

32 In the 1550s, Valentin Mennher published handbooks on bookkeeping that were based on a precursor or crude form of double-entry bookkeeping. Between 1560 and 1563, he adopted the variety that was depicted in Ympyn's handbook. See Raymond De Roover, 'Aux origines d'une techniques intellectuelle: la formation et l'expansion de la comptabilité à partie double', *Annales d'histoire économique et sociale* 9 (1937), 171–298, 286; P.G.A. de Waal, *Van Paciolo tot Stevin: een bijdrage tot de leer van het boekhouden in Nederland* (Roermond: Romen, 1927), 124–125. For a detailed overview of the (varying) contents of other Antwerp instructional guides on accounting, see de Waal, *Van Paciolo tot Stevin*, 89–277.

33 Ympyn, *Nieuwe instructie*, fol. 1r.

34 Ympyn, *Nieuwe instructie*, fol. 4r.

35 John B. Geijsbeek, *Ancient Double-Entry Bookkeeping* (Denver, CO: John B. Geijsbeek, 1914), 113; Basil Yamey, 'Pacioli, Manzoni, Oldcastle and Ympyn re-visited', in Esteban Hernández-Esteve and Matteo Martelli (eds.), *Before and After Luca Pacioli* (Conference publication, Florence, 2011), 290. The dialectical relation between bookkeeping tracts and practice in the later fifteenth and the sixteenth centuries is detailed in David Oldroyd and Alisdair Dobie, 'Bookkeeping', in John R. Edwards and Stephen P. Walker (eds.), *The Routledge Companion to Accounting History* (London: Routledge, 2009), 95–119, 103–108.

36 Ympyn, *Nieuwe instructie*, fol. 4r.

37 Gelderblom also refers to 'a legal tract published in Antwerp in 1584', which 'underlined that merchants had to use double-entry bookkeeping to preserve the evidential value of their ledgers'. See Gelderblom, *Cities of Commerce*, 98. The reference is to Wilhelm F. Lichtenauer, *Geschiedenis van de wetenschap van het handelsrecht in Nederland tot 1809*

Ympyn presented a rational method of keeping books, which when applied, would be beneficial. However, if a merchant were to use double-entry bookkeeping too loosely, inconsistencies might trigger allegations of fraud and cumbersome procedures,[38] with reputational damage resulting from such practices. Warning of this possibility was given more in terms of a caution, though, rather than as a standard of formal requirements. Ympyn's advice could be stringent, but even in that case he referred to best practices, not to norms. Not only was his advice not reflecting official law, it was not based on the customs of merchants either. Best practices could gain recognition among experts, but opinions could still differ. Even those practices considered 'best' by specialists were not phrased or conceived of as being mandatory or delineating in any way. They were directive, not normative. Ympyn intended to guide, not to hold up a yardstick.

4 Hearing the Author's Voice: Individual Advice versus Norms and Best Practices

The aforementioned conclusions concur with other guidebooks concerning business practice. In many of the merchant-orientated manuals printed at Antwerp, the advice of the author is not a reflection of customs, and at times

(Amsterdam: Noord-Hollandsche Uitgevers, 1956), 69. In Lichtenauer, a collection of *consilia* by Elbertus Leoninus is cited: *Centuria consiliorum* (Antwerp, 1584), 80 (cons. 12, 22). At the place referred to, it is mentioned that '*libri ... more mercatorum non fuerunt scripti, & quod inter mercatores nulla fides secundum stilum & morem illorum adhiberi illis possit*'. This is Leoninus' opinion, not that of the Antwerp aldermen. Leoninus refers in his *consilium* to general principles on the possible fraudulent nature of errors in books. It is not clear whether double-entry bookkeeping was at stake in the case for which the *consilium* was drawn up.

38 This was also observed by Raymond De Roover. See Raymond De Roover, *Jan Ympyn: Essai historique et technique sur le premier traité flamand de comptabilité (1543)* (Anvers: Veritas, 1928), 24: 'L'*aspect juridique de la comptabilité* n'a *pas échappé à Jan Ympyn, qui se montre constamment préoccupé d'augmenter les garanties de sincérité et de prévenir les fraudes dans les livres de commerce. Il ne manque pas de faire force recommandations et de prémunir les commerçants contre certaines pratiques qui pourraient mettre en doute l'authenticité des écritures*'. In this respect, a mention in another accounting manual is interesting: in his 1563 treatise on bookkeeping, Valentin Mennher warned merchants not to cross out erroneous entries '*anderst warden sie fur falsch geachtet, und haben im Rechten kain kraft*' ('otherwise they will be considered false, and will have no value in court'). See Valentin Mennher, *Buech halten, Kurtz begriffen durch zway buecher* (Antwerp, 1563), fol. 2r.

not even of practices among merchants, even though wording could appear normative.

In 1590, for instance, a merchant manual was published in Amsterdam by an unknown author, called *Tresoir van de maten* ('Treasury of measures'). Despite its place of publication, its contents clearly reflect mercantile practices of Antwerp. As is known, following the upheaval of the Dutch Revolt, many merchants had left the Southern Netherlands and Antwerp in particular, taking refuge in the North and often in Amsterdam. These immigrants naturally brought with them their business expertise. The author of *Tresoir* was possibly one of them. *Tresoir van de maten* contains sections on marine insurance, which had been practiced to a considerable extent in Antwerp since the 1530s. Though not commonly discussed in *ars mercatoria*-guidebooks published in the city,[39] *Tresoir* lists some advice in matters of marine insurance. For example, it warns merchants not to sign insurance contracts for voyages for which neither the port of departure or the port of arrival were in the Low Countries, because it was to be feared that news would arrive too late, and for such insurances, fraud could easily be orchestrated.[40] *Tresoir* also states that one should not insure ships left unspecified in the insurance contract, or ships for which the name of the captain was excluded.[41] These lines of advice appear as somewhat out-of-touch, though, with mercantile realities at that time. In the third quarter of the sixteenth century, both long-distance insurance policies as well as insurance contracts in which the captain was named, albeit with the additional clause 'or anyone else', were commonly signed in Antwerp.[42]

These sections of *Tresoir* are written in instructional language that indicates exercising caution and avoiding risk. In this respect, *Tresoir* corresponds to Ympyn's *Nieuwe instructie*. However, *Tresoir* also contains one reference to what from the description can be interpreted as referring to a custom. It states that marine insurance of 'leaky merchandise' is not to be practiced, but that in case of (intentionally inflicted) damage to such cargo, for the purpose of saving the

39 In his 1563 manual on bookkeeping, Valentin Mennher added some examples of entries reflecting the payment of a premium for marine insurance. See de Waal, *Van Paciolo tot Stevin*, 138–139. Examples of a charter party and a bill of lading can be found in John Weddington, *A breffe instruction, and manner, how to kepe, marchantes bokes, or accomptes …* (Antwerp, 1567), fols. 36v–37r. The letter book by Meurier, containing an insurance contract, is the only example. It will be discussed hereafter.

40 *Tresoir vande Maten, van Gewichten, van Coorn, Landen, vande Elle ende natte Mate, oock vanden Gelde ende Wissel, ende ander practycquen ende vergaderinghen, seer profytich ende gevoechlyck* (Amsterdam, 1590), 140.

41 *Tresoir*, 140.

42 De Groote, *De zeeassurantie*, 100–101, 110–111.

ship, the general average (also called gross average) is 'always' applied, except for when 'no average is agreed upon'.[43] The wording of the passage ('always') hints at a shared practice (a custom), or a mandatory official rule found in legislation or imposed through judicial practice, providing that this general average (also) applies to merchandise such as oil and wine. However, neither official law nor mercantile customs referred to this practice in such detail. The Municipal Court of Antwerp stipulated as a general rule that damages that had intentionally been inflicted in order to save the vessel or its cargo were to be borne collectively by all owners of the hull and of the merchandise transported with the ship.[44] This 'general average' contrasted with 'particular average', which referred to damages caused by accident or storms and not by deliberate action. In the case of particular average, costs could not be recovered, except for when the shipmaster could be accused of negligence or fault.[45] There are no sources that stated that this recuperation also applied to perishable merchandise. Still, from the general official rule referred to, in addition to a lack of detail as to exceptions, it can be deduced that leaky cargo could indeed be remunerated on the basis of general average. The mention that 'no average' could be provided, most likely in the chartering or carriage contract, might refer to an older practice of shipmasters and charterers taking on contractual liability for damages even when caused by accident or weather conditions.[46]

Even so, in spite of some similarities to rules on general average, the words of the author of *Tresoir* do not represent common insurance practices and the laws regulating them. Insurance of 'leaky' cargo was also possible by law. According to the Antwerp municipal law books of 1570 and 1582, insurance coverage of such shipments was allowed, on the condition that the composition of the cargo was explicitly mentioned in the insurance contract.[47] A princely ordinance of January 1571 regarding marine insurance confirmed this rule.[48]

43 *Tresoir*, 140.

44 E.g. AMA, V1235, fol. 26v (1517).

45 De Groote, *De zeeassurantie*, 19–20.

46 Dave De ruysscher, 'Antwerp 1490–1590: insurance and speculation', in Adrian Leonard (ed.), *Marine insurance: international development and evolution, 1300–1700* (London, 2015, in the press).

47 'Deterioration' was even mentioned as an insurable peril according to the 1570 and 1582 law. See *Costuymen 1570*, 602; *Costuymen 1582*, 402 (s. 4), 404 (s. 13). See also *Costuymen 1608*, 216–218 (leaky goods can be insured, if mentioned in detail in the contract).

48 A 1598 Amsterdam ordinance also provided for this same rule (coverage is possible, if the leaky merchandise or victuals are mentioned in the insurance policy). See Johan P. van Niekerk, *The Development of the Principles of Insurance Law in the Netherlands from 1500 to 1800*, 2 vols. (Johannesburg: Juta, 1998), 1:292–293.

In practice, the nature of insured freights was often not detailed in the insurance contract,[49] but this is not the situation referred to in the *Tresoir*. Furthermore, the author of *Tresoir* seems to have missed the fact that general average was often combined with marine insurance, and that this practice was also lawful. If merchandise was thrown overboard, in order to elevate the hull of a stranded ship, for example, then the marine insurers of the jettisoned cargo could not waive their contractual liability by pointing to the captain.[50] What the aforementioned passage in *Tresoir* might hint at is that in average calculations, damage to merchandise was not always taken into account, even when the leaky merchandise had been jettisoned so as to save the ship.[51] Yet in that case, *Tresoir* states a contrary rule, and then it still overlooks the relevance of insurance. It was actually much safer to insure 'leaky' cargo than to rely on any general average. While *Tresoir* in this regard did use normative wording, it was actually phrasing advice in a different way to the description in contemporary customs and official law.

A comparable conclusion can be drawn from the advice in *Tresoir* that transferable acknowledgments of debt (bills obligatory, called *obligaties*) 'must' mention the cause of the debt.[52] It had formally been accepted by the Antwerp aldermen that this was not required: 'abstracted' *obligaties* were also considered lawful and legally valid.[53] Again, it seems that the author of *Tresoir* was being cautious, but that he was not referring to a custom or other rule when using such normative phrasing. Furthermore, it is very unlikely that the lines on *obligaties* and average of leaky merchandise in *Tresoir* reflect the norms of Amsterdam instead of Antwerp. In 1590, Amsterdam official law concerning mercantile contracts was still sketchy. A bylaw on the topic of marine insurance was only passed in 1598, making allowances for the insurance of perishable merchandise, on the condition that it was mentioned in the

49 De Groote, *De zeeassurantie*, 99–100 (listing vague descriptions of insured freights in sixteenth-century Antwerp insurance contracts).

50 Van Niekerk, *The Development*, 1:78–79.

51 A. Weytsen, *Een tractaet van avarien, …* (Haarlem, 1631), 6–8. Weytsen is not explicit, but one can think of some reasons for these reservations. Proof of causality between the act of damaging and the damages to perishable cargo is likely to have been difficult. Especially when the ship was delayed, it could be suspected that the merchandise had expired before it was thrown overboard. It goes without saying that foodstuffs that were over date were probably the first to be discarded into the ocean in case of stranding.

52 *Tresoir*, 188.

53 AMA, V69, fol. 25v. (April 19, 1559), V69, fol. 59v. (June 21, 1567) and V70, fol. 19v. (August 6, 1575).

insurance contract.[54] This stipulation was the same rule as that which applied in Antwerp before then. Even before 1598, the sections in the Antwerp municipal law book concerning marine insurance had been used in Amsterdam.[55] In addition, transferable bills obligatory handed out to the bearer were very common in Holland at around the time when *Tresoir* was being written.[56] It is very likely, then, that Antwerp rules on this mercantile document were exported to the city on the Amstel before the writing of *Tresoir*, even though there is no evidence of an official rule in Amsterdam hinting at 'abstracted' *obligaties* before the 1630s.[57]

All this documentation yields obvious *caveats* as to any possible links between business practices, norms concerning trade and the prescriptive contents of *ars mercatoria*-literature. What was written in merchant guidebooks did not reflect *per se* official law or mercantile custom, and not even practices. Other manuals containing, for instance, translations or models of letters, also include examples of *obligaties* in which the cause of its issuance was mentioned, for example.[58]

Some of these instructional tracts include full contracts that were not commonly drawn up between merchants. Instead, they contain what according to the author was an ideal contract, even when it was sometimes presented as a specimen taken from business practice. An example of such illustrations can be found in a letter manual by Gabriel Meurier that was published in Antwerp in 1558.[59] It contains a contract of marine insurance, under the heading *Lettres d'assuerances* ('letters of insurance'). The author presents the agreement as

54 van Niekerk, *The Development*, 1:292.

55 Dave De ruysscher, 'Antwerp Commercial Legislation in Amsterdam in the 17th century: Legal Transplant or Jumping Board?', *The Legal History Review* 77 (2009), 459–479, 464, 472–473.

56 J.M.F. Fritschy, 'Holland's Public Debt and Amsterdam's Capital Market', in Carmen Sanz Ayán and Bernardo J. García García (eds.), *Banca, crédito y capital: La Monarquía Hispánica y los antiguos Países Bajos (1505–1700)* (Madrid: Fundación Carlos Amberes, 2006), 39–59, 53.

57 De ruysscher, 'Antwerp Commercial Legislation', 474. After establishing the Exchange Bank in 1609, transferable bearer bills were denounced by the Amsterdam administrators. This was not the case before that time.

58 Nicolas Berlaimont, *Dictionariolum hexaglosson cum colloquiis aliquot sex linguarum …* (Antwerp, 1585) fols. 157v–161v; Jean Bourlier, *Stile et maniere de composer lettres missives avec plusieurs reigles & argumens à ce convenables: ensemble obligations, quitances, & lettres de change, le tout à l'utilité d'un chacun* (Antwerp, 1566), 172–178.

59 Gabriel Meurier, *Formulaire de missives, obligations, Quittances, letters de change, d'asseurances, & plusieures Epitres familières, messages, requêtes, & instructions notables …* (Antwerp, 1558), fol. 13r–14v.

having been drawn up at Antwerp; the text mentions Lazarus Tucher, a well-known Antwerp merchant, as the insured party, and provides for the insurance of shipments from Antwerp to Lisbon. The contract contains some clauses that were quite common around 1558, such as references to the customs of Antwerp and London, and references to the insurance of the perils of man and sea. It even paraphrases a custom concerning the mandatory payment by underwriters within two months after their summons to do so. Merchants considered this norm to be a *consuetudo* that bound insurance underwriters, and it had been acknowledged by the Municipal Court of Antwerp well before 1558.[60] Nevertheless, there are also some strange sections in Meurier's contract. For example, it was not common to list the composition of insured freights in detail:[61] Meurier's text of the agreement mentions *cuivre, toyles, cire & autres marchandises*. Moreover, it lists barratry among the risks covered by the insurance underwriters. This provision entailed that conduct by the shipmaster and his crew leading up to damages of insured freights was considered insurable. However, in this period, the 1550s, many merchants vacillated over the issue as to whether such insurance was possible.[62]

It is possible that Tucher's contract was genuine, and that it had been somewhat exceptional. However, a 'reproduction' of a bill obligatory in another part of Meurier's book, in the form that according to Meurier was commonly used by the clerks of the Antwerp aldermen,[63] leaves less room for doubt in this regard. Contracts, agreements and promises could be submitted to the municipal offices in Antwerp for registration. In the 1550s, filing such records was no longer necessary for the evidential value of documents, but it was still commonly done. Meurier's *obligatie* is very detailed: it contains the reason for its writing (a loan), the addition that the debtors would pay at first invitation, and a provision of collateral in the form of a house, the location of which is described in detail. Moreover, the *obligatie* mentions that the debtors abandon invoking legal arguments when being asked to pay up. None of these features were

60 Already in the 1530s, the Antwerp administrators labelled this rule as being 'old law'. See Oskar De Smedt, 'De keizerlijke verordeningen van 1537 en 1539 op de obligaties en wisselbrieven. Eenige kantteekeningen', *Nederlandsche Historiebladen* 3 (1940), 15–35, 19.

61 De Groote, *De zeeassurantie*, 99.

62 Guido Rossi, *Insurance in Elizabethan England: the London Code* (Cambridge: Cambridge University Press, 2015), 173–176 (the pages refer to a manuscript version). The regional diversity was seen at Antwerp in the 1550s and thereafter, when draft legislation was debated over among legislators and merchants. See Dave De ruysscher and Jeroen Puttevils, 'The Art of Compromise: Legislative Deliberation on Marine Insurance Institutions in Antwerp (*c.* 1550–*c.* 1570)', *BMGN-Low Countries Historical Review* (2015), in press.

63 Meurier, *Formulaire de missives*, fol. 22v–23 r.

common in contemporary *obligaties*, and some of them were never stated.[64] It seems that for this text, and maybe also with regard to the insurance contract mentioned, Meurier mingled actual mercantile practices with his own insights so as to make his argument.

Meurier and Ympyn both presumed, upon their licence as authors, to present a picture of mercantile techniques and arrangements as they saw fit, and in the form that they believed was best. The individuality of authors is thus a variable to be taken into account here. Merchant guidebooks were often written by teachers,[65] and their function as supplementary materials for students can be understood from remarks in the introductory sections of these manuals. It was commonly stressed, for example, that the author of the manual could be consulted with further questions and that he could provide personal assistance.[66] The promotional value of course books is not to be underestimated either. The common granting of printing privileges, for short periods of time (four to five years, with a monopoly and copyright for the printer) also points in the direction of 'authorship'.[67]

5 The Normative Value of Practice, Best Practices and Advice

Merchant manuals provided basic information on the outlines of contracts and arrangements that were used among merchants in Antwerp. Jan Ympyn, for example, distinguishes between different types of bills of exchange. He paraphrases Pacioli on the matter but in so doing also provides a blueprint for the applications of bills of exchange in practice.[68] Another example is Maarten van Dijck's 1591 *Chijferboeck* ('Book of numbers'), which lists questions of mathematics, but at the same time gives a very detailed overview of

64 Puttevils, 'The Ascent of Merchants', 247. The author systematically studied 1,132 bills obligatory handed out in Antwerp between 1490 and 1587.

65 Henry L.V. De Groote, 'De zestiende-eeuwse Antwerpse schoolmeesters', *Bijdragen tot de geschiedenis* 19 (1967), 179–318 and 20 (1968), 5–52; Meskens, *Practical Mathematics*, 44–47.

66 E.g. Valentin Mennher, *Buechhalten* (Antwerp, 1560), introduction '*warin ich jedem mit meiner hilff Persønlichen kan dienen*'.

67 Some of the writers of Antwerp-printed merchant guidebooks, such as Michiel Coignet, combined the publication of bookkeeping treatises with the writing of manuals on instruments for seafaring and other purposes. See Meskens, *Practical Mathematics*, 122–130, 139–160.

68 Ympyn, *Nieuwe instructie*, fols. 13v–15v. Critical is De Roover, *Jan Ympyn*, 22–24.

mercantile arrangements and of their possible use.[69] Examples of book entries in bookkeeping manuals not only served to teach the technique of bookkeeping, but also provided information as to mercantile contracts and how they should be practiced. In his 1537 manual, Gielis van den Hoecke states that partnerships (*compagnieën*) are set up for a specific period of time (*metter tyt*) or with indeterminate duration (*sonder tyt*).[70] Similarly, a passage on future sales of grain (i.e. sales against prices fixed but payable in the future, for merchandise that is not yet available) in the above-mentioned *Tresoir* combines factual information on prices and best practices with data on the essentials of the arrangement. It mentions, for example, that a sum of money, called *stellegelt*, had to be paid in case the purported buyer withdrew from the future contract at around the projected time of delivery, because the market price was lower than the price that had earlier been agreed upon.[71]

Still, it would go too far to consider all of these references as indicating law. In sixteenth-century Antwerp, law could take the form of official law, when rules were imposed with legislation or through the judgments of courts. Legislation comprised bylaws, statements and *turbe*-inquiries that were drafted or supervised by the administrators of the city, as well as princely ordinances. Moreover, law could be a custom, which was a repeated practice that was shared because it was felt that it had to be followed.[72] In theory, enforcement of customs could be informal (through exclusion from an organization, for example), but it could also happen by means of official sanctions. In that case the custom would have been acknowledged within the sphere of the official law.[73] Law is here defined as normative: it stipulates what is to be or can be done; it is mandatory in the sense that non-compliance or transgression of limits has group- or community-related and reputational consequences. From that perspective, the above-mentioned advice, guidelines and references to

69 Marten van den Dycke, *Chijferboeck, inhoudende veelderley subtile exempelen, question ende vraeghen, dienende totter comenschappen ende andersins, seer nut ende profitelyck voor alle cooplieden van wat digniteyt conditie oft qualiteyt darse syn, ende beminders der selver vrijer consten* (Antwerp, 1591).

70 Cited in Jan A. Goris, *Étude sur les colonies méridionales* (Louvain: Uystpruyst, 1925), 105, note 3; and Puttevils, 'The Ascent of Merchants', 214.

71 *Tresoir*, 193.

72 On the sources of law in sixteenth-century Antwerp, see Dave De ruysscher, 'From Usages of Merchants to Default Rules: Practices of Trade, *Ius Commune* and Urban Law in Early Modern Antwerp', *The Journal of Legal History* 33:1 (2012), 3–29, 5–8.

73 On possible overlap between official law and customs of merchants, see Dave De ruysscher, 'Normative Hybridity in Antwerp Marine Insurance (*c.* 1650–*c.* 1700)', in Seán Donlan and Dirk Heirbaut (eds.), *Legalities and Complexities, c. 1550–1850* (Berlin, in press).

techniques and practice are not law, since they do not in any way impose or delimit conduct. Considering Ympyn's instructions against the backdrop of bookkeeping in the first half of the sixteenth century leads to the conclusion that he was presenting one method of double-entry bookkeeping, according to his own insights. Variation in the techniques presented, along with a lack of detailed regulation from the authorities, demonstrates that the contents of Ympyn's tract were not mandatory but merely informative and directive. The same can be said of Meurier's 'examples' of mercantile documents, which do not always refer to practice, and thus lay outside the views shared among merchants trading in Antwerp.

The counter argument which could be taken against these arguments is that much of what these authors described was law, if one is prepared to expand upon what is understood under the concept of 'law'. Following on from the work of such scholars as Eugen Ehrlich and Lon Fuller, law might be defined in terms of conventions, of stable interactional expectations.[74] Such conventions may formulate conduct in negative ('do not') or positive terms, leaving open a choice ('if, it is possible to'). If resulting from a definition of law as consisting of conventions, then best practices and instructions regarding reputational harm do have the potential to be labelled as legal. Moreover, the fact that merchants were a recognized group within society, and were sometimes organized into associations, might argue for considering certain aspects of their interactions to be law.[75] Nevertheless, what all these mentioned theories have in common is that, according to them, not all expectations are 'stable' (Fuller) or apt to establish 'common patterns of behaviour' (Ehrlich). Directions and instructions, therefore, are in themselves not sufficient to be labelled as law in this regard.

In order to qualify as law in the broader sense mentioned above, advice must reflect what merchants can expect from each other. Some of the mentioned data on mercantile contracts (e.g. *stellegelt*) indeed refers to practices that were known in the market and shared among traders. If the term *stellegelt* was mentioned in an agreement, it is fairly likely that merchants knew what this meant. In a situation where the buyer pulled out of a future contract, a sum had to be paid to the seller. For other data mentioned, as found in merchant guidebooks, legal contents in a broader sense are less obvious. This is

74 Eugen Ehrlich, *Fundamental Principles of the Sociology of Law* (Cambridge, Mass.: Harvard University Press, 1936); Lon L. Fuller, 'Human interaction and the law', *American Journal of Jurisprudence* 14 (1969), 1–36 (custom and law in general arise from the stabilization of interacting expectancies so that conduct is directed by these expectancies).

75 Proponents of a *ius mercatorum* in this sense are, for example, Umberto Santarelli and Giovanni Cassandro.

because, for the aforementioned (broad) qualification as law, it must be determined whether the instructions found in these handbooks conformed with practice, and whether practice was so uniform and stable that it could be taken as being normative.

In this respect, it seems that not many mercantile conventions, in line with guidelines in instructional tracts, but also more generally speaking, existed. In court proceedings before the Municipal Court of Antwerp, advocates debating questions of mercantile arrangements very rarely referred to customs.[76] The same can be seen at so-called *turbe*-inquiries, which were organized by the aldermen-judges of Antwerp in order to state a rule of municipal law under the label of a (official) *consuetudo*. These sessions were examinations at which invited witnesses answered precise questions as to the conditions of an alleged *consuetudo*. Yet very few merchants were called upon to attend *turbe*-inquiries, even when the issue concerned mercantile contracts.[77]

Granted, there was some pressure from legal professionals and administrators, but this was minimal. Merchants, along with their advocates, were not restrained in any way from bringing up mercantile customs. The procedural framework of rules that applied in the Municipal Court of Antwerp supported references to customs. According to the Romano-canonical norms that were applied in the Antwerp court, customs filled in gaps in contracts, and they had priority over rules that were found in academic doctrine. Only legislation, which during Antwerp's Golden Age was minimal for mercantile and other subjects, put contrary custom aside. Moreover, the threshold for speaking of a custom was very low, according to late medieval and early modern doctrine: repeated practices were held to be normative (thus, valid and binding) if they were based on the implied consent as to their normativity (*tacitus consensus*) of a group of people.[78] Although advocates occasionally stretched the scope and contents of rules of academic and municipal law in order to make them encompass mercantile practice, it seems that this was not done often. Even the merchants testifying at Antwerp *turbe*-inquiries referred to mercantile norms as belonging to municipal law, and did not merely phrase them as customs of their own.[79] Moreover, upon close scrutiny, it has become clear that late

---

76 See Dave De ruysscher, 'L'interprétation des contrats commerciaux à Anvers (*c.* 1490–*c.* 1540)', in Boris Bernabé (ed.), *L'interprétation du droit* (Besançon, 2015, in the press).

77 I developed this argument in De ruysscher, 'From Usages of Merchants to Default Rules', 3–29.

78 See footnote 5.

79 De ruysscher, 'From Usages of Merchants to Default Rules', 26–28.

medieval and sixteenth-century legal treatises and *consilia* list few customs relating to merchants and mercantile contracts.[80]

Even though more research is needed in this regard, it is not unlikely that merchants trading in sixteenth-century Antwerp and other cities and regions did not consider many practices to be normative – not even best practices or instructions referring to them. Maybe they did not need many conventions to do business. Correspondence might have gone a long way in detailing what was expected; trade was largely a matter of 'facts and figures' as well. When disputes arose, the academic and local official law then provided more arguments than the few customs that existed among merchants. This was use of law *ex post*; yet even in that case, it is a fair estimate to state that before the end of the sixteenth century, lawsuits between merchants did not turn into debates over juristic issues very often.[81] *Ex ante* references to external law among merchants seems to have been even rarer. For most of the sixteenth century in Antwerp, deliberately leaving out details in agreements with regard to rules that could afterwards be reconstructed and imposed by judges was indeed possible, but it seems to have been more a mere theoretical possibility.[82]

6 Conclusion

The materials analysed in this chapter provide a glimpse into the instructional and normative purposes of merchant manuals. It is evident that some of their contents were stricter than the framework of official law and even went against merchants' practices and common dealings. Ympyn's treatise and others contain prescriptive parts that were advice, however, rather than a reflection of

80 Ch. Donahue, 'Medieval and Early Modern Lex Mercatoria: An Attempt at the Probatio Diabolica', *The Chicago Journal of International Law* 5 (2004), 21–38, 32 (referring to Straccha's *De Mercatura*, 1553); Carlos Petit, 'Del vsvs mercatorvm al uso de comercio: Notas y textos sobre la costumbre mercantil', *Revista da Faculdade de Direito* 48 (2008), 7–38, 10, footnote 3 (referring to Pedro de Salazar, *De usu et consuetudine et de stilo curiae regalis*, 1579). In *consilia* written in the sixteenth-century Southern Low Countries, there are some references to customs of merchants, but one gains the impression from published *consilia* that they were not too abundant either. See Alain Wijffels, 'Business Relations Between Merchants in Sixteenth-Century Practice-Orientated Civil Law Literature', in Vito Piergiovanni (ed.), *From lex mercatoria to commercial law* (Berlin: Duncker & Humblot, 2005), 255–290.

81 AMA, V1231–1242.

82 The policy of crafting default rules of contract appeared only rather late in Antwerp, starting around 1550. See De ruysscher, 'From Usages of Merchants to Default Rules', 28.

rules set forth by legislation or custom. Merchant guidebooks must be considered for the individual thoughts and choices of their authors, as a consequence, and are not always paraphrasing the ideas of a merchant community. This chapter, then, provides a clear warning against viewing this *ars mercatoria*-literature as a historical source of conduct and of normative ideas concerning trade. In fact, the limited value of mercantile guidebooks in this respect adds to other evidence pointing in the direction of limited juridification of commerce, even in the sixteenth century. Not only was official law rather minimal, it seems that even the normative practices of merchants were not abundant. Antwerp records dating from the 1500s demonstrate that the customs of merchants were seldom mentioned in court-related documents and inquiries into customs; in addition, academic literature does not mention them very often. Both the nature of commerce as well as a mercantile culture that carefully administered business provide arguments for this legal situation. An overarching academic and local law, which was imposed through judgments and by legal professionals, offers a possible explanation for the low number of customs found in official documents; however, the latter were not brought forward, not even by merchants, in a setting that was generally custom-friendly. One can speculate that the historiography concerning trade norms in the later Middle Ages and early modern period will benefit from a more modest approach towards normative practices of merchants, which have often been inflated to transnational legal levels. In this regard, pursuing a broad perspective on the features of interactions in commerce clearly seems to be a prescription for modesty.

CHAPTER 8

Sources of Commercial Law in the Dutch Republic and Kingdom

Boudewijn Sirks

1 Introduction

In his *Quaestiones Juris Publici* I.21, Bijnkershoek states at the beginning: *In regnis et reipublicis, quae commerciis exercendis student, contractu assecurationis nullus hodie est frequentior, excepta emptione venditione, locatione conductione.* 'In kingdoms and republics which are keen on exercising trade, there is with the exception of sale and hire no contract more in use than that of insurance'.[1] After giving a historical outline of how this contract was developed, he deals with the question of whether one may insure enemies' cargo. That is understandable in the context of the *Quaestiones Juris Publici*, which are mainly on war and the legal complications for belligerents (including letters of marque and reprisal), but one wonders how the legal construction took shape. In his *Quaestiones Juris Privati*, published posthumously in 1744, the entire fourth part is dedicated to problems of insurance law.[2] Thus Bijnkershoek identifies three contracts as being specific for commerce: sale, hire (and contracting), and insurance. He distinguishes these within the context of the general body of private law, and he was no exception in this respect.

2 Sources of Commercial Law up to 1809

A commercial law separate from private law by being applicable to a special group, founded on a special body of rules, and applied by special courts, did not come into existence in the Northern Netherlands until 1811. But there were regulations specific for commerce,[3] particular contracts important for

1 Cornelii van Bynkershoek, *Quaestionum Juris Publici libri duo* (Leiden, 1737), 152–153.

2 Bynkershoek, *Quaestionum*, 517–744.

3 Every town and province had its own laws and bylaws, and the States-General did too. These were published, often in a collection, such as 'placaatboeken'. In the *Groot Placaet-boeck, vervattende de placaaten* [...] *van de* [...] *Staaten Generaal* [...] *en de Staten van Holland en*

 | DOI 10.1163/9789004363144_009

commerce (as Bijnkershoek states), some legal works focusing on commercial themes, jurisprudence dealing particularly with commerce, and even some courts dealing with mostly commercial activities. For the period up to 1809, W.F. Lichtenauer has given an excellent survey of all these, written in a lively style.[4] For the nineteenth century, from 1809 onwards, Van Oven's study is fine but focuses primarily on the science of commercial law.[5] Lichtenauer, on the other hand, first offers a general survey of the law (Ch. II), then a description

---

Westvriesland; mitsgaders van de [...] *Staten van Zeeland*, 9 vols. (Leiden, Amsterdam, 1658–1796), with a *Repertorium* (Amsterdam, 1797), one finds the regulations for the Republic and its commercially most important provinces of Holland and Zeeland. Some regulations may be found on the website *Regelgeving in de Nederlanden* (http://www.geneaknowhow.net/regel/nederlanden.htm).

4 Wilhelm F. Lichtenauer, *Geschiedenis van de wetenschap van het handelsrecht in Nederland tot 1809* (Amsterdam: Noord-Hollandsche Uitgevers, 1956). The author relates the wish of the Dutch Association of Lawyers in 1883 to relinquish the differentiation between private and commercial law, and remarks that if the views of Molengraaff held (that commercial law was non-existent before the introduction of the Code of Commerce in 1811), his work would resemble a charcoal drawing of a negro by night. But Lichtenauer rejects this view as being unrealistic. With the new codification of private law in the second half of the twentieth century, the Code of Commerce was to be abolished and commercial law incorporated in the new Civil Code. Yet Lichtenauer was right: commerce retains a special place, with all of book 8 dedicated to transportation and means of transport, while some international treaties rule commerce still; book 9, on intellectual property – a new but very important subject for commerce – will not be discussed at all due to the many international regulations which rule this subject. Thus this will stay outside of the Civil Code. W.F. Lichtenauer (1900–1987) studied law at Leiden from 1918 till 1922, and defended his doctoral thesis in 1932, entitled *De vernietigende verjaring en aanverwante rechtsfiguren beschouwd naar wezen, begrenzing en onderlinge verhouding*, under the supervision of Prof. E.M. Meijers. He was an erudite and very energetic man, employed first in the Chamber of Commerce of Rotterdam 1922–1951 (lastly as General Secretary, but remaining a member until 1961), CEO of a transport enterprise 1951–1956, General President of the important Scheepvaart Vereniging Zuid 1956–1961 (and in these functions he was important for the rebuilding of Rotterdam after the war), i.a. Member of the First Chamber of Parliament 1956–1961, and Member of the Raad van State 1961–1973. He was also a keen historian and participated in many cultural and social institutions. 'Obituaries: R.A.D. Renting, 'Lichtenauer, Wilhelm Franz (1900–1987)', in *Biografisch Woordenboek van Nederland*, http://resources.huygens.knaw.nl/bwn1880-2000/lemmata/bwn4/lichten [12-11-2013], also one in *Jaarboek van de Maatschappij der Nederlandse Letterkunde* (1988), 168–176.

5 A. van Oven, *Geschiednis van de wetenschap van het handelsrecht in Nederland in de 19e eeuw* (Amsterdam: Noord-Hollandsche, 1968). Van Oven gives short scholarly biographies of twelve important scholars, before turning to commercial law arranged according to subject. There is no survey of sources, courts, jurisprudence, nor a separate list of publications. It is more in line with the setup of the series, of course.

of the legal science and foreign influences (Ch. III), followed by an inventory of sources of commercial law (Ch. IV: scholarly literature, literature of practice, jurisprudence, register books, formularies, orations, statutes, treaties, and customs), and finally the *jus singulare* of commerce (Ch. V). The list of literature pp. 215–236 provides the reader with what is likely a complete survey of writings on or connected with commercial law.[6]

There is no pressing need to redo the work of Lichtenauer, and since his work is written in Dutch, I shall relate the essence of his study as regards sources. Under the authors of general works, Grotius figures highly (pp. 85–104). The subjects Lichtenauer deals with for Grotius are: interest; bottomry; intermediaries; bills of exchange, assignments, commercial paper; commercial sale; maritime law (i.e., transportation etc., except average); company law; insurance law; average; insolvency (although summarily). Other authors of note are S. à Groenewegen van der Made,[7] S. van Leeuwen,[8] and J. Munniks (maritime law).[9] Authors on the same level as Grotius are C. van Bijnkershoek (pp. 109–110, insurance law),[10] D.G. van der Keessel (pp. 113–115),[11] and J. van der Linden (pp. 116–117).[12] For monographs Lichtenauer mentions Weytsen

6 Lichtenauer took the trouble to peruse not just publications by professors and practitioners, but also all dissertations at Dutch universities. A researcher can now avail himself of the bibliographies of Dutch authors insofar as they were a professor at a Dutch university for at least five years (see note 42). It is possible that some works may still turn up, through this channel, but which was unknown to Lichtenauer. Yet these bibliographies do not cover dissertations unless the author became a professor at a Dutch university for at least five years, or a practitioner who published more. Thus Lichtenauer's survey remains indispensable, the more so since he has valued the publications.

7 Simon à Groenewegen van der Made, *Tractatus de Legibus Abrogatis et inusitatis in Hollandia vicinisque regionibus* (Leiden, 1649). Where necessary and possible, bibliographical data have been updated in the following with the help of the bibliography of Dutch authors who were not connected to a Dutch university (see note 42).

8 Simon van Leeuwen, *Het Rooms-Hollands-regt* (Leiden, Rotterdam, 1664); many reprints.

9 Johannes Munniks, *Handleiding tot de hedendaagsche Rechtsgeleerdheid, der Vereenigde Nederlanden, naar de order van het Romeinsche recht* (Amsterdam, 1776).

10 Lichtenauer based himself on Bynkershoek, *Quaestiones*, and the first three volumes of Bijnkershoek's *Observationes Tumultuariae* (see note 35).

11 Dionysius G. van der Keessel, *Praelectiones iuris hodierni ad Grotii Introductionem ad jurisprudentiam Hollandicam* (Amsterdam: Balkema, 1961–1975); Dionysius G. van der Keessel, *Theses selectae juris Hollandici et Zeelandici* (Leiden, 1800). Lichtenauer still had to consult the manuscript for the *Praelectiones*.

12 Joannes van der Linden, *Regtsgeleerd, practicaal en koopmans handboek, ten dienste van regters, practizijns, kooplieden en allen die een algemeen overzicht van regtskennis verlangen* (Amsterdam: Allart, 1806). Van der Linden also published translations of Pothier's

(pp. 120–121, maritime law),[13] Van Glins (pp. 122–123, on the ordinance of Philip II of 1563 on maritime law),[14] Heineccius-Reitz (p. 125, bills of exchange),[15] Roccus-Feitama (p. 126, insurance),[16] and Banck-Wegern (p. 127, insolvency).[17] Of the dissertations Lichtenauer mentions, *inter alia*,[18]

Traité des Obligations, *Traité du contrat de société*, and *Traité du contrat de change*: all important for commerce. He also made a good translation of the Code Civil when this law book was imposed upon the Dutch in 1811.

13 Q. Weytsen, *Een tractaet van avarien, dat is ghemeene contributie vande koopmanschappen ende goederen inden schepe bevonden om te helpen dragen 't verlies van eenighe kooplieden ofte schippers goeden, gewillichlijck gebeurt, om lijf, schip ende goet te salveeren* (Haarlem, 1631; the reprints of 1651 and later contain additions by S. van Leeuwen); Latin edition, with additions by M. de Vicq: *Tractatus de avariis, id est communi contributione mercium rerumque in navi repertarum ad sarciendum damnum bonis mercatorum sive nautarum quorundam ultro illatum, eum in finem ut vita, navis ac reliqua bona salva evadant ... denuo perlustratus atque allegatione legum, jureconsultorum, edictorum, placitorum, ordinationum, statutorum etc., una cum necessariis quibusdam observationibus confirmatus et ditatus per D. Simonem a Leeuwen ... Latina vero toga indutus atque amplissima dote observationum adauctus, studio atque opera Matthaei de Vicq J.U.D.* (Amsterdam, 1672).

14 Taco van Glins, *Aenmerckingen Ende Bedenckingen over de Zee-rechten, uyt het Placcaet van Koninck Philips uytgegeven den lesten Octobris 1563* (Amsterdam, 1727).

15 *Grondbeginselen van het wisselrecht,* in't *Latyn saamgesteld door ... J.G. Heineccius naar de zevende uitgaaf vertaald, en met de noodige aanmerkingen verrykt en opgehelderd, door Karel Koenraad Reitz...; waarachter gevoegd zyn eene verhandeling over de feilen en gebreken in den wisselhandel, door de heeren Heineccius en Lochau; ; eene boekzaal van het wisselrecht, door den heer Eisenhart; ; een aanhangsel van eenige wisselwetten...*, 2nd ed. (Middelburg, 1774).

16 Francesco Rocci, *De Navibus et Naulo Item de assecurationibus Notabilia Editio nova* (*A. Westerveen*) (Amsterdam, 1708), translation: *Franciscus Roccus ... deszelfs Merkwaardige aanmerkingen, vervat in twee tractaaten ... uyt het Latyn en Italiaans, als mede het reglement der assurantien en haveryen van de stad Hamburg, uyt het Hoogduyts vertaalt ... door Mr Johan Feitama* (Amsterdam, 1741).

17 Daniel Wegern, *De Bancciruptoribus Dissertatio, editio auctior* (Franeker, 1650). It is ascribed to L. Banck, his promotor; but Feenstra does not express himself on this point in the bibliography of Franeker professors (see note 42), 15.

18 Lichtenauer does not provide us with the number of dissertations at the five Dutch universities he perused. That number is not inconsiderable. On page 134 he mentions that he found some 200 dissertations which he suspected were on commercial law, of which some 160 indeed dealt with this subject. This suggests that he perused catalogues, and more than these 200. The exact number of dissertations submitted at the Dutch universities during the Republic is not yet known (a list is being made) but certainly exceeded by far the number of 200. In view of his personality and scholarly training it is likely that Lichtenauer did check more than 200, but how much more remains open.

A. Brouwer on bills of exchange;[19] J. van Ghesel, M. den Beer and E.F. Harckenroth on insurance;[20] D. van Goens on monopolies of publishers;[21] P.G. Donker and C. Pruimers on market law;[22] eight dissertations on jettison;[23] H. Tollius on average;[24] W.C. Boey on shipwrecking;[25] A. Sandra, on insolvency;[26] and also P. Stellingwerff and C.J. Vaillant.[27]

In the category of monographs Phoonsen on the law of bills of exchange (*wissels, wisselbrieven*) figures highly. His 'Wissel-Stijl' became an authority.[28] Another authority was Verwer with his book on maritime law (particularly on average and bottomry).[29]

There existed, in the first instance, courts which dealt with subjects which were specific for commerce: the 'Camere van Asseurantie' (Insurance Chamber) in Amsterdam since January 1598, also competent for average cases since Dec. 1598, and the 'Commissarissen voor zeezaken' (Commissioners for Sea Cases) since 1641; similarly there was a college of Commissioners for Sea Cases in Rotterdam since 1604, which also sat on insurance cases. Dordrecht had a court, the 'Waterschepenen', later 'Watergeregt' (Aldermen's Water Bench).[30]

---

19 Arnold Brouwer, *De litterarum cambialium acceptatione* (Groningen: J.J. Homkes et H. Eekhoff, 1804).

20 Jacobus van Ghesel, *De assecuratione* (Leiden, 1727); M. den Beer, *De assecurationibus* (Utrecht, 1729); Eilardus F. Harckenroth, *De assecuratione, et Bodemeria* (Utrecht, 1756).

21 D. van Goens, *De Monopoliis* (Utrecht, 1743).

22 P.G. Donker, *Tractatus Juris Belgici de Jure Nundinarum* (Leiden, 1752); C. Pruimers, *De nundinis, earumque jure ex institutis romanorum, et patriis* (Groningen, 1774) (law of the province of Overijssel).

23 By H. van der Hoop, P. van der Schelling, Th. Beckeringh, H.M. Barels, W.E. van Brakel, F. Wolff, C. Wagee Schuman, W.A. Alting Lamoral van Geusau, see Lichtenauer, *Geschiedenis*, 132–133.

24 H. Tollius, *De contributione, juxta legem Rhodiam de jactu facienda* (Harderwijk, 1770).

25 W.C. Boey, *De Jure circa naufragas* (Leiden, 1761).

26 A. Sandra, *De Pacto debitoris obaerati cum majore parte cum creditoribus, ex jure romano ac zelandico* (Leiden, 1777).

27 C. Stellingwerff, *De Jure Navium* (Franeker, 1750); C.J. Vaillant, *De usufructu navium* (Leiden, 1802).

28 J. Phoonsen, *Wissel-Stijl tot Amsterdam* (Amsterdam, 1676), many reprints and translations into German and French; see Lichtenauer, *Geschiedenis*, 136–138.

29 Adriaen Verwer, *Nederlants see-rechten, averyen en bodemeryen, begrepen in de gemeene costuimen vander see, de placcaten van keiser Karel den vijfden 1551 en koning Filips den II 1563,'t tractaet van Mr Quintyn Weitsen van de Nederlantsche avaryen ende daerenboven in eene verhandelinge nopende het recht der Hollantsche bodemeryen, verklaert met aenteikeningen, ook met keurige bijlagen en 't laetste nieuw-gemaekt* ... (Amsterdam, 1711).

30 Lichtenauer, *Geschiedenis*, 142.

Archives exist from these courts,[31] but unfortunately little is known about arbitration, which was, however, practiced.[32]

Regarding collections of judgments, which also contain commercial cases of course, a description of published and unpublished collections has been made by Meijers in 1918 and not much has been added to the list;[33] but several have been published (Loenius-Boel, Z. Huber, Schomaker, Schrassert; *Utrechtse Consultatiën, Hollandse Consultatiën*).[34] Among them are the famous Observationes of Bijnkershoek and Pauw, an indispensable source of judgments of the Supreme Court of Holland and Zeeland for the period of 1704–1787.[35] In their summaries the two usually mention the decisions in first and second instance, which are also important of course: but not in all cases did parties decide to take the long and costly road to the Supreme Court and so deviating views on a lower level may have been more common than we would be led to believe, as we shall see, and consequently were more important for daily life. It would be good to make a comparison between, for example, the *Schepenbank* of Amsterdam or Rotterdam and the *Hoge Raad* to find the number of appealed cases. A number of cases deal with commerce.[36] Two collections are

31 Lichtenauer, *Geschiedenis*, 143–145.

32 Lichtenauer, *Geschiedenis*, 145–146.

33 E.M. Meijers, 'Uitgegeven en onuitgegeven rechtspraak van den Hoogen Raad en van het Hof van Holland, Zeeland en Westfriesland', *Tijdschrift voor Rechtsgeschiedenis* 1 (1918), 400–421. Reprint in *Études d'histoire du droit*, tome 2 (Leyde: Universitaire Pers Leiden, 1973), 3–20.

34 See Lichtenauer, *Geschiedenis*, 146–148.

35 Pieter Ockers: Helene C. Gall (ed.), *Regtsgeleerde decisien, Aan de raadsheer Pieter Ockers toegeschreven aantekeningen betreffende uitspraken van het Hof (1656–1669) en de Hoge Raad (1669–1678) van Holland, Zeeland en West-Friesland* (Amsterdam: Cabeljauwpers, 2002) with the review by A.J.B. Sirks, 'De Decisiën van Pieter Ockers (1628–1678)', in *Tijdschrift voor Rechtsgeschiedenis* 71 (2003), 197–210; Bijnkershoek and Pauw: E.M. Meijers, A.S. de Blécourt and H.D.J. Bodenstein, *Cornelii van Bijnkershoek Observationes Tumultuariae*, I 1704–1714 (Haarlem [1923–]1926); idem, with T.J. Dorhout Mees, F.J. de Jong, B.M. Telders, II 1714–1724 (Haarlem 1934); E.M. Meijers, A.S. de Blécourt, F.J. de Jong, K.N. Korteweg, G.J. ter Kuile, W.S. van Spengler, B.M. Telders, III 1724–1735 (Haarlem 1946); E.M. Meijers, H.F.W.D. Fischer, M.S. van Oosten, IV 1735–1743 (Haarlem 1962); H.F.W.D. Fischer, W.L. de Koning-Bey, L.E. van Holk, H.W. van Soest, *Wilhelmi Pauw Observationes Tumultuariae Novae* I 1743–1755 (Haarlem 1964); R. Feenstra, W.L. de Koning-Bey, L.E. van Holk, H.W. van Soest, II 1756–1770 (Haarlem 1967); *idem.*, III 1771–1788 (Haarlem 1971).

36 Indices to the *Observationes* provide first of all the said published volumes (note 35), and further: *Index in Observationes tumultuarias Cornelii van Bijnkershoek et Wilhelmi Pauw, naar het handschrift uitgegeven door A.J.B. Sirks* ('s-Gravenhage 2005) (the index made and used by Bijnkershoek and Pauw themselves); M.S. van Oosten, *Systematisch Compendium*

particularly focused on commerce: Barels' *Advijsen* of 1781, and the *Verzameling van Casus Positiën* (Collection of cases) of 1793/4.[37]

Due to the constitution of the Dutch Republic (a loose confederation of seven provinces and one land, each again consisting of autonomous and semi-autonomous jurisdictions; and of three (later four) conquered parts, governed by the States-General) there existed a multitude of statutes, laws, bylaws etc. on commerce, each having force in a specific area. It is impossible to mention all here. On a general level, several *ordonnances* of Charles V and Philip II created some unity, such as the placates of these two rulers on insurance,[38] or the placates of the latter on average.[39] There were initiatives to codify, but nothing came of these. Customary maritime law as comprised in the Rules of Antwerp or Wisby was received in practice or used as inspiration.[40]

Lichtenauer's study has not been surpassed, but some recent works have provided much more information on specific subjects. The two works of J.P. Van Niekerk on the history of insurance law contain references to all legislation, judgements and authors who wrote on insurance in the Dutch Republic (and contrary to the potential suggestion in title, present day Belgium is not included). These surveys to one specific part of commercial law help in approaching other parts of commercial law as well.[41] As regards specific works on sale or hire (and contracting), the bibliographies of professors at Dutch universities in the period 1585–1815, all published, may provide information,

---

der Observationes Tumultuariae van Cornelis van Bijnkershoek (Haarlem, 1962); P. van Warmelo, *Registers op die Observationes tumultuariae van Cornelis van Bijnkershoek en van Willem Pauw*, s.d., s.l.

37 J.M. Barels, *Advysen over den koophandel en zeevaert* (Amsterdam, 1781); *Verzameling van Casus Positiën, voorstellingen en declaratiën betrrekkelijk tot voorvallende omstandigheden in den koophandel, van tijd tot tijd binnen deeze stad beoordeeld en ondertekend*, 2 vols. (Amsterdam, 1793,1794); see Lichtenauer, *Geschiedenis*, 148–149.

38 See *Groot placaetboeck, vervattende de placaten van de Staten Generael ende van de Staten van Holland en West-Vrieslandt…*, vol. 1 ('s-Gravenhage, 1658), 387ff.

39 Ordonnance of 1563, see preceding note.

40 Lichtenauer, *Geschiedenis*, 153. For example, *Rechten ende costumen van Antwerpen. Met verscheyde aenteyckeninge, verrijckt door C. Gabri*, was published in 1639 in Amsterdam.

41 J.P. van Niekerk, *An Introduction to and Some Perspectives on the Sources and Development of Roman-Dutch Insurance Law with Appendices Containing the More Important Roman-Dutch Insurance Legislation* (DPhil., University of South Africa, Department of Mercantile Law, Pretoria, 1988) and voluminous and complete J.P. van Niekerk, *The Development of the Principles of Insurance Law in the Netherlands from 1500 to 1800* (Johannesburg: Juta, 1998). See further F. Stevens, 'The Contribution of Antwerp to the Development of Marine Insurance in the 16th century', in Marc Huybrechts (ed.), *Marine Insurance at the Turn of the Millennium*, vol. 2 (Antwerpen: Intersentia, 2000), 15–20.

while the final volume provides the bibliographies of authors not attached to a Dutch university (including practitioners).[42] Regarding other specific areas, Christiaan Brom's Frankfurter dissertation of 2007 gives a fine survey of the scholarly points of view combined with the line followed by the Supreme Court in matters of sale (the Court was conservative, in agreement with theory).[43] Punt's Leiden dissertation of 2010 deals with the company law of Holland as treated in the jurisprudence of the same Supreme Court.[44] More study would be desirable, for example a study on the practice of contracting out army supplies, combined with research into the social and financial background of the contractors. The Dutch Republic had a large standing army and its supply must have been of commercial importance.[45] Likewise, a study of the law of insolvency (*cessio bonorum*) would be useful; there is enough jurisprudence on this, as there is on bills of exchange, cession and bottomry.[46]

---

42 Margreet Ahsmann and Robert Feenstra with the cooperation of R. Starink, *Bibliografie van hoogleraren in de rechten aan de Leidse Universiteit* (Amsterdam: Noord-Holland, 1984). Additions (and corrections) to be found in volumes II, III and IV, see notes 2–4.; Margreet Ahsmann with the cooperation of Robert Feenstra and C.H.J. Jansen, *Bibliografie van hoogleraren in de rechten aan de Utrechtse Universiteit* (Amsterdam: North-Holland, 1993). On pages 33–52 and 171–184 additions to vol. I (Leiden). Additions to vol. II to be found in volumes III and IV; Robert Feenstra with the cooperation of Margreet Ahsmann and Theo Veen, *Bibliografie van hoogleraren in de rechten aan de Franeker Universiteit* (Amsterdam: Koninklijke Nederlandse Akademie van Wetenschappen, 2003). On pages XXIV–XXXIV additions to vol. I (Leiden) and II (Utrecht). Additions to vol. III to be found in vol. IV.; B.S. Hempenius-van Dijk, with the cooperation of R. Feenstra, J.H.A. Lokin and A.L. Hempenius, *Bibliografie van hoogleraren in de rechten aan de universiteiten van Groningen en Harderwijk tot 1811* (Amsterdam: Koninklijke Nederlandse Akademie van Wetenschappen, 2013). On pages XXX–XXXVII additions to volumes I (Leiden), II (Utrecht) and III (Franeker). Finally volume V: Robert Feenstra, Douglas J. Osler, Bibliography of jurists of the Northern Netherlands active outside the Dutch universities to the year 1815, Amsterdam: Amsterdam University Press, 2017.

43 Christian Brom, *Urteilsbegründungen im 'Hoge Raad van Holland, Zeeland en West-Friesland' am Beispiel des Kaufrechts im Zeitraum 1704–1787* (Frankfurt am Main: P. Lang, 2007).

44 Hendrik M. Punt, *Het vennootschapsrecht van Holland: het vennootschapsrecht van Holland, Zeeland en West-Friesland in de rechtspraak van de Hoge Raad van Holland, Zeeland en West-Friesland* (Deventer: Kluwer, 2010).

45 On the 'Staatse Leger' see Olaf van Nimwegen, *De subsistentie van het leger: logistiek en strategie van het Geallieerde en met name het Staatse leger tijdens de Spaanse Successieoorlog in de Nederlanden en het Heilige Roomse Rijk (1701–1712)* (Amsterdam: De Bataafsche Leeuw, 1995).

46 Van Oosten (note 36) has a chapter on the law of insolvency as dealt with in the jurisprudence of the Supreme Court (§§83–88), and three paragraphs on the other three subjects mentioned (§§56, 57, 58). The indices of the published volumes of the *Observationes* are also extensive.

3 Judgments as a Source

As already indicated above, judgments were also formative for the law of commerce. Although they were, until the beginning of the nineteenth century, promulgated without motivation, the published collections of judgments did contain the views of the court and in this way shaped commercial law too. But the way a court reached a decision in the 17th and 18th century differed from later periods and we often see concurring or diverging views within the court, and sometimes also what appears to be a contradiction in the judgments of the same court. To illustrate and explain this, I shall discuss two cases of insurance law, of which Van Niekerk wrote that it was difficult to reconcile the decisions of the Supreme Court. They show us the restrictions of using judgments as sources, and the restrictions of literature. These are *Observationes Tumultuariae* 909 of 1712 and 1290 of 1716, and both, in reworked form, were included in Bijnkershoek's *Quaestiones Juris Privati* of 1744 in 4.5 and 4.6.

The first case concerned the voyage of a ship with a cargo of coal from Newcastle to St. Malo and then to Rotterdam. The cargo was not of great value but nevertheless had been insured in Rotterdam for 2000 guilders, which covered the expected ('imagined') profit. The Rotterdam law on insurance forbade this and therefore the insurer, Isaac Rodrigues Mendes, waived the law (*ius renunciaverat*). The insured party, Adriaen van Nimmegen, had to get a passport, because of the war with France (this was the Spanish Succession war, in which the UK and the Republic fought against France) and he was provided with one for free sailing from Scotland to France and back. During the trip the ship was taken by privateers from Dunkirk and sold, with the cargo. Van Nimmegen claimed the sum of 2000 guilders from Rodrigues Mendes' heirs. The heirs protested. Insuring expected profit was forbidden by the Sea Laws of Philip II and the law of Rotterdam, and agreements against these were invalid by these laws *ipso iure*. The purpose of these laws was to prevent fraud, and that insured parties were indemnified for their loss, rather than to make a profit which would be impossible to estimate anyway. For this, one has to resort to a guarantee. Van Nimwegen argued that custom could set aside statutes, and that it was a frequent use to insure expected profit and that the estimate was to be paid out.

The majority of the judges were of the opinion that the waiver was valid and that an insurer who went back on his word acted in bad faith, which was unacceptable. The minority thought otherwise. Though merchants often concluded such agreements, it did not yet imply a custom. For that, a judgment was required, and moreover, a custom could create law, but could not abrogate an express law. A judge could not set aside an express statute.

The passport had been insufficient, since the ship had not sailed from Scotland. The seizure of it had therefore been legitimate. Bijnkershoek thought that this also proved Van Nimmegen's fraudulent intent. But again a majority of judges considered it sufficient that it had happened on the route from Scotland to St. Malo.

The second case, four years later, again concerned the voyage of a ship, this time from Amsterdam to Norway, and from there to Cadiz. After it had left Larkol in Norway, it got into a storm, ran into another ship and was wrecked, but did not sink. The Amsterdam insurers ordered the captain and owners of the ship to collect the ship and sell the remains, while the insurers accepted to compensate the loss. Cited before the court to pay on the basis of this letter and not on basis of the insurance contract, the insurers raised all kinds of futile objections, which were accepted by the Insurance Chamber and the *Schepenbank* in Amsterdam, but were all rejected by the Court of Holland and the Supreme Court. But one point was raised which troubled the Supreme Court. It was evident that the insurance contract was applicable. The law of 1563 related to cargo. The statute of 1570 forbade the insuring of a ship for more than 2/3 of its value. That was understandable if the owners also managed the ship; otherwise the managers had grounds to be insured for the full value. According to Bijnkershoek, since hardly any ship owner exercised the management, it was understandable that the new Rotterdam insurance statute simply allowed the insuring of a ship. Here Amsterdam had still the old rule, the ship had been insured for a sum, estimated at the time of the insurance as over 2/3 of its value. Some judges argued therefore that the excess was not valid, and the clause was void in as far as it exceeded the statute. Others argued that commercial custom had set this prohibition aside, and that often a clause was added stating that if something went against a statute, parties renounced the statutory rule. Besides, the Amsterdam judges used to disregard this stipulation. Bijnkershoek reiterated the arguments against these views: the custom had not been properly established, the statute was clear, and declared such agreements void. This time there was a majority for this and the judgement of the Court was confirmed with 4 against 3, and the compensation for the ship was reduced to 2/3 of the estimated value.

According to Van Niekerk these judgments are difficult to reconcile on principle.[47] He took into consideration the fact that decisions were taken by majority vote. Yet it pays to consider also the individual opinions of the judges. It appears that in the first case, eight judges were sitting (the ninth, Keetlaer, was absent). Five judges accepted the custom, and three rejected it. In the time

47 van Niekerk, *The Development*, vol. 1, 267.

between the two cases, four years, two judges had died. Of the two who had died, one who had rejected the custom was replaced by somebody who wavered; the place of the other judge had not yet been filled. The judge absent in 1712 was also against accepting the custom. In the second case, 7 judges sat, the president being absent. He had accepted the custom. Had all judges kept to their opinion, the decision would have been again in favour of the custom in 1716, but one judge had now changed his mind. We do not know why De Roovere did this, but perhaps it was due to the the fact that the prohibition was abolished in Rotterdam. In any case, we see that in the way the Supreme Court reached its decision, as in cases where there was no great majority, the outcome could depend very much on incidental issues such as illness. One has to bear that in mind when evaluating court decisions. The judges themselves did not rashly change their view, regardless of the way it was founded.

There is another aspect to this. The entire discussion was not about whether insurance contracts could comprise *lucrum cessans* or cover the full value of a ship, which is something that might be expected. According to Stracca,[48] Santerna and Scaccia,[49] that was possible. Santerna distinguished finely between different formulations in the contract. If the insurer promised to guarantee the safety of the goods upon arrival in the harbour of destination, the price of the goods there was to be taken. If the owner rather focused on the loss as such, then apparently he did not consider the *lucrum cessans*.[50] But this approach

48 Benvenuti Stracchae, *De Assicurationibus Tractatus* (Venice, 1569), Glossa sexta, 9.

49 Sigismundi Scacciae, *Tractatus de commerciis et cambio* (Cologne, 1620), 30, or his *Tractatus de commerciis et cambio* (Cologne, 1670), 169–170. Scaccia rather gives a survey of Stracca and Santerna.

50 Petrus Santerna, *Tractatus perutilis et quotidianus, de Assecurationibus et Sponsionibus Mercatorum* (Antwerp, 1554), Tertia pars, 40, 41 states it clearly: [40] *Qualiter autem fiat existimatio praedictarum mercium in casu adventus periculi, an debeat haberi respectus ad tempus infortunii et naufragii, vel ad tempus emptionis, quando dominus eas emit, vel ad tempus, quo potuerant vendi si navis salva ad portum fuerat, et videbatur quod ad tempus infortunii per l. ii § Sed in his D. ad l. Rho. item quia ut supra alias dixi iste contractus assecurationis est conditionalis, et per consequens debet inspici tempus conditionis periculi not. in l. quotiens in die, de verbo. obliga. et l. si Calendis, de re iudica. Breviter puto dicendum, quod aut quis promittit salutem mercium in certo loco* [41] *ut puta Ulisbonae, et tunc eius loci existimatio inspicienda est. l. fin. D. de triti. cond. aut non promisit dare merces salvas in certo loco, sed tantum aestimationem vel valorem mercium in casu periculi, scilicet si navis periret, ut fieri solet. Etiam inspici debet tempus obligationis, et sic prout tunc valebant debet fieri estimation l. fundum Cornelianum D. de nova. cum concor. Ratio est, quia tunc aestimatio debetur iure obligationis, et sic videtur permitti id quod tunc valebant, ut ibi declarant. Gl. Item ille qui procurat in adventu periculi aestimationem rerum suarum, videtur magis providere damnum, ne patiatur in amissionererum, non autem considerat lucrum: et per*

was not favoured in Holland: we do not see this interpretation raised. Due to the fact that the statute of Philip II and the local statutes of Amsterdam and Rotterdam declared agreements which were contrary to their rules void, the discussion was reduced to the question of whether a custom could set aside express statutory law. No recourse had to be taken to the literature on the point. There, the thinking went further, as Van der Keessel's discourse on insurance shows.[51]

It is not my aim to redo the work of Van Niekerk. His works deal extensively and in a detailed manner with points of insurance law. But I hope that the two cases demonstrate the way the courts worked and that discussing the opinion of the Court is not such an easy task. As regards commerce, the fact that Bijnkershoek considered regarding the insurance of his times, that is, the first half of the eighteenth century, as the most important contract in commerce after sale and hire, reveals a great deal. If it were indeed so important, it also meant that the financial trade was very important. Without sufficient capital insurance, it is difficult to practice. Insurers need to spread the risks and to have sufficient buffers.

4 Commerce in the Second Half of the Eighteenth Century and the Move to Codification in 1809

Notwithstanding Bijnkershoek's words, commerce and industry experienced a gradual decline in the second half of the eighteenth century, due to several causes. One was that Dutch trade had profited in the 17th century from the weak economic situations of England and France. Once these countries began to protect their own markets by import duties, and encouraged their own industries, this changed. It implied a relative decline of the Dutch share in European trade. In the middle of the eighteenth century requests were sent to the States-General for support by way of prohibitions, to protect their own industries too. The Prince of Orange submitted a plan for economic reforms

---

consequens venit illud, in quo tunc damnum sentire potest quando stipulator, et non venit lucrum, ad hoc facit bonus tex. In l. ii § portio autem D. ad l. Rho. De iac. non ob. l. 2 § Sed in his allegata, quia ibi aestimatio debetur loco rei, ut probatur, eadem l. i par. sed in iis, quia fit exoneratio collationis, si res iactae apparuerint, et ideo non immerito consideratur tempus iacti, et non tempus emptae, sed quando vendi possunt, nec obstat h. l. quotiens, quia licet iste contractus.

51 D.G. van der Keessel, *Praelectiones iuris hodierni ad Grotii Introductionem ad jurisprudentiam Hollandicam*, vol. V (Amsterdam: Balkema, 1961–1975), 122ff; D.G. van der Keessel, *Theses selectae juris Hollandici et Zeelandici* (Leiden, 1800), §717, nr. 10.

in 1751.[52] The main causes for the economic decline were the high import and export duties. The remedy suggested was to alleviate the duties for those goods which were necessary for the inland industries.[53] The plan was never realised, as the confederal structure of the Republic obstructed any implementation. Though the VOC still had a monopoly on the East India trade, the revenues from this source dwindled too, and the company came into severe financial difficulties. Its servants still made huge gains, which were transferred to the Netherlands, leading to immense private fortunes. It is no wonder that one trade flourished in the Netherlands: the banking industry. It became a banking centre, which during the Batavian Republic and the Kingdom of Holland served as a transfer table for European financial affairs.[54]

In 1795 the stadholder was chased away and the Republic of the Seven United Provinces became the Batavian Republic. Although there was much discussion about whether this should be a unitary or more decentralised state, there was unanimity that there should be an end to the particularistic fragmentation and that general statutes should govern all. Further, the Batavian government wanted to stimulate the economy. The Constitution of 1789 indeed contained several sections to this end,[55] as did the later Constitution of 1805.[56] It stipulated freedom of traffic, and consequently tolls were abolished as far as possible and substituted by import duties.

It is not so easy to check all regulations and measures issued in the period of the Batavian Republic (1795–1806), the Kingdom of Holland (1806–1810) and the French occupation (1810–1813). There is, first of all, Luttenberg's register of

---

52 See Hendrik C. Diferee, *Studiën over de Geschiedenis van den Nederlandschen Handel* (Amsterdam: Akkeringa, 1908), 9–46: I. Een onuitgevoerde maatregel tot herstel van den Koophandel in de achttiende eeuw.

53 See also Adam Smith, see O.I.M. Ydema, 'Op zoek naar draagkracht. Belastingen vóór, tijdens en na de tijd van Lodewijk Napoleon', in J. Hallebeek and A.J.B. Sirks (eds.), *Nederland in Franse schaduw: Recht en bestuur in het Koninkrijk Holland (1806–1810)* (Hilversum: Verloren, 2006), 101–123, 102.

54 This and the following is drawn from A.J.B. Sirks, 'De gevolgen van de inlijving van Nederland bij het Franse Keizerrijk in 1810 voor handel en nijverheid', in A.M.J.V. Berkvens, J. Hallebeek and A.J.B. Sirks (eds.), *Het Franse Nederland: de inlijving 1810–1813. De juridische en bestuurlijke gevolgen van de 'Réunion' met Frankrijk* (Hilversum: Verloren, 2012), 297–314.

55 Sections 47, 48 and 49 formulated the intention to mitigate the worst poverty and its consequences (beggary, foundlings), and Sections 50 till 55 to stimulate trade and industry. All, however, had still to be worked out and implemented.

56 *Staatsregeling 1805*, Sections 65 and 67: departmental and local taxes may not obstruct transit, import or export of products.

statutes, decrees etc. for 1796–1813, which in each case refers to the source.[57] Then there are collections of legislation, with registers, up to the end of the Napoleonic kingdom.[58] Other collections are more manageable, but are not

57 G. Luttenberg, *Register der wetten en besluiten betrekkelijk het openbaar bestuur in de Nederlanden sedert den jare 1796 tot 1813* (Zwolle, 1834; 2nd rev. and extend. edition Zwolle: Doijer, 1843–1851; available in Google Books). Luttenberg has arranged the statutes and decrees according to subject, and within these titles chronologically, with reference to the source. The source, again, is yet to be found.

58 J.A. de Chalmot, *Verzameling van placaaten, resolutien en andere authentyke stukken. Betrekking hebbende tot de gewigtige gebeurtenissen sedert den maand September MDCCXCIII bevoorens en vervolgens, in het gemeenebest der Vereenigde Nederlanden voorgevallen*, 50 vols. (Kampen, 1787–1793); J.A. de Chalmot, *Nieuwe verzameling van placaaten, resolutien en andere authentyke stukken. Betrekking hebbende tot de gewigtige gebeurtenissen sedert MDCCXCIII in het gemeenebest der Vereenigde Nederlanden voorgevallen*, 2 vols. (Kampen, 1793–1794). Registers on these: J.A. de Chalmot, *Verzameling van placaaten, resolutien en andere authentyke stukken enz. betrekking hebbende tot de gewigtige gebeurtenissen, in de maand september MDCCLXXXVII en vervolgens, in het gemeenebest der Vereenigde Nederlanden voorgevallen. Algemeen register*, vols. 1–9 (Kampen, 1789); J.A. de Chalmot, *Tweeledige registers over de vyftig deelen van de Verzameling van placaaten, resolutien en andere authentyke stukken enz. betrekking hebbende tot de gewigtige gebeurtenissen, in de maand september MDCCLXXXVII alvoorens en vervolgens, in het gemeenebest der Vereenigde Nederlanden voorgevallen*, 6 vols. (Kampen 1794), on vols. 1–50. This series of publications covers the period 1787–1794, that is, the prelude to the Batavian Revolution of 1795. For the period after this, I found regarding the province of Friesland: *Verzaameling van placaaten, proclamatien, notificatien, door het Committé Revolutionair, de Provisioneele en volgende Representanten, aanvang nemende met het laatste Placaat der Geremoveerde Staats-Leden, zijnde het begin der revolutie; dus van den 7 februari 1795 tot den 23 juni 1796 ingesloten*, vol. 1 (Franeker, 1796; subsequent 13 volumes over 1796–1810, Franeker 1796–1810). Vol. 1–2 issued by the Committé revolutionair; v. 3–10, by the Departementaal bestuur van Friesland; v. 11–14, by Zijne Majesteit den koning van Holland, ministers van rijk, landdrost- ambt van Friesland. This collection includes the legislation of the (unitary) Republic and the Kingdom of Holland in as far applicable (also) to Friesland. For the province of Limburg, already annexed in 1795 as the French department of Basse-Meuse: Hendrik A. Kamphuis, *De invoering van wetgeving in het Franse departement Nedermaas gedurende het eerste Directoire: inleiding en regestenlijst van afgekondigde rechtsvoorschriften 1 oktober 1795–19 maart 1797* (Ph.D., Rijksuniversiteit Limburg, Maastricht, 1995). Also: *Recueil des lois et actes généraux du gouvernement, en vigueur dans le royaume des Pays-Bas, et publiés depuis le 10 juillet 1794; avec une notice des principales lois publiés pendant la réunion des diverses parties du royauyme à la France et des changemens survenus dals cette partie de la législation, et un supplément, en forme de dictionnaire alphabétique, dans lequel toutes les dispositions des lois, décrets et arrêtés relatifs à chaque matière, sont indiqués avec orde et succintement analysées*, Ser. 1, vol. 1 – Ser. 3, vol. 20 (Bruxelles, 1819–1830). A *Dictionnaire raisonné des matières comprises dans le Recueil des lois (première série)* was published in

complete, both for the period 1798–1810[59] and for 1810–1813.[60] However, since they provide easy access to the texts, they can have advantages over Luttenberg, or can supplement his work. Because many special local and provincial regulations were to be substituted by national regulations, because the government wanted to stimulate trade and industry, and because many revolutionaries wished to reform society, we find amongst the issued legislation of state and provinces much which is of importance for commerce. The same is true for the moment of annexation: again many rules of an administrative nature, now from France, applied to trade and industry. This is not the place to give examples, as they can be found in the sources mentioned and in literature.[61] Of the several collections of jurisprudence, a general register exists.[62]

Brussels, 1824. Further, in 1827 a *Table chronologique* on the first twelve volumes of the Ser. 3 was published in Brussels.

59 For the period 1795–1798 there is no collection available. For the period Jan. 22, 1798–July 10, 1810 (the end of the Kingdom of Holland and the annexation by France) there is J. van de Poll, *Verzameling van vaderlandsche wetten en besluiten, uitgevaardigd sedert 22 Januarij 1798 tot 10 Julij 1810, in zooverre zij ook, sedert de invoering der nieuwe wetgeving in Nederland, middelijk of onmiddellijk van toepassing zijn* (Amsterdam, 1840). It is a very useful collection, also because Van de Poll adds a summary to certain subjects of the previous abolished regulations and the vicissitudes of the regulation after July 10, 1810. However, Van de Poll only included regulations still applicable after the French occupation was shaken off in 1813. What was introduced and abolished between 1798 and 1810 found no place, unless included in a summary.

60 The French legislation became applicable upon the annexation in one fell swoop, and is neatly collected in L. Rondonneau, *Collection des lois françaises, constitutionnelles, administratives, judiciaires, commerciales, militaires et religieuses, actuellement en vigueur dans l'empire, et déclarées par les décrets des 8 novembre 1810, 6 janvier et 19 avril 1811, exécutoires dans les départemens de la Hollande, et autres réunis à la France depuis 1810: mises en ordre et conférées entre elles avec une table chronologique à chaque volume et une table générale alphabétique et analytique des matières à la fin du dernier volume*, 6 vols. (Paris: Ange Clo, 1811). Of course the sovereign prince William began at once in 1813 with introducing new regulations, so that after some time a mixture of old French law and new Dutch law existed. This led to a collection of French law, still applicable in 1839: J. Fortuijn, *Verzameling van wetten, besluiten en andere regtsbronnen van Franschen oorsprong, in zooverre deze, ook sedert de invoering der nieuwe wetgeving, in Nederland van toepassing zijn*, 3 vols. (Amsterdam: J. Müller, 1839). Again it is possible that French law was introduced after 19 April 1811 and was abolished before 1839, but this is not recorded here.

61 See A.J.B. Sirks, 'De gevolgen van de inlijving van Nederland', 297–314, with examples of the changes in commerce, during and after the French annexation.

62 L.Th. Grave van Nassau la Leck, *Algemeen beredeneerd register op alle de voornaamste rechtsgeleerde advysen, consultatien, avertissementen, decisien, observatien en sententien* (Utrecht, 1778); after this followed J. Van der Linden, *Verzameling van merkwaardige*

These regulations supplanted many which had existed before in matters of commercial importance. One main difference now of course was that they imposed uniform rules where previously provincial and local rules had reigned. An example of such a general regulation, this particular one introduced with the annexation, is the imperial decree of 15 August 1810, which dealt with the release of harmful fumes from workshops.[63] First, one now needed a licence to set up such a shop. Three classes were distinguished: workshops which had to be kept far away from homes; workshops which did not have to be that far away yet required special precautions to prevent harm; and workshops which could stay where they were, but remained under supervision. This must have led in several cases to higher costs for the entrepreneur.

The Constitution of 1798 had expressed a desire for the codification of the civil laws (*burgerlijke wetten*) in its Section 28. The place of commercial law in the system was not clear. The Cras committee, charged with codifying these, included for example the rules on insurance and average in the code of private law, but others proposed a separate draft for sea law and insurance (the draft of Walraven).[64] Between 1801 and 1804 no work was done at all. Louis Napoleon (king from 1806 till 1810) in 1808 charged Joannes van der Linden with drafting a new civil code.[65] And although in his *Rechtsgeleerd Practicaal* this jurist had proposed that commercial law should be dealt with separately, in his draft of a civil code he integrated commercial law under obligations. His draft, however, became superfluous upon Napoleon's introduction of his civil and other codes, including *the Code de commerce*, in force since 1807. Under pressure from his brother to introduce this code, Louis Napoleon had to change his course. He had to cede to his brother's wish, but at the same time he wanted to adapt these codes to the circumstances in Holland. He had just appointed a new committee (Committee Van Gennep) which had to formulate the commercial law in

---

gewijsden der gerechtshoven in Holland (Leiden, 1803). See also W.J. Zwalve, C.H.J. Jansen, Publiciteit van Jurisprudentie, Deventer: Kluwer 2013.

63 Rondonneau, *Collection des lois françaises*, 2:297–302.

64 For the draft of Walraven, see Carel van Nievelt, *Bronnen van de Nederlandse codificatie van het zee- en assurantierecht, 1798–1822* (Leiden: New Rhine Publishers, 1978), XIX–XLVII.

65 For Joannes van de Linden (1756–1835) see R. Feenstra, 'Joannes van der Linden', in M. Stolleis (ed.), *Juristen: Ein biographisches Lexikon von der Antike bis zum 20. Jahrhundert* (München: Beck, 2001), 390–391; for his draft: J. Th. de Smidt (ed.), Joannes van der Linden, *Ontwerp Burgerlijk Wetboek 1807–1808* (Amsterdam, 1967); company law, law of bills of exchange, maritime law (insurance, average, bottomry and shipping) are treated of in resp. titles 8, 10 and 11 of the third book, On Personal Rights (*Van de Personele Reghten, of Regten tot eene Zaak*); for his draft of commercial law, based on the draft of Walraven, see Nievelt, *Bronnen van de Nederlandse codificatie*, XLVIII–LVI.

the context of the civil code. The committee now proposed to make a separate commercial code, and accordingly their charge was changed. The committee, consisting of A. van Gennep, M.S. Asser and J. van der Linden, submitted their draft of a *Wetboek van Koophandel voor het Koningrijk Holland* on 8 June 1809.[66] Introduction was probably planned after the introduction of the adaptation of the Code Napoleon, the *Wetboek Napoleon ingerigt voor het Koningrijk Holland* on 1 May 1809. But by 1 July 1810 Louis was forced to abdicate and on 9 July 1810 Holland was annexed. On 1 January and 1 March 1811 the French legislation came into force. Until that moment all *ancien régime* regulations had retained force if they had not been abolished. The annexation, however, meant a real breach with the past. With it came the *Code de commerce*, be it with the addition of an authenticated translation; and with it came also the division between citizens and merchants, and the separate tribunals for commerce (until then the judicial system of the *ancien régime* had continued).[67]

This meant a serious setback. The French Code was mainly based on the royal *Ordonnance Savary* of 1673. Criticism arose at once. The structure was not scholarly based, it lacked general principles, it lacked a logical structure, and it did not show much progress since the Code Savary. It did not take account of the economic changes since 1673, the industrial revolution, as was apparent from its scant treatment of anonymous companies. It is significant that it did not inspire any foreign code, contrary to the civil code.[68] Worst of all, the banking industry, insurance, shipping, transportation of passengers, shipwrecking, etc.: none of these subjects were dealt with in the *Code de Commerce*.[69] These

66 *Het eerste ontwerp van een Nederlandsch Wetboek van Koophandel, zamengesteld op last van Koning Lodewijk Napoleon door A. van Gennep, M.S. Asser en J. van der Linden.* Op nieuw uitgegeven met eene voorrede van Mr T.M.C. Asser (Amsterdam, 1866).

67 The French *Code de Commerce* had gained force of law on 10 resp. September 11, 1807 and was published on 20 resp. September 21, 1807. See for this R.J.Q. Klomp, *Opkomst en ondergang van het Handelsrecht* (Nijmegen: Ars Aequi Libri, 1998), 5–14. Dutch edition: *Wetboek van den Koophandel voor het Fransche rijk, vertaald door J. van der Linden* (Amsterdam, 1808).

68 The criticism, pronounced in Belgium on the occasion of the bicentenary of this code, is basically that no account was made of the economic changes since the seventeenth century; for example, anonymous companies still needed authorisation by the public authorities. See P. van Ommeslaghe, 'Rapport introductief', in Jean-Pierre Buyle et al. (eds.), *Bicentenaire du Code de commerce: Tweehonderd jaar Wetboek van Koophandel* (Brussel: Larcier, 2007), 12–13.

69 As Asser wrote, *Het eerste ontwerp van een Nederlandsch Wetboek van Koophandel, zamengesteld op last van Koning Lodewijk Napoleon door A. van Gennep, M.S. Asser en J. van der Linden. Op nieuw uitgegeven met eene voorrede van Mr T.M.C. Asser*, vi–vii: *'De kassierderij, benevens het kassiers- en ander handelspapier, de assignatiën, de algemeene regelen van*

were subjects of utmost importance for Holland and had been, unsurprisingly, dealt with excellently in the Dutch drafts. The *Code de commerce* did not provide the Dutch economy with the instruments it needed to recover and develop. In view of the draft of 1809 one would expect that after the French were gone, this draft would have become law in or after 1815; but the political changes obstructed the introduction of a new code every time. The union with the Southern Netherlands in 1815 made creating a code necessary which was also acceptable for the Southerners. This code was ready in 1830, but due to the separation of Belgium in the same year it became outdated. Consequently a new commercial code did not come into existence before 1838, partly inspired by the draft of 1809 to remedy the gaps mentioned.[70] In the period following the Code, a discussion arose about whether commercial law should remain a separate area or fuse with private law. What was the value of keeping commercial law apart? It culminated in two pieces of advice for the yearly meeting of the Association of Dutch Jurists (*Nederlandsche Juristenvereeniging*) in 1883, in which the two authors, A.F.K. Hartogh and W.P.L.A. Moolengraaff, argued for removing the distinction. After that, the general opinion was that this should be the line to follow. In 1934–35 the division between citizens and merchants, and with it the special commercial courts, was abolished. In 1947 the Parliament ordered the recodification of private law, with the inclusion of commercial law in the new Civil Code. Despite this wish, the new Dutch Civil Code does not comprise all commercial law. A part of it, maritime law, is still in the Code of commerce; the idea of including intellectual property in the new Civil Code in a Book 9 has been relinquished, since this subject is often ruled by international treaties, as are other parts of commercial law. As regards jurisprudence, publication of this, and thus of judgments on commercial law since 1813, came into being only hesitatingly. Some journals were founded whose editors planned to discuss cases judged; in practice it hardly happened. Only the *Bijdragen tot Regtsgeleerdheid en Wetgeving*, published 1826 till 1838, was particularly active.[71] A systematic collection and publication did not start until W.Y. van Hamelsfeld, judge in the Supreme Court (*Hoog Gerechtshof*), began

het verzekerings-contract, de brand-, landbouw- en levensverzekering, de reederijen, de passagiers op buitenlandsche zeereizen, de leer der schipbreuken, strandingen en zeevonden, de schepen en vaartuigen die de rivieren en binnenwateren bevaren, dat alles was in het Fransche wetboek in het geheel niet behandeld' and a number of other subjects were very poorly treated.

70 *Wetboek van Koophandel* ('s-Gravenhage, 1838).

71 See for a survey of journals W. Zwalve and C. Jansen, *Publiciteit van Jurisprudentie* (Deventer: Kluwer, 2013), 180–225.

his *Verzameling van gewijsden van het Hoog Gerechtshof te 's-Gravenhage* in 1826.[72] The promulgation of the civil code in 1838 led to a flood of journals, of which two specialised in jurisprudence: the *Weekblad van het Regt* and the *Nederlandsche Regtspraak*. From 1913 onwards the *Nederlands(ch)e Jurisprudentie* appeared, which became the foremost journal of jurisprudence. Next to these the collection of judgments of the Supreme Court, initiated by J. van den Honert Thz, must certainly be mentioned. The judgments were divided into six categories, one of which included commercial law.[73]

As to the science of commercial law since 1809, Van Oven has mentioned that for the period after the promulgation of the Commercial Code of 1838 there were a number of scholars who influenced the views on commercial law: J. van der Linden, J.D. Meijer, A.C. Holtius, J. van Hall, A. de Pinto, G. Diephuis, J.G. Kist, G.J. Hingst, J.A. Levy, T.M.C. Asser, W.P.L.A. Molengraaff, and some others. It was rare for them to be specialists in commercial law, and their sphere of action was usually private law. Further, Van Oven notes, for the second half of the nineteenth century, a shift from a legal historical to a dogmatic approach for commercial law. He presents in his study a thorough description and analysis of various themes of commercial law.[74]

---

72 Willem Y. van Hamelsveld and Petrus van Hamelsveld, *Verzameling van gewijsden van het Hoog Gerechtshof te's-Gravenhage*, 6 vols., judgments from 1823 onwards (Delft: J. Allart, 1826–1834); 2nd series: W.Y. van Hamelsveld and P. Simons, *Nederlandsche Pandecten, of Verzameling van gewijsden van het Hoog Gerechtshof te 's-Gravenhage*, 10 vols., judgments from 1814 onwards (Delft, 1827–1844).

73 J. van den Honert Thz., *Verzameling van arresten van en Hoogen Raad der Nederlanden, Burgerlijk regt, regt van koophandel en burgerlijke regtsvordering*, 68 vols. (Amsterdam, 1839, 1840–1902).

74 A. van Oven, *Geschiedenis van het handelsrecht in de 19e eeuw* (Amsterdam: Noord-Hollandsche,1968).

CHAPTER 9

The Files and Exhibits of the Imperial Chamber Court and Aulic Council as Sources of Commercial Law

Anja Amend-Traut

1 Introduction

As part of the general project 'The Making of Commercial Law' this chapter describes a significant phenomenon of the common practice: how commercial law came into existence in the Holy Roman Empire during the Early Modern period. Only occasionally and in specific fields such as the law on bills of exchange we can find legal rules that were passed following the formal legislative procedure. But mainly, commercial law was developed in alternative ways – through the daily practice of the merchants as consuetude, or as the products of judicial work. Court documents are a worthwhile topic for spotting those forms and manifestations of commercial law as complementary sources, and are therefore an important component of the key concern upon which this book aims to elaborate.

The two supreme courts of the Holy Roman Empire of the German Nation, the Imperial Chamber Court (*Reichskammergericht*) and the Aulic Council (*Reichshofrat*), were at work altogether for more than three hundred years. However, to answer the question of to what extent their work can be considered as a source of commercial law, or more precisely to what extent their work produced sources of commercial law, the following distinctions need to be made. The Imperial Chamber Court was installed in 1495 to ensure the 'Eternal Public Peace' (*Ewiger Landfrieden*) as part of the Imperial Reform adopted at the Imperial Diet at Worms in 1495 under the Emperor Maximilian I, and acted exclusively as a judicial body.[1] The Aulic Council, newly instituted in Vienna on the basis of the regulations of Maximilian I's court of 1497[2] and in contrast

* A German-language version with slight modifications is published in *ZNR* 37 (2015), 177–205.

1 Strictly speaking, the court was merely reformed, given that the Chamber Court was its forerunner. Still a fundamental work on the institution of the Imperial Chamber Court, see Rudolf Smend, *Das Reichskammergericht, 1. Teil: Geschichte und Verfassung* (Weimar: Böhlau, 1911), 3.

2 Printed with remarks in Thomas Fellner and Heinrich Kretschmayr, (eds.), *Die Österreichische Zentralverwaltung. 1. Abt. Von Maximilian 1. bis zur Vereinigung der österreichischen*

 | DOI 10.1163/9789004363144_010

to the Imperial Chamber Court, was solely dependent upon the Emperor both with regard to its location and its members, and he did not merely act as a chief justice, but also as head of the Empire and a supreme feudal lord. Thus, is was not only a supreme court, but it also acted as a legislator, an imperial fief authority, and as an advisory body for legal cases involving political factors.[3] Therefore, the files and exhibits examined here affect two spheres of legal sources, namely court rulings and legislation. This chapter then deals with sources as produced by or before the two courts, but not with historical sources or legal sources as such. Owing to their different functionality, the sources produced insofar also reveal different states of aggregation of commercial law, which shall hereinafter be investigated.

2 The Term Commercial Law

At first, a dividing line needs to be drawn to determine to what extent the files of the Imperial Chamber Court and those of the Aulic Council can be referred to at all as sources of commercial law. For this purpose, the literature on the laws of merchants emerging since the sixteenth century is essentially not followed, because it limited their explanations to the area of private merchant law – to individual discourses[4] or comprehensive works[5] on laws relating to bills of exchange, insurance or bankruptcy. Rather, the following expositions are based on the broader concept of *ius singulare mercatorum* as first introduced by Johann Marquard in his dissertation published in 1636[6] and which – since the 1920s denominated as economic law[7] – also covers public law regulations, *inter*

---

und böhmischen Hofkanzlei (*1749*), *2nd volume of records 1491–1681* (Wien: Holzhausen, 1907), No. 4, 6–16. Online http://www.literature.at/viewer.alo?objid=19475&viewmode=fullscreen&rotate=&scale=5&page=1 (last visited on January 6, 2018).

3 For an introduction to the institution, see Oswald von Gschließer, *Der Reichshofrat. Bedeutung und Verfassung, Schicksal und Besetzung einer obersten Reichsbehörde von 1559–1806* (1942; repr. Nendeln: Kraus-Reprint, 1970).

4 Matthias Bode, *Dissertatio Juridica de cambiis, ...*(Marburg: Chemlin, 1646); Wolfgang Adam Lauterbach, *De jure in Curia Mercatorum usitato* (Tübingen, 1655). Further evidence on the law on bills of exchange can be found in Anja Amend-Traut, *Wechselverbindlichkeiten vor dem Reichskammergericht: Praktiziertes Zivilrecht in der Frühen Neuzeit* (Köln: Böhlau, 2009).

5 Sigismund Scaccha, *Tractatus de commerciis et cambio* (Rome: Brugiottus, 1619); Benvenuto Straccha, *Tractatus de maercatura seu mercatore* (Lyon, 1558).

6 Johann Marquard, *Dissertatio politico-historico-iuridica de jure mercatorum singulari ... sub praesidio ... Petri Theodorici* (Jena, 1636).

7 In this regard see Heinz Mohnhaupt, Justus Wilhelm Hedemann und die Entwicklung der Disziplin 'Wirtschaftsrecht', *ZNR* 25 (2003), 238–268, 243–247.

alia also addressing issues of personal safety on trade fairs and markets, the subsidy and contribution system, but also on procedural law.[8] This is also clear insofar as the merchants often enjoyed privileges, and the jurisprudence of the seventeenth to the nineteenth centuries only occasionally structured the material according to content, i.e. 'public law and private law issues overlapped in the privileges'.[9]

Against the background of what Karl Otto Scherner called the 'correlation of economy, social structure and law',[10] it is only logical to understand the term commercial law hereinafter as merchants' law (*Kaufmannsrecht*), given that the primary focus of the considerations is on a particular group of persons resorting to the mercantile profession. Marquard grants this profession a special legal status[11] – a concept that experienced a renaissance as a so-called subjective system in the nineteenth century and which superseded the internationally most widespread objective system focusing on the commercial transaction as such.[12]

8 On the order of material in Marquard see Heinz Mohnhaupt, 'Jura Mercatorum' durch Privilegien: Zur Entwicklung des Handelsrechts bei Johann Marquard (1610–1668), in Gerhard Köbler (ed.), *Wege europäischer Rechtsgeschichte: Karl Kroeschell zum 60. Geburtstag* (Frankfurt am Main: P. Lang, 1987), 308–323, 316–318.

9 Heinz Mohnhaupt, 'Privatrecht in Privilegien', in *Vorträge zur Geschichte des Privatrechts in Europa* (Frankfurt am Main: Vittorio Klostermann, 1981), 58–75, 62.

10 Karl Otto Scherner, 'Zum Sonderrecht der Kaufleute bei Johann Marquard', in Hans-Peter Haferkamp and Tilman Repgen (eds.), *Usus modernus pandectarum: Römisches Recht, Deutsches Recht und Naturrecht in der Frühen Neuzeit, Klaus Luig zum 70. Geburtstag* (Köln: Böhlau, 2007), 199–217, 206.

11 The author himself describes this as a novelty: Marquard, 'Dissertatio', *Prooemium*, without page numbers; repeated in Johann Marquard, *Tractatus de iure mercatorum et commerciorum singulari* published in 1662 (1662; repr. Frankfurt am Main: Vico, 2008), 19, Lib. I., Cap. I., 3, fn. 2ff.

12 On this, see Joachim Rückert, 'Handelsrechtsbildung und Modernisierung des Handelsrechts durch Wissenschaft zwischen ca. 1800 und 1900', in Karl Otto Scherner (ed.), *Modernisierung des Handelsrechts im 19. Jahrhundert*, (Heidelberg: Verlag Recht und Wirtschaft, 1993), 19–66, 62–65. On the relationship between trade law and civil law see Peter Raisch, *Geschichtliche Voraussetzungen, dogmatische Grundlagen und Sinnwandlung des Handelsrechts* (Karlsruhe: C.F. Müller, 1965), 3–9, 18–34. Further substantiations can be found in Mohnhaupt, 'Jura Mercatorum', 312, fn. 21. On the term merchants' law (*Kaufmannsrecht*) as counterpart to case law as interpretation of statutory right for the 19th century see Peter Collin, 'Schwurgerichte und andere Formen der Laienbeteiligung: staatsfremde Normativitäten und gesellschaftliche Selbstregulierung im staatlichen Organisationsgehäuse', in Peter Collin (ed.), *Justice without the State within the State* (Frankfurt am Main: Klostermann, 2016) 223–241, here 236 with further substantiation.

Whether formed as *ius singulare* or as *privilegium*,[13] both deviations from *ius commune* were of a legislative nature,[14] at least as far and for as long as they complied with *utilitas publica*.[15] However, due to the alignment of the special legal position to a mutual performance relationship as construed by Marquard, the privileges could hardly be revoked.[16]

Finally, some further examples will be given beyond the line drawn, to reflect the entire spectrum of the sources that can be traced back to the two central institutions under discussion here, and which report on the extent to which they influenced the trading activities of individual persons, groups of persons, or entire imperial estates.

3 Court Rulings in Different States of Aggregation – The Imperial Chamber Court

The reader of Supreme Court files may come across court rulings in different forms. If a regulation had already been in existence, whether as codified law or as customary law, then it was possible that the courts simply applied that law. In that case, the files merely indicate the legal source and thus cannot be referred to or treated as the original source of that law.

However, it is a different case where the court used a standard already given only as a basis for its own judgment in further development of the law. Then, the ruling of the Imperial Chamber Court constituted a harmonising meta-level in an area of territorially divergent legal sources, as for example was the case with the law on bills of exchange.

We can certainly ascribe a legal source character to the file material if no standard had been available for the conflict that was to be resolved. In that situation, the court acted in a law-creating capacity. In such a case, the Supreme Court rulings acted as a harmonising meta-level in an area which previously had not been subject to any standards or where such standards were at least not on record.

---

13 'The demarcation and definition on the basis of Roman Law' was thus 'inconsistent and uncertain', see Mohnhaupt, 'Privatrecht', 67, with individual substantiations.

14 With regard to the privilege, this goes back to Bartolus: '*Est privilegium lex scripta contra ius commune*'. On the legal source character of privileges see in more detail Mohnhaupt, 'Privatrecht', 59.

15 In summary, see Scherner, 'Zum Sonderrecht', 202–204. More details on special privilege law and its theoretic foundation can be found in Thomas Duve, *Sonderrecht in der Frühen Neuzeit: Studien zum ius singulare und den privilegia miserabilium personarum, senum und indorum in Alter und Neuer Welt* (Frankfurt am Main: Klostermann, 2008), 12–25.

16 Marquard, *Dissertatio*, Thesis IV, at the end. Id., *Tractatus*, Lib. IV, Cap. III, 489, no. 53, 54. For more details on the contractual character see Mohnhaupt, 'Jura Mercatorum', 315f., 321.

The Aulic Council also created laws when granting privileges or making trade policy decisions other than for a singular dispute, which to varying degrees – compromises, imperial decrees, mandates, and the like – were of a normative nature.

The different possibilities shall be illustrated by means of examples.

3.1 *Files of the Judicial Body as Source of Commercial Law*

The classification of the Supreme Court files made so far can first be distinguished in terms of whether they relate to a decision of the ruling panel itself – the Imperial Chamber Court or Aulic Council –or to exhibits submitted to the files by the parties or consulted during the course of the proceedings. Then, the pending proceedings take an intermediary role – it was not the court itself that produced the source, but owing to the case heard before it, a commercial expert opinion for instance was drawn up, or prior to that a law faculty had been requested to submit the reasons for their doubts or the reasons for the decision (*rationes dubitandi et decidendi*).

a Decisions

Regarding the rulings, the decision of the ruling panel itself can constitute an original commercial law source that was generally applied.[17] It is true that the judgments in question, if made[18] or known[19] at all, are of a minor independent

17 The view was still held by Adolf Stölzel, *Die Entwicklung der gelehrten Rechtsprechung*, 2 vols. (Berlin: F. Vahlen, 1910), 2:125, according to which the view that the Imperial Chamber Court had no significance beyond its own rulings can be considered as refuted.

18 More recent research works have turned away from the focus on judgments, and analyse the value of judicial activities for an amicable outcome to the proceedings, thus e.g. for the Imperial Chamber Court: Anja Amend-Traut, 'Brüder unter sich – die Handelsgesellschaft Brentano vor Gericht: Elemente privater Konfliktlösung im Reichskammergerichtsprozess', in Albrecht Cordes and Serge Dauchy (eds.), *Eine Grenze in Bewegung: Öffentliche und private Justiz im Handels- und Seerecht* (München: R. Oldenbourg Verlag, 2013), 91–116; Anja Amend-Traut, 'Konfliktlösung bei streitigen Wechseln im Alten Reich: Der Kaufmannstand zwischen der Suche nach Alternativen zur gerichtlichen Geltendmachung von Forderungen und strategischer Justiznutzung', in Rolf Lieberwirth and Heiner Lück (eds.), *Akten des 36. Deutschen Rechtshistorikertages Halle an der Saale* (Stuttgart: Steiner, 2008), 153–175; Anja Amend-Traut, 'Wie Prozesse enden können – alternative Formen der Beendigung reichskammergerichtlicher Verfahren', in Albrecht Cordes (ed.), *Mit Freundschaft oder mit Recht? Inner- und außergerichtliche Alternativen zur kontroversen Streitentscheidung im 15.–19. Jahrhundert* (Köln: Böhlau Verlag, 2015). The contributions to the present conference material are also on this issue.

19 In trials decided by final judgment, the tenor of those judgments is often unknown because the judgment books and the books of records are kept separate to the actual case files. The judgment books, however, are incomplete. The only portfolios preserved are

value as judicial records, because the ruling sentences themselves did not yet contain their underlying reasons. *Vis-à-vis* the parties, this was generally prohibited.[20] Their scope and depth of content, however, can frequently be reconstructed by means of various records accrued during the proceedings, for example the legal elaboration drawn up by the reporting assessor.[21] Irrespective of this fact it is known that contemporaries[22] ascribed a high level of significance to the rulings of the Imperial Chamber Court, even if this thematically has so far been researched in a context different to that of interest here.[23] At first, this applies with regard to the comments of contemporary lawyers, who like Johannes Limnaeus equated the significance of the decisions of the Imperial Chamber Court with the imperial constitutional laws such as the imperial enactments and the Golden Bull,[24] or in any case ascribed them force of law. According to Hermann Conring, territorial manorial courts treated the Imperial Chamber Court judgments like mandatory regulations.[25] Also, cases have been documented in which Supreme Court decisions changed the

---

those of 1573–1601, 1630–1688, 1693–1704, and 1711–1806. More details on this in Amend-Traut, *Wechselverbindlichkeiten*, 48.

20 Heinrich Gehrke, *Die privatrechtliche Entscheidungsliteratur Deutschlands: Charakteristik und Bibliographie der Rechtsprechungs- und Konsilienliteratur vom 16. bis zum Beginn des 19. Jahrhunderts* (Frankfurt am Main: Vittorio Klostermann, 1974), 23ff.; Wolfgang Sellert, 'Zur Geschichte der rationalen Begründung zivilrechtlicher Entscheidungen gegenüber den Parteien am Beispiel des Reichskammergerichts und des Reichshofrats', in Hugo de Schepper (ed.), *Höchste Gerichtsbarkeit im Spätmittelalter und der Frühen Neuzeit: Internationales Rechtshistorisches Symposium, Amsterdam 1.–3. Juni 1984* (Amsterdam: Faculteit der Rechtsgeleerdheid, 1985), 61–70; Wolfgang Sellert, 'Zur Geschichte der rationalen Urteilsbegründung gegenüber den Parteien insbesondere am Beispiel des Reichshofrats und des Reichskammergerichts', in Gerhard Dilcher and Bernhard Diestelkamp (eds.), *Recht, Gericht, Genossenschaft und Policey: Studien zu Grundbegriffen der germanistischen Rechtshistorie* (Berlin: Schmidt, 1986), 97–113, 104.

21 Generally, on the value of Imperial Chamber Court files in terms of legal history see Peter Oestmann, 'Die Rekonstruktion der reichskammergerichtlichen Rechtsprechung', in Anette Baumann et al. (eds.), *Prozessakten als Quelle* (Köln: Böhlau, 2001), 15–54; Amend-Traut, *Wechselverbindlichkeiten*, 50–57.

22 On the question of whether the Imperial Chamber Court rulings in the nineteenth century were adopted see Bruno Heusinger, *Vom Reichskammergericht, seinen Nachwirkungen und seinem Verhältnis zu den heutigen Zentralgerichten* (Karlsruhe: Müller, 1972), esp. 33f.

23 More details on this in Amend-Traut, *Wechselverbindlichkeiten*, 50f.

24 Johannes Limnaeus, *Juris publici Imperii Romano-Germanici libri IX*, 3 vols. (Strasbourg, 1629–34), 1:Lib. I, Cap. 3, German trans. Michael Stolleis, *Geschichte des öffentlichen Rechts in Deutschland*, 3 vols. (München: Beck, 1988), 1:152.

25 Michael Stolleis (ed.), Hermann Conring, *Der Ursprung des deutschen Rechts* (Frankfurt am Main: Insel Verlag, 1994), 230, who in this context refers to the Würzburg Council.

opinion previously prevailing in literature.[26] In their expert reports, law faculties pointed out the relevant findings of the Imperial Chamber Court, and for private expert opinions people sought the advice of assessors at the Imperial Chamber Court.[27] The efficacy generally ascribed to Imperial Chamber Court judgments among lawyers is also evident from the fact that they were adopted by territorial law collections[28] and commentaries, and that the significance ascribed to them was equal to that of laws. The introduction to Johan Philipp Orth's commentary on the Frankfurt Reformation states that 'for better explanation and understanding' of Frankfurt Law, 'both old and new statutes, responsa, deductions and other documents' had to be attached. Correspondingly, it would not be rare that 'dark and difficult passages' in a code of law were interpreted in the light of a decision passed by one of the two supreme courts, and thus were implicitly declared as generally binding.[29] The pleadings of the parties prepared by authorised advocates also contain numerous references to Imperial Chamber Court judgments regarding a relevant subject matter of dispute when it came to convincing the reader – i.e. primarily the reporting assessor – of the correctness of the defended legal view.

In addition, collections of decisions are at least as indirect records part of the sources of commercial law under examination here, because they frequently extend beyond a mere summary of the legal dispute and are then enriched with the compiler's critical reflection on the legal issue and his personal evaluation. Above all, however, they only enabled a reception of the Imperial Chamber Court decisions, because otherwise they would not have entered the public domain, because the official oath which judges at the Imperial Chamber Court had to take obliged them to secrecy. The standing rules of the Imperial Chamber Court stipulated that 'the judges and assessors under their vows and oaths taken must forever keep strictly secret anything deliberated, voted on and judged, and not disclose it to anyone'.[30]

In the eighteenth century, this benefit was emphasised by Johann Stephan Pütter, who pointed out that the observations were 'full of useful legal rules

26 Andreas Schwennicke, *'Ohne Steuer kein Staat': Zur Entwicklung und politischen Funktion des Steuerrechts in den Territorien des Heiligen Römischen Reichs (1500–1800)* (Frankfurt am Main: Vittorio Klostermann, 1996), 33, 272ff., esp. 275.

27 Substantiations in Oestmann, 'Rekonstruktion', 31.

28 One example from Lübeck can be found in Oestmann, 'Rekonstruktion', 30.

29 Johann Philipp Orth, *Nöthig- und nützlich-erachtete Anmerckungen über die im Zweyten Theil enthaltene Acht erstere Tituln Wie auch viele andere aus den übrigen Theilen dahin gehörige Tituln und Stellen Der so genannten Erneuerten Reformation Der Stadt Franckfurt am Mayn* ..., 6 vols. (Frankfurt am Main, 1731–75), 1:preface, IIf.

30 RKGO 1555 Part I Title 13 § 16, in Adolf Laufs, *Die Reichskammergerichtsordnung von 1555* (Köln: Böhlau, 1976), 97.

and almost consistently so concise and thorough that it is not surprising that they have become almost universally accepted all over Germany as if they were laws and that they enjoy a high reputation to this date'.[31] Also the first author to be named here, Joachim Mynsinger von Frundeck,[32] justified his publication by pointing out that he was concerned with the general benefit rather than with secrecy.[33] Later assessors followed Mynsingers example and published extensive decision literature; the best known among them are Andreas Gail (1526–1587)[34] and, around 200 years later, Johann Ulrich von Cramer (1706–1772).[35] The significance of the publication of the statements of reasons for the history of private law was already emphasised in the past with the aim of promoting the strengthening of the Imperial Chamber Court judicature and the adoption of the Roman-Canonical Law.[36] The process in terms of historical reception, however, is at least equally remarkable with regard to commercial law questions answered beyond ordinary law, namely by the consultation of legal sources of particular laws or the court's creation of new laws. The literature on the law on bills of exchange, for example, provides a great deal of evidence for the reception of Imperial Chamber Court decisions.[37]

31 Johann Stephan Pütter, *Litteratur des Teutschen Staatsrechts*, 4 vols. (Göttingen: Wittwe Vandenhoeck, 1725–1807), 1:§ 52, 123.

32 *Responsorum iuris, sive consiliorum decades decem, sive Centuria integra* (Basel, 1566); *Singularium observationum imperialis camerae ut centuriae VI.* (Helmstedt, 1599). On this person, see Anja Amend-Traut, 'Reformer, Gelehrter, Dichter. Zum 500. Geburtstag Joachim Mynsingers von Frundeck (1514–88)', *ZEuP* 22:2 (2014), 337–348.

33 Joachim Mynsingers von Frundeck, *Singularium observationum iudicii imperialis camerae (ut vocant) centuriae quatuor. Additvs Est Rervm Et Verborum memorabiliu[m]* ... (Basel, 1566), cited from Karl Zippelius, 'Ein Juristenleben im 16. Jahrhundert: Joachim Mynsinger von Frundeck', in Jean-François Gerkens (ed.), *Mélanges Fritz Sturm*, 2 vols. (Liège: Éditions Juridiques de l'Université de Liège, 1999), 1:959–970, 964.

34 For a biographical study see Anja Amend-Traut, 'Gail, Andreas (1526–87)', in Albrecht Cordes et al. (eds.), *Handwörterbuch zur deutschen Rechtsgeschichte* (*HRG*), vol. I, 2nd ed. (Berlin: Erich Schmidt, 2008), cols. 1913f.

35 Andreas Gail, *Practicarum observationum*, (trans.) Thobias Loncius, *Deß Keiserlichen Cammer Gerichts Sonderliche Gerichtsbreuche vnnd Rechts Regeln: in zweyen Büchern sein ordentlich zusam verfasset* ... (Hamburg: Moller, 1601, later, unchanged edition Munich, 1673); Johann Ulrich von Cramer, *Wetzlarische Nebenstunden, worinnen auserlesene beym Höchstpreißlichen Cammergericht entschiedene Rechts-Händel zur Erweiter- und Erläuterung der Deutschen in Gerichten üblichen Rechts-Gelehrsamkeit angewendet werden*, 32 vols. (Ulm, 1755–73).

36 Amend-Traut, 'Reformer', 343.

37 For example, in Johann Adam Beck, *Wechsel-Recht In sich begreiffend, so wohl die Persohnen, welche diesem Recht unterworffen sind, als auch die verschiedene Arten und Gattungen derer Wechsel und Wechsel-Brieffen, ...zu observiren ist, ...* (Nürnberg: Lochner, 1729), Cap. XIII, § 18., n. 4ff., 408f.

An example of a customary commercial law matter adopted and frequently confirmed by rulings – ultimately by the Supreme Court – is the question of repayment modalities of overdue debts. This also in particular affected commercial transactions, especially when the redemption of loans or bills of exchange were concerned. In this respect, the Supreme Court rulings followed the medieval tradition of the *communis opinio* entirely, therein following the opinions of the lawyers of the *usus modernus*. If, according to those, a specific type of coin had been contractually promised as a means of payment, the creditor could request repayment in the same coin at the value given at the time of the conclusion of the contract. Debasements of coinage, which were the order of the day during the so-called 'Kipper and Wipper time' and often resulted in court action, were thus to the debtor's detriment.[38] In a dispute about the amount of the liabilities to be settled under a loan, which was brought before the Imperial Chamber Court, it was stated that according to '...general reasonable custom', the redemption of debts 'had to be made at the value of the money provided at the time of lending'. This was said to correspond to the appropriate style and daily observance of the Imperial Chamber Court (*unsers Kayl. Cammergerichts wohlerbrachter styli und täglicher observanz*).[39]

A frequently cited decision later on,[40] where the Imperial Chamber Court took a law-creating decision in favour of prospering trade, dealt with the question of whether and under which conditions bills of exchange could also be settled in the form of a current account. Generally, bills of exchange had to be settled in cash.[41] Two trading partners named Hauer and Pörtner were in

38 This aspect is discussed extensively, with a number of Imperial Chamber Court decisions and further substantiations from applicable literature, in Anja Amend-Traut, 'Geld regiert...' Frühneuzeitliche Geldpolitik im Lichte zeitgenössischer Rechtsprechung, in Ignacio Czeguhn (ed.), *Recht im Wandel – Wandel des Rechts, Festschrift für Jürgen Weitzel zum 70. Geburtstag* (Köln: Böhlau, 2014), 367–408, 391–406; Anja Amend-Traut, 'Monetary and Currency Problems in the Light of Early Modern Litigation', in Wolfgang Ernst and David Fox (eds.), *Money in the Western Legal Tradition: Middle Ages to Bretton Woods* (Oxford: Oxford University Press, 2016) 295–316.

39 From the parties' file in the Imperial Chamber Court proceeding: Princely Castell archive KA no. B VII 1 4, lawyer's pleading of 1636, unbound. The case file can be found at the Central State Archive Munich (HStA), n. 15248. This is recorded in: Manfred Hörner (resp.), *Bayerisches Hauptstaatsarchiv, Reichskammergericht. n. 1840–2129* (*lit.* C) (Munich, 1995), n. 1885.

40 Thus inter alia at Cramer, *Nebenstunden*, 13:Part 49, IV.

41 Besides that, set-off could also be imagined; Amend-Traut, *Wechselverbindlichkeiten*, 293–296.

regular business contact, had annual turnovers of several ten thousand florins with each other, and were also otherwise in a 'current account' relationship. They had mutually agreed to settle accounts through an annual 'general invoice', where all given invoice positions should be set off against each other. A separate assertion of individual claims, including claims under bills of exchange, was excluded. Such an obligation normally conflicts with the special features of bills of exchange, which can be immediately liquidated within the scope of a summary procedure and permit only those objections which are provable without further investigation. In accordance with this principle, the first reporter of the defendant dealing with the matter at the Imperial Chamber Court wanted to oblige the defendant to pay the disputed bills of exchange, which he had drawn on the claimant, and to evaluate the remaining facts as inconclusive (*das übrige aber als ohngeständig zu besserem Beweiß*).[42] The majority of the members of the assessors' committee, however, held 'that such opinion ... did [not] conform with the usual local custom between merchants'. Merchants constantly 'in trade and account' with each other were obliged to draw up general statements of accounts upon the request of the respective other party. Conversely, they were then not entitled to assert claims under 'due bills of exchange *paratam executionem*'.[43] The acknowledgement of individual debt positions, however, did not amount to the admission of a final payment obligation, but was made in reliance on the balancing of the mutual claims.[44] If, on the other hand, the possibility were granted to assert individual claims – in court – in the case of such trade relations, the ultimate question would only be which of the parties would 'first go to court' and request the acknowledgement of the mutual liabilities. This was hardly beneficial to trade.[45] This evaluation was shared by a whole range of expert opinions (*Pareres*) 'of many famous merchants and traders',[46] which the court also explicitly took as a judgment basis. Based on these considerations, and in fact in consideration of the provability of all requirements for a full balancing and a positive result for the defendant, the Imperial Chamber Court dismissed the claim for relief of the Amsterdam merchant Hauer[47] and ordered him 'to present the requested general invoice of 1736, and to confirm it with his trade book'.[48]

42 Cramer, *Nebenstunden*, 13:Part 49, IV, § 4, 57ff., here 61, and in the *rationes decidendi*, 78.
43 Cramer, *Nebenstunden*, 13:Part 49, IV, § 5, 61f.
44 Cramer, *Nebenstunden*, 13:Part 49, IV, § 6, 63.
45 Cramer, *Nebenstunden*, 13:Part 49, IV, § 7, 63.
46 Cramer, *Nebenstunden*, 13:Part 49, IV, § 11, 80, 83.
47 Thus expressly in Cramer, *Nebenstunden*, 13:Part 49, IV, § 7, 63.
48 Cramer, *Nebenstunden*, 13:Part 49, IV, § 11, 76.

Here, as also in other disputes, it becomes apparent that in matters of commercial law the Imperial Chamber court,[49] but also other supreme courts,[50] were not necessarily following judicially rigid constructions, but rather orientated itself towards commercial practice and sought pragmatic solutions to maintain the '*commercium inter mercatores*, and its structure'. For the lack of a law 'that ordered otherwise'[51] they explicitly followed 'solely ... natural standards of reason and fairness'[52] (*nach der natürliche*[*n*] *Vemunft und Billichkeit*) or the common good.

Accordingly, there were situations where individual merchants, and moreover the entire mercantile profession, benefited from the consistent ruling of the Imperial Chamber Court; its rulings often had a harmonizing effect beyond the territorial boundaries, especially where particular provisions were different or regulations were entirely missing, namely in commercial law matters and more specifically in issues relating to bills of exchange.[53]

b Enforcement Measures

In contrast, two further examples will show that the Imperial Chamber Court's course of action – which incidentally was also that of the Emperor by means of his subordinated authority, the Aulic Council[54] – against emancipated member of the Empire could also have a detrimental economic effect on them. Thus, trading partners – especially cities, but also individual merchants and trading companies – could be ordered by the Supreme Court to break off or undermine the business relations to the convicted persons. Of course, in actual fact a large group, consisting of uninvolved persons, was also affected by these decisions, and therefore the overall economic power of the Empire was weakened.

In 1497, the Imperial Chamber Court outlawed the Cities of Danzig and Elbing, after these had taken 44 ships loaded with grain from the merchant Thomas Jadeck and then disregarded the subsequent Imperial Chamber Court jurisdiction. First, the City of Lübeck complained about being threatened by economic damage, because goods of its merchants with a value of about 70,000 Talers and a majority of their ships were located in the outlawed cities. The matter was then heard before the Imperial Diet at Freiburg in 1498. Although

49 On this see Amend-Traut, *Wechselverbindlichkeiten*.

50 Thus, for example, in Alain Wijffels, 'Gelehrtes Recht und Wirtschaftsordnung: Niederländische "Bierkriege" im 15. und 16. Jahrhundert', *ZNR* 25 (2003), 177–203, 201, proven for the Grote Raad van Mechelen.

51 Thus the *rationes decidendi*, in Cramer, *Nebenstunden*, 13: Part 49, IV, § 11, 80.

52 Cramer, *Nebenstunden*, 13:Part 49, IV, § 7, 64f. On the use of such guiding concepts and classification patterns see Amend-Traut, *Wechselverbindlichkeiten*, 417–422.

53 On this, cf. Amend-Traut, *Wechselverbindlichkeiten*.

54 More details on this aspect are set forth in Section 4.2.

it was recognised there that it '[would be] disgraceful to the Empire and the Chamber Court to set aside the judgments', the Emperor ultimately suspended the enforcement measures by ordering the Imperial Chamber Court 'to stop action in disputes regarding these two cities, no matter what was concerned, and not to take further action against them without imperial order'.[55] Various cities, including Augsburg, Frankfurt, Leipzig, Lübeck, and Nuremberg then resumed their business relationships with the previously outlawed. The trials which the Imperial Chamber Court then instigated against these cities and individual merchants and trading companies for disregarding the ban imposed on them was again quashed by the Emperor[56] – 'in the interest of the merchants and trade of the German nation'.

The protagonists of the dispute had already and for a long time lost sight of the mercantile aspect; the constitutional and legal policy dimension of the incidents made them to the subject matter of the hearings at the Mainz Convention in 1517 and the Augsburg Diet in 1518. The imperial estates gathered denounced the deficiencies and infirmity of the judiciary; it happened again and again that Imperial Chamber Court decisions were disregarded in such a manner that this 'amounted to contempt ... of the court and German nation: ... the outlawry and repeated outlawry, although properly and duly obtained, was little respected; rather the outlawed were tolerated ... reprieved, which all resulted in deprivation and disadvantage especially to the winning parties'.[57] Thus, the imperial estates criticised the Emperor who opposed the orders of the court staffed with the cooperation of the imperial estates and enforced his will in the form of a dictum (*Machtspruch*) – even if in doing so he actually pursued superior economic interests of the Empire. In the end, they 'humbly asked' Maximilian 'to execute the given judgments in accordance with the imperial rules, as is proper'.[58]

In 1509, the court, upon the successful action of the two imperial curates of the Cities of Verona and Vicenza and according to the subsequent disobedience to the judgment, outlawed the City of Venice.[59] The legal dispute was preceded by the occupation of these cities by Venice. As a result of the outlawry, any exchange of goods with the Swabian imperial cities which 'at these times

55 Johann Heinrich Harpprecht, *Staats-Archiv Des Kayserl. und des H. Röm. Reichs Cammer-Gerichts Oder Sammlung Von gedruckten und mehrentheils ungedruckten Actis Publicis...*, 6 vols. (Ulm, 1757–68), 3:142; Imperial letter to the Chamber Court, August 4, 1518, *ibid.*, 325f.

56 On the facts in the case, see Harpprecht, *Staats-Archiv*, 3:141–145.

57 Harpprecht, *Staats-Archiv*, 3:144.

58 Recess at Augsburg 1518, § 10.

59 Further evidence in Harpprecht, *Staats-Archiv*, 3:87f.

had the most flourishing trade with Italy' largely broke down. At first, the Imperial Cities asked the Imperial Chamber Court for help, because the 'prohibition did not most severely damage the enemy cities, but rather the German imperial state itself, commerce and trade were in a bad condition, ...which made the imperial hereditary lands themselves suffer and perish'. The Imperial Chamber Court, however, saw itself as being incapable of departing from its decision once taken. Thereupon, the league of cities turned to Emperor Maximilian I, who in 1510 and 1511 ordered the Imperial Chamber Court and the imperial fiscal prosecutor to allow the exchange of goods between Swabian merchants and trading companies to and from Venice, with an imperial escort, but 'with the exception of the Duke [of Venice] and his people'.[60]

With the imperial outlawry, the two cases document a measure still imposed in later periods by the Imperial Chamber Court against cities or territories, where the forum had no other means of action/response due to the distance between the Empire and the defendants, or the defendants' distance from the imperial administration of justice. Those actually affected by the outlawry, however, were the merchants. Once the outlawry was passed, the Imperial Chamber Court felt bound to its pronounced word in the interest of the reliance of the beneficiary on the legal force of the Supreme Court's decisions. As a logical consequence, the 'Chamber Court's world-renowned love of justice'[61] was not only confined to a favourable effect on trade and the economy.

3.2 *Exhibits*

Apart from the court decisions themselves, the exhibits contained in the files of the supreme courts constitute further commercial law sources. These were produced on the occasion of the legal dispute and during the course of the Supreme Court proceeding taken to its files. Among these are the reasons for the decisions and the concerns (*rationes decidendi et dubitandi*) of lower courts and evaluating law faculties[62] and especially the so-called *Pareres*, i.e. commercial expert opinions.[63]

---

60 Quotations and a summarising description in Harpprecht, *Staats-Archiv*, 3:66f. and 3:88f. Letter to the Imperial Chamber Court, February 21, 1511, Harpprecht, *Staats-Archiv*, 3:262f.

61 Harpprecht, *Staats-Archiv*, 3:143.

62 On this see also Anja Amend, 'Die Inanspruchnahme von Juristenfakultäten in der Frankfurter Rechtsprechung', in Anja Amend et al. (eds.), *Die Reichsstadt Frankfurt als Rechts- und Gerichtslandschaft im Römisch-Deutschen Reich der Frühen Neuzeit* (München: R. Oldenbourg, 2008), 77–96, with further substantiations.

63 The fundamental research of these expert opinions has so far been a desideratum in Germany. For France, see Édouard Richard, 'A l'orée du droit des marchands: Les parères',

a *Pareres*

The commercial expert opinions were recognised not only among the merchants themselves, but were generally adopted by legal literature, and references to their content were made by law faculties, lower courts and also the Imperial Chamber Court.[64] This in particular applies to disputes for which the available particular law regimes and sources of ordinary law offered no solution, but which at the same time were matters of everyday commercial practice. The *Pareres* were frequently included as collections in printed handbooks on commercial practice or added to law collections.[65] Textbooks on the law on bills of exchange point out their quality as a guideline for the judge: They would 'constitute in commercial matters what otherwise in legal disputes was a legal opinion, ...but should in such matters that concern a legal provision also not be disregarded improperly'.[66]

The judges were not supposed to simply follow the *Pareres*, but 'where peculiar commercial courts were not mandatory' and given that 'in matters of bills of exchange a lot originated from mercantile style and custom', the merchants were well advised 'to inform and instruct the judge in important cases having a

Revue d'Histoire des Facultés de Droit 33 (2014), 155–217. The most recent and authoritative work on the practice of legal opinions in the Early Modern Age by Ulrich Falk, *Consilia: Studien zur Praxis der Rechtsgutachten in der frühen Neuzeit* (Frankfurt am Main: Vittorio Klostermann, 2006), leaves out the entire area of commercial law. The doctoral project of Sonja Breustedt/Ffm., 'Pareres der "löblichen Kaufmannschaft" zu Frankfurt am Main. Handelsrechtliche Konfliktlösung im 18. Jahrhundert' is a first attempt. However, the study is based on the collections of the Institute of City History/Frankfurt am Main, which does not have any conclusive collection of expert opinions. The project 'Die Nürnberger Handelsgerichtsbarkeit. Handelsgerichtliche Gutachten in der Frühen Neuzeit' recently sponsored by the German Research Foundation (DFG) and headed by Anja Amend-Traut aims to interpret and analyse the collection of sources that have been conclusive for several centuries and which reflect the activities of the Nuremberg Director of Trade. On this see http://www.jura.uni-wuerzburg.de/lehrstuehle/amend-traut/die-nuernberger-handelsgerichtsbarzeit/.

64 The acceptance of the Councils – with a focus on Roman and Canonical law – has recently been emphasised by Eberhard Isenmann, 'Plenitudo potestatis' und Delegation: Die höhere und höchste Gewalt in Rechtsgutachten vornehmlich für deutsche Städte in Spätmittelalter und früher Neuzeit, in Gerhard Dilcher and Diego Quaglioni (eds.), *Die Anfänge des öffentlichen Rechts, 3. Auf dem Weg zur Etablierung des öffentlichen Rechts zwischen Mittelalter und Moderne* (Bologna: Mulino, 2009), 197–241, 100.

65 For example in Johann Gottlieb Siegel, *Corpus juris cambialis* (Leipzig: Heinsius, 1742).

66 Beck, *Wechsel-Recht*, Cap. XIV, § 4, note 8, 412f. To that effect also Paul Jacob Marperger, *Neu=eröffnetes Handels=Gericht/oder Wohlbestelltes Commercien-Collegium* ... (Hamburg, 1709), III. Cap., 68.

wider impact on the mercantile community by means of expert opinions from expert merchants and traders residing in different towns (then called *Parere*), to shorten extensive circuitousness of the procedures'.[67]

Accordingly, a guideline on the law on bills of exchange states with regard to the *Pareres* that it was recommendable 'that every court commonly considered them if demanded by the judge with intend to examine the custom and usage of bills of exchange according thereto'.[68]

And in fact, university judicial councils took note of the expert opinions and, if applicable, recited them. Thus, a collection of expert opinions of the law faculty of Halle states with regard to a *Parere* of the Leipzig masters of the retail merchant guild on the law on bills of exchange that 'some months ago this law faculty had also affirmed this opinion in a dispute submitted for decision'.[69] Also lower courts and in the end the Imperial Chamber Court dealt with *Pareres* either when they were submitted to the files as evidence by the parties in pending court proceedings,[70] or when the Imperial Chamber Court itself requested such expert opinions.[71]

A further case in addition to that already described above, whereupon the instigation of one of the parties' *Pareres* was used as a commercial law source

67 Jacob Friederich Ludovici, *Einleitung zum Wechsel-Prozeß*, 9th ed. (Halle, 1743), Cap. XII, § IV, 373.

68 Philipp Carl Scherer, *Handbuch des Wechselrechts, worinnen theils die Art und Weise, wie die Wechselgeschäfte zu behandeln und zu beurtheilen, gezeigt, theils die vielen Abweichungen der Wechselgesetze unter sich dargestellt werden zum Gebrauch für Rechtsgelehrte aus allen Ständen absonderlich auch für Kauf= und Handelsleute und alle diejenigen, welche sich mit Wechselgeschäften abgeben*, 3 vols. (Frankfurt am Main, 1800–1), 2:326.

69 Carl Gottlieb Knorre, *Rechtliche Abhandlungen und Gutachten* (Halle: Hemmerde, 1757), II. Rechtsfrage, 28–44, here § 14, 42f., note 24.

70 Besides, a dispute could be settled solely with the help of the *Pareres* without being bound to a strict judicial procedure. Within the scope of a research area examining the history and culture of the contested decision of legal conflicts and its consensual resolution – decisively the LOEWE-project focused on 'extrajudicial and judicial conflict resolution' – see Sonja Breustedt, 'Kaufmännische Pareres – Gutachten als Konsens und Beweismittel im 17. und 18. Jahrhundert', in Albrecht Cordes (ed.), *Mit Freundschaft oder mit Recht? Inner- und außergerichtliche Alternativen zur kontroversen Streitentscheidung im 15.–19. Jahrhundert* (Köln: Böhlau Verlag, 2015), examine the significance of the *Parere* in this context.

71 Regarding a *Parere* requested by the Leipzig Trade Guild from the Imperial Chamber Court in the middle of the eighteenth century see Johann Ulrich von Cramer, *Observationum juris universi ex praxi recentiori supremorum imperii tribunalium haustarum...*, 6 vols. (Wetzlar/I, II, Ulm/ III–VI, 1758–72), 1:Obs. CCXI, 491ff.

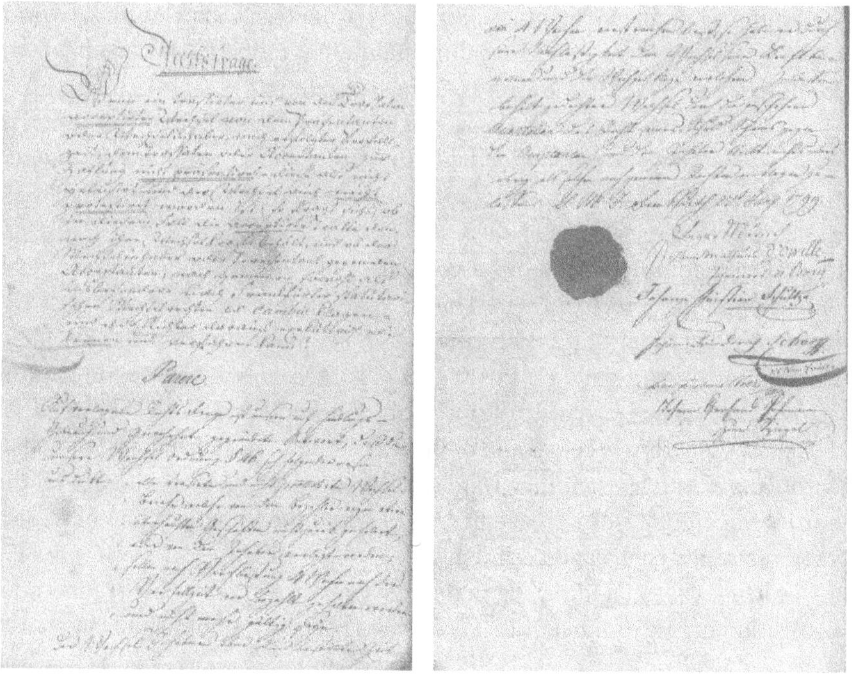

CHART 9.1 *Example of a* Parere *from:* ISG *Frankfurt M.,* RGK *n. 332, [Q] 26. In 1799 the Frankfurt merchants were asked, if an accepted bill of exchange remains in full force and effect after the agreed day of expiry, when it is neither presented nor protested, or if the claim has to be sued by ordinary law rulings.*

in a supreme court proceeding,[72] dealt with the question of whether a shareholder could validly oblige the company and his co-shareholders by entering into liabilities on bills of exchange. In this respect, individual laws on bills of exchange as well as court practice and scientific research were in disagreement. The highly respected and very wealthy trading company Gebrüder Heese[73] was sued after the eldest of three brothers had entered into a multitude of liabilities on bills of exchange without the knowledge of the other two. Between May 1792 and April 1793, he issued several bills of exchange for approx. 5.000 Carl d'or in the name of the company,[74] and the younger brothers refused to pay on

72 ISG Frankfurt a. M. RKG n. 796 and 798; within the course of the proceedings, the two legal actions were combined.

73 At the time when the trading company was taken over by the founder's sons in 1792, the company assets amounted to 488.162 florins. Further details on the family Heeser Alexander Dietz, *Frankfurter Handelsgeschichte*, 4 vols. (Frankfurt am Main: H. Minjon, 1910), 4-1:267, 315f., 329.

74 On May 6, 1792 on the order of Löw Isaak Elias for 450 Carl d'or, on January 5, 1792 for 793 Carl d'or by the order of Wolf Seligmann Oppenheimer, on April 12, 1793 for 1,000 Carl d'or

the due dates. The creditors did not accept the reason they stated, namely that the bills of exchange had been signed by the eldest brother without their 'prior knowledge' and that the 'monies had not been credited to the trading assets'.[75] They then entered a protest about the bills of exchange and subsequently sued. Without waiting for the final decision of the Frankfurt lower court, the creditors resorted to the Imperial Chamber Court.[76] In their interrogations, the younger brothers stated that they had not had any knowledge of the transactions and that the relevant money had not flowed into the joint business, which was why 'neither ratification nor payment by bill of exchange could take place'.[77] Section 7 of the Frankfurt exchange law principally provided for joint liability for liabilities on bills of exchange. However, this regulation could be understood only in the light of the restriction provided for under Frankf. Ref., P. II Tit. 23 § 9.[78] According to that, the company incurs liabilities only if negotiations take place 'in the name of such company by one of them (upon consent of prior knowledge of the others) or by their acknowledged and known agent'. However, given that the eldest brother had neither expressly in the articles of association nor implicitly been granted power of attorney to 'borrow monies which the company did not need',[79] they did not have to assume responsibility for the liabilities. The special law could reach only so far as the Frankfurt Reformation, which generally regulated company law, allowed it. The existence of the trading company alone, according to that, should not suffice to oblige its co-shareholders by the actions of one single person in general and in particular also under the law on bills of exchange. Part of the relevant literature on the Frankfurt law also interpreted the relationship between the standards concerned in a similar way,[80] or at least established that the unlimited liability of the company as ordered in Section 7 *Bills of Exchange Act 1739*, i.e. without

to Samuel Schuster and on January 15, 1793 for 750 Carl d'or to Callmann Meyer Amschel, ISG Frankfurt a. M. RKG,. 798, [Q] 7. In addition, bill of exchange claims for 280, 700 und 896 Carl d'or, inter alia asserted by Beer Abraham Stiebel and David Seidel in 1794, ISG Frankfurt a. M. RKG n. 796, [Q] 5.

75 ISG Frankfurt a. M. RKG n. 796, [Q] 4, ISG Frankfurt a. M. RKG n. 798, [Q] 5.

76 ISG Frankfurt a. M. RKG n. 798, [Q] 15.

77 ISG Frankfurt a. M. RKG n. 798, [Q] 13.

78 ISG Frankfurt a. M. RKG n. 798, [Q] 115, fol. 7^{r}.

79 ISG Frankfurt a. M. RKG n. 798, [Q] 115, n. 11, fol. 5^{r}.

80 Johann Ludwig Span, *Der freien Stadt Frankfurt am Main Wechsel-Recht. Aus dasigen Statutis, sonderlich der jüngsten Wechselordnung de 1739, methodice verfasset und mit dem gemeinen Wechsel-Recht überall verglichen, folglich zugleich als eine Einleitung zu dem letztern eingerichtet, auch mit einem vollständigen Register versehen* (Frankfurt am Main, 1752), Cap. 17, § 119.

the acting shareholder being granted special power beforehand, 'was not provided for in ordinary laws'.[81]

To refute this special law starting point and its interpretation, the creditors presented as many as three consistent *Pareres* to the Imperial Chamber Court from the leagues of merchants in Leipzig, Vienna, and Hamburg. According to them, the defence that the co-shareholders had no knowledge of the obligation, or that the money had not flowed into the company's coffers, was inadmissible at least in matters concerning bills of exchange. The holder of a bill of exchange could, without further requirements, demand settlement from the company, because it was 'joint *in solidum*' in cases such as the one under discussion.[82] This view held by the Leipzig expert opinion was shared by that from Hamburg, which was signed by almost 50 merchants and trading companies: 'When a trading shareholder signs bills of exchange in the name of the trading company he was entitled to manage, then the trading company incurs joint liability and must not be heard with the mentioned defence'.[83]

Finally, the Vienna Merchants believed that Art. 29 of their Exchange Act complied 'with exchange laws adopted [in] all countries', according to which each merchant was bound when the representation had been properly shown beforehand, either by the granting of *Prokura* (a registered statutory power of representation), power of attorney or, as here, by publication of the company and its shareholders. The trust created by the company among third parties had to be 'steadfastly maintained' and could not be unsettled by such defence.[84] Apart from the Leipzig Reformation Tit. 18 L. 3. § 1, the Hamburg Town Charters P. 2 Tit. 10. Art. 8, and Section 8 of the Vienna Exchange Act, the town charters of Florence, Genoa and Mantua also provided that each shareholder of a trading company was 'without differentiation … bound in solidum … under the contract entered into by the other, thus in consideration of the joint company…'. Also, legal scholars partly followed this line of argumentation that it had to be presumed 'that the shareholders had so to speak instructed and authorized each other what was contained in their company's contract'.[85]

81 Orth, *Anmerckungen*, 4:527.

82 *Parere* of the Leipzig Merchants of October 19, 1793, ISG Frankfurt a. M. RKG n. 798, [Q] 24.

83 *Parere* of the Hamburg Merchants of October 23, 1793, ISG Frankfurt a. M. RKG n. 798, [Q] 28.

84 *Parere* of the Vienna Merchants of October 24, 1793, ISG Frankfurt a. M. RKG n. 798, [Q] 27.

85 Beck, *Wechsel-Recht*, Cap. I, § 37, n. 1–4, 34f.; Lauterbach, *De jure in Curia Mercatorum usitato*, §§ 152ff.; Wolfgang Adam Lauterbach, *Sociorum obligatione quae oritur ex conventione cum extraneis inita* (Tübingen, 1668), Cap. V., § 47, 49f.; Orth, *Anmerckungen*, 4:527. On the entire contentious issue also Christoph Franck, *Institutiones iuris cambialis ex legibus cambialis diversarum gentium indole negociationis moribus ac iure communi NOVA METHODI…*, 2nd ed. (Jena, 1737), lib. I., Sect. I., tit. VIIII., th. XV., 126.

They thus complied with the needs and requests of the merchants, who always demanded the simplest possible liability benchmark and a quick processing of business transactions.

The plea presented by the Heeser brothers themselves looked rather insufficient in comparison to the weighty arguments of the appellants, even if they attached a petition of the Frankfurt League of Merchants to their pleading, in which 148 merchants, trading companies and banks, including Brentano, Bethmann, Passavant, and Städel, affirmed that the two younger Heeser brothers enjoyed the best reputation in Frankfurt and elsewhere and that the company had not in any way needed to borrow the sued-for monies by bills of exchange.[86]

The view held by the Imperial Chamber Court on the issue raised can only be speculated upon, because the parties ultimately ended the legal action by a settlement agreement whose content, however, has an indicative effect. The settlement contained a promise of 'satisfaction by settlement' to the creditors of the bills of exchange on delivery of the bills of exchange.[87] This example clearly shows that Supreme Court files are suitable sources for imparting information on commercial law issues, and thus indirectly explain commercial law aspects.

It therefore appears, based on the commercial expert opinions, that commercial law institutions, namely customary institutions, were equally implemented, developed and spread in the form of a knowledge transfer. Individual works on lower instances have already shown in what form and to what extent especially instituted commercial courts or commercial committees based there were used for commercial law matters as an essential feature of early modern regulatory authority in order to guarantee legal certainty.[88] The Imperial Chamber Court as a supreme court played a special role in this respect, because it could substantially contribute to legal harmonisation due to its scope of application throughout the Empire, all the more in a legal area which otherwise often had a restraining effect on trade because of its particularly high legal fragmentation. While the expert opinions were on the one hand primarily drawn up by merchants for merchants, they were on the other

86 Of October 12, 1793, ISG Frankfurt a. M. RKG n. 798, [Q] 114, Subadj. Litt. B ad n. 7.

87 Settlement of March 18, 1795, ISG Frankfurt a. M. RKG n. 798, [Q] 124, n. 796 [Q] 49.

88 Helmut G. Walther, 'Die Rezeption Paduaner Rechtswissenschaft durch die Aufnahme Paduaner Konsilien in die Nürnberger Ratschlagbücher', in Irmgard Baumgärtner (ed.), *Consilia im späten Mittelalter* (Sigmaringen: Thorbecke, 1995), 207–224; Simona Cerutti, *Giustizia sommaria: Pratiche e ideali di giustizia in una società di ancien régime* (Milano: Feltrinelli, 2003); Amalia D. Kessler, *A Revolution in Commerce: The Parisian Merchant Court and the Rise of Commercial Society in Eighteenth-century France* (New Haven, Conn.: Yale University Press, 2007).

hand also consulted beyond the concrete case of application for deciding on similar cases, so that a generally applicable commercial law beyond particularities could emerge based on the *Pareres*, backed up by the ruling bodies – first and foremost the Imperial Chamber Court. However, a systematic examination as to whether this working hypothesis is viable, taking it further than the individual cases examined here, is yet to come.

b Considerations by Law Faculties

The legal discussions and decision proposals of the law faculties involved in lower court procedures by the submission of files, which were frequently appended to the Imperial Chamber Court files as part of the *acta priora*, and also constitute sources which are relevant here, are to be evaluated in a similar way, because it can be frequently observed that the Imperial Chamber Court adopted the considerations of the law faculties. One example in this respect is the case of Bourne *versus* Küchler, which dealt with the limitation of a guarantee of a bill of exchange (*Wechselbürgschaft*).[89] The guarantee of a bill of exchange, also called a surety (*Aval*), was the obligation of a third party to pay the sum stated on the bill of exchange in case of late payment. This third party could commit itself on the bill of exchange itself, separately to the acceptor, the drawer, or the endorser.[90] If he did not do so, and the guarantee was declared in a separate deed, it was questionable whether legal consequences should depend on the regulations applicable to bills of exchange or on those of ordinary law. Thus, it was particularly controversial whether the limitation of the guarantee should depend on the generally applicable regulations of ordinary law on the statute of limitations, or on any special regulations of the law on bills of exchange.[91] The obligation under common guarantees was subject

89 Further details in Amend-Traut, *Wechselverbindlichkeiten*, 284–289; Anja Amend, 'Gerichtslandschaft Altes Reich im Spiegel einer Wechselbürgschaft', in Anja Amend et al. (eds.), *Gerichtslandschaft Altes Reich: Höchste Gerichtsbarkeit und territoriale Rechtsprechung* (Köln: Böhlau, 2007), 7–15.

90 Further details in Jacob Friederich Ludovici, *Einleitung zum Wechsel-Prozeß*, 9th ed. (Halle, 1743), IV. Cap., § XCIII; Jaques Savary, *Le parfait Negotiant*, 4th ed. (Lyon: Chez Jacques Lyons, 1697), 1. Part, Liv. III, Chap. VI, 174f., Chap. VII, 184f. On the historic development of the guarantee of a bill of exchange, see Georg Schaps, *Zur Geschichte des Wechselindossaments* (1892; repr. Leipzig: Zentralantiquariat der Deutschen Demokratischen Republik, 1975), § 9, 48ff.

91 This problematic issue is dealt with in particular by Johann Ludwig Hetzler in his disputation *De Differentiis Juris Romani et Juris Cambialis Hodierni in Fidejussione* (Strasbourg, University Diss., 1775), here § XII, 31. Reference to it is also made by Küchler in his publication '*Actenmäßige Beleuchtung in bey Hochansehnlichem Schöffenrath zu Frankfurt am*

to the thirty-year limitation of claims according to ordinary law.[92] What then, if a guarantee relating to a debt on a bill of exchange was in dispute, but was not a 'guarantee of a bill of exchange' in the narrow sense? In this respect, a legal dispute arose in the 1770s between Claude Bourne and Johann Wilhelm Küchler. In this legal dispute, seven years had gone by since the bill of exchange had been protested before a claim was asserted against the guarantor, Küchler.[93]

The decision of the Imperial Chamber Court substantially followed the considerations of the law faculty Frankfurt an der Oder, which acted for the lower instance. Upon its *rationes dubitandi et decidendi* which were available to the Imperial Chamber Court as part of the preliminary files, the guarantee of the bill of exchange was considered as being 'entirely expired' (*völlig erloschen*). The reasons were primarily based on Article 20 of the French *Ordonnance du Commerce* of 1673. The short – three-year – limitation of guarantees relating to bills of exchange was expressly oriented towards the functional capacity of trade. The carelessness of a holder of a bill of exchange would be too well supported if he were granted a 30-year period for asserting his claim against a guarantor of a bill of exchange. 'It was not uncommon that the children and grandchildren were requested to pay the debts of their parents and grandparents, of which they did not even have knowledge, and were by this hardship forced into tearful ruin through no fault of their own'.[94] The objection that the French regulation was not applicable here, because it required that it had to be a special bill guarantee, and that the guarantee in dispute was not noted down on the bill of exchange itself but was issued as a separate deed, was

Mayn rechtshängigen Sachen des Lyoner Gallonen-Fabricanten Claude Bourne, Klägern; contra den Handelsmann Johann Wilhelm Küchler zu Frankfurt, Beklagten. Gegen das von dem Bourne in den Druck gegebene Memoire und weiter nachgefolgte Fait, als ein ausführlicher und gewissenmäßiger Unterricht zu näherer Belehrung des Publici entworfen und zum Druck befördert' (Frankfurt, 1775), in ISG Frankfurt a. M. RKG n. 947, [Q] 34, here § 145, 51.

92 On the development of the Roman legal institution see Max Kaser, *Das römische Privatrecht*, 3 vols. (München: Beck, 1955–1959), 3:3. Cap. 2, 46f. A summary with further substantiations can be found in Ekkehard Kaufmann, 'Verjährung', *HRG*, vol. V (Berlin: Schmidt, 1998), cols. 734–7.

93 On the facts, see in particular the publication of Küchler contained in the files, ISG Frankfurt a. M. RKG n. 949, [Q] 34.

94 Thus Küchler's ornate translation of the French commercial law scholar Savary, ISG Frankfurt a. M. RKG n. 949, [Q] 34, § 149, 53. The latter (see above, n. 90) in this regard states: '*Il y a plusieurs exemples des inconveniens qui en sont arrivez, dont plusieurs familles ont esté ruinées...*', 174.

countered by the law faculty by stating that Art. 20 did not contain such restriction, but referred 'simply to the caution given for the coincidences of bills of exchange'.[95] By its judgment, the Imperial Chamber Court released Küchler from all payment obligations.[96] It agreed with the views of the law faculty and thus with the regulations under the *Ordonnance*, but without explicitly declaring them to be applicable.

This shows that the Supreme Court was open to searching for models and explanations beyond territorial boundaries to arrive at practically oriented solutions in cases of commercial law. Roman Law did not enable a satisfactory, i.e. practicable result, so that the court adopted the considerations of the law faculty which on its part took recourse to the content of the regulations of the *Ordonnance du Commerce*. This was created in addition to the two further partial codifications *Ordonnance civile* and *Ordonnance de la Marine* under Ludwig XIV and his minister Jean Baptiste Colbert (1619–1683) and superseded both Roman Law and domestic law. A generally applicable, commercial law beyond particularities could also develop on the basis of decision proposals drawn up by law faculties mainly in lower instance proceedings, due to the fact that a higher court adopted the evaluations and applied them to further relevant cases.

4 Legislative Measures

In addition to their function as judicial bodies, the two institutions under consideration here also acted in a broader sense in a legislative capacity. A further approach was deliberately followed here, which did not necessarily run through a formal legislative procedure in compliance with eligible admissibility criteria.

4.1 *Common Orders* (Gemeine Bescheide) *of the Imperial Chamber Court*

Thus, the Imperial Chamber Court also produced – albeit only occasionally – sources of commercial law in the form of so-called Common Orders, which regulated the free trade of goods. This source genre, recently compiled in an edition of Peter Oestmann,[97] proves very impressively that the Imperial

95 ISG Frankfurt a. M. RKG n. 949, without [Q], file number 1465, C., from fol. 15^{v}.

96 Of September 7, 1778, ISG Frankfurt a. M. RKG n. 949, [Q] 107, fol. 5^{v}.

97 Peter Oestmann, *Gemeine Bescheide: Teil 1: Reichskammergericht 1497–1805* (Köln: Böhlau Verlag, 2013).

Chamber Court did not create legal sources solely by legal interpretation and development in the form of court decisions to be taken, but that in addition it also created laws on its own accord and directly, without having been acknowledged as a legislative instance beside the Emperor and the Empire.

The Common Orders primarily contained procedural and administrative supervisory instructions for future court practice. However, in individual cases Common Orders are on record which contain commercial law references. Just like the commercial ordinances worked out by the Aulic Council based on the Emperor's stipulations, they constitute edicts according to contemporary view.[98] Three Common Orders prescribe codes of conduct for officials (*Kamerale*),[99] subject to punishment in case of violation, requesting proper market conduct *vis-à-vis* the domestic population and prohibited the so-called '*Fürkauf*',[100] i.e. usurious trade. Thus, the contractual freedom of the addressees was limited – guided by welfare state considerations.[101] One of the three Common Orders states: 'As in purchasing food and other items required in the house, proper behaviour has to be observed in all respects so that nobody shall refuse to pay sellers a fair price, depending on the season, but also no excessive price shall be paid, the members of the Imperial Court are hereby seriously instructed not to cause any price increase to the detriment of both other inhabitants and themselves by hasty purchases or excessive offers, and to cooperatively report any excessive purchase price claims to the market master correspondingly instructed here by the honourable council'.[102] It had to be ensured that the court and its staff, mostly more solvent than the local city residents, did not fall into disrepute through excessively expensive business transactions. Increases in the prices of goods should not be attributable to any misconduct by members of the court.

These regulations, which at first glance seem to suggest commercial law aspects, must not hide the fact that neither its addressees were traders or merchants, but officials (*Kamerale*), nor that the economic actions described in the notices were actions within the scope of an enterprise. Given that thus neither

---

98 Thus also Oestmann, *Gemeine Bescheide*, 582.

99 Common Orders of August 22, 1607, February 10, 1690, and October 4, 1690. With individual substantiations set forth in Oestmann, *Gemeine Bescheide*, n. 99, 299f., n. 221, 575f., n. 225, 581f.

100 On this, Albrecht Cordes, 'Fürkauf', *HRG*, vol. 1, 2nd ed. (Berlin: Schmidt, 2008), cols. 1876–8.

101 Oestmann, *Gemeine Bescheide*, 71.

102 Common Order of February 10, 1690. With individual substantiations set forth in Oestmann, *Gemeine Bescheide*, n. 221, 575f.

in subjective nor objective terms[103] any commercial law matter was covered by the Common Orders, these also cannot be seen as sources of commercial law.

4.2 *Privileges – The Aulic Council as Executive Body*

Although German court rulings in the late Middle Ages and early Modern Age were marked by the Emperor's supreme jurisdiction over the Empire which was in existence until 1806, many imperial estates had since 1495 successfully sought to gain partial or full sovereignty of their own jurisdiction. This could be achieved in two ways: on the one hand, a request could be addressed to the Imperial Vice-Chancellor or – this was common practice – an application for the granting of corresponding privileges was filed with the Imperial Aulic Council in its capacity as imperial authority.[104] Once privileged in such a way, the process of law at an imperial court was excluded – except for denied or delayed administration of justice and nullity complaints.[105] From the various appeal privileges, those ones which denied an appeal for specific subject matters are of special interest here. In particular, the commercial cities of Augsburg, Bremen, Hamburg and Nuremberg insisted on being granted a privilege of exclusion from any appeal (*privilegium de non appellando*) for commercial or trade matters. These constitutional procedural law regulations, however, were

103 In this respect see the statements on sect. 2.

104 For the term of legal source (*Rechtsquelle*) and its various interpretations see Heinz Mohnhaupt, 'Die Edition von Privilegien als *Rechtsquellen* in Deutschland und in ihrer europäischen Perspective', Krakowskie Studia z Historii Państwa i Prawa 7.3(2014), 419–432, 420–422. Due to the legislative nature of the privileges, these could be issued only by a legislator – princely sovereign, pope or in particular, as here, the Emperor. According to the general view held in Imperial publications, however, a reservation applied only to 'divine and natural laws', anything prohibited by imperial laws or constitution, or also in favour of the '*iura quaesita* of a third party', so for example Carl Friedrich Häberlin, *Repertorium des Teutschen Staats und Lehnrechts*, 4 vols. (Leipzig: Weidmann, 1782–95), 4:§ 10, 289. Thus, to the extent that the constitutional status of an imperial estate was not affected, the Emperor was unrestrictedly entitled to granting privileges; see also Mohnhaupt, 'Privatrecht', 61. By derivation, the Imperial Vice-Chancellor or the Aulic Council were internally responsible, Johann Jacob Moser, *Neues teutsches Staatsrecht*, 24 vols. (1766–82; repr. Osnabrück: Zeller, 1967), 5:Cap. 16, § 112, 529. According to the findings of Friedrich Lehne, 'Zur Rechtsgeschichte der kaiserlichen Druckprivilegien', *MIÖG* 53 (1939), 323–409, 349, the files handed down indicated an overall 'large elasticity of the competences'.

105 In summary, see Ulrich Eisenhardt, *Die kaiserlichen privilegia de non appellando* (Köln: Böhlau, 1980), 25–27 with further substantiations. However, access to an imperial court nonetheless often remained impossible when the territorial court official delegated his supervision of the courts to a supreme territorial court; on this recently see Stefan Andreas Stodolkowitz, 'Rechtsverweigerung und Territtorialjustiz: Verfahren wegen iustitia denegata vel protracta am Oberappellationsgericht Celle', *ZRG.GA* 131 (2014), 130–181.

of course not addressed to the individual traders, but to the imperial cities. Thus, the trade guild was only indirectly affected by these special rights. The first privilege of this kind was granted in 1508 to the City of Nuremberg for 'purchase and sale disputes' (*Kaufhändel*).[106]

Given that 'the daily crafts and merchants in the City of Bremen had so much expanded and increased on land and on the water', the Bremen Council felt that the proper administration of the City's interests was being threatened. For the 'legal disputes between the foreign merchants trading here' as also for any transactions between them and the citizens and residents of Bremen, the establishment of a new branch of court for disputes resulting from such transactions was applied for 'for the common good' (*zum gemeinen nutz*). Such a branch of court should be staffed by 'two or three honourable sensible men [from among the Council members], together with one legal scholar'. In 1541 the City obtained the privilege for all relevant disputes with 'a principal sum not exceeding six hundred florins in gold' for which henceforth no appeal to any imperial court was admissible.[107] The Augsburg privilege excluded any matters relating 'generally to actions by merchants, their exchange and mercantile transactions' from appeal,[108] a further Nuremberg privilege 'disputes in respect of currency', i.e. coinage disputes,[109] and the benefit granted to the City of Hamburg related to all decisions in disputes regarding claims documented by deeds, 'commercial establishments, companies, bottomry, currency exchange, insurances' and all disputes arising in connection with commerce and trade among the merchants.[110]

At first glance, the granting of such rights, through which the Emperor relinquished his court supremacy and thus an essential part of his sovereign power, seems to be hardly comprehensible. This is also reflected in various expert opinions of the Aulic Council on petitions for the granting of appeal privileges; the expert opinion on the petition of the City of Bremen for an extension of its privilege, for example, states that, as was commonly known, the 'appeal

106 Privilege for Nuremberg of March 14, 1508, city archive Nuremberg B 11 n. 385.

107 The original of July 15, 1541 is part of the wartime losses. The certified copy of April 5, 1661 has been preserved, StaatsA Bremen, Privilegarium collationatum 1663 (compilation of the Bremen privileges confirmed by the imperial court chancery in Vienna in 1661) StAB 2-P.1. – 118 fol. 96^{r}–100^{v}.

108 *Privilegium de non appellando* v. September 4, 1627, StA Augsburg, Deeds 913, fol. 6^{r}, repeated in 10^{r}, 12^{v}.

109 *Privilegium de non appellando* of November 3, 1629, in an entry in the book of copies (Kopialbuch) from the seventeenth century: Extensio Privilegii Appellationis Für die Statt Nürnberg, 1630, StadtA Nürnberg, A 6 n. 729.

110 *Privilegium de non appellando* v. March 31, 1634, StA Hamburg, Threse C 7 fol. 5^{v}, 6^{r}.

privileges granted in former times already restricted the imperial office more than too much, and that the true foundation of the heavily declining supreme imperial authority had to be respected'.[111]

However, the reasons given in the granting of privileges provide an insight into the overriding interests which the Emperor also pursued for the Empire: Thus, the confirmation of the privilege granted to the City of Augsburg by Emperor Ferdinand II states that 'it would be highly detrimental and harmful for it as one of the leading commercial cities (in which, according to the rights also described in imperial decrees, the disputes between merchants and other disputes, where the consequences and circumstances would result in damage in case of a delay, should be decided on rapidly and shortly, *ex aequo et bono*...) if the principle of good faith in matters of obligations, trade and transactions were diminished from day to day and the danger were obviously given that the decrees of the magistrate do not retain their real authority, and illiquid persons and delinquent debtors then cause damage to many poor widows and orphans by fraud and improper actions, others besides them become illiquid and cause trouble, disturb the exactness of commercial records, thievishly collect outstanding debts, misappropriate goods of value, look for the opportunity to escape and finally cause irreparable damage to all creditors concerned, so that because of the aforementioned circumstances ... in order to further the common good and to cause domestic and foreign persons to act more carefully, the trade and the financial standing of the merchants of the City of Augsburg has to be strengthened'.[112] It had of course also been noticed at the Emperor's Court that especially in commercial disputes, delays had to be avoided, especially if there were clear time limits to the presence of the disputing parties during trade fairs. A dispute, however, was regularly considerably extended by a

111 Concept of April 14, 1768, HHStA (=Haus-, Hof- und Staatsarchiv of Vienna), RHR, Priv. de non appell., KARTON 2. Similarly already the expert opinions on the applications of the Dukes of Mecklenburg of August 9, 1629 and of October 19, 1651, Konzepte, RHR, Priv. de non appell., KARTON 5, Konv. 1 and 2, on the applications of the landgrave of Hessen-Darmstadt of October 29, 1630, of July 12, 1631 and of February 27, 1635, Konzepte, HHStA, RHR, Priv. de non appell., KARTON 4, Konv. 3, on the application of Hamburg of March 28, 1634, 2 Konzepte, HHStA, RHR, Priv. de non appell., KARTON 4, Konv. 1, on two applications of Nuremberg of January 23, 1657 and of May 16, 1659, Konzepte, HHStA, RHR, Priv. de non appell., KARTON 6, on the application of the Archbishop of Cologne for the Hildesheim monastery of December 15, 1664, Konzept, HHStA, RHR, Priv. de non appell., KARTON 4, Konv. 2, and on one application of Frankfurt of April 26, 1743, Konzept, HHStA, Reichskanzlei, Priv. de non appell., KARTON 3, Konv. 4.

112 *Privilegium de non appellando* of September 4, 1627, StA Augsburg, Deeds 913, fol. 4^v, 5^r.

lengthy legal process at one of the two imperial courts. To maintain a flourishing trade, the prerequisites for the swift handling of contradictory procedures had to be created locally. The Bremen merchants also sought an appeal privilege to accommodate the interests of out-of-town merchants, who 'were not insignificantly interested' in a beneficial law for their trade, i.e. in achieving a swift completion of a legal dispute. In contrast, all complications 'clearly impaired the common benefits'.[113] This aspect of increasing the attractiveness of a trading place, particularly also for strangers, was already evident in the deeds of the so-called founding towns since the twelfth century.[114]

A result of this imperial privilege was that the administration of justice in disputes with commercial or economic implications should be substantially territorialised – at least *de jure* – according to the ideas of the sovereigns.[115] In the 1980s, Eisenhardt had already analysed the special influence of the appeal privileges on the forming and application of domestic law in a commercial law context.[116] However, it has not yet been conclusively clarified whether this was actually the case, and whether an independent commercial law which adapted to the respective market conditions could be maintained and developed in the commercial cities despite the otherwise Romanising tendencies[117]

---

113 See above n. 107.

114 Primarily to be named here is the market privilege for Freiburg i. Br. of 1120 (under dispute) and the Berner Handfeste (Charter of Bern) of 1218. More details on the Freiburg privilege Karl Kroeschell, *Deutsche Rechtsgeschichte (bis 1250)*, 3 vols., 13th ed. (Köln: Böhlau, 2008), 1:237–242, 249–251. A critical examination of it by Marita Blattmann, *Die Freiburger Stadtrechte zur Zeit der Zähringer: Rekonstruktion der verlorenen Urkunden und Aufzeichnungen des 12. und 13. Jahrhunderts*, 2 vols. (Freiburg i. Br.: Ploetz, 1991), vol. 1. A translation of the text of the Bern deed in Hans Strahm, *Die Berner Handfeste* (Bern: Huber, 1953), 152–181.

115 This connection is also pointed out by Mohnhaupt, 'Privatrecht', 65, with further substantiations.

116 Ulrich Eisenhardt, 'Überlegungen zu der Frage, ob die Befreiung von der höchsten Reichsgerichtsbarkeit in einigen deutschen Reichsstädten die Entwicklung eines von der Rezeption des römischen und kanonischen Rechts im Wesentlichen unbeeinflussten partikularen Handelsrechts ermöglicht hat', in Hugo de Schepper (ed.), *Höchste Gerichtsbarkeit im Spätmittelalter und der Frühen Neuzeit: Internationales Rechtshistorisches Symposium, Amsterdam 1.–3. Juni 1984* (Amsterdam: Faculteit der Rechtsgeleerdheid, 1985), 89–103; id., *privilegia*, 56.

117 Cf. Art. 3 RKGO of 1495, according to which common law was presumed to be known to the court, while the parties had to submit the applicability of particular law regulations. Stating that in the territories the Imperial Chamber Court most often enforced common law to the detriment of a particular law and ultimately ousted domestic law

which can be observed in the supreme court rulings. To date, there are no studies on lower court rulings in the commercial law matters of the privileged cities.[118] Ebert-Weidenfeller proved for Hamburg at least that the decisions of the Hamburg Higher Court were essentially confirmed by the Imperial Chamber Court,[119] whereby 'the autonomy of shaping the law in the territory was essentially furthered by the Imperial Chamber Court practice'.[120] And with regard to the law on bills of exchange, it could be shown that the Imperial Chamber Court regularly confirmed decisions of the Frankfurt lower courts, when they dealt with the interpretation of the particular law on bills of exchange.[121] These findings, however, are less attributable to the imperial privileges as commercial law sources, and more to the fact that the Roman Law particularly did

---

in legal practice, Bernhard Diestelkamp, 'Die Bedeutung des Reichskammergerichts für die Rechtsentwicklung im Heiligen Römischen Reich Deutscher Nation. Eine (Zwischen-) Bilanz', in Jörg Wolff (ed.), *Kultur- und rechtshistorische Wurzeln Europas* (Mönchengladbach: Forum Verlag Godesberg, 2006), 459–474, 462ff. Meanwhile, more recent studies have proven that this has not always been the case in legal practice: on a commercial law matter Anja Amend-Traut, *Wechselverbindlichkeiten*; further, Peter Oestmann, *Rechtsvielfalt vor Gericht: Rechtsanwendung und Partikularrecht im Alten Reich* (Frankfurt am Main: Klostermann, 2002).

118 For Nuremberg, the project 'Die Nürnberger Handelsgerichtsbarkeit. Handelsgerichtliche Gutachten in der Frühen Neuzeit' headed by Anja Amend-Traut has taken up this work, sponsored by the German Research Foundation (DFG).

119 The fact that the number of 'commercial disputes' referred to the Imperial Chamber Court from the Imperial City of Hamburg was not significantly reduced even after the privilege had been granted might in particular be based on the controversial definition of the term commercial dispute: Harscher von Almendingen, 'In wie fern erklären die Reichsgesetze überhaupt und die Hamburger Appellationsprivilegien insbesondere Handlungssachen für inappellabel?', in *Reichskammergerichtliche Miscellen* 2 (1806), 1–11, 9f., who states that despite the Hamburg privilege for commercial matters, disputes relating to bills of exchange were continuously heard before the Imperial Chamber Court. This statement has meanwhile been confirmed by the data presented by means of the statistical analysis of the entire file collection of the Imperial Court: Anette Baumann, *Die Gesellschaft der Frühen Neuzeit im Spiegel der Reichskammergerichtsprozesse: Eine sozialgeschichtliche Untersuchung zum 17. und 18. Jahrhundert* (Köln: Böhlau, 2001), 43. The so-called Kameralliteratur, i.e. the literary genre dealing specifically with the supreme jurisdiction of the Old Empire, contains references to Hamburg proceedings dealing with bills of exchange, see for example Cramer, *Nebenstunden*, 14:Part 56, V, 2–4. More details in Andreas Ebert-Weidenfeller, *Hamburgisches Kaufmannsrecht im 17. und 18. Jahrhundert* (Frankfurt am Main: P. Lang, 1992), 35–46, 253–261; Amend-Traut, *Wechselverbindlichkeiten*, 166f.

120 Ebert-Weidenfeller, *Kaufmannsrecht*, 291.

121 Amend-Traut, *Wechselverbindlichkeiten*.

not offer any suitable instruments for resolving individual disputes, either for Hamburg mercantile law in particular, or for the law on bills of exchange in general.[122]

Finally, at this point reference shall be made to the debit commissions of the Aulic Council. Upon their establishment, direct imperial territories were put under compulsory administration, particularly due to financial mismanagement.[123] Apart from an expert opinion of the Aulic Council of 1653, the legal basis was provided by the Aulic Council Rules and the Latest Imperial Recess. The 'furthering of justice and salvation of the distressed' were explicitly named as reasons.[124] The – not undisputed – competence of the Emperor was for these cases also essentially derived from his office as chief justice,[125] because the commissions of the Aulic Council in general, i.e. also with regard to debt management, should support the Emperor in this judicial function. At the same time, however, the concern for the members of the Empire praised in the electoral capitulations played as much of a role as his position as supreme feudal lord did as far as imperial estates were concerned, or his position as town lord when imperial cities were concerned.

The network of regulations going back to the activities of these 'institutionalised and in their course largely uniform'[126] commissions is, however, only then a commercial law source when as an exception it was addressed to a merchant or his enterprise. Without any doubt, however, their main emphasis was on the attentive interest in the economic restructuring of the territories concerned and the protection of the people from an over-indebtedness of the sovereigns, as they were the ones primarily threatened by its consequences.

122 More details Amend-Traut, *Wechselverbindlichkeiten*, 422–429.

123 Finally in this respect see Leopold Auer, 'Zwangsverwaltungen in den Territorien des Alten Reiches: Zu den reichshofrätlichen Debitkommissionen im 18. Jahrhundert', in Fabian Frommelt (ed.), *Zwangsadministrationen: Legitimierte Fremdverwaltung im historischen Vergleich (17.–21. Jh.)* (Berlin: Duncker & Humblot, 2014), 45–62.

124 Individual evidence in Auer, 'Zwangsverwaltungen', 49.

125 More details in Heinrich Wilhelm Bergsträßer, *Merkwürdige Reichshofraths-Gutachten mit Gesichtspunkten für den Leser*, 4 vols. (Frankfurt, 1792–5), 2:183–198, here in particular 183f., even though the Aulic Council speaker reporting on the mentioned case agreed with the debtor's objection that all affairs of clemency remain with the emperor ('*alle Gnadensachen und Strafen* [*seien*] *als Effecten ihrer Landesregierung, mithin nicht ad Camerale gehörig*': '*Hierinnen muß nun meines Orts derselben beyfallen. Gnadensachen gehören gemeiniglich zur Chatoulle und verbleiben des Regenten Handgelder*'), *ibid.*, 192f.

126 Auer, 'Zwangsverwaltungen', 56.

4.3 *The Aulic Council as a Political Advisory and Administrative Body*

The Emperor not only interfered with the rulings of the Imperial Chamber Court as already described above.[127] At the level of economic policy, the Emperor also tried to maintain commodity trading and to further commercial capital by means of the Aulic Council. He did this by various kinds of trade policy decisions (compromises, imperial decrees, mandates, and the like), which arose from individual legal disputes and acquired, or could have acquired, normative character.

Thus, in the fifteenth century a taxation of trade capital and commodities was dismissed on the occasion of a discussion about an empire-wide tax, because the merchants liable to pay tax only had insufficient cash reserves – due to the paying out of considerable cash amounts to the coffers of the papal court and the imperial court, but also to Venice and other countries, and in addition due to the commercial habit of handling transactions through trade credits and non-cash payment options, so-called clearings, 'so that there was not enough money in the country to obey to the imposition, even if transactions were handled in cash'. This would endanger the existence of merchants and the groups corresponding with them, and deprive them of their bases.[128]

Other internal imperial efforts in promoting trade were also successful. Thus, in a dispute between Hamburg and Magdeburg on the one hand and the Dukes Heinrich and Wilhelm the Younger of Braunschweig-Lüneburg on the other, the Emperor succeeded in conciliating the parties' differences by means of a compromise after setting up a commission 'for amicable and legal trading'.[129] The case dealt with the freedom of the two Hanseatic cities to navigate on the Elbe, which had been blocked by the Dukes in 1567/68. The Dukes had demanded that the traded goods be unloaded in Lüneburg and further transported by land. The declared intention of the negotiations, with the involvement of the Aulic Council, was to reach a decision giving due regard to the 'common good'.[130] This successful conciliation procedure also had the character of a legal source, due to its sustainable and intergenerational effect – not only *inter partes*, but *inter omnes*; all merchants who wanted to use this trade route travelling to and from Hamburg and Magdeburg during the following

127 In this respect see the statements in Section 3.b.

128 Johannes Janssen, *Frankfurts Reichscorrespondenz*, 2 vols. (Freiburg: Herder, 1863–72), 2, 1:348. On that see also Eberhard Isenmann, 'Reichsfinanzen und Reichssteuern im 15. Jahrhundert', *ZHF* 7 (1980), 1–76, 129–218, here 178f. with further substantiations.

129 HHStA, RHR, Antiqua, 12/4a, inv. n. 192, imperial privileges to the cities of Hamburg, fols. 39^{r}–42^{v}, and Magdeburg, fols. 43^{r}–45^{v}, notification about the establishment of a commission, fol. 205^{r}.

130 HHStA, RHR, Antiqua, 12/4a, inv. n. 192, fol. 117^{r}.

time successfully invoked the regulation brought about with the Emperor's help.

The currently ongoing indexing work on the Aulic Council's file materials[131] also reveals the abundance of petitions by which individual merchants or trading companies applied for the granting of special commercial privileges, such as trade, factory,[132] inventor, or printing privileges,[133] regarding coins, customs, market and trade fair,[134] trade monopolies or moratoria,[135] especially since they are only occasionally published in the large law collections of the *Ancien Régime*.[136] The granting of such privileges was principally subject to considerable restrictions, on the one hand 'because the right to grant privileges is attached to the legislative power', which, however, could not be exercised by the Emperor without the cooperation of the imperial estates.[137] On the other hand, privileges and 'monopolies granted for particular types of medicines,

131 On the currently ongoing interpretation project of the Academy of Sciences in Göttingen, in cooperation with the Commission for the History of Austrian Law of the Austrian Academy of Sciences and the Austrian State Archives (Haus-, Hof- und Staatsarchiv), see Tobias Schenk, 'Ein Erschließungsprojekt für die Akten des Kaiserlichen Reichshofrats', *Archivar* 63 (2010), 285–290.

132 Gustav Otruba, 'Von den "Fabriksprivilegien" des 17. und 18. Jahrhunderts zum "Österreichischen Fabrikenrecht" 1838', *Scripta Mercaturae* 10:2 (1976), 75–108.

133 The latter were examined by Lehne, 'Druckprivilegien', inter alia on the basis of the Aulic Council records, here in particular 348f., 360–372. Of recent date – with the focus on case files – see Thomas Gergen, 'Auseinandersetzungen um Kölner Druckprivilegien vor dem Reichshofrat', a paper given at the conference 'In letzter Instanz. Appellation und Revision im Europa der Frühen Neuzeit' (Vienna, September 7–9, 2011); Thomas Gergen, 'Kopierschutz im Alten Reich. Prozesse (insbesondere Appellationen und Vollstreckungsersuchen) über Kölner Druckprivilegien (*privilegia impressoria*) vor dem Reichshofrat in Vienna', in Èva Jakab (ed.), *Geistiges Eigentum und Urheberrecht aus der historischen Perspektive, Internationaler Kongress vom 17.–19. Mai 2012 an der Staats- und Rechtswissenschaftlichen Fakultät der Universität Szeged* (Lectiones Iuridicae) 10 (Szeged, 2013), 9–26.

134 For further details about the *privilegia de nundinis* see Johann Jacob Moser, *Teutsches Staats-Recht*, 50 vols., 2nd ed. (1737–53, repr. Osnabrück: Zeller, 1968), 5:Cap. 84, 303–324.

135 Particularly in times of economic crisis, such as for example the 30-year war, debtors – including in particular merchants or trading companies – applied for such protection of the assets against quick seizure by creditors in order to prolong their payment period and to be able to continue participating in economic life and contributing to 'the common good'. On the moratoria see Moser, *Neues teutsches Staatsrecht*, 5:Cap. 15, § 93, 389–396. On the older history of the institution see Adolf Mayer, 'Studien über das Moratorium des Altertums und Mittelalters im Rahmen der gleichzeitigen Kreditwirtschaft', in *Jahrbücher für Nationalökonomie und Statistik* 108 (1917), 417–477.

136 This was already pointed out by Mohnhaupt, 'Privatrecht', 63.

137 Häberlin, *Repertorium*, 4:§, 4, 285.

pills, balm, rosemary quintessence and the like to the persons trading in them' violated the prohibition of monopolies laid down in Art. 7 Section 3 of the electoral capitulation. However, imperial publications held the view that the granting of such liberties by the Emperor was permissible if and to the extent that the imperial estates did not raise any objections.[138]

Due to the fact that they were effective for and against everybody during the period of their binding force, these privileges may easily be referred to as commercial law sources.[139] This finding has subsequently been transferred to privileges for using trademarks, and linked to that generalised for another field of the commercial law.[140]

Only one example shall be mentioned: Peter von Hame, who came from Brussels, was upon his request granted the imperial privilege in 1665 for distributing the water of an acidic spring, i.e. the spring of a mineral water, in Eger for ten years.[141] His application was supported by the Dean and the faculty of medicine in Vienna, to 'have the poor patients feel health and the good effect and operation [of the water]'.[142] The extent of the binding force provided by such privilege, the profitability of such trade privileges to the beneficiary, and the severe impact on others is reflected by the subsequent intensive endeavours of the mayor and the municipal council of the City of Regensburg regarding this 'gift of God'. They stated that the imperial privilege conflicted with earlier privileges granted to them by the Bohemian Crown. They therefore asked for either its cancellation or at least for the express release of the City of Regensburg and its citizens from the penal provisions established in the privilege.[143]

In this context, the efforts to found a so-called privileged trading company between the Holy Roman Empire of the German Nation and Spain have to be pointed out. On the one hand they were intended to help return the

138 Häberlin, *Repertorium*, 4:§ 5, 286 with further substantiations.

139 Heinz Mohnhaupt, 'Erteilung und Widerruf von Privilegien nach der gemeinrechtlichen Lehre vom 16. bis 19. Jahrhundert', in Barbara Dölemeyer and Heinz Mohnhaupt (eds.), *Das Privileg im europäischen Vergleich,* vol. 1 (Frankfurt a.M.: Klostermann, 1999), 93–121, 109.

140 Anja Amend-Traut, 'Sich der Concurrenz erwehren…'. Kaufmännischer Wettbewerb unter höchstgerichtlicher Kontrolle (16.–18. Jh.), in Eva Schumann (ed.), *Justiz und Verfahren* im Wandel der Zeit. Gelehrte Literatur, Gerichtliche Praxis und bildlicher Symbolik. Festgose für Wolfgang Sellert zum 80. Geburtstag (Berlin: De Gruyter, 2017), 55–82.

141 Privilege of September 7, 1665, HHStA, RHR, Antiqua, 2/2, inv.n. 19, fols. 5r–7v, 12r–14v.

142 Quotation RHR, Antiqua, 2/2, inv.n. 19, fol. 6r. Intercession letter in HHStA, RHR, Antiqua, 2/2, inv.n. 19, fols 46r–47v.

143 Aulic Council record of proceedings, HHStA, RHR, Antiqua, 2/2, inv.n. 19, fols. 16r–17v.

secessionist Dutch provinces to the Spanish Crown and to restore or preserve the highly sensitive religious balance of Europe during the Thirty Years War. These military and political interests however were on the other hand linked to economic interests. The Emperor expected a reliable maritime trade partner to open up a market previously largely closed to the Empire. As shown in the Aulic Council files, the legal instrument used for this purpose was again not the *Ius Commune*, but the principle of specific law. The draft contract for a planned trade cooperation as the actual core of these varied strategic considerations provides insight into the legal structure of the early privileged trading companies, showing surprising parallels to the laws of modern corporations.[144] This treaty would have been easily classified as a legal source for commercial law due to its privilege nature – the matter concerned was the granting of staple right[145] for the Hanseatic cities – particularly because it was well suited to serve as a model for further establishments of this kind due to its legal precision and balance. However, the venture ultimately failed due to the lack of willingness to cooperate shown by the Hanseatic Cities, so that the 'maritime projects of the Habsburgs were abandoned forever'.[146]

On the other hand, the efforts of the imperial authority to turn around the brittle trade treaty with Great Britain for the benefit of the Empire showed no

144 For further detail see Anja Amend-Traut, 'Der Reichshofrat und die Kapitalgesellschaften: Die Bemühungen um eine Handelscompanie zwischen den Hansestädten und Spanien', in Anja Amend-Traut, Albrecht Cordes and Wolfgang Sellert (eds.), *Geld, Handel, Wirtschaft: Höchste Gerichte im Alten Reich als Spruchkörper und Institution* (Berlin: De Gruyter, 2013), 61–89; Anja Amend-Traut, 'The Aulic Council and Incorporated Companies: Efforts to Establish a Trading Company between the Hanseatic Cities and Spain', *Annales Universitatis Scientiarum Budapestinensis De Rolando Eötvös Nominatae* 53 (2012), 203–283.

145 Apart from numerous territorially concentrated studies on staple right, see in general Max Hafemann, *Das Stapelrecht: Eine rechtshistorische Untersuchung* (Leipzig: Duncker & Humblot, 1910), here in particular 29; Otto Gönnenwein, *Das Stapel- und Niederlagsrecht* (Weimar: Böhlau, 1939); Ulf Dirlmeier, 'Mittelalterliche Zoll- und Stapelrechte als Handelshemmnisse?', in Hans Pohl (ed.), *Die Auswirkungen von Zöllen und anderen Handelshemmnissen auf Wirtschaft und Gesellschaft vom Mittelalter bis zur Gegenwart. Referate der 11. Arbeitstagung der Gesellschaft für Sozial- und Wirtschaftsgeschichte vom 9. bis 13. April 1985 in Hohenheim* (Stuttgart: Steiner, 1987), 19–39. Substantiations on individual staple rights and corresponding literature are available through the 'Gemeinsame Portal zu Bibliotheken, Archiven und Museen', BAM-Portal on https://www.deutsche-digitale-bibliothek.de/searchresull?isThumbnailFiltered=true&gueri=stapelrecht (last visited on January 6, 2018).

146 See also Franz Mareš, 'Die maritime Politik der Habsburger in den Jahren 1625–1628', *MIÖG* 2 (1881), 49–82, 77.

effect.[147] Thus, the Emperor did in fact grant the request of the Hanseatic Cities to expel the Merchant Adventurers.[148] Within the course of several centuries, the English overseas merchants had formed ever more closely knit ties, and through trading privileges and contracts had been able to procure for themselves nearly the same position in the Empire as the local continental Europeans had. On the other hand, the renewal of trade privileges in favour of the Hanseatic Cities in Great Britain had been denied by Elisabeth I. However, the imperial mandate was never enforced due to the different economic interests in the Empire.[149]

The imperial order of 1600 to the United States of the Netherlands to withdraw announcements directed against the Hanseatic Cities and published within the Empire, in which trade with Spain and Portugal had been regulated and contravention was prohibited on pain of force, also had a normative significance, but again the imperial order could not be enforced.[150] Incidentally, it becomes clear here that under Rudolph II (1552–1612)[151] imperial policy was still extremely reserved when it came to taking external political risks at the insistence of individual subjects of the Empire, especially where their special economic interests were concerned.

In contrast, some decades later, sanctions imposed especially in times of war and crises could severely affect both the foreign opponent and the internal imperial trade sector.[152] In order to weaken the opponent as severely as possible, the imperial authority also repeatedly issued orders relating to 'commerce'. As *iura singularia* they can also be counted among the legal sources of

147 For further details see Nils Jörn, 'Die Auseinandersetzungen zwischen Hanse und Merchant Adventurers vor den obersten Reichsgerichten im 16. und 17. Jahrhundert', *Zeitschrift des Vereins für Lübeckische Geschichte und Altertumskunde* 78 (1998), 323–348, 333; Amend-Traut, 'Reichshofrat', 71f.

148 In this regard, see the petition to withdraw the imperial trade permit by the imperial fiscal prosecutor Dr Johann Wenzel, HHStA, RHR, Antiqua, 27/1, 28/1, 29/2, 29/3, 29/4, 29/5, 29/6, 29/7, 29/8, 29/9, 29/10, 29/12, 29/13, 29/20, 29/21, 29/22, 29/26, 29/27, 30/3, inv.n. 385, 393–401, 403, 404, 411–413, 417, 418, 428. In summary Anne F. Sutton, 'The Merchant Adventurers of England: Their origins and the Mercers' Company of London', *Historical Research* 75 (2002), 25–46; Jörn, 'Merchant Adventurers'.

149 HHStA, RHR, Antiqua, 29/17, inv.n. 408, fols. 1^r–2^r, 5^r. In summary see Jörn, 'Merchant Adventurers', 339–347.

150 HHStA, RHR, Antiqua, 29/32, inv.n. 423, fols. 1^r–3^v.

151 For a biography see Volker Press, 'Rudolf II. 1576–1612', in Anton Schindling and Walter Ziegler (eds.), *Die Kaiser der Neuzeit 1519–1918: Heiliges Römisches Reich, Österreich, Deutschland* (München: Beck, 1990), 99–111.

152 This was pointed out by Harpprecht, *Staats-Archiv*, 3:87, and Smend, *Reichskammergericht*, 111f., the letter with regard to the imposition of the imperial ban against individual trading towns by the Imperial Chamber Court; in this respect see further details in Section 3.1.b.

interest here, but unlike the privileges, they were not addressed to individual persons or groups of persons, but were classified as common law regulations. According to a contemporary definition, the *iura singularia* were to be understood as 'those regulations of common law, which contain an exception to the rule of older and stricter law, either for a particular age, gender, status or class of person or for a particular class of objects or for all and every subject, insofar as a particular case is given'.[153] Reference was also made to a 'rule established in the law of nations that the enemy shall not be provided with weapons, war ammunition and other necessaries required for warfare'.[154]

The ban on trade mostly imposed on merchants had been generally legitimated since the mid-seventeenth century at the latest. In this context, in particular[155] the 'thorough idea of the nature of the German commerce and its prohibition regarding France and the Spanish countries' of 1693[156] has to be pointed out, which dealt in great detail with the most varied trade transactions – thus, the export of 'sewing needles and pins' was also explained[157] – and only the trade with 'innocent' goods continued to be allowed. These orders were, without any doubt, of a normative nature; they were generally pronounced, brought into force, and were subject to penalty.

5 Conclusion

Imperial estates and especially subjects like the fore mentioned merchants regularly obtained help and support from the emperor if they could not enforce their trade interests. Commercial law was mainly developed not by regarding the formal legislative procedure, but through alternative ways such as judicial practice. The court documents presented here demonstrate different forms

153 Christian Friedrich von Glück, *Ausführliche Erläuterung der Pandecten nach Hellfeld…*, 34 vols, 2nd ed. (Erlangen, 1790–1830), 1:4. Tit., § 98, 558.

154 Harpprecht, *Staats-Archiv*, 3:87.

155 Further orders were issued in the years 1705, Kayserl. Majest. Commercien-Ordnung was vor Handels-Waaren ins Römische Reich passabel…, bei: Christian Leonhard Leucht, *Europäische Staats-Cantzley darinnen zum Behuff der neuesten politischen-, Kirchen- und Reichshistorie was sowohl in Religions-Angelegenheiten merckwürdiges vorgefallen als in Staats- und Reichs-Geschäfften vor kurztem abgehandelt worden und zum Vorschein gekommen ist*, 115 vols. (Frankfurt am Main, 1697–1734), 10:402–437, and 1734, see Leucht, *Staats-Cantzley*, 64:486ff.

156 Order of November 6, 1693 with annexes, printed in Leucht, *Staats-Cantzley*, 9:647–714.

157 Leucht, *Staats-Cantzley*, 9:662.

and manifestations of commercial law as complementary sources. Not only the petitioners and beneficiaries benefited from this. The commercial law sources generated by the Imperial Chamber Court and the Aulic Council also primarily had a positive effect on the Emperor and the Empire. This applies both with regard to their effect in terms of the political stabilisation of sovereign power, and legal harmonisation and with regard to their often economically profitable effect.

CHAPTER 10

Legal, Moral-Theological, and Genuinely Economic Opinions on Questions of Trade and Economy in Fifteenth- and Early Sixteenth-century Germany

Eberhard Isenmann

1 Introduction

In the collections of late medieval *consilia* I have examined in archives and public libraries, mainly those of Nuremberg, Augsburg, Eichstätt, Ulm and Tübingen, I could find only a relatively small number of legal opinions concerning commercial law either in a narrow and specific sense, or a wider sense. What exactly can be considered to be commercial law, or even law concerning commerce, is quite a difficult question.[1] Expert opinions on specific cases and particularly produced for litigation cannot by themselves give a more or less comprehensive definition or explanation, so therefore, different sources, such as laws, contemporary tracts, manuals and handbooks, must be consulted in order to create a structural basis for the issue and to state the opinions in an adequate context, not least in an international context.

2 Commercial Law and Law Concerning Commerce

With regard to the highly fragmented historical situation of earlier commercial law, a useful place to start and a basis for possible comparisons with the present

1 General overviews on commercial law: Levin Goldschmidt, *Universalgeschichte des Handelsrechts*, vol. 1 (Stuttgart: F. Enke, 1891); Hansjörg Pohlmann, 'Die Quellen des Handelsrechts', in Helmut Coing (ed.), *Handbuch der Quellen und Literatur der neueren Europäischen Privatrechtsgeschichte*, 3 vols. (München: C.H. Beck, 1973), 1:801–832; Karl Otto Scherner, 'Die Wissenschaft des Handelsrechts', in Helmut Coing (ed.), *Handbuch der Quellen und Literatur der neueren Europäischen Privatrechtsgeschichte*, 3 vols. (München: C.H. Beck, 1973), vol. 2, part 1, 797–997; Siegbert Lammel, 'Die Gesetzgebung des Handelsrechts', in Helmut Coing (ed.), *Handbuch der Quellen und Literatur der neueren Europäischen Privatrechtsgeschichte*, 3 vols. (München: C.H. Beck, 1973), vol. 2, part 2, 571–1083; on trade and commercial law: Eberhard Isenmann, *Die deutsche Stadt im Mittelalter 1150–1550: Stadtgestalt, Recht, Verfassung, Stadtregiment, Kirche, Gesellschaft, Wirtschaft*, 2nd ed. (Wien: Böhlau Verlag, 2014), 881–995.

 | DOI 10.1163/9789004363144_011

normative system would be to go cautiously back, but avoiding severe or uncontrolled anachronisms. That would also mean progressing from the general to the particular. Because medieval and early modern lawyers included precise economic aspects in their legal advice, or added moral-theologian considerations or discussed merely economic facts and operations, we must analyse the respective relationships between law, moral theology and economy. These different or interdependent aspects lead to the framing of the theme. In the following study, some expert opinions are only listed and mentioned with their subjects, but others are discussed in some detail as part of the argument, in order to get some insight into the legal technicalities and the intellectual qualities of the work. The specific value of these opinions, furthermore, consists of the possibility of seeing how the law and ethical norms are applied in cases of everyday transactions, as well as in the big business of large trading companies.

Commercial law today is part of private law, a special right of the merchants and the merchant profession, regulating the merchants' rights in their interrelationships. In Germany, it is set out in the Commercial Code (*Handelsgesetzbuch* – HGB) and in the Introductory Law (*Einführungsgesetz*) to the Commercial Code (EGHGB), which are directed to the specific requirements and needs of the legal and economic relationships. Commercial law has, amongst its aims, enabling fast business processing, legal clarity, publicity, creditor protection, self-responsibility, release from strict formal requirements and the use of its own commercial courts. The Civil Code (*Bürgerliches Gesetzbuch* – BGB), with regard to the Commercial Code, is applicable as a subsidiary, and its legal regulations are applied only if not otherwise specified in the Commercial Code, but it supplements the Commercial Code in important cases such as the proxy, the general partnership, the limited partnership and the right of purchase and sale.

The applicability of the Commercial Code (HGB) depends on the status of the merchant who in the Code means any person carrying on a mercantile trade (§ 1); at least one of the contracting parties involved in the transactions, must be a merchant. But it applies, deviating from the stricter sense of the term, to craft, industry and other economic branches with trade components. The legal regulations for merchants also apply to trading companies (§ 6). As between merchants all acts and omissions must be interpreted as regards their significance and effect with reference to mercantile usage (*Gebräuche*) and customs (*Gewohnheiten*) (§ 346).[2]

---

2 Cf. already previously Benvenuto Straccha, *Tractatus de mercatura seu mercatore* (1533), published 1552 in Venice, *De probationibus*, fol. 286r: *Observare etiam oportet consules nostros mores, et consuetudines mercatorum, ut inter mercatores in quottidiano casu ex facto*

The present link between the Commercial Code with its special intentions and range and the Civil Code, shows that different legal sources come together, and it is therefore not possible to find a substantial narrow definition according to Ockham's razor. For our topic, for example, as will be shown below, laws against restraints of competition by monopolies and cartels play an important role. But the intention of commercial law is to meet the profession's specific needs and requirements – resulting from organisational and economic conditions or constraints, and the desire for legal certainty. The applicability of the customs and usages of trade and the combination of different legal sources – or on a more abstract level the interaction between mandatory law (*ius cogens*), non-mandatory law (*ius dispositivum*) and subsidiary law (*subsidiäres Recht*) and the *aequitas mercatorum* as an interpretive principle – are common developmental instances giving rise to similarities between the past and the present.[3] However, the earlier legal regulations often were locally isolated, highly casuistic, and positioned in only imperfect systemic contexts without the internal cohesion of modern codifications.[4] Therefore, our topic needs to take the broad concept of law concerning commerce.

---

consultus, inquit Phil[ippus] corn[ides] in consi[lio] cccxix, nu. 12. uol. iij. https://books.google.de/books?id=_gU6AAAAcAAJ&printsec=frontcover&hl=de&source=gbs_ge_summary_r&cad=0#v=onepage&q&f=false. On the impact of the *consuetudines* see also Ulrich Zasius; Eberhard Isenmann, 'Wirtschaftsrecht und Wirtschaftsethik um 1500: Theologische und juristische Konsilien zum Barchenthandel in der Reichsstadt Ulm', in Rolf Lieberwirth and Heiner Lück (eds.), *Akten des 36. deutschen Rechtshistorikertages: Halle an der Saale, 10.–14. September 2006* (Baden-Baden: Nomos, 2008), 195–259, 257. According to Goldschmidt it was a principle of Roman law that *consuetudo* and *usancia* had to be respected first. Goldschmidt, *Universalgeschichte des Handelsrechts*, 305.

3 With a certain pathos, Levin Goldschmidt declares: 'In der Gestaltung seines Rechts aus eigensten Bedürfnissen und Anschauungen heraus liegt die Größe und für alle Zeit vorbildliche Bedeutung des mittelalterlichen Kaufmannsstandes'; Goldschmidt, *Universalgeschichte des Handelsrechts*, 142. On general methodological, functional and factual considerations concerning relations between past and present, see Eberhard Isenmann, 'Kann das Mittelalter modern sein? *Vormoderne* und *Moderne – Alterität* und *Modernität*', in Jan Broch and Markus Rassiller (eds.), *Protomoderne: Schwellen früher Modernität* (Würzburg: Königshausen und Neumann, 2008), 27–82; Eberhard Isenmann, '"Liberale" Juristen? Zur Konsiliartätigkeit Nürnberger Ratsjuristen im ausgehenden Mittelalter', in Franz Fuchs (ed.), *Medizin, Jurisprudenz und Humanismus in Nürnberg um 1500* (Wiesbaden: Harrassowitz, 2010), 241–314, 241–254.

4 Levin Goldschmidt comes to the conclusion that in the Middle Ages, besides the universal imperial, i.e. the Roman law, and the ecclesiastical law, in the Romance part of Europe from local urban statute law and more or less local trade custom according to the merchants' needs and opinions 'a hardly less universal commercial law' had developed. But he adds that:

In the late Middle Ages and the Early Modern Period the Roman-canon *ius commune*, local statute law as *ius proprium*, statutes of local merchants' colleges, privileges granted by superior authorities, (immemorial) customary law, common usages and good morals (*bonae mores*) were the materials of commercial regulations concerning purchase and sale, forward transactions, usury, bills of exchange, merchants and trading companies, the partners' liability, bookkeeping, market rights and market participants, customs and the regulations of national and international fairs, currency exchange and commercial brokers, maritime law and insurance. The common civil law of the *ius commune* was subsidiary when corrected, replaced or completed by local statutes, customary law and commercial usages.[5] With respect to the general regulations of the common law, mercantile law was the merchants' *ius speciale*, with the effect of a privilege. It was a question of whether local customs on principle needed to be proven or even corroborated *iudicio contrario* (*contradicto*). They were restricted to the one place, but they were extended by a legal transfer from one city to the other and, according to Goldschmidt, tended to universality.[6]

Customary law, usages and *mores* are mentioned in a general way in *consilia*, but are rarely produced in detail, and are not explicitly and substantively analysed, because the learned Jurists tried to find decisions and solutions to legal questions by quoting Roman-canon law, the glosses, the commentaries – and other *consilia*. But it was always a requirement that mercantile matters should be judged *ex aequo et bono* without juridical subtleties and legal quibbling

---

'*Immerhin darf bei der Eigenthümlichkeit mittelalterlicher Rechtsbildung und Rechtsüberlieferung der Gedanke der Universalität nicht zu sehr gepreßt werden; wichtiger als der statistische Aufweis partikulärer Gleichförmigkeit ist die Auffindung ursprünglich vielleicht örtlich vereinzelter Keime späterhin vollentwickelter Rechtsgedanken*'. Goldschmidt, *Universalgeschichte des Handelsrechts*, 240. On his concept of universality and the relationship between universal history and national history, see *ibid.*, 40–47. On this topic see the contribution of Albrecht Cordes in this volume. On objections against the thesis of Harold J. Berman, *Law and Revolution: The formation of the western legal tradition* (Cambridge, Mass.: Harvard University Press, 1983), 333, that in the late eleventh and twelfth centuries 'the basic concepts and institutions of modern western mercantile law – *Lex mercatoria*, "the law merchant" – were formed, and even more important, [...] first came to be viewed as an integrated, developing system – a body of law', see Albrecht Cordes, 'Auf der Suche nach der Rechtswirklichkeit der mittelalterlichen Lex mercatoria', *Zeitschrift der Savigny-Stiftung für Rechtsgeschichte: Germanistische Abteilung* 118 (2002), 168–184.

5 Goldschmidt, *Universalgeschichte des Handelsrechts*, 124–131; Eltjo Schrage, 'Mercatura honesta: "Mercator vix aut numquam potest Deo placere"', *Fundamina: The Journal of Legal History* 8 (2002), 190–202, 199–201.

6 Goldschmidt, *Universalgeschichte des Handelsrechts*, 124.

(*apices iuris*), and were to aim at the facts, the circumstances and the *veritas negotii*.[7] With regard to purchase and sale transactions, greater formlessness and – on promissory notes – short disposals based on trust were conceded, but in exchange law the simple form was simultaneously combined with a strict enforceability of the bills receivable (*rigor cambialis*).[8] More autonomy by the parties was allowed with respect to the contractual penalties,[9] and the *pactum nudum*, not actionable under ancient Roman law, was now appreciated,[10] whereas canon law lessened the actual or alleged harshness and formalism of Roman law. Municipal books and trading books with confidence (*fides*) were to facilitate the proof. Trading companies were in Germany not regulated by positive partnership law before the local Nuremberg reform of municipal

7 Goldschmidt, *Universalgeschichte des Handelsrechts*, 303; Eberhard Isenmann, 'Wirtschaftsrecht und Wirtschaftsethik', 257 (Ulrich Zasius); Straccha, *Tractatus de mercatura seu mercatore*, Titulus de probationibus, fol. 244v: *In curia mercatorum aequitatem praecipue spectandam, et ex bono et aequo causas dirimendas esse et de apicibus iuris disputare minime congruere.* Cf. *ibid.*, fol. 271r (*veritas negotii*); fol. 284v: *Nota tex[tum] contra ignaros, imperitosque mercatores, qui se aequitatis magistros esse credunt, et inquiunt Iuriscon. cauillationes concupiscere, et sequi, mercatores uero aequitatem.* [...] *quid sit rigor, qui aequitati opponitur* [...]. *Sed illud nos non negabimus quaestiones mercatorum ex bono, et aequo cognoscendas esse, in quo genere plerunque sub autoritate iuris scientiae pernitiose erratur* [...]; passim. On the relation between *aequitas* (*ex circumstantiis*) in human mind and found in law, see fols. 285rv, nu 5, and on methodological provisons to be observed, fol. 285v, nu 5: *Credimus tamen ex arbitrio a lege dato consulibus mercatorum, quod ex bono et aequo procedant. Si aequitas in iure scripta reperiatur, licet non in specie sed vel in genere, vel etiam in simili posse consules de similibus, ad similem procedere ubi casus qui in controversiam venit. l. comprehensus speciatim non esset* [...]*; si aequitas reperitur scripta in iure licet non in specie in simili, tamen ad cavendum posse compellere, de similibus ad similia procedendo. At si iudes* [*iudex*] *moveretur aequitate, quaedam nec in eo casu scripta ne in simili ad cavendum neminem esse cogendum* [...].

8 Eberhard Isenmann, 'Gelehrte Juristen und das Prozeßgeschehen in Deutschland im 15. Jahrhundert', in Franz-Josef Arlinghaus et al. (eds.), *Praxis der Gerichtsbarkeit in europäischen Städten des Spätmittelalters* (Frankfurt am Main: Vittorio Klostermann, 2006), 305–417, 340–341 (According to a lawsuit in the Imperial Chamber Court in 1493); comprehensive on the topic is Anja Amend-Traut, *Wechselverbindlichkeiten vor dem Reichskammergericht: Praktiziertes Zivilrecht in der Frühen Neuzeit* (Köln: Böhlau, 2009).

9 On contractual penalties in cases of *mora* see Straccha, V, *Titulus de contractibus mercatorum*, fols. 77v–78v.

10 Straccha, v, fol. 77r: *At in curia mercatorum in qua quaestiones sunt de bono et aequo, huiusmodi exceptio quod ex pacto nudo actio non oriatur reijcitur, quinimmo ex ea agi posse receptum est.* Cf. fol. 248v.

statutes in 1479,[11] but there it was on a basis similar to modern commercial law on *ius cogens* with regard to the licit purpose of the company and in relation to third parties, *ius dispositivum* with regard to the company's internal relationship and subsidiary regulations, if there existed no contractual provisions on matters concerning the company's autonomous legal possibilities.[12] This legal reformation introduces with the essential and defining features of general partnership the notion of an external relationship, defines the debts of the company, prescribes joint and unlimited liability of the partners, and suggests the repartition of the company's debts *pro rata* according to the partners' capital contributions or in another manner. It gives rules for the legal status of the partners' heirs, accounting, determination and distribution of profits, and the liquidation of the company. Roman law is in this reform recognisable with regard to the licit purpose of the company,[13] and also when an excessive unequal distribution of profit and losses, according to the *societas leonina*, is forbidden[14] and a partner transacting business is not liable for detriments, if he had exercised due 'diligence as in own matters', *diligentia* (*qua*) *quam in suis*.[15] Later in 1564, the principle of limited liability with respect to not working partners of a company according to a single privilege, which Emperor Frederick III had already granted to the city of Nuremberg in 1464, was inserted into the third Nuremberg Reformation.[16] We can see how this element of a local commercial law now became gradually more general, being adopted in

11 '[Neue] Reformation der Stadt Nürnberg', 30. Titel, in Franz Beyerle, Wolfgang Kunkel and Hans Thieme (eds.), *Quellen zur neueren Privatrechtsgeschichte Deutschlands*, 1. Halbbd. (Weimar: H. Böhlaus Nachfolge, 1936), 73–76.

12 Mechthild Isenmann and Eberhard Isenmann, 'Das Innenverhältnis einer spätmittelalterlichen Handelsgesellschaft und die Ausweitung interner Konflikte – Hans Arzt und Gesellschaft, Anton Paumgartner und die Reichsstadt Nürnberg (1447–1471)', *Vierteljahrschrift für Sozial- und Wirtschaftsgeschichte* 101 (2014), 432–487, 436–450.

13 D. 17.2.57 (Ulpian): [...] *esse verum, si honestae et licitae rei societas coita sit.*

14 D. 17.2.29.2.

15 'Reformation der Stadt Nürnberg', 30. Titel, 9. Gesetz, 76. Cf. D. 16.3.32; D. 18.8.6; D. 10.2.25.16. Cf. on this principle Mathias Schmoeckel, Joachim Rückert and Reinhard Zimmermann (eds.), *Historisch-kritischer Kommentar zum BGB, vol. 3: Schuldrecht: Besonderer Teil § 433–853* (Tübingen: Mohr Siebeck, 2013), 1, Rn 21 (Martin Josef Schermaier); Mathias Schmoeckel, Joachim Rückert and Reinhard Zimmermann (eds.), *Historisch-kritischer Kommentar zum BGB, vol. 3: Schuldrecht: Besonderer Teil § 433–853* (Tübingen: Mohr Siebeck, 2013), 2, Rn 101, 104, 108 f., 111 f., 124 (Susanne Lepsius).

16 Elmar Lutz, *Die rechtliche Struktur süddeutscher Handelsgesellschaften in der Zeit der Fugger*, vol. 1 (Tübingen: Mohr, 1976), 141–153; Albrecht Cordes, 'Transfer einer Rechtsidee: Gesellschaftsrechtliche Haftungsbeschränkungen in Florenz und Nürnberg im 15. Jahrhundert', in Marcel Senn and Claudio Soliva (eds.), *Rechtsgeschichte und Interdisziplinarität*

the same wording for the Frankfurt Reformation of 1578. The other reforms and codifications of municipal law at the turn of the fifteenth and sixteenth century in contrast to the Nuremberg statutes contained only legal regulations concerning the merchant's basic transaction of purchase and sale.

3 Substantial Affinities between Expert Opinions and Handbooks: Benedetto Cotrugli and Benvenuto Straccha

According to medieval definitions, which start from the object of trade, a merchant (*mercator, negotiator*)[17] is a person who buys a thing in order to sell it without a change in its form as a *res integra* und *immutata*;[18] according to the French Code Civil, the merchant per definition trades in movables, but according to the definition of the German Commercial Code (HGB), he carries out a mercantile trade which leads to the expiry of the status of a merchant when the enterprise is abandoned.

For further questions on trade and commercial law, we can consult two different handbooks of the fifteenth and sixteenth centuries in their approaches and objectives. One was written by the educated merchant Benedetto Cotrugli (1416–1469), and the other by the experienced lawyer Benvenuto Straccha (1509–1556).

Benedetto Cotrugli, an early precursor of Jacques Savary, was originally from Ragusa (Dubrovnik), but from 1451 on he went about his trade based in Naples. In 1458 he wrote his *Libro dell'arte di mercatura*,[19] which was not printed until 1573 in Venice. Other than the Bible, sources he quotes in his work include Augustine and Thomas Aquinas, Greek and Latin literature and philosophy (Aristotle, Cicero and Seneca), canon law, the canonist Hostiensis and the moral theologian Raymundus a Pennaforte.

(Bern: P. Lang, 2001), 243–254; Mechthild Isenmann and Eberhard Isenmann, 'Das Innenverhältnis einer spätmittelalterlichen Handelsgesellschaft', 442–450.

17 Straccha notes that *negotiari* as the generic term is broader than *mercari*. Straccha, *Tractatus de mercatura seu mercatore*, I, fol. 5r.

18 Decretum Gratiani, Dist. 88 c. 12 Palea: *Sed omnes homines videntur esse mercatores. Ostendam ergo quis non est negotiator, ut qui talis non fuerit, eum intelligas esse negotiatorem. Quicumque rem comparat, non ut ipsam rem integram et immutatam vendat, sed ut materia sibi sit inde aliquid operandi, ille non est negotiator. Qui autem comparat rem, ut illam ipsam integram et immutatam dando lucretur, ille est mercator qui de templo eiicitur.*

19 Ugo Tucci (ed.), Benedetto Cotrugli Raguseo, *Il libro dell'arte di mercatura* (Venezia: Arsenale, 1990), with a comprehensive introduction of the editor, 3–128.

In the first of the four books, Cotrugli defines trade as an *ars* or *disciplina*, names the circle of persons allowed to trade, justifies in a scholastic argument the general purpose of trade which is to maintain the human race, and adds that the merchant's personal hope is that of profit.[20] He presents three basic business types: (1) The bartering (*Del vendere a baratto*) of goods (*cose*) for goods, or goods for goods with an additional charge on the side; (2) the cash transaction (*Del vendere a danari contanti*), which is free from any doubt, holds no danger, and offers certain profit on the basis of a just price; and (3) futures (*Del vendere a termine*), which are a discussed source of controversy among theologians and lawyers, and which are necessary in situations with a lack of coins (*pecunia numerate*), and which require good faith (*buono credito*).[21]

Then Cotrugli deals with the collecting of outstanding receivables at maturity on the basis of the debt register, *però che al mercante il perdere tempo et danari è una medesima cosa*:[22] and, with regard to payment behaviour, the payment of debts, on which depend good reputation (*bona fama*) and creditworthiness (*credito*),[23] before turning to the deposit (*disposito*) and pledge (*pegno*).[24] He explains the bill of exchange in the form of a draft (*lectera di cambio di luogo a luogo*) in detail and didactically, and gives examples, and he calls the bill the most important and necessary functional element, without which trade cannot be carried out. He emphasizes the outstanding importance of bookkeeping with *ricordanze*, *giornale* and *libro grande*, and explains, even before Fra Luca Pacioli dealt with the subject, with instructive examples, the principle of double-entry bookkeeping.[25] In addition, he considered it necessary to suspend all commercial transactions and contract conclusions every seventh year – analogous to the Biblical history of the creation (Genesis 2, 2–3) – and to draw up a balance sheet and strike a balance.[26] A chapter is devoted to marine insurance. The chapter on matters forbidden to the merchant does not contain

20 […] *mercatura è arte o vera disciplina intra persone ligiptime giustamente ordinata in cose mercantili, per conservatione del'humana generation, con isperanza niente di meno di guadagno*; Cotrugli, I, cap. 2, 139, 139–141. The merchant takes hard physical exertions and spends the greatest possible diligence to make a large profit (*fare gran proficto*) as the personal aim of the *arte mercantile*, I, cap. 3, 144–145.

21 Cotrugli, *Dell'arte di mercatura*, I, cap. 5–7.

22 Cotrugli, I, cap. 8, 156, 156–157.

23 Cotrugli, I, cap. 9, 157–158.

24 Cotrugli, I, cap. 12, 170–171.

25 Cotrugli, I, cap. 13, 171–175.

26 Cotrugli, I, cap. 19, 182–183. Short rules for a balance are attached to the final chapter of book 10, 255.

legal regulations but rather, general moral-ethic and economic-ethical rules of behaviour.

The other three books move away from the legal and technical side of trading and are devoted to the practice of religion by giving alms, the question of usury with regard to conscience, the virtues and specific qualities of the honourable merchant and his household (as Leon Battista Alberti did). Cotrugli transfers economic-ethical postulates together with a virtue doctrine into his manual for merchants. The contents of the first book are elements we can assign to a mercantile law and business administration, concerning business types, credit, the choice of merchandise, insurance, resource allocation, correspondence, record keeping and accounting.

Benvenuto Straccha's *Tractatus de mercatura seu mercatore*, written in 1533 and published 1552 in Venice, is a comprehensive compendium of civil and mercantile law, underpinned by a large scholarly juridical apparatus. The patrician and humanist Straccha worked as a lawyer in Ancona and combines scholarship and professional practice on the basis of daily commercial experiences (*vidi et audivi*) in his handbook, and inserts his own legal opinions into his tract. Discussing current legal questions – *quottidianum et frequens est* – within his scholarly treatise, this shows very close affinities with the genre of legal opinions. He answers fundamental as well as very specific issues on the basis of Roman-canon law, and compares or mentions statutory regulations of cities and merchants' colleges and the judicial decisions of several places like Ancona, Antwerp, Florence, Siena, Perugia, Bologna, Milano, Venice, Rome or Naples. In some respects, his opus tends towards a comprehensive tract on universal, but not consistently universal, commercial law. This is why Straccha was accepted in Europe as an authority on commercial law until the nineteenth century.

Straccha contrasts the *mercator* with the craftsman and retailer, and calls commerce a *professio*, *ars* and *officium*. He defines *mercatura* – following explicitly the Decretum Gratiani and Andreas Alciatus[27] – as a frequently exercised barter or purchase [and sale] of goods without changing or dividing them in form, in order to make a licit gain,[28] and he mentions the

27 Alciatus, commentary on D. 50.16.206: *Mercator est qui negotiationis exercendae quaestusque faciendae causa merces emit ut vendat. Quapropter qui semel emit pannos, ut venderet, mercator non est, quia in eo deficit exercitium.* See Schrage, 'Mercatura honesta', 198.

28 *Mercatura est officium, quod ratione quaestus liciti exercetur in permutandis emendisque frequenter mercibus, illis non mutata per se forma nec minuatim distrahendis.* Straccha, *Tractatus de mercatura seu mercatore*, I, fol. 22r, nu 74; identical is the definition of *mercator*: *Mercator est, qui negotiationes seu negotiationum exercendarum, quaestusque liciti*

merchants' registration on a wooden panel (*albus*) or in a matriculation register.[29] However, to use the merchant's *immunitas a muneribus publicis* and other privileges, trade must be actually exercised.[30] Like Cotrugli he excludes all noblemen apart from clergy and soldiers from trade; the noblemen would lose their nobility by engaging in commercial activities. The articles making up merchandise are all kinds of movables, on principle.

Straccha is still concerned with a large range of traditional arguments accumulated from canon law and moral theology, and is particularly concerned with the prohibition of usury, which was committed by taking loan interest. He justifies the activity of the merchant, following Aquinas,[31] against the verdict of Pseudochrysostomus.[32] Profit, according to Aquinas, too, is certainly the purpose of trade, but it is not the final purpose (*finis ultima*); it is only the merchant's necessary aim (*finis necessaria*) to maintain himself and his family and household (*ad sui et suae familiae sustentionem*).[33] Merchants are useful and necessary because they provide daily food, and no town or region is self-sufficient, but needs the help of the other.[34]

Well versed in the practice of trade in Ancona and frequently asked for advice, the lawyer Straccha deals with merchandise, the accounting books resulting from custom and statutes, accounting regulations, the merchant's books

faciendi causa frequenter merces permutat seu emit, ut easdem non minuatim, nec mutata per se forma distrahat. Idem, I, fol. 4v. Defined are the professional grand merchants, those of long-distance trade. Considered economically, craftsmen sell their products and therefore are involved in trade, too. This took into account for example Robert Joseph Pothier in his *Traité de la procédure civile* (Lyon: Duplain, 1776), cinquieme partie, chap. 1, 282: *On apelle Marchands ceux qui achetent pour revendre, les artisans qui achetent de la matière pour employer aux ouvrages qu'ils vendent sont aussi reputés Marchands*. See Schrage, 'Mercatura honesta', 201. Our Commercial Code (HGB) is also not restricted to sole merchants.

29 Straccha, *Tractatus de mercatura seu mercatore*, I, fol. 19v.

30 Straccha, I, fols. 6rv.

31 Summa Theologiae, Secunda pars secundae partis, quaestio LXXVII, articulus IV, co. Straccha, I, fols. 9rv.

32 *Eiiciens Dominus vendentes et ementes de templo* [Matthew 21, 12–13; Mark 11, 15–17; Luke 19, 45–46; John 2, 13–16] *significavit, quia homo mercator vix, aut numquam potest Deo placere. Et ideo nullus Christianus debet esse mercator, aut, si voluerit esse, proiiciatur de ecclesia Dei* [...]. *Quemadmodum enim qui ambulat inter duos inimicos, ambobus placere volens, et se commendare, sine maliloquio non potest* [...] *sic qui emit et vendit sine mendacio et periurio esse non potest*. Decretum Gratiani, Paleae to canon 12 of the 88. Distinctio.

33 Straccha, *Tractatus de mercatura seu mercatore*, I, fols. 9v–10r, nu 29.

34 Straccha, II, fols. 34rv, nu 16.

and their faith (*plena fides*) due to the *lex municipalis*, the mercantile customs, and the statutes of the merchants' *licita collegia* as the *ius proprium inter collegiatos* in matters concerning the *mercatura* and their *officia*. These statutes need no confirmation by the authorities, but they must not contain things which are naturally and obviously unjust, or which contradict public law and oppose the whole *civitas*. Straccha discusses the contracts approved by the custom of the merchants and the place, the difference between simple *nuda pacta* and actionable *contractus*, the promises (*sponsiones*)[35] and the partnerships (*societates*).[36] He also deals with trademarks, mandate (*mandatum*), the *mandatarius* or *procurator* and commission business. Merchandise forms a field of its own, that is as a rule, all movables, but with some objects being *extra commercium*.[37] Straccha devotes space to the function of jurists and the constitution of the *collegium mercatorum*, the powers of the elected consuls, then the settlement of disputes by experienced *boni viri* and the consuls of the merchants' *collegium* explaining with reference to the obligations the statement of claim (*petitio, libellus*), the exceptions (*exceptiones*), and pieces of evidence (*probationes*). Other subjects considered are insolvency and bankruptcy, the escape of debtors, safe conduct (*salvus conductus*) for debtors, agreements between creditors and debtors, the impact of the majority ratios in the creditors' meeting, and the testamentary restitution of usurious profits. Finally he deals with maritime trade and marine insurance.

4 Substantial Intersections between the *Consilia* and Late Scholastic Tracts

Apart from economic manuals and legal handbooks, scholastic tracts on contracts, just price and usury form a third category and show major intersections with legal opinions, because all of them have similar subjects and refer partly to the same sources. Court decisions declaring or producing commercial law,

---

35 Straccha, V, fols. 104r–122v. A verbal *stipulatio*, explained in legal opinions, was one of the objects of the Cologne civil action between Johannes von Wipperfürt, called Rosenkranz, and the merchant Gerhard vom Viehof 1449–1451. Gerhard had among other things promised to regard Johannes as his son and to help him in his business paying bills and selling merchandise. Historisches Archiv der Stadt Köln, Zivilprozesse, Nr. 149, fols. 137v, 151v, 154v; see Eberhard Isenmann, 'Gelehrte Juristen und das Prozeßgeschehen', 387–388.

36 Straccha, *Tractatus de mercatura seu mercatore*, V, fols. 81r–83r.

37 Straccha IV, fols. 66v–75v.

such as the decisions of the Lübeck City Council[38] and the later merchants' opinions (*Parere*),[39] should at least be mentioned.

We have to take into consideration the fact that legal opinions can be traced back to concrete conflicts and litigations, and therefore deal with contentious legal aspects of economic activities, being primarily questions of the general law of obligations and of procedural law. These conflicts are mainly based on economic and legal relations between private persons who are merchants as well as non-merchants. In the question of whether a contract is permissible or not, contracts become a socio-political, public and theological dimension. The law of contracts then is not only a matter concerning learned jurists, but concerning jurists, moral theologians and philosophers together, as the minster priest Dr *utriusque iuris* Ulrich Krafft tells us in a legal opinion (*Ratschlag*) for the Swabian imperial city of Ulm.[40]

Philosophers, primarily meaning Aristotle, discuss the *iustitia commutativa*; lawyers stress the *aequalitas dati et accepti* and the rule of the *laesio enormis*; moral theologians know the relevant positions of Roman and canon law just as the lawyers do, but according to Bible and canon law they introduce the aspect of sin, deadly sin and salvation into the judgement of economic activities and refer, besides the secular and ecclesiastical *forum contentiosum*, to conscience and the *forum internum* demanding the restitution of profits made by usury.[41] From the Late Ancient Church Fathers and the Early Middle Ages onwards up to Luther and the humanist Erasmus of Rotterdam, trade and merchants

38 Wilhelm Ebel, *Lübisches Kaufmannsrecht vornehmlich nach Lübecker Ratsurteilen des 15./16. Jahrhunderts* (Göttingen, 1951).

39 Eva-Christine Frentz, 'Kaufmännische Gutachten – Parere – im Hamburgischen Seeprozeß', *Zeitschrift für Neuere Rechtsgeschichte* 10 (1988), 151–178; Sonja Breustedt, 'Kaufmännische Pareres – Gutachten als Konsens und Beweismittel im 17. und 18. Jahrhundert', in Albrecht Cordes (ed.), *Mit Freundschaft oder mit Recht? Inner- und außergerichtliche Alternativen zur kontroversen Streitentscheidung im 15.–19. Jahrhundert* (Köln: Böhlau Verlag, 2015), 261–268; see further the contribution of Anja Amend-Traut in this volume.

40 Eberhard Isenmann, 'Wirtschaftsrecht und Wirtschaftsethik', 205–206. Generally on the topic see further Wim Decock, *Theologians and Contract Law: The Moral Transformation of the Ius Commune (ca. 1500–1650)* (Leiden: Martinus Nijhoff, 2013); Nils Jansen, *Theologie, Philosophie und Jurisprudenz in der spätscholastischen Lehre von der Restitution: Außervertragliche Ausgleichsansprüche im frühneuzeitlichen Naturrechtsdiskurs* (Tübingen: Mohr Siebeck, 2013).

41 Winfried Trusen, 'Zur Bedeutung des geistlichen Forum internum und externum für die spätmittelalterliche Gesellschaft', *Zeitschrift der Savigny-Stiftung für Rechtsgeschichte: Kanonistische Abteilung* 76:1 (1990), 254–285; Winfried Trusen, *Gelehrtes Recht im Mittelalter und in der frühen Neuzeit* (Goldbach: Keip, 1997), 47*–78*.

were suspected of avarice, usury, fraud, and generally of sin and immorality.[42] Regarding the moral theologians, *consilia* with regard to market, just price and usury must be compared with international scholastic tracts from Aquinas and Henry of Gaunt to Johannes Gerson, Antoninus of Florence, Bernardinus of Siena, Richard of Middletown or the German scholars Heinrich Langenstein, Johannes Nider, Heinrich of Oyta, Gabriel Biel and Konrad Summenhart and later those of Johann Eck and Martin Luther.[43] For pastoral care and practical economic advice in the confessional, the matters were prepared in penitential handbooks.[44] The tracts of the moral theologians combine legal and ethical norms with knowledge of contemporary commercial business practices, economic empiricism and analysis. This is why Joseph A. Schumpeter and, with some major reservations, Raymond de Roover could regard some moral theologians to be the first economists, though the medieval scholars primarily aimed at the just social and spiritual order and the pastoral care of salvation (*cura animarum*). They were economists, though they did not examine economic processes as autonomous subjects, and despite their legal and very formalistic point of view and their strong focus on the permissiveness of contracts.[45]

42 Harald Siems, *Handel und Wucher im Spiegel frühmittelalterlicher Rechtsquellen* (Hannover: Hahn, 1992); Schrage, 'Mercatura honesta', 190–202; E. Isenmann, *Die deutsche Stadt im Mittelalter*, 968–972.

43 Winfried Trusen, 'Äquivalenzprinzip und gerechter Preis im Spätmittelalter', in Franz Mayer (ed.), *Staat und Gesellschaft: Festgabe für Günther Küchenhoff zum 60. Geburtstag am 21. August 1967* (Göttingen: Schwartz, 1967), 247–263; Trusen, *Gelehrtes Recht*, 531*–547*; Winfried Trusen, '*De contractibus mercatorum*: Wirtschaftsethik und gelehrtes Recht im Tractat Johannes Niders (†1438)', in *Ius et commercium: Studien zum Handels- und Wirtschaftsrecht: Festschrift für Franz Laufke zum 70. Geburtstag* (Würzburg: Holzner, 1971), 51–71. See further Joseph Höffner, *Wirtschaftsethik und Monopole im 15. und 16. Jahrhundert*, 2nd ed. (Darmstadt: Wissenschaftliche Buchgesellschaft, 1969), 84–164; John W. Baldwin, *The Medieval Theories of the Just Price: Romanists, Canonists, and Theologians in the Twelfth and Thirteenth Centuries* (Philadelphia: American Philosophical Society, 1959); Raymond de Roover, 'The Concept of the Just Price: Theory and Economic Policy', *Journal of Economic History* 18 (1953), 418–434.

44 Odd Langholm, *The Merchant in the Confessional: Trade and Price in the Pre-Reformation Penitential Handbooks Studies* (Leiden: Brill, 2003).

45 Joseph A. Schumpeter, *Geschichte der ökonomischen Analyse*, vol. 1 (Göttingen: Vandenhoeck & Ruprecht, 1965), 143: '*Innerhalb ihres Systems von Moraltheologie und Recht erlangte die Wirtschaftslehre* [*der Scholastiker des 14. bis 17. Jahrhunderts*] *ihre klar umrissene, wenn nicht sogar eigenständige Existenz, und die Scholastiker sind mehr als jede andere Gruppe die "Begründer" der Wirtschaftswissenschaft geworden*'. On the moral theologians' analytical, logical and scientific method, deriving general principals from empirical cases – despite their normative motive and question, see Schumpeter, *Geschichte der*

The core of their discussion was the just and licit contract, but it must be conceded that 'the merchant's business consists of contracting'.[46]

5 Types of Expert Opinions Concerning Trade and Economy

Legal and economic counsels were produced for parties in litigation, for the judgement of courts, for the legal and political advice of city councils and territorial princes, and in favour of urban and princely economic and commercial policies, trading companies or their competitors. Several jurists in the early sixteenth century participated with legal and economic opinions in the economic-ethical controversies about five per cent interest-bearing investments in companies, initiated by the Ingolstadt professor of theology Dr Johannes Eck, and later in the Imperial Diet's legislation on monopolies and other questions of trade. Thus they took part in a limited public discussion.

If we differentiate between (1) legal opinions mainly based on Roman-canon law and (2) *consilia* to a large extent based on moral theological tracts, we can add as a further category (3) legal and economic expert opinions of lawyers and political committees preparing legislative projects, namely under the final purpose of just price and more generally against the outsized economic power of large trading companies, of cartels, syndicates or monopolists. As a final category, despite these legislative activities aiming at economic restrictions and at nearly the same time, in 1518 and 1527, (4) purely economic proposals were made by experts on how to create monopolies and cartels in the Saxon tin trade[47] or to gain control of the middle European trade with several metals.[48] But in one of these economic projects it was expressly requested that a scholar's opinion should additionally be sought, proving that the monopolistic trade, because of the alleged sustenance of the poor and other positive impacts, could be done without burdening the conscience.[49]

ökonomischen Analyse, 148–150. On De Roover's opinions on the issue see Julius Kirshner, 'Raymond de Roover on Scholastic Economic Thought', in Julius Kirshner (ed.), *Business, Banking, and Economic Thought in Late Medieval and early Modern Europe: Selected Studies of Raymond de Roover* (Chicago: University of Chicago Press, 1974), 15–36.

46 Goldschmidt, *Universalgeschichte des Handelsrechts*, 305.

47 Jakob Strieder, *Studien zur Geschichte kapitalistischer Organisationsformen: Monopole, Kartelle und Aktiengesellschaften im Mittelalter und zu Beginn der Neuzeit* (München: Duncker & Humblot, 1914), Nr. 16, 420–424.

48 Strieder, *Studien*, Nr. 21, 432–435.

49 Strieder, *Studien*, Nr. 16, 422.

6 Matters of Legal Opinions

Because companies in cases of internal conflicts avoided the judgements of ordinary courts and preferred to resolve them by extrajudicial settlements, litigation and subsequently getting expert opinions was mostly limited to disputes within merchants' families concerning testaments and heredities.[50] But, we find in the library of Dr Konrad Peutinger a *consilium* concerning the legal capacity of a simple-minded partner of the Vöhlin company (Leonard Vöhlin),[51] and another concerning the question of the entitlement of interests on a capital invested in the commercial company of Hans Imhoff for thirty-eight years, which had now been inherited by Peter Imhoff from his mother.[52]

6.1 *Mandate and Commission*

Two Nuremberg legal opinions (dated to about 1474) in Latin concern a loan contract between the Augsburg merchant Ulrich Arzt and a creditor, V.[53]

---

50 As an example: Legal opinion of Johannes Gossolt declaring that the testament of the Memmingen merchant Erhard Vöhlin senior (†1484/85) is valid and cannot be contested by his son Leonhard Vöhlin; Hans-Jörg Künast and Helmut Zäh, (eds.), *Die Bibliothek Konrad Peutingers: Edition der historischen Kataloge und Rekonstruktion der Bestände Bd. 2: Die autographen Kataloge Peutingers: Der juristische Bibliotheksteil* (Tübingen: Niemeyer, 2005), Nr. 962.17, 158–159; Universitätsbibliothek Tübingen, Mc 63, fols. 178r–182r. On the topic: Katharina von Ciriacy-Wantrup, *Familien- und erbrechtliche Gestaltung von Unternehmen der Renaissance: Eine Untersuchung der Augsburger Handelsgesellschaften zur frühen Neuzeit* (Berlin: Lit, 2007); Silke Pettinger, *Vermögenserhaltung und Sicherung der Unternehmensfortführung durch Verfügungen von Todes wegen: Eine Studie der Frühen Augsburger Neuzeit* (Berlin: Lit, 2007); Britta Schneider, 'Reich statt Augsburg: Fuggersche Generationenkonflikte vor Gericht', in Mark Häberlein et al. (eds.), *Generationen in spätmittelalterlichen und frühneuzeitlichen Städten (ca. 1250–1750)* (Konstanz: UVK Verlagsgesellschaft, 2011), 117–131.

51 Legal opinion of the Ingolstadt jurist Gisbert von Stoltzenburg (between 1484 and 1495); Künast and Zäh, *Die Bibliothek Konrad Peutingers*, Nr. 962.10, 157. Benvenuto Straccha discusses the question which persons must not trade and mentions particularly such of insound mind (*mente capti*); Straccha, *Tractatus de mercatura seu mercatore*, III, fols. 52v–53v.

52 Legal opinion of Konrad Peutinger (about 1500); Künast and Zäh, *Die Bibliothek Konrad Peutingers*, Nr. 962.12, 158.

53 Legal opinion of Dr Conrad Schütz, jurist of the Nuremberg City Council, concerning the causa Ulrich Arzt; Staatsarchiv Nürnberg, Reichsstadt Nürnberg, Rep. 51, Ratschlagbücher, Nr. 6*, fols. 442r–448v; another *Consilium in idem* [causa] of an unknown jurist: fols. 445r–448v. On the matter of the procurators' mandate see in general Straccha, *Tractatus de mercatura seu mercatore*, V, *Titulus mandati*, fols. 85r–100r.

M., the procurator of V., had confessed that he had received the loan as the obligation's solution from G., the procurator of Artzt, but then he had fled, misappropriating the money. He had, instead of a general and free mandate, only a limited mandate issued to negotiate in a certain place (in the city of Ulm) and with certain persons. The question was whether the principal (*dominus*) V. was obliged by his procurator and had to ratify the agreement, when his procurator negotiated in a different place and with persons not included in the mandate. A further matter in question was whether the principal, in case of doubt, had to ratify an agreement (*gesta*) or if a *tacitum mandatum* was to presume, when he had in the past ratified an agreement negotiated in a different location than that indicated in the mandate. Or, was M., negotiating beyond his mandate, presumed to be contracting in his own name? Discussing many very special aspects of the case and the need for proofs, the jurists explained among other things that if the *procurator* or *gestor negotiorum* had exceeded his mandate, the principal was not obliged to ratify the agreement unless the procurator had concluded the contract, turning it *in utilitatem domini*.

In 1499/1500 two very similar Latin *consilia* dealt with the question of whether the heads of the Company of the tin trade in Meißen were allowed to refuse a partner, who for more than a year had invested 2.000 florins to profit and loss.[54] He was listed in the partners' register (*Matrikel*) and his capital contribution figured in the account book (*liber rationum*) as participating in the profit determination and distribution. But his capital had been accepted only by delegated agents of the company, *institores* or *famuli*, having only limited

54 One legal opinion comes personally from the person concerned, the Braunschweig legal advisor (syndic) Dr *utriusque iuris* Christoph Kuppener (1466–1511), the other from Dr *utriusque iuris* Tilemann Brandes (Strieder: Brandner), *Praepositus* of Sancta Crucis in Hildesheim. Strieder, *Studien*, Nr. 14, 416–418; Nr. 13, 415–416. Copies of the opinions are handed down in the *Juridicus Liber* of Kuppener, (formerly) Königliches Staatsarchiv Königsberg, Msc, A 34, fols. 199–202 (Dr Kuppener), 204–208 (Dr Brandes); the *liber* is now to be found in Geheimes Staatsarchiv Preußischer Kulturbesitz (GStA PK) Berlin, XX. HA (Digitalisierte Archivalien). Strieder has omitted the opinions' scholarly apparatus including the solutions of the different legal questions and the case. On several issues and problems concerning mining companies and the law of partnership – capital investment, obligatory capital increase (*Zubuße*) concerning mining shares (*Kuxen*), profit and loss determination, mutual compensation of *debitum ad debitum* and *damnum ad lucrum*, the nature of a societas (*vinculum fraternitatis et aequalitatis*), equality and *societas leonina*, the whereabouts of books, correspondence etc. after the end of a company – see the two legal opinions in Henning Goden, *Consilia* (Budissinae, 1563), Nrs. LXXXV–LXXXVI. On the related features of a *societas omnium bonorum* of brothers see *ibid.*, Nr. LXXXVII.

mandate, as the refusing chief partners (*domini*) alleged.[55] Both *institores* were fugitives and could not be questioned.

The legal opinions follow this argumentative line: *Prima facie* it is valid that a partnership agreement comes into existence by consent (*consensus*) and that it is dissolved by renouncement (*renuntiatio*) and death, but it must be a simultaneous consent (*simultaneus consensus*) which between absentees can only be made by an envoy (*nuntius*) or by a letter (*epistola*). In the present case, however, both the agents who made contracts appeared, and had purchased and sold for many years. The agents were not entitled, had no *potestas*, to accept capital and to admit someone into the company (*societas*); without a legitimate and sufficient mandate an act is *nullus*. But the chief partners are not able to evidence by documents that the agents were not empowered to do so; their testimony would not be valid, because it would be in their own case. However, the following is considered to be crucial: from the entry in the partners' register a legal presumption results that the person concerned is co-partner (*consocius*).[56] Furthermore, the capital contribution is recorded in the accounting book and it participated in the company's profit distribution. This is not a loan (*mutuum*) which must not bear interest, but a contribution to profit and loss to be used in favour of the company and its negotiations, creating a partnership ratio (*ius societatis*). Even if the agents had only a certain, limited and insufficient mandate, it is valid if the chief partners had knowledge of it and tolerated it. The main argument is that knowledge (*scientia*) and connivance (*patientia*) of a person entitled to prohibit, *pro consensu habetur*.[57] It is a tacit consent (*tacitus consensus*), and as a company can be dissolved by tacit consent, it can in the same way

55 Cf. the legal opinions on procuration and mandate in Goden, *Consilia*, Nr. LXXXV (*De procuratore ad negotia*); Nr. XCI (*De mandato*). On the matter see further Straccha, *Tractatus de mercatura seu mercatore*, V, *Titulus mandati*, in particular with regard to the power of the procurator, 88r.

56 Cf. on this issue the legal opinion in Goden, *Consilia*, Nr. LXXXVIII, Nr. 12: *Liber in quem consortes scribuntur, probat.*

57 *Igitur in proposito domini ex contractibus institorum suorum per scientiam et pacientiam suam preiudicarunt; ad quod optime facit singulare verbum Inno*[*centii*] *in* [*c. 33 X 1.3*], *ubi voluit quod si dominus scit causam suam agi a falso procuratore sibi preiudicat si non contradicat et sibi imputet, nam ex voluntate sua creditur agere, cum potuerit prohibere et non prohibuit, debuit enim protestari quod factum talis praesenti procuratoris displiceret, quam sententiam Inno*[*centii*] *approbant Archi*[*diaconus*] [*Guido de Baysio*] *et Jo*[*annes*] *An*[*dreae*] *in* [*c. 4 VI° I.19*]. GStA PK Berlin, XX. HA, Msc, A 34, fols. 205v–206r (Dr Brandes). On this issue see Straccha, *Tractatus de mercatura seu mercatore*, V, *Titulus mandati*, fol. 91v, nu 18.

be agreed (*contrahitur*). The complementary sentence reads: *Non improbare est aliquam approbare, per Bar*[*tolum*] *in* [*D. 46.8.12.1*]. If a principal knows that his *procurator* has exceeded the limits of his mandate and has tolerated it, he is considered to consent,[58] and to extend the mandate,[59] and thus he is prejudged. *Sciencia et paciencia in rebus incorporalibus multum operatur* [D. 39.3.8; D. 39.3.19].

Similar issues concerning a quite different case are treated in a legal opinion commissioned by the merchant Bartholomaeus Welser the Elder (1484–1561)[60] whose disobedient sun Bartholomaeus Junior, travelling in a company via Lyon through France to Paris, instead of going back via Lyon to Antwerp as ordered, had begun to lend money in his own and his father's company name without its knowledge, will and commission – and was also wasting it. The younger Welser had no commission with the company, no mandate or power of procuration to raise, lend and accept money, or to sell and to conduct business in any way. Recognising his son's licentiousness much earlier, the father had created an ordinance in his company which restricted his son's expenditure to the most necessary items (clothing), and explicitly forbade his son from transacting any business. Moreover, he had openly protested that he would not settle any more of his son's debts. Nevertheless, he sought to steel himself against the potential claims of creditors by a legal opinion.

The instructed lawyer refused six conceivable arguments of creditors; some concerned the legal question of mandate, commission and power. Because Welser Junior had not any mandate and power, either openly or tacitly, Welser Senior and the company had no knowledge of the lending and therefore did not tolerate it, and the existence of mandate and power had to be proved. The following arguments in favour of the creditors were refused: if a person declares that he is the procurator of another person and the other person does not contradict, it is presumed that it is his will, and that the notifying person had his will and commission to make a (preliminary) decision to his disadvantage.[61] Welser Junior, it may be argued, is a commissioned agent (*institor*) or

58 *Quando dominus sciuit procuratorem suum habentem mandatum excedere fines mandati nam tunc si patitur videtur consentire* [Alexander de Imola ad D. 42.1.63]. GStA PK Berlin, XX. HA, Msc, A 34, fol. 206r.

59 *Ideo paciendo quod delegatus excedat fines mandati delegatorii videtur delegans ampliare mandatum, per* [*D. 14.1.1.5*]; *ibid.*

60 Staats- und Stadtbibliothek Augsburg, 2° Cod. Aug. 386, fols. 447r–454v (German text with a scholarly apparatus in Latin).

61 *Ibid.*, fol. 448v. The lawyer translates the legal term *praejudicare* into German *nachteil thun schöpfen.*

factor of the company with the company's commission to purchase and sell. If a person (informally) notifies that he is acting as a deputy, and the superior or principal, knowing this, does not contradict it and tolerates it, then the action is as valid as if the principal had tacitly placed him in office, even though the commission had not been proved. If a person acts in the name of another and the other tolerates it, this person is considered to have gained power, even though there was no notification of such a power. Power and commission are indeed presumed by knowledge and toleration, but without a proof the presumption does not last.[62]

6.2 *Bookkeeping and Proof in Court*

In 1477, the Bavarian councillor Dr Johannes Pirckheimer, originally from Nuremberg, discussed in a legal opinion for the Nuremberg council the question whether in litigation, a plaintiff was obliged to disclose his account books in order to prove a sale transaction.[63] Pirckheimer explains that the exercise of trade does not legally require bookkeeping, but a merchant is obliged to enter a transaction in his account book and disclose it if he keeps such a book by usage (*pfleg*) and custom (*gewonheit*), and if the party of a contract had demanded the entry.

62 But if someone should be obliged to take action, in law generally *taciturnitas* and *patientia* as such and by themselves do not work; they work in specific cases where personal presence is required or connivance (*taciturnitas*) caused an obligation. If a person is constituted to be procurator in absence, the procurator must not act if he had not got a verbal commission before or had received a letter of attorney or was informed by a messenger, and when he had accepted the commission. If these prerequisites were not met, the principal was not obliged to accept the negotiation result or to ratify it. *Ibid.*, fols. 452rv.

63 *Consilium in materia editionis/ An reus compellat actorem ad tradendum suos libros racionum*; Staatsarchiv Nürnberg, Ratschlagbücher, Nr. 2*, fols. 88v–90r (German text with a Latin apparatus). See Eberhard Isenmann, 'Recht, Verfassung und Politik in Rechtsgutachten spätmittelalterlicher deutscher und italienischer Juristen, vornehmlich des 15. Jahrhunderts', in Hartmut Boockmann et al. (eds.), *Recht und Verfassung im Übergang vom Mittelalter zur Neuzeit*, II. Teil (Göttingen: Vandenhoeck & Ruprecht, 2001), 47–245, 188–193. The obligation to hand over and disclose books and records (*editio*) was later regulated in the Nüremberg reform of the municipal statutes of 1479, printed in 1984. Gerhard Köbler (ed.), *Reformation der Stadt Nürnberg* (Gießen: Arbeiten zur Recht- und Sprachwissenschaft, 1984), VIII, 2, 128 (fol. 64b). On correct and careful bookkeeping, the account books (*libri rationum*) and their faith (*fides*) see Straccha, *Tractatus de mercatura seu mercatore*, II, fols. 42r–47r, nu 51–70, particularly on their *editio* fols. 45v–46r, nu 68, fol. 46v, nu 70.

Furthermore, a short *responsum* by an unknown Nuremberg jurist offers answers to the question of under which conditions the *privatae scripturae* of merchants submitted in court had full probative force.[64]

6.3 *The Trademark of a Company*

When the brothers Hieronymus Imhoff (Augsburg) and Sebastian Imhoff (Nuremberg), who were partners of their cousins in the old Imhoff company, separated around 1548 from the company, founding a new one with the same merchandise trade, the question arose – and resulted in a legal opinion – of which of the both companies should in future have the right to use the company's traditional trade mark.[65] The legal issue was already a scholarly matter, and was generally formulated by Bartolus in his tract *De insigniis et armis* of 1357.[66] We can observe the informative process of how this issue became the subject of a later specific German dispute in the mid-sixteenth century, and that the late medieval tract served as the main argumentative basis and already offered the solution to the legal question raised in our legal opinion.[67] The topic had also been dealt with, about fifteen years earlier, in Straccha's tract of 1533/1552, particularly with reference to Bartolus and Petrus de Ubaldis.[68] The Bartolus' tract thus proved to be of high importance for international commercial law.

According to the legal opinion for the Imhoff case, the trademark was used to seal the mercantile correspondence and to mark barrels, bales and individual

64 Staatsarchiv Nürnberg, Ratschlagbücher, Nr. 6*, fol. 91r; Eberhard Isenmann, 'Recht, Verfassung und Politik', 192–193. On the *fides* of *scripturae privatae mercatorum* according to statutes and in the court of the *consules mercatorum* see Straccha, V, fol. 248rv.

65 Germanisches Nationalmuseum Nürnberg, Historisches Archiv, Imhoff-Archiv I, Faszikel 30, Nr. 29, fols. 1r–10r. The legal opinion is written in German, but its scholarly apparatus is in Latin; no author and date, but after 1548.

66 Osvaldo Cavallar, Susanne Degenring and Julius Kirshner, *A Grammar of Signs: Bartolo da Sassoferrato's Tract on Insignia and Coats of Arms* (Berkeley: University of California, 1994), appendix 1, 109–121.

67 Besides the tract of Bartolus in the legal opinion are quoted the tracts of Petrus de Ubaldis, *Tractatus de duobus fratris*, p. II, qu. 11; see Cavallar, Degenring, Kirshner, *A Grammar of Signs*, Appendix 4, 163–178; Guilelmus de Montserrat, *Tractatus de successione regum* and particularly Barthélémy de Chasseneuz, *Catalogus gloriae mundi* (1529), further commentaries of Petrus de Anchorano, Baldus de Ubaldis, Antonius de Butrio, Guilelmus Benedictus, Nicolaus de Tudeschis (Panormitanus), Joannes de Platea, Lucas de Penna, Roffredus Beneventanus.

68 Straccha, *Tractatus de mercatura seu mercatore*, II, fols. 47v–56r, 54r–55v (*Signum finita societate, seu divisa apud quem remaneat*).

goods so that they could be correctly assigned at the customs clearance.[69] Derived from the company's progenitor, the trademark was used in the next generation by Endres Imhoff and his brothers. The trade operated under the name of the elders, who were considered to be the seniors and the heads of the company. Some years later, some of the brothers withdrew from trade, retired from the company and did not use the trademark further, but kept for the future the coat of arms and the seal of the lineage. The remaining brothers transmitted the trade to their sons, who also functioned as the seniors of the company. The sons of the retired brothers, Sebastian and Hieronymus Imhoff, again joined the company of their present cousins as merchant assistants, and became partners later for four years or more, but then separated and founded a similar trade using the old trademark. This led to confusion at customs and toll stations and at other places with regard to the goods and customs debts of the two companies. But no side was willing to give up the traditional trademark.

The starting point of the legal opinion was the statement that the parties in dispute were related in the same degree, and the ancestor and his sons had, after long-term use by prescription, acquired the exclusive right to use the trademark and could therefore refuse the use to third parties and prohibit it by rights. Unlike the genealogical coat of arms, the trademark, which is used for commercial business, is not inherited and is bound to trading activities. If no agreement was concluded on the trademark, the younger cousins who had started the new trade were to cede it to the older ones, because if a company is split up, the trademark remains in the exclusive use of the senior or principal of the original company.

Furthermore, the father's side of the younger cousins has lost the trademark by non-use and the termination of the company (*renuntiatio societatis*), whereas the fathers of the older cousins had continuously pursued the trade, were the seniors and the heads of the company, and the company was named after them. If all partners have the same status, the decision is based on which of them had invested the major capital. This applies to the older cousins in this case who moreover continued in the business of the old, original company. The trademark had already acquired credibility and faith, before the younger cousins had joined the company; the younger cousins had neither increased nor reduced it. For these reasons, the older cousins could refuse the younger ones the use of the trademark on the loss of their merchandise and the

69 Cf. Ebel, *Kaufmannsrecht*, 26–32; Evamaria Engel, 'Signum Mercatoris – Signum Societatis. Zeichen und Marken im Wirtschaftsleben deutscher Städte im Spätmittelalter' in Gertrud Blaschitz et al. (eds.), *Symbole des Alltags – Alltag der Symbole* (Graz: Akad. Druck- u. Verl.-Anstalt, 1992), 208–231; Wolfgang von Stromer, 'Zeichen des Wirtschaftslebens', ibid., 233–243.

penalty of forging (*sub poena falsi*); they could legally force them to abandon the trademark and take another one. However, if all the parties had the same status and conditions, the lot had to decide.

The process of a legal action can have consequences for the current commercial activities. In the case of dispute, the older cousins were to take due care that they did not file their suit for the *petitorium*, but only for the *possessorium retinendae* and support their claim on the *possessorium*,[70] because if they asserted the *petitorium*, they would not be permitted to use the trademark in the meantime until the end of the litigation, for the reason that they had admitted that the younger cousins were using and were in *possessio vel quasi* of the sign, rather than themselves.

Sebastian and Hieronymus Imhoff changed their trademark, adding an 'S' for Sebastian to the traditional trademark in terms of the former legal opinion, but when both part of them separated in 1559, among other issues, the future use of the trade mark resulted again in a severe dispute lasting around ten years.[71] Sebastian Imhoff called on his brother to waive the trademark, whereas Hieronymus proposed that the lot should decide. But Sebastian did not accept. Basically, the former *consilium* already offered a legal solution for this issue, as well.

6.4 *Carrier and Customs Fraud*

Some *consilia* are concerned with customs and the freedom of trade routes. In around 1470 no fewer than five legal opinions were prepared concerning a customs fraud committed by a shipmaster carrying wine on the Danube in the service of the Nuremberg patrician Nikolaus Groß. The cargo was seized at the Free City of Regensburg by the Bavarian customs officer, and was to be transferred to another part of the Bavarian judicial district on the order of his

70 *Sed experiatur remedio possessorio, presertim retinendae possessionis adversarium velut turbatorem repellendo*; Germanisches Nationalmuseum Nürnberg, Historisches Archiv, Imhoff-Archiv I, Faszikel 30, Nr. 29, fol. 10r.

71 Manfred Hörner (ed.), *Bayerisches Hauptstaatsarchiv Reichskammergericht: Bd.13: Nr. 5283–5568 (Buchstaben I und J)* (München: Generaldirektion der Staatlichen Archive Bayerns, 2006), 14–15. The dispute and the issue of the trademark are briefly mentioned in Mark Häberlein, 'Frühneuzeitliche Handelsgesellschaften zwischen Markt und Recht', in Thomas M.J. Möllers (ed.), *Vielfalt und Einheit: Wirtschaftliche und rechtliche Rahmenbedingungen der Standardbildung* (Baden-Baden: Nomos, 2008), 127–147, 134. In detail on the dispute, see Mechthild Isenmann, *Strategien, Mittel und Wege inner- und zwischenfamiliären Konfliktlösung oberdeutscher Handelshäuser im 15. und 'langen 16. Jahrhundert'* (forthcoming), chap. 3.1: 'Die Gebrüder Sebastian und Hieronymus Imhoff aus Nürnberg und Augsburg. Vermittlung als Strategie'.

colleague in Straubing.[72] The questions under discussion were whether the freight as the principal's property or a part of it was legally forfeited to the Bavarian Duke Albert as the sovereign owner of the customs, and whether the carrier and not the owner of the cargo had to pay extra customs according to the real value of the wine, or whether the amount of the customs should be doubled as a punishment. A further question was whether the Bavarian customs officer in Regensburg was allowed to seize the cargo within the city and transfer it arbitrarily against the asserted owners' will and request, and which court would be the competent court in the case of litigation.

6.5 *Freedom of the* Via Publica – *Insolvency*

Since the middle of the fifteenth century at the latest, the idea already existed that the German nation constituted a virtually unified economic area, but commercial trade was obstructed by the fragmentation of the Empire into emerging and closing territorial states. When Duke Albert of Bavaria forbade the transport of salt through his territory, particularly in the direction towards Nuremberg, and when even then merchants were captured and their goods seized, in 1477 the jurist of Nuremberg City Council, Dr Conrad Schütz, provided a legal opinion against the duke's actions.[73] He conceded that the duke as well as the city of Nuremberg were to impose for their dominions an export ban on salt or on other merchandise for their own needs and necessity, but not the prohibition of the transit trade in several directions, infringing the freedom of the common, the public or imperial roads. Princes and cities as owners of the regal rights of customs and escort were obliged to protect, pacify and maintain the roads. No one but the Emperor had the authority to impose an *interdictum prohibitorium*. Anyone obstructing or blocking the free use of the road had to pay compensation for the detriment resulting from the loss of business opportunities. A *via publica* or imperial road was defined by the (written) laws in this way: that its ground and land was common and not owned by anyone in particular. Nevertheless its reason, nature and quality were devoted to the private persons' benefit and promotion, so that everyone could carry their merchandise back and forth on the road in order to seek their own profit. Therefore, Nuremberg City Council and anyone who may have a grievance

72 Staatsarchiv Nürnberg, Ratschlagbücher, Nr. 6*, fols. 296v–297v, 371r–374r (Dr Johannes Pirckheimer), 374r–378r (Dr Seyfrid Plaghal), 377r–378r (Dr Wilhelm von Werdena, Dr Ludwig zum Paradies), 391v–400v (Dr Martin Mair).

73 Edited in Eberhard Isenmann, 'Reichsstadt und Reich an der Wende vom späten Mittelalter zur frühen Neuzeit', in Josef Engel (ed.), *Mittel und Wege früher Verfassungspolitik* (Stuttgart: Klett-Cotta, 1979), 9–223; Anhang Nr. 4, 207–212.

was allowed to claim by an *actio popularis* that transgressors must lift the prohibition and remove their obstructions at that time and for the future. It was possible to achieve an interdict of the Emperor even against a prince, but it was extremely difficult to enforce it, if the Emperor or territorial neighbours were not interested as actual opponents or enemies of the prince concerned.

Questions of the law of obligations with regard to barter, purchase and sale transactions (*emptio/venditio*) or loans could of course concern professional merchants and non-merchants as well. When a citizen of Ulm did not repay the credit owed to an Augsburg merchant at the due date and escaped into the church asylum in Ulm, heavily indebted and insolvent, but with ready money and valuables, three jurists of the Nuremberg City Council – Dr Seyfrid Plaghal, Dr Conrad Schütz and Dr Peter Stahel – together produced a legal opinion for the City Council of Ulm.[74] They discussed among other matters the arrest of persons and goods, whether one could avoid debtor's prison by a *cessio bonorum*[75] and leaving the city until the debt was paid, the statutes concerning the *fugitivi*, and the difference between the bankruptcy law of the Roman-canon law and of the municipal statutes, which preferred the citizens of Ulm to foreigners, who had to be content with the remaining bankruptcy assets.[76]

In another case, a Nuremberg jurist made references to the Antwerp enforcement and bankruptcy law which would be handled swiftly and without legal quibbles, *de bono et aequo* and according to the principle of priority: *qui prior est in tempore, prior sit iure.*[77] There is also a short legal opinion on the *salvus conductus* of insolvent debtors who escaped the city and then petitioned

74 E. Isenmann, 'Gelehrte Juristen und das Prozeßgeschehen', 340–355.

75 *Ibid.*, 349–350. In detail on the *cessio bonorum* and on the fraudulent bankrupts see (primarily following Baldus) Straccha, *Tractatus de mercatura seu mercatore, De conturbationibus sive decoctoribus tractatus*, fol. 177r: *Falliti sunt infames, et infamissimi* [...]. *Adeo quod propter dolum suum non videntur beneficium cessionis habere, quod est subsidium miserorum, sed non praesidium dolosorum* [...]; fol. 185r: [...] *cum decoctores beneficium cessionis non habeant, et in carcerem detrudi possint.* A person, however, going bankrupt *fortunae vitio*, does not commit an offence and is *civiliter* admitted to the *cessio bonorum*; fol. 214r. Straccha's definition of a bankrupt is: *Decoctor est, qui fortunae vitio, vel suo, vel partim fortunae, partim suo vitio non solvendo factus foro cessit.* Fol. 173v.

76 E. Isenmann, 'Gelehrte Juristen und das Prozeßgeschehen', 351–352.

77 Legal opinion of Dr Peter Stahel (1494); Staatsarchiv Nürnberg, Ratschlagbücher, Nr. 5*, fols. 85r–86v; E. Isenmann, 'Gelehrte Juristen und das Prozeßgeschehen', 351, n. 151. On the rule *qui prior est in tempore, potior est in iure, ut in reg. qui potior de reg. iur in vj.* see Straccha, *Tractatus de mercatura seu mercatore, De conturbationibus sive decoctoribus*, fols. 234v, 236r–237r.

for a temporary conduct in order to make arrangements for debt relief with the creditors in the city.[78]

6.6 *Contracts, Just Price and Usury*

The great topics of the series of *consilia* since 1500 were usury, i.e. interest payment on loans, and the market power and its abuse by financially strong trading companies, syndicate agreements, cartels and monopolistic market-dominating positions. Usury, the repayment of a loan (*mutuum*) *ultra sortem*, was a centuries-old subject of Council decrees, canon law, moral theological tracts and secular legislation and even today is still producing an extensive, and barely manageable, research literature.[79]

---

78 E. Isenmann, 'Recht, Verfassung und Politik', 126, n. 280. On the debtor's escape and *salvus conductus* in the case of the Nuremberg merchant Anton Paumgartner see Mechthild Isenmann and Eberhard Isenmann, 'Das Innenverhältnis einer spätmittelalterlichen Handelsgesellschaft', 479. On *salvus conductus* cf. Straccha: *securitas seu salvus conductus a creditoribus uel praeside provincie decoctori concessus quibus modis defendi oppugnariue possit.* Straccha, *De conturbationibus sive decoctoribus tractatus*, VI: *Tractatus de pactis conventis inter creditores et decoctores*, fols. 220rv; see further the complete tract, fols. 202v–212v. On insolvency, the *fugitivi* and bankruptcy acts see Friedrich Hellmann, *Das Konkursrecht der Reichsstadt Augsburg* (Breslau: M. & H. Marcus 1905); Walter Schorr, *Zwangsvollstreckung und Konkurs im Recht der freien Reichsstadt Nürnberg* (Nürnberg: Frankenverlag L. Spindler, 1961); Werner Ogris, 'Konkurs', in Adalbert Erler, Ekkehard Kaufmann and Wolfgang Stammler (eds.), *Handwörterbuch zur deutschen Rechtsgeschichte*, vol. 2 (Berlin: Erich Schmidt, 1978), cols. 1083–1084; Reinhard Hildebrandt, 'Zum Verhältnis von Wirtschaftsrecht und Wirtschaftspraxis im 16. Jahrhundert: Die Fallitenordnungen des Augsburger Rates 1564–1580', in Anita Mächler et al. (eds.), *Historische Studien zu Politik, Verfassung und Gesellschaft: Festschrift für Richard Dietrich zum 65. Geburtstag* (Bern: Herbert Lang, 1976), 153–160; Hans-Rudolf Hagemann, *Basler Rechtsleben im Mittelalter*, vol. 2 (Basel: Helbing & Lichtenhahn, 1987), 117–139; Ulf Heppekausen, *Die Kölner Statuten von 1437: Ursachen, Ausgestaltung, Wirkungen* (Köln: Böhlau, 1999), 116–147; Mark Häberlein, *Brüder, Freunde und Betrüger: Soziale Beziehungen, Normen und Konflikte in der Augsburger Kaufmannschaft um die Mitte des 16. Jahrhunderts* (Berlin: Akademie Verlag, 1998), 323–326, 331–337.

79 Wilhelm Endemann, *Studien in der romanisch-kanonistischen Wirthschafts- und Rechtslehre bis gegen Ende des siebzehnten Jahrhunderts*, vol. 1 (1874, repr. Aalen: Scientia, 1962); Terence P. McLaughlin, 'The Teaching of the Canonists on Usury (XII, XIII and XIV Centuries)', *Medieval Studies* 1–2, 1 (1939), 81–147 and 2 (1940) 1–22; Benjamin Nelson, *The Idea of Usury: From Tribal Brotherhood to Universal Otherhood*, 2nd ed. (Chicago: University of Chicago Press, 1969); John T. Noonan, *The Scholastic Analysis of Usury* (Cambridge Mass.: Harvard University Press, 1957); John Gilchrist, *The Church and Economic Activity in the Middle Ages* (New York: St. Martin's Press, 1969); Odd Langholm, *The Aristotelian Analysis of Usury* (Bergen: Universitetsforlaget, 1984); Odd Langholm, *Economics in the*

Economically, the prohibition of usury was grounded on the Aristotelian-Thomistic concept of money as a mere means of exchange and measure of value being consumed by its use, the sterility of money being not capital, and the doctrinaire refusal to make a difference between consumptive loans granted in cases of crisis and need – as a commandment of Christian neighbourly love – and productive credits to merchants or entrepreneurs who make profits by this inflow of additional capital. However some authors like Petrus de Olivi, Bernhardinus of Siena and Antoninus of Florence and particularly Konrad Summenhart, accepted that money invested in an enterprise by labour and trade could produce profit. The wide interpretation concerning the *interesse* of *lucrum cessans*[80] – tending to opportunity costs – and the modest and licit interest of Roman law of eight per cent among merchants on loans granted for business purposes[81] opened an approach for differentiating between consumptive and productive loans, as later Calvinists such as Carolus Molinaeus (1500–1566) and particularly Claudius Salmasius (1588–1653) clearly did.[82]

The ban on usury gave rise to a serious economic and political controversy and a critical situation in the Swabian city of Ulm in 1500. A popular form of

---

Medieval Schools: Wealth, Exchange, Value, Money and Usury According to the Paris Theological Tradition, 1200–1350 (Leiden: Brill, 1992); Odd Langholm, 'The Medieval Schoolmen (1200–1400)', in S. Todd Lowry and Barry Gordon (eds.), *Ancient and Medieval Ideas and Concepts of Social Justice* (Leiden: Brill, 1998), 439–501; Amleto Spicciani, *Capitale e interesse tra mercatura e povertà nei teologi e canonisti dei secoli XIII–XV* (Rome: Jouvence, 1990); Julius Kirshner, 'Storm over the Monte Comune', *Archivum Fratrum Praedicatorum* 53 (1983), 219–276; Hans-Jörg Gilomen, 'Wucher und Wirtschaft im Mittelalter', *Historische Zeitschrift* 250 (1990), 265–301; Gerhard Rösch, 'Wucher in Deutschland 1200–1350: Überlegungen zur Normdidaxe und Normrezeption', *Historische Zeitschrift* 259 (1994), 593–636; Lawrin Armstrong, *Usury and Public Debt in Early Renaissance Florence: Lorenzo Ridolfi on the Monte Comune* (Toronto: Pontifical Institute of Mediaeval Studies, 2003). On the question of usury and just price in Germany's municipal statutes see E. Isenmann, *Die deutsche Stadt im Mittelalter*, 957–972, 982–985. On the historical shift of the issues and the connection to the legal system of the German *Bürgerliches Gesetzbuch*, see Hans-Peter Haferkamp, 'Sittenwidriges Rechtsgeschäft, Wucher', in Mathias Schmoeckel, Joachim Rückert and Reinhard Zimmermann (eds.), *Historisch-kritischer Kommentar zum BGB, Bd. 1: Allgemeiner Teil §§ 1–240* (Tübingen: Mohr Siebeck, 2003), 708–752, § 138.

80 See in the case of Ulm, with regard to merchants, the opinions of the theologian Dr Georg Northofer, the jurist Dr *utriusque iuris* Paulus de Citandinis and Dr *legum* Ulrich Zasius. Stadtarchiv Ulm, A (Reichsstadt) 2963, fols. 27r, 57v; Eberhard Isenmann, 'Wirtschaftsrecht und Wirtschaftsethik', 213, 249–250, 255–256.

81 According to Andreas Alciatus, see Schrage, 'Mercatura honesta', 199.

82 Noonan, *The Scholastic Analysis*, 367–373; Schumpeter, *Geschichte der ökonomischen Analyse*, 151; Kirshner, 'Raymond de Roover', 30–31.

trade in the city at the time was the so-called fustian exchange – *Barchentwechsel, wechsel, cambium* – which basically meant that bleached white fustian was exchanged for the same quantity of raw fustian, with an extra charge in money, but the raw fustian not yet produced was later delivered, together with the charge, on a fixed date. The question of whether the contract was legally permitted or usurious led to comprehensive discussions, which went far beyond the mere question of usury.[83] The issue started when the mighty priest of the minster of the Swabian city of Ulm Dr *utriusque iuris* Ulrich Krafft accused a common type of business of being usurious and demanded that the city council prohibited it by a by-law. The burgomaster Dr *iur.* Mattheus Neithart feared that it would lead to the loss of employment for common and poor people, business opportunities for the higher social classes, and a strong slump in the urban tax revenues. Therefore, he sought the external expert opinions of moral theologians and learned jurists from the University of Freiburg im Breisgau, supported by several other scholars of the upper Rhine and Lake Constance region. The result was five great expert opinions and twenty major or minor opinions of 25 scholars altogether; the case produced a volume of 162 pages.[84] This impressive action is exceptional, showing the application and function of legal opinions in a virulent political and economic confrontation, the clash between the ethical rigour of the minster's priest, and the secular government's responsibility for the common good.

The experts justified in their opinions the merchants' business of buying cheap and selling at a higher price with reference to costs, labour and risk, operating costs such as rents for storerooms and salaries for the employees, and the merchants' trade profits with the maintenance of his household and family, his ability to distribute alms among the poor and by his services to the *bonum commune* in procuring necessary goods from one country to the other, especially in times of shortage. They explained the notion of contract with regard to its *substantialia* – the essential parts creating the contract's existence, without which it cannot persist; its *naturalia* – elements concluded from the contract, which can be altered by an explicit agreement; and its *accidentialia* – elements based only on an explicit agreement; and dealt with different types of contracts: the contracts of exchange (barter), of purchase and sale, and the mixture of both, loan contracts and innominate contracts *do ut des*.

---

83 On the following see E. Isenmann, 'Wirtschaftsrecht und Wirtschaftsethik', 201–258 (with numerous legal *allegationes* and quotations from the gloss and the commentaries).

84 Stadtarchiv Ulm, A (Reichsstadt) 2963; Eberhard Isenmann, 'Wirtschaftsrecht und Wirtschaftsethik', 195–259.

This discussion was important because it was argued that if there was literally or conceptually no loan contract (*mutuum*), one could not commit usury. Loans were explained in connection with the compensation of credit risks, the claims of *damnum emergens* and *lucrum cesssans* in case of debtors default, further subtle claims of damage (*interesse*) – *interesse timoris, interesse pudoris* – the fungibility (*functio*) of goods with regard to the discharging effect of payments, the principle of generic obligation, or the meaning of the *aequalitas bonitatis* and the *bonitas intrinsecum* of things and goods.

A major part of the expert opinions is devoted to the estimate of the value of goods, the factors of price formation,[85] and the just price being mainly the current market price. The just price otherwise cannot be fixed point-like, but needs a certain range; a *moderata laesio* is allowed, but the *laesio enormis* of more than a half (*ultra dimidium*) requests an adjustment or allows the withdrawal from the contract.[86] The human need (*indigentia humana*) with reference to Aristotle and subjective utility according to time, place and different circumstances create the price; further pricing factors are rarity, abundance, deficiency, fertility or infertility. With regard to utility as the source or cause of value, utility is not the characteristic of the goods themselves;[87] it was, speaking anachronistically, a neo-classical position. The subjective utility or the *particularis affectio* of the individual buyer for the object result from his reasonable *indigentia, utilitas* and *commoditas*. Another matter is the competitive price, the common estimation of value and the common market price, the *communis cursus* according to Roman law: *res tantum valet quanto communiter vendi potest*.[88] But sellers and buyers may both, however, take advantage of the other in the price negotiations (*invicem decipere, circumvenire*), but without fraud.[89] In case of doubt, experienced *boni viri* know the just price.

Beyond these very learned, scholastic and analytical considerations and together with them, the *communis consuetudo mercatorum*, the *longissima consuetudo*, the *communis opinio*, the *observantia patriae* are also of great importance for the legal and moral permissibility of contracts and business

---

85 Konrad Summenhard (*Septipertitum opus de contractibus*, Hagenau 1500, tr. III, q. 56) e.g. is able to distinguish 16 pricing factors to be observed, if prices should be legally fixed; Trusen, 'Äquivalenzprinzip', 259–261.

86 C. 4.44.2 and 8; c. 3 X 3.17; c. 6 X 3.17, c. 11 X 3.13.

87 E. Isenmann, 'Wirtschaftsrecht und Wirtschaftsethik', 235–236; cf. Schumpeter, *Geschichte der ökonomischen Analyse*, 144.

88 D. 13.1.14 and the gloss of Accursius ad D. 35.2.63 pr. v. *funguntur*.

89 D. 4.4.16.4 (Ulpian); D. 19.2.22.3 (Paulus). On *circumvenire* and *deceptio* see Straccha, *Tractatus de mercatura seu mercatore*, II, fol. 32rv, nu 6: *Idque iure etiam pontificio intra dimidiam concedit* [*c. 3 X 3.7*].

practices, and are accepted as a proper sphere of common rule-setting and law-making as a kind of *ius proprium* besides *ius commune*.[90]

Furthermore the consent and approbation of contracts and practices by the upper class of urban society (*optimates*) and the heads of the community need to be considered. And it is important that a practice does not harm anyone, but on the contrary benefits the poor and lower classes (*proletaria plebs*) giving them a means of subsistence. Contracts, as legal interpretation rules, have to be interpreted *bona fide*, with the doubt in *bonum, non in malum*; they have to be judged *ex aequo et bono* and not according to subtleties of law. But extrajudicial decisions on the just price in cases of doubt, as a highly pragmatic and common rule, shall be made by *probi et honesti viri* experienced in business affairs. The merchant's freedom of disposition and quasi-proprietary autonomy within the limits of the permitted was grounded on the sentence of Roman law, quoted by Ulrich Zasius and Konrad Peutinger, that the merchant is *suae rei moderator et arbiter*.[91] A certain freedom of action was, in the view of Zasius, also granted by a general but rebuttable presumption in favour of the merchant's business purposes being licit and legal.[92]

7 Great Legal, Moral-Theological, and Economic Discussions

7.1 *Partnership Agreement or Usurious Loan? The Five per Cent Investments and the Triple Contract*

A series of international legal opinions was prepared between 1512 and 1516 on the question of whether the fixed interest-bearing capital contributions of five per cent invested in trading companies, as was widespread in Augsburg, the seat of the largest trading companies, were usurious or not. From the traditional point of view they were; but the theologian of the University of Ingolstadt Dr *theol.* Johann Eck (Johann Maier), a student of the moral theologian Konrad Summenhart (Tübingen) and the jurist Ulrich Zasius (Freiburg i. Br.), first engaged by Jakob Fugger, tried to prove in 1514 by two expert opinions that this investment contract was substantially a partnership agreement (*societas*) – characterised by the usufruct of the capital – and not a usurious

90 E. Isenmann, 'Wirtschaftsrecht und Wirtschaftsethik', 257.

91 C. 4.35.21; C. 1.9.9; E. Isenmann, 'Wirtschaftsrecht und Wirtschaftsethik', 255; Clemens Bauer, 'Conrad Peutingers Gutachten zur Monopolfrage: Eine Untersuchung zur Wandlung der Wirtschaftsanschauungen im Zeitalter der Reformation', *Archiv für Reformationsgeschichte* 45 (1954), Teil I: 1–43, 31.

92 C. 4.32.17, Baldus ad C. 4.32.23; E. Isenmann, 'Wirtschaftsrecht und Wirtschaftsethik', 257.

loan, characterized by the transfer of the capital possession. To this purpose, Eck converted sophisticatedly and fictitiously the one contract into a triple contract (*contractus trinus*),[93] which consists of three allegedly harmonising special contracts, each single one being licit. (1) The first contract with a merchant, which can be denounced quarterly, is a partnership contract (*societas*), in which the partner, inexperienced in trade and seeking an investment opportunity, invests only capital and not labour as well; he invests only to make profit and not to make a loss and is in no way liable for debts towards external creditors; (2) the second contract is the investor's sale of his uncertain future profit to the merchant and partner for a lower certain profit (*venditio lucri incerti*) legally considered to be the 'sale of a right (*ius*)'; (3) the third contract is an insurance of the investor's principal (*assecuratio capitalis*) taken out with the merchant to the debit of the investor's certain profit.[94] The sale of the uncertain profit and the insurance reduce the investor's profit to a net return of five per cent, which is absolutely fixed in advance.[95] It was, as Eck notes, a

93 Ernest van Roey, 'Le contractus germanicus ou les controverses sur le 5% au XVI siècle en Allemagne', *Revue d'histoire ecclésiastique* 3 (1902), 901–946; Noonan, *The Scholastic Analysis*, 202–229; Johann Peter Wurm, *Johannes Eck und der oberdeutsche Zinsstreit 1513–1515* (Münster: Aschendorff, 1997). The legal opinion of Eck, *Consilium in casu quinque de centenario* is edited in Wurm, *Johannes Eck*, 223–283. It was preceded by the *consultatio in causa quinque de centum a Mercatore* of the ducal-Bavarian councillor of Augsburg origin Dr *utriusque iuris* Sebastian Ilsung, who considered the investment to be licit according to the construction of the triple contract, and an opposing opinion of the Nuremberg Dr Anton Kress rejecting the investment to be usurious. The study by Wurm, as such very competent, suffers from the fact that the author reports the positions of Eck containing logical and economic inconsistences, uncritically, while he polemically depreciates the short but quite remarkable replies of Zasius. On the later discussion of the *contractus trinus*, particularly by the Jesuist Leonhardus Lessius (1554–1623) from Antwerp, see Wim Decock, 'In Defense of Commercial Capitalism: Lessius, Partnerships and the Contractus Trinus', *Max Planck Institute for European Legal History: Research Paper Series* 4 (2012), 1–35.

94 The capital of A is strangely enough insured with the partner B, who already is bearing the risk for his own and the contributed capital, too, being obliged on principle to refund the whole contribution which can be reclaimed by A every day or quarterly. In so far as an insurance was unnecessary, and in a case of insolvency and bankruptcy, of course it was useless. For logical and economic reasons the insurance must be taken out with C, but already Konrad Summenhart in his *De contractibus licitis atque illicitis tractatus* (Venice, 1580) had accepted the insurance with B in *tractatus* VI, *quaestio* 97.

95 Eck's argumentative efforts to reject the charge of usury must logically fail on the base of a quantitative calculation, because the 5% are absolutely fixed, whereas the unknown uncertain profit is variable and can tend towards zero. Eck presents the following simple calculation as an example: The joint profit of both partners from the capital investment

summa maxime legalis et apud nos consuetudinalis. These five per cent cases correspond with the usual interest rate of perpetual, but redeemable annuities (*wiederkäufliche Renten*). But the capital contribution was not such a licit annuity, and the five per cent were not accepted under the name of an annuity.[96] The five per cent contract was customary in Augsburg, as Eck alleged, for around 40 years. Considered in detail, within Eck's fictitious construction, the trade profit on the basis of an alleged partnership characterized by profit and loss is, changing its nature, transformed into a capital gain with fixed interests. As such, Eck's opponents could regard the contribution as being an interest-bearing and therefore usurious loan (*mutuum*).[97]

The bishop of Eichstätt, to whose diocese the University of Ingolstadt belonged, prohibited a public disputation on the topic, and Dr Eck transferred it to the University of Bologna. In the library of Konrad Peutinger there survive five expert opinions for and against the permissibility of the five per cent contract, including two of Bologna legal scholars.[98] Ulrich Zasius in 1515 contributed a

---

is 20%, divided by half it is 10% per person. The compensation for the risk of capital and uncertain profit deducted, remain 5%. Wurm, *Johannes Eck*, 261. On the capital insurance Eck elaborates without regarding the sale of the uncertain profit: *Si negotiatio est talis qualitatis, quod assecuracionem capitalis inueniret soluendo tria aut quatuor pro centenario, et tamen pro lucro societatis communiter esset recepturus sex vel octo, et sic conueniret cum socio, quod solum daret sibi tria vel quatuor pro lucro et eum de capitali assecuraret, talem assecurationem opinatur licitam*. Wurm, *Johannes Eck*, 242. Eck takes the calculation example of Angelus Carletus de Clavasio who was the first to apply capital insurance to the *societas* in his *Summa angelica de casibus conscientiae* (1485). In Eck's great tract on interests of 1515 the uncertain profit is on sale for 7% and the capital is insured for 2% or 3%. The remaining 5% would require a certain but pretended uncertain profit of about 15% of the capital contribution. Wurm, *Johannes Eck*, 112. The triple contract is not a real contract, but only a construction to justify an unnamed type of transaction based on a merely fictitious calculation within the circular system of the canonistic and moral theologian usury doctrine, in many cases, economic facts put aside.

96 Wurm, *Johannes Eck*, 114, 118. On the legal nature, canonical justification and economic function of medieval (and early modern) annuities see the overview in E. Isenmann, *Die deutsche Stadt im Mittelalter*, 544–549, 949–955.

97 If the contract is regarded to constitute a *societas*, one can compare it – anachronistically – in some isolated features with the modern German silent partnership (*stille Gesellschaft* §230 HGB), which is not a veritable trading company, but a pure, '*Innengesellschaft*', and rather a contractual obligation, because the capital contribution passes into the property of the business proprietor. This transfer again characterizes a loan in the medieval understanding.

98 Künast and Zäh, *Die Bibliothek Konrad Peutingers*, Nr. 972.3 (Sebastian Ilsung, 1512/13); Nr. 972.4 (Anton Kress, before September 1513); Nr. 972.5 (Carlo Ruini, Bologna 1515/16);

short negative statement in the form of a private letter on the opinion of his former student Eck, rejecting the construction of the *contractus trinus* and considering the five per cent contract to be a usurious loan.[99] Other opinions of universities and humanists such as the Nuremberg Dr *theol.* Johannes Cochlaeus on Eck's opinion and his theses for the disputation held in Bologna were added.[100] Incidentally, Peutinger blamed the clergy, possessing most of the licit annuities, of committing a tyranny of conscience by his verdict of usury on the capital contributions to trade companies. These were the remaining form of investment necessary to the lay populace for its economic and social purposes. He agreed with Eck in principle, but – cutting the Gordian knot – he did not deal with the question of usury and supplemented his argument that virtually no alternative investment form existed with the apodictic assertion that there was no law forbidding the five per cent contributions.[101] Pope Sixtus V condemned the triple contract in 1586, but the discussion went on.

7.2 *Trading Companies, Monopolies, and Cartels: Opinions of Jurists, Burghers, City Councils, and Diet Committees*

This disputes on the triple contract had aspects related to another discussion by expert opinions on the large trading companies and their monopoly position, insofar as it was alleged that the five per cent investments contributed to

---

Nr. 972.6 (Johannes Crotus de Monteferrato, [Bologna] 1516); Nr. 972.7 (Johannes Eck, 11. September 1514).

99 The statement is edited in Steven Rowan, *Ulrich Zasius: A Jurist in the German Renaissance, 1461–1535* (Frankfurt am Main: Vittorio Klostermann, 1987), Appendix 1, 227–231. Rowan reports upon, but does not analyse, the case, 112–117. In particular, Zasius characterizes the *societas* and the purchase contract in a different way with regard to its *substantia* and *natura*; he analyses the transfer of the capital's *dominium*, the sale contract with the necessary elements of consensus, price and merchandise and the insurance of the capital risk with deviating results and rejects the threefold construction as being a monster and actually a usurious *mutuum*. The wording of Eck was misleading: Gaius *paciscitur cum Ticio, ut capitali saluo accipiat pro porcione lucri sui incerti quinque florinos de centum annuo* [...] and: *Illud lucrum iam sic fixum ex venditione lucri incerti non est lucrum sociale, sed est pretium, pro quo vendidit ius suum sociale.* Wurm, *Johannes Eck*, 224, 241. See further Pietro Nervi, 'L'umanesimo giuridico in Germania: Le 'usurae' nella dottrina di Ulrich Zasius (1461–1535)', *Annali dell Istituto storico italo-germanico in Trento: Jahrbuch des italienisch-deutschen historischen Instituts in Trient* 25 (1999), 63–92.

100 Wurm, *Johannes Eck*, 192–200 (Dr *theol.* Johannes Cochlaeus). Wurm does not use the two contradictory *consilia* from Bologna handed down in Peutinger's collection.

101 Letter Peutinger's to Eck December 19, 1514. Erich König, (ed.), *Konrad Peutingers Briefwechsel* (München: Beck, 1923), Nr. 153, 250–251; this argument is repeatedly used by Eck and Peutinger and in the Augsburger opinion of 1522 (see below note 108).

the creation of great commercial capitals enabling monopolies. But this discussion became an independent subject when from 1512 until 1532 and later on until 1548, a series of Imperial Diets on the German princes' initiative intended to create laws to prohibit the large companies of upper Germany, particularly the outstanding ones of Augsburg. The companies were blamed for establishing monopolies and price-cartels manipulating prices, and therefore damaging the common good.[102] On the basis of the future monopoly laws the local authorities and subsidiary the Imperial attorney, the *procurator fiscalis* (*Reichskammerprokuratorfiskal*), should prosecute monopolistic contracts and practices, but he already proceeded with legal actions on the basis of the Cologne Diet's resolution of 1512 – regardless of legislative results during the discussions' main phase – in 1523 against the Nuremberg Imhoff company and the Augsburg Jacob Fugger, Andreas Grander, Christof Herwart, Ambrosius Höchstetter, Bartholomäus Welser and Andreas Rem, co-partners included. In 1529 and 1530 he brought actions against Bartholomäus Welser, the brothers Andreas und Lukas Rem and Elisabeth Pfister, the widow of Christof Herwart.[103] In view of this dangerous situation, lawyers prepared legal opinions on procedural law.[104] The accused were threatened by severe penalties, but the

102 Fritz Blaich, *Die Reichsmonopolgesetzgebung im Zeitalter Karls v. Ihre ordnungspolitische Problematik* (Stuttgart: G. Fischer, 1967); Fritz Blaich, *Die Wirtschaftspolitik des Reichstags im Heiligen Römischen Reich* (Stuttgart: G. Fischer, 1970); Karin Nehlsen-von Stryk, 'Das Monopolgutachten des rechtsgelehrten Humanisten Conrad Peutinger aus dem frühen 16. Jahrhundert', *Zeitschrift für Neuere Rechtsgeschichte* 10 (1988), 1–18; Bernd Mertens, *Im Kampf gegen Monopole: Reichstagsverhandlungen und Monopolprozesse im frühen 16. Jahrhundert* (Tübingen: Mohr, 1996). Infringements on competition rules are today not issues of commercial law, but concern the particular laws against restriction of competition. The modern Welfare economy according to the Neoclassics (Alfred Marshall, *Principles of Economics* (London: Macmillan, 1890)) brings back economy into the sphere of ethics. Monopolies reduce the 'consumer surplus' and lead to an individual 'deadweight-loss', because they disturb the optimality conditions of perfect competition. The consumer surplus results from the difference between the maximum amount the consumers would be willing to pay and the current market price. According to Schumpeter the late scholastic economic sociology with its notion of common good in the utilitarian sense understood as 'satisfaction of the individuals' economic needs recognized by the observer's reason or *ratio recta* – apart from the technical side – is identical with the welfare concept of the modern Welfare Economics, e.g. of Prof. Pigous. Schumpeter, *Geschichte der ökonomischen Analyse*, 143.

103 On the lawsuits for monopolistic behaviour see Mertens, *Im Kampf gegen Monopole*, 118–148.

104 Legal opinion of the jurist Dr Simon Pistorius; Staats- und Stadtbibliothek Augsburg, 2° Cod. Aug. 402, fols. 179r–186r; two opinions of Dr Peutinger; 2° Cod. Aug. 386, fols. 211r–213r; 2° Cod. Aug. 402, fols. 169r–172r.

actions proved to be unsuccessful due to the Emperor's interventions and an alleged delaying of files.

The discussion in the Imperial Diets on monopolies and illicit cartel agreements gave rise to expert opinions on several stages and of different types. (1) Urban jurists such as Konrad Peutinger and others prepared legal and economic opinions in favour of the trading companies and cities, and urban representatives presented (2) their cities' opinions for the Diet's proceedings. (3) Smaller committees consisting of deputies of the Diet's three 'estates' (*Stände*) or *curiae*, who were often jurists in a large number, elaborated several expert advices for the Diet's legal policy (*Ratschläge*) to be forwarded to (4) a larger committee which then presented its report to the so-called *Reichsregiment*, a governing and advisory body composed of representatives of electors, princes and cities under the Imperial procurator's presidency and acting during the absence of the Emperor from the German nation residing in Spain.

The most comprehensive advice was the report (*Ratschlag*) concerning monopolies and commercial abuses with 42 articles worked out by the small committee of the second Nuremberg Diet in 1522/23.[105] It later became the basis for the large monopoly-committee of the Augsburg Diet in 1530 and its report. Three questions of the *Reichsregiment* concerning the big companies were the very basis and starting point of the great report of 1522/23. It was asked (1) whether the companies were detrimental to the Holy Empire and common good and therefore should be abolished; (2) whether they should be totally abolished without any differences between companies or whether they should be only limited and 'a measure should be put to them'; and (3) by what means restrictions should be done.[106] Cities like Ulm, Frankfurt am Main, Nuremberg and Augsburg were invited to submit the opinions of some burghers to the Diet.

The Augsburg City Council was not satisfied with the deputed burghers' opinion and report[107] and presented instead a longer and more substantial opinion, whose authors are unknown.[108] Experts in Augsburg were at this time the jurists Dr Peutinger and Dr Rehlinger and the merchant Ulrich Arzt. The second Augsburg opinion for the *Reichsregiment* gave an overall view of the trade's problems and specific features in important regions of Europe. It

105 Adolf Wrede (ed.), *Deutsche Reichstagsakten: Jüngere Reihe, Deutsche Reichstagsakten unter Kaiser Karl* V., vol. 3 [RTA JR III] (1901, repr. Göttingen: Vandenhoeck & Ruprecht, 1963), Nr. 104, 571–599 (1522 Dec.–1523 Jan.).

106 RTA JR III, Nr. 100, 556 (Nov. 6, 1522).

107 RTA JR III, Nr. 102, 558–561 (Nov., 1522).

108 RTA JR III, Nr. 103, 561–571 (Nov., 1522).

justified the Augsburg five per cent investments increasing the companies' capital, using the same argument that Johannes Eck and Peutinger offered: the clergy had acquired and bought up nearly all real estates and rents so that the investment was the only remaining possibility to meet by its return the social needs of wide circles of the population. And it spoke out against any limitation of the companies' principal (*hauptsumma*) and operating capital (*handlunggelt*) with reference to the common Papal and Imperial law. The 'common law(s)', the Roman-canon law – regarded as a universal commercial law – by natural and reasonable grounds allow the trade and business of all companies, and do not impose a restriction of their capital, and this is already customary at all times and all over the world. Furthermore the common laws clearly allow one person who does not work in the company to invest his money, and to reward another part who does work in the company, from the company's realized gain.

The city of Ulm sent a short statement proposing that a company should be restricted to father, son and son-in-law as partners, with a maximum capital of 1.000 florins. Maximum prices on important goods such as metals, spices, cloths and alike, should be set, if grievances went on.[109] The opinion of the Frankfurt council was to abolish the well-known big companies completely, to fix prices and to prohibit the acceptance of third persons' contributions (*frembd gelt*) and to operate with such.[110]

In Nuremberg, the Council's jurist Dr Christoff Kress had earlier elaborated a predominantly economic expert opinion,[111] which was discussed in the City Council and then presented to the *Reichsregiment*. This opinion is very important, because 15 articles of the critical committee's report of 1522/23 – and later that of 1530 – originate in the exact wording from this opinion.[112] We can see that Dr Kress and the Nuremberg Council, declaring for the limitation of the companies' economic power, did not argue in favour of big business, but were – as were the City Councils of Ulm and Frankfurt – rather antipodes of Augsburg and its big companies. Furthermore, the detailed proof of raising prices for spices and some other merchandise in the period from 1510 to 1522,

109 RTA JR III, Nr. 101, 556–558 (Dec. 4, 1522).

110 RTA JR III, 556–557, n. 3; Lutz, *Die rechtliche Struktur*, 90, n. 321.

111 Staatsarchiv Nürnberg, Reichsstadt Nürnberg, Ratskanzlei, A-Laden 150, Nr. 18, fols. 2r–12r, 1–21 (*in consilio* October 4, 1522). The advice is to my knowledge unpublished and is not mentioned in contributions on the topic.

112 The adoptions by the committee's report concern the articles 9–12, 14, 18–22, 25, 26, 37–39. Nuremberg was in the committee represented by the merchant and city councillor Sigmund Fürer. RTA JR III, 290.

inserted into the report of 122/23, came from lists provided by Nuremberg merchants.

The Diet's committees with regard to legislation had to clarify the question of which of the companies and which contractual trading strategies and commercial practices with what kind of goods were abusive, and had to be subsumed under the facts of monopoly and cartel and had to be prohibited by law. This required a conceptual juridical discussion connected to an analysis of economic issues. With the background of popular current opinions and above all the princes' and nobles' hostile attitudes to capitalism and the major cities' economic and financial power, the direct motif of action for the legal policy was the stipulation Charles V made at his election in 1519, which was to prohibit the big, financially strong trading companies of Upper Germany, considered to act as price-driving and against the common good. Key aspects were price increases particularly affecting the common man as a result of price dictation, and manipulation of the companies and the assumption that capital strength and monopolization were directly related.

The Diet's committees, with regard to the facts of monopolies, went on from the traditional prohibitions of pre-emption and buying-up complete stocks and legally referred to Roman law, the prohibition of monopolies and cartels by Emperor Zeno in 483 (C. 4.59). In modern terms they dealt with price cartels, supply monopolies and exclusivity agreements (with the king of Portugal). In their opinion – and that of the moral theologians[113] – the facts of monopoly were also given, if not all goods were in one single hand and only a quasi-monopoly existed; a marked-dominating position enabling the exercising of a price dictate and manipulation was sufficient.

Dr Konrad Peutinger[114] and other Augsburg jurists prepared legal opinions and the committees of the Imperial Diets made legislative proposals in the form of legal and economic expert opinions. Peutinger, related to the Höchstetter and related by marriage to the Welser, was the main protagonist defending the great Augsburg mercantile and banking houses and the interests of the

113 Raymond de Roover, 'Monopoly Theory prior to Adam Smith: A revision, 1951', in Julius Kirshner (ed.), *Business, Banking, and Economic Thought in Late Medieval and early Modern Europe: Selected Studies of Raymond de Roover* (Chicago: University of Chicago Press, 1974), 273–305, 280; see also Odd Langholm, 'Monopoly and Market Irregularities in Medieval Economic Thought: Traditions and Texts to A.D. 1500', *Journal of the History of Economic Thought* 28 (2006), 395–411.

114 On Peutinger see in general Erich König, *Peutingerstudien* (Freiburg i. Br.: Herder, 1914); Heinrich Lutz, *Conrad Peutinger: Beiträge zu einer politischen Biographie* (Augsburg: Verlag Die Brigg, 1958).

city of Augsburg. From 1499 to 1530 – in 1499, 1522/23, 1524/25, 1526, 1530 – he produced six expert opinions, legal advices and memoranda,[115] and additionally two legal opinions on procedural law concerning the fiscal's actions against Augsburg companies.

Peutinger had in 1499 already elaborated an expert opinion on the copper syndicate of 1498/1499, between the companies of the Fugger, Herwart, Gossembrot, Paumgartner and Knoll.[116] In his legal opinion, written for the Fugger opponents within the syndicate who were damaged by Fugger's sales and price manipulations, he denied that the prohibition of monopolies and cartels by Roman law was under consideration, taking the view that only unseemly agreements (*illicitae conventiones*) were forbidden. This means contracts violating the common good and equity. In 1522/23 Peutinger presented a translation of the Greek word and a simple definition of the term of monopoly. A monopoly is given if one or more persons get common consumer goods into one hand with the intent of selling them as the sole supplier at their discretion, and in order to dictate the purchase price and not to sell cheaper.[117] The monopoly committee of the Diet in 1530 also did not start from an absolute monopoly of one sole supplier, but enumerated several kinds of goods such as spices, ore, metal and cloths with regard to monopolistic practices. A monopoly in its opinion was established by massive pre-emption and was possibly maintained by specific associations, agreements – cartels, syndicates – or companies, indenturing the seller to sell the merchandise exclusively to them, or to sell it to later buyers but not cheaper.[118]

Peutinger however in 1523 had the concept of monopoly in his interpretation of Zeno's law limited to daily consumer goods necessary for life (*res viles*) such as grain and wine, items the common and poor man could not live without, and materials needed by the simple manual worker and workman to earn their living. Mining products such as the metals gold and silver and luxury goods like expensive spices, particularly pepper and saffron, bought only by

115 Apart from the opinion on the copper syndicate, all opinions are edited in Bauer, 'Conrad Peutingers Gutachten', Teil I: 1–43; cf. Teil II: 145–196 (Bauer on the topic).

116 *Consilium in causa societatis cupri*; Staats- und Stadtbibliothek Augsburg, 2° Cod. Aug. 398, fols. 189r–198v (autograph fair copy by Peutinger); Cod. Aug. 404, fols. 190–197 (draft). The contract (May 12, 1498) and the amendments (September 2, 1499) are printed in Richard Ehrenberg, *Das Zeitalter der Fugger: Geldkapital und Kreditverkehr im 16. Jahrhundert*, vol. 1, 3rd ed. (Jena: G. Fischer, 1922), 417–420; see also Mertens, *Im Kampf gegen Monopole*, 27–29; Nehlsen-v. Stryk, 'Die Monopolgutachten', 6–8.

117 Bauer, 'Conrad Peutingers Gutachten', 8.

118 Bauer, 'Conrad Peutingers Gutachten', 16–17.

the rich, were excluded.[119] Thus Peutinger framed a restricted social concept of monopoly, protecting the poor, who were supposed not to need pepper in their necessary consumer goods,[120] but excluded them from higher demands. Nicole Oresme (c. 1320–1382), San Antonino of Florence (1389–1459) and San Bernardino of Siena (1380–144) had already condemned monopolies and cartels, the latter especially if temporary or more permanent cartels 'involved victuals or other necessities and thus placed an excessive burden on the poor'.[121] Irrespective of the concept of monopoly, Peutinger denied that the incriminated big companies in the pepper trade strove for monopolistic positions or held them, because they depended on the arbitrary contractual behaviour of the king of Portugal, who unilaterally disposed of the pepper as a mighty monopolistic supplier, a *venditor unicus*.

Zeno's law also prohibited restricted labour practices, illicit agreements between craftsmen; nobody could was permitted to finish the work of another originally commissioned to do or to take on his work order. This corresponded later with similar practices by medieval guilds. Peutinger took the Imperial prohibitions, in a paradoxical turn, as an opportunity to propagate everyman's fundamental freedom to buy and sell as well as to order and accept works.[122]

Price cartels and monopolies were to be prohibited, according to authors of the early and late fifteenth century, such as the author of the *Reformatio Sigismundi* and the Strasbourg minster preacher Dr Johann Geiler of Kaysersberg (1445–1510),[123] but they were already prohibited by Roman law (C. 4.49), which was generally the applicable law in the Roman-German Empire. The anti-capitalist *Reformatio Sigismundi* of 1439, published 80 years later in the early 1520s in several prints because of its contemporary topicality, had demanded the destruction of the large trading companies by force if needed. Such demands immediately became politically virulent when Charles V in 1519 promised to proceed against the financially mighty and selfish companies. The resolution made by the Diet of Cologne and Trier in 1512 during the reign of Maximilian I referred in its monopoly prohibition concerning all commercial

---

119 Bauer, 'Conrad Peutingers Gutachten', 11–12.

120 1526: [...] *dummodo non infringantur nec tollantur nec frivolae monopoliorum* (*et praecipue cum nihil contra pauperes, eorum victum et usum moliantur*) *obiectioni respondere cogantur*. Bauer, Nr. III, 16.

121 De Roover, 'Monopoly Theory', 279–8.

122 *In summa in kauffen, verkauffen, arbeit zue bestellen oder auf sich zu nehmen, soll yderman frey sein: Hostiensis* [*ad c. un. X 1.3*], *Bartolus* [*ad C. 1.3.48, D. 47.22*]; Bauer, 'Conrad Peutingers Gutachten', Nr. II, 13 (1522/23).

123 E. Isenmann, *Die deutsche Stadt im Mittelalter*, 969–970.

goods (spices, ore, wool cloths and the like) to the law of Emperor Zeno as 'common written imperial law' and defined the noxiousness of monopolies to the public by the ability to dictate prices arbitrarily.[124]

Monopolies and cartel agreements existed above all in the mining sector. The Toledo edict petitioned by an Augsburg legation and enacted by Charles V on 13 May 1525 created an exception area for the monopoly prohibition concerning ores and metals: The mines were a great gift of God and a usability for the German nation, but in order to construct and maintain them, high investments and continuously high selling prices were necessary. Such prices could be best guaranteed when the products with regard to the first buyer were not sold 'to many hands', but to one hand or a few ones. A high price was not detrimental, because the largest share of the products were exported and the common man did not need them for his necessary demands. On the other hand, the German nation, being in competition with other nations, would suffer considerable disadvantages, if the mines were not promoted by exemption from the monopoly prohibition, and thereby a shortage of metal would occur.[125]

This was also the argumentative line of Peutinger, who in addition was of the opinion that in view of the large variety of mines at different places, monopolization to one hand by companies and syndicates was not possible.[126] When Duke George of Saxony in 1520 granted a monopoly on tin by privilege to a tin trading company of merchants, among others the Augsburg Welser, he justified the granted monopoly with the current drop in prices and the resulting danger that mines could go to ruin to the detriment of the territory, and had to cease operations, so that the people could no longer earn their living there.[127] The monopoly committee of the Augsburg Diet in 1530 confirmed the benefit from the mines, but complained that the export of large quantities of gold and silver bullion was leaving the Empire in exchange for more harmful than useful merchandise; and it criticized pre-emption and the monopoly of companies of the tin trade in a general way.[128]

124 Johann J. Schmauß and Heinrich C. von Senckenberg (eds.), *Neuere und vollständigere Sammlung der Reichs-Abschiede* [...], vol. 2 (Frankfurt a. M.: Koch, 1747), 1244.

125 The edict of Toledo is printed in Strieder, *Studien*, 375–381. According to modern ideas a monopoly of only short duration with its profit maximization may have positive effects, if it enables technical progress and other innovations.

126 Bauer, 'Conrad Peutingers Gutachten', 33, cf. 24 (petition).

127 Strieder, *Studien*, Nr. 17, 424–427. Duke Georg of Saxony had already in 1500 granted a monopoly privilege for three years to the 'Gesellschaft des Zinnkaufs'. Strieder, *Studien*, Nr. 15, 418–420.

128 Bauer, 'Conrad Peutingers Gutachten', 18–19.

While Diets were discussing a prohibition of monopolies, in Saxony, economic expert's opinions were prepared on how the tin trade monopolies could be created and how the control over the Central European metal trade was to gain.[129] Duke George of Saxony had granted monopolies on the tin trade in 1500 and 1520 even before the Toledo edict of 1525, and the Roman-German, Hungarian and Bohemian King Ferdinand I assured the recipient of his monopoly privilege of 1549 on the Bohemian tin trade, the Augsburg Conrad Mair, help and promotion, if he were sued in the Imperial Chamber court or charged by the Imperial fiscal.[130]

The committee's report of 1530 attacked not only unfair trade practices but also the organisation of the 'selfish companies' pressing the poor merchant and the small trades men by pre-emption, establishing many branches (*Faktoreien*), and their methods of transacting business – without travelling, and by letters and commercial correspondents – in order to increase the volume of business. The poor merchants and small tradesmen depended on the companies and had to buy from them, whereas the companies sold their merchandise on credit and beat the reasonable prices of the merchants so that the merchants also had to cut their prices, and repurchase merchandise through straw men. Instead of one company, twenty or thirty well-situated merchants, who had to travel, could earn their living. This idea was based on the old *Nahrungsprinzip* of the craft guilds, it is the repartition of an assumed volume of earning opportunities between several persons to ensure them a reasonable living appropriate to their social standing. This principle was now applied to the free trade, as it first had demanded the *Reformatio Sigismundi* in 1439.[131]

The question in 1522/23 and 1530 was whether all companies tended to monopolies and corresponding practices, and whether the big trading companies should be totally abolished or, instead of this rigorous intention, only their

129 Strieder, *Studien*, Nr. 21, 432–435. On March 10, 1525 Charles V signed in Madrid a law elaborated in Augsburg by Dr Peutinger or Dr Johann Rehlinger and submitted by an Augsburg legation. The law is printed in König, *Peutingerstudien*, 169–174. It prohibited to get merchandise into one hand for the purpose of dictating prices and exclusivity contracts. But the law otherwise allowed merchants and companies a 'completely free' trade at all times and in all places without the restriction of the principal, the investments of the partners and the acceptance of borrowed third-party money. After a provisional rejection, Peutinger had elaborated a memorandum as an instruction for the Ausgsburg legation and an *informatio* for the imperial councillors. Staats- und Stadtbibliothek Augsburg, 2° Cod. Aug. 403, fols. 336–358; Mertens, *Im Kampf gegen die Monopole*, 74, n. 294.

130 Strieder, *Studien*, Nr. 29, 445.

131 E. Isenmann, *Die deutsche Stadt im Mittelalter*, 262–61, 986–987.

capital stock should be reduced and limited to amounts between 20.000 and 50.000 florins;[132] the number of the branches outside the company's domicile should be limited to three, and whether in order to guarantee the capital restriction an accounting to the authorities should be performed periodically. Fixed interest bearing contributions were to be prohibited in order to prevent an increase in capital and the possibility of monopolization as well as forbidden usurious contracts. Maximum prices, possibly in consideration of the different transport distances (1532), should be applied to spices, cloths and similar merchandise. Also, merchants of foreign nations should be subject to capital restrictions and legal maximum prices.

7.3 *The Legal, Economic and Social Opinions of the Lawyer Dr Konrad Peutinger*

Konrad Peutinger presented his arguments in a polemical counter opinion to the advice of the small committee on monopolies of 1523,[133] in a short memorandum on monopolies and trading companies of 1526,[134] and in a petition of the City of Augsburg to Charles V with regard to the committee's report of 1530[135] with an enclosed memorandum dated to August/September 1530.[136] Since the report of 1530 is largely based on the advice of 1523, he commented twice, to a great extent, on the same issues.

Peutinger did not consider monopolies in his narrow interpretation of the notion as legal or justifiable, but with regard to the restrictions of the Diet's committees he defended in favour of big business – companies and potent excellent merchants – the freedom of the price formation process in a dynamic economy, free movement of the merchants and the freedom of any negotiation, because free negotiation promoted the benefit of the *res publica* more than an economy restricted by coercion, as daily experience teaches. His arguments are legal, empirically based on data and experience, of evident nature (*auditum et visum est*), economic-analytical and sociological ones. Against economic restrictions and coercion, and in favour of liberty, he asserts, in general statements and only very rarely giving legal references in particular, the permission of companies and trading activities by *ius*, *ius*

132 Examples of capital stocks and profit rates of companies and merchants: E. Isenmann, *Die deutsche Stadt im Mittelalter*, 914–916.

133 Bauer, 'Conrad Peutingers Gutachten', Nr. I, 3–7.

134 Bauer, 'Conrad Peutingers Gutachten', Nr. III, 14–16.

135 *Ratslag der Monopolia halb* (August 12, 1530); Bauer, Nr. IV, 16–22; Nr. V, 22–28 (Augsburg petition).

136 Bauer, 'Conrad Peutingers Gutachten', Nr. VI, 28–43.

commune, *aequitas*, *consuetudo*, (*honestus*) *usus mercanciarum* (*negotiationum*), *bonae mores* and *ratio*, or he invokes only the fact that they are in no way and nowhere forbidden.

Peutinger's economic and social arguments are in detail that the raising of a great capital is not forbidden by any kind of law. Accepting great capital contributions does not induce *per se* a monopolistic strategy on principle, because economic engagements at many different places and in remote nations lead to the division and diversification of business and to a diverse allocation of the capital stock. Therefore the number of external branches should not be limited to three, but on contrary rather increased to a hundred. Everybody knows that the greater the capital and the quantity of goods, the greater the profit (*utilitas*). Thus, wealth is directed to Germany and remains here, the revenues of the rulers and authorities increase and private persons obtain benefits, too. With regard to the costs resulting from long distances, customs and expenses on *salvus conductus*, only great companies, but not minor merchants with their small quantities, are able to carry out international long-distance trade by importing and exporting.[137] The mining sector needs rich and financially strong persons, companies and joint ventures (*coniciones*).[138] Continuously high prices are needed, but monopolization in one hand is not possible.[139] Commercially powerful merchants may not be blamed for exporting *bona moneta* in gold and silver to foreign nations, because they use bills of exchange, whereas minor merchants are not capable of doing so and must trade with specie.

Nobody in society from the princes down to the peasants is prohibited to enrich himself, to set up funds, or take profits by his assets and to promote his own benefit (*utilitas propria*) in an honest manner, and every political community (*res publica*) is interested in wealthy subjects. Therefore major companies are allowed to trade and contract with a capital stock of more than 50,000 florins and without capital restrictions at all, if they do not offend in anything against legal prohibitions and their acts conform to law. A capital control by an obligatory and sufficient accounting is not only impossible every year according to the *consuetudo* and *usus negotionum*, but hardly possible every two years, if business should not be interrupted and one has time for such annoying accounts at all. Foreign companies moreover cannot be subjected to capital

137 In the second Augsburg advice of 1522 is noticed: Great merchants must do the great transactions, because common merchants are not able to cope with them by their means. RTA JR III, Nr. 108, 564.

138 Bauer, 'Conrad Peutingers Gutachten', 15 (1526).

139 Bauer, 'Conrad Peutingers Gutachten', 33, 24.

restriction, capital control by accounting and legally fixed prices, as intended by the Diet's committee.

With regard to the capital contributions to companies bearing annual interests, Peutinger avoids the usual discussion on usury and confines it to the statement that they do not contravene *ius commune*, and merchants and companies are not prohibited to accept money for their trade against adequate and honourable returns in the form of a callable loan or in another honourable way. Accepting the interest-bearing money of clients, companies help those persons who cannot trade themselves or are not economically active people such as noblemen, orphans or burghers, who can make their living only by the shrinkage and loss of their capital or by (ground) rents and returns on capital, and for various reasons cannot invest ready money to profit and loss or in real estates or annuities. The investors can call in their contributions and take their adequate yields, for example under social aspects in order to provide for their daughter's dowry or their son's *donatio propter nuptias*.

Legal prices as maximum prices fixed by public authorities and imposed on all goods would be against the *ius commune* and prevent business at all. Price fluctuations and unequal selling prices according to the changeable course of time are natural; and nobody would take on labour, danger and risk, if he cannot hope to make profits because of fixed prices. Pricing depends on the seller's personal living conditions and necessities. The seller must sometimes sell dearer, sometimes cheaper; he sells for ready money or on credit, or he demands not money but goods. One merchant sells faster, the other slowly, depending on the number of buyers and as his experience teaches him, and depending on the crop yields and the supplied quantity. If maximum prices are fixed, it may happen that the seller does not get the price appropriate to him, or he has to sell for less than the purchase price.[140] Higher prices are not generally and primarily caused by monopolies, and prices for handicraft products have increased, too. A merchant who, for example, has metals to sell, must bring them to the places where he can expect to get his best prices.

The lawyer and humanist Peutinger shows in his counsels – in a defending position – the economic life of merchants and companies determined by God's will, a fateful rotating *fortuna* and changeable course of time (*nihil enim in mundo stabile esse potest*), by risk, danger to life and goods, labour, human experience, competence, success and failure, profit and loss and free disposal of his property. Monopolies – in a narrow interpretation – are indeed prohibited by Roman law, but Peutinger invokes law in general, Roman-canon law, customary law and *usus* primarily to assert that trade must be free, economic

140 Bauer, 'Conrad Peutingers Gutachten', 32, 40–41.

restrictions were against the law and the commercial practices in question were not prohibited by law and were permitted by commercial *consuetudo* and *usus*. Again and again he draws attention to the competition by large trading companies of other nations damaging the German nation and common good, if the intended economic restrictions would be put into law and practice. Ethical limits for legally permitted enrichment are not drawn.[141] Peutinger paints a picture of a free risk society discussing the argument that many companies have become bankrupt and it was not only these which had suffered detriment, but they had damaged others, too. Bankruptcies are no reason for prohibiting big companies. Peutinger's arguments are lapidary: Fortuna's wheel just is turning; nobody is forced to invest his money in a company, but it is his own decision (*arbitrium*); *unde volenti non fit iniuria*.[142]

Contrary to the report of the committee, Peutinger does not admit that the companies give cause for turmoil and riots in cities.[143] Where economically powerful merchants exist, there, as a rule, livelihood (*victus*) and income of all crafts increase.[144] Wealth and means promote peace and tranquillity, scarcity and poverty cause discord and disturbance of the peace.[145]

To seek one's own benefit (*proprium commodum*) is *de iure* not only in business, but also in all other actions permitted, and prohibited to nobody. It is not only permitted for the economically active merchants and companies, but also for non-active persons, the idlers (*otiosi.*). Under economic-social aspect the merchants' and companies' self-interest and the common good of all people, rich and poor, and particularly the fiscal interests of the ruling public authorities, are in harmony with each other; possible inconsistencies are not considered.

---

141 In the second Augsburg advice of 1522 Peutinger states: The merchant's trading does not tolerate limits; the richer merchants are and the greater their number is, the greater is the trading volume, the more are the trade transaction and the more is the common profit promoted; if trading would not be free, one would look for something else or totally stop it; if a merchant with his company having more means beyond a legally fixed capital, what should he do with the loose money? RTA JR III, Nr. 108, 564.

142 Cf. D. 47.10.1.5 (Ulpian). The sentence, concerning the freedom of the human will, had in its variations become a kind of commonplace in legal and moral theologian literature; cf. Langholm, *The Merchant in the Confessional*, 163, 223.

143 Bauer, 'Conrad Peutingers Gutachten', VI (1530). In the true sense, pre-emptions of companies raising prices were meant, rather than the companies as such.

144 The Augsburg City Council stated in the advice of 1522: The activities of great, rich and powerful merchants are followed by a great business of crafts. RTA JR III, Nr. 108, 564.

145 Bauer, 'Conrad Peutingers Gutachten', VI (1523).

According to the scholastic teleology, from the intention of self-interest (*Eigennutz*) the common good, as it was a necessary prerequisite for licit contracts and business enterprises, could never emerge. The *bonum commune* or *utilitas publica* had absolute priority over the *privatum commodum*; at best the justified, but not autonomous, self-interest was included within the common good, the undisputed ultimate objective (*causa finalis*).[146]

Peutinger dissolved this stringent teleology starting from the readily available compatibility and interdependence of private and public interest and formulating, as one of the first, the later Adam Smith phenomenon of the 'invisible hand'. When people trade freely but within the limits of the law and the elemental moral law, and when they pursue their own benefit (*propria utilitas*, *proprium commodum*) and advantage taking labour and danger to person, life and goods; then – due to the intertwining of the economy – it will emerge the lasting advantage of the others as the common good of all economically active men, of ruling authorities and communities. And even if mining and metal trade are operated in a monopolistic way, the common good of the community will arise miraculously (*mirum in modo*) as a result.[147]

146 Eberhard Isenmann, 'The Notion of the Common Good, the Concept of Politics, and Practical Policies in Late Medieval and Early Modern German Cities', in Elodie Lecuppre-Desjardin and Anne-Laure van Bruaene (eds.), *De Bono Communi: The Discourse and Practice of the Common Good in the European City (13th–16th c.)* (Turnhout: Brepols, 2010), 107–148. On the increasing normative acceptance of self-interest (Eigennutz) in social and economic relations see Winfried Schulze, 'Vom Gemeinnutz zum Eigennutz: Über den Normenwandel in der ständischen Gesellschaft der Frühen Neuzeit', *Historische Zeitschrift* 243 (1986), 591–626.

147 Bauer, 'Conrad Peutingers Gutachten', 37, 33, cf. 25, 26, 33, 41; Teil II, 192–195. See the resumee in Clemens Bauer, 'Conrad Peutinger und der Durchbruch des neuen ökonomischen Denkens in der Wende zur Neuzeit', in Hermann Rinn (ed.), *Augusta 955–1955. Forschungen und Studien zur Kultur- und Wirtschaftsgeschichte Augsburgs* (München: Verlag Hermann Rinn, 1955), 219–228, 224, 226. This is not the place to discuss the interesting question of whether Peutinger, defending the Augsburg commercial interests as a lawyer informed in economy, is one of the intellectual founders of a new attitude to business and of economic individualism.

CHAPTER 11

The Birth of Commercial Law in Early Modern Sweden: Sources and Historiography

Heikki Pihlajamäki

Introduction

Rules governing business and merchants emerged separately from other branches of law in some European countries during the early modern period. France is the major example. A commercial court was established in Paris in 1563, and it was followed by two statutes, *Ordonnance sur le commerce* (1673) and *Ordonnance de la marine* (1681). Although the statutes were incomplete, and in practice needed to be complemented by *ius commune* and mercantile custom, this was nevertheless an important milestone on the way towards a separate commercial law. In most countries, both procedural and substantial norms regulating commercial relations were placed under contract law and procedural law until the late eighteenth century. The Prussian Code of 1794 (*Allgemeines Preussisches Landrecht*) first introduced a separate chapter on commercial law and in fact started what became a virtual wave of commercial law codifications in the nineteenth century.[1] Following international examples, most of the Swedish early modern legal rules that today would be observed under the label of commercial law were classified under maritime law (*sjörätt*), private law (*privaträtt*), or the law of negotiable instruments (*växelrätt*). Maritime law, in particular, was one of the developing fields of law in the seventeenth century because it was through sea trade that Swedish merchants most frequently came into contact with foreign merchants and their legal regulations.

Despite the anachronism attached to it, commercial law nevertheless serves well as a descriptive historical concept. It gathers together various legal norms and practices related to different aspects of commercial life, such as company law, the law of commercial instruments, transport law, insurance law, insolvency law, and the law of obligations (between merchants). Most importantly, commercial law serves as what comparative lawyers call *tertium comparationis*

1 Johannes Flume, 'Law and Commerce: The Evolution of Codified Business Law in Europe', *Comparative Legal History* 2:1 (2014), 45–83, 50; Dave De ruysscher, *Gedisciplineerde vrijheid: Een geschiedenis van het handels- en economisch recht* (Antwerpen: Maklu, 2014), 19–25.

 | DOI 10.1163/9789004363144_012

or a common denominator. It enables us to compare legal phenomena by placing them under a common umbrella, even though the legal phenomena may originally have carried different labels in different jurisdictions.

The history of Swedish commercial law remains largely unexplored by modern research, and this is partly simply because commercial law has never before been taken as the common umbrella concept. This does not mean that some of the problems, which can be understood as part of commercial law, have not been dealt with. Although it cannot alone, of course, remedy this problem, this article at least aims to introduce the central sources available and to establish some legal changes pertinent to the seventeenth-century Swedish business relations.

The plan of this article is as follows. Part 1 acquaints the reader with what little literature exists, and with the picture that this literature creates of the history of Swedish commercial law in the early modern period. We will see that the picture is full of lacunae and is poorly updated vis-à-vis the flourishing literature of the past few decades in the field elsewhere. This is largely, as stated above, due to the lack of a common *tertium comparationis*. The Swedish historians who have been interested in commercial phenomena have not identified the object as belonging to commercial law. Part 2 describes some of the essential features of the political, social and legal context necessary for the understanding of the legal change involved. As with any legal history, the history of commercial law can only be understood within the complex network of social relations that surround it. Part 3 introduces the reader to an early modern body of law which can meaningfully be said to have constituted the early modern Swedish commercial law. An essential question here is to what extent and how the commercial law of the European commercial centres influenced the statutory law and legal practice (of both courts and private entities) in Sweden. Part 4 concludes the essential findings of the article. The conclusion will lead to another question: what kind of a connection did the general Swedish legal development of the sixteenth and seventeenth century towards a 'pre-positivistic' legal order – in which statutory law came to rule from early on over other legal sources – have on commercial law, if any? Did the Swedish commercial law emerge 'from above' instead 'from below'? The article will ask whether Swedish early modern commercial law was essentially a creation of the state rather than of the merchants themselves.

1 The Historiography of Swedish Commercial Law

The history of Visby Town Law has occupied a prominent place in the historiography of Swedish commercial law. The German legal historian Karl von Amira in his *Altschwedisches Obligationenrecht* showed the connections of the Visby law to the laws of Hamburg and Lübeck.[2] Most the research of the early nineteenth century followed Amira, for example Björkander, Holmbäck, and Westman, who all emphasized the influence of the surrounding Gotland (*Gutalagen*) in addition to that of German law.[3] In the 1950s, Hasselberg then claimed that the influence of German town law was not as decisive as had thitherto been claimed, but that most of the influences would have come from other parts of Scandinavia.[4]

It is not important here to determine whether they were exactly right or wrong. Instead, it is interesting to note that Visby Town Law remained the focal point of research interest for a long time, and even that research has not attracted new scholars in half a century. A major exception is the anthology that Kjell Åke Modéer in 1981 edited on the Sea Law of 1667.[5] In his book on the reception of Roman law in the practice of Svea High Court of 1967, Stig Jägerskiöld also discusses some commercial cases presenting them as examples of learned Roman law.

The history of transport insurance has attracted more attention than other central areas of commercial law. Söderberg's *Försäkringsväsendets historia* [History of insurance] (1935) was based on original sources – court records and business archives – and remains the best work on transport insurance.[6] The first transport insurance that Söderberg mentions is the insurance taken in 1615 by a Dutch merchant De Geer, on whom E.W. Dahlgren wrote a biography, who probably took out his insurance in Amsterdam. The premium that De Geer and another Dutch merchant named De Besche paid for their insurance in 1615–1618 was 2¼ per cent of the cargo value. According to the prevailing opinion, the sea insurance paragraphs of the Swedish Sea Law of 1667 followed the Dutch model, by and large, as well *Guidon de la mer* (Ch. 1–4, 7, 12 and 15).[7]

2 Karl von Amira, *Nordgermanisches Obligationenrecht I: Altschwedisches Obligationenrecht* (Leipzig: Veit & Comp., 1882), 7–8.

3 Adolf A. Björkander, *Till Visby stads äldre historia: ett kritiskt bidrag* (Uppsala: Almqvist & Wiksell, 1898), 7–8; Åke Holmbäck, *Ätten och arvet enligt Sveriges medeltidslagar* (Uppsala: Almqvist & Wiksell, 1911), 191; K.G. Westman, *De svenska rättskällornas historia* (Uppsala: Almqvist & Wiksell, 1912), 27.

4 Gösta Hasselberg, *Studier rörande Visby stadslag och dess källor* (Uppsala: Almqvist & Wiksell, 1953), 354.

5 Kjell Åke Modéer (ed.), *1667-års sjölag i ett 300-årigt perspektiv: ett rättshistoriskt symposium i Göteborg den 16–18 mars 1981* (Stockholm: Institutet för rättshistorisk forskning, 1981).

6 Tom Söderberg, *Försäkringsväsendets historia i Sverige intill Karl Johanstiden* (Stockholm: P.A. Nordstedt & Söners Förlag, 1935).

7 G. Granfelt, 'Om försäkringsaftalets uppkomst och utveckling', *Tidskrift utgiven av juridiska föreningen i Finland JFT* (1908), 1–111, 40.

Finland was an integral part of the Swedish realm for roughly eight centuries, before Sweden had to cede it to the Russian Empire in 1809, and Finnish legal historians have always written about Swedish legal history as being their own. Themes of early modern commercial law, however, have not been an issue for Finnish scholars either. Again, exceptions prove the rule. In 1882, Axel Lille devoted a chapter to transport insurance in his book on the history of insurance.[8] Ragnar Hemmer, in a textbook from 1967, briefly mentions that commercial transactions favoured the reception of Roman law, because foreigners were often involved in them, but he leaves the theme of commercial law at that.[9]

2 The Economic, Social, and Legal Contexts

The Swedish economic history of the early modern period has been fairly well researched. Eli Hekscher, Stellan Dahlgren, Eric Thomson, and others have mapped out the development of Swedish commerce in the seventeenth century, and demonstrated how commerce gradually grew to support the growing great power. In economic terms, seventeenth-century Sweden came to depend on the Netherlands, the centre of European commerce. Since the late sixteenth century, Amsterdam had developed into the most important commercial centre in Western Europe. In 1570, the share of Dutch ships sailing through the Sound was 60 per cent, and at the beginning of the seventeenth century the number was close to three fourths.[10] The Dutch invested capital in Sweden and introduced technological innovations and know-how in the iron industry, manufacturing, and other fields.[11]

During the late sixteenth and seventeenth centuries, Sweden grew from a peripheral northern kingdom to a European military might, able to exert its influence not only in northern and north-eastern Europe but also in the

8 Axel Lille, *Försäkringsväsendet: dess historiska utveckling och nationalekonomiska betydelse* (Helsingfors: Frenckell, 1882).

9 Ragnar Hemmer, *Suomen oikeushistorian oppikirja: 3, Varallisuusoikeuden historia* (Helsinki: Lainopillisen ylioppilastiedekunnan kustannustoimikunta, 1967), 40.

10 Kristof Glamann, 'European Trade 1500–1750', in Carlo M. Cipolla (ed.), *The Fontana Economic History of Europe: The Sixteenth and Seventeenth Centuries* (London: Fontana, 1974), 427–526, 441–443.

11 On Sweden on the semiperiphery of the world economic system, see Immanuel Wallerstein, *The Modern World System I: Capitalist Agriculture and the Origins of the European World Economy in the Sixteenth Century* (New York: Academic Press, 1974), 107–108, 214–221, 349.

territories of the Holy Roman Empire of the German Nation. Sweden was eager to match its military success in the European war fields with corresponding advances in the economic and cultural spheres.[12] The different spheres were unavoidably linked to one another. Armies do not march without money. Arts and higher learning were also needed, and not only to show off an image of a cultural nation to the rivals in the south. University-trained officials, knowledgeable in languages and law, were necessary to help Sweden in its diplomatic relations and to polish the national administrative and economic machinery into such a shape that they would effectively yield the necessary support for the war machine. This was the logic of an expanding early modern state.[13]

Culturally, Sweden never rose to quite to the same level with its military might, but remained a European periphery. The Swedish castles on the shores of Lake Mälaren, easily reached by waterways from Stockholm, were and still are beautiful constructions, showing off the wealth of their owners. Although the difference between this Swedish heartland and most of the other parts of the realm is striking, in comparison to their counterparts in France or Germany, these dwellings of the Swedish nobility remained second-class creations. The resources were still not sufficient to allow true competition.

Law followed along much the same lines. Research has shown how the Swedish sixteenth- and seventeenth-century legal elite sought to bring law closer to the European *ius commune*. This involved staffing the newly founded high courts – themselves a legal transplant – with learned jurists,[14] and introducing legal novelties of European origin in statutory law. The same occurred in all major fields, such as private law,[15] criminal law,[16] procedural

12 Stellan Dahlgren, 'New Sweden: The State, the Company and Johan Risingh', in Stellan Dahlgren and Hans Norman (eds.), *The Rise and Fall of New Sweden* (Uppsala: Almqvist & Wiksell, 1988), 1–43, 2.

13 On the logic of early modern state expansion, see Ralph Tuchtenhagen, *Zentralstaat und Provinz* (Wiesbaden: Harrassowitz, 2008), 440.

14 See Mia Korpiola, 'A Safe Haven in the Shadow of War? The Founding and the *raison d'être* of the New Court, Based on its Early Activity', in Mia Korpiola (ed.), *The Svea High Court in the Early Modern Period: Historical Reinterpretations and New Perspectives* (Stockholm: Institutet för rättshistorisk forskning, 2014), 55–108.

15 See Elsa Trolle Önnerfors, *Justitia et prudentia: Rättsbildning genom rättstillämpning, Svea hovrätt och testamentmålen* (Stockholm: Institutet för rättshistorisk forskning, 2014).

16 See Heikki Pihlajamäki, '*Executor divinarum et suarum legum*: Criminal Law and the Lutheran Reformation', in Virpi Mäkinen (ed.), *Lutheran Reformation and the Law* (Leiden: Brill, 2006), 171–204.

law,[17] and *Polizeirecht*.[18] Swedish legal literature was born in the seventeenth century, although the literature remained insignificant in both quantity and quality up until the mid-nineteenth century.[19]

Swedish early modern law, however, ought not to be seen as poor copies of their European models, any more than Swedish economic solutions should. Instead, they should be viewed as practical adaptations of those models to the Swedish circumstances. Most importantly for law, Sweden lacked the finances necessary to maintain a corps of professional lawyers, who would have been able to make a living as advocates. In comparison to elsewhere, the bourgeoisie and the nobility were small, which meant that having the judiciary very much relied on the peasantry. Because of this, no deep-level *Rezeption* could occur. Related to this and again unlike elsewhere, the Swedish legal culture remained simple, as far as legal sources and the judiciary are concerned. Royal statutory law gained a supreme position over the other legal sources from very early on, leaving urban law, feudal law, customary law, and legal literature as relatively insignificant.[20] The founding of the high courts from 1614 onwards turned the Swedish judicial system into a rather neat hierarchical system in a couple of decades, whereas judicial complexities known from just about everywhere else[21] remained exceptional.[22]

---

17 Heikki Pihlajamäki, 'Gründer, Bewahrer oder Vermittler? Die nationalen und internationalen Elemente im Rechtsdenken des Olaus Petri', in Jörn Eckert and Kjell Å. Modéer (eds.), *Juristische Fakultäten und Juristenausbildung im Ostseeraum: zweiter Rechtshistorikertag im Ostseeraum: Lund 12.–17.3.2002* (Stockholm: Institutet för rättshistorisk forskning, 2004), 29–38.

18 Toomas Kotkas, *Royal Police Ordinances in Early Modern Sweden: The Emergence of Voluntaristic Understanding of Law* (Leiden: Brill, 2014).

19 See Lars Björne, *Patrioter och institutionalister, Den nordiska rättsvetenskapens historia I: Tiden för 1815* (Lund: Institutet för rättshistorisk forskning, 1995), 22–50, 69–145; and Lars Björne, *Brytningstiden, Den nordiska rättsvetenskapens historia II: 1815–1870* (Lund: Institutet för rättshistorisk forskning, 1998), 151–198.

20 Heikki Pihlajamäki, "Stick to the Swedish Law': The Use of Foreign Law in Early Modern Sweden and Nineteenth-Century Finland', in Serge Dauchy, W. Hamilton Bryson, and Matthew C. Mirow (eds.), *Ratio decideni: Guiding Principles of Judicial Decisions, Volume 2: 'Foreign' Law* (Berlin: Duncker & Humblot, 2010), 169–185.

21 See Dirk Heirbaut and Seán Donlan (eds.), *The Law's Many Bodies: Studies in Legal Hybridity and Jurisdictional Complexity*, c. 1600–1560 (Berlin: Duncker & Humblot, 2015).

22 For Swedish feudal courts during the early part of the seventeenth century, see Heikki Pihlajamäki, 'On Forgotten Jurisdictional Complexities, The Case of Early Modern Sweden', in Dirk Heirbaut and Seán Donlan (eds.), *Jurisdictional Complexities* 127–144.

3 The Sources of Swedish Commercial Law

3.1 *Statutory Law*

As shown above, the early modern history of Swedish commercial law centred on topics such as Visby Town Law, sea law, and the reception of Roman law. The historians of Visby Town Law restricted themselves to textual comparisons between the law itself and its foreign counterparts. This was also the methodology employed in the historical articles in Modéer's anthology. Indeed, it is clear that the Sea Law of 1667 was the most important statute of Swedish commercial law produced in the early modern period. The Sea Law therefore deserves some more attention here. In addition to the fact that it was much influenced by Dutch law, the Swedish Sea Law of 1667 was also a codification of rules that had developed during the course of the seventeenth century. The Sea Law thus codified previous developments, not only those of legal practice but also those of statute law. Indeed, there is more and plenty of legislative material to be taken into consideration. A survey of these materials should begin in the late middle ages. A privilege given to the City of Stockholm in 1436 states that whenever the town court was dealing with legal cases, which 'are not described and printed in law books, (the judges) may decide the case upon their oath and according to their best conscience, and the decision shall be equally lawful as written law'.[23] A privilege given by King Eric XIV of 1563, again to Stockholm, was almost identical.[24]

Cases which could not be decided according to statutory law were thus to be decided according to conscience. It is typical of international commercial disputes that more space was given to conscience, custom, and the type of sources, which allowed for flexibility. Other interpretations are possible, of course, since the privilege letters do not say anything about commercial cases

---

23 'Item vare thet sva, at nokre rætte fore kome, som eigh finnas bescrifne ok uth trychte i laghbokinne, thöm mugha the rætta uppa thera edh effter thera bætsta samvit, oc skula stadhughe oc faste blifva som annor bescrifven lagh'. Document 2, Riksrådets privilegiebref, Stockholm den 1 maj 1436, *Stockholms stads privilegiebref I* in Karl Hildebrand (ed.), *Urkunder till Stockholms historia* (Uppsala: K. HumanistiskaVetenskaps-samfundet, 1900), 2–7.

24 'Till thet 25, schole borgmestere och rådh udi Stocholm, när några saker för rätte komme, som icke finnes i lagen uttrychte, ransake och döme ther um effter theres bäste samvet, och schall then dom blifve så fast som någen annen'. Document 35, Erik XIV:s privilegier, Stockholm den 12 april 1563, *Stockholms stads privilegiebref I* in Karl Hildebrand (ed.), *Urkunder till Stockholms historia* (Uppsala: K. Humanistiska Vetenskaps-samfundet, 1900), 56–63, 61.

specifically. I think it is nevertheless highly probable that commercial cases were at stake here.

This becomes even more probable when one looks at the privilege letter which King John III issued in 1570 to the City of Stockholm. The contents of the privilege letter were otherwise similar to the two described above (the use of conscience in cases of statutory lacunae), except that these cases were now always to be appealed to the King and his Council. Even more interesting from the point of view of this article is the following part of the privilege: 'when foreign cases are to heard, investigated, and judged, half domestic and half foreign (judges) shall be used, so as to have the cases investigated more ably, and so that foreigners would have nothing to complain about some injustice'.[25] Again, commercial cases are not specifically mentioned, but it is hard to think of any relevant class of legal cases other than mercantile ones, in which foreigners would frequently be involved and in which their law (or 'foreign' law in general) would come into question as the applicable set of norms.

Statutory material from the Swedish west coast offers similar evidence. When the town of Gothenburg was being founded in the early seventeenth century, representatives of King Charles IX travelled to Amsterdam to negotiate the conditions on which Dutch immigrants would agree to move to the town. They presented the King's negotiators a list of 21 demands, which they wanted to have guaranteed as privileges. The model behind these demands was the Amsterdam town privileges. Some of the privileges had to do with the immigrants' legal position, and they were to ensure a legal immunity in relation to Swedish law. The town law was to consist of the laws approved by the new inhabitants themselves and Roman law. Legal documents were to be drafted in Dutch, and the cases decided by the town court were not to be appealed to anyone but the king himself.[26] The King confirmed the privileges in

25 'Till thet 15, schole borgemestere och rådh udi Stocholm, när några saker for rätte komme, som icke finnes i lagen uthtrychte, ransake och dömme ther um effter theris bedzte samveth. Och schal then dom blifve så fast som någen annen, doch ath appellation altidh må ske under oss och vårt elschelige rikis rådh effter Sverigis lagh; och när några främmende saker schole förhöres, ransakes och dömmes, dhå schal ther till brukes halffparten uthländske och halffparten inländske, på thet alle saker thäss schickeligere schole förhandlede varde, och ath the fremmende icke schole hafve sigh till ath beclage um någen orätt'. Document 38, Johan III:s stadgar, Stockholm den 10 mars 1570. Document 35, Erik XIV:s privilegier, Stockholm den 12 april 1563, *Stockholms stads privilegiebref I* in Karl Hildebrand (ed.), *Urkunder till Stockholms historia* (Uppsala: K. Humanistiska Vetenskaps-samfundet, 1900) 71–81,76.

26 Emil Wolff, *Studier rörande Göteborgs äldsta författning* (Göteborg: Bonnier, 1894), 6–13.

this form, in German, but because the founding of Gothenburg was postponed until later – for other reasons – the privileges never entered into force.

The only other town with comparable privileges in Sweden was Landkrona, a town situated in Scania, which had been ceded to Sweden in 1658. It was the intention of the new rulers to make the town a commercial centre for the southern part of the realm.[27] In the privileges of 1663, merchants were accorded exceptional rights when compared to other Swedish towns. Once a week, 8 to 10 'reliable and honest men' (*cordate och ärlige män*) were to convene under the leadership of the merchant burghermeister to solve commercial disputes, if both parties were willing to let them do so.[28] Unfortunately no records are preserved of this judicial organ, which seems to have amounted to not much less than a merchant court.

In an international comparison, southern Europe seems different to northern continental Europe. In Italy, Spain, and France, merchants themselves were active in shaping the rules of commercial law. This was done in the merchant-run *consulados* and in the merchant courts, which emerged in many parts of southern Europe from the late middle ages onwards. The rulers were much less active in the field. The situation in north-western Europe turned out to be largely the opposite. In Holland and England, no separate courts developed for mercantile affairs. Instead, ordinary courts of law usually handled commercial cases. Merchant law developed, instead, often by way of procedural privileges. It is interesting that seventeenth-century Sweden still wavered between these two models, not automatically accepting the north-western model of ordinary courts.

The powerful foreign merchants had an interest in securing commercial dispute resolution for themselves, and they managed to do that to some extent in the early seventeenth century. The procedure of commercial law cases thus became an issue. The Svea High Court handled commercial affairs by way of appeals, but it was criticized for not being expert enough in commercial matters. The drafters of the Sea Law of 1667 agreed on the need for a speedier procedure in sea law cases than in normal cases. The chief draftsman of the law was the Dutchman Hendrik Moucheron, who in his draft proposed a separate maritime court. The idea caused some discussion in the Council of the Realm. Some councillors thought that no ordinary appeals to a high court should be

27 See Harald Nilsson, *Landskrona 1413–1963: en historisk-topografisk bekrivning* (Landskrona: Landkrona stad, 1963).

28 Landskrona Privileges 14.3.1662, § 29; Ernst Fredrik Ivar Lagerwall, *Öfversigt af förordningar rörande Sveriges Handel och öfriga Stadsnäringar under Karl x Gustaf och Karl xi:s förmyndare, 1654–1672* (Upsala: Schultz, 1869), 81.

allowed, but only an extraordinary remedy (*beneficium revisionis*) as in all other cases.[29] The Council finally decided that a maritime court be founded in Stockholm, but the question of the appeals instance was left open.[30]

A specialized maritime court was established in Stockholm in 1665 with the Dutchman Hendrik De Moucheron as its president and four others (Johan Risingh, Matthias Törnecrantz, Daniel Young, and Hans Olofsson) as assessors. The new court, however, never began to function as its cases were instead referred to ordinary lower courts. Their decisions could then be appealed to the Commercial Collegium (*Kommerskollegium*), which then became a second-instance court for matters maritime and those cases involving bills of exchange. De Moucheron became an assessor of the Collegium.[31] The Commercial Collegium's history as a commercial high court ended up being short-lived, however, because of the commercial downturn that Sweden faced in the 1670 because of wars. The Commercial Collegium lost its independence and was merged into a department of the Chamber Collegium (*Kammerkollegium*). One of the consequences of the merger was that the jurisdiction of the Commercial Collegium was returned to the Svea High Court. The Commercial Collegium nevertheless functioned as the commercial high court for over ten years (1667–1678), and has a well-preserved archive as part of the Swedish State Archives. It has not yet been systematically researched from the point of view of legal history. Tom Söderberg's valuable study on the insurances from 1935 demonstrates, however, that practically all insurances in late seventeenth century were taken abroad. Insurance forms that the Sea Law of 1667 either failed to mention or expressly forbid nevertheless occurred frequently in the documents. Such insurances included ship instruments and the hire of personnel as insurance objects, in addition to which insurances were taken against slavery.[32]

29 The institution of *beneficium revisionis* was regulated in the Article 35 of the Judicial Procedure Act (*Rättegångsprocessen*) of 1615, see Johan Schmedeman (ed.), *Kongl. stadgar, förordningar, bref och resolutioner, ifrån åhr 1528, in til 1701 angående justitie och executions-ährender etc.* (Uppsala, 1706), 161.

30 Johan August Posse, *Bidrag till svenska lagstiftningens historia från slutet av sextonde århundradet till till stadfästelsen af 1734 års lag* (Stockholm: P.A. Norstedt & Söner, 1850), 178–179.

31 Joh. Ax. Almquist, *Kommerskollegium och riksens ständers manufakturkontor samt konsulstaten: administrativa och biografiska anteckningar* (Stockholm: P.A. Norstedt & Söner, 1912–1915), 20–21.

32 See Tom Söderberg, *Försäkringsväsendets historia i Sverige intill Karl Johanstiden* (Stockholm: Norstedt, 1935), 138–140.

The eighth book of the Sea Law nevertheless created a flexible procedure for the first instance. In the cities, maritime cases were taken directly to the upper town courts. The lower courts were thus bypassed and time was saved. Plaintiffs had the right to take appropriate property of the defendants as a guarantee, if the defendant was a foreigner. The plaintiff could even arrest the defendant, if he had no property or if there was a danger of escape.

In addition to the Sea Law of 1667 and the town privileges, a large amount of other statutory material pertaining to commercial relations was issued during the sixteenth and seventeenth centuries. This can best be described as falling into the category of police law (*Polizeirecht*), and it is in fact best found in the collections such as Anton von Stiernman's *Samling utaf kongl. bref, stadgar och förordningar angående Sweriges rikes commerce, politie och oeconomie uti gemen, uppå hans kongl. maj:ts nådigesta befallning giord ifrån 1523 I–VI* (1747–1775) and Johan Stiernman's *Justitiewercket*. Few of the statutes issued in these collections have anything to do with international commercial law as it is understood here in the narrow sense (see the Introduction), and thus the statutes do not concern negotiable instruments, company forms, or insurance as such. Most of the statutes to do with commerce set out the basis for the mercantilist society, controlling who is to trade when and where, customs, and so on. From the point of view of the merchant organizing this everyday business activity, these regulations were of the utmost importance and failure to comply with them might result in fines and loss of business.[33]

As was typical for Holland and for much of the north-western part of the European mainland, commercial law in Sweden was also developed by way of privileges. Company law is a good example, as the first commercial companies were created by privilege (Privileges for the Commercial Company of 1619).[34] Models of company management developed throughout the seventeenth century and were eventually extended to cover a wider range of commercial activity in the nineteenth century.

3.2 *Legal Practice*

Legal practice shows that practices specific to merchant relations were developing not only by way of statutory law but also in the practice of early modern Swedish courts. One such institution that seems to have developed in legal practice is that of 'good men' (*gode män*). Good men or similar institutions with different names already existed, certainly, in early medieval law all over

33 On the Swedish police law pertinent to commercial relations, see Kotkas, *Royal Police Ordinances in Early Modern Sweden*, 59–67, 131–149.

34 Stierman I: Privilegier för Koop-Handels Compagniet (1.3.1615), 660–667.

Europe.[35] In Swedish provincial laws just as in many other parts of the Europe, good men appeared as some kind of inspectors, assisting the court in various tasks such as determining land borders. The Visby Town Law recognized good men in the role of arbitrators. The Law states (II.9., *Saken to goden lyden to latende*) that whenever two or more men had a legal problem, it could left to good men to decide the matter. It was enough that one of the parties wished this. If the good men were 'such men that the decision could be entrusted upon them', their decision would be binding. If, however, the parties or one of them did not think the good men were trustworthy, the party in doubt had to swear this upon oath. If a party consented to the jurisdiction of the good men, he could still refuse to let them decide a case up to three times; the fourth time, the good men could decide regardless of his consent.

As far as evidence was concerned, Roman-canon law is specifically referred to in the Visby Town's Law's chapter on the good men (*gode män*): it says that in the good men's procedure 'full proof through witnesses' was needed. It makes sense that this was stated clearly, for medieval Swedish laws typically consisted of evidence rules from different time periods. Since all provincial laws are post-1215 (after IV Lateran Council), ordeals no longer feature in these laws. Instead, oath procedures dominate, with elements of Roman-Canon rules of procedure popping up here and there. The more recent the law, the more Roman-canon procedural laws are found. It is, however, typical of medieval provincial laws that the rules of evidence are specified in connection to each and every chapter or paragraph, because so many variations of the theme were possible. Therefore, it is logical that the chapter on good men should also say something about evidence.[36]

The jurisdiction of good men in the Visby Town Law was not, at least according to the text of the law, limited to any special group of cases. The law gives the picture that good men could be used for all kinds of legal disputes. This would tune well with the comparative picture of good men. They had been known all over Europe from the early middle ages onwards. Depending on which part

35 The terms *boni vires*, *rachimburgi*, *prud'hommes*, *goede mennen*, among others, are more or less identical. See 'Conclusion', in Wendy Davies and Paul Fouracre (eds.), *The Settlement of Disputes in Early Modern Europe* (Cambridge: Cambridge University Press, 1986), 207–240, 216–217; and Karin Nehlsen-von Stryk, 'Boni homines', in Albrecht Cordes et al. (eds.), *Handwörterbuch zur deutschen Rechtsgeschichte* (HRG), vol. 1, 2nd ed. (Berlin: Erich Schmidt, 2008), 644–645, www.HRGdigital.de/HRG.boni_homines.

36 In early sixteenth-century Antwerp law, the finding of facts was customarily commissioned to *geode mennen* or *boni vires*. See Dave De ruysscher, 'From Usages of Merchants to Default Rules: Practices of Trade, *Ius Commune* and Urban Law in Early Modern Antwerp', *Journal of Legal History* 33:1 (2012), 3–29, 13.

of Europe one talks about, good men could serve as judges, mediators, arbitrators, evaluators, witness of different kinds, and experts in border disputes. They could come from all social classes but were men of good repute and experience, and in possession of at least some land. The institution of good men features commonly in Swedish medieval legislation as well, usually as evaluators or experts in border disputes.

This was no longer the case in the early modern period. In the legal practice of the sixteenth and seventeenth centuries, the institution of good men appears to be commonly used as experts in merchant cases, whereas the other functions of good men have disappeared.[37] At the request of a court, good men read account books in order to determine a state of complex economic relations between merchants. Judicial sources contain evidence of good men sometimes also deciding cases as extrajudicial arbitrators before the cases ended up in court – because one of the parties was not happy with the good men's decision.

It is difficult if not impossible to assess how large a proportion of merchant cases was decided in mediation as against regular court procedure, because no original sources of the good men's procedure exist. Instead, in order to catch at least occasional glimpses of the good men's arbitration activities we need to rely on other sources for information. Thus in 1650 the Lower Town Court (*kämnerrätt*) of Turku decided a case between Thomas Jerfvi and Anders Marten. By the scant description of the court protocol it is not easy to determine whether both parties were merchants, but judging by the circumstances it seems probable. The minutes mention a 'contract' being made between the two men on 17 May 1648. Thomas had purchased beverages from Anders's cellar, for which Anders had presented Thomas with a bill for 2391 copper coins. Thomas did not think he owed Anders anything (his arguments do not appear in the protocol) and had taken the case to good men. They had recommended that Thomas pay 1562 copper coins as a compromise. Not consenting to this, Anders sued Thomas and claimed for the whole sum of the original bill. The court decided in favour of the plaintiff.[38] Similarly, in a case between Benedict Kedings and his father Christian Kedings, the good men had attempted to solve the litigious debt payments between the parties. The good men, however, had not reached

37 This is not the place to discuss the disappearance of good men from their other functions, but it is most probably connected to the strengthening ties of local courts to the crown and the corresponding weakening of local communities' influence on judicial decision-making.

38 The Lower Town Court of Turku, January 26, 1650, digital archive, 31–33. The Upper Town Court (*rådstuvurätten*) confirmed the decision on February 18, 1650.

an acceptable solution, which led Benedict to take the case to court. The courts also called upon a group of good men (Jochim Mergentia, Alexander Matsson, Jacob Erichsson, and Peter Black). They were probably different to the first set of good men, although this cannot be concluded from the records.[39]

An example of good men acting as a court's experts is taken from the records of Turku Upper Town Court from the year 1640. Thomas Martin had sued Anders Martin for unpaid debts. Anders brought to court a list of property items, with which he intended to pay the debt. The good men were entrusted with evaluating the value of the goods to determine whether it was sufficient for the payment.[40]

In most cases, the names of good men do not figure in the records. From the few cases in which names appear, it may be concluded that good men were chosen because of their commercial expertise or social standing, or probably usually both combined.

Judging by the rarity of commercial cases in the general courts, it seems that many or perhaps even most business cases were decided out of court. Sometimes these cases were, however, handled by the lower court. One often gets the picture that the court was used as a last instance or pressure device, when all other means had failed. Insurance as a theme emerged in the case of Peter Jesenhausen, who in 1642 sued his factor in Lübeck, Johan Prussman, because Jesenhausen had not received payment for the goods (tar and salmon) sent to Lübeck from Turku. It turned out that Prussman had not received the goods, because the shipper Christian Keding, although he had taken the goods to be shipped, had not transported them. With a sea letter proving this, Keding was held liable. In addition, Prussman wanted Jesenhausen to pay for the insurance which Prussman had taken to secure the goods that were to be shipped back from Lübeck to Turku.[41] Insurance was one of the issues in a case between Herman von Borgen and Rötgert Platzmann as well. Platzmann (together with Henrik von Broken and Peter Ruuth) had asked Borgen to arrange Borgen's contact in Amsterdam, Daniel Rulandt, to ship goods to Viborg. The ship sank, but only von Borgen received money from the insurance. Platzmann thought Borgen should have arranged for Platzmann's insurance as well. Borgen – and the Court – thought otherwise, since Platzmann had not specifically asked Borgen to arrange for the insurance, nor had Platzmann paid for the insurance (*asserantzpenningar*).[42]

39 Turku Upper Court 9.3.1650, 44–45 digital archive.

40 Turku Upper Town Court 2.11.1640, digital archive, 24.

41 Sylvi Möller, *Suomen tapulikaupunkien valtaporvaristo ja sen kaupankäyntimenetelmät 1600-luvun alkupuolella* (Helsinki: Suomen historiallinen seura 1954), 153.

42 Viborg Town Upper Court May 20, 1639, digital archive, 64–66.

International commerce sometimes raised questions of jurisdiction. In the previously discussed case of Platzmann, Ruuth and von Broken had sued both von Borgen and Rulandt in Viborg. The Court, when deciding the case in favour of von Borgen, did not solve the case *qua* Rulandt, but instead advised the plaintiffs to turn to a court in Amsterdam. In another case from Viborg, Mårten Munstens came to court stating that a representative of a Lübeck shipper, Lorents Hoon, had come to him asking for payment, which was based on a decision of a Lübeck court. Munstens asked the Upper Town Court to overrule the Lübeck decision, which he believed was unlawful. The court did not take a stand on the matter.[43] These two cases at least suggest that Swedish courts were reluctant to decide cases involving foreigners (foreigners residing abroad), not to mention overturning foreign court decisions. It is indeed not difficult to think that such judicial activism might have harmed commercial relations.

An important part of commercial law and of the everyday life of the merchant consisted of the activities of the urban commercial administration controlling trade. It was important for the merchants to comply with the rules concerning customs duties and other payments, lest they ran the risk of being fined. The protocols of the town courts offer a good insight into these practices, because the cases needed to go through law courts. The picture that the court protocols give is thus more complete, as far as commercial control is concerned, than that which regards legal problems between merchants themselves, which often failed to reach the court room but were settled completely or partly extrajudicially.

Commercial inspectors (*handelsinspektör*) were central figures in administering control measures.[44] Rotgerd Cass was the Commercial Inspector in Vyborg and he was particularly active in the 1650s. Many of Cass's cases ended up in court as well, and his actions were not always well received. In January 1650, Cass charged the nobleman Bernhardt Lewers in the Vyborg Upper Town Court with not paying due charges in tar handling. Lewers turned the charges against Cass himself, claiming that Cass was not aware of all noble privileges. The court accepted this charge and sentenced Cass to a harsh fine of 100 silver dollars for causing difficulty for Lewers' business.[45]

Not all of Cass's actions ended this way though. In April of the same year, Cass charged the merchant Anders Skarpenbergh with selling trinkets without paying customs. In addition to this, he had refused to open the doors of his

43 Viborg Town Upper Court, Feb 8, 1640, digital archive, 72.

44 On commercial inspectors (*handelsinspektör*, *handelsuppsyningsman*), see J.W. Ruuth, *Viborg stads historia* (Helsingfors: Helsingfors centraltryckeri och bokbinderi, 1906), 334.

45 http://digi.narc.fi/digi/view.ka?kuid=1199560 (digital archive, 96–133).

warehouse to Cass and his assistants. When they finally managed to enter the warehouse, Cass and the assistants found the trinket merchandise which had not been stamped for paid customs. Skarpenbergh was sentenced to a fine of 40 marks.[46]

3.3 *Legal Literature*

Major legal writers were scarce in early modern Sweden. Of the few, Johannes Loccenius, who was of German-origin, touched upon commercial questions more than others. His *De iure maritime & navali* (1652) contained chapters on maritime insurance, transportation contracts, and companies, and there was as chapter on procedural questions regarding litigation arising from maritime contracts and commercial contracts. Loccenius, as in his other writings as well, makes frequent allusions to German, Dutch, and other European sources. In *De iure maritime*, he refers to Pedro de Santarem's (Pedro Santerna Lusitano) *Tractatus de assecurationes*, to Hugo Grotius, to Vinnius, and to the Amsterdam and Antwerp statutes.[47]

David Nehrman (1695–1769) was by far the most renowned Swedish legal writer of the eighteenth century. In his *Inledning til then Swenska Jurisprudentiam Civilem* of 1729 (Introduction to Swedish civil law), Nehrman explains the Swedish system of company law. The company (*societas*, Sw. *bolag*) consisted of two or more people, who wished to set together their 'property or work' in order to take care of commerce or other business. Whatever profit the undertaking produced was divided between the partners, either in equal or unequal shares. According to Nehrman, several different kinds of *societates* could be distinguished, such as village association (*byalag*), *värnelag*, and *medrederskap*. Nehrman suggests that not all commercial companies fit the category of *societas*, however, but that the specific customs and royal statutes need to be taken into account. A lawful contract of *societas* could be oral, but Nehrman advised that it be made in written form for the sake of the proof. The contract needed to include provisions, among other things, on how much and what the partners invested in the company, what their duties were, how profit was

46 http://digi.narc.fi/digi/view.ka?kuid=11199613 (digital archive, 149–152). Similarly, Cass vs. Anthonius Borehardt in a case of textiles, http://digi.narc.fi/digi/view.ka?kuid=11199625 (digital archive, 161–163 and 192; Cass vs. the Lübeck merchant Henrich Thomasson, http://digi.narc.fi/digi/view.ka?kuid=11199642 (digital archive, 178); Cass vs. Bertill Ruuth, a Lübeck merchant, for trading illegally in Viborg, http://digi.narc.fi/digi/view.ka?kuid=11199691 (digital archive, 229–230); and Cass vs. Johas Fåhl and Anthonius Borehard, http://digi.narc.fi/digi/view.ka?kuid=11199642 (digital archive, 178).

47 Johannes Loccenius, *De iure maritime & navali* (Stockholm, 1652), 18, 22, 29, 52, 55, 57, among many others.

divided and how the company was dissolved. Nehrman refers to the Roman law prohibition of *societas leonina* (D. 2.29.) but states that in Swedish law such a company is not necessarily always unlawful. A blacksmith, for instance, may want to enter into such a contract with his children. If someone is allowed to donate his property away, asks Nehrman, why should he not be allowed to enter a contract of *societas leonina* as well? However, if someone is persuaded into such a contract, it is void. Nehrman follows the *ius commune* insofar as the company debts are concerned. If all partners engage in a debt *in solidum*, they are also responsible for it. If, however, one partner alone had entered a contract, the company was responsible only if the contract pertained to a function to which the contracting partner had been entrusted (*lex praepositionis*). The law was the same if the company had benefited from the contract (Kongl. Bref til G. Hoff=R den 12 Junij 1673).[48] Otherwise Nehrman does not touch commercial matters.

The actual Swedish legal writers thus did not devote much ink to commercial questions as a separate theme. In addition to books of law, merchant handbooks contain valuable information on commercial law, although one should be cautious not to treat them as normative sources, but rather as descriptions of good merchant practice. The most important of the Swedish merchant handbooks was Erik Zettersténs' work *Om allmänna handelshistorien och köpmanna-Wetenskapen* (*On the General History of Trade and Merchant*'s *Knowledge*) of 1769.[49] Zettersten's book thus came late in comparison to merchant manuals elsewhere in Europe. Before domestic manuals began to emerge, foreign manuals were used. Merchant families spent considerable amounts of money on foreign literature, including legal literature.[50] Studies of merchant libraries have shown that Swedish merchants frequently owned – and thus probably consulted as well – Dutch, English, German, and French handbooks. The Helsinki-based merchant Carl Jacob Dobbin owned over 450 titles, among which were Jacques Savary's *Le parfait négociant* (first printed in

48 David Nehrman, *Inledning til then Swenska Jurisprudentiam Civilem* (Lund: Ludwig Decreaux, 1729), 210–229.

49 In general, see Jyrki Hakapää, 'From Popular Law Books to Rarities of Economics: Merchants' Professional Literature in the Latter Half of the 1700s in Helsinki', in Cecilia af Forselles and Tuija Laine (eds.), *The Emergence of Finnish Book and Reading Culture in the 1700s* (Helsinki: Finnish Literary Society, 2011), 55–69.

50 Christina Dalhede, *Handelsfamiljer på stormaktstidens Europamarknad II: Resor och resande i internationella förbindelser och kulturella intressen, Antwerpen, Lübeck, Göteborg och Arborga* (Partille: Warne, 2001), 476, according to which merchant families were 'carriers of culture'.

1675), the best known of all European handbooks, and Josh Gee's *The Trade and Navigation of Great-Britain Considered* (1755).[51]

4 Conclusions

In this study, I have approached the question of early modern commercial law from the point of view of Sweden, a peripheral region of Europe with relatively little sources. Learned commentaries of commercial law are scarce, court cases rarely refer to any legal sources, and legal literature and merchant manuals are rare. It is time to attempt an answer to the questions I posed at the beginning. In addition to showing upon what sources such a study can be based, I have also sketched some lines of legal change based on what I can say at this point, and based on previous studies by other people and on the basis of the sources I have studied myself.

Was there something which could conveniently be called commercial law in early modern Sweden? As my examples from both legal practice, statutory law and legal literature from the seventeenth century show, rules governing relations between merchants had developed in Sweden by the seventeenth century. To what extent the origins of those rules lay in the Middle Ages is a question I have left aside for now. Did European models influence Swedish commercial law? They certainly did, both as far as the procedures and the substantial contents of the law are concerned, and both as regards legal literature, practice, and statutory law.

Swedish legal literature received influences from European legal literature on matters merchant – just as it has shown to have done regarding other matters. To what extent and how these influences were customized to Swedish circumstances is an important question left unanswered in this survey. If commercial law followed the same model as private law, criminal law, or procedural law in general, one might assume that its rules were adopted in Sweden in a simplified form, without the finesses that ultimately only learned lawyers could have mastered – and of which there was a lack in Sweden.

The institution of good men found in the legal practice was clearly not a Swedish invention, but was used elsewhere as well. Separate merchant courts were discussed as an alternative, and they were even established in some towns by way of privilege. The Commercial Collegium operated as an appeals instance for commercial cases for about a decade. The great line of legal change was, however, towards the model of north-western Europe, in which general

51 Hakapää, 'From Popular Law Books to Rarities of Economics', 61–62.

courts handled all merchant cases as well. This was probably the situation by the end of the seventeenth century and certainly by 1734, when the Swedish Law of the Realm was given.

Finally, did seventeenth-century general Swedish legal development touch upon law merchant in some way, and if it did, how? The answer seems quite evident to me: commercial law was drawn into the same current of setting the law straight and attempting to place it into the straight-jacket of pre-codifications. The Swedish royal power had few competitors from the reformation onwards: neither the towns nor the nobility could stand up against the crown. When ecclesiastical power was turned over to the crown after the Reformation, the Swedish crown was amongst the most powerful in Europe.[52] This came to be reflected in the judicial structure as well. From the early seventeenth century onwards, all courts finally became part of the same hierarchy, which culminated in the crown.

In many fields of law, the centralizing royal power of late seventeenth century wanted to clarify the law and codify it. The doors that still seemed to have been left open for foreign influences in the legal procedure in the early part of seventeenth century, were closed as the seventeenth century drew to its close. Commercial law and the Sea Law of 1682 was no exception. The Sea Law was in fact the first in the line of important 'codifications' of Swedish law in the seventeenth and eighteenth centuries. It was followed in 1682 by the War Articles, in 1719 by the Form of the Government, in 1723 by the Diet Statute and finally in 1734 by the Swedish Law of the Realm. This is important to note, because the Sea Law was clearly one in a series of statutes, which aimed at setting the Swedish law straight at the statutory level in all materials.[53]

This triumph of statutory law can probably best be explained in terms of politics: the period 1680–1719 was one of royal absolutism, when the pre-eminence of royal statutory law suited its interests well. The Law of 1734 as a product slightly out of place is actually not a true reflection: the preparations for the Law had already begun in 1686. The codification of rules developed in legal practice and previous statutory law thus not only concerned mercantile law, but was rather an overarching phenomenon spanning all across Swedish law. The pre-eminence of statutory law can, furthermore, be explained by an

52 See the articles in Virpi Mäkinen (ed.), *Lutheran Reformation and the Law* (Leiden: Brill, 2006).

53 The concept of codification is difficult and will not be discussed here. See Heikki Pihlajamäki, 'Private Law Codification, Modernization and Nationalism: A View from Critical Legal History', *Critical Analysis of Law* 2:1 (2015), 135–152.

almost complete lack of competing legal sources – which were very much the order of the day elsewhere in Europe.[54]

How well, again, the statutory law managed to describe or even to steer legal practice, is another matter. Assuming again that commercial law followed the course of other fields, one might suppose that statutory law was fairly successful. However, without larger empirical studies I would hesitate to offer this as much more than a hypothesis.

54 See Pihlajamäki, 'Private Law Codification, Modernization and Nationalism'.

CHAPTER 12

Svea Court of Appeal Records as a Source of Commercial Law: The Founding Year of 1614

Mia Korpiola

1 Introduction

The Svea Court of Appeal was founded in Stockholm, the capital of the Swedish realm, in 1614 by King Gustav II Adolf (r. 1611–1632) as the first royal Court of Appeal in the realm.[1] The establishment of this important tribunal has been called 'without doubt one of the most significant internal occurrences during the reign of Gustav Adolf'.[2] Between 1614 and 1623, when the next court of appeal was established in Turku/Åbo, the Svea Court was the appellate tribunal of the whole country, which had about 1,1–1,2 million inhabitants.[3]

* Previous versions of this essay have been presented at the workshop 'The Making of Commercial Law: Common Practices and National Legal Rules from the Early Modern to the Modern Period' in Helsinki on 5 March 2014 ('Serving Commercial Interests? International Trade Disputes and the Founding of the Svea Court of Appeal in 1614'), and the conference on the historiography and sources of commercial law in Helsinki on 1 September 2014 ('Svea Court of Appeal Records as a Source of Commercial Law: The Founding Year of 1614'). I would like to thank the participants for their kind feedback and suggestions. I would also like to acknowledge with thanks the comments and suggestions for further literature I received from Steve Murdoch (St. Andrews) and Jussi Sallila (Helsinki). The work for this article was largely funded by the Academy of Finland through the research group 'The Making of Commercial Law: Common Practices and National Legal Rules from the Early Modern to the Modern Period', but parts of the article were also written in the congenial and inspiring atmosphere of the Centre for Advanced Study at the Norwegian Academy of Science and Letters.

1 On the history of the Svea Court of Appeal, see in particular Sture Petrén, Stig Jägerskiöld and Tord O:son Nordberg, *Svea hovrätt: studier till 350-årsminnet* (Stockholm: Norstedt, 1964); and Mia Korpiola (ed.), *The Svea Court of Appeal in the Early Modern Period: Historical Reinterpretations and New Perspectives* (Stockholm: Institutet för Rättshistorisk Forskning, 2014).

2 Nils Ahnlund, *Gustav Adolf den Store* (Stockholm: Svenska Kyrkans Diakonistyrelses Bokförl., 1932), 185: '*Rättegångsreformen är utan tvivel en av de betydelsefullaste inre tilldragelserna under Gustav Adolfs regering*'.

3 The Swedish population is difficult to estimate. However, it has been assessed that Sweden proper had about 800,000 inhabitants in 1571 whereas Finland had about 300,000 inhabitants. For discussion on the Swedish population estimates, see Eli F. Heckscher, *Sveriges ekonomiska historia från Gustav Vasa*, 1:1 (Stockholm: Albert Bonniers Förlag, 1935), 29–31, esp.

 | DOI 10.1163/9789004363144_013

The establishment of the court and the reasons behind it have been discussed by researchers over many decades.[4] One of these is Sture Petrén, who wrote in 1966 that the needs of the changing commercial law had been a major impetus behind the establishing of the Svea Court of Appeal.[5] According to Petrén, the Swedish 'judicial procedure [was adjusted] to changing habits of life and commercial usages [… that hampered] social and economic progress'.[6] He pointed out in particular the difficulties foreign merchants had in collecting their debts in Sweden because of what he called the 'parochiality' of medieval Swedish law. With this, he meant the mid-fourteenth-century town law of King Magnus Eriksson (r. 1319–1364) that governed commercial relations, but disregarded 'the usages guiding the international merchant […] in the conduct of his trade. Nor did the rules of procedure applicable to lawsuits make it easy for a foreigner to obtain justice in the courts'.[7] He also linked the establishment of the Court to the 'increasing economic contacts with the outer world' and the need for 'foreign capital and technical assistance for its incipient industrialization and for the more efficient exploitation of its natural resources'.[8] Indeed, the Swedish economic historian Eli Heckscher has assessed that '[i]t can safely be said that neither before nor later did foreigners contribute more to Swedish economic development' than in the seventeenth century.[9]

In addition, Petrén maintained that foreigners lacking 'well-developed networks of local contacts' faced greater difficulties than did 'native litigants' to 'obtain justice'. Occasionally, this kept Swedish diplomacy busy, as tradesmen from other countries struggled to have their debtors pay the debts, and protested against the hindrances in their way. Petrén further claimed that the Swedish

---

30; and for Finland, Kyösti Kiuasmaa, 'Valtaistuinriitojen ja uskonpuhdistuksen aika', in Yrjö Blomstedt et al. (eds.), *Suomen historia. 2: Keskiaika, valtaistuinriitojen ja uskonpuhdistuksen aika, kansankulttuurin juuret* (Espoo: Weilin & Göös, 1985), 229–345 at 337.

4 Esp. J.E. Almquist, 'Bidrag till frågan om Svea hovrätts uppkomst', *Svensk Juristtidning* 25 (1940), 468–478; Sture Petrén, 'Kring Svea hovrätts tillblivelse', *Svensk Juristtidning* 30 (1945), 171–184; Sture Petrén, 'Hovrättens uppbyggnad 1614–1654', in Sture Petrén, Stig Jägerskiöld and Tord O:son Nordberg, *Svea Hovrätt: studier till 350-årsminnet* (Stockholm: Norstedt, 1964), 3–117.

5 Sture Petrén, 'The Reform of the Swedish Judiciary under Gustavus Adolphus', in Morris D. Forkosch (ed.), *Essays in Legal History in Honor of Felix Frankfurter* (Indianapolis: The Bobbs Merrill Company, 1966), 263–274.

6 Petrén, 'The Reform of the Swedish Judiciary', 263.

7 Petrén, 'The Reform of the Swedish Judiciary', 264.

8 Petrén, 'The Reform of the Swedish Judiciary', 266–267.

9 Eli F. Heckscher, *An Economic History of Sweden*, (trans.) Göran Ohlin (Cambridge, Mass.: Harvard University Press, 1954), 101.

crown was not perceived to be a reliable debtor, causing the creditworthiness of the country to suffer.[10]

In this essay, I will take Sture Petrén's assertions as my starting point, and explore them by focusing particularly on the records of the Svea Court of Appeal in the founding year of 1614. Looking at the Svea Court records as a source of commercial law will enable me to answer two main questions: what kind of commercial cases the Court dealt with, and what the 1614 records tell us about the activities of the court in commercial cases. Thereby, I will test Petrén's thesis about providing foreigners with remedies for commercial disputes being the *raison d'être* of the establishment of the Court in Stockholm in 1614. The exigencies of international trade and new economic contacts for this will also be assessed.

In order to investigate Petrén's thesis, I will be looking at the Svea Court of Appeal records of the founding year of 1614. My main sources for the court's activities in its first year are its register of outgoing letters[11] and records, including judgments.[12] These sources cover the Court's first two law terms or 'judicial sessions', i.e. May-July and September-November 1614.[13]

2 Commerce and Foreign Tradesmen in Sweden

The Swedish economy, which was relatively autarkical, was dominated by agriculture. In 1559, the main import products for Sweden proper were various types of cloth (*c.*35 per cent), salt (*c.*25 per cent) and hops (*c.*19 per cent) for brewing ale. Iron (*c.*29 per cent) was the most important export product, followed by leather and hides (18.7 per cent) and butter (17.5 per cent). Copper, which became the leading export product by the early 1600s, had only a modest

10 Petrén, 'The Reform of the Swedish Judiciary', 264–265.

11 Riksarkivet [The National Archives], Stockholm, Sweden (hereafter RA), Svea Hovrätt (Svea Court of Appeal, hereafter SH), Huvudarkivet (Main Archive, hereafter HA), B I a:1.

12 RA, SH, HA, A I a 1:1. It is worth noting that the archival labelling of the records is misleading. Under 'Records of civil litigation' (*protokoll i civila mål*) for 1614, one not only finds the day-to-day minutes of the court's two sessions, but also signed copies of all the letters of judgement as well as summaries of the causes. These not only involved civil cases, but also criminal cases regardless of whether they had been initiated *ex officio* or by private accusations.

13 Art. 20, Rättegångs-Ordinantie (1614), Ordinance of Judicial Procedure (hereafter RO 1614), in Johan Schmedeman (ed.), *Kongl. stadgar, förordningar, bref och resolutioner ifrån åhr 1528, in til 1701* (Stockholm, 1706), 141: from 1 May to 29 June (*ifrån Walburgis och intil Petri Pauli*) and 8 September to 11 November (*ifrån mårmesso in til Martini*).

role (under six per cent).[14] Since the Middle Ages, the Crown had enjoyed regalian rights on silver, but in the sixteenth century it attempted to expand such old and more limited rights into a monopoly on other products such as copper, furs and iron as well.[15]

Stockholm was by far the most dominant port and trading town in the Swedish reign. By Continental standards, it was a smallish capital, having only about 7,500~8,000 permanent inhabitants in 1582. Thus, it was comparable to Northern German towns of middling size such as Rostock and Wismar.[16] The urban population of Sweden was small, comprising about five per cent of the whole population. For Sweden proper, there may have been about 38,000 town dwellers in the 1570s, and thus, the total urban population in Sweden and Finland may have been around 50,000~55,000.[17] Tradesmen formed a major part of burgher householders from which the mayors and town councillors (*rådsmän*) were recruited, and they dominated the administration of medieval Swedish towns.[18] This picture remained largely the same in the early modern period. In 1582, the town of Stockholm had 1,260 households, a third of which (396) were burgher households. Within these, tradesmen formed the biggest group (44 per cent), and it has been estimated that all in all, about 14 per cent of the Stockholm population were pursuing commerce.[19] In the 1620s, Stockholm still only had about 10,000 inhabitants, but the town was growing quickly, increasing almost four-fold to *c.*40,000 by 1660.[20]

---

14 Heckscher, *Sveriges ekonomiska historia*, 39–40, 55, appendix 5. In Turku, the principal Finnish port, the main import products (based on their value in Swedish marks) in 1559 were salt (*c.*45 per cent), cloth (*c.*12 per cent) and hops (*c.*3.7 per cent). Lacking mining resources, the main export products consisted of butter (*c.*38 per cent), hides (*c.*34 per cent), horses (*c.*13 per cent) and fish (*c.*6 per cent), Mika Kallioinen, *Kauppias, kaupunki, kruunu: Turun porvarisyhteisö ja talouden organisaatio varhaiskeskiajalta 1570-luvulle* (SKS: Helsinki, 2000), 191.

15 Birgitta Odén, *Kronohandel och finanspolitik 1560–1595* (Lund: Gleerup, 1966), 307–311, 317–318.

16 On the population of Stockholm in 1582, Birgitta Lager, 'Stockholms befolkning på 1500-talet', in Ingrid Hammarström (ed.), *Historia kring Stockholm – Vasatid och stormaktstid* (Stockholm: Wahlström och Widstrand, 1966), 13–34 at 18. However, if the royal court sojourned in Stockholm, the population could go up 9,000~9,500.

17 Heckscher, *Sveriges ekonomiska historia*, 32–33; Kiuasmaa, 'Valtaistuinriitojen ja uskonpuhdistuksen aika', 327.

18 Marko Lamberg, *Dannemännen i stadens råd: Rådmanskretsen i nordiska köpstäder under senmedeltiden* (Stockholm: Stockholmia förlag, 2001), 54–56.

19 Lager, 'Stockholms befolkning på 1500-talet', 19–20.

20 Gösta Selling, 'Stormaktens huvudstad', in Ingrid Hammarström (ed.), *Historia kring Stockholm – Vasatid och stormaktstid*, (Stockholm: Wahlström & Widstrand, 1966), 47–64 at 49.

The later Middle Ages had witnessed rivalry and even violence in Swedish towns between Germans and Swedes, and town administration was accommodated to include both groups with fifty-fifty participation. However, for political reasons, this rule was revoked in 1471 when foreigners were forbidden to participate in town administration.[21] The number of German burghers in Sweden seems to have declined in Stockholm between 1460 and 1525, reducing their proportion of the whole population to only around two per cent by 1525. A similar trend showing a quick decline of both the absolute and proportional number of German burghers was also visible in Turku/Åbo. The decline has at least partly been attributed to King Gustav I Vasa's (r. 1523–1560) restriction of freedom from customs only to those merchants who resided permanently in the Swedish towns.[22]

The iron and copper production and transport of goods from European trading centres to and beyond the mining district in Central Sweden provided lucrative trading possibilities not only for the Swedish but also for foreign merchants in the latter half of the sixteenth century. In fact, the biggest exporters were foreigners – mostly Germans – even though the role of Dutchmen and Scots grew during the later sixteenth century. Stockholm was by far the most important port exporting iron and copper.[23] The main ports or regions exporting goods to Sweden proper in 1615 were Lübeck (*c.*40 per cent), Danzig (*c.*16 per cent) and Holland (*c.*15 per cent). In Stockholm, Lübeck was less dominant, while the role of Danzig and Holland was slightly bigger. England and Scotland together formed almost one-tenth of the value of the Swedish import in 1610.[24]

In 1582, only around 15 per cent of the permanent (*bofast*) inhabitants of Stockholm were foreigners. Germans formed by far the biggest group of these – 12 per cent of the Stockholm households. Most of the Germans were artisans, but there were also several successful tradesmen. The number of Dutch, English and Scottish entrepreneurs and tradesmen was increasing in the last decades of the sixteenth and early seventeenth century, and some of them, such as the Dutch Willem de Wijk (d. 1597)[25] and the Scot Blasius Dundee (Dundi,

21 Lamberg, *Dannemännen*, 58, 61–65; Kallioinen, *Kauppias, kaupunki, kruunu*, 133–135, 140–142.

22 Lamberg, *Dannemännen*, 58–59; Kallioinen, *Kauppias, kaupunki, kruunu*, 138–140.

23 Heckscher, *Sveriges ekonomiska historia*, 102–110, 157, 269; Maj-Britt Nergård, *Mellan krona och marknad: utländska och svenska entreprenörer inom svensk järnhantering från ca. 1580 till 1700* (Uppsala: University of Uppsala, 2001), 71–72, 76, 79–83.

24 Heckscher, *Sveriges ekonomiska historia*, 45–50, appendix 5.

25 On de Wijk, see Nergård, *Mellan krona och marknad*, 67–83; Birgitta Lager, 'Wijk, Willem (Welam) de (van)', in Nils Bohman (ed.), *Svenska män och kvinnor 8: Biografisk uppslagsbok* (Stockholm: Albert Bonniers Förlag, 1955), 362–363; E.W. Dahlgren,

d. 1621), were very successful. Blasius Dundee traded in foreign luxury goods such as wine, spices and bitter oranges (*pomerans*), and he became one of the wealthiest tradesmen in Stockholm.[26] Thus, foreign tradesmen could both make and lose their fortunes in Sweden.

3 Commercial Litigation, Citations, and Letters of Judgement

When commercial cases were heard at the Svea Court of Appeal, it issued both citations and letters of judgement as in any other instances of litigation. However, the records of the Svea Court of Appeal demonstrate that it handled very little commerce-related litigation in its first year. Few cases in the first year were new appeals from the lower courts, while those cases that had been or were referred to the Court of Appeal by the king from the Council of the Realm were usually not commercial. Consequently, only a small number of commercial cases ended up with letters of judgement in contrast with the twenty or so debt reminders and rescripts recorded for 1614.

One of these cases was to prove complicated, involving parties from both Germany and London. This contract case involving money (Humphrey Streit vs. Jacob Ballie and Lorentz Schröder) was initiated that year, and went on for some years, possibly partly because it was so international. Two German merchants' apprentices (*köpsven*),[27] James Baley (*Jacob Ballie*, who was actually

'De uppländska bruken Österby, Forsmark, Leufsta och Gimo under äldsta tider (intill 1627)', *Med hammare och fackla: Årsbok utgiven av Sancte Örjens gille* 1 (1928), 1–88 at 10–23.

26 On Dundee, see F.U. Wrangel, 'Blasius Dundie', *Stockholmiana I–IV: Ny upplaga jämte tillägg* (Stockholm: P.A. Norstedt & Söners Förlag, 1912), 41–55; Gunnar Bolin, 'Blasius Dundi (Dundie, Dundey, Dondey, Dondy)', *Svenskt biografiskt lexikon* [hereafter SBL] 11 (Stockholm: Bonnier, 1945), 525–528. See also Steve Murdoch, 'Community, Commodity and Commerce: The Stockholm-Scots in the Seventeenth Century', in David Worthington (ed.), *British and Irish Emigrants and Exiles in Europe, 1603–1688* (Leiden: Brill, 2010), 31–66 at 34–47.

27 King Magnus Eriksson's mid-fourteenth-century Town Law regulated and limited the trading competences of apprentices depending on the property they possessed; see Köpmålabalken (Chapter on Trade, hereafter K) 14, Åke Holmbäck and Elias Wessén (eds.), *Magnus Erikssons stadslag i nusvensk tolkning* [hereafter MESL] (Stockholm: Nordiska bokhandel, 1966), 119; K 14–15, Elias Wessén (ed.), *Söderköpings lagbok 1387 utgiven efter den medeltida laghandskriften och med en inledning* (Stockholm: Institutet för rättshistorisk forskning, 1971), 57–58.

Scottish, not German),[28] and Lorenz Schröder, had sold a considerable amount of lead to Humphrey Streit, a London merchant. As was customary in commercial circles, the apprentices or assistants of merchants represented their masters and performed a great number of various tasks for them.[29] According to the sales contract, Baley and Schröder were to receive a 'manuscript' in return – possibly an IOU – issued by Ernest Kleinfeld of Danzig, amounting to 1,190 *dalers*. However, they claimed that they had not received the manuscript on the appointed day and that Streit still owed them the sum. Streit countered by claiming that the document was still in Danzig, consigned to a notary. In the Court of Appeal, the case revolved around the question of whether the manuscript was genuine or not. Streit had to place a very high one-thousand-*daler* caution. If the document was a forgery, Streit also risked having to pay the plaintiffs some damages as 'assessed by good men'. If it was authentic, Baley and Schröder were to compensate Streit his damages, again determined by 'good men'.[30]

It is difficult to know what the expression 'good men' means, as its contents seem to vary. In the case of Anna, widow of Hans Karkman against Baron Erik [Gustavsson] Stenbock's (1538–1602) heirs, the expression (*gode män som retten bekläde*) would seem to refer to the town councillors sitting in session at the town court.[31] On the other hand, in another debt case from the town court of Stockholm, the court observed that the 'parties seemed willing to settle'. Therefore, it appointed two 'good men'. One of these, Michel Melitz, was probably German, and Jacob Makler (possibly James Maclean) was a Scot, and they were to determine the going rate of exchange for Lübeck marks in Swedish marks, on which there was disagreement.[32] Thus, both nationalities seem to have been represented in the nominated two 'good men' as mixed panels with

28 Baley had been involved in a case in which Salomon Standow, originally of Danzig, was accused of slander in the town court of Stockholm, 10 May 1615, *STb från år 1592*, 85–86.

29 Gunnar Mickwitz, *Aus Revaler Handelsbüchern: Zur Technik des Ostseehandels in der ersten Hälfte des 16. Jahrhunderts* (Helsinki: Societas Scientiarum Fennica, 1938), 116–125; Sylvi Möller, *Suomen tapulikaupunkien valtaporvaristo ja sen kaupankäyntimenetelmät 1600-luvun alkupuolella* (Helsinki: SHS, 1954), 123–125, 170–172, 235–242; Kallioinen, *Kauppias, kaupunki, kruunu*, 56, 98, 117; Carole Rawcliffe, 'That Kindliness Should be Cherished More, and Discord Driven Out: The Settlement of Commercial Disputes by Arbitration in Later Medieval England', in J. Kermode (ed.), *Enterprise and Individuals in Fifteenth-Century England* (Stroud: Sutton, 1991), 99–117 at 108.

30 31 Aug. 1614, *STb från år 1592*, 8, 38–39; RA, SH, HA, A I a 1:1, 19–20, 27 Oct. 1614, 131v–132v, 135r, 171v, 223r.

31 8 Nov. 1615, *STb från år 1592*, 158.

32 22 June 1615, *STb från år 1592*, 90–91.

equal numbers of representatives of both, a practice which seems to have been customary in commercial disputes.[33]

In a third case, a complex debt and pledge case, 'good men' had been used by the first-instance tribunal, the Stockholm Town Court, in order to adjust or moderate (*jäncke*) the interest (*jnteresse*) mentioned in the promissory note between the parties.[34] Count Per Brahe the Elder (1520–1590),[35] one of the leading sixteenth-century noblemen and nephew to King Gustav I Vasa, maintained in his *Oeconomia*, which was a book for the education of young noblemen and management of noble estates, that a 5 or 6 per cent interest was reasonable, while he defined a 10–12 per cent interest as usurious.[36] Indeed, 6 per cent seems to have been the going interest rate in Stockholm, judging by certain cases referred to in the Town Court.[37]

However, there were also some cases labelled as disputed contracts by the Svea Court of Appeal. One involved a contract between Jöns Eskilsson, a ship's captain, and Bertil Farenheide (also *Vorenheijde*), a German merchant's apprentice. The latter took the burgher's oath in Stockholm on 10 May 1615.[38]

---

33 Rawcliffe, 'That Kindliness Should be Cherished More', 100, 102, 104, 111.

34 1 March 1613, *STb från år 1592*, VII, 240–241.

35 On Brahe, see, e.g., Georg Landberg, 'Per Brahe, d.ä'., *SBL* 5 (Stockholm: Bonnier, 1925), 641–658; Bo Eriksson, *I skuggan av tronen: En biografi över Per Brahe d.ä.* (Stockholm: Prisma, 2009).

36 John Granlund and Gösta Holm (eds.), Per Brahe, *Oeconomia eller Hushållsbok för ungt adelsfolk* (Stockholm, 1971), 67–68.

37 27 Oct. 1604, *STb från år 1592*, 5, 336. Toini Aunola's research on the trade and credit relations between farmers and merchants in later eighteenth-century Northern Ostrobothnia indicates that a 5–6 per cent interest rate for debts was common. However, no interest was charged on accounts receivables as long as an IOU had not been written on them; see Toini Aunola, *Pohjois-Pohjanmaan kauppiaiden ja talonpoikien väliset kauppa- ja luottosuhteet 1765–1809* (Helsinki: SHS, 1967), 307–308. Ilmakunnas has also reported of interest rates of 5 or 6 per cent for loans taken by aristocrats in eighteenth-century Sweden: Johanna Ilmakunnas, *Kuluttaminen ja ylhäisaatelin elämäntapa 1700-luvun Ruotsissa* (Doctoral dissertation, University of Helsinki, 2009), 129–132. However, in some credit relationships in the Baltic Sea area, interest rates could sometimes even be higher, up to 23 per cent per annum, especially if the creditor carried the risk of the goods during the carriage in contracts involving the sale of shipped goods; Kallioinen, *Kauppias, kaupunki, kruunu*, 206; Mickwitz, *Aus Revaler Handelsbüchern*, 109, 113–114; Möller, *Suomen tapulikaupunkien valtaporvaristo*, 255, 257, 260–262. See also Heckscher, *Sveriges ekonomiska historia*, 198–200; Leif Runefelt, *Hushållningens dygder: Affektlära, hushållningslära och ekonomiskt tänkande under svensk stormaktstid* (Doctoral dissertation, Stockholm University, 2001), 209–210.

38 17 Feb. 1613, *STb från år 1592*, VII, 237–238; 10 May 1615, *STb från år 1592*, 61.

On 30 May 1614, Jöns Eskilsson had presented the Court of Appeal the sentence from the Stockholm Town Court that he had wagered against. As the defendant Farenheide was not present at court, the case was postponed.[39] David Wexell owed them 800 *dalers* that waited for them in Finland, which was where Farenheide had sent his representative, Hans Grönwald. They had agreed to share the sum fifty-fifty, and both were to answer for the costs. However, both the Stockholm Town Court and the Court of Appeal declared that Farenheide had breached the contract by keeping the whole sum for himself. Jöns Eskilsson, the plaintiff, was to receive half of the sum in accordance with the contract, and the execution of the sentence was ordered.[40] However, such disputes were infrequent in 1614.

4 'Access to Justice' and Commercial Disputes in the Svea Court Records of 1614

In his essay, Petrén argued – surely correctly – that foreign tradesmen may have had greater difficulties than Swedes in collecting debts owed to them because of the antiquated methods of proof (compurgation and oath-helpers) and the lack of powerful connections and local networks.[41] In Sweden – as in many other countries – foreign merchants faced certain restrictions as to their travelling and doing business. While allowing visiting foreign traders (Swe. *gäst*; Finn. *kesti*) to enter Swedish towns with the new sailing season, the mid-fourteenth-century Town Law of King Magnus Eriksson had forbidden them from travelling inland to 'pursue commerce or recover debts'. Any offence of that kind was to be punished with a forty-mark fine and a forfeiture of the sum collected or traded.[42]

However, to ensure that non-resident foreign visitors were granted justice, a member of the Council of the Realm, together with a high-ranking prelate, a member of the archiepiscopal chapter of Uppsala, was to preside over

39 RA, SH, HA, A I a 1:1, 30 May 1614, 17. On the legal wager, a sort of an appeal, see e.g. Mia Korpiola, 'General Background: From Judicial Crisis to Judicial Revolution through the Svea Court of Appeal?' in Mia Korpiola (ed.), *The Svea Court of Appeal in the Early Modern Period: Historical Reinterpretations and New Perspectives* (Stockholm: Institutet för Rättshistorisk Forskning, 2014), 21–50, 36–37.

40 17 Feb. 1613, *STb från år 1592*, VII, 237–238; RA, SH, HA, A I a 1:1, 7 June 1614, 29v–30r; RA, SH, HA, B I a:1, 7 June 1614, 29r–29v.

41 Petrén, 'The Reform of the Swedish Judiciary', 264–265.

42 K 30-30:1, Holmbäck and Wessén, *MESL*, 126–127; K 31, Wessén, *Söderköpings lagbok 1387*, 64.

a biannual court session on Whitsunday and St. James' Day (25 July). Then, both visiting tradesmen (*gäster*) and townspeople were to be guaranteed justice against 'noblemen and clerics and any other people in the land that they cannot get justice of'. Moreover, the sentence had to be given within a fortnight after the case had to be heard.[43] Thus, unlike the German merchants in Bergen or Novgorod who were restricted to their own Hanseatic *Kontor* with internal government, norms and jurisdiction as well as an appeals system to Lübeck, foreign merchants were allowed to settle freely in Stockholm and other towns, but only under Swedish law and the Swedish judiciary.[44]

Visiting foreign tradesmen were considered in medieval jurisprudence to be *miserabiles personae*, persons without protection whose rights had to be safeguarded by the either the temporal or secular ruler. Also, in Sweden, visiting foreign merchants were placed under the special protection of the king and the local bishop, and both together could provide justice for them and for other groups of people who were unable to have justice on the basis of the argument of *ex defectu justitiae*.[45] The growing presence of foreign tradesmen from various countries may have prompted King John III (r. 1568–1592) to issue a special clause in the privileges of the town of Stockholm regarding disputes involving foreigners in 1570. In it, he addressed the question of access to justice for foreigners. When 'foreign' (*främmende*) cases were heard, the panel of judges was to be constituted fifty-fifty of foreigners and Swedes 'so that all the matters be more competently negotiated and so that the foreigners should not have cause to complain of any injustice'. Moreover, all cases so decided could always be 'appealed' (*appellation altidh må ske*) to the king and his council in accordance with the law of Sweden.[46]

Yet, most of the commerce-related cases at the Svea Court of Appeal in 1614 involved Swedes, or people whose names point to them being naturalised foreigners. For example, the Stockholm tradesman Daniel Brandes may have been German originally. Blasius Dundee, who had taken the burgher's oath in Stockholm in 1583, was Scottish, as was Colonel Patrick Rutherford, who was

43 K 30:2, Holmbäck and Wessén, *MESL*, 127; K 31, Wessén, *Söderköpings lagbok 1387*, 64.

44 Wilhelm Ebel, *Forschungen zur Geschichte des lübischen Rechts 1: Dreizehn Stücke zum Prozeß- und Privatrecht* (Lübeck: Archiv der Hansestadt, 1950), 10, 13.

45 On jurisdiction *ex defectu justitiae* and over *miserabiles personae*, see R.H. Helmholz, *Spirit of Classical Canon Law* (Athens, GA: University of Georgia Press, 1996), 118–144.

46 Karl Hildebrand and Arnold Bratt (eds.), *Stockholms stads privilegiebref 1423–1700*, Johan III:s stadgar, Stockholm, 10 March 1570, 76: *'när några främmende saker schole förhöres, ransakes och dömmes, dhå schal ther till brukes halffparten uthländske och halffparten inländske, på thet alle saker thäss schickeligere schole förhandlede varde, och ath the fremmende icke schole hafve sigh till ath beclage um någen orätt'.*

employed by the king and settled in Sweden, and who also had many links to Scottish tradesmen. The Gävle burgher Andrew Littlejohn (*Anders Litteljehn*) may have been originally English or Scottish and the same applies to Paul Young (*Poul Joungh*), a burgher of Nyköping, and William Russell (*Willam Russil*), burgher of Arboga, who owed John Dundee money. 'Hans Finlodh', burgher and inhabitant of Hedemora, may have been of foreign origin – possibly Scottish (John Finlay?). By contrast, Henry Guthrie (*Henrick Gÿttrj*) probably a Scot, was referred to as a foreign merchant (*en främmande Köpman*).[47] The London tradesmen John Cootes (*Johan Kout*)[48] and Humphrey Streit (*Humfridh Streitt*)[49] also appear in the commercial cases of the Svea Court of Appeal in 1614. It is more difficult to identify German or Danish tradesmen based on their names. However, Bertil Rödker was expressly mentioned as being a foreign merchant, probably German.[50]

More generally, it has been assessed that 'longstanding credit-giving and the difficulties in getting liquid funds were typical features of still relatively undeveloped Swedish commerce'.[51] This applied particularly to the nobility. As elsewhere, the Swedish nobility was often cash-poor and required credit to provide funds for sudden expenses and major acquisitions, e.g., in connection with a royal visit, trips abroad, weddings or funerals. In the mid-sixteenth century, the highest echelons of the Swedish aristocracy used only a moderate portion of the profit of their estates for building projects and luxury consumption, such as costly imported textiles and cloth.[52] Nevertheless, this trend of following Continental fashion and the lavish consumption habits of foreign nobility became all the more pronounced in the latter half of the sixteenth century and in the course of the seventeenth century.[53] Count Per Brahe the Elder condemned

47 RA, SH, HA, B I a:1, 14 Oct. 1614, 52r and 24 Nov. 1614, 75v–76r.

48 RA, SH, HA, B I a:1, 10 Dec. 1614, 81v.

49 E.g., RA, SH, HA, A I a 1:1, 19 Oct. 1614, 131v–132v.

50 RA, SH, HA, B I a:1, 13 July 1614, 27r.

51 Bolin, 'Dundi', 526.

52 Olle Ferm, *De högadliga godsen i Sverige vid 1500-talets mitt – geografisk uppbyggnad, räntestruktur, godsdrift och hushållning* (Stockholm: Riksantikvarieämbetet, 1990), 314, 359–360, 368–369, 372–373.

53 In an article, Margareta Revera has discussed the growing consumption of luxury items by the Swedish nobility in the course of the seventeenth century, especially its latter part. But she points out that the luxury consumption was already considerable in the 1620s and 1630s among the highest aristocracy, see Margareta Revera, 'En barock historia: Om den 1600-talslyxen och dess plats i samhällsomvandlingen', in Gudrun Ekstrand, *Tre Karlar: Karl X Gustav, Karl XI, Karl XII* (Stockholm: Livrustkammaren, 1984), 113–135, esp. 117–120; and also Möller, *Suomen tapulikaupunkien valtaporvaristo*, 220–221. On luxury

the 'unnecessary and superfluous splendour' of the time. Brahe claimed that the consumption of extravagant clothes, jewellery, furniture, foodstuff and alcohol, as well as gambling, had spread to Sweden particularly since the 1560s and the reign of King Erik XIV (r. 1560–1568), in contrast to the previous more parsimonious habits of King Gustav Vasa. To Brahe's more sober thinking, such 'overabundance [was] more princely than noble' and threatened eventually to ruin the country.[54]

Although there is something of the older generation lamenting over the frivolity of youth in Brahe's moralist writing, in real life, the more extravagant consumption habits or the vicissitudes of the period could lead noblemen and women to have to pawn their jewellery or silverware.[55] It also led to the indebtedness of the nobility to merchants and artisans. Olof the Tailor (*Oloff Skräddare*) complained to the Court of Appeal that Lady Elisabet Grip had for many years owed him a sum of money that she had failed to pay him. The Court of Appeal provided him with a letter of exhortation (*Mane Breff*) urging her to recompense him 'voluntarily and without any long delay'.[56]

Despite royal assistance, certain Swedish court cases demonstrate that it could be onerous, even physically dangerous, to attempt to collect debts from Swedish noblemen. Richard Peterson (*Rickert Petterßon*), a taverner from Stockholm, attempted to collect a long-standing debt from the Brahe family in 1615. Peterson had to show the IOU of Count Erik Brahe (1552–1614), son of Per Brahe, on 300 barrels of grain, signed in 1594. But matters had been complicated by the fact that Brahe had gone into exile in 1600 and had never returned. The bailiff of Brahe's estranged widow, Countess Elisabet of Braunschweig-Lüneburg (1553–1618), claimed that the debt had been prescribed, as it had not been claimed from the Countess before. This Peterson denied: he had reminded the Count of the debt in 1595 and 1600, but he had only received fair promises (*godh ordh*) of payment. After Erik Brahe had left the country, he had approached the Countess at the Castle of Visingsborg in an attempt to collect the debt. He had stood the whole day in the hall (*förstuffuen*) of the castle in the freezing cold, but had not been allowed to meet her, nor had he been

consumption among eighteenth-century aristocrats, see Ilmakunnas, *Kuluttaminen ja ylhäisaatelin elämäntapa*, esp. 188–218. The Swedish economic historian Eli Heckscher has dated the commencement of the luxury consumption of the aristocracy to the latter half of the sixteenth century; Heckscher, *Sveriges ekonomiska historia*, 99.

54 Granlund and Holm, Per Brahe, *Oeconomia*, 74.

55 E.g., Ilmakunnas, *Kuluttaminen ja ylhäisaatelin elämäntapa*, 134, 207–208; SST från år 1592, VI, 23 Sept. 1609, 256–257.

56 RA, SH, HA, B I a:1, 24 Dec. 1614, 84v–85.

paid.[57] Richard Peterson goes to show that the Swedish court system did not necessarily have any automatic prejudice against naturalized aliens, while he had faced difficulties in collecting debts from powerful members of the elite. Moreover, Sigfrid Nilsson – probably of Stockholm – had to face threats and intimidation from the noble Erik Tönnesson [Tott] when attempting to recover the longstanding debt of his late father Tönne Eriksson [Tott] (1553–1608) on which immobile property had been pawned.[58]

Petrén's argument of foreigners being underdogs applies to all European countries. Moreover, the problems of strangers or foreigners were certainly not only limited to commercial disputes, but were even more acute in criminal cases in which compurgation was still one of the most common means of proof. For example, Captain Alexander Ferne (in the court records usually *Capiten Farij*) was first accused of homicide in the Stockholm town court, and was later also sentenced at the Svea Court of Appeal in 1614. Ferne was a Scot who, together with another man, had assaulted and killed a compatriot, a Scottish soldier (*drabant*), on a street in Stockholm. The Court of Appeal insisted that Ferne provide twelve compurgators to support his innocence of stabbing the soldier to death with his sword. Ferne announced that he would be unable to find them 'because he was a stranger'.[59]

However, even if aliens may have felt the lack of contacts and acquaintances more acutely than natives, all strangers and newcomers to a town – even Swedes – could have difficulties in making their debtors pay. Indeed, the Svea Court records suggest that even Swedish merchants could have similar problems in obtaining justice if they lived in another jurisdiction and did not have local support for their debt suit or trade dispute. In fact, the Svea Court of Appeal register of 1614 indicates that Måns Nilsson, burgher and town councillor of Stockholm, and before him, his wife, had been for thirteen years trying to collect, both in person and through their representatives (*fulmechtige*), a debt owed to them by Lars Olofsson of Arboga, who had since died. The Court of Appeal observed that justice demanded that both courts did what their calling and office required them to do. The royal justices wrote to the town court of Arboga finally to examine and adjudicate the case by 29 June (feast of

57 The Stockholm town court considered that there had been no prescription and sentenced the debt to be paid, 6 Nov. 1615, *STb från år 1592*, VIII, 156. On Erik Brahe, see S. Tunberg, 'Erik Brahe', *SBL* 5 (Stockholm: Bonnier, 1925), 658–660. For another foreign merchant attempting to collect a debt from the Brahes and ending up incarcerated and manhandled, see Eriksson, *I skuggan av tronen*, 341–344.

58 RA, SH, HA, B I a:1, 27 Oct. 1614.

59 RA, SH, HA, A I a 1:1, 70. See also 10 May 1615, *STb från år 1592*, 6.

St Peter and Paul), as Count Magnus Brahe 'seriously exhorted' and 'ordered on the behalf of His Royal Majesty, Our Most Gracious King and Lord'. The Arboga magistrates were also threatened with 'the punishment that the law decrees' in case of any further delays.[60]

Daniel Brandes (*Daniel Brandt*), a Stockholm burgher, had similar problems, having not managed to get money out of his debtors despite the debt reminder (*manebrev*) obtained from the king. Consequently, he had to request that the Court of Appeal issue a precept (*Förschrifft*) to all governors, crown officials and district judges to help him recover his debts from his several noble and commoner debtors. While these were exhorted to pay Brandes their debts, all officials were to assist him in obtaining his rights. Any protesting debtors had to appear at the Svea Court of Appeal on 8 September that year.[61] The above-mentioned Blasius Dundee of Stockholm requested a so-called letter of exhortation (*Mane Breff*) from the Court of Appeal for his many noble creditors.[62] Sven Gunnarsson, burgher of Enköping, also faced difficulties in receiving payment of the debts owed to him in the mining district: his servant had been badly beaten, and the culprit had even absconded with some iron belonging to Sven.[63] Thus, debt collection could be onerous for Swedes, naturalized foreigners and aliens alike, and the Court of Appeal emphasized that its duty was to help everyone, both foreigners and Swedes, to receive justice.[64]

5 Debt Reminders and Rescripts: Court of Appeal Remedies in Commercial Disputes

What kind of remedies could the Court of Appeal provide in commercial disputes? Basically, there were no special categories for commercial disputes in comparison with other litigation, apart from the so-called *manebrev*. These were royal reminders or debt collection notices, requested by the creditor, which reminded the debtor of the debt and exhorted him or her to pay it and to satisfy the supplicant or answer to the complaint in court. The Court provided debt reminders even outside its ordinary court terms. Consequently, the service was available all year round.

60 RA, SH, HA, B I a:1, 27 May 1614, fol. 3–4.

61 In the records, what Brandes was asking was called a 'debt collection letter' (*een förfordringz Schrifft*), RA, SH, HA, A I a 1:1, 30 May 1614, 17; RA, SH, HA, B I a:1, 30 May 1614, 5r–5v.

62 RA, SH, HA, B I a:1, 22 Nov. 1614, 73–73v.

63 RA, SH, HA, B I a:1, 30 May 1614, 4r–4v.

64 RA, SH, HA, B I a:1, 15 Oct. 1614, 54v.

In the autumn of 1614, the Court of Appeal decided on its notarial fees, which were the prices of the documents it issued. A rescript (*Förschrifft*) cost only one *daler*, making it the cheapest document issued (in comparison to the three-*daler* fee for a letter of judgement on paper).[65] The letters reminding people of debts probably cost the same, making either a worthwhile investment, if its authority helped the creditor collect the debt without resorting to the courts or to catch the fugitive debtor.

An example of such a situation was the reminder that the Court of Appeal sent to 'Claes Christiernsson' – possibly the aristocratic Klas Kristersson Horn (1587–1651), whose father, Kristiern Klasson Horn (1554–1612), Councillor of the Realm, had died a few years earlier.[66] The late Kristiern Klasson Horn owed Bertil Rödker 150 *dalers*. As Klas Kristersson's siblings were either legally incompetent to answer in court as minors, or did not have the money to satisfy the creditor, Rödker had been forced to wait to have the debt paid until he himself arrived in Sweden. The Court of Appeal exhorted Horn either to pay the debt or to answer in court to the plaintiff's claim.[67] It may be that the two-month delay between Rödker's appearance in court and the issuing of the actual reminder was caused by the Court of Appeal's wish that private debt reminding should first take place and prove unsatisfactory before the Court took action.

In addition to these authoritative debt collection notices from petitioners to individual debtors, the Court of Appeal also granted supplicants' rescripts (*förskrift*) to local governors, officials or courts, with an order to assist the petitioner as the recipient's office required and to help the petitioner to his or her rights. These rescripts came in two types: general rescripts to local governors and officials to help a person to his/her rights, and particular ones ordering them for example to investigate and judge a claim, arrest certain property or capture a fugitive debtor.

Sometimes the titles (esp. *manebrev* and *förskrift*) are confused, partly at least due to vacillating terminology on the part of the Court. For example, the Scottish merchant Henry Guthrie, called 'a foreign tradesman' in the source, requested the Court of Appeal to give him 'a prescript or letter of exhortation' against Johan Melchersson who owed him three hundred *dalers*. The Court of Appeal finally granted this request in a letter dated on 19 December 1614, more than two months later. What he received was a special rescript addressed to

65 Fees of the Court of Appeal, 1 Sep. 1614, RA, SH, HA, E I:1b, 75r.

66 Anonymous, 'Horn', *SBL* 19 (Stockholm, Bonnier, 1971–1973), 343–353. On Krister Klasson Horn, *ibid.*, 347 and on Klas Kristersson Horn, *ibid.*, 347–348.

67 Svea Court of Appeal to Claes Christiernsson, 13 July 1614, RA, SH, HA, B I a:1, 27r.

the governor of the Kopparberg region to catch and detain the fugitive debtor if he appeared in the region.[68]

A couple of observations are necessary to clarify the kind of source to which we are referring here. Firstly, the debt reminders and prescripts issued by the Court of Appeal usually tell us very little about the business transactions behind the debt. Thus, from the perspective of the Svea Court, they are debt collections. One does not necessarily find out what kind of credit or commercial transactions had been made. Even the one dispute registered as a contract dispute involved the collection of a sum of money.[69] However, for those cases that went on to become litigation at the Svea Court, one can find stacks of original documents tied together in books in the series *Liber causarum*. Some international commercial law suits in this series could be very complicated and also involve documents in German and Latin.

The Court of Appeal probably handled so many commerce-related supplications in 1614 because it had been delegated some tasks from King Gustav II Adolf who was abroad in Estonia managing a military campaign against Russia. Such supplications were normally likely to have been addressed to the King (and his Council), and handled by the Royal Chancellery. Wherever the King resided, he could expect petitioners, asking him for a letter helping creditors to collect debts from debtors. For example, when Gustav II Adolf travelled to the Livonian war zone via Finland in 1614, he was approached by Gregorius Martini Teit (*c.*1560–1615), vicar of Turku. Teit had many debtors around the country and he needed a royal letter in order to facilitate his efforts in debt collection.[70] Teit is just one example to show that in a country without banking systems such as Sweden, persons from many different societal groups could be involved as creditors in credit transactions in practice.

The number of creditors requesting royal debt reminders was such that some years later, in 1619, King Gustav II Adolf complained about the problems relating to the collection of debts in trade and commerce in the country. The King considered himself as being over-burdened by tradesmen complaining to him about debts other merchants and the elite (*ståndzpersoner*) owed them. Indeed, the King claimed to be bothered and overwhelmed by daily requests for debt reminders from merchants all over the country. Although the King

68 Svea Court of Appeal to Edvert Halvarsson on behalf of Henry Guthrie, 19 Dec. 1614, RA, SH, HA, B I a:1, fol. 83r; RA, SH, HA, A I a 1:1, Oct. 1614, fol. 122r. Cf. RA, SH, HA, B I a:1, 22 Nov. 1614, 73r–73v.

69 RA, SH, HA, A I a 1:1, 7 June 1614, 29r–29v.

70 Simo Heininen, 'Teit, Gregorius Martini', in Matti Klinge et al. (eds.), *Suomen Kansallisbiografia* 9 (Helsinki: SKS, 2009), 695–696 at 696.

acknowledged the importance of commerce for society (*Commercia* [...] *eliest* nervi societatis civilis *äre*), he wanted to be rid of endless complaints. Thus, he authorized that these disputes could be resolved in Stockholm, conveniently situated for all parties, either by the Svea Court of Appeal, or by the trading company in question. Gustav II Adolf issued certain rules for procedure in some cases and attempted to make the collecting of debt from noblemen more efficient by making it possible for local governors to make distraints on noble property and ordering that interest be paid.[71] Thus, debt cases were to obtain an even more pronounced future role in the Svea Court of Appeal.

6 The Court of Appeal, Arbitration, and Account Books

The Rules of Procedure for the Svea Court of Appeal, published in 1615, ordered that the Court in all cases was to seek actively and facilitate settlements and amicable compromises between the parties before anything else was done in the case. However, the statute conceded that not all cases could or were to be arbitrated.[72] While the rules were only officially signed by King Gustav II Adolf in 1615, some version of them had already been in use in Stockholm since the summer of 1614.[73]

The regular extent and frequency of arbitration cannot be determined by the Svea sources even if the court sometimes delegated some tasks to 'good men' as has been discussed above. However, it may be assumed that private negotiations between the parties, possibly also arbitration attempts, preceded court proceedings. In fact, arbitration was often used in medieval and early modern commercial and credit disputes because of the greater flexibility and speed involved. The possibility of choosing the arbitrators, of having more technical expertise at the panel, or of freely assessing evidence may also have been worthwhile aims.[74] Moreover, the Swedish early seventeenth-century merchant community shared the values of the famous Czech pedagogue Johannes Amos Comenius (1592–1670) who wrote in his famous best-selling *Orbis Sensualium Pictus* (first published in 1658): 'The best Law, is a quiet agreement, made either by themselves, betwixt whom the suit is, or by an Umpire. If

71 Statute on the Payment of Debts, 15 Aug. 1619 in Schmedeman, *Kongl. stadgar*, 183–185.

72 23, Rättegångs Process 1615, in Schmedeman, *Kongl. stadgar*, 158.

73 RA, SH, HA, B I a:1, 28 June 1614, 15v–16v.

74 Rawcliffe, 'That Kindliness Should be Cherished More', 98–103; Craig Muldrew, 'Interpreting the market: the ethics of credit and community relations in early modern England', *Social History* 18:2 (1993), 163–183 at 179.

this do not proceed, they come into Court [...]'.[75] Yet, it has been observed for some towns in Europe that 'the initiation of litigation must have been a fairly normal part of the process of the process of recovering debts or resolving disputes over payment' – perhaps an invitation to an out-of-court settlement. In fact, almost all of the cases were dropped after the first stage.[76]

According to its Rules of Procedure, only cases with a high enough economic interest could be appealed to the Court of Appeal. The limits were one hundred *dalers* from Stockholm and fifty *dalers* from the rest of the country.[77] This may have provided an extra incentive to have smaller cases settled locally by arbitration and/or by a court. However, the Court of Appeal seems not to have refused any case on the basis of too small an interest in its first year. Moreover, as it accepted to handle cases because of alleged denial of justice (*denegatio justitiae*), it provided remedies even in cases which were not appealable.[78]

On occasion, the Court of Appeal took even more active measures in attempting to arrange credit relations to the advantage of all parties concerned. For example, in October 1614, Anna, the wife of Hermann Takelborgh, appeared in court demanding payment of a 148-*daler* debt from the wife of Daniel Wagner. The Court sent three of its judges down to town in order to try to have the parties reconciled through 'good men'.[79] Probably as a consequence of the Court's active mediation, the following day, the Court sent its secretary Jakob Simonsson to the creditors of Herman Takelborgh to find out the extent of his debts and to try to negotiate a respite until the midsummer of 1615 so that Takelborg could get money from his own debtors, who indeed had promised payment by that date.[80] Similarly, when Blasius Dundee made a supplication to the Court of Appeal, referring to his own economic difficulties and the many debts owed to him, the Court took active measures to aid the merchant in distress. The vice president and two other judges were sent to town to go through

75 English translation by Charles Hoole from 1777: *Joh. Amos Comenii Orbis Sensialium Pictus* [...] *Joh. Amos Comenius's Visible World: or, A Nomenclature, and Pictures of all the Chief Things that are in the World, and of Men's Employments therein* [...]. Translated into English by Charles Hoole, 12th ed. (London: S. Leacroft, 1777), 160–161. The simultaneous Latin version: '*Optimum Jus, est placida convention, facta vel ab ipsis, inter quos list est, vel ab Arbitro. Hæc si non procedit, venitur in Forum*'.

76 Craig Muldrew, 'Credit and the courts: debt litigation in a seventeenth-century urban community', *Economic History Review* 46:1 (1993), 23–38 at 27–28; Rawcliffe, 'That Kindliness Should be Cherished More', 100.

77 Rättegångs Process 1615, in Schmedeman, *Kongl. stadgar*, 154–155.

78 RO 1614, in Schmedeman, *Kongl. stadgar*, 136.

79 RA, SH, HA, A I a 1:1, 4 Oct. 1614, 114v.

80 RA, SH, HA, A I a 1:1, 6 Oct. 1614, 118v.

Dundee's account books to ascertain his demands towards his debtors for future decisions by the Court of Appeal.[81] Thus, the Court of Appeal assumed the role of a dynamic and benevolent arbitrator in these cases.

We know from scattered references that several Swedish merchants kept account books and that they were referred to as evidence of debts at least in the fifteenth century.[82] Even if the account and copy books of tradesmen had legal relevance as evidence in court, particularly if they were carefully and unequivocally kept, the custom of account-keeping was not yet very well-developed in sixteenth- and early seventeenth-century Sweden. In fact, Gunvor Kerkkonen, who analysed the account books of the Tallinn merchant Helmich Ficke (d. 1542), has observed that they contain 'a jumble of data', having a character 'something between a journal and an accounts ledger'.[83] Its notices 'can hardly be characterized as real account books. Rather, they are formed by short jotted memorial notices over owed debt, that is, debt books. Completely comprehensible can they hardly have been for anyone else than for the writer/merchant himself as he had the whole context clear in his consciousness'.[84] Observations about the poor quality and informality of debt accounts and account books have also been made concerning early modern England.[85] Double-entry bookkeeping, known in Italy from the early 1300s, spread slowly to the north, even among Hanseatic traders. The Swedish crown started to use double-entry

81 RA, SH, HA, A I a 1:1, 5 Nov. 1614, 199v–200r.

82 30 Jan. 1464, Erik Noréen and Torsten Wennström (eds.), *Arboga stads tänkebok*, vol. 1 (Uppsala: Almqwist & Wicksell, 1935), 197: '*klarlegir oc lyuslegir j hans rækinskap stodh scrifuat*'; 21 Sept. 1492, doc. 4436, Reinhold Hausen (ed.), *Finlands medeltidsurkunder* 5 (Helsingfors, 1928), 363–364 at 364: '*myn reckensbuch*'; 22 May 1503, doc. 4973, Reinhold Hausen (ed.), *Finlands medeltidsurkunder* 6 (Helsingfors, 1930), 259: '*ær honom skillogh lxxxiiij mark swenska, som han klarligha kan bewisa met hans rækenskapz bock*'. See also 29 Apr. 1455, Reinhold Hausen (ed.), *Finlands medeltidsurkunder* 4 (Helsingfors, 1924), 65–67 at 67: '*dat steit all in mineme bocke gescreven*'; Axel Grandell, *Äldre redovisningsformer i Finland: En undersökning av den företagsekonomiska redovisningens utveckling i Finland intill 1800-talets slut* (Helsingfors, 1944), 30–31. See also Wilhelm Ebel, *Bürgerliches Rechtsleben zur Hansezeit in Lübecker Ratsurteilen* (Göttingen: Musterschmidt Wissenschaftlicher Verlag, 1954), 12; Ebel, *Forschungen zur Geschichte*, 72–77, 122–134.

83 Gunvor Kerkkonen, *Borgare och bondeseglare: Handelssjöfart på Reval genom och i SV-Finlands skärgård under tidig 1500-tal: Kring tvenne skuldböckers notismaterial detaljutredningar och reflexioner* (Helsingfors: SHS, 1977), 14. See also Mickwitz, *Aus Revaler Handelsbüchern*, 17.

84 Kerkkonen, *Borgare och bondeseglare*, 15. On similar notions of late medieval Swedish account books as 'relatively simple and undeveloped', see Grandell, *Äldre redovisningsformer*, 33, 41–45.

85 Muldrew, 'Interpreting the market', 173.

bookkeeping in 1625, and it was also known in some Finnish merchant circles in the 1620s.[86]

Blasius Dundee seems to have had his documentation in order, as he referred to the 'clear and pure manuscripts [meaning IOUS] of his debtors'. But he seemed almost apologetic when he not only referred to the fact that the debts were long-standing, but also to his advanced age and long weakness and illness: 'he has not much else to live on than what he can collect' from those owing him money.[87] After receiving the exhortation letter of the Court of Appeal, Blasius Dundee's representative collected the debt owed to him by Count Erik Brahe from his only legitimate child and heir, Beata Margareta Brahe (1583–1645). Dundee's IOU, signed by the Count, was dated 1594. Countess Brahe was represented by the attorney of her husband, Baron Gustav [Eriksson] Stenbock (1575–1629).[88]

At the same time, the above-mentioned Anna, widow of Hans Karkman, was also collecting the debt owed, by presenting an IOU signed by Baron Gustav Stenbock's late father as early as 1571. The debt of over 1,600 marks had been unpaid for more than four decades. Nevertheless, Stenbock refused to honour the IOU claiming not to know the signet, hand or signature. Yet, the court confirmed it and ordered the debt to be paid. One hindrance to the payment of the late Erik Stenbock's debts may have been the fact that he had died in exile in Denmark, a political refugee due to the political turbulences of the 1590s and early 1600s. His county and his estates had been confiscated by this time. However, his son Gustav had been allowed to return to Sweden and to succeed to his father's former barony in 1603, becoming Councillor of the Realm in 1611.[89] As Möller has argued, credit could be given to domestic debtors for long periods, even decades, while international credit relations tended to be more short-term.[90]

The Enköping burgher Sven Gunnarsson owed 500 *dalers* to Colonel Patrick Rutherford who turned to the Court of Appeal. Sven Gunnarsson was willing

86 Mickwitz, *Aus Revaler Handelsbüchern*, 188–190; Möller, *Suomen tapulikaupunkien valtaporvaristo*, 81–85; Grandell, *Äldre redovisningsformer*, 57–58, 62. On the history of double-entry bookkeeping, see e.g. James Aho, *Confession and Bookkeeping: The Religious, Moral, and Rhetorical Roots of Modern Accounting* (Albany: State University of New York Press, 2005), 10, 31–34, 55–56, 63–79.

87 RA, SH, HA, B I a:1, 22 Nov. 1614, 73r–73v.

88 8 Nov. 1615, *STb från år 1592*, 158.

89 *Ibid.* On Erik Stenbock, see Lars-Olof Larsson, 'Erik Gustafsson (Stenbock)', *SBL* 33 (Stockholm: Riksarkivet, 2007–2011), 269–271, and on his son Gustav, see Hans Gillingstam, 'Stenbock, släkt', *ibid.*, 247–265 at 251–252.

90 Möller, *Suomen tapulikaupunkien valtaporvaristo*, 259.

to pay, but unable to do so, as Henry Cato (*Henrich Cato*), a Västerås burgher possibly of Scottish origin, in turn owed him money. But Cato had absconded – nobody knew where he had gone. However, some copper belonging to him was kept at the public weighing house (*wågen*) of Uppsala. Rutherford asked for an arrest of this property owned by Cato until the debt Sven Gunnersson owed him had been paid. This the Court granted.[91]

Several of the cases indicate that the debt had been owed for many years already. Obviously, court proceedings were perceived as a final resort when informal exhortations and means of debt collection had failed. Even more generally, the correspondence and activity of the Court indicate awareness that claiming debts could be slow and onerous and that delays in the process could hamper the claimant's own creditworthiness, threaten his livelihood and plunge him into bankruptcy. In a few instances, the Court refers to a chain of credit: the failure of someone to collect debts owed to him (or her) would lead to his bankruptcy. A chain reaction could take place, and the creditor urgently needed help from the authorities so that he himself did not go under.[92]

7 The Svea Court of Appeal and Norms Controlling Trade

There are some other things the Svea Court of Appeal sources can tell regarding attitudes towards commercial law. One of these is related to the protests and disturbances at the town hall of Stockholm when the new royal Trade and Sailing Ordinance of 1614 was being publicly read out.[93]

The issuing of the Trade and Sailing Ordinance of 1614 was justified with a reference to the great disorder regarding trade in the Swedish towns that was impoverishing them, and the declared aim of the new norm was the reverse, to make the towns and their burghers wealthier.[94] Some of the rules involved

91 RA, SH, HA, B I a:1, 13 July 1614, 26v–27r.

92 RA, SH, HA, B I a:1, July 1614, 28v; RA, SH, HA, B I a:1, 19 Dec. 1614, 82v. See also 6 Nov. 1615, *STb från år 1592*, VIII, 156–157.

93 For the ordinance see Handels och Seglations Ordning och Stadga, 10 Feb. 1614, Anders Anton von Stiernman (ed.), *Samling Utaf Kongl. Bref, Stadgar och Förordningar etc. Angående Sweriges Rikes* Commerce, Politie *och* Oeconomie *Uti Gemen, Ifrån Åhr 1523 in til närwarande tid* 1 (Stockholm: Kongl. Tryckeriet, 1747), 591–602. On the economic police ordinances in Sweden in the sixteenth and seventeenth centuries, see Toomas Kotkas, *Royal Police Ordinances in Early Modern Sweden: The Emergence of Voluntaristic Understanding of Law* (Leiden: Brill, 2014), 59–71, 131–152.

94 Prologue, Handels och Seglations Ordning och Stadga, 10 Feb. 1614, von Stiernman, *Samling Utaf Kongl. Bref* 1, 591.

the enforcing of a division of Swedish towns into staple towns (*Sjöstädher*) and inland towns (*Upstäder*). The rudiments of this policy were already visible in the mid-fifteenth-century town law.[95] As only staple towns were permitted to trade freely directly overseas, this increased their role and wealth, as much of the foreign trade had to pass through them.[96] While Stockholm was one of the winners from this division, many tradesmen and the burghers of Stockholm more generally considered the statute as being against their interests. The relationship between King and town was strained, as the town had to pay extra taxes and costs because of the shipping of troops overseas, extraordinary levies for warfare, and the upkeep of billeted soldiers. The conflict was evident, and the burghers out-and-out refused to pay certain exertions demanded by the crown. As a result, first Axel Oxenstierna (1583–1654), Chancellor of the Realm, appeared in person at the town court to rebuke the burghers and later, King Gustav II Adolf himself sent for the mayors and town councillors in order to reprimand them for their unwillingness to contribute to the ransoming of the fortress of Älvsborg, which had been recently been lost to the Danes in war.[97]

The Ordinance also limited the possibility for all foreigners to do business in Sweden: sailing and trading was only permitted in certain nominated towns including Stockholm.[98] The crown threatened any disregarding foreigners with the confiscation of their vessel and goods, three-quarters to the fisc and one quarter to the closest staple town as the injured party. The statute came into force eight weeks after it had been issued.[99] Foreigners were also forbidden to sail or travel to other towns, or to the Swedish mining regions, either during markets or otherwise in order there to 'buy or trade or to demand payment of debts'. Trading directly with nobles or commoners in the countryside was also forbidden, as foreigners had to operate via the closest staple town and its burghers. Their measures used for sale and trading locations were also restricted. These norms did not remain dead letters, but they were enforced in practice as

95 K 33:3, Holmbäck and Wessén, *MESL*, 131.

96 2–9, Handels och Seglations Ordning och Stadga, 10 Feb. 1614, von Stiernman, *Samling Utaf Kongl. Bref* 1, 592–597. On the royal trade policy in the sixteenth and seventeenth centuries, see also e.g. Möller, *Suomen tapulikaupunkien valtaporvaristo*, 9–19; Heckscher, *Sveriges ekonomiska historia*, 243–245, 250–253.

97 Piia Einonen, *Poliittiset areenat ja toimintatavat: Tukholman porvaristo vallan käyttäjänä ja vallankäytön kohteena* (Helsinki: SKS, 2005), 104–105, 175–185.

98 These towns were Stockholm, Nya Lödöse, Kalmar, Gothenburg, Söderköping, Norrköping, Nyköping, Västervik, Tälje, Gävle, Turku, Viborg and Tallinn (Räfle).

99 1, Handels och Seglations Ordning och Stadga, 10 Feb. 1614, von Stiernman, *Samling Utaf Kongl. Bref* 1, 592.

the seventeenth-century examples indicate.[100] The 1614 Trade and Sailing Ordinance also confirmed the rule that foreign merchants were only allowed to spend six weeks in one of the Swedish staple towns. The foreigner disregarding the statute had to pay eighty marks for each extra week, half to the crown and half to the town in question.[101] However, the government could grant exceptional dispensations from this rule.[102]

This six-week time limit had been mentioned in the Trade Ordinance of 1594 as being based on 'law and old custom'.[103] In fact, the six-week limitation had first been included in the 1537 treaty between Sweden and Lübeck, while it had been repeated several times (in 1573, 1577, 1580 and 1585). Judging by the repetitive statutes, the norms had not been strictly enforced in practice.[104] The Estates of Sweden had dealt with the problem of the unfair competition by foreign tradesmen in its decisions at the Diet of Stockholm in 1602, confirming the licit sojourn of foreign tradesmen in towns to six weeks. If someone wished to extend his stay, he was to apply for burgher status and perform the duties accordingly. The same problems continued and involved foreign merchants' apprentices, and new ordinances were given for the better observance of the rule.[105]

The 1614 Trade and Sailing Ordinance also forbade Swedish burghers from trading on commission for foreigners, or as the Ordinance expressed it, 'allowed themselves to be used as hirelings for the foreigners' for a 'petty gain' in illicit trade in towns, the countryside or mining districts. Such an offence was punishable for both parties, the foreign owner of the goods and the Swedish factor or mercantile agent, who acted on commission, with confiscation of the money and goods as well as an eighty-mark fine.[106] By contrast, earlier in the

100 10, Handels och Seglations Ordning och Stadga, 10 Feb. 1614, von Stiernman, *Samling Utaf Kongl. Bref* 1, 597–598. For legal practice, see Möller, *Suomen tapulikaupunkien valtaporvaristo*, 117–126.

101 10, Handels och Seglations Ordning och Stadga, 10 Feb. 1614, von Stiernman *Samling Utaf Kongl. Bref* 1, 598.

102 RA, SH, HA, A I a 1, 1 July 1614, 65r.

103 Ordinantia om Kiöphandelen etc., 1594, von Stiernman, *Samling Utaf Kongl. Bref* 1, 417–427, here 427.

104 Heckscher, *Sveriges ekonomiska historia*, 247.

105 E.g., Sveriges Rijkes/ Ständers/ Beslut,/ Som af them frijwilligen och een/helleligen gjordt och samtyckt är,/ Uthi Stockholm then 17. Junij,/ Åhr etc./ 1602,/ Stockholm, Andrea Gutterwitz, [1602], fol B iij; Bref för Stockholmz Stadh, att främmande Kiöpswänner intet måge wara öfwer 6. wekor i Rijket etc., 4 Jan. 1612, von Stiernman, *Samling Utaf Kongl. Bref* 1, 564–565.

106 18, Handels och Seglations Ordning och Stadga, 10 Feb. 1614, von Stiernman *Samling Utaf Kongl. Bref* 1, 601; Möller, *Suomen tapulikaupunkien valtaporvaristo*, 124–136.

sixteenth century, trading on commission had been practiced in Sweden.[107] This naturally curtailed the trading opportunities of foreigners and forced them to settle in one of the staple towns and acquire burgher rights there in order to pursue trade without restrictions as to nationality.[108] Alternatively, they could send their own apprentices as their factors to Sweden.

Judging by the correspondence of the Svea Court of Appeal, some fleeing or hiding debtors were quick to attempt to profit from the disadvantages and travel restrictions the Ordinance imposed on foreigners attempting to collect credit owed them. This dodging tactic was mentioned by the Court.[109] However, representatives or attorneys could be appointed. Consequently, the London tradesman John Cootes (*Johan Koutz*) authorized the Scottish Colonel Patrick Rutherford (1577–1618)[110] to act as his representative in collecting the 150 *dalers* from his debtors.[111] Rutherford seems to have been regularly used as an advisor, representative and factor by Englishmen and Scots, as he had been in Sweden for years. He had probably acquired knowledge of the 'local language, customs and laws' of Sweden – skills necessary for a successful factor.[112] As Rutherford resided in Sweden permanently, he was not hampered by the sojourn or travelling restrictions hindering foreign merchants. John Dundee (*Hans Dundj*), another Scot, needed to appoint a representative for the same purpose as Cootes, debt collection, before having to leave the country as required by 'the Ordinance' [Trade and Sailing Ordinance of 1614].[113] Perhaps for a foreign tradesman with many commercial or credit relations in Sweden, becoming a burgher in a Swedish town was a way of overcoming this practical difficulty.[114] Then,

107 Kerkkonen, *Borgare och bondeseglare*, 23–24.

108 E.g., Sylvi Möller has observed (in *Suomen tapulikaupunkien valtaporvaristo*, 45–61) that judging by the family names, the number of foreign merchants – particularly German, but also Dutch and Scottish – grew in the course of the seventeenth century in Turku and some other Finnish towns.

109 RA, SH, HA, B I a:1, 15 Oct. 1614, 54r.

110 On Rutherford, see e.g. Stefan Palm and Ola Undin, 'A Note on the Scots in 17th Century Sigtuna', *Northern Studies* 43 (2012), 110–127 at 113–115. See also Colonel Patrick Rutherford (record ID: 6633) on The Scotland, Scandinavia and Northern European Biographical Database (SSNE), accessed on 5 Jan. 2018, on: http://www.st-andrews.ac.uk/history/ssne/item.php?id=6633&id2=6633.

111 RA, SH, HA, B I a:1, 10 Dec. 1614, fol. 81v.

112 Steve Murdoch, *Network North: Scottish Kin, Commercial and Covert Associations in Northern Europe* (Leiden: Brill, 2006), esp. 145–161.

113 Svea Court of Appeal to Hans Persson, 24 Nov. 1614, RA, SH, HA, B I a:1, fol. 75v–76r.

114 The court records of Stockholm contain lists of people who took the burgher's oath and many of the names seem to point towards German, Scottish and English origins, 10 May 1615, *STb från år 1592*, 61–62.

they were no longer referred to as foreigners but as burghers of the town in question.

After the issuing of the 1614 Ordinance, the burghers of Stockholm immediately asked King Gustav II Adolf to clarify its text and dispense with some of the norms. While all the norms regulating and restricting the activities of foreigners in Sweden were upheld, the King commanded all provincial governors and the keepers of his castles that nobody was to suffer from injustice because of the restrictions.[115] Obviously, there was cause for discontentment even in Stockholm. Even if the mayors of Stockholm attempted to calm down the situation and supplicate the king, the three ring-leaders, the Stockholm burghers Nils Kuure, Tomas Eriksson and Petter Knävelkamp, ended up in gaol and were sentenced for the tumult.[116]

The royal inspectors (*Opsynings-Männerne*) were ordered to observe vigilantly that foreigners did not break the restrictions imposed on them by the Ordinance.[117] However, the permitted six-week stay of foreign tradesmen in Sweden was extended temporarily by two weeks to eight weeks in Gustav II Adolf's Explanatory Decree of the Trade Ordinance, issued on 23 February 1615.[118] Moreover, the permitted sojourn was permanently confirmed as being eight weeks in the 1617 Trade Ordinance.[119]

The mid-fourteenth-century town law had already limited trade from boat to boat in Sweden, and only certain merchandise could be sold or bought directly from a ship instead of in the public marketplace. Moreover, the trading area in Stockholm had also been restricted.[120] Suspicions of smuggling – especially of copper which was so crucial for the Swedish economy – and corruption in the customs office of the Stockholm port had also come out around 1614. This was something that the Swedish government took very seriously. The port of Stockholm was by far the most important harbour in Sweden, not only according to statistics in the 1630s, but during the whole of the seventeenth century. It alone handled two-thirds of all import and export to and from Sweden and

115 Resolution för Stockholms Stadh på några Punchter, som i Handels-Ordningen blifwa förklarade etc., 25 Feb. 1614, von Stiernman, *Samling Utaf Kongl. Bref* 1, 612–614.

116 RA, SH, HA, A I a 1:1, 8 and 27 Oct. 1614, 155v–158v, 171v.

117 Instruction för Opsynings-Männerne N.N. öfwer Handels-Ordinantien, 14 May 1614, von Stiernman, *Samling Utaf Kongl. Bref* 1, 614–619, esp. 615, 617.

118 Förklarings Placat öfwer några Puncter i Örebro Handels-Ordinantie, 23 Feb. 1615, von Stiernman, *Samling Utaf Kongl Bref* 1, 655–660, at 657.

119 14, Ordinantie, huruledes Kiöphandelen af Rijksens Inbyggiare så wäl som fremmande drifwas skal, 12 Oct. 1617, von Stiernman, *Samling Utaf Kongl. Bref* 1, 690–704 at 699.

120 K 15–17, Holmbäck and Wessén, *MESL*, 120–121.

at times, its role increased to three-fourths.[121] The way the captains of foreign ships and tradesmen were to act in declaring their goods openly was regulated in a statute from 1604, based on the suspicion that much of the imported goods had already been secretly unloaded from the ship before reaching the quay. A skipper or tradesman caught smuggling goods into Sweden in this way, in defiance of the proper procedure laid out for foreigners importing goods, was to forfeit both vessel and goods.[122]

This was precisely what the case in 1614 was about. It was investigated thoroughly by the Svea Court of Appeal even if the matters at hand had already taken place some years earlier in 1609. The Swedish crown was very concerned about the control of commerce and trade. Indeed, this was of paramount concern for fiscal interests, and the early 1600s witnessed an increasing number of statutes on custom duties and excise taxes.[123] In fact, the Swedish economic policy had relied increasingly on the revenue raised by customs and excises since the reign of Gustav Vasa – and relied even more heavily on it in the seventeenth century. In the 1614 Customs Ordinance, the King lamented the great fraud that had 'recently taken place and which still continued daily' in customs and excises.[124] He may indeed have been talking of this particular case.

Many rounds of witness hearings were organized in the Court in order to find out how high officials had been aware of the smuggling and accepted bribes. The activities of the German Remer Remersson and the night-time goings-on on his ship were particularly investigated. It transpired that the higher naval official (*holmamiral*) Anders Cordeel,[125] and two lower customs officials (*brokikare*, lit.

121 Eli F. Heckscher, *Sveriges ekonomiska historia från Gustav Vasa*, 1:2 (Stockholm: Albert Bonniers Förlag, 1936), 386–387.

122 Öpet Breff om fremmande, som komme til Stockholm, at the ingalunde fördriste sigh stighe op från skiepett etc., 14 Sept. 1604, von Stiernman, *Samling Utaf Kongl. Bref* 1, 485–486. See also *Förordning huru handlas skal medh the fremmande skiepp, som hijt til Stockholm ankomma*, 23 Apr. 1604, *ibid.*, 481–482.

123 E.g., Customs and Excise Ordinances (*Tull och* Accis *Ordning*) of 1612 and 1613 and Customs Ordinances (*Tull-Ordning*) of 1614, von Stiernman, *Samling Utaf Kongl. Bref* 1, 568–583, 602–611.

124 Kallioinen, *Kauppias, kaupunki, kruunu*, 81–83; Heckscher, *Sveriges ekonomiska historia* 1:2, 285–286; Customs Ordinance (*Tull-Ordning*) of 1614, von Stiernman, *Samling Utaf Kongl. Bref* 1, 603.

125 On 8 September 1611, Anders Cordeel had already been court-martialled and sentenced to death by a military court for failure to obey the King's orders while he was captain of certain vessels during the war against Denmark. See Jonas Hallenberg, *Svea rikes historia under konung Gustaf Adolf den stores regering* 2 (Stockholm: Johan A. Carlbohm, 1790), 822–824.

wharf inspector) Abel Jöransson, whose son had been living at Remer Remersson's house in Lübeck, and Peder Pedersson, were convicted of corruption and misconduct.[126] Remersson admitted to the smuggling of cloth, but only of one bolt of cloth, while it was claimed that he had also smuggled some copper out of the country.[127] Nevertheless, a witness statement claimed that the clandestine unloading of cloth averting customs had taken three to four hours in the night. Even when the Court of Appeal bluntly asked why Remersson was unwilling to tell the truth and confess in detail the whole extent of his activities in smuggling and illicit trading, he stayed mute because of solidarity between merchants. As he himself put it: 'I cannot be a traitor to merchants'.[128]

Obviously, Remer Remersson considered that in order to maintain his good name and reputation as well as his trustworthiness – all essential for the success of a merchant – he could not denounce other merchants whose activities were not completely above board. In fact, the merchant community operated upon trust, reputation and reliability. Moreover, mutual solidarity within the merchant community was also an important virtue.[129] However, this did not prevent judgement, and on 22 June, Anders Cordeel was fined 18 *dalers* by the King's own decision, whereas five days later Peder Pedersson and Abel Jöransson were fined 50 *dalers* each. Remer Remersson was convicted of smuggling goods into the country, but also of secretly smuggling out some copper, and was fined 200 *dalers*.[130]

8 Conclusion

As the records of the Svea Court of Appeal have demonstrated, most of the commercial cases in 1614 involved credit reminders and rescripts to local

126 Anders Cordeel had accepted bribes for that some goods had secretly been loaded at night from Remer Remersson's ship sailing from Lübeck. Moreover, he had wrongfully got hold of the ship's inventory of transported cargo (*skiepzrullen*) and concealed it as well as an attempt to silence whistle-blowers both by violence and money. All this was against Cordeel's oath of loyalty and office. Peder Pedersson and Abel Jöransson had also turned a blind eye to the smuggling and illicit trade of smuggled goods.

127 RA, SH, HA, A I a 1:1, 1 June 1614, 3–4 June 1614, fols. 19r–29r, 35r–36v, 47v–52r, 83r–83v.

128 RA, SH, HA, A I a 1:1, 1, June 1614, 20r: *'Jagh kan icke wara Köpmans förrädare* [...]'.

129 In general, see e.g. Muldrew, 'Interpreting the market', 177–179; Aho, *Confession and Bookkeeping*, 68; Kallioinen, *Kauppias, kaupunki, kruunu*, 243–244, 251; Runefelt, *Hushållningens dygder*, 43–59; Jarkko Keskinen, *Oma ja yhteinen etu: Kauppiaiden keskinäinen kilpailu ja yhteistyö Porin paikallisyhteisössä 1765–1845* (Turku: University of Turku, 2012), 60–63 and *passim*.

130 RA, SH, HA, D VIII a 1, Fine records of the first law term of 1614, 22 and 27 June 1614, unpaginated; RA, SH, HA, A I a 1:1, 1 June 1614, 83r–83v, 84v.

governors, officials and courts to help a particular creditor to obtain justice. The Court of Appeal probably received a number of such cases because it was authorized to do so during the absence of the king, as some years later the king had to delegate them permanently to it. There was very little commercial litigation in 1614 which is understandable, and the number of such cases obviously grew with time. Nevertheless, an analysis of the records of the Svea court for a longer period would throw much more light on this. Yet, even this material suffices to observe that commercial disputes – international or domestic – were not the moving force behind establishing the court.

While foreign tradesmen did encounter difficulties in collecting debts, so did the Swedes. Indeed, one of the main things mentioned as the new court's duties was providing justice to all. The 1614 ordinance establishing the Court of Appeal and the king's authorization to its judges did not refer to foreign parties at all, but rather stressed the interest of providing justice to the king's subjects. It has been suggested that in 'obligations contracted over long distances', information about the other party and, subsequently trust, may have been 'in a much more fragile state' while the pressure of the merchant community may have been less strict.[131] This – in connection with the complexity of the financial arrangements in such cases – may have increased the likelihood of litigation in cases involving foreign trade.

Admittedly, a major problem relating to the Swedish local lay-dominated court system involved fugitive criminals and unwilling debtors who evaded the clutches of creditors, victims and crown officials attempting to bring them to justice. As justice delayed was justice denied, and as the image of the king as a guarantor of justice for all his subjects was affected by unresolved cases, it was in the interests of the king and his councillors to improve the effectiveness of the justice system. This was also important for the King's reputation in foreign countries in the early 1610s as Sweden was tottering on the verge of bankruptcy. It urgently needed loans and credit from abroad – especially from the Low Countries – for paying its war indemnity to Denmark, and Swedish creditworthiness was questioned. Thus, unlike late medieval England, there were not attempts to out-and-out forbid trade on credit with foreign merchants, or prosecute and punish merchants defying the norms.[132] Foreign trade and credit were vital for the Swedish crown, and the growing presence of foreign traders did not cause such resentment that would have resulted in domestic

131 Muldrew, 'Interpreting the market', 181.

132 Wendy Childs, '"To oure losse and hindraunce": English Credit to Alien Merchants in the Mid-Fifteenth Century', in J. Kermode (ed.), *Enterprise and Individuals in Fifteenth-Century England* (Stroud: Sutton, 1991), 68–98.

protectionism and regulation against overseas trade on credit. On the other hand, foreigners were not to be favoured at the expense of the Swedish taxpayers, and towns were complaining of how foreign merchants were evading the taxes, levies and other burdens and were thus distorting the competition.

Nevertheless, based on the records, foreign merchants faced a problem that Swedish tradesmen did not encounter, namely, the temporal restrictions of sojourn. As they were not allowed to stay for longer than six weeks, these restrictions on sojourn hampered their possibilities in using the ordinary legal procedures offered in Sweden, and was explicitly mentioned in some of the rescripts and debt reminders.[133] Moreover, their right to travel in Sweden in order to claim debts owed to them had been severely curtailed by the 1614 Ordinance, forcing foreigners to authorize agents or attorneys to act for them. Yet, some such restrictions were also issued for Swedish merchants.[134]

In connection to Sture Petrén's assertion that foreign tradesmen may have had special difficulties in getting to their rights, it must be pointed out that as their cases often had supraregional connections, they may have especially needed supraregional remedies or authorities. Julia Maurer has pointed out for the *Kammergericht*, the precursor of the Imperial German *Reichskammergericht*, that between 1451 and 1493, merchants were the social group that most often took their case to the *Kammergericht*. Moreover, their cases were usually 'strictly juridical' (*schlicht juristische*), as opposed to being cases of a political nature. These merchants came from a vast area ranging from Italy and Slovenia to the Baltic Sea. Thus, Maurer points out that merchants may have preferred to turn to a supraregional court (*überregionale Gerichtsinstanz*) instead of local, and possibly less advantageous, courts.[135] This plausible argument can be supplemented by observing that the remedies offered by such a court were probably more effective, and the royal authority of the court may have been an extra bonus.

In Sweden – as in many other countries – foreign merchants faced certain restrictions as to their travelling and doing business. Their position was traditionally such that they were especially considered to be under the special protection of the territorial ruler who defended the *miserabiles personae* and guaranteed them peace and justice. Thus, those merchants, who sought assistance from the authority of the king, and later more permanently, his royal Court of Appeal, were building on a long established tradition.

133 E.g., RA, SH, HA, B I a:1, 13 July 1614, 27r. See also *ibid.*, 10 Dec. 1614, 81v.

134 E.g., Möller, *Suomen tapulikaupunkien valtaporvaristo*, 207–208.

135 Julia Maurer, 'Die Köningsgericht und sein Wirken von 1451 bis 1493', in Bernhard Diestelkamp (ed.), *Das Reichskammergericht: Der Weg zu seiner Gründung unde die ersten Jahtzehnte seines Wirkens (1451–1527)* (Köln: Böhlau Verlag, 2003), 79–115, at 91, 102–103.

CHAPTER 13

Tracing the Speculation Bubble of 1799 in Newspapers, Court Records, and Other Sources

Margrit Schulte Beerbühl

1 Introduction

'People here seem to have lost their heads and I do not see that any appropriate measures are taken to stop the evil'. The Frankfurt banker Simon Moritz Bethmann wrote these remarks from Hamburg in October 1799.[1]

What could have happened to cause people in the Hansetown to be paralysed and unable to know what to do? A few weeks before, early in September, a speculation bubble had begun to burst. Within the next six weeks, 136 merchant and banking houses in Hamburg went bankrupt for about 68 million Mark Banco. The crisis soon swept over Europe and shortly after the beginning of the New Year reached the towns on the east coast of the United States.[2]

The speculation bubble of 1799 was not the first one. During the eighteenth century Europe had witnessed a number of bubbles: John Law's Mississippi swindle of 1719, the South Sea Bubble of 1720, as well as the bubble of 1763 to name only the well-known ones. The bubbles did not leave Hamburg a mere spectator to events. In the 1763 commercial and financial bubble more than 90 merchant houses in Hamburg were affected. What was different in 1799? A new situation arose as, for the first time, Hamburg became the epicentre of the bubble. The earlier crises had all been based abroad, and contemporaries such as the economist Johan Georg Büsch (1728–1800) had already witnessed the 1763 crisis. Büsch wrote a book on the 1799 crisis, which he entitled 'the big trade confusion'.[3] He described the one of 1799 as a serious illness that raged

1 *'Hier scheinen die Menschen alle Köpfe verloren zu haben und ich sehe nicht, dass zweckmäßige Mittel genommen werde, um dem Unheil Gränzen* [sic] *zu setzen'.* Stadtarchiv Frankfurt am Main, Bethmann Records, letter book of Simon Moritz Bethmann, Hamburg, to Simon Moritz Bethmann in London October 8, 1799 (both had the same Christian names).

2 Margrit Schulte Beerbühl, 'Die Hamburger Krise von 1799 und ihre weltweite Dimension', *Hamburger Wirtschafts-Chronik, Neue Folge* 10 (2012), 85–110.

3 Johann Georg Büsch, *Geschichtliche Beurtheilung der großen Handelsverwirrung im Jahre 1799, nebst Anmerkungen mit besonderer Bezugnahme auf die Krisis von 1857* (Hamburg: Hoffmann und Campe, 1858).

 | DOI 10.1163/9789004363144_014

in den Eingeweiden der Handlung [raged in the bowels of trade], compared to the crisis of 1763 which he described as a *vorübergehenden Krampf* [temporary convulsion].[4] In his still valuable 'history on commercial crises', economic historian Max Wirth similarly came to the conclusion that the crisis of 1799 affected the economy much more severely than the earlier one had done. 'In 1763' he resumed, 'only a few commercial branches were affected, while in 1799 all commercial manufacturing branches were severely hit'.[5] Büsch as well as Wirth were among the very few who mention that the 1799 bubble was not just a local affair, but also affected places like London and Denmark.

Apart from these two publications, the crisis of 1799 is hardly mentioned in modern economic history literature. If it is mentioned at all in economic history or in local histories on Hamburg, it is seen as a short-lived, peripheral and local event.

There are a few reasons for the neglect of studies on the 1799 event. Firstly, there is the long-held and still to some extent, prevailing concept of economic crises that distinguishes between pre-modern agricultural and food crises on the one hand and modern ones of the capitalist economy on the other hand. The latter are seen as a sign of economic growth and are recurrent phenomena. They are generally followed by more or less severe economic recessions and unemployment. The speculation bubbles of the eighteenth century are attributed a certain transitory character, but even in a recent study they are still described as 'comparatively harmless [...] not affecting the economic everyday life'.[6] Secondly, the French Revolutionary and Napoleonic Wars as well as the early spread of industrialisation have absorbed the attention of historians.

Another and third reason is the dominating focus, for at least half a century, if not much longer, on the history of achievements and the successful entrepreneur. In 1985 Julian Hoppit had already demanded that historians should not neglect the history of economic failures. 'Failures' he argued, 'are much commoner than success, at any period [...] that enterprise can be properly understood only when due regard is paid to bankruptcy and that the undoubted success of business expansion over the century has to be placed in the context of the possibility and reality of such bankruptcy'. Moreover, 'studying the patterns of bankruptcy evidence [...] adds detail and substance to the pictures of growth, decay and structural change'.[7] In the wake of 2008 and the fall of

4 Büsch, *Handelsverwirrung*, 87f.

5 Max Wirth, *Geschichte der Handelskrisen* (Frankfurt am Main, 1890), 107.

6 Werner Plumpe, *Wirtschaftskrisen: Geschichte und Gegenwart* (München: Beck, 2010), 41f.

7 Julian Hoppit, *Risk and Failure in English Business 1700–1800* (Cambridge: Cambridge University Press, 1987), 1.

the Lehman Brothers' bank, a new and intensified interest in the history and causes of economic failures has arisen. Meanwhile, a vast literature has been published. The overwhelming majority deals with the crises in the twentieth and the twenty-first centuries, while the number of publications on the early modern period is still limited.[8]

The speculation bubbles of 1719 and 1720, and the earlier Tulip Mania in 1637, have found some attention, as they were the first bubbles based on speculation in financial papers. The crises of 1763 and 1799 differ from them, as they were caused by speculations on goods and overtrading in bills of exchange. The 1763 crisis started with the breakdown of the De Neufville bank in Amsterdam and then spread to Hamburg, Berlin, Sweden and other places. Among the reasons that caused the burst were the end of the Seven-Years War, accompanied by a wrong assessment of the post-war economic development, and a currency reform which led to a liquidity squeeze. Dutch and Anglo-American scholars have dealt with various aspects of this crisis. Unlike this crash so far no academic research has been done on the 1799 speculation crisis.[9]

A study on its geographic dimension, economic and legal implications may shed new light on the interconnectedness of the late eighteenth-century world. Moreover, during the crisis, new legal and political instruments were developed that had a far-reaching impact on the handling of later bubbles, on the modernization of the bankruptcy laws, and the practice of conflict regulation.

Although it cannot be dealt with in this paper, it may be kept in mind that the eighteenth century was a period of growth and fundamental economic changes. It saw the coming of the industrial revolution and a rapid expansion

8 Mark Häberlein, *Brüder, Beziehungen, Normen und Konflikte in der Augsburger Kaufmannschaft um die Mitte des 16. Jahrhunderts* (Berlin: Akademie Verlag, 1998); Thomas Max Safley (ed.), *The History of Bankruptcy. Economic, social and cultural implications in early modern Europe* (London: Routledge, 2013); Ingo Köhler and Roman Rossfeld (eds.), *Pleitiers und Bankrotteure, Geschichte des ökonomischen Scheiterns vom 18. bis 20. Jahrhundert* (Frankfurt am Main: Campus, 2012); Dorothee Guggenheimer, *Kredite, Krisen und Konkurse* (Zürich: Chronos, 2014).

9 On the 1763 crisis see, among others, the Dutch publications of Johannes Gerard van Dillen, 'De Beurscrisis Te Amsterdam 1763', *Tijdschrift voor Geschiedenis* 37 (1922), 241–253; Isabel Schnabel and Hyun Song Shin, 'Liquidity and Contagion, The Crisis of 1763', *Journal of the European Economic Association* 2 (2004), 929–968; on the effects on Berlin, Stephan Skalweit, *Die Berliner Wirtschaftskrise von 1763 und ihre Hintergründe* (Stuttgart: Kohlhammer, 1937); W.O. Henderson, 'The Berlin Commercial Crisis of 1763', *Economic History Review, New Series* 15 (1962), 89–102; on Hamburg, Johan Georg Büsch, *Versuch einer Geschichte der Hamburgischen Handlung nebst 2 kleinere Schriften verwandten Inhalts* (Hamburg: Hoffmann, 1797).

of trade across the Atlantic and towards Asia. The slowness of communication and transport systems and the frequent wars of the century, moreover, increased not only the prospects of large gains but also of risks. Furthermore, recurrent overexpansion of credit added to the growth of failures.

In the following, I am going to present some preliminary results of an ongoing project on the speculation bubble of 1799, in which I want to highlight the new geographical dimension and the institutional developments that were initiated during the speculation bubble. Firstly, I will start to review information based on selected statistical material derived from court records on the development of bankruptcies in the 1790s, and delineate to what extent they reveal the bubble. A few remarks on the trend in bankruptcies in the 1790s will follow. Information on the dimension of panic, public discourse as well as political measures affecting commercial law cannot be derived from legal records, therefore I will turn to the media i.e. the newspapers in the next part of this paper. They are an important source on the geographical dimension of the crisis. It is only through them that we can get an impression of the far-reaching dimension of the bubble, the panic and the public debate. Thereafter, I will add some remarks on the contemporary bankruptcy law and the practice of dealing with the unfortunate merchants. Finally, I will question the distinction between pre-modern and modern crises.

2 Bankruptcy Registers of Selected Towns

Bankruptcy data for the eighteenth century have been compiled for various European countries. Information on this data varies very much depending on the country, the law and the type of entries. Local figures are selected for Hamburg, Bremen, Amsterdam or Stockholm. For London, the leading economic and financial centre of the second half of the century, no separate statistics have been compiled, only for England as a whole. About 52 per cent of all bankruptcies in England occurred in London in the first half of the century, and slightly less than that in the second half.[10] Moreover, only traders and merchants could come under the English bankruptcy laws, while in other countries other occupations are included. Although the English statistics are not strictly comparable, they provide an insight into the general trend and on the question of to what extent the numbers reveal the 1799 crisis.

While the bankruptcy registers of Amsterdam, Stockholm and England start either shortly before the turn of the eighteenth century or slightly later,

10 Hoppit, *Risk and Failure*, 63.

the records in Bremen only start in 1729, and in Hamburg they begin even later. In London, *The London Gazette*, a semi-official paper launched in the 1660s, began to publish bankruptcies from the 1680s. However, it mentions only a few cases before the turn of the century. *The Docket Books*, the first official register for filing bankruptcies begin in 1710 and are entry books. They are not an unproblematic source, because unlike in other countries debtors could not voluntarily declare bankruptcy in England but could only do so at the request of the creditor. After the first entry in the docket books mentioning the name and location of the debtor, quite frequently the case was not further pursued and no bankruptcy commission installed. Three tables of adjusted bankruptcy trends for England have been published based on *The London Gazette*, the *Docket Books* and the *Gentleman's*. However, they do not differ fundamentally.[11] My remarks are based on the latest compilation by Julian Hoppit. A printed list of failures for Amsterdam was compiled by Oldeweit. The figures are based on the records of the desolate *Boedelskamer*.[12] Although some big failures do not appear in the records, they seem to be more comprehensive than the English ones. A database of all failures have been put online for Stockholm.[13] It suggests that the number of big international merchants was rather low in the eighteenth century, and the majority belonged to other occupations. For Bremen no published list exists. A manuscript register mentioning the name of the bankrupt and the sum for which he failed starts in 1729.[14] For Hamburg, a bankruptcy list was compiled and published by Ernst Baasch that starts only in 1772.[15] It is based on a register of names of bankrupts that was put up at the exchange. In line

11 Norman J. Silberling, 'British Prices and Business Cycles, 1779–1850', *Review of Economic Statistics* 5, Supplement 2 (1932), 223–247; Thomas S. Ashton, *An Economic History of England: The Eighteenth Century* (London: Methuen, 1955), table xvi; Hoppit, *Risk and Failure*, appendix i.

12 W.F.H. Oldeveit, 'Twee eeuwen Amsterdamse faillissementen en het verloop van de conjunctuur (1636 tot 1838)', *Tijschrift vor Geschiedenis* 75 (1962), 421–435 (I would like to thank Joost Jonker for referring me to that article).

13 www.tidigmodernakonkurser.se; see also Klas Nyberg and Hakan Jakobsson, 'Negotiations, credit and trust in Northern Europe: institutional efficiency in the handling of bankruptcies in late eighteenth century Stockholm', in Albrecht Cordes and Margrit Schulte Beerbühl (eds.), *Dealing with Economic Failure: Between Norm and Practice (15th to 21st Century)* (Frankfurt am Main: Peter Lang, 2015), 97–114.

14 Staatsarchiv Bremen (StA), 2–D.11.b.1.b: Verzeichnis der eröffneten Konkursverfahren, vols. 1–8.

15 Ernst Baasch, 'Aus einer hamburgischen Fallitenstatistik des 18. Jahrhunderts', *Vierteljahrschrift für Sozial und Wirtschaftsgeschichte* 15 (1919), 533–545.

with the Hamburg bankruptcy law of 1753, the list also records whether it was a deceitful, an unfortunate, or a frivolous failure. Without presenting a detailed analysis of the scope and limitations of the several lists in this paper, some significant trends will be delineated.

3 Trends in Bankruptcies in the Eighteenth Century

During the eighteenth century, bankruptcy numbers increased considerably in various European countries. They rose conspicuously in the second half of the century. In England, bankruptcies averaged between 172 to 278 per year in the first half of the century and from 1766 onwards the numbers never fell below 350 per year.[16] In Stockholm, the average yearly bankruptcy rate was about 50 before the middle of the eighteenth century. After the middle of the century it rose to more than 100, and from the 1780s onwards usually did not fall below 150 per year.[17] In Amsterdam, bankruptcies remained below a hundred per year, in the first half of the century. From the late 1770s onwards they averaged about 150. For Bremen no real trend can be perceived.[18]

The outbreak of the French Revolution and the Coalition Wars (or French Revolutionary and Napoleonic Wars) caused a surge of failures across Europe. In Amsterdam, numbers already peaked in 1789. That year saw the highest number of failures in the century with altogether 224 bankruptcies. They fell to 197 in the next year. For the remaining years of the century they remained much lower.[19] In England, Hamburg and Bremen figures peaked at the time of the outbreak of the first Coalition War between 1792 and 1794.[20] Only Stockholm diverged from this picture. The Swedish capital had the highest failures of the century with 205 bankruptcies in 1799 to be surpassed in the following year with 214.[21]

Except for Stockholm, none of the records reveal any indication of the 1799 bubble. Moreover, the registers for England record the lowest number of the decade, and those for Hamburg based on the *Fallitenanschlag* (Baasch), the

16 Margrit Schulte Beerbühl, *The Forgotten Majority: German Merchants in London, Naturalization and Global Trade 1660–1815* (New York: Berghahn Books, 2015), 198.

17 Nyberg and Jakobsson, *Negotiations*, 2.

18 StA Bremen: Verzeichnis der eröffneten Konkursverfahren.

19 Oldeveit, 'Amsterdamse faillissementen'.

20 In England, the highest number for the whole century is recorded for the year 1793, with 1276 failures. According to the compilation by Ernst Baasch, the numbers for Hamburg reached the highest level in 1794 with 104 bankruptcies, and in Bremen in 1792 with 17 failures.

21 www.tidigmodernakonkurser.se.

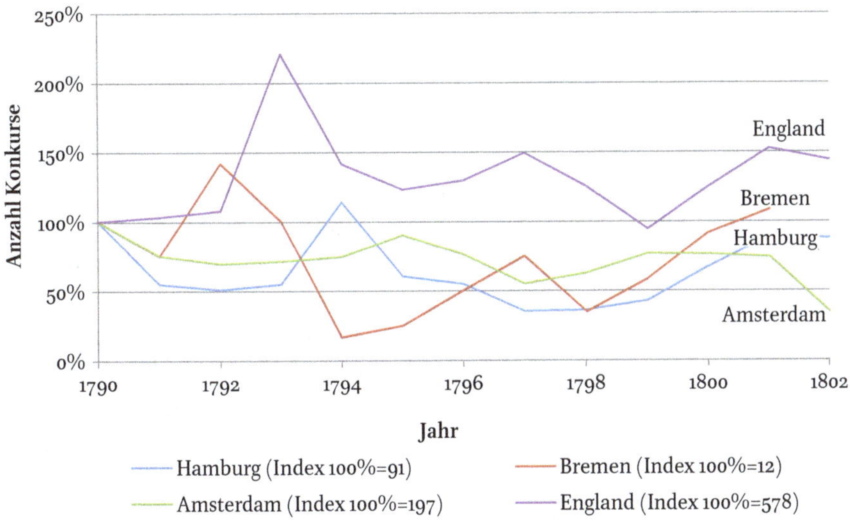

CHART 13.1 *Bankruptcy trend 1790–1802.*

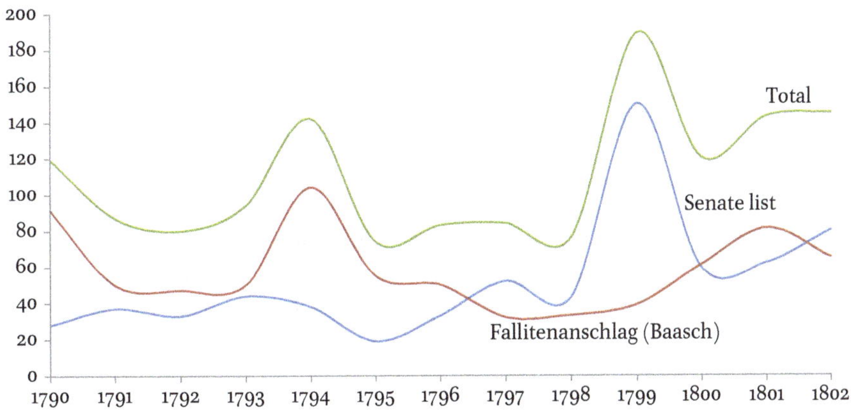

CHART 13.2 *Bankruptcy trend of the Hamburg bankruptcy registers 1790–1802.* Blue= court of commerce, red= Fallitenanschlag, green = total

second lowest one. Surprisingly, none of the big failures are mentioned in that Hamburg register. Oddly enough, Ernst Baasch, one of the leading historians on the history of Hamburg and the director of the library of the Chamber of Commerce in the past, did not mention in the above-mentioned publication that two further bankruptcy registers existed, one that started to record bankruptcies from 1754 onwards established by the Senate, and a separate list for the year 1799 only.[22] These registers provide a completely different impression.

While the above-mentioned list by Baasch does not reveal the crisis nor the names of the big merchant- and banking-houses, the other lists clearly indicate the bubble, and reveal the names as well as the amount of debts of the big bankrupts. The Senate list mentioned 150 failures for 1799.

Economic theory on the difference between the pre-industrial and capitalist speculation bubbles generally put forward that the early modern bubbles did not have any grave consequences for the economy as a whole. Comparing the development of both Hamburg lists, i.e. the one by Baasch and the Senate one, suggest that the crisis had more severe effects than has been so far assumed. The *Fallitenanschlag* (Baasch) does not mention the occupation of the bankrupts; however, a search through available directories of Hamburg suggest that they belonged to the class of lower tradesmen and craftsman, including a few of the learned professions. This group of bankrupts became affected in the aftermath of the crisis. The numbers of failures from this group rose from the rather low figure of 39 in 1799 to 61 in 1800 and 81 in 1801.

A diverging picture also emerges for London, if we extrapolate the German houses in London and those London houses dealing primarily with the European mainland. German merchants in London made up the largest Christian immigrant group in the eighteenth century, and in the 1790s the number grew rapidly due to the loss of the Amsterdam market after the occupation by the French revolutionary troops in 1795. Looking at the fate of this group in 1799 an unusually high number stopped payment.[23]

Although at least some of the data provides an indication of the 1799 crisis, it does not reveal the causes of the speculation crisis nor the panic it created. This gap can be filled to a considerable extent by reports in contemporary newspapers. Moreover, it is only from the newspapers that we get an impression of the geographical dimension of the speculation bubble.

4 The 1799 Bubble in the Newspapers

In the context of this article, and also due to the high number of contemporary newspapers as well as the limited availability, only a few samples can be given.

22 Commerzbibliothek Hamburg, S/1295 Verzeichnis der Fallimenten vom Jahre 1799; Staatsarchiv Hamburg (StA Hamburg) 222–3 A2.4 *Handelsgericht* vol. 1. The chamber of commerce (Handelsgericht) was only established in Hamburg in 1813, but as the records are found among those of the Handelsgericht, I refer to them under that denomination.

23 Schulte Beerbühl, *Forgotten Majority*, 200.

In all, it seems that German newspapers only cautiously and hesitantly reported on the Hamburg events, as will be shown below. Censorship may also have contributed to it to some extent. The only exception was the *Allgemeine Zeitung*. English newspapers, however, began to publish on the topic from very early on.

The first signs of a coming crisis already showed in July and August in Hamburg, when the number of failures started to rise. Nearly every day in August, one of the smaller houses stopped, as the Hamburg lawyer Ferdinand Beneke noted in his diary.[24] It took a dramatic turn early in September, when between 10–13 September several big mercantile houses in Hamburg failed, and about the same time two big merchant houses in London. From then on until the second half of October, merchant houses in Hamburg and London broke down like houses of cards. The crisis soon spread to Bremen, Lübeck and cities like Frankfurt, Augsburg or Leipzig; it reached Amsterdam, Copenhagen, Brussels, Russia and the U.S. after the turn of the century.

The *London Evening Mail* published an article on 13 September reporting on the many failures in Hamburg and the effects on the houses in London and on the London exchange. *The Times* followed with a similar report the next day. From then on, the leading London newspapers published almost daily about the spread of the failures. The *Morning Chronicle*, the *Observer*, *The Times* and other papers also began to publish the names of the bankrupts, including the sums for which the Hamburg houses failed. The largest ones were:

H.D. Goverts	3.000.000 Mark Banco
De Dobbeler & Hesse	2.500.000 Mark Banco
Wolf, Leven & Popert	2.700.000 Mark Banco
J.D. Rodde	2.200.000 Mark Banco
Berend Roosen	1.500.000 Mark Banco
Hinr. Kleinwort	1.400.000 Mark Banco
Henckel & Eimbcke	1.300.000 Mark Banco[a]

a Compiled from the above-mentioned newspapers.

Among the German newspapers, the liberal *Allgemeine Zeitung* edited by Johann Friedrich Cotta[25] was one of the first to report on the crisis. While some of the other German newspapers were very selective in their news on the topic, the *Allgemeine Zeitung* reported on it very extensively and openly.

24 Frank Hatje et al. (eds.), *Ferdinand Beneke (1774–1848): Die Tagebücher, Erste Abteilung: 1792–1801* (Göttingen: Wallstein, 2012).

25 It was one of the most important daily newspapers published by Johann Friedrich Cotta (1764–1832) in Tübingen. From 1807 onwards it was published in Augsburg.

On 23 September it started with a long and detailed article on the causes of the crisis, attributing them to an excessive speculation caused by enormous gains made in colonial articles such as sugar, coffee or tobacco the year before, but also to the loss of markets in Russia, Holland and Sweden. According to the report, the price for sugar had fallen by 50 per cent and tobacco by as much as 60 per cent. It further mentions the amount of debts of some houses, without mentioning any names. The author of the article concludes his report in fearing the worst even for solid and old established houses. The first news about failures in Bremen appears on the 28 September. The report mentions that one of the biggest mercantile houses was saved by the mutual support of Bremish merchants. In all, the *Allgemeine Zeitung* was a very well informed paper. Only in English papers is a reference found about the bankruptcy of the Leipzig merchant house of G.H. Wagner junior, for 205.387 Mark Banco.[26] Nothing is mentioned on the shock the news of the Hamburg failures created among the Polish and Russian merchants who were visiting the Leipzig fair.[27]

Frankfurt newspapers, such as the *Frankfurter Journal* or the *Frankfurter Kaiserl. Reichs-Ober-Post-Amts-Zeitung*, kept calm until very late, that is, until the middle of October.[28] They hardly mention any of the bankrupt firms in Hamburg. Only when a well-established merchant house in Augsburg went bankrupt they informed the public about it in a short notice, but did not provide any information at all on the fear and panic that the Hamburg event had on the mercantile community of Frankfurt on Main.[29] Surprisingly detailed information on Frankfurt is found in some English newspapers. The *Oracle and Daily Advertiser* remarked on 19 October that 'the general calamity [...] was rapidly extending to other trading towns on the Continent', including Frankfurt and reports that eleven mercantile houses in Frankfurt had stopped payment. Other English journals further referred to frequent meetings among the merchant and bankers of Frankfurt held in the Town Hall. They appointed a committee to adopt measures speedily. Among other subjects discussed was a temporary suspension of bills of exchange, even of those drawn, accepted and endorsed by Jewish houses.[30] Frankfurt had a large and established Jewish community and the Jewish merchants were commercially closely connected to the Jewish merchant houses in Hamburg. As leading Jewish houses in Hamburg had

26 *Evening Mail*, November 1–4, 1799; *Courier and Evening Gazette*, November 2, 1799.

27 See for that more explicitly Schulte Beerbühl, 'Hamburger Krise', 93f.

28 The *Frankfurter Journal* started to report on the Hamburg crisis on October 14, and the *Frankfurter Kaiserl. Reichs-Ober-Post-Amts-Zeitung* on October 11, 1799.

29 *Frankfurter Staats-Ristretto*, October 15 and 24, 1799.

30 *Oracle and Daily Advertiser*, November 7, 1799.

failed, the merchants in Frankfurt dreaded that as soon as the Jewish houses at Frankfurt were drawn into the crisis, many Christian houses would follow.

The *Allgemeine Zeitung* and English newspapers also spoke of the effects of the crisis on the sugar merchants in Liverpool as well as on the planters on the sugar islands in the Caribbean.[31] American newspapers started to report on the failures in Europe, with a delay of about two months due to the contemporary slowness of transport and communication systems. The first news were simple reprints of the English ones. However, they soon began to comment on the Hamburg crisis. As the German states had become the second largest market for American goods, the *New Hampshire Sentinel* feared that due to the price drop of American goods, such as Maryland and Virginia tobacco, sugar, coffee and cotton, the American merchants would be the worst victims of the bankruptcy wave.[32]

In the newspapers on both sides of the Atlantic a debate also arose as to measures to be taken to calm the crisis and to restore credit. *The Times* had already reproached Hamburg of its inactivity

> The state and Government of Hamburg being composed of several enlightened merchants, must in their wisdom have foreseen such a crisis, although they might not be able to ascertain the exact period [...]. Some months before the present failures broke out, the entire stagnation of the most current West-India produce of coffee and sugars should have put the Mercantile Public on its guard, to calculate and estimate the chances of speculation, sales, and consumption. The principal merchants pretty well knew the extent and overflow of the market, together with the extent of their engagements, or their acceptances running thereon. That period should have been seized for the establishment of a Public Loan and Discount Society, which, no doubt would have saved many respectable houses from falling. The above establishments having been adopted too late....[33]

This reproach is only partly justified. The failures of many houses were caused by a liquidity squeeze, and the Admiralty of Hamburg had already made one million Mark Banco available in May to alleviate the liquidity bottleneck.[34]

---

31 *St. James Chronicle and the British Evening Post*, October 3, 1799; *Morning Chronicle*, October 1, 1799; also *Allgemeine Zeitung*, October 16, 1799.

32 *New Hampshire Sentinel*, December 14, 1799, 1.

33 *The Times*, October 19, 1799, S. 2, col. d.

34 StA Hamburg, 321–322 vol. 17, Journal der Darlehnskasse des Admiralitätskollegiums 1763–1800, 1799: fol. 1.

However, the sum was much too low, once the bankruptcy wave had started to unfold. One of the central questions discussed was whether political institutions should step in to calm the panic and restore confidence. The already mentioned Büsch remarked that 'extraordinary cases need extraordinary means of support', meaning that political decisions should be taken by the Hamburg Senate.[35] Similarly, also in Britain and the U.S. demands arose that governments should intervene. An interesting comment appeared in the *New York Gazette* late in November 1799: 'friendship and interest' it remarked, were generally the best assistants for merchant houses in difficulties, however, 'when inconsiderate speculation […] have produced a public crisis like the present, both friendship and private interest are by far too feeble to stop the evil. Public interest and credit being at stake, public-spirited measures ought to be speedily adopted'.[36]

In Britain also a discussion arose in Parliament as to whether Parliament should provide financial help to the sugar merchants in Liverpool and the planters on the Caribbean islands. Colonel Gascoyne, the MP for Liverpool, as well as Alderman Lushington for the planters of several Caribbean islands, petitioned Parliament for a loan of half a million pounds in the form of exchequer bills to overcome the liquidity squeeze and to enable the merchants and planters of St. Vincent and Grenada to fulfil their monetary obligations.[37] They pledged goods to a value of 2.5 million pounds as security. A debate arose about the petition as it was thought of as being of 'a novel nature' that Parliament should intervene.[38] Among the opponents to the proposed bill was William Pitt.[39] However, the argument that the Liverpool sugar merchants and the Caribbean planters were innocent victims of the Hamburg speculators and the fact that the state would not suffer any losses given the value of goods as security, meant that even Pitt finally agreed, and the bill was passed within a short time.[40] The *Morning*

---

35 Büsch, *Handelsverwirrung*, 130: '*außerordentliche Fälle bedürfen auch außerordentliche Hülfsmittel* [sic!]'.

36 *New York Gazette and General Advertiser*, November 26, 1799, 2.

37 *Morning Chronicle*, October 1, 1799; *Morning Herald*, October 1, 1799; *Parliamentary Intelligence*, October 1, 1799; *Morning Post and Gazetteer*, October 1, 1799; 'Parliamentary Proceedings', *Oracle and Daily Advertiser*, October 1, 1799.

38 *Morning Chronicle*, *ibid.*

39 *St. James's Chronicle or the British Evening Post*, October 1–3, 1799.

40 *ibid.* 'Mr. Pitt said […] he had objected to this claim in the first instance, as he had ever entertained a strong prepossession against blending the publick resources with any private interests. But this, on a review, appeared to him to be a case of great distress, not arising from any improper speculation, and one in which without any risk to the Publick, the

Chronicle commented on Pitt's change of opinion with the following ironic words:

> It seems that the Minister, though, somewhat stiff in his opinions, is occasionally open to conviction. He was extremely averse to support the Liverpool petition in the first instance. Mr. Pitt has always been a great authority for changing opinions, and his reputation in this way will assuredly increase.[41]

To restore confidence in the market, the Hamburg Senate finally decided on various measures. The Hamburg Admiralty increased the sum of one million Mark Banco, which it had made available in May, to three million. A discount bank and a loan bank were instituted with a capital of more than six million Mark Banco, the bankruptcy law was temporarily suspended and a new institution was created. Failed merchants were put under 'administration', i.e. an institution was established at the Senate, composed of some leading merchants who were not threatened by the bubble. Failed merchants who came under administration were allowed to continue their trade under the control of the administrators. Thereby, they did not suffer the dreadful social consequences of a bankruptcy. This novel measure was to have far-reaching effects. It became a crucial instrument to overcome the 1856/7 speculation crisis.

All these measures adopted in Hamburg 1799 were insufficient to restore trust in the markets. *Die Allgemeine Zeitung* already assumed at the beginning of October that the Hamburg crisis would force the English prime minister William Pitt to take up measures in order to stop the further spread of the crisis, and above all to stabilize the exchange rate, for the pound sterling had dropped by more than 30 per cent, but it questioned whether Pitt would be able to supply a sufficient sum of silver to be sent to Hamburg in order to stop the further fall of the exchange rate.[42] Only eight days later it hailed that the Bank of England had consented to export bullion worth 1.75 million pounds.[43] The ship *Lutine*, with bullion on board, left Yarmouth on 9 October.

This measure received considerable attention in the newspapers. Even the Frankfurt papers that had remained silent until the middle of October began to report on it. Already the news that the ship had left Yarmouth contributed

greatest benefit may be rendered to individuals'. See also *Morning Chronicle*, October 4, 1799.

41 *Ibid.*

42 *Allgemeine Zeitung*, October 10, 1799.

43 *Allgemeine Zeitung*, October 18, 1799.

in calming the panic, although the ship never arrived in Hamburg. She was shipwrecked on the first night after her departure near the island of Terschelling. Ship, men and money were lost.[44] The *Lutine* was not the only ship laden with money for Hamburg.[45] A further ship laden with bullion on board had already arrived for Thornton & Power in Hamburg, before news of the shipwreck came in.[46]

5 Legal Records and the Entanglement of the Commercial World

Although the newspapers are the only source which reveal the spread of the crisis, the monies involved, and the public measures taken to overcome the panic, they tell us little about the fate of the bankrupts and the financial entanglements that led to the 'tsunami' of failures.

In view of the significant growth of risk and failure, new bankruptcy laws had been passed throughout Europe at some point during the eighteenth century. It was generally felt that the old early modern bankruptcy laws, which regarded bankruptcy as a crime that had to be punished respectively with imprisonment and social marginalization, were no longer adequate to deal with economic failure. Although legislators did not relinquish punishment, they increasingly created rules that aimed at encouraging composition between debtors and creditors through the courts. Throughout the eighteenth century, a lively legal activity can be seen developing to cope with the requirements of a rapidly commercializing and industrializing society.[47]

In Hamburg a new bankruptcy law was passed in 1753, after more than fifty years of discussion. Unlike many other countries, which only divided bankrupts in two groups – the innocent bankrupt who failed due to external and adverse circumstances, and the fraudulent bankrupt – the new Hamburg law inserted a third category: the frivolous bankrupt, who failed because he did not keep his books properly, or overextended his business.[48] Except in the

---

44 *The Times*, November 4, 1799; *Frankfurter Kaiserl. Reichs-Ober-Post-Amts-Zeitung*, November 4, 1799; see also Frederick Martin, *The History of Lloyd's and of Marine Insurance in Great Britain* (London: Macmillan & Co., 1876), 183–210.

45 *Evening Mail*, November 1, 1799.

46 *The Times*, November 4, 1799.

47 Albrecht Cordes and Margrit Schulte Beerbühl (eds), *Dealing with Economic Failure: Between Norm and Practice (15th to 21st Century)* (Frankfurt am Main: Peter Lang, 2016).

48 The tripartite division was not completely new. The old Venetian bankruptcy law already distinguished these three types of bankrupts.

case of a fraudulent bankruptcy, it encouraged the judges to jostle the parties into composition. Although the 1753 law was not reformed before the middle of the next century, discontent with the existing laws led to frequent smaller amendments to adjust the law to the swiftly altering economic situations. The growing perception that composition should be encouraged becomes particularly apparent in Bremen. Early in the century, the city government had passed a law that declared secret compositions, e.g. outside the court, as illegal. By the end of the century the Senate not only abolished this law, but declared private compositions as being legal.[49]

Given the efforts of the legislators to adapt to changing circumstances, the question on the practice of dealing with bankrupts arises. Bankruptcy records, as far as they have survived, are a particularly valuable source, revealing an invaluable insight into the geographical dimension of a business and the interconnectedness of the commercial world of the late eighteenth century. However, information about the outcome is limited. Furthermore, they only reflect those unhappy victims who could not agree on a composition with their creditors. There is no way of evaluating the volume of private arrangements outside the courts.

In Hamburg, a large number of the bankruptcy records and other sources were destroyed by the big fire of 1842; the wars of the twentieth century and also decisions by archivists to get rid of records in order to find room for new ones added to the losses. The survival of extensive bankruptcy records from some of the failed London houses may compensate a little for the losses, and provide together with the newspaper reports, a more comprehensive picture of the far-reaching interconnectedness and the commercial shifts in the 1790s.

Given the outbreak of the French Revolution and the Wars, many young German merchants had left Hamburg and had settled in London. Within very few years their businesses expanded enormously. The surprising boom was mainly caused by the occupation of the Netherlands and Amsterdam by the French Revolutionary Army in 1795. Trade shifted to the north German ports. Hamburg, Bremen and even smaller ports such as Emden experienced a surprising prosperity. Money, credit and bills of exchange that had been traded in Amsterdam shifted to Hamburg and the relations between London and Hamburg intensified rapidly. Thus, houses in either city were more or less simultaneously forced to stop payment.

Reciprocal reproaches make it difficult to decide where it started and who set the ball rolling. Büsch and other Hamburg merchants reproached the German house of Persent & Bodecker in London, while *The Times* and other English

49 Staatsarchiv Bremen, 2-D.11.a.5, 'Accorde heimliche'.

newspapers reproached the Hamburg merchants and its Senate. American newspapers additionally blamed the English government.[50]

The bankruptcy records of Persent & Bodecker in London show that the situation became critical after the Hamburg house of Milow had failed.[51] Only a day after Persent & Bodecker had stopped payment, the Anglo-German house of Cox & Heisch also suffered the same fate. They were forced to go to the court in London, when shortly afterwards De Dobbeler & Hesse in Hamburg failed for several million Mark Banco. According to The Times 'De Dobbeler and Hesse's bankruptcy involves the greatest number of sufferers in this country'.[52] It created a chain reaction and panic in London as well. 'Such is the consternation which these failures [in Hamburg] have occasioned on our own Exchange' wrote *The Times* on 19th Oct 1799, 'that it has been agreed to draw no more bills on Hamburg for the present. Indeed any transaction of this nature must be attended with ruin'. Only a day before *The Times* had reported on the suspension of Hamburg bills, and one of the leading merchant and banking houses in London, that of Battier & Zornlin, had also stopped payment.[53]

Persent & Bodecker failed for about 300 000 pounds, probably even much more.[54] Like many other houses at that time, Persent & Bodecker were not only commodity merchants but also acted as accept bank. When it failed, it had accepted bills for more than £274,000. More than 80 business partners of the firm lived in Hamburg and Bremen. The largest partners in Hamburg were De Dobbeler, Henckel & Eimbcke, Eimbcke & Hereshoft, Luis & Jencquel, C.C. Schutt and Gaedechens. All named houses belonged to the big bankrupts. Persent & Bodecker had had a far-reaching trading network. It had business partners, among others, in Bielefeld, Brunswig, Cologne, Stuttgart, Berlin, Königsberg, Danzig and Hirschberg in Silesia, also in Russia, Sweden, the Netherlands, Spain, Portugal, Italy and Demerara in South America.[55] The Anglo-German house of Cox & Heisch in London had similarly traded to a large extent with the above-mentioned Hamburg firms. It failed for about £200,000.

Although the bankruptcy records of the Anglo-Swiss firm Battier & Zornlin have survived, they do not contain a balance sheet which reveals the sum for which it failed.[56] The large volume of letters arriving at the Chancery Court

50 Büsch, *Handelsverwirrung*, 41f., 65f.,

51 The National Archives, Kew (TNA), Bankruptcy records, B3/ 3862.

52 *The Times*, September 30, 1799.

53 TNA, Docket books, B4/25 No 368.

54 According to Büsch the house failed for £900 000, the balance sheet in the bankruptcy records only mention the sum of slightly below £300 000. Büsch, *Handelsverwirrung*, 64; TNA B3/3862.

55 Demerara today British-Guayana.

56 TNA B3/ 205–6; see also Hoppit, *Risk and Failure*, 156–160.

with claims from abroad suggest that Battier & Zornlin belonged to the very large merchant-bankers of the capital. Its bankruptcy drew new and wider circles. The above-mentioned bankrupt house of Schwarz & Co in Augsburg was not the only firm which had to sustain losses from Battier & Zornlin, but a further eight Augsburg banking houses also lost out.[57] Although we know the amount of losses they had to suffer from the London bankruptcy, we cannot evaluate consequences for these banking houses, as we do not know much about them. We also do not know whether the bankrupt bank of Schwarz & Co caused a further wave of failures. Its 340 creditors were dispersed in particular in the southern parts of Europe and even in the New World. Some among them had to suffer heavy losses, if not failure.[58]

As they were of Swiss descent, many partners of Battier & Zornlin lived in Basle. A number of Basle women had invested money in the house of Battier & Zornlin which they had to write off. We do not know about the economic and social consequences of the bankruptcy of Battier & Zornlin on the city of Basle. It was occupied by the French in that year. That event has probably overshadowed everything else in the research on the city. A considerable number of claims against Battier & Zornlin reached the Court of Chancery from banks in Vienna, Milan, from the Royal Prussian Bank of Franconia at Fürth and from the U.S.

These examples may suffice to show the interrelatedness of the international trade and the avalanche a bankruptcy could set off.

As mentioned, the London bankruptcy files tell us little about the outcome of a bankruptcy procedure. The files predominantly inform us about outstanding debts and credits, the collection of debts and dividends. There is, however, another group of legal records, which tells us something about the outcome of bankruptcy proceedings. Already in 1706, a law was passed that allowed a debt-free restart after a bankruptcy, if four fifths of the major creditors consented. The bankrupt then received a certificate of conformity. From 1734 onwards a register of certificates exists that records the names of the bankrupts who received such a document.[59] In her study on the registers, Sheila Marriner came to the conclusion that only between 57 and 62 per cent received a certificate.[60] It is not possible to evaluate how diligently the books were kept. It also seems that those who took their case out of the courts and came to a private agreement were either not recorded or are lost. According to Simon

57 Among them were the bankers Benedikt Adam Liebert, Francis Jaccond the younger, Gabriel Savaron and others (TNA, B3/205–6).

58 Staats- und Stadtbibliothek Augsburg, 2 Aug 286–2.

59 TNA B6/1–10.

60 Sheila Marriner, 'English Bankruptcy Records and Statistics before 1850', *Economic History Review* 33 (1980), 351–366.

Moritz Bethmann of London, bankrupts easily received a certificate once a composition was arranged between debtors and creditors.[61] In the case of another German merchant house in London, we know of a private arrangement out of the courts, but no certificate could be found. In all, certificates were issued much more quickly after the surge of failures in 1793 than before, as has been shown elsewhere.[62]

Nevertheless, the fate of the unfortunate debtors varied considerably and depended much on the debtors' reputation and embeddedness in a social network, but even then a recalcitrant creditor could prevent a composition or have a debtor imprisoned. Those cases, of which we have information about the results of a bankruptcy procedure, reveal a wide range of options from debtors' prison to a successful restart. One of the unfortunate London merchants of German birth, who was thrown in prison for eighteen months, was Simon Moritz Bethmann, the cousin of the above-mentioned Frankfurt banker of the same name.[63] After he had stopped payment in 1799, creditors and representatives of the debtor tried to come to a composition in private meetings lasting more than a year. The obstinate refusal of a creditor prevented an arrangement, so that a formal bankruptcy procedure started in the autumn of 1800. It was finally closed only in 1851.[64] After Bethmann was released from prison, he left London for Germany.

Others restarted very quickly. Of Persent & Bodecker we know that Persent entered a new partnership that was, however, dissolved shortly after the turn of the century. Cox & Heisch continued their partnership. They became engaged in successful undercover trading enterprises during the Napoleonic Wars, for which they got licences from the British government. Similarly, another German merchant in London had a successful restart after his failure in 1799, while his former partner had to face a second bankruptcy in 1804, after the occupation of part of the German coast by French troops.[65]

Information about the fate and future of the merchants in Hamburg are rare and dispersed in a variety of different types of sources. Biographical and

---

61 Stadtarchiv Frankfurt, Bethmann Records, Simon Moritz Bethmann, London to his father October 1 and 11, 1799; see also British Parliamentary Papers, 'Report from the Select Committee on the Bankrupt Laws: With the Minutes of the Evidence', (July, 1817), 90f., 112.

62 Schulte Beerbühl, *Forgotten Majority*, 224f.

63 Wolfgang Henninger, *Johann Jakob von Bethmann 1717–1792: Kaufmann, Reeder und kaiserlicher Konsul in Bordeaux* (Bochum: N. Brockmeyer, 1993), 528–529.

64 TNA B3/209.

65 See more explicitly Schulte Beerbühl, *Forgotten Majority*, 217–219, 225–6; Margrit Schulte Beerbühl, 'Ostfriesische Kaufleute und Unternehmer in London 1760–1814', *Emder Jahrbuch* 84 (2004), 99–137.

surviving business records of other merchants may contain some information. Given the large number of big failures in Hamburg the *Allgemeine Zeitung* was sceptical that it would be easy for the unfortunate to find a new living, because the usual avenues were closed:

> ...where would the ruined beings get the first funds for starting again a business? They cannot count on the support of prosperous friends, for most of them suffered heavy losses and have to be on the guard themselves. Formerly an unfortunate merchant in Hamburg could take up one of the side lines of business like broker, clerk, etc. Unfortunately even some among them are without a living now and every philanthropist shudders to think about the fate of this city, which had been a resort for many unfortunate.[66]

Evidently, whoever saw a chance of coming under 'administration' availed himself of the opportunity, for the Hamburg lawyer Ferdinand Beneke commented 'the latest fashion to go bankrupt is to apply for administration'.[67]

The above-mentioned institution of 'administration' for bankrupt merchants in Hamburg was only open to those who only suffered under a temporary liquidity squeeze, but had enough assets. Others were granted credit from the Hamburg Admiralty, from solvent partners, or sold part of their assets and estates to satisfy their creditors. According to Vincent Nolte, a young merchant who worked as an employee in the mercantile house of his father in Hamburg at that time, the big merchants soon started trading again.[68] His father was saved from bankruptcy by a credit from Francis Baring.

Given the abovementioned sum for which the Hamburg merchants failed, the speculation crisis threatened Hamburg's economy and the free state of Hamburg. In order to prevent a state bankruptcy it made every endeavour to restore peace and economy. However, only the big merchants and bankers

---

66 '*...allein wo werden diese jetzt ruinirten Menschen wieder die ersten Fonds zur Betreibung von Geschäften hernehmen? Auf Unterstützung wohlhabender Freunde ist wenig zu rechnen, da die meisten selbst sehr empfindliche Verluste gelitten haben, und auch auf ihrer eigenen Hut seyn müssen. Ehedem pflegte ein unglücklicher Kaufmann in Hamburg ein NebenGeschäft des Handels zu ergreifen, und Makler, Buchhalter u. der. zu werden; allein von diesen werden durch diese Zeitläufte auch schon mehrere ausser Brod gesezt, und es schaudert jeden Menschenfreund bei dem Andenken an das Schicksal dieser guten Stadt, dem bisherigen Zuflucht Ort so vieler Unglücklichen*'. *Allgemeine Zeitung*, October 10, 1799.

67 Frank Hatje and Ariane Smith (eds), *Ferdinand Beneke (1774–1848), Die Tagebücher: Erste Abteilung 1792–1801* (Göttingen: Wallstein Verlang, 2012), Sept 21, 1799.

68 Vincent Nolte, *The Memoirs of Vincent Nolte* (New York: G.H. Watt, 1934), 36.

could avail themselves of the credit facilities granted by the Admiralty and the new administration procedure.

A feature of modern business cycles is a severe economic depression in the aftermath of bubbles. A few contemporary statements suggest that the crisis was followed by a steep decline in the economy. According to the wife of a Hamburg merchant, house prices had rocketed before the burst of the bubble, and luxury articles had risen considerably but plummeted during the crisis.[69] In other regions of Germany, merchants reduced their orders, e.g. for textiles, by 50 per cent, which of course had repercussions on weavers and spinners.[70] It also had grave effects on the new industrial areas of England: 'The manufacturing towns are in a state of idleness and starvation, never before experienced in England. [....] The manufacturing interests have felt so severely the bankruptcies in our own and various capitals of Europe'.[71]

More detailed research is still needed to evaluate the economic effects of the bubble, although it may be difficult to evaluate, as the war overshadowed and influenced economic development.

6 Conclusion

In this paper I have dealt in detail with the various sources on the Hamburg speculation bubble of 1799 in order to uncover its geographical size and the financial interlacement. The effects of the bubble were possibly also felt in further regions not covered by this article. There are indications that it was even felt in Asian countries, which still need research.[72] Only by combining the various sources, such as newspapers, economic and legal sources, as well as private documents, does the dimension become visible. Given its scale and structure, the crisis threatened various local and regional economies. The panic it created forced politicians in several countries to intervene in order to subdue the panic, thus creating new institutions and instruments to overcome the crisis.

69 Sophie Reimarus in Heinrich Sieveking, 'Das Handelshaus Voght und Sieveking', *Zeitschrift des Vereins für Hamburgische Geschichte* 17 (1912), 54–128, 106.

70 Ernst August Delius, a leading textile merchant and entrepreneur in Bielefeld, reduced its orders by about 50%. Similarly, Kriedte mentioned in his study on the silk industry in Krefeld and surroundings, that trade and industry stagnated. Peter Kriedte, *Taufgesinnte und großes Kapital* (Göttingen: Vandenhoeck & Ruprecht, 2007), 361.

71 Letter of an Englishman to the *Herald of Liberty*, May 19, 1800.

72 *The Lloyd's Evening Post* already mentioned many failures in Constantinople on September 2, 1799. It is not clear whether there is any connection to the early Hamburg failures, or if they originated from other causes.

The 1799 bubble also reveals that bankruptcy procedures as well as dealing with bankrupts had changed considerably by the end of the eighteenth century. During that century many European countries had begun to modernize the bankruptcy laws as a consequence of the rapid expansion of commerce, wars and growing risks in long-distance trade. Given these developments, a growing awareness can be seen in that contemporaries began to consider bankruptcies not only as fraudulent and criminal activities, but also as an integral part of economic life. At least from the sixteenth century onwards legislators in many countries distinguished between unlucky and fraudulent bankrupts. In Hamburg, the Senate introduced a third category, that of the frivolous (*leichtsinnig*) bankrupt in 1753, who failed as a result of disorderly bookkeeping or excessive speculation. He envisaged milder penalties than the fraudulent and in his case, as in that of the unfortunate merchant, the law encouraged arbitration.[73] Although other countries kept to the two categories of bankrupts, they also, as in the Netherlands or Sweden, increasingly encouraged arbitration.[74]

Despite endeavours to adjust bankruptcy laws to an expanding economy, a gap remained between the practice of conflict regulation and law. The laws still contained traditional regulations that threatened the unfortunate with prison and even capital punishment. That gave room for a variety of outcomes, depending on the causes of a failure, the social embeddedness of a bankrupt or its lack of it. Notwithstanding the modernization of law, the Western countries had to face a new phenomenon in the eighteenth century: that of speculation bubbles sweeping across countries like tsunamis in ever widening circles. In the last year of the century, the bubble acquired a worldwide dimension for the first time.

During the early modern period, debtors and creditors had endeavoured to settle a bankruptcy by composition whenever possible. In a bubble such as the one of 1799, private arrangements could be one option, but could not stop the panic. The breakdown of leading mercantile houses and accept banks initiated a discussion on whether politics should intervene or not, that is, the question on the 'lender of last resort'.[75] As it was necessary to calm the panic, liquidity

73 Der Stadt Hamburg *Neue Fallitenordnung auf Befehl des Hochedl. Raths publicirt den 31. Aug. 1753 nebst den Additional-Artikeln und den das Fallitwesen betreffenden neueren Conclusis und Verordnungen* (Hamburg 1823). It may be that the older Venetian bankruptcy law served as a model for the Hamburg law. It also distinguished three types of bankrupts.

74 See Nyberg and Jakobsson, *Negotiations*.

75 The role of 'the lender of last resort' to provide liquidity is still a controversial issue among modern economic theorists.

had to be made available, and the governments saw themselves as forced to develop new instruments and institutions to overcome the panic, which like the 'administration' in Hamburg, became important instruments in overcoming the crisis.

To sum up, dimension, structure, political issues and institutions established in 1799 foreshadow some more modern developments, and they question the still-prevailing division between pre-modern and modern crises. Taking the eighteenth century as a whole, it would be preferable to regard the era as a transitory period in the history of financial crises, and also in legal history dealing with economic failures and bankrupts.

CHAPTER 14

The Rise of Usages in French Commercial Law and Jurisprudence (Seventeenth–Nineteenth Centuries): Some Examples

Edouard Richard

1 Introduction

Given the subject of this paper, it deliberately spans a broad timeframe. Indeed, it is when we observe the permanence of commercial practices, their existence before as well as after the legal upheaval caused by the victory of post-revolutionary *légicentrisme*,[1] that the nature, role and revelation of commercial practices become interesting as objects of study. In the nineteenth century, rather than drying up, these practices found new well-springs. There followed an impressive acceleration of the traditional manoeuvring between legislative and regulatory rules in a nineteenth-century France that was prone, however, to sanctifying standards, particularly civil standards. How then did commercial practice manage to take hold? Through what channels (jurisprudence, law or simple fact) did it manage to become established in business? Its strength is such that it even managed to become established *contra legem*, in the face of a political establishment incapable of containing it (as was the case with the Stock Exchange). Behind this question lies a wider debate about identifying the most common *modus operandi* of commercial law formation and tracing its development, and defining this particular branch of the law of obligations – hitherto neglected until modern times – as a separate field. Then, there is the important question we must now ask ourselves concerning the relationship between law and economics. Did France not consummate a divorce between these two subjects back in the early nineteenth century?

It is sometimes difficult for the French traditionalist and the Romanist school of understanding obligations to admit that obligations may have efficiency (before the judge) even if they are not based upon some amount of legal formalism. Because commercial usages do not necessarily refer to pre-established rules, law merchant is frequently devoid of formalism. It does not really matter if the law remains silent, but sometimes usages are *contra legem*.

1 The French doctrine of legislative supremacy.

 | DOI 10.1163/9789004363144_015

Whenever their existence is based upon economic necessities, the question is whether negating the authority of commercial usages because of their lack of formalism makes any sense. One should not forget that before being included in our law, many legal institutions had been created by the Roman *praetors*, who based their *formulae* on pre-existing commercial practices. The logic of the facts, economic necessities, preceded rules. The French *légicentrisme*, particularly after the Revolution, seemed to have forgotten this.

2 The Examples

Studying the impact of usages or customs in the world of business reveals the strength, and indeed the weakness, of the link between law and economics. We could almost illustrate this by one example alone, by recalling the age-old, totally ineffectual censure of usury by any number of jurists and canon lawyers. Yet interest-bearing loans became legal reality during the French Revolution. Usury is a practice *contra legem* which has become law. Like it or not, this usage is fact, a practical and economic reality. In this, it follows the traditional pattern of creating behaviours.

However, the specificity of commercial usage is that it almost always concerns money. Consequently it has to a certain extent become victim to a kind of presumption of immorality, for the merchant and his commercial activities are traditionally tainted with suspicion: a reaction which is doubtless more marked in Catholic countries.

The tolerance, and in particular the recognition, of a usage in case law assumes in general and in principle that those who follow it keep within the limits of what they are entitled to do. Once those limits are crossed, one enters into the realm of fraud.[2] But there are cases where even fraud as defined by existing rules of law cannot prevent a usage from being followed, or prevent it from developing in such a way that the legislator is eventually forced to recognize its existence and incorporate it from then on into normative provisions.

The most common way of acknowledging a usage can be seen as positive. It can be found first of all in the opinions of the trial judge which indicate the existence of such and such a usage specific to a particular corporation, professional branch or type of activity. The legislator may, on occasion, be obliged to draw conclusions from this, and confirm the existence of these usages in a legally-binding text.

2 This can be compared to the border crossing of the *sollertia*.

But a usage can also be acknowledged negatively, that is, by admissions of defeat on the part of the public authorities. To explain the point more fully, the defeat is the inability of the authorities to regulate or outlaw a usage, as if a stone placed in the middle of a torrent would stop the current. The usage, propelled by the economic necessity from which it draws its strength, navigates its way around the obstacle, overcomes it and in certain cases, eliminates it.

2.1 *First Example*

The law's incapacity can clearly be reflected in the paucity of legislative measures. This was evidently the case before, as under the Ordinance of 1673, but also after, if one considers the obvious gaps in the 1807 Commercial Code.[3] In this type of case where the law says nothing and makes no prohibitions, usages fill the empty space, *sine lege*.

There's a notable example of this in Old French Law when Colbert's Ordinance (1673) intervened to recognize and regulate officially the practice of sponsorships which had, until then, been treated as a mere usage.

However, the powerlessness of the law is most often revealed in a more implicit fashion. What about the silence of the royal legislator in this same ordinance, which required publication only of those companies made up of merchants and traders?[4] Clearly, this measure did not concern sponsorships, which were usually composed of merchants and non-merchants. The unstated objective was to protect the reputation of the noblemen who were accustomed

3 The silence of the 1807 Code said it all about the law's incapacity to embrace commercial affairs. There was no mention of banking or mainland insurance operations, nothing about business assets, industrial property, about the institution of the Paris Stock exchange, nothing about chambers of commerce, and so forth. Consequently, the door was wide open to a whole plethora of practices, simply because of this lack of regulation.

4 Article 2 of Part IV of the Ordinance deliberately stipulated: 'Extracts from the registers of merchant and trader companies concerning retail or wholesale shall be held in the commercial court'.... The constitution of partnerships between merchants and non merchants was not therefore legally subject to the duty of public notification. So the concern for security championed so strongly by the commentators of the Ordinance of Savary had become a forgotten virtue. The reader of *Le Parfait Négociant* (*The Perfect Trader*) is left dumbfounded on this point: '...better leave things as they were before the ordinance, so as not to prevent persons of quality coming into the trade partnerships, since they are of such benefit to the State and to the public as we have said above, and it should left be up to those debtors who have gone bankrupt to let their creditors know of any partnerships they have contracted, or up to the due diligence of the creditors to discover if there are no such partnerships'. Jacques Savary, *Le Parfait Négociant* (Genève: Droz, 2011), 77.

to investing as sponsors without wishing this to be known. Hypocritical capitulation of the law confronted with practice and faced with economic necessity.[5]

2.2 *Second Example*

There is another flagrant example of the law capitulating in the face of the economic logic borne by usages. The decree of the King's Council of 14 July 1787[6] handed over to the Parliamentary Court (civil section) elements relating to litigation on unlawful trade in company stock by private shares (prohibited by the Council decree of 1724-09-24[7]). In so doing, the Council divested itself of this litigation, for it no longer had the material means to deal with the problem. The practice of trade in securities, which alone guarantees the smooth flow of capitalism, forced the law to bend to the proof of material fact. The real impossibility for justice to prevent such trade was evidence of the emergence of usages *contra legem*. This decision by the state power recognizes usage negatively, through a sort of resignation ('I cannot regulate on this') and also somewhat positively, for it was jurisprudence that first indicated the existence of this practice. The usage ultimately prevailed after the collapse of the *Ancien Régime*, when the principle of stock-market dealing in the securities of companies was accepted.

5 Clearly the developing economy could not dispense with the still notable sources of finance emanating from capital held by the nobility.

6 On July 14, 1787 King Louis XVI returned litigation on speculation to the ordinary judges: 'I acknowledge that speculation cannot be stopped by my direct supervision or by that of my council. If those who indulge in it for profit use means contrary to probity and proscribed by the law, the courts shall be their natural judges and shall suffice to repress them. Should they use legal means, they are still reprehensible, but like all those whose actions run contrary to moral standards without being against the law, they must be abandoned to the remorse, shame and misery to which shall lead sooner or later, and with only some rare exceptions, speculation unfettered by extreme greed. [...] The Stock Exchange, in its very institution must be the theatre of good faith and trust, must not offer up the spectacle of ruinous indiscretion, equally harmful to public credit and individual fortune'. Oscar de Vallée, *Les manieurs d'argent: Etudes historiques et morales 1720–1882* (Paris: C. Lévy, 1882), 286–287. On the 1780s speculation, and particularly under Calonne, see studies of Jean Bouchary, *Manieurs d'argent à Paris à la fin du XVIIIe siècle* (Paris: Librairie des sciences politiques et sociales, M. Rivière, 1939–43).

7 The Council Decree of 24 September 1724 had, in creating the Stock Exchange, strictly regulated the stock market by restricting it from the outset to authorised companies (i.e. privileged companies). So State supervision of these corporations was exercised through the control of the stock market. To contain the excesses of speculation (bearing in mind the failure of John Law's system), all negotiations were to be paid up within twenty-four hours, putting paid to the futures market and the practice of short selling.

2.3 *Third Example*

Keeping to the same theme, the introduction of limited liability clauses in the great private companies of the late eighteenth century, also *contra legem*,[8] was bound to hold sway for obvious economic reasons. For the first time in history there emerged entities in which limited liability concerned all the actors associated, even the trustee, leaving behind the model of partnerships constituted by shares.[9] Thus, and highly significantly, the Gorneau project,[10] followed by the Commercial Code of 1807, were to confirm the appearance in law of new types of companies which would not be called public limited companies until the 1807 Code, and the principle of whose existence had been previously denied in law.

Economic growth was based on limiting liability, so the law was powerless to stop it. Consequently, in the two cases to which we have referred, the usage, based on the requirements of economic reality, ended up forcing itself upon the legislator at the end of a three-stage process. First, the powerless legislator condemns a practice and refers it to the judges. Secondly, jurisprudence assumes its role of revealing and even sanctioning the usage. Finally, the increasing number of cases forces the legislator to ratify what he cannot control, pushed into this position by economic reality. The law is powerless to curb an economic reality in any lasting fashion. The divorce between law and the economy always ends up with the economy winning, as illustrated by usages.

2.4 *Fourth Example*

The corporate interest clause is another illustration of a usage that the legislator, unable to counteract the economic need represented by this practice, was incapable of containing. We know that the interest clause was present in the

---

8 We must admit some hesitation at this point about the aptness of employing the expression *contra legem*, considering that the ordinance of 1673 mentioned nothing about this possibility or even about the fact that companies may be constituted by shares. Should we then say *sine lege*? We think not, because of the spirit of commercial practices in which, until the 1780s, we can find no occurrence of a limited liability concerning every associate.

9 It seems that the first occurrence of this kind of clause can be observed in the fifth article of the statutes of the *Société des mines du Bourbonnais* (May 18, 1786) in which we read: '*...que les fonds seuls de cette entreprise seront et demeureront uniquement à tous les évènements...*' The same clauses appeared a few months later in the *Fonderies royales d'Indret et Mont Cenis* (*Le Creusot*) and one year later in the *Société pour l'exploitation de bains orientaux* (art. 15). A number of other examples are mentioned by Henri Lévy-Bruhl, *Histoire juridique des sociétés de commerce en France aux* XVII*e et* XVIII*e siècles* (Paris: Domat-Montchrestien, 1938), 247–248.

10 See in this present volume the article by Olivier Descamps on the Gorneau project.

so-called 'privileged' or colonial trading companies, and this with the full blessing of the authorities.[11] Its practice was justified by the length of time it took for any profits to emerge. In order to reassure the investors, it was necessary to offer them some remuneration in advance of receiving the profits. However, this money was taken from the company's share capital, which endangered the whole structure of the company itself. It is true that the state assumed the role of sponsor, and guaranteed the operation. But with the legalization of purely private companies, notably public limited companies, in 1807, we can witness the Council of State progressively banning the use of these interest clauses which, by reducing the share capital, risked endangering the security guarantees the company's social capital was supposed to offer third-party investors.[12] But while receiving pre-profit interest was gradually prohibited (with notable exceptions for the railway companies[13]), the idea remained that it was still possible to remunerate shareholders with interest, on condition, however, that there were profits in advance, which was called the 'first dividend' clause. After all, was it right to prohibit the free distribution of a share of the gains when the company was making a profit?

But, more than this, in 1867[14] the *Cour de Cassation* itself considered that the perception of an interest in a sponsorship by share may be acceptable, even when there were no benefits to justify its existence, and merely because this practice was permitted by usage.[15]

---

11 See Lévy-Bruhl, *Histoire juridique*, 225–227.

12 We should also note the emergence, in 1827, of what we still call 'obligations' (bonds). This allowed companies to give interest to people who were only lenders, distinguishing them from shareholders, which is something that had never been done before.

13 This is understandable in the case of large companies which, having lengthy works to carry out (building railways, opening up isthmuses) would leave their shares unproductive for a long time if they had to wait to make profits in order to remunerate them, which would put off subscribers. Apart from this, the clause barely merits any encouragement. Edmond-Eugène Thaller, *Traité élémentaire de droit commercial, à l'exclusion du droit maritime* (Paris: Rousseau, 1904), 219.

14 We have to remember here that sponsorships by share were not under the control of the Council of State.

15 Civ., May 8, 1867, *DP*, 1867.1.193. This was, moreover, legitimized by the fact that those small shareholders, owners of share capital, saw their funds more exposed than owners of industrial, dividend or premium shares. Hippolyte-Ferréol Rivière, *Commentaire de la loi du 24 juillet 1867 sur les sociétés* (Paris: Marescq, 1868), 142. But above all, and this is the determining factor, the lawfulness of the interest came from the fact that they could be considered as a social security contribution or payroll tax, independent of any entitlement to a share in profits. '...and the receivers of a company that then went bankrupt could not pursue the restitution of pre-paid interest, basing this on the fact that when

The persistent acceptance of this practice by some authorities meant that they were still accepting a conceptually challenging confusion of types between the company and the loan: two very distinct contracts, however, in their causes as well as in their consequences. There again, economic necessity (that is, the motivation of investors attracted by receiving interest) prevailed over the will to rationalize and categorize which underlies all legal and regulatory frameworks. Through good times and bad, the clause persisted, even through legislative provisions. Indeed the Act of 7 March 1925 establishing SARL (limited liability companies) in France would accept it, with a number of conditions.[16] However, the criticisms levelled against it ending up winning in the end, notably by underlining the dangers. Today, this kind of clause is strictly forbidden.[17]

The same can be said for the introduction (albeit measured) in 2011 in French law of *la fiducie* or the trust. This proves yet again that economic necessity can overturn the very foundations of French law, which had traditionally always defended the principle of the unity of heritage and rejected any notion of constituting a patrimony by appropriation. The manifest influence of comparative law on the introduction of the trust into our law is also worth underlining.

---

the payment was made, there was not profit to distribute'. Rivière, *Commentaire*, 142. v. Req. May 19, 1847; November 25, 1861; and in particular, Civ. May 8, 1867, DP, 1867.1.193, see Beudant and S. 1867. 1. 23. In 1899 the Supreme Court would finally reach a compromise solution: the clause was a conditional recovery of capital when there was insufficient yearly profit to complete the interest. (Civ. rej., November 7, 1899, *D.* 1900. 1, 513 and see Thaller; *Pand. Franç.* 1901, 1, 320, and see Champcommunal; *S.* 1901, 1, 513 and see Wahl; Arthuys, 'Examen doctrinal, jurisprudence commerciale', *Rev. Crit.* (1901), 321; see also Labbé, *S.*, 1878, 2, 225).

16 The interest clause was accepted, but only for the period of time necessary to carry out the works which, according to the object of the company, had to precede the start of transactions, and under the further condition that the clause had to be published and that the amount of interest be included in the start-up costs. Paul Didier, *Droit commercial*, vol. 2, 2nd ed. (Paris: PUF, 1997), 365.

17 The fixed interest clause, prohibited since the act of July 24, 1966 (today art. L. 232–15 al. 1 C. com). Although the new preference shares established in French law by the Ordinance no. 2004–604 of June 24, 2004, gave certain special advantages to their owners, they could on no account allow the payment of fixed interest. (Article L. 232–15 of the French Commercial Code – a fixed percentage of the investment realised, like the interest rate for a loan, cannot be provided for). One of the most noteworthy innovations made by Ordinance no. 2004–604 of June 24, 2004 (Décret d'application n°2005–112 of February 10, 2005) was the establishment of preference shares inspired by the Anglo-Saxon preferred stocks.

2.5 *Fifth Example*

Stock exchange transactions are highly indicative of the strength of usages, because of the fact, once again, that they force themselves upon the authorities, notwithstanding the various prohibitions that have been expressly emitted. We have seen that only authorised companies' securities could be traded (1724); usage killed off the ban and, after the Revolution, it became legal to trade in the securities of any listed company, whether authorized public limited companies or partnerships limited by shares. Only brokers were authorized to trade in company securities on the Stock Market. However, a clear shortage of brokers led to the emergence of unauthorized dealers (*la coulisse*) who carried out the same operations (and even more) as the brokers and were able to do so thanks to the tolerance of the government.[18] From the legal point of view, such tolerance was completely incomprehensible, particularly when you consider the 'Jansenist' severity of the Napoleonic codes. However, in economic terms, it was absolutely necessary because of the feeble number of brokers.[19] And what about the futures market, or short sales transactions? These have always been officially prohibited[20] but practice and usages simply ignored

18 The brokers' monopoly on negotiating listed securities had, since 1817, been challenged by unofficial brokers operating over the counter. For the development of the market in the nineteenth century, see Carine Romey, 'Les transformations de l'activité boursière', in Pierre-Cyrille Hautcoeur (ed.), *Le marché financier français au XIXe siècle*, vol. 1 (Paris: Publication de la Sorbonne, 2007), 273–312, p. 100 sq., then p. 273 sq. and part. p. 298 sq., and also p. 411 sq.

19 Notwithstanding some interim phases of legal rigour, the public authorities tended to abandon the question. It is highly symbolic in this respect that as early as 1834, stock brokers no longer came under the responsibility of the Home Office, but of the Ministry of Trade and Industry. Nelly Hissung-Convert, *La spéculation boursière face au droit 1799–1914* (Paris: LGDJ, 2009), 240.

20 In principle, futures markets had been prohibited by article 7 of the Decree of Council of August 7, 1785. Thus, markets not preceded by a deposit 'are undertakings without cause and substance [which] have no value in law, occasioning an infinity of insidious operations that tend to distort the course of government securities, giving an overblown value to some and using others in a way that could devalue them; this results in disordered speculation which puts at risk the fortune of those imprudent enough to indulge in it, encourages greed to pursue immoderate and risky profit and substitutes illicit trafficking for authorised negotiations'. But, with an eye to realism, the Decree of Council of September 22, 1786 authorised markets to be delivered within two months, under penalty of being declared void. These texts were not rescinded by Revolutionary legislation.

On July 14, 1787 King Louis XVI returned litigation on speculation to the ordinary judges: 'I acknowledge that speculation cannot be stopped by my direct supervision or by that of my council. If those who indulge in it for profit use means contrary to probity and proscribed by the law, the courts shall be their natural judges and shall suffice to repress

the ban until 1885, when the legislator ended up conceding and authorising futures and short sales,[21] despite the collapse of the General Union.[22]

2.6 *Sixth example*

The sixth example to be considered is just as remarkable, but for slightly different reasons. It involves the silence of the law, and also demonstrates the incapacity of the civil law to adapt to economic demands, hence once again the need to make business law more independent.

Indeed, trading in business assets (the notion of *fonds de commerce* had been created by Parisian practice in the 1780s) and the protection of creditors in respect of movable property are an example of a usage emerging *sine lege* this time. Normally, only immovable, real estate transfers were subject to mandatory disclosure under the Civil Code. Business assets, considered as movable property, were therefore not covered by the rules on disclosure.[23]

---

them. Should they use legal means, they are still reprehensible, but like all those whose actions run contrary to moral standards without being against the law, they must be abandoned to the remorse, shame and misery to which shall lead sooner or later, and with only some rare exceptions, speculation spurred on by extreme greed. [...] The Stock Exchange, in its very institution must be the theatre of good faith and trust and must not offer up the spectacle of ruinous indiscretion, equally harmful to public credit and individual fortune'. Vallée, *Les manieurs d'argent*, 286–287.

21 In a word, the system introduced by the 1885 decree legitimised a 'mongrel system' where the complicity of the authorities allowed unofficial traders to negotiate annuities, even, perfectly legally. Abel Waldmann, *Ministère obligatoire des agents de change, critique de la jurisprudence de l'arrêt de cassation du 1er juillet 1885* (Lyon: A. Rey, 1904), 40.

22 The Act of March 28, 1885, passed in the aftermath of the *Union Générale* scandal and the various financial disruptions that had punctuated the early days of the opportunistic republic. This text legalised futures markets and, in its third article, rescinded the provisions of Articles 421 and 422 of the French Penal Code, considering as gambling 'sales or procurements of effects which the buyer or seller does not have at their disposal'. Article 420 of the same Code sanctioned all gambling on increases and decreases in public [but not private] securities. See Edouard Richard, 'Un exemple de l'application conjuguée des articles 76 C. com. et 419 C. pén. à l'épreuve de la révolution industrielle: une véritable question de susceptibilité', *Revue historique de droit français et étranger* 3 (2012), 421–450.

23 Maurice de Pindray, *Etude sur l'utilité d'une réforme de la législation en matière de Fonds de commerce* (Paris: Administration du répertoire générale pratique du notariat, 1905), 2: '... with no legislative provision for the sale of these funds, their sale is governed by ordinary law rules concerning movable property. In a private sale, no particular form is required for the sale to be valid; it can even take place orally (Paris, January 19, 1859, November 12, 1860; *Journ. Trib. com.*, 1859, 335, and 1861, 69). The sale is definitive, in accordance with ordinary law, at the moment the seller and buyer agree on the price and other ancillary conditions: nature of the price, payment dates, prohibition for the seller to undertake an identical commercial activity within a given radius, etc'.

The business could consequently be transferred without the creditors being informed about it, denying them the possibility to challenge payment of the transfer sale price.[24] That price could, in fact, have been reduced in order to protect a proportion of the bankrupt's assets from the aforementioned creditors.[25] It has been judged many times that there was an obligation for the seller to inform creditors of his selling operation.[26] Parisian traders (and also traders from some other towns[27]) established the practice, however, of publicizing transfers even without being ordered to do so by the law, in order to guarantee the security of the transferor's creditors.[28] This heralded the emergence of a system of self-protection in the field of commerce[29] and this practice was

24 Pindray, *Etude sur l'utilité d'une réforme*, 2: '…consequently, in law and according to current legislation, agreement and tradition suffice to realize the sale of a business. Once the agreement is concluded and the tradition carried out, the sale is complete, and no one can protest, not even the seller's suppliers or creditors, who were unpaid when the business was transferred'.

25 All too often, unfortunately, the sale of a business is carried out to the detriment of the seller's creditors. 'It does happen that unscrupulous traders with problems transfer their business, get paid for it and keep the money illegally while feigning insolvency and enriching themselves to the detriment even of those who may have filled their shops with goods that remain unpaid for'. (Exposé des motifs de la proposition de loi de MM. Mazeau et Dièt z-Monnin). It could in fact be argued that Article 1167 of the Civil Code allows creditors to have fraudulent acts that infringe their rights annulled, but in practice they are loath to take such steps (procedure, costs …) cf. Pindray, *Etude sur l'utilité d'une réforme*, 3.

26 Seine, 5 February, 1859; 29 May, 1878; 30 June, 1881; 4 August, 1886; 4 June, 1888; Bordeaux 27, August 1883. In particular, Paris (3e ch)., 18 February 1882, *Journal du Palais*, 1883. 1. 475; and *Sirey*, 1883. 2. 91.

27 Pindray, *Etude sur l'utilité d'une réforme*, 4: 'This usage exists, notably in Paris, Lyon, Marseille, Amiens, Cambrai and Rouen. (Pandectes, Fonds de commerce, n° 392 et suiv.). In Algeria, a decree of the Governor dated December 19, 1831, stated that the buyer of a business would be responsible for any debts contracted by the seller in relation to that business, unless the sale had been notified to the public by means of bills and posters and that an extract of the Act of Sale had been registered with the Court of justice. This decree was rescinded on September 15, 1874. Allow us here, in passing, to regret its repeal'.

28 Pindray, *Etude sur l'utilité d'une réforme*, 4: 'With the aim of suppressing these iniquities and giving some guarantee against bad faith, a usage is established in the absence of legal prescriptions, by virtue of which the buyer of a buyer of a business may only pay for it ten days after having published his purchase in a number of publications. During this ten-day period, the seller's creditors may file opposition to payment by the purchaser, who could be made to pay twice if he hands over payment to his assignor without the said notification or prior to the expiry of the ten-day period'.

29 On the strength of these kinds of practices see particularly Charles Leon Lyon-Caen and Louis Renault, *Traité de Droit commercial*, Tome 3, 2nd ed. (Paris: Pichon, 1889), 177–178.

sometimes recognized by the courts.[30] We can clearly see here the incapacity of the Civil Code, still turned towards immovable property, to correspond to economic needs. Perhaps we have here the vestiges of that old medieval adage, *res mobilis res vilis* (a movable object is without value)?[31] In any case, there was a lively debate. Some went so far as to assign an obligatory character to this usage, in the absence of any proof that it was *contra legem*. Others considered that, on the contrary, constituting a resale in clear favour of creditors conflicted with the wording of Article 2279 of the Civil Code. Once again, case law had to assume the role of declaring the existence of the usage, which ended up becoming law.

3 To Conclude

There is also a very French characteristic in respect to the law of obligations which concerns the near absolutist primacy of Roman law before the

30 Trib. Civ. Seine 31 mars 1868 et 8 octobre 1866, *Sirey*. 1869. 2.56; 1870. 2. 333; *Journal du Palais*. 1869. 234 et 1870. 1200.

31 Pindray, *Etude sur l'utilité d'une réforme*, 5–6: In 1885, MM. Mazeau et Dietz-Monnin introduced into the Senate a Bill whose object was the public notification of the sale of businesses. It read thus: 'The following provision is added to article 109 of the Commercial Code: Any sale or transfer of a business shall, at the instigation of the purchaser, be published in the form of an extract or notice in a publication pertaining to the commercial court where the transferred business is found or, failing that, in a local publication designated each year by the court. This publication shall contain an address for service in the jurisdiction; it shall be renewed on the fifth and the tenth day after the first insert. Any creditor of the seller may, during fifteen clear days after publication, file his opposition to payment at the address stipulated. Any purchaser who, without notification or prior to the expiry of the fifteen-day period, pays the seller, will remain liable to third parties'. In the explanatory statement, those responsible for the Bill noted that the absence in our law of special provisions relating to the sale of businesses can be explained by the 'limited importance of movable property in France when the Commercial Code was issued, and by commercial practices at that period, when businesses stayed in the same hands for a long time'. These considerations, which were certainly true a hundred years ago, are totally false today and are manifestly opposed to the current state of society and commercial practices. Movable property, which was more or less inexistent in 1805 has proliferated to such an extent that today it has overtaken in value the immovable property or, to be more precise, land property, that alone had constituted the fortunes of the French in the late eighteenth century. Also, at that time, when commercial life was calm and without vicissitudes, business establishments (few in number but secure) formed family patrimonies that it was customary to hand on from generation to generation with never a thought of adding something new to them or giving them greater vitality.

Revolution and then of the Civil Code over all other sources of law.[32] From 1804 onwards, civil usages were wiped out and commercial usages viewed with distrust, for the majority thinking was that these practices were *de facto* rather than *de jure*. Moreover, the 'nationalization' of the law from the seventeenth century, and the idea that this should serve as the unchallengeable foundation of French law, contributed to the fracture between the law and the economy.[33] Usages, which derived traditionally from 'international' practices, were considered suspect in a period when France claimed to exert some sort of legal Magisterium both within and beyond its frontiers.[34] If we sum up the common characteristics of commercial usage we find that: (1) it's a fact; (2) it often

32 Article 7 Act of 30 ventôse, year XII: 'From the day these laws become binding, Roman laws, ordinances, general and local customs, statutes and rules shall cease to have the force of ordinary or special law in those matters which form the object of the said laws comprising the present code'.

33 In addition, in his *Etudes de droit commercial* (1833), Frémery regrets that 'For two hundred years, real commercial law, the slow, successive work of unanimous traders whose sources can be found in the scattered monuments of their custom, has been divided and torn to shreds by the legislators of diverse nations and instead of a single, great, universal commercial law such as commerce had produced, we have French commercial law, English Commercial law and Spanish Commercial law'. A. Fremery, *Etudes de Droit commercial* (Paris: Alex-Gobelet, 1833), 19. Similarly in Emmanuel Delamare and Le Poitvin, *Traité théorique et pratique de Droit commercial*, t. I (Paris: Hingray, 1861), 29. Delamarre and Le Poitvin write: 'Inspired by equity and interest alone, commerce would perhaps have grasped and developed in a uniform manner the true character of standard transactions, had the work of unity not been interrupted. Incapable of appreciating its advantage, every legislator of the period, dominated by national jealousies and a selfish policy and believing they could monopolize trade, consequently regulated it. Each people wanted its own trade and its own commercial legislation, and because of principles that were over exclusive, national law often distorted contracts formed by the law of nations (*ius gentium*)'. Francesco Galgano, *Lex mercatoria* (Bologna: Il mulino, 2001), 109: '*La lex mercatoria si statalizza: si converte nei codici di commercio, con quali ciascuno Stato impone una propria visione del diritto regolatore degli scambi*'.

34 See Auguste Vavasseur, *Traité des sociétés civiles et commerciales*, t. 1 (Paris: Marchal et Billard, 1896), VI–VII: 'Alongside this law [Act of 24 July 1867 concerning joint stock companies] which had been in existence for barely ten years, a whole body of doctrine and case law has been formed; more rarely, there has also been a set of foreign laws, enacted after ours and often inspired by them, which will provide us with the used service that we ourselves provided them; for more than once these foreign laws will have underlined the imperfections of French law by correcting them, and more than once they will have highlighted its obscure provisions. But there will never be much opportunity to draw at these foreign wellsprings and French case law will remain the principal source of information for those commenting on our laws'.

comes from an international practice; (3) it brings into play questions related to money; and (4) it is deployed by people of whom we are suspicious (see the 1807 Code). All these elements explain how it was sidelined as a source of law by French jurists who tended to consider the Civil Code as the French Civil Constitution.[35] And even when the law did admit the use of custom and usages, it always accorded them a very subordinate role. While Article 1873 of the Code stated clearly that 'the provisions in this Title apply to commercial companies only in respect of the points which do not contravene commercial laws and usages', article 18 of the Commercial Code went on to stipulate that 'Company statutes are regulated by the civil law, by the laws specific to commerce, and by conventions between the parties'. The pre-eminence of the civil law was obvious. Yet its philosophy was by no means the same. The Civil Code was made for the head of a family wanting to acquire some real estate, not for merchants subordinating property to trade. This led to a cruel lack of pragmatism. Drawing strength from its actuality, hard economic fact made light of all the philosophy, and the legislator bowed to its authority.[36]

35 The wish to reduce the Civil Code to the simple rank of written reason and divest it of its character of Supreme Law [was] to break the bond between our codes and throw ourselves into the elusive and the arbitrary. M. Troplong, *Revue de Législation et de jurisprudence*, t. 16, 47. See also Gabriel Massé, *Le droit commercial dans ses rapports avec le droit des gens et le droit civil*, 2nd ed. (Paris: Guillaumin, 1861–1862).

36 Nineteenth-century commercial lawyers assimilated usage and trade custom in order to claim for them an eminent place amongst the sources of commercial law. In practice, their role was, in this century of industrial revolution, to prove even more important in the huge growth of what was not yet labelled 'business law'. The legislator's readiness to be guided by usages from the second half of the nineteenth century onwards (under the guise of controlling them, moreover) shows how important their role actually was, even though officially they kept a minor place in the hierarchy of legal sources. See on this point Jean Hilaire, *Introduction historique au droit commercial* (Paris: PUF, 1986), 109–111. See also Edouard Richard, 'A l'orée du droit des marchands: les parères', *Revue d'histoire des facultés de droit et de la culture juridique* (2014), 155–217.

CHAPTER 15

On the Origins of the French Commercial Code: Vicissitudes of the Gorneau Draft

Olivier Descamps

1 Introduction

On 9 November 1799, the *coup d'état* brought General Napoleon Bonaparte to power as First Consul of France. One of his numerous ambitions was to reform French society, and in particular to make the legal system uniform, and so a movement of codification began, with the creation of a commission of four jurists. The French civil code had known a long working process before its enactment in 1804.[1] In April 1801, a committee was created with the aim of proposing a complete commercial codification.[2] It was a kind of revolution, because of the failure of attempts to reform the commercial law during the French Revolution, and that was the reason why merchants worked on the basis of the old ordinances rather than starting afresh with a new approach to commercial law.[3] After eight months, a first draft was ready,[4] and it was named the Gorneau Draft, after its main author, and a process with different stages was initiated.[5] The minister of justice sent this document to the commercial courts and higher jurisdictions (*cours d'appel, Tribunal de cassation*). But trade was also dependent on the Home Office's competence[6] so that the minister sent also the draft to the *Chambres de commerce* and *conseils de commerce* with the obligation to give observations within two months. Three members of the Gorneau

1 Jean-Louis Halperin, *L'impossible Code civil* (Paris: PUF, 1992).

2 Philippe Paschel, 'La commission du 13 germinal an XI (1801) chargée d'établir un projet de Code de commerce', *Revue Historique de Droit français et étranger* (1995), 559–568.

3 Joël Monéger, 'De l'ordonnance de Colbert de 1673 sur le commerce au Code de commerce français de septembre 2000', *Revue international de droit économique* 2 (2004), 171–196, 171.

4 *Projet de Code de commerce présenté par la commission par le gouvernement le 13 germinal an IX* (Paris, Imprimerie nationale, Frimaire an X).

5 Fabien Valente, 'La naissance du Code de commerce napoléonien', in Corinne Saint-Alary-Houin (ed.), *Qu'en est-il du Code de commerce? États des lieux et projections: Actes du colloque des 27 et 28 octobre 2007* (Toulouse, LGDJ, 2009), 15–38, 16.

6 Anne Lefebvre-Teillard, 'Cambacérès et le Code de commerce', in Bernard Teyssié et al. (ed.), *Le Code de commerce, 1807–2007: livre du bicentenaire* (Paris, Dalloz, 2007), 3–17, 4, n. 7.

 | DOI 10.1163/9789004363144_016

commission collected all the criticisms and prepared a reviewed version. Unfortunately, the process was slowed down because Napoleon wanted, above all, a civil code in order to establish a new society, and so the Gorneau draft was not the priority of the First Consul.[7] As a result, the text was ignored for a period of five years. But one factor encouraged Napoleon to relaunch the process: in 1805–1806, an important economic crisis triggered many bankruptcies.[8] The emperor decided to take action against the fraudulent bankruptcies, and deemed it to be the right moment to complete a commercial codification.[9] It is possible to compare Napoleon's actions in this case with Colbert's actions to gain control over the French economy during the second part of the seventeenth century, who also wished to have.[10] Colbert, *contrôleur général des finances* under the reign of Louis XIV between 1665 and 1683, organized the French trade with several ordinances. Discussions on Napoleon's commercial code took place between November 1806 and August 1807; the French commercial code or *Code de commerce* was enacted in September 1807, and came into force on January 1, 1808.

If we focus more precisely on the process, it can be seen that it was a complex one. There were four drafts made during the Napoleonic period. The Gorneau draft, ready in 1801, was the first. A second document was proposed by the *Chambre de commerce* of Lyon in 1802.[11] This text was written by a committee comprised of seven members: two judges in the commercial jurisdiction and five members of the *Chambre de commerce*; based on the Gorneau version, it was a specific approach with several innovative propositions.[12] The observations collected about the Gorneau draft then gave rise to a new version: the so-called reviewed Gorneau draft. Finally, a fourth text was presented by the *Chambre de commerce* of Paris in 1804. Some famous commercial experts contributed to the preparation of the provisions: Nicolas Frochot, the *Préfet de la Seine* that is to say the main representative of State in the *Départements*,

---

7 Jean Tulard, 'Code civil', *Dictionnaire amoureux de Napoléon* (Paris: Plon, 2012).

8 Romuald Szramkiewicz and Olivier Descamps, *Histoire du droit des affaires* (Paris: LGDJ, 2013), 350.

9 Philippe Paschel, *La portée de la codification dans l'histoire du droit commercial français* (Thèse, Université Panthéon-Assas, 1993), 50–51.

10 Jean Hilaire, 'Propos historique sur le Code de commerce de 1807 et l'avenir de la codification', *Bicentenaire du Code de commerce 1807–2007*, sous l'égide de l'Association du bicentenaire du Code de commerce, (Paris: Dalloz, 2008), 69–85, 70.

11 Fabien Valente, 'Une découverte récente: le projet de Code de commerce lyonnais (1802)', *Vie et sciences économiques* 136–137 (1993), 117–122.

12 Fabien Valente, *Le code de commerce au XIXe siècle* (Thèse doctorat, Université Jean Moulin, 1992).

merchants (among others Vital Roux, a selfmade man who worked at the Delessert Bank), bankers (including Benjamin Delessert, founder of the Delessert Bank), and three regents of the *Banque de France* (Jean-Charles Davillier, Louis-Victor Moreau and Louis-Charles Thibon).[13] The document consisted of a preamble and two parts. The first part of this document deals with the form and effects of the transactions, and the second relates to the commercial jurisdiction, insolvencies and bankruptcies. The authors of this version were largely inspired by the reviewed Gorneau draft, although their ideas appeared to be more severe. In previous documents, a biennial stocktaking was required, but members of the *Chambre* asserted the necessity to do it annually. Other provisions indicated the desire for improving the morals of business. The need for swift justice and the respect of discretion explained that the contributors wanted arbitration to be obligatory. They also defended the independence of commercial law in relation to the civil law. In fact, the draft tried to correct inconsistencies found in previous texts. Among the nineteen provisions of the first part, eleven were included in the final version of the code. But there existed a second part with important aspects in relation to insolvencies,[14] bankruptcies and commercial courts. Circumstances justified the attention given to these issues. The war against Great Britain led to terrible impacts on the French economy, and that was the reason why the number of insolvencies increased and impacted confidence in business circles. The *Chambre* aimed to avoid a legal reaction with a narrow scope; the main goal was ensure that commercial transactions took place. It was necessary to punish dishonesty in contracts regarding trade, and there was an intention of preventing the risk of bad faith. In connection with this, several provisions reinforced conditions for revealing the existence of insolvency. Members of the *Chambre* developed the idea of limiting interventions by public authorities in general trade, and this step was carried out by initial discussions before the institutions (*Conseil d'Etat, Tribunat* and *Corps legislatif*). The same scheme was followed when it came to dealing with the study of the last version of the Gorneau draft: the presentation of one book or one title, with its justifications (*ratio legis*), discussions, explanations and vote. The aim of such a codification was not to follow an economic liberalism but rather to intensify state control in a difficult period of crisis.[15]

13 Romuald, Szramkiewicz, *Les régents et les censeurs de la Banque de France nommés sous le Consulat et l'Empire* (Genève: Droz, 1974), *passim.*

14 Robert Bigo, 'Les rédacteurs du Code de Commerce', *Revue historique de droit français et étranger* (1929), 426.

15 Anna Klimaszemska, 'General principles in the commercial code of France of 1807', *Journal of European History of Law* 2 (2011), 91–94.

In connection with these different aspects, it is necessary to study the Gorneau draft and its complete conception, which will be done in Section 2, before explaining its specific fate in Section 3 of this study.

2 Conception of the Gorneau Draft

On 3 April 1801, a commission was established in relation with the French Home Office, with the aim of preparing the draft. The decree asserted the obligation to insert into the future code all provisions regarding maritime trade. A few weeks later, a first document was released, focusing on the main questions in relation to all commercial matters. In fact, the preparation shows a transaction between the past and the contribution of the recent period (2.1.), but the content reveals many weaknesses. These aspects will be discussed in the following Sections (2.2.).

2.1 *The Preparation of the Draft*

The commission was comprised of seven members. Philippe-Joseph Gorneau (1733–1810),[16] the president of this committee, was a merchant, with political experience, and he was in fact a member of a chamber during the *Directoire* era. His judicial competences as a judge at the *Cour d'appel* in Paris, and his consultation as a professional when the Miromesnil draft was prepared within 1778–1782,[17] made him highly qualified for the specific work he had to prepare. Gorneau himself had a noted reputation on commercial issues. Another important member was Philippe Legras (1763–1824), an ex-prosecutor at the *Parlement* in Dijon. Legras developed an interesting analysis on a codification about insolvency and bankruptcy. Another member with an important place in the commission was Vital Roux (1766–1846). A merchant by trade, he was also a banker and represented the famous Delessert Bank in Lyon and Paris. Vital Roux exercised the functions of judge at the Parisian commercial court. In the field of trade issues, he had written a remarkable book, *De l'influence du gouvernement sur la prospérité du commerce*, published in 1800. In the first part of his book, Roux proposed a complete public law on business, and dealt

16 Jean-Louis Halpérin, 'Gorneau Philippe-Joseph', *Dictionnaire historique des juristes français: XIIe–XXe siècle*, sous la direction de Patrick Arabeyre, Jean-Louis Halpérin et Jacques Krynen (Paris: PUF, 2015).

17 Henri Lévy-Bruhl, *Un projet de Code de commerce à la veille de la Révolution, le projet Miromesnil (1778–1779)* (Paris: Cujas, 1932). Michel Reulos, 'Une source du Code de commerce: le projet Miromesnil', *Revue trimestrielle de droit commercial* (1948), 224–229, 224.

with the redaction of this in the second part of the book. For instance, he recommended the creation of business schools, the establishment of a minister of trade – something which was non-existent at this time – and he was very keen on the separation between commercial law and civil law. In order to achieve this distinction, Roux suggested making the commercial courts independent of the civil jurisdictions. He had no hesitation in asserting the necessity of including criminal provisions regarding business in the future code. Within the committee, he represented bankers, textile manufacturers and, in particular, the commercial customs of Lyon, the place of the junction between French law, Italian law and Swiss law. He knew Legras' *opus* and considered a code as a means of making trade more efficient. Pierre Vignon (1736–1823) was a merchant and from 1798–1823, the president of the Parisian commercial court; he defended the idea of a large section concerning the trade courts' competences.[18] Also among the contributors was Jacques-Augustin Mourgues (1734–1818), a specialist in maritime issues with administrative experience; he was responsible for the harbour of Cherbourg, and for the Home Office in 1792. Mourgues was also known for his scientific knowledge, and he developed works on agriculture and participated in the creation of statistics as a subject area. The commission was also comprised of less known members such as Alexandre Boursier, a merchant and judge at a commercial court, and Coulomb, an ex-judge. The two final members, Azuni and Bertrand, had been chosen because of their competences in maritime law. The draft was ready in eight months, which suggests that the Miromesnil draft was the basis of the work.

The structure of the draft was comprised of 485 provisions distributed over three books. The first Book,[19] divided into ten sections, opens with general provisions. Then, there are sections regarding companies, brokers and dealers, trade stock exchange, purchases and sales, and negotiable instruments. The second book,[20] comprised of thirteen sections, deals with maritime matters. There are articles about the sale of ships or their seizure, and several provisions were interested in the owners of ships or in the personality of the captain. There are also diverse provisions on specific maritime institutions or notions. For instance, many rules handled issues with sailors, the contracts in relation with the maritime trade – the marine bill of lading – chartering, insurance contracts and the specific liability relating to these matters. But other themes

18 Philippe Paschel, *La portée de la codification dans l'histoire du droit commercial français* (Thèse, Université Panthéon-Assas, 1993), 33.

19 *Projet de Code de commerce présenté par la commission par le gouvernement le 13 germinal an IX*, 139–140.

20 *Projet de Code de commerce*, 141.

were dealt with: freight, maritime loan, maritime liability regarding the issue of throwing items overboard, and prescriptions. The third book,[21] with fifteen sections, brings together provisions on insolvency and its procedure and bankruptcy, the latter considered to be more serious than the former; commercial courts and their jurisdictions, and imprisonment for the non-payment of debts. In this general overview, it can be noted that the Gorneau draft was inspired by the Miromesnil draft, that is to say, indirectly, by the old ordinances.

2.2 *The Content of the Draft*

It is impossible to present all the aspects of this first version of a commercial code. Some points, however, are very significant and deserve to be examined in more detail. For example, the Draft was responsible for the introduction of the maritime matters. This is an important evolution in comparison with the past, and also in comparison with the ordinance of 1681. This approach in the Draft testifies to the desire to gather together all the topics in relation to trade, and in this sense, maritime matters became a branch of commercial law. In fact, the aim was to standardize and to unify.

In relation to the companies, we can observe the choice to maintain the existence of partnerships and to introduce incorporated companies.[22] More specifically, there were four kinds of companies developed in the text: general partnership (*société en nom collectif*); limited partnership (*société en commandite simple*); participating partnership (*société en participation*); and incorporated company (*société par actions*).[23] This was the first time that the limited company appeared firmly in an Act. One provision indicates that 'the incorporated company is anonymous'.[24] The redaction of this provision shows the way that this kind of company was perceived; it was a not very well known practical creation, and it is also clear from the work that all the members of the commission had a negative opinion about it.[25] In general, limited companies were

---

21 *Projet de Code de commerce*, 142–143.

22 Edouard Richard et al. (eds.), *Droit des affaires: Questions actuelles et perspectives historiques* (Rennes: Presses universitaires de Rennes, 2004), 340, n. 729.

23 Art. 13: 'The Law recognizes four kinds of commercial companies: general partnership; limited partnership; participating partnership; incorporated company'. *Projet de Code de commerce*, 41.

24 Art. 20: 'Incorporated company is anonymous; it is only known by a relative qualification of its corporate purpose. Its capital was composed of a determined number of shares. It is governed by administrators who are shareholders or employees. It existed without a governmental authorization. The liability of shareholders is limited to the value of their shares'. *Projet de Code de commerce*, 42.

25 Anne Lefebvre-Teillard, *La société anonyme au XIXe siècle* (Paris: PUF, 1985), 2.

ignored by a large part of the commercial doctrine in the *Ancien regime*,[26] but it was covered by some – for example, the famous Jacque Savary[27] gave the first definition of the idea, describing it as the company 'done under no name'.[28] This kind of company suffered because of its secretiveness,[29] and none of its elements revealed its existence.[30] Nevertheless, the development of this structure was current in international trade at the time, especially between France and the Ottoman Empire.[31]

Article 20 of the draft seemed to introduce a confusion between the limited partnership and the limited company, both gathered under a common category: the incorporated company. The writers of this first version had made every effort to clarify definitions of the companies and to ensure more strictness in the company law. They defined each company and made it easier to know the name of shareholders via the name of the company. In this way, it was possible to know those who were responsible *in solidum* and *in infinitum*. This was the reason why the word anonymous, reserved for the participating partnership, was given to the incorporated company.[32] This was not a novelty. As a matter of fact, the monarchical government had intervened in the constitution of incorporated companies in order to support them and to promote their optimal development. The French king bestowed privileges, and the legislative way was the only method of obtaining them. We can also see a British influence regarding the idea of control. The multiplication of these sorts of companies, without any specific guidance, led to many scandals, with a governmental reaction. In the Bubble Act, enacted in 1720, incorporated companies were forbidden, with some exceptions. The central power could allow them via a charter, and that is why this structure was called charted or incorporated companies. The writers of the first version were all too familiar with the vicissitudes of the long historical evolution regarding these types of companies.

---

26 Henri Lévy-Bruhl, *Histoire juridique des sociétés de commerce en France au XVIIe et XVIIIe siècle* (Paris: Domat-Montchrestien, 1938), 42.

27 Jean Hilaire, 'Savary Jacques', *Dictionnaire historique des juristes français*, sous la direction de Patrick Arabeyre, Jean-Louis Halpérin et Jacques Krynen (Paris, PUF, 2015).

28 Edouard Richard (ed.), Jacques Savary, *Le parfait négociant* (Genève: Droz, 2011).

29 Henri Lévy-Bruhl, 'Les différentes espèces de société de commerce en France au XVIIe et XVIIIe siècle', *Revue historique de droit français et étranger* 16 (1938), 314–318.

30 Jean Hilaire, *Introduction historique au droit commercial* (Paris, PUF, 1986), 192–193.

31 Victor Simon, 'Le rôle des sociétés anonymes d'Ancien régime dans le commerce entre la France et l'Empire ottoman', *Revue historique de droit français et étranger* 92:1 (2014), 37–54, 40–41.

32 Lefebvre-Teillard, *La société anonyme*, 4.

In this draft, we can also note other important provisions, including those on the admission of the loan interest. Few years ago, the interdiction of this contract was a real issue, because there was a need to finance the economy. Debates existed between the sixteenth and the eighteenth century focusing on the reiteration of the prohibition of usury by the Bull *Vix pervenit* in 1745. This opinion constituted an obstacle to the development of the trade. That was the reason that many authors defended the idea of a moderate usury, but the Pope did not accept this possibility.[33] In the Gorneau draft, one provision admits the contract,[34] and this decision constituted a real innovation. Another important aspect was the control on the insolvency procedure. In the past, many frauds were possible because of the direction left to the creditors, and there was often a collusion between the insolvent merchant and some creditors, to the detriment of the others, which was the reason why a proposal to create a specific function during the insolvency procedure was suggested. In the title dedicated to the insolvencies, a *commissaire du gouvernement*, representing the State, should control all the stages of the procedure. Instituted before the commercial court, this administrative officer had to observe different formalities. Within 24 hours of the declaration of insolvency, he was to affix the seals' stores, movable property and personal items of the insolvent debtor (art. 357). He was to perform all the necessary acts to maintain all the creditors' and debtors' rights (art. 358). The *commissaire du gouvernement* was to observe a whole range of acts that the insolvent debtor had to carry out.

Finally, an extension of the commercial courts' jurisdiction was established in article 447. These institutions exercised their jurisdiction over the contracted commercial transactions, which could be concluded verbally, by a private deed, by a public agreement, by a bill of exchange, or by a promissory note. The courts were also competent to appraise legal actions against stockbrokers and brokers who committed negligence in their profession. The main role was to follow the insolvencies and the procedure in relation to this situation. This point was very important regarding the expansion of the commercial courts. The first version of the Gorneau draft followed this same process until a reviewed one was created.

33 Paola Vismara, *Oltre l'usura: La chiesa moderna e il prestito a interesse* (Soveria Mannelli: Rubbettino, 2004); Paola Vismara, *Questioni di interesse: La Chiesa e il denaro in età moderna* (Milano: Bruno Mondadori, 2009).

34 Art. 71: 'The interest rate is determined in the field of trade as in matter of goods'. *Projet de Code de commerce*, 52.

3 The Fate of the Draft

When the text was ready, Bonaparte had it sent by different ministers to the courts. As a matter of fact, all the jurisdictions were expected to criticize the structure and the content of the Gorneau draft. The objective was to prepare possible modifications for improving the first version. In sum, the observations of the main jurisdictions (3.1.) would be the way to a definitive document, the so-called reviewed Gorneau draft (3.2.).

3.1 *Observations of the Main Jurisdictions*

We can distinguish the general approach of the observations, issued from different jurisdictions, and the one proposed by the commercial court of Lyon in collaboration with the *Conseil de commerce.* 389 observations were gathered, distributed in three important books. Among the most important ones, we can highlight many criticisms. Looking at the sections about purchases and sales, the concept of evidence given by a broker was denounced by the courts, because the way of proving had the power to ruin a merchant, although a possible collusion with a so-called purchaser did exist. The section on the loan at interest was criticized because the redaction of the provision was considered to be unclear as there was no indication of the rate, and the detailed rules for determining it were not indicated either. Some courts asserted in their criticisms that the rigour of the insolvency procedure could have been accidental rather than deliberate, and in the extension of the commercial courts' jurisdictions over the insolvency, many criticisms were made on the lack of technical skills in these tribunals in civil matters. In effect, there were many consequences in relation to civil institutions, for instance the dower or the dowry of the merchant's wife. But, it should also be noted that some jurisdictions defended this expansion, particularly the fact that commercial court judges were not paid by the litigants as they had been before under the old civil courts.

Among one of the most criticised topics in the Gorneau draft was the creation of the *commissaire du gouvernement*, a kind of government representative. Among all the commentaries, a trend seems to emerge clearly: they all stated that the concept of a government representative was opposed to the simplicity of the commercial procedure. He would be a permanent judge before the temporary one. A real risk existed that he might want to influence decisions of the court. Moreover, the status of this civil servant, appointed by the central power, could be in contradiction with the election of the commercial court's magistrate. It seemed to the observers that too many powers given by the law could lead to the risk of abuses. Regarding his competences, the *commissaire du gouvernement* could control creditors, and this possibility appeared dangerous. However, there were observations in favour of this new civil servant as well. The trade which this kind of administrative officer could control its business ethics would be in the interest of the state. Effectively, he could prevent embezzlements and punish torts.

The jurisdiction of Lyon organized its observations by writing a new draft with a specific structure. This text, prepared with the *conseil de commerce*, is comprised of 324 articles.[35] In order to avoid references to the civil code under discussion, the document integrated the civil rules regarding the commercial law into its new version. In concrete terms, many new provisions completed the first book of the Gorneau draft in this respect with articles on the separate ownership of property, commission agents, and several in relation to the companies. In connection with this noticeable topic, provisions dealt with the relationships between members of companies with commitment with third parties or with aspects of the companies' demise. It is interesting to note that the obligations of commission agents were precisely conceived. They should perform as a *vir bonus* or a reasonable person. Their liability could be triggered if their acts overstepped the commission, and if the orders were not clear, the situation would be interpreted in favour of the commission agent. When it came to the companies, the will for insuring the legal certainty led to envisaging the end of the structure at the first written request if the statutes did not exist, or if a member had died. The *intuitus personae* was highlighted, no matter what kind of company it was. Some provisions were to ensure that the capital would be paid. For instance, a delay in the payment of contributions in cash should be submitted to an interest. During the life of the company, if any provisions were not dedicated to rule the topic, the draft foresaw a distinction between the acts for current management executed only by one associate, and those regarding immovable property that required the express consent of all the partners. When it came to the acts with third parties, a principle of joint liability was asserted. Regarding the sharing of benefits and losses, if any provisions did not foresee the repartition, it should be proportional to the contributions. Several possibilities for the termination of the company were considered. In the first case, the end point could be reaching the expiry of the period for which the contract was signed. Second, the termination of the company could occur as a result of a loss of capital which could then give rise to a crisis, leading to a justification for closing down all the activities. Thirdly, the cessation should occur in case of *mort civile* affecting a member. In the case of the death of a member, the same result was to be applied.

35 Valente, 'La naissance du Code de commerce napoléonien', 31.

The forced arbitration was conceived with more flexibility, that is to say, it became optional. Members of this institution could propose to end the partnership in which they were participating. Effectively, this sort of company had one major disadvantage: it was far too ephemeral. The draft dealt with the bill of exchange, and did away with the *distancia loci*. Moreover, it developed a severe concept of bankruptcy. A further inconvenience was the lack of commercial jurisdiction for the start of the procedure. That was the reason why the draft suggested that a justice of the peace should be instituted in places where there was no commercial court. The goal was to avoid any delay in the process. Astonishingly, this draft did not seem to influence the reviewed Gorneau draft.

3.2 *The Reviewed Gorneau Draft*

Three members of the Gorneau committee were appointed in order to analyse all the observations. Gorneau, Vital-Roux and Legras modified the first draft, taking into account most of the criticisms. On the basis of the considerations, a new version was written which comprised of 485 provisions, distributed over three books. In fact, many articles from the first version were modified or deleted, and many others were maintained without modifications, or were added but without giving a number to the provision.[36] The first book, which had no title, was comprised of general provisions; the second book was concerned with maritime matters; and the last book focused on insolvencies and the commercial courts. The draft preserved many previous ideas. The text was published[37] and analysed by the Parisian *Chambre de commerce* on its own initiative, and the members of this institution attempted to propose solutions for preventing insolvencies and abuses. In fact, like the *Chambre de commerce* of Lyon, the Parisian *Chambre* gave its own views in 1804.[38] A committee of sixteen members was established under the president of the *Chambre* and *préfet*, Frochot, and the committee was comprised of different people, among them Vignon and Vital Roux, two writers of the Gorneau draft. The commission worked on the latter and on an insolvencies draft proposed by the *Conseil general de commerce*. The document, comprising of 497 articles, was divided into three books, without titles, and was preceded by a preamble. The Parisian text, like the text presented by the *Chambre de commerce* of Lyon, was a synoptic table with the Gorneau draft's provisions, the observations gathered by members of the

36 Valente, 'La naissance du Code de commerce napoléonien', 33.

37 *Révision du projet de Code de commerce précédé de l'analyse raisonnée des observations du Tribunal de cassation, des Tribunaux d'appel et des Tribunaux et Conseils de commerce* (Paris, an XI).

38 *Observations de la Chambre de commerce de Paris sur la révision du projet de Code de commerce* (Paris: Stoupe, An XII).

Parisian *Chambre* and its own provisions for a new version. In the preamble, it was asserted that the commercial legislation should be divided in two parts. The first part[39] addressed the form and the effects of commercial transactions, rights and duties of merchants. The second[40] was interesting both from the point of view of the judges' powers, and also in the jurisdictions' competences and insolvencies. In general, this draft did not make great modifications to the Gorneau version. Some ideas, already proposed by the *Chambre de commerce* of Lyon, were reiterated: for instance, the inclusion of civil rules in relation to commercial matters was reasserted, as was the suppression of the *distancia loci* in the bill of exchange. This possible comparison can be explained in the fact that each committee had several members in common: Vital Roux, and Vignon, among others. The *Chambre* of Paris had a very important debate on the possibility of creating a *commissaire du gouvernement* near the commercial courts. This issue seemed to give rise to real opposition. It created a situation where many proposals were made inside the *Chambre de commerce* of Paris before a common opinion could be agreed upon, and the result was a conditional acceptance. Even then, however, modifications were suggested on three points.[41] First, regarding their competences, there was a question about their power. The reason for creating this post of *commissaire du gouvernement* was justified by the multiplication of insolvencies and scandals, and so it appeared necessary to have a person who could conduct the bankrupt's affairs. In this situation, it would be important to defend the creditors' interests and to reduce the influence of the go-betweens. The members suggested that this expert could be called the *commissaire aux faillites*, a title which limited the field of his powers. Another advantage to having this kind of professional was to propose a help to manage all the business. But members of the Parisian *Chambre de commerce* asserted that if the increase of abuses justified severe repression, it would not be imperative in the ordinary field of commercial litigations. On the contrary, the influence of the *commissaire du gouvernement* on judges could be dangerous and could generate many conflicts. Moreover, one officer only would not be sufficient, and could not respect the duties of the office. The second modification that the members discussed was the topic of the *commissaire du gouvernement*'s wage and it was decided that it would be better to avoid appointing an administrative officer. At the same time, they were aware of the difficulties in finding the right person. This aspect led them to consider the method of appointment. A comparison with the unpaid judges of the commercial courts was suggested, and this allowed them to affirm the

39 *Observations*, 3.

40 *Observations*, 3.

41 *Observations*, 114.

obligation to choose the expert from among the well-known merchants. But, finally, this draft did not have any influence on the reviewed Gorneau draft.

For a long time, the authorities were not interested in the commercial codification process. Their preference was to develop the civil code, because the latter could change French society, and the business topics did not interest to the public authorities. But the approach changed, and the process was accelerated because of the increase in bankruptcies without any punishment. Bonaparte decided to fire the minister of finance, and summoned members of the *Conseil d'État* in charge to discuss legislative drafts. Bonaparte asked for a severe legislation against insolvencies, something which he confused with bankruptcies, in order to stop the extent of these problems. An answer indicated to the Emperor a fact that he ignored: the existence of a commercial code draft with rigorous provisions against insolvencies. He required the immediate resumption of the process. Discussions took place between November 1806 and August 1807 during 61 sessions. Bonaparte presided over only four sessions, among which three considered the insolvencies. In comparison, he attended almost 80 sessions of the 110 discussions for the civil code. During the debate, some of the aspects were modified. As a matter of fact, in regard to companies, there were discussions about the interest in preserving the category of incorporated company that could be included in the limited partnership. There were contests against the preservation of the participating partnership, because it was considered as being too short-lived. In the *Code de commerce*, we can observe the existence of three kinds of companies: a general partnership, an incorporated company, and a limited partnership. When it came to the insolvencies, the reviewed draft preserved the *commissaire du gouvernement* but reduced his powers to that of a kind of curator and the defender of a non-represented creditor. Before the *Conseil d'État*, a debate took place concerning the creation of an insolvency's curator. Many sessions were dedicated to discuss the problems raised by this kind of function. Risks of collusion between the insolvent merchant and the curator were evoked, as well as between this curator and creditors. One of the main aspects was to sideline the creditors over the management of their business. All these reasons led to the creation of a new function: a *juge-commissaire*, an official receiver with the mission of watching the administration after the insolvency.

4 Conclusion

At the end of the process, which was an easier process before the different assemblies (*Tribunat, Corps legislative* and *Senat*) than the process for the discussions over the civil code,[42] five laws were enacted in September 1807 and they were gathered in a commercial code on 15 September. The commercial code came into effect on January 1, 1808. It was composed of 648 provisions divided into four books. The initial structure was the same in the final version. In comparison with the civil code, the commercial code was more concentrated. In fact, this aspect led to criticisms that this codification was really incomplete,[43] particularly on the theme of purchases and sales. Only one provision dealt with this crucial contract for business. The code was also criticised because it did not take into account the recent developments in business matters. For instance, securities were evoked only *via* provisions on shares in the section concerning the limited companies. There were no rules regarding the organisation of stock exchange or banking activities, apart from the bill of exchange. The subjects of business (*fonds de commerce*) and industrial property were totally ignored. Some flaws seemed to result from the confusion between civil and commercial legislation. The writers of the civil code considered that the trade transactions should be ruled by the commercial legislation, whereas those working on the commercial code were highly uncertain of the civil one.[44] Finally, this codification appeared as a work which had been enacted because of specific circumstances: the multiplication of bankruptcies, and an economic crisis. The weaknesses of the commercial code led to a phenomenon of decodification later on, but despite this, as the great French legal historian, Jean Hilaire, stated, the commercial code constituted a real turning point, a symbol of a new legal system, and it established a new hierarchy of norms with the Act in the highest place.[45]

---

42 Szramkiewicz and Descamps, *Histoire du droit des* affaires, 351, n. 719.

43 Hilaire, *Introduction historique au droit commercial*, 87.

44 Hilaire, *Introduction historique au droit commercial*, 88, n. 46.

45 Hilaire, *Introduction historique au droit commercial*, 90, n. 48.

CHAPTER 16

Court Records as Sources for the History of Commercial Law: The *Oberappellationsgericht Lübeck* as a Commercial Court (1820–1879)

Peter Oestmann

1 Introduction

This paper reflects the *Oberappellationsgericht* of Lübeck, the high court of appeal of the four free German cities. Without a doubt, it was the most important court for developing the practice of a scientific commercial law. In the German discussion on the history of commercial law in the nineteenth century in general, three aspects stand out in this context: firstly, the modern science of commercial law established by Thöl and Goldschmidt[1] around 1850; secondly, the 1861 enacted commercial code (*Allgemeines Deutsches Handelsgesetzbuch*) as a first codification for the whole of Germany;[2] and thirdly, the court practice of the most famous commercial court, the *Oberappellationsgericht Lübeck* as the high court of appeal of the four free cities. In fact, commercial law and particularly the decisions of the Lübeck court were important steps on the way to the unification and modernisation of German law. This brief picture, then, shows not only the sources, persons and details of the commercial history, but in addition, draws the bigger lines of German legal history on the whole.

2 Commercial Law as a Pacesetter for the Modernisation of Law

In the nineteenth century, commercial law was the pacesetter for the modernisation of law. The high court of appeal in Lübeck has always been held

1 Overview of the scientific literature and the codification of the ADHGB by Mathias Schmoeckel, *Rechtsgeschichte der Wirtschaft: Seit dem 19. Jahrhundert* (Tübingen: Mohr Siebeck, 2008), 95–106, n. 145–163.

2 Christoph Bergfeld, 'Handelsrecht (Deutschland)', in Helmut Coing (ed.), *Handbuch der Quellen und Literatur der neueren europäischen Privatrechtsgeschichte*, vol. III/3 (München: Beck, 1986), 2853–2968; Thomas Henne, 'Handelsgesetzbuch', in Albrecht Cordes et al. (eds.), *Handwörterbuch zur deutschen Rechtsgeschichte* (HRG), vol. 2, 2nd ed. (Berlin: Schmidt, 2012), cols. 712–714.

 | DOI 10.1163/9789004363144_017

fondly in exactly this way. Therefore, it might be useful to emphasize that throughout history, commercial law was often an indication of the progress and change in the prevailing law system. Some short remarks may illustrate this. Already in the fourteenth century, a discussion had been started regarding a contract's validity in a case where the parties did not use the traditional Roman formalistic figures of a stipulation. In court, defendants sometimes pleaded that the contract did not contain a stipulation, and therefore they were not willing to pay. Bartolus de Sassoferrato wrote that those pleas were not valid amongst merchants.[3] The origin of the freedom of design as part of the freedom of the contract is found not only in the canon law, but mainly in the commercial law, and this expanded into all of civil law in the sixteenth century.[4]

In the nineteenth century, the consequences of the expansion from commercial affairs to general laws can be observed in several fields of law and politics in Germany. In 1834, some decades before Germany was united as a nation, the toll union (*Deutscher Zollverein*) was founded. Therefore, even before state unity was achieved, economic unity existed in a toll free internal market.[5] The Pan-German codification movement showed a similar picture. In 1848, one of the first legislations the German Confederation (*Deutscher Bund*) enacted for the German states was a law for bills of exchanges (*Wechselordnung*).[6] In 1861, the parliament in Frankfurt passed a general German commercial code (*Allgemeines Deutsches Handelsgesetzbuch*), but it was not directly applicable in all German federal states. However, the 39 different states introduced this law in their own territories. In the years after 1861, the commercial law thereby became harmonised via legislation throughout Germany (and

3 Reinhard Zimmermann, *The Law of Obligations: Roman Foundations of the Civilian Tradition* (Cape Town: Juta, 1990/1992), 540.

4 Rudolf Meyer-Pritzl, '§§125–129. Form der Rechtsgeschäfte', in Mathias Schmoeckel, Joachim Rückert and Reinhard Zimmermann (eds.), *Historisch-kritischer Kommentar zum BGB (HKK), Vol. 1: Allgemeiner Teil: §§ 1–240* (Tübingen: Mohr Siebeck, 2003), 498–531 (500–508), n. 5–24; Sibylle Hofer, '*vor § 145. Vertrag*', in Mathias Schmoeckel, Joachim Rückert and Reinhard Zimmermann (eds.), *Historisch-kritischer Kommentar zum BGB (HKK), Bd. 1: Allgemeiner Teil: §§ 1–240* (Tübingen: Mohr Siebeck, 2003), 818–836, n. 1–34.

5 Dietmar Willoweit, *Deutsche Verfassungsgeschichte Vom Frankenreich bis zur Wiedervereinigung Deutschlands*, 7th ed. (München: Beck, 2013), § 30 n. 13–14, § 32 n. 6; Gerhard Lingelbach, 'Zollverein', in Adalbert Erler, Ekkehard Kaufmann and Dieter Werkmüller (eds.), *HRG*, vol. 5, 1st ed. (Berlin: Schmidt, 1998), cols. 1769–1772.

6 Kurt von Pannwitz, *Die Entstehung der Allgemeinen Deutschen Wechselordnung: Ein Beitrag zur Geschichte der Vereinheitlichung des deutschen Zivilrechts im 19. Jahrhundert* (Frankfurt am Main: P. Lang, 1999).

including Austria).[7] In this aspect, the standardisation of the commercial law was the first step to unifying the whole civil law. The Empire founded in 1871 had in its constitution the competence only to enact legislation in the law of obligation, not in the civil law as a whole. For codifying the German civil law, it was necessary to change one section of the constitution via the so-called Lex Miquel-Lasker.[8] Hence, the German BGB was not enacted before 1896, 35 years later than the commercial code.[9] The highest court for commercial litigation was founded in 1870, whereas the *Reichsgericht*, the highest court for the second German Empire (*Kaiserreich*), was instituted not before 1879.[10] In every aspect, the commercial law was fully developed before the civil law.

This finding can probably be transferred to the modernism of the twentieth century. Individual communities such as the European Coal and Steel Community mark the beginning of the European unification movement. A few years later, the European Economic Community (1957) followed. Significantly, after about 1967, the name 'European Community' became prevalent in practice. With that, it was hinted that the aspirations for unification spread from the economy to other sectors. When the name of the European Community was changed to 'European Union' in 1992, the change displayed linguistically to everyone that the Union's focus had shifted from the joint coordination of agricultural and economic politics, to general political

7 Alexander Brix, *Das allgemeine Handelsgesetzbuch vom Standpunkt der österreichischen Gesetzgebung* (Wien, 1864).

8 Reinhard Zimmermann, 'Das Bürgerliche Gesetzbuch und die Entwicklung des Bürgerlichen Rechts', in Mathias Schmoeckel, Joachim Rückert and Reinhard Zimmermann (eds.), *Historisch-kritischer Kommentar zum BGB (HKK), Vol. 1: Allgemeiner Teil: §§ 1–240* (Tübingen: Mohr Siebeck, 2003), 1–33 (8–9), n. 11.

9 Short overview by Hans Schlosser, *Neuere Europäische Rechtsgeschichte: Privat- und Strafrecht vom Mittelalter bis zur Moderne*, 2nd ed. (München: Beck, 2014), 279–296; Sources: Benno Mugdan (ed.), *Die gesammten Materialien zum Bürgerlichen Gesetzbuch für das Deutsche Reich*, 5 vols. (Berlin: Decker, 1899); Horst Heinrich Jakobs and Werner Schubert (eds.), *Die Beratung des Bürgerlichen Gesetzbuchs in systematischer Zusammenstellung der unveröffentlichten Quellen*, 6 vols. (Berlin: Walter de Gruyter, 1978/90).

10 Ulrike Müßig, 'Handelsrechtseinheit durch Höchstgerichtsbarkeit: Die Entstehung des Bundes- bzw. Reichsoberhandelsgerichts', in Albrecht Cordes and Serge Dauchy (eds.), *Eine Grenze in Bewegung: Private und öffentliche Konfliktlösung im Handels- und Seerecht/Une frontière mouvante: Justice privée et justice publique en matières commerciales et maritimes* (München: R. Oldenbourg Verlag, 2013), 265–292; sources collected by *Werner Schubert, Die deutsche Gerichtsverfassung (1869–1877)* (Frankfurt am Main: Klostermann, 1981).

affairs.[11] The project of a comparative history of commercial law – to which this essay hopes to contribute a little – intends to shed light on such overall developments. Therefore, to encourage future discussions, the findings shall be concretised further: unification and modernisation of law often originate in the area of economy and commerce. Only later do they spread to the entire legal system. Therefore, the history of commercial law is a sensible and well-suited indicator for forward-looking movements in law. The high court of appeal in Lübeck is one significant example which can demonstrate this situation.

3 Jurisdiction in Germany at the Turn of the Nineteenth Century

Dealing with the Lübeck court of appeal, this paper focuses on the field of jurisdiction. But there existed no commercial courts in most of the German federal states. The French-influenced commercial courts introduced during the time of the French occupation were abolished after 1813, apart from in Hamburg, which was one of the few states which maintained special commercial courts in the nineteenth century.[12] Traditionally, the German cities of the early modern period knew the *Zunftgerichte* (courts dealing with legal disputes about crafts), and may have been somewhat familiar with *Marktgerichte* or so-called *Wettegerichte* (courts dealing with legal disputes about trade); all of them were local courts, often without reference to the territorial lord. In comparison to the ordinary civil courts, such courts were interested in efficiency and consensus. Therefore, the courts focused on pragmatic settlements without long-winded legal verdicts. For this reason, there were often special *privilegia de non appellando limitata* (privileges for the prohibition of appeal) in commercial matters; in many places, it was forbidden to appeal against the verdicts of those commercial courts.[13] Special high courts for commercial matters had not been conceived of, but the highest courts of the old German Empire sometimes dealt with commercial matters.[14] In part, the

11 Hans Hattenhauer, *Europäische Rechtsgeschichte*, 4th ed. (Heidelberg: C.F. Müller, 2004), 869–882; Uwe Wesel, *Geschichte des Rechts in Europa: Von den Griechen bis zum Vertrag von Lissabon* (München: Beck, 2010), 656–670.

12 Jan Jelle Kähler, *Französisches Zivilrecht und französische Justizverfassung in den Hansestädten Hamburg, Lübeck und Bremen (1806–1815)* (Frankfurt am Main: P. Lang, 2007), 294–295.

13 Philipp Nordloh, *Kölner Zunftprozesse vor dem Reichskammergericht* (Frankfurt am Main: P. Lang, 2008).

14 See the paper by Anja Amend-Traut in this volume; also Robert Riemer, *Frankfurt und Hamburg vor dem Reichskammergericht: Zwei Handels- und Handwerkszentren im*

jurisdiction in commercial matters was seen as *Policeyrecht* with a prohibition of appeal.[15]

The German court system changed totally after 1806.[16] Before 1806, the *Reichskammergericht* and the *Reichshofrat* existed as the two highest courts for appeals above the territorial courts. Their high status was due in part because of prohibitions of appeal, especially in the electorates. However, in most territories it was possible to appeal, and even if a *privilegia de non appellando illimitata* existed, a claim would have been possible in cases of justice denied or delayed.[17] Therefore, the territories of the Holy Roman Empire could not become sovereign before 1806.

The change came after the fall of the first German Empire. The superior Federal states had their own high courts, usually called *Oberappellationsgericht*. The congress of Vienna decided that there had to be three levels of courts. As some of the 39 Federal states had not many inhabitants, the constitutional act of 1815 (*Bundesakte*) declared that states with fewer than 300,000 inhabitants were allowed to build their highest courts together.[18] For the former imperial cities, there was another exception to the *Bundesakte*: the remaining four free cities of Frankfurt, Bremen, Hamburg and Lübeck had the explicit competence to create their own highest court together. The *Bundesakte* decided that if the territory of jurisdiction in which the highest court worked had fewer than

Vergleich (Köln: Böhlau, 2012); Anja Amend-Traut, Albrecht Cordes and Wolfgang Sellert (eds.), *Geld, Handel, Wirtschaft: Höchste Gerichte im Alten Reich als Spruchkörper und Institution* (Berlin: De Gruyter, 2013); Anja Amend-Traut, *Wechselverbindlichkeiten vor dem Reichskammergericht: Praktiziertes Zivilrecht in der Frühen Neuzeit* (Köln: Böhlau, 2009).

15 Heinz Mohnhaupt, '"Jura mercatorum" durch Privilegien, Zur Entwicklung des Handelsrechts bei Johann Marquard (1610–1668)', in Gerhard Köbler (ed.), *Wege europäischer Rechtsgeschichte: Karl Kroeschell zum 60. Geburtstag* (Frankfurt am Main: P. Lang, 1987), 308–323; now in Heinz Mohnhaupt, *Historische Vergleichung im Bereich von Staat und Recht: Gesammelte Aufsätze* (Frankfurt am Main: V. Klostermann, 2000), 349–369.

16 Bernhard Diestelkamp (ed.), *Das Reichskammergericht am Ende des Alten Reiches und sein Fortwirken im 19. Jahrhundert* (Köln: Böhlau, 2002); Eric-Oliver Mader, *Die letzten 'Priester der Gerechtigkeit': die Auseinandersetzung der letzten Generation von Richtern des Reichskammergerichts mit der Auflösung des Heiligen Römischen Reiches Deutscher Nation* (Berlin: Akademie Verlag, 2005).

17 Peter Oestmann, 'Rechtsverweigerung im Alten Reich', *Zeitschrift der Savigny-Stiftung für Rechtsgeschichte, Germanistische Abteilung* 127 (2010), 51–141; Stefan Andreas Stodolkowitz, 'Rechtsverweigerung und Territorialjustiz. Verfahren wegen iustitia denegata vel protracta am Oberappellationsgericht Celle', *Zeitschrift der Savigny-Stiftung für Rechtsgeschichte, Germanistische Abteilung* 131 (2014), 128–181.

18 For example: Ulf Häder, *Das gemeinschaftliche Oberappellationsgericht thüringischer Staaten in Jena: ein Beitrag zur Geschichte des Gerichtswesens im 19. Jahrhundert* (Frankfurt am Main: P. Lang, 1996).

300,000 inhabitants, the court would have to ensure its quality by guaranteeing the transmission of files to a university in order to consult qualified and academically trained judges in every case.[19] In the time of separation of power, the legal scholarship discussed this transmission.[20]

According to this compromise in the Vienna act, the four free cities agreed to establish such a high court of appeal.[21] The conciliation dragged on for years and was under much pressure to succeed; failing that, their judiciary would have been weakened, as other *Oberappellationsgerichte* would have been competent for their matters. Finally, Lübeck was chosen as the location for the new institution. Lübeck was the smallest of the four free cities.[22] However, as a former Hanseatic town, it had a great tradition of medieval statutory and customary law, its own scientific legal literature since the middle of the seventeenth century,[23] and limited administrative power so that the court could work without any political pressure.

4 *Oberappellationsgericht Lübeck*

4.1 *History and Constitution of the Court*

The high court of appeal started its work in October 1820. The celebration of the official opening was held in November 1820. In this year, the court wrote its first court order – only as a draft, but still influential. This regulation was finally repeated and enacted as a formal law in 1831.[24] However, the principles of the organisation and the procedural law did not change during this period.

19 Deutsche Bundesakte art. XII, in Karl Zeumer (ed.), *Quellensammlung zur Geschichte der Deutschen Reichsverfassung in Mittelalter und Neuzeit*, 2nd ed. (Tübingen: Mohr, 1913), 543.

20 Peter Oestmann, 'Aktenversendung', in Albrecht Cordes et al. (eds.), *Handwörterbuch zur deutschen Rechtsgeschichte* (*HRG*), vol. 1, 2nd ed. (Berlin: Schmidt, 2008), cols. 128–132.

21 The discussions about the foundation of the new court can be seen in Katalin Polgar, *Das Oberappellationsgericht der vier freien Städte Deutschlands (1820–1879) und seine Richterpersönlichkeiten* (Frankfurt am Main: P. Lang, 2007); Antjekathrin Graßmann, 'Die Anfänge des Oberappellationsgerichts der vier freien Städte Deutschlands in Lübeck', in *Schleswig-Holsteinische Anzeigen: Justizministerialblatt in Schleswig-Holstein, Teil A. Sonderheft 'Obergerichtsbarkeit in Schleswig-Holstein'* (Glückstadt, 1988), 24–27.

22 Information about the history of the city of Lübeck can be found in Antjekathrin Graßmann (ed.), *Lübeckische Geschichte*, 4th ed. (Lübeck: Schmidt-Römhild, 2008).

23 See the impressive bibliography collected by Wilhelm Ebel, *Jurisprudencia Lubecensis: Bibliographie des lübischen Rechts* (Lübeck: Schmidt-Römhild, 1980).

24 Friedrich Bluhme (ed.), *Gerichtsordnung für das Oberappellationsgericht der vier Freien Städte Deutschlands nebst den darauf bezüglichen Gesezen der einzelnen Städte und den*

The court had one president.[25] During the whole period of nearly sixty years, the high court had only three presidents. The first was Georg Arnold Heise, who presided over the court from 1820 until 1851.[26] Carl Georg Wächter, a famous scholar, succeeded him in 1851 but worked only until 1852.[27] The third president was Johann Friedrich Martin Kierulff who stayed in Lübeck from 1853 until 1879.[28] All of them had been professors of civil law before their appointment to become judge in Lübeck. In addition, all of them had previous experience of the practical work of a court. Heise had studied in his youth at the *Reichskammergericht* in Wetzlar and had worked on cases which the University of Göttingen had to decide via transmissions of files. Wächter had worked at the appeal court of Leipzig. Kierulff had been judge and afterwards vice president of the highest court of Mecklenburg. These presidents' careers show the very close connection between practice, and university scholarship, which was the basis for the famous reputation of the Lübeck court and the high regard in which it was held.

Next to the president, six (sometimes seven) judges worked at the court. The entry requirement was legal training, and several of the judges had also been professors before. Altogether, 26 judges worked at the court between 1820 and 1879. Many of them wrote instructive literature on legal history, especially on the history of the Low German customary law of Lübeck and Saxony. Others wrote about the medieval canon law and edited critical versions of the *Lex Salica* and other early medieval sources. One judge was expert in French civil

---

allgemeinen Verfügungen des Gerichts (Hamburg: Fr. Perthes, 1843). This edition also provides the draft of 1820 and other remarks.

25 Further information about the organisation of the court is presented by Horst Greb, *Die Verfassung des Oberappellationsgerichts der vier freien Städte Deutschlands zu Lübeck* (Göttingen, 1967).

26 Wilhelm von Bippen, *Georg Arnold Heise: Mittheilungen aus dessen Leben* (Halle: C.A. Schwetschke, 1852); Markus Braunewell, *Georg Arnold Heise: Biographie und Briefwechsel mit Savigny und anderen* (Diss. jur. Frankfurt am Main, 1999); Polgar, *Oberappellationsgericht*, 166–179.

27 Bernhard Windscheid, *Carl Georg von Waechter* (Leipzig: Duncker & Humblot, 1880); Bernd-Rüdiger Kern (ed.), *Zwischen Romanistik und Germanistik: Carl Georg von Waechter (1797–1880)* (Berlin: Duncker & Humblot, 2000), 49–63; Christoph Mauntel, *Carl Georg von Wächter (1797–1880): Rechtswissenschaft und Frühkonstitutionalismus* (Paderborn: Ferdinand Schöningh, 2004); Polgar, *Oberappellationsgericht*, 179–189.

28 Jörn Eckert, 'Johann Friedrich Martin Kierulff (1806–1894): Vom Universitätsprofessor zum Präsidenten des Oberappellationsgerichts zu Lübeck', in Jörn Eckert, Pia Letto-Vanamo and Kjell Åke Modéer (eds.), *Juristen im Ostseeraum: Dritter Rechtshistorikertag im Ostseeraum, 20.–22. Mai 2004* (Frankfurt am Main: P. Lang, 2007), 31–43; Polgar, *Oberappellationsgericht*, 189–197.

law, and another on the system of the Roman digests. Even in Germany, where the intellectual level of courts and the quality of the judges was quite high, the *Oberappelationsgericht Lübeck* was extraordinary and was therefore known as 'Germany's erudite court' (*Deutschlands gelehrter Gerichtshof*). The famous jurist for civil law, Rudolf von Jhering, was responsible for this apellation. In 1879, when the court was suspended and transferred into the *Hanseatisches Oberlandesgericht Hamburg*, Jhering wrote an obituary for the judge Agathon Wunderlich with the oft-cited sentences: 'One could thus call the *Oberappellationsgericht* of Lübeck Germany's erudite court, and in this Court the German science splendidly passed the test of collaboration with legal practice: both practitioners and theoreticians acknowledged the Court's decisions, true masterpieces both as to their form and as contents, achievements that in just a few pages could outweigh thick legal monographs'.[29]

One secretary and two members of the chancellery completed the court's staff. The secretary also had to have studied law. In fact, he was responsible for writing the concepts of the decisions. The judges told him how to decide the case, and the secretary formulated the details. Some other court systems continue to use this model today, in particular the Swiss Federal court.[30] However, the instructions of the judges could be compared with the final judgement as the reasoning of the judges is preserved.

4.2 *Procedural Law and Principles*

The court's procedural law seems old fashioned at first glance,[31] as the procedure was completely written. When the court's modernity in commercial matters is considered, there also only substantive legal questions could be asked.

---

29 Rudolf von Jhering, 'Agathon Wunderlich: Ein Nachruf', *Jahrbücher für die Dogmatik des heutigen römischen und deutschen Privatrechts* 17 (1879), 145–157, 156, in the German original: '*So konnte man das Lübecker Oberappellationsgericht als den gelehrten Gerichtshof Deutschlands bezeichnen, und die deutsche Wissenschaft hat die Probe, zu der sie hier in Verbindung mit der Praxis berufen ward, mit Ruhm bestanden; die Lübecker Urteile gehörten zu denjenigen, denen der Praktiker wie der Theoretiker in gleicher Weise Anerkennung zollte, es fanden sich darunter wahre Meisterstücke, gleichmäßig nach Form und Inhalt, Leistungen die auf ganz wenigen Seiten ganze dickleibige juristische Monographien aufwogen*'.

30 Christoph Leuenberger, 'Die Zusammenarbeit von Richter und Gerichtsschreiber: Überdenken im Zeichen der zunehmenden Belastung der Gerichte', *Schweizerisches Zentralblatt für Staats- und Verwaltungsrecht* 87 (1986), 97–113, 97 [online version: https://www.google.de/?gws_rd=ssl#q=gerichtsschreibe+schweiz+bundesgerich, visited 26.3.2015].

31 Nora Tirtasana, *Der gelehrte Gerichtshof: Das Oberappellationsgericht Lübeck und die Praxis des Zivilprozesses im 19. Jahrhundert* (Köln: Böhlau, 2012).

The procedure was not only written, but the law of evidence was still dominated by the so-called statutory theory of proof (*gesetzliche Beweistheorie*): these traditional features of the Lübeck procedure set it apart from contemporary French procedure. Only in some criminal cases in the later period of the court were oral hearings introduced. Therefore, it is a typical detail that some rooms had to be rebuilt in the courthouse in 1864/1866.[32] In fact, there were only small rooms and previously there was no place for visitors, parties and procurators. The written lawsuits were a survival from the early modern period. In addition, the organisation of the folders with their quadrangles and nominations of the single statements was also traditional.

However, one other point makes this different to most of the courts in the eighteenth century. In the four cities, it was possible to appeal against an interlocutory judgement, something which was under discussion elsewhere in the jurisprudence. According to most theories, the appeal against an interlocutory judgement would have been allowed only if the interlocutory had the same binding force as a final judgement.

Concerning this aspect, there was extensive discussion in the jurisprudence and different evaluations, all based on whether their origin lay in canon or statutory law.[33] In Lübeck, the court mainly decided on appealed interlocutory judgements for better evidence.[34] Here, it did not use the modern concept of free appreciation of evidence, but followed the traditional legal theory of evidence: the courts of first and second instance decided which party had the burden of proof, which proof had to be adduced, which testimony or witness had to be produced and lastly, the outcome of it.[35] Against these decisions,

32 Polgar, *Oberappellationsgericht*, 86.

33 Helpful on contemporary problems concerning the appeal against interlocutory decisions are some papers in Leopold Auer and Eva Ortlieb (eds.), *Appellation und Revision im Europa des Spätmittelalters und der Frühen Neuzeit* (Wien: Verl. der Österr. Akad. der Wiss., 2013); Steffen Schlinker, 'Die prozessuale Funktion der sententia interlocutoria im spätmittelalterlichen gelehrten Zivilprozess', *Zeitschrift der Savigny-Stiftung für Rechtsgeschichte* 127, *Kanonistische Abteilung* 96 (2010), 152–185; Peter Oestmann, 'Ludolf Hugo und die gemeinrechtliche Appellation', in Peter Oestmann (ed.), *Ludolf Hugo, Vom Missbrauch der Appellation* (Köln: Böhlau, 2012), 1–43, 12–13.

34 Peter Oestmann, 'Seehandelsrechtliche Streitigkeiten vor dem Oberappellationsgericht der vier freien Städte Deutschlands (1820–1848)', in Albrecht Cordes and Serge Dauchy (eds.), *Eine Grenze in Bewegung: Private und öffentliche Konfliktlösung im Handels- und Seerecht/Une frontière mouvante: Justice privée et justice publique en matières commerciales et maritimes* (München: R. Oldenbourg Verlag, 2013), 221–264, 262.

35 Concerning the law of evidence in the nineteenth century, see Thomas Drosdeck, 'Entwicklung des Beweisrechts im 19. Jahrhundert: Zum Stand des Forschungsprojekts', *Ius*

the parties appealed – as shown – frequently to avoid disadvantages and prejudices.

Therefore, the first result presented in this paper might be that the *Oberappellationsgericht* in Lübeck decided mainly on appeals against interlocutory decisions, which the court could decide efficiently (often taking less than a year). All research concerning the substantial law, especially the commercial law, has to view the situation from the procedural side in order to see the substantial nucleus. On the other hand, the jurisdiction over interlocutory questions had the very considerable advantage that nearly every case in the court was decided in a quite short time, very often in less than a year.

4.3 *No Specialised Commercial Courts*

Regarding this procedural frame, the *Oberappellationsgericht* was not a commercial court in a strict literal sense, but was rather a typical high court of appeal with a broad competence in all appealable civil and criminal law cases.[36] However, contemporaries regarded this court specifically as the most important commercial court of the nineteenth century, because it had jurisdiction over the population of four trade cities. Therefore, it is no surprise that the court did not decide the everyday cases of the rural population, but rather focused on commercial disputes fitting into the four cities' social structure. The files of Frankfurt alone show more than 250 commercial companies, some of them with more than ten lawsuits.[37] Particularly in comparison to the number of inhabitants, the *Oberappellationsgericht* had to decide many and even more commercial cases in daily practice than any other German court at the time.

A second provisional result might be that commercial disputes were not exceptional cases, but rather were regular affairs at the *Oberappellationsgericht*. Hence, the decisions of the court solved the specific problems of the commercial

---

Commune 19 (1992), 205–216; André Gouron, Laurent Mayali, Antonio Padoa Schioppa and Dieter Simon (eds.), *Subjektivierung des justiziellen Beweisverfahrens: Beiträge zum Zeugenbeweis in Europa und den USA (18.–20. Jahrhundert)* (Frankfurt am Main: Vittorio Klostermann, 1994).

36 In the early modern period, the appeal against penalties was mainly forbidden in Germany, *inter alia* by a *Reichsabschied* in 1530 and the authority of Benedikt Carpzov. To the contrary, the appeal against criminal procedures and the revision by a second instance courts of appeal were common in the nineteenth century. For the earlier period, see Christian Szidzek, *Das frühneuzeitliche Verbot der Appellation in Strafsachen: Zum Einfluß von Rezeption und Politik auf die Zuständigkeit insbesondere des Reichskammergerichts* (Köln: Böhlau, 2002).

37 Inge Kaltwasser, *Gesamtinventar der Akten des Oberappellationsgerichts der vier Freien Städte Deutschlands*, vol. 6 (Köln: In Kommission bei Böhlau, 1994), 1491–1497.

law with the general system of the civil law, and incorporated them. The details of the commercial law were examples of principal legal problems, fitting well with the main movements in the contemporary scholarship.[38] The legal literature mostly tried to build a system of modern Roman law or a system of today's law.[39] The method used by the *Oberappellationsgericht* to integrate commercial law into civil law followed the ideas of the contemporary scholarship exactly. The connection between the scientific method at the universities and the method of the court's practice was close enough to reduce the reciprocal correlations between literature and court – between theory and practice.[40] In fact, the personal exchange between the universities and the court supports this idea.

4.4 *Sources for the History of Commercial Law*

The main aim of this volume is to extend the knowledge about the sources of commercial law in European legal history. For the *Oberappellationsgericht Lübeck*, there exist three different groups of records for reconstructing the practice of commercial law in the nineteenth century. Therefore, this paper will not focus on the general development of the science of commercial law and the dogmatic distinction between commercial law and civil law, but rather will present three concrete sources to reconstruct the legal practice of the *Oberappelationsgericht.*

a) Published Court Decisions

First, there are published court decisions. In the early modern period, courts were not to justify their decision in front of the parties. So, it was forbidden to give the opinions of the court to the litigants.[41] However, many judges often

---

38 The special example of the commercial law is dealt with by Joachim Rückert, 'Handelsrechtsbildung und Modernisierung des Handelsrechts durch Wissenschaft zwischen ca. 1800 und 1900', in Karl Otto Scherner (ed.), *Modernisierung des Handelsrechts im 19. Jahrhundert* (Heidelberg: Verlag Recht und Wirtschaft, 1993), 19–66.

39 Joachim Rückert, Savignys Dogmatik im 'System', in Andreas Heldrich et al. (ed.), *Festschrift für Claus-Wilhelm Canaris zum 70. Geburtstag*, vol. 2 (München: Beck, 2007), 1263–1297; now in Joachim Rückert, *Savigny-Studien* (*Savignyana 9*) (Frankfurt am Main: Vittorio Klostermann, 2011), 153–193.

40 The general problem is explained by Joachim Rückert, 'Theorie und Praxis' am Beispiel der Historischen Rechtsschule, mit einem Ausblick bis heute, in Claes Peterson (ed.), *Rechtswissenschaft als juristische Doktrin: Ein rechtshistorisches Seminar in Stockholm 29. bis 30. Mai* 2009 (Stockholm: Institutet för rättshistorisk forskning, 2011), 135–193.

41 *Stefan Hocks, Gerichtsgeheimnis und Begründungszwang: Zur Publizität der Entscheidungsgründe im Ancien Régime und im frühen 19. Jahrhundert* (Frankfurt am Main: Vittorio Klostermann, 2002).

published their votes and opinions. Soon, the extensive literature about legal practice embraced several hundred titles in the old German Empire.[42] Courts had mostly not published official volumes of legal practice before 1800, when the *Reichskammergericht* began to publish their decisions,[43] but even then they were published without the *rationes decidendi*. The *Oberappellationsgericht Lübeck* therefore existed and made its decisions in a transitional period.[44] Remarkably, the court published its decisions together with the opinions and reasons (20 years after the court had begun to practice). In addition, the publication usually separated the judgements according to the city from which the appeal had come.[45] Therefore, there is a substantial amount of published material, but the downside is that it is not very easy to use.

The first volume was published in Frankfurt in 1845. This was followed one year later by Bremen in 1846, which presented the material from 1840 up to 1845. After that five other edited volumes appeared containing Bremensia up

42 Very helpful: Heinrich Gehrke, *Die privatrechtliche Entscheidungsliteratur Deutschlands: Charakteristik und Bibliografie der Rechtsprechungs- und Konsiliensammlungen vom 16. bis zum Beginn des 19. Jahrhunderts* (Frankfurt am Main: Vittorio Klostermann, 1974).

43 *Vollständige Sammlung aller im Jahre [1800–1801] bey dem Höchstpreislichen Kaiserlichen und Reichs-Kammergerichte ergangenen Urtheile und Decrete, auch gemeinen Bescheide und entweder in den Proceß einschlagenden, oder sonst zur Bekanntmachung geeigenschafteten conclusorum pleni* (Wetzlar, 1800/01); later under the new title *Sammlung aller im Jahre [1802–1804] bey dem höchstpreislichen kaiserlichen und Reichs-Kammergerichte ergangenen Haupt- oder sonst eine praktische Ansicht gewährenden Urtheile und Decrete, auch gemeinen Bescheide und geeigenschafteten conclusorum consilii pleni; nebst fordersamster Bemerkung des Kammergerichtlichen Personals und der sich daby von Zeit zu Zeit ergebenden Veränderung* (Wetzlar, 1802/04).

44 Filippo Ranieri (ed.), *Gedruckte Quellen der Rechtsprechung in Europa (1800–1945)*, 2 vols. (Frankfurt am Main: Vittorio Klostermann, 1992).

45 These collections have confusingly similar titles: *Sammlung der Entscheidungsgründe des Oberappellationsgerichts der vier freien Städte in bremischen Civil-Rechtssachen*, vols. 1–5 (Bremen, 1846/66); *Sammlung der Erkenntnisse und Entscheidungsgründe des Ober-Appellations-Gerichts zu Lübeck in hamburgischen Rechtssachen nebst Erkenntnissen der früheren Instanzen*, together 8 vols., in detail with different titles (Hamburg 1849/64); Christian August Thomas Bruhn (ed.), *Sammlung der Entscheidungen ds Oberappellationsgerichts zu Lübeck in Lübecker Rechtssachen*, 2 vols. (Lübeck, 1858); Agathon Wunderlich (ed.), *Die Jurisprudenz des Oberappellations-Gerichts der vier freien Städte Deutschland in bürgerlichen Rechtssachen aus Lübeck*, 2 vols. (Bremen, 1866); Johann Jacob Römer (ed.), *Sammlung der Entscheidungen des Oberappellationsgerichts zu Lübeck in Frankfurter Rechtssachen mit Berücksichtigung der Erkenntnisse der früheren Instanzen*, 4 vols. (Frankfurt am Main: Boselli, 1854/58); *Sammlung der Entscheidungen des Oberappellationsgerichts der vier freien Städte zu Lübeck in Frankfurter Rechtssachen*, 8 vols. (Frankfurt am Main: Sauerländer, 1855/67).

to 1865/66. In Hamburg, a first volume of decisions was published in 1856, with material beginning in 1848. The first volume of Lübeck judgements was published in 1858. These first volumes included the older decisions, sometimes from the 1820s and 1830s. Afterwards, it became common to publish new volumes of decisions every year, with individual volumes for each of the four cities. In 1866, this regularity ended, because the third and last president of the court, Johann Friedrich Kierulff, started a new volume with judgements from all four cities. As Frankfurt had been annexed by Prussia in this year, there were only three Hanseatic cities left, and the court modified its name. The volume of decisions by Kierulff became the official collection, including decisions from 1871 to 1872, and was the last one published in 1874.[46]

Altogether, there are 36 volumes of published decisions, mostly chronologically and geographically separated, and they show the development from the old-fashioned private editions of judges, to the official announcements of the court. Heinrich Thöl, professor of commercial law in Göttingen, for example, published some well-chosen decisions in 1857, because he thought they were important for the contemporary legal scholarship.[47] In the later years, the court edited the material officially, rather than under the names of individual judges. The motivations (*Entscheidungsgründe*) were mostly published in abridged versions, but they contained all the central points the court found. Therefore, it became possible to discuss the legal problems and practical solutions on the basis of the decisions and the issues they were founded upon.

In addition, many decisions were published in the law journals of the nineteenth century. The *Seuffert's archive* in particular, which was one of the famous journals of the time,[48] published many of the *Oberappellationsgericht*'s decisions. The journal was founded mainly to publish the decisions of the German high courts concerning aspects of the contemporary *ius commune* (*heutiges gemeines Recht*). The editor, Johann Adam Ritter von Seuffert, hoped that the judgements of the different German courts gave important examples for the unification of law. Hence, he did not publish decisions of regional legal

---

46 Johann Friedrich Kierulff (ed.), *Sammlung der Entscheidungen des Oberappellationsgerichts der Vier Freien Städte Deutschlands zu Lübeck*, vols. 1–2 (Hamburg: Mauke, 1866/67); Johann Friedrich Kierulff (ed.), *Sammlung der Entscheidungen des Ober-Appellationsgerichts der Freien Hansestädte zu Lübeck*, vols. 3–7 (Hamburg, 1869/74).

47 Heinrich Thöl (ed.), *Ausgewählte Entscheidungsgründe des Oberappellationsgerichts der vier freien Städte Deutschlands* (Göttingen: Dieterich, 1857).

48 Overview of the contemporary legal journals in Michael Stolleis (ed.), *Juristische Zeitschriften: Die neuen Medien des 18.–20. Jahrhunderts* (Frankfurt am Main: Vittorio Klostermann, 1999).

disputes or laws, but rather judgements with potential to influence all German courts. The *Oberappellationsgericht Lübeck* had this potential, and therefore its decisions were often published.

It seems that the journal and the decisions contained within it became a timeless reference work for many readers and judges of other courts. In 1863, the *Seuffert's archive* edited a repertory of the first 15 volumes of the journal with the decisions of the *Oberappellationsgericht Lübeck* only.[49] It is interesting evidence for the court's extraordinary importance to erudite contemporaries; they wanted to get information about the court's jurisprudence as soon as possible. Other contemporary courts were not found in the inventories of the *Seuffert's archive*.

For contemporaries, there were no special repertories or registers, e.g. search tools for legal decisions, or for judgements dealing with commercial law. An important exception is a collection of decisions concerning exchange matters from 1858.[50] Presumably there was no need for a more differentiated publication of the judgements. The published abstracts in the *Seuffert's archive* always contain references about the legal problems which the court had to decide. Therefore, the connections with commercial law became clear. The court's published decisions (sometimes with short summaries) made it clear, too, whether a case fell under the auspices of the commercial law or not. Indeed, the reconnection with the plurality of statutes and municipal courts of the different four free cities hindered a systematic analysis. However, after scrutiny, it is clear that most of the important decisions were at least published in part. The publication showed very clearly whether they were commercial law disputes. But one note is essential: because there was more scientifically influenced commercial law in the nineteenth century, with its specific journals and specific scholarly law books,[51] the published judgements are themselves not strictly separated into civil and commercial law. Both contemporaries and today's legal historians have to search for the commercial law principles from a large number of cases. There were no special chambers or senates for commercial matters at the *Oberappellationsgericht Lübeck*. Hence, the source

49 *Chronologisch-alphabetisches Verzeichniß der bei dem Oberappellations-Gericht zu Lübeck verhandelten in Band I-XV von 'J.A. Seufferts Archiv für Entscheidungen der obersten Gericht in den deutschen Staaten' mitgetheilten Rechtssachen* (Stuttgart, ca. 1863).

50 *Die Jurisprudenz des Oberappellations-Gerichts der vier freien Städte Deutschlands in Wechselsachen 1821–1857. Nebst Anhang aus der Jurisprudenz des Handels- und Obergerichts zu Hamburg in Wechselsachen. November 1855–1857* (Frankfurt am Main, 1858).

51 The commercial law journal *Zeitschrift für das gesamte Handelsrecht*, founded in 1858 and edited by Lewin Goldschmidt, was especially important. The journal still exists today.

material shows in a straightforward manner that commercial law was naturally understood as being part of the general civil law.

b) Court Files in the Archives of the Former Free Cities

Court files are the second group of sources for the commercial law of the *Oberappellationsgericht Lübeck*. From the earliest days of the court's work, the file numbers were quite modern and professionally organised. The folders were given title pages with the number of the case and the city from which the appeal came. The parties' written statements, or to be more precise the procurators' or advocates' statements, were much shorter then than they were in the eighteenth century; the terminology and the argumentation were precise. On average, an ordinary folder was only a quarter of the extent of a folder from the former *Reichskammergericht*,[52] which makes working with the files easier. The folders were used and appreciated by contemporaries, as well as by Heinrich Thöl, one of the most important professors of commercial law in the nineteenth century. Born in Lübeck in 1807,[53] he was settled in Göttingen in 1830 and wrote a monograph about bills of exchanges and endorsements. He dedicated his work to Friedrich Cropp, a judge from the *Oberappellationsgericht Lübeck*.[54] Starting in 1836, Thöl spent several of his holidays in Lübeck, working with the folders of the court. He praised the quality of the written statements as well as the high level of the decisions. When he wrote his important textbook on commercial law, which was first published in 1841, one of the main bases of his dogmatic principles were the continuous decisions of the *Oberappellationsgericht* in their '*unvergeßlichen Meisterschaft*' (memorable masterpiece).[55] For one of the most important scholars, the basis for his research in commercial law were the files of the court.

52 Inge Kaltwasser, *Inventar der Akten des Reichskammergerichts 1495–1806: Frankfurter Bestand* (Frankfurt am Main: Kramer, 2000), 33.

53 Sketch of his life by Gerhard Ahrens, 'Heinrich Thöl – ein vergessener lübeckischer Ehrenbürger', *Zeitschrift des Vereins für Lübeckische Geschichte und Altertumskunde* 86 (2006), 99–113; from the older literature, see Ferdinand Fehling, *Zur Erinnerung an Professor Heinrich Thöl* (Lübeck, 1893); Bernd-Rüdiger Kern, 'Thöl, Johann Heinrich', in Adalbert Erler, Ekkehard Kaufmann and Dieter Werkmüller (eds.), *HRG*, vol 5, 1st ed. (Berlin: Schmidt, 1998), cols. 179–182.

54 Heinrich Thöl, *De verbi an ordre cambiis vel indossamentis inserti vi atque effectu* (Göttingen, 1830); '*Viris illustrisimis splendidissimis doctissimis Friderico Cropp supremi provocationum tribunalis quod Lubecae viget consiliario et Car. J.A. Mittermaier (...) patronis suis summa observantia colendis praeceptori pie reverendo*'.

55 Heinrich Thöl, *Das Handelsrecht*, vol. 1 (Göttingen, 1841), Vorwort (preface *De verbi an ordre cambiis vel indossamentis inserti vi atque effectu*).

After the closing of the court in 1879, the folders were divided and sent to the cities from which the initiating appeal came, and that is where they still are today.[56] Nowadays, one finds the records in the town archives of Frankfurt and Lübeck and in the state archives of Bremen and Hamburg. The files are divided into three sections. The first and most relevant section contains the civil litigations. Next there is a second, smaller section with criminal proceedings, and the third section contains only commercial litigations decided by the *Oberappellationsgericht Lübeck* after 1870, when it was already subordinate to the newly founded German commercial court (*Reichsoberhandelsgericht*) in Leipzig.[57]

The largest number of files is preserved in Hamburg, which has 2100 civil files. Frankfurt has 1700 files, Lübeck 720, and Bremen 620. Altogether, there are 5300 records of civil proceedings between 1821 and 1879. Because the *Bundesoberhandelsgericht* and the *Reichsoberhandelsgericht* were founded in 1870/71, the most interesting files derive from the fifty years before the unification of the German jurisdiction. Between 1994 and 1996, a modern inventory was made and published in six volumes. Unfortunately, the description of the files is very short, sometimes only one word. However, on one special point the authors of the repertory were extraordinarily attentive. First, they noted the names of all the commercial companies in the Frankfurt files, and secondly they also listed the names of all ships, which were matters in disputes.[58] So we know that the proceedings in the North German cases concerned more than 300 ships.

The commercial law of the *Oberappellationsgericht Lübeck* was often maritime trade law.[59] Looking at the courts' decisions, the technical innovations of the time become clear – for example, the replacement of sailing ships by steamships. Unsurprisingly, the technical developments caused new legal difficulties. The heat in the steamships' hold sometimes scorched the goods. On the other hand, the steamships could then cross the Baltic Sea even in late autumn. In earlier times, trade had usually been forbidden between November and February.[60] But now the trade season was extended, and therefore the spare time that ships had staying in harbour was reduced enormously. In the

56 All details can be found in Klaus-Joachim Lorenzen-Schmidt and Inge Kaltwasser, *Gesamtinventar der Akten des Oberappellationsgerichts der vier Freien Städte Deutschlands*, 6 vols. (Köln: In Kommission bei Böhlau, 1994/96).

57 Müßig, 'Handelsrechtseinheit'.; Thomas Henne, 'Bundesoberhandelsgericht', in *HRG*, vol. 1, 2nd ed. (Berlin: Schmidt, 2008), cols. 715–716.

58 E.g. Lorenzen-Schmidt and Kaltwasser, *Gesamtinventar*, vol. 3, 200–203.

59 Some examples in Oestmann, 'Seehandelsrechtliche Streitigkeiten', 228–263.

60 Albrecht Cordes, 'Flandrischer Copiar Nr. 9. Juristischer Kommentar', in Carsten Jahnke and Antjekathrin Graßmann (eds.), *Seerecht im Hanseraum des 15. Jahrhunderts: Edition*

decades before the modernisation of steamships the winter weather had always been an important factor in ships' delay and timing. Now this point was no longer important.

In modern German law, maritime trade is an exotic matter of dispute. Today, the most widespread edition of the modern commercial code, the so-called '*Schönfelder*', does not even include the section about maritime trade legislation. The common user no longer has any interest in this. By contrast, the *Oberappellationsgericht Lübeck* had to judge mainly on matters of maritime trade, as three of the four cities were harbour cities.

Before the announcement of the decision, one of the six judges was appointed as the consultant (*Referent*).[61] He took the folder home and worked on his opinion. Usually he fixed the *species facti*, the arguments of the parties, and came to his own proposal. In addition, he mostly drafted the wording of the decision and sketched out the main points of the later opinion. These opinions are now part of the files, even if the parties had no possibility of seeing them. The dates in the files show when the appointed judge took the folders home and how quickly he worked. After the referent had finished his work, Georg Arnold Heise, the first president of the court, took the same folders home and worked on a second opinion – he did this nearly every day for the whole 30 years. It seems almost unthinkable, but the folders give the evidence: the president really prepared nearly every decision on his own, whereas the other six judges alternated with each other. It is not certain whether Wächter and Kierulff continued Heise's tradition. However, the files from the first three decades of the court show that the president really worked much more than his colleagues did. Therefore, it is easily understandable that the dogmatic positions and opinions of Heise determined the practice of the court extraordinarily broadly.

In his scientific work, Heise often used the phrase 'in the nature of things' (*kraft Natur der Sache*).[62] The court's decisions contain this phrase, too. Therefore,

---

und Kommentar des Flandrischen Copiar Nr. 9 (Lübeck: Schmidt-Römhild, 2003), 119–144, 126.

61 Tirtasana, *Der gelehrte Gerichtshof*, 120–125.

62 Christoph Bergfeld, 'Handelsrechtliche Entscheidungen des Oberappellationsgerichts der vier freien Städte Deutschlands', in Karl Otto Scherner (ed.), *Modernisierung des Handelsrechts im 19. Jahrhundert* (Heidelberg: Verlag Recht und Wirtschaft, 1993), 67–87, 81; Boto Kusserow, *Das gemeinschaftliche Oberappellationsgericht der vier freien Städte Deutschlands zu Lübeck und seine Rechtsprechung in Handelssachen* (Diss. jur. Kiel, but printed in Düsseldorf, 1995), 214; Kirsten Kraglund, *Familien- und Erbrecht: Materielles Recht und Methoden der Rechtsanwendung in der Rechtsprechung des Oberappellationsgerichts der vier Freien Städte Deutschlands zu Lübeck* (Frankfurt am Main: P. Lang, 1991),

this may show Heise's influence on the judgements. During his work as professor, Heise lectured on commercial law. However, the lectures were published for the first time in 1858, several years after Heise's death.[63] In the opinions, Heise wrote the same finding for different cases. During his lifetime, his judgements and not his books were consequently the basis of his reputation as a scholar of commercial law.

According to the fact that only one judge signed the draft version of the decision, it is quite possible to see the personal views of the court members and to imagine the legal discussions among the assessors. Without any doubt, the files of the *Oberappellationsgericht* are the most important sources of legal practice for the history of commercial law in the nineteenth century.

c) Scholarly Literature by Court Members

Next to the published decisions and the court files, the third group of sources are the judges' scientific works. The most important of these, the *Juristische Abhandlungen mit Entscheidungen des Oberappellationsgerichts der vier freien Städte Deutschlands*,[64] are two volumes by Georg Arnold Heise and Friedrich Cropp. Published in 1827 and 1830, the books do not contain only published decisions, but rather have erudite comments on different legal difficulties concerning commercial law and also on the law of succession and civil procedure law. The articles comprise around 30 pages filled with literature and legal sources of Roman law, and also the foreign law of other states. The decisions of the *Oberappellationsgericht* itself were simply examples for practical disputes. The two volumes belonged to the first published works written by court members, and were often used and quoted in the nineteenth century. In Gerhard Ahrens's opinion, contemporaries looked forward to seeing a serialized continuation of the volume, and felt its need sorely. Therefore, the edition of judgements by Heinrich Thöl became an alternative to the volumes.[65] This modern interpretation might be correct. Without any doubt, Heise and Cropp started a rather original genre of outstanding scientific literature, which would not be superseded.

136–141; John Karl-Heinz Montag, *Die Lehrdarstellung des Handelsrechts von Georg Friedrich von Martens bis Meno Pöhls: Die Wissenschaft des Handelsrechts im ersten Drittel des 19. Jahrhunderts* (Frankfurt am Main: P. Lang, 1986).

63 Agathon Wunderlich (ed.), *Heise's Handelsrecht, Nach dem Originalmanuskript* (Frankfurt am Main: Sauerländer, 1858).

64 Georg Arnold Heise and Friedrich Cropp, *Juristische Abhandlungen: mit Entscheidungen des Oberappellationsgerichts der vier freien Städte Deutschlands*, 2 vols. (Hamburg: Friedrich Perthes, 1827/30).

65 Ahrens, 'Heinrich Thöl', 109.

d) Commercial Law in the System of Civil Law

Both the volumes of Heise/Cropp and the files show the endeavour to integrate the special problems of commercial law into a general system of civil law. When the court had found a solution for a special question, the judges compared their result with the international literature and law. There were references to French, English and American literature, to Roman and Canon law of course, and lastly to particular medieval customs.[66] In cases of insurance, the court often quoted the insurance decree of Hamburg,[67] even if it was a case appealed from Lübeck. Hence, the generalisation process led to a dogmatic system in the court, almost without the need for written law. In 1861, when the general German commercial code was enacted, it even followed the remains of the *Oberappellationsgericht Lübeck* in many ways. For instance, the sections concerning the conclusion of the contract, added to the commercial code in 1861, originated from the court's judgement on many points.[68] So the practice influenced the later codification. Truly, the codification of law changes the character of law fundamentally, simply because of the new hierarchy of legal sources.[69] However, the German BGB continued its tradition by adopting the instructions concerning the conclusion of contracts.[70]

The late Rudolf von Jhering and other jurists used to speak about a so-called *Begriffsjurisprudenz* (jurisprudence of concepts), when they wanted to criticize the contemporary romanistic science of the pandectistic civilian scholarship. But the negative connotation of the term is not good.[71] The jurisprudence of principles describes the nineteenth century more exactly and in

---

66 Examples in my study: Oestmann, 'Seehandelsrechtliche Streitigkeiten', 231–232, 249, 257–258.

67 Thomas Dreyer, *Die 'Assecuranz- und Haverey-Ordnung' der Freien und Hansestadt Hamburg von 1731* (Frankfurt am Main: Lang, 1990).

68 Diethard Bühler, *Die Entstehung der allgemeinen Vertragsschluß-Vorschriften im Allgemeinen Deutschen Handelsgesetzbuch (ADHGB) von 1861: Ein Beitrag zur Kodifikationsgeschichte des Privatrechts im 19. Jahrhundert* (Frankfurt am Main: P. Lang, 1991).

69 This is the main subject in several works by Pio Caroni, e.g., *Gesetz und Gesetzbuch: Beiträge zu einer Kodifikationsgeschichte* (Basel: Helbing & Lichtenhahn, 2003).

70 Peter Oestmann, '§§ 145–156: Vertragsschluß', in Mathias Schmoeckel, Joachim Rückert and Reinhard Zimmermann (eds.), *Historisch-kritischer Kommentar zum BGB (HKK), Vol. 1: Allgemeiner Teil: §§ 1–240* (Tübingen: Mohr Siebeck, 2003), 837–880; Matthias Janko, *Die bewußte Zugangsverzögerung auf den Todesfall: Ein Beitrag zur sogenannten 'postmortalen Willenserklärung'* (Berlin: Duncker & Humblot, 2000).

71 Hans-Peter Haferkamp, *Georg Friedrich Puchta und die 'Begriffsjurisprudenz'* (Frankfurt am Main: Vittorio Klostermann, 2004).

a better way.[72] The *Oberappellationsgericht* conforms to this jurisprudence. In its commercial disputes, the court could integrate details into wider contexts to create homogenous supra-regional law. The court's regional sphere of influence could not hinder its actual impact. The modernisation of commercial law and additionally its connection with the civil law were interesting for all, even those coming from other German states. The *Oberappellationsgericht* became a groundbreaking and scientifically accredited court, particularly because it broke through the particular limitations and boundaries of legal sources. So it received high esteem throughout nineteenth-century Germany.

5 Research Dealing with the *Oberappellationsgericht Lübeck*

The legal historical research on the *Oberappellationsgericht Lübeck* could not keep up with the speed of indexing of the files. There are older works based on the Court's commercial law practice, such as Boto Kusserow's dissertation in 1964[73] and Christoph Bergfeld's essay in 1993.[74] However, since the complete general inventory had been published in 1994/96, there were only very few studies based on the folders in the archives.

Dealing with the constitution of the court and its judges, Katalin Polgar published a work in 2007.[75] On the lower court's procedural law and the decisions of the *Oberappellationsgericht* concerning procedural questions, Nora Tirtasana read a great deal of files and provided a useful monograph in 2012.[76] In the same year, Tim Borgers published a dogmatic historical study concerning the judging of the court in stock law, including commercial law.[77] Clara Günzl is currently working on a study of the methods of judicial decision making in the nineteenth century with a special focus on the Lübeck court.

Of course, most of the files have not yet been the subject of scientific research. It was a Japanese legal historian who found an essential case. The *Oberappellationsgericht* dealt with a foundation of legal capacity by will in

72 Peter Landau, 'Puchta', *Neue Deutsche Biographie* 20 (2001), 757–759; Thomas Henkel, *Begriffsjurisprudenz und Billigkeit: Zum Rechtsformalismus der Pandektistik nach G.F. Puchta* (Köln: Böhlau, 2004), 107–108.

73 Kusserow, *Oberappellationsgericht.*

74 Christoph Bergfeld, 'Handelsrechtliche Entscheidungen', 67–87.

75 Polgar, *Oberappellationsgericht.*

76 Tirtasana, *Der gelehrte Gerichtshof.*

77 Tim Borgers, *Das Oberappellationsgericht zu Lübeck und seine Rechtsprechung zum Aktienrecht: Eine Auswertung der Rechtsprechung unter Berücksichtigung der aktienrechtlichen Literatur des 19. Jahrhunderts* (Hamburg: Kovač, 2012).

the so-called 'Städel-case' (*Städel-Fall*), a legal dispute from Frankfurt in the nineteenth century.[78] The Japanese researcher wondered why the file was still unused, although the inventory had been published more than twenty years earlier.[79] The spotlighting case represents characteristically the research on the German court practice in the nineteenth century. Thinking about the eighteenth century, more source-based research exists and has done so for several years. A study group comprised of Ulrike Müßig, Martin Löhnig, Ignacio Czeguhn and others will at the very least undertake research on the German organisation and constitution of courts in the time of the German Confederation.[80] Currently, it is unclear whether any works on the history of commercial law will follow.

6 Conclusion

The decisions of the *Oberappellationsgericht Lübeck* became well known long before the scholarly literature on commercial law. The important textbook written by Thöl was published in 1841, and the works of Goldschmidt from 1850 onwards. In 1858, Goldschmidt said in the first volume of his 'journal for the whole commercial law' (*Zeitschrift für das gesamte Handelsrecht*) that bit by bit, the court's case law became well known among the scholars of commercial law.[81] In any case, he recognised it as one of the main sources for the scientific literature.

78 Hans Kiefner, 'Das Städel'-sche Kunstinstitut. Zugleich zu C.F. Mühlenbruchs Burteilung eines berühmten Rechtsfalls', *Quaderni Fiorentini per la storia del pensiero giuridico moderno* 11/12 (1982/83), 339–397; Hans-Jürgen Becker, 'Der Städel-Paragraph (§ 84 BGB)', in Gottfried Baumgärtel (ed.), *Festschrift für Heinz Hübner zum 70. Geburtstag am 7. November 1984* (Berlin: De Gruyter, 1984), 21–33.

79 Ryuichi Noda, 'Zum Städelschen Beerbungsfall', paper at the Rechtshistorikertag Tübingen 2014 (forthcoming in *Zeitschrift der Savigny-Stiftung für Rechtsgeschichte: Germanistische Abteilung*).

80 Antonio Sánchez Aranda and Martin Löhnig (eds.), *Justizreform im Bürgerlichen Zeitalter: Rechtsentwicklungen in Spanien und Deutschland* (Regenstauf: Gietl, 2013); Ignacio Czeguhn and Antonio Sanchéz Aranda (eds.), *Vom Diener des Fürsten zum Diener des Rechts: Zur Stellung des Richters im 19. Jahrhundert* (Regenstauf: Gietl, 2011); Ignacio Czeguhn and José Antonio Péres Juan (eds.), *Reflexiones sobre la Justicia en Europa durante la primera mitad del siglo XIX: Überlegungen zur Justiz in Europa im 19. Jahrhundert* (San Vicente, Alicante: Club Universitario, 2011).

81 Levin Goldschmidt, 'Ueber die wissenschaftliche Behandlung des deutschen Handelsrechts und den Zweck dieser Zeitschrift', *Zeitschrift für das gesamte Handelsrecht* 1 (1858), 1–24, 16; overview of journals concerning commercial law by Christoph Bergfeld,

As mentioned, in German legal history, there are only a few studies dealing with the *Oberappellationsgericht* and its judgements on commercial affairs. The court system of the early modern period is much better known than that of the period between 1806 and 1879. For the past couple of decades, legal histories that concentrate on substantive law only have appeared to be less and less interesting or helpful. The so called *Dogmengeschichte*, the history only of the dogmatical forms and figures of some articles and sections, detached from every social and historical background, is no longer very convincing, and is probably obsolete.[82] On this point the history of commercial law certainly has a serious methodological problem. But the sources of the practice are wide open and easy to use. Therefore, a great deal of work could and should be done.

'Handelsrechtliche Zeitschriften', in Michael Stolleis (ed.), *Juristische Zeitschriften: Die neuen Medien des 18.–20. Jahrhunderts* (Frankfurt am Main: Vittorio Klostermann, 1999), 259–276.

82 The last small textbook for students was published more than thirty years ago: Heinrich Mitteis and Heinz Lieberich, *Deutsches Privatrecht: Ein Studienbuch*, 9th ed. (München: C.H. Beck, 1981).

Index of Names

Index of Places

Index of Subjects

www.ingramcontent.com/pod-product-compliance
Lightning Source LLC
LaVergne TN
LVHW010639300926
849161LV00005B/983
9789004360457